Ohio

Ohio

A History of the
Buckeye State

Kevin F. Kern
and
Gregory S. Wilson

WILEY-BLACKWELL

A John Wiley & Sons, Inc., Publication

This edition first published 2014
© 2014 John Wiley & Sons, Inc.

Registered Office
John Wiley & Sons, Ltd, The Atrium, Southern Gate, Chichester, West Sussex, PO19 8SQ, UK

Editorial Offices
350 Main Street, Malden, MA 02148-5020, USA
9600 Garsington Road, Oxford, OX4 2DQ, UK
The Atrium, Southern Gate, Chichester, West Sussex, PO19 8SQ, UK

For details of our global editorial offices, for customer services, and for information about how to apply for permission to reuse the copyright material in this book please see our website at www.wiley.com/wiley-blackwell.

The right of Kevin F. Kern and Gregory S. Wilson to be identified as the authors of this work has been asserted in accordance with the UK Copyright, Designs and Patents Act 1988.

Library of Congress Cataloging-in-Publication Data

Kern, Kevin F. (Kevin Frederic)
  Ohio : a history of the Buckeye State / Kevin F. Kern and Gregory S. Wilson.
    pages   cm
  Includes bibliographical references and index.
  ISBN 978-1-118-54829-5 (hardback : alk. paper) – ISBN 978-1-118-54843-1 (paperback : alk. paper) – ISBN 978-1-118-54832-5 (epub) – ISBN 978-1-118-54840-0 (mobi) – ISBN 978-1-118-54847-9 (vitalsource) – ISBN 978-1-118-54854-7 (epdf) – ISBN 978-1-118-54858-5 (coursesmart)
  1. Ohio–History.   I. Wilson, Gregory S.   II. Title.
  F491.K47 2014
  977.1–dc23

                                    2013020167

A catalogue record for this book is available from the British Library.

Cover image: Aerial view of Serpent Mound State Memorial, Ohio. © Tom Till/SuperStock/Corbis
Cover design by Simon Levy

Set in 10.5/13pt Minion by SPi Publisher Services, Pondicherry, India

1   2014

Contents

List of Figures   viii
Acknowledgments   xii

1   Ohio Before Ohio: State Geology and Topography   1
    Geology   2
    Topography   7
    Importance of Ohio Geology and Topography   13

2   The First Ohioans: Prehistoric Ohio   20
    Paleo-Indian Period (c. ?–c. 11,000 years ago)   22
    The Archaic Period (c. 11,000–c. 2,800 years ago)   24
    The Woodland Period (c. 3,000–c. 1,000 years ago)   29
    Late Prehistoric Period (c. 1,100–c. 400 years ago)   42

3   The Middle Ground: European and Native American
    Interaction in Ohio   47
    Early Effects of European Contact   49
    Ohio as "The Middle Ground"   52
    Colonial Wars and Life in Middle Ground Ohio   54

4   War and Peace: The End of "Middle Ground" Ohio   67
    The Resistance of 1763   68
    Lord Dunmore's War   75
    The American Revolution   79
    The Western Confederacy and the End of the Middle Ground   87

5   The Ohio Experiment: Formation of the Northwest Territory,
    Early American Settlements, and Statehood   100
    Clearing Title and Related Problems   101
    Organizing Ohio and the Birth of the Public Land System   102
    Early Ohio Settlements   113
    From Territory to State   117

6   A Community of Communities: Early Ohio Society   125
     Demographics   126
     Social Conflict   138
     Reform   141

7   Revolutions: Early Ohio Economic Developments   160
     Early Ohio's Economy   161
     Economic Revolutions   166

8   From Periphery to Center: Early Statehood and National Politics   185
     Early Statehood Politics   186
     The War of 1812   192
     State and National Politics, 1815–36   200
     Political Ascendance and its Problems   206
     Sectional Politics and the End of the Second Party System   208
     The Constitution of 1851   210

9   Ohio Must Lead! The Civil War and Reconstruction   214
     Ohio and Sectional Conflict   216
     Ohio and the Civil War   222
     Ohio's Civil War Contribution: A Summary   234
     The Reconstruction Period, 1865–77   240

10   Why Ohio? Late Nineteenth-Century Politics and Presidents   247
     Why Ohio?   247
     State Politics   249
     Ohio's Presidents from Hayes to McKinley   256

11   The Making of an Industrial State: 1865–1920   280
     Industrialization   281
     Location and Transportation   283
     Natural Resources   287
     Finances, Entrepreneurs, and Innovation   288
     People   294
     Industrial Work and the Rise of Organized Labor   307

12   Urban Life, Leisure, and Political Activism: 1880–1920   316
     Urban Life and Leisure   317
     Urban Political Reform   324
     Women's Activism   331
     Education   336
     Conclusion   338

13   Reform and the Great War: 1912–1920   340
     The 1912 State Constitution   341
     The 1912 Elections   343
     The Flood of 1913   347
     Ohio and the Great War   349
     The 1920 Election   358
     Summary   359

14 Boom, Bust and War: 1920–1945   361
    The Economy and Politics in the 1920s   363
    Social and Cultural Conflict   366
    Literary Critics of Ohio   370
    The Great Depression and the New Deal   376
    World War II   387
    At War's End   393

15 Affluence and Anticommunism   396
    The Postwar Boom   397
    Migration and the Changing Cities   404
    The Cold War and Ohio Politics   411
    Conclusion   424

16 Rebellion and Reaction: The 1960s   426
    The Struggle for Black Equality   427
    Carl and Louis Stokes   434
    Resurgence of Women's Activism   436
    Emerging Environmental Issues   440
    Escalation: Vietnam and Politics   444
    Campus Unrest and the Kent State Shootings   451

17 Ohio since 1970   457
    Stagnation and Decline   458
    Politics in the 1970s and 1980s   467
    Towards the Future: Ohio since the 1990s   476
    Summing Up: Ohio as America   485

Index   490

List of Figures

Map of the United States		xv
Map of the highways of Ohio		xvi
1.1	Geologic map and cross-section of Ohio	3
1.2	The extent of shales in Ohio	6
1.3	Landscape during maximum advance and after retreat of ice	9
1.4	Glacial grooves on Kelleys Island in Lake Erie	11
1.5	Elevation map of Ohio	12
2.1a–b	Atlatl and bannerstone	26
2.2	Miamisburg Mound in Miamisburg, Ohio	33
2.3	The Adena Cultural Complex and the Hopewell Complex	34
2.4a–c	Artifacts from Hopewell mounds	37
2.5	The Newark Earthworks	38
2.6	Teosinte and maize	43
2.7	Serpent Mound near Peebles, Ohio	45
3.1	Beaver fur hats	48
3.2	White trader with Native American trappers	54
3.3	Contest for control in the Ohio Country, 1741–63	56
3.4a–b	Captain Pierre-Joseph Céloron de Blainville reinforcing French claims to territory by burying an inscribed lead plate	61
3.5	General Braddock's retreat from the Battle of the Monongahela, July 9, 1755	64
3.6	General Jeffrey Amherst	65
4.1	Gnadenhutten monument	68
4.2	The return of captives to Colonel Henry Bouquet after the Resistance of 1763	73
4.3	The Ohio country during the revolutionary era, 1774–83	77
4.4	Early national conflict with Native Americans, 1785–95	89

4.5	Miami Chief Mishikinakwa	91
4.6	Broadside from 1791 with news of St. Clair's disastrous defeat	94
4.7	The Battle of Fallen Timbers	97
4.8	Signing of the Treaty of Greenville	98
5.1	State land claims and cessions to the federal government, 1782–1802	102
5.2a–b	Numbering under the Land Ordinances of 1785 and 1796	104
5.3	Diagram of the Seven Ranges—the first government survey in Ohio	107
5.4	Ohio during the territorial period, 1788–1803	110
5.5	The Virginia Military District's (VMD) use of irregular-shaped units	111
5.6	Fort Harmar	115
5.7	Governor Arthur St. Clair	118
5.8	Thomas Worthington	119
6.1	Migration and settlement patterns, 1788–1850	133
6.2	Charles Grandison Finney, "The Father of Modern Revivalism"	142
6.3	Zoarites	144
6.4	The Commercial Hospital and Lunatic Asylum for the State of Ohio	146
6.5	Frances Dana Gage	147
6.6	Oberlin College	148
6.7	The "Old Stone School" in Akron	152
6.8	McGuffey's *Reader*	153
6.9	*The Philanthropist*	156
7.1	A "shinplaster"—worthless paper money	164
7.2	Steamships on the Ohio River in 1929	167
7.3	Major Ohio roads and canals, 1850	168
7.4	The Ohio and Erie Canal	170
7.5	The growth around the canal in 1860s Akron	174
7.6	The meatpacking process, Cincinnati	179
7.7	Boy coal miners	181
8.1	The Ross County Courthouse, later the first Ohio Statehouse	186
8.2	The Black Laws	190
8.3	Tenskwatawa, also known as Lalawethika or The Prophet	193
8.4	Ohio during the War of 1812	196
8.5	Perry's victory	199
8.6	Campaign ribbon for the election of William Henry Harrison	207
9.1	The 127th Ohio Volunteer Infantry (later designated the 5th U.S. Colored Troops) at its training base in Delaware, Ohio	216
9.2	Oberlin rescuers pose at the Cuyahoga County Jail	221
9.3	The "Black Brigade"	225
9.4	Clement Laird Vallandigham	228
9.5	Ohio during the Civil War	233
9.6	Salmon Chase "greenback"	236
9.7	The trio of generals from Ohio, "Honor to the Brave," 1865	239
9.8	Ulysses S. Grant	243

10.1   Eliza Jane Trimble Thompson (1816–1905), also known as
       "Mother Thompson," circa 1900   251
10.2   Women kneel in front of J.C. Mader's Saloon in Bucyrus, during
       the temperance crusade of 1873–74   252
10.3   Wayne Wheeler   253
10.4   Jacob Coxey, taken about the time he led his march to
       Washington D.C. in 1894   255
10.5   Coxey's Army, in Hagerstown, Maryland on their way to
       Washington D.C.   256
10.6   Campaign banner for the 1876 Republican presidential ticket of
       Ohio governor Rutherford B. Hayes and New York Representative
       William A. Wheeler   264
10.7   Garfield's assassination, photos taken and assembled
       by Charles Milton Bell   269
10.8   Campaign poster from 1900 supporting the re-election
       of William McKinley with new vice presidential candidate
       Theodore Roosevelt   277
11.1   Hulett Ore Unloader.   286
11.2   John Henry Patterson (1844–1922)   289
11.3   Charles Kettering (1876–1958)   291
11.4   The Wright brothers   293
11.5   Isaac Meyer Wise   300
11.6   Walter Black (1920)   304
11.7   Harry C. Smith (1863–1941)   305
11.8   Photograph of child labourer Harry McShane by Lewis Hine (1908) 310
12.1   The Cincinnati Reds in 1869   320
12.2   Jim Thorpe   323
12.3   Samuel "Golden Rule" Jones (1846–1904)   325
12.4   Tom Johnson of Cleveland (1854–1911)   328
12.5   Postcard from 1915 depicting the Seal of Ohio and a woman's
       face framed by the sun   334
12.6   Hallie Quinn Brown   335
13.1   James Middleton Cox   346
13.2   A rescue boat built by NCR employees in action in Dayton
       during the 1913 flood   348
13.3   "Doughboys" from Grove City at Camp Coëtquidan in France, 1918   351
13.4   The 372nd Infantry Regiment in a victory march held in
       Columbus in April 1919   352
13.5   A propaganda poster for Liberty Bonds issued during World War I 356
13.6   Poster produced during World War I to promote "Americanization"
       of immigrants   357
14.1   Warren G. Harding on a camping trip in Maryland with Henry Ford,
       Thomas Edison, and Harvey Firestone in 1921   364
14.2   KKK in Akron's centennial parade, 1925   369

14.3	Louis Bromfield at Malabar Farm	373
14.4	A "Hooverville" in Circleville, south of Columbus, 1938	379
14.5	Akron police clash with striking rubber workers from Goodyear, May 1938	385
14.6	Mural in a Cleveland barbershop depicting the movement of African Americans out of the South and into the city, 1952	386
14.7	Paul Tibbets in the B-29 bomber *Enola Gay*	388
14.8	Women employed in a manufacturing plant in Cleveland during World War II	391
14.9	The Tuskegee Airmen	394
15.1	John Glenn sitting outside the *Friendship 7* space capsule	400
15.2	Larry Doby, the American League's first black player, with Lou Boudreau and Hank Greenberg, 1948	401
15.3	Shoppers crowd a recently opened Big Bear supermarket in Columbus, 1952	402
15.4	The "Moondog Coronation Ball" in 1952	405
15.5	George DeNucci	413
15.6	Pamphlet issued as part of the campaign to defeat the proposed right-to-work law, 1958	418
15.7	James Rhodes	421
16.1	Fannie Lou Hamer leading a group of civil rights workers in song during the Freedom Summer campaign	429
16.2	Hough riot, July 1966	433
16.3	Carl and Louis Stokes	434
16.4	Toledo native Gloria Steinem	438
16.5	The Cuyahoga River fire of 1952	443
16.6	Congressman John Ashbrook	446
16.7	National Guard troops march towards Taylor Hall in their efforts to dispersethe rally on the Kent campus on Monday May 4, 1970	453
17.1	Rita Dove, Poet Laureate of the United States	458
17.2	U.S. Steel's Ohio Works in Youngstown	467
17.3	Ohio governors George Voinovich, Richard Celeste, James Rhodes, and John Gilligan, 1994	472
17.4	Cartoon capturing the popular view of Kasich's plan to end collective bargaining for public employees in Ohio	483
17.5	Rally against Kasich's proposed measure, February 2011	484
17.6	Support given to the Republican Party in Ohio 1980–2010	486

Acknowledgments

Although this book may have only two authors, literally hundreds of people have contributed to it in one way or another. In some ways, this makes writing the acknowledgments section more daunting than writing certain chapters: the text of every historical survey probably neglects to mention figures who ought to have been included, but most of those people are usually immune from feeling undeservedly slighted. To anyone not mentioned below who deserves to be, please accept our apologies, and we will endeavor to include you in future editions.

Contributing most visibly to the look and experience of the book was the Ohio Historical Society, which supplied the lion's share of images and was supportive of the project above and beyond what we had even hoped it would be. In particular we'd like to thank Janice Tallman who went the extra mile in securing images and getting permissions and Jillian Carney, who approved the entire set for our use. Thanks, too, to Victor Fleisher and his staff at the University of Akron Archives for their help in supplying images at extremely short notice.

We have been extremely fortunate to find ourselves surrounded by colleagues in the historical community who have made this project much less difficult than it might have been otherwise. First and foremost, George Knepper has been of inestimable inspiration and gracious support to us ever since we took over teaching Ohio History upon our arrival at the University of Akron (UA). The fact that it has taken two of us to do this gives some indication of the size of the shoes we have been trying to fill. Similarly, Andrew Cayton's (Miami University) research and writing should be an inspiration not just to all Ohio historians, but also to all historians anywhere. The field is fortunate to have a scholar of his caliber bend his considerable talents its way, just as we are fortunate that he has generously shared his time and expertise with us. We also must thank Bil Kerrigan (Muskingum University) and Donna DeBlasio (Youngstown State University), who provided invaluable suggestions after reading an earlier draft of this manuscript. We would also like to thank our colleague in the Political Science Department at the University of Akron, John Green, who took time out from his many media interviews during election seasons to offer advice and suggestions for research. Finally, we would like to offer our sincerest gratitude to our colleagues in the History Department at the University of Akron during the years this manuscript was in preparation: Shelley Baranowski, T.J. Boisseau, Connie Bouchard, Rose Eichler, Lesley Gordon, Michael Graham, Steve Harp, Walter Hixson, Janet Klein, Mike Levin, Elizabeth Mancke, Martha Santos, Michael Sheng, Martin Wainwright, Zachery Williams, and Gang Zhao. The fact that we have had the good fortune to work every day with such talented historians and collegial supporters has made our time at UA something approaching a dream job.

We would also like to thank our students in our Ohio History classes and Greg's Public History classes at the University of Akron. While you learned from us (we hope), you may not have realized that we learned from you as well. Not only have your thousands of term papers and other class projects contributed to our understanding of Ohio history, your course evaluations and individual meetings with us have helped us understand the best ways to form an Ohio History learning community every semester.

The people most directly responsible for the production of this book, though, are the truly gifted people at Harlan-Davidson/Wiley with whom we have the great privilege to work over the past few years. Sincere thanks to Annie Jackson and Carol Thomas who had this project put on their respective plates relatively late in the process but nevertheless pushed it through with utmost professionalism and stunning alacrity. Linda Gaio and Andrew Davidson probably deserve a page of acknowledgments of their own for their tireless efforts on this project (and their incredible patience with us). There is no one else with whom we would have rather worked to bring this book to fruition, and we feel that any thanks we could possibly give to them would still be insufficient.

In addition to the many people we must jointly thank, both Greg and Kevin also would like to express sincerest thanks to a number of people who have inspired us individually. Dr. G. Richard Kern instilled an intense interest in history in his son from a very early age and provided a wealth of material for him when he first began to teach Ohio History. He is still Kevin's favorite historian. Kevin's mother, Marilyn Ruth Rayle Kern, has not only always been tremendously supportive of his every endeavor, but also always reminded him (as Macaulay said) that "no one who is correctly informed as to the past will be disposed to take a morose or desponding view of the present." His brother Christopher Garrett-Kern and his sisters Kathleen Kern and Carolyn Schlicher have long been the most supportive siblings one could ever wish for, even if he does not tell them nearly enough. Without even knowing it, Kevin's daughter Jennifer-Carolyn and son Kenton have kept him going on many days when he might have otherwise quit. And last, sincerest thanks and love must go to Kevin's wife Kristie, who bore the burdens of the countless late nights and weekends Kevin devoted to the project with grace and endless patience. With no offense intended to Greg, Kevin thinks that his life with Kristie has been his greatest and most satisfying collaboration.

Greg became interested in Ohio history by working on his dissertation (later book), which dealt in part with deindustrialization in Ohio and the nation. He then began teaching at the University of Akron, taking over the Ohio History course (along with Kevin) from the legendary George Knepper. He also worked with Kevin to start the

Northeast Ohio Journal of History. Starting the journal and teaching the course – and doing so in the former rubber capital of the world, helped fuel the desire to contribute to a new book on Ohio's history.

Perhaps the single most important intellectual and professional activity that inspired Greg's work was his great fortune of having co-written and helped to run three Teaching American History grants. Work on these TAH projects and with the many people who made them possible deepened his knowledge and enthusiasm for Ohio history, and teaching and learning more generally such that this book and these grants are intertwined. Funded through the federal Department of Education, these programs brought K–12 teachers together with historians and professional staff from historical sites and organizations to train teachers in U.S. history content. The funding for the program ended in 2012. The grants used Ohio history as a lens to examine how events at the state and local levels intersected with national and international events. It modeled the way Greg teaches Ohio history and has inspired so many aspects of this book. He is deeply indebted to the K–12 teachers with whom he worked on these grants. Through the many journeys they made together across Ohio and points east, they continued to amaze him with their enthusiasm, passion for learning, dedication to their craft, and their sense of humor. The current project director, Erin Stevic, has brought so much enthusiasm and knowledge of Ohio history and material culture to the project and made Greg think in new ways about teaching and learning history. A special thanks goes to the former project director, Sharon Hays, who passed away in 2012; she combined skill, grace, and patience with a deep knowledge of history and enthusiasm for learning. The partners over all three grants at the Akron Public Schools, the Cuyahoga Valley National Park, the National Constitution Center, the Ohio Historical Society, the Summit County Educational Service Center, and the Stark County Educational Service Center – especially Jody Blankenship, Mark Butler, Pat Clayton, Betsy Hedler, Dave Irvine, Gail Martino, Adam Motter, and James "Kimo" Tichgelaar taught him so much about teaching, learning, and Ohio history. The grant evaluators, Doug Clay, Carole Newman, and Isadore Newman, added further to his knowledge and understanding. Finally, Greg thanks all of the staff and volunteers at the many sites we visited in Ohio, Maryland, Pennsylvania, Virginia and Washington D.C. and the many scholars who led seminars and workshops. Without them, neither these grants nor this book would have been possible.

On a personal level, Greg's wife, Laura Hilton deserves his deep thanks – and a medal. She endured many days and nights of being a "grant widow" as he traveled with teachers during the academic year and in summers as part of the TAH projects. Busy with her own professional concerns as a historian and department chair, she – almost always with great patience – listened to ideas, offered criticism, and provided the support and encouragement he needed to see the book (and the grants) through. Greg and his wife share the joy and work of marriage, which includes taking care of their daughter, Kate, who grew up with this book and the grants as they evolved over several years since her birth in 2007. She always appreciated the gift items Greg brought back from sites around Ohio and elsewhere, and the stories he would tell her about where he'd been, even if she never quite understood why – sometimes – getting the book finished and traveling for work were more important than playing school or flying like Supergirl.

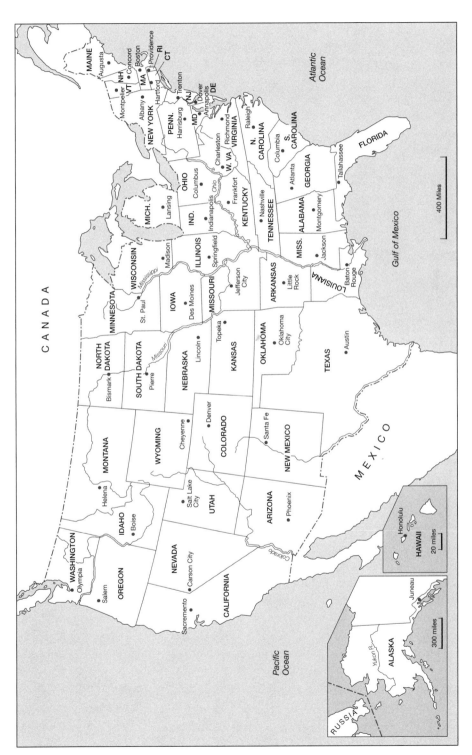

Map of the United States.

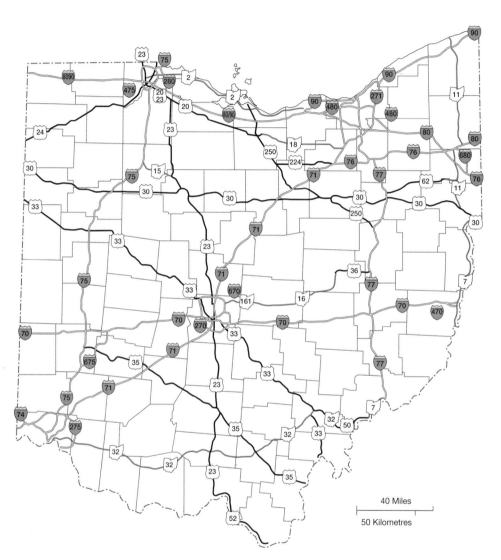

Map of the highways of Ohio.

1

Ohio Before Ohio
State Geology and Topography

The history of Perry County, which sits in predominantly rural south central Ohio, is in many ways representative of the history of the state as a whole. The northern half underwent several phases of glaciation while the southern half lies in the more rugged unglaciated Allegheny Plateau. Lying just to the south of the famous prehistoric Newark Earthworks and Flint Ridge quarries, the county has numerous Woodland-period mounds as well as much older outcrops of the Flint Ridge and Upper Mercer flints that Ohio's earliest inhabitants prized highly. The county boasts several locations on the National Register of Historic Places, including Somerset's Saint Joseph's Church (the state's first Catholic Church) and Somerset's Old Courthouse (the oldest continuously used public building in the Northwest Territory). Although agriculture has always been important to the county other commercial pursuits have traditionally driven its economy. The National Ceramic Museum and Heritage center in Roseville celebrates only one of the many industries that once flourished in the area. Salt-making, centered in McCuneville, was the county's first industry, followed soon thereafter by lime production in Maxville. By the middle of the nineteenth century mining started in earnest, and for a while Perry was the largest coal-producing county in the state, with major operations in the "black diamond" region of Shawnee, Congo, and New Straitsville. This combined with locally produced lime and the iron ore, found primarily in the southern part of the county, gave rise to a significant smelting industry with as many as seven blast furnaces operating within the county by the late 1800s. Commercial production of gas and oil in Corning and Junction City had augmented this economic boom by the early 1890s with the county reaching its peak population in the 1920s. As with the rest of the Appalachian region, Perry County faced increasingly difficult times starting with the Great Depression and has never fully recovered

Ohio: A History of the Buckeye State, First Edition. Kevin F. Kern and Gregory S. Wilson.
© 2014 John Wiley & Sons, Inc. Published 2014 by John Wiley & Sons, Inc.

from the decline of its mining and iron industries. By the late twentieth century the county experienced increasingly low median incomes and high unemployment. Nevertheless, the county is still home to some of its historic industries, including the ceramic manufacturers Petro Ware in Crooksville and CertainTeed Corporation/ Ludowic Roof Tile in New Lexington (the world's largest roofing tile firm).

However well Perry County may represent the highs and lows of Ohio's social and economic development it is an even better exemplar of the significance of Ohio's geology to its development. The flint obtained from Flint Ridge, which was such a valuable resource for early Native American groups, was a product of a unique set of silicon dioxide deposits made during the Pennsylvanian period. The saltwater that created Perry County's early salt mining industry was a remnant of Silurian period seas that covered the area, and one can trace its lime industry to the shells of the creatures that lived in those seas. The clays that formed the basis of the county's enduring ceramic industry—as well as the bricks that make up Saint Joseph's Church and Somerset's Old Courthouse—were drawn from deposits made by Mississippian and Pennsylvanian seas and by glaciers that came hundreds of millions of years later. The iron ore processed by Perry County blast furnaces, as well as the coal that made them run, came from the Pennsylvanian period, while the limestone used as flux to remove impurities from the iron came primarily from the Devonian and Mississippian periods. Life forms from these periods probably formed the gas and oil that Ohioans began to use in the late nineteenth century. The 21 percent of Perry County's land that is used for agriculture has a complex geological signature with the rich soil having developed from both the erosion of ancient rock strata and relatively more recent glacial deposits. Although most residents there probably give it little thought, Perry County's history has been at least half a billion years in the making.

This case study of just one of Ohio's eighty-eight counties shows how important an understanding of Ohio geology is to understanding its history. To comprehend what happened to Ohioans through the ages, it is first necessary to appreciate what went on beneath their feet. Their stories and lives, explored in this book, are inextricably entwined with the nature of the land.

Geology

The substructure of Ohio can be thought of as a kind of multilayered cake that has been pushed up from the bottom and shaved off the top, leaving slanting edges of layers exposed on the surface. This differential exposure has given different regions of Ohio different surface rock types and resources. Each of these exposed strata, plus others that remain buried far beneath the surface, are the product of millions of years of geological processes. Figure 1.1, a geologic map of Ohio, shows the formations beneath Ohioan's feet.

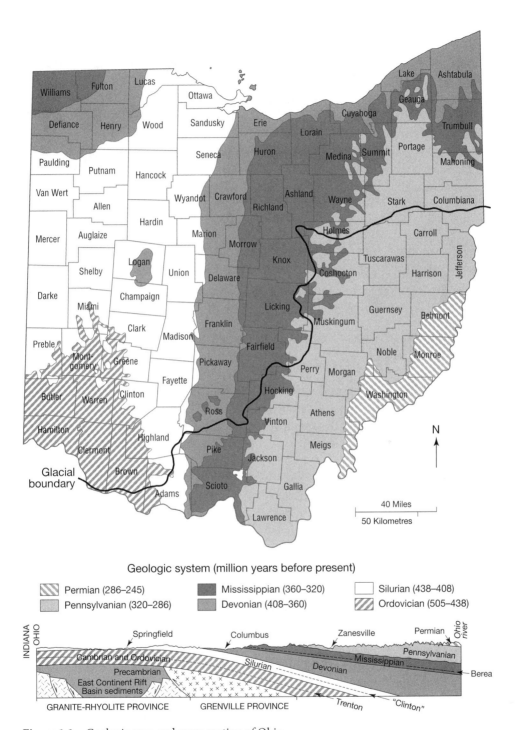

Figure 1.1 Geologic map and cross-section of Ohio.

Source: Ohio Department of Natural Resources, Division of Geological Survey

Precambrian era

The oldest, "basement," layer of Ohio's substructure is a several-mile-thick and multilayered sheet of igneous and metamorphic rocks laid down between 1.5 billion and 800 million years ago. The most notable feature of this layer is the eastern edge of the "Granite-Rhyolite Province," an uprising or "superswell" in the earth's mantle under what is now Ohio and states farther west. This extending and splitting of the crust created a deep feature called the East Continent Rift Basin. At about the time that the superswell activity ceased, the continent that would become North America—of which Eastern Ohio lay on the edge—collided with another protocontinent to the east. The impact caused significant compression of the crust, the formation of faults, and a prehistoric range (known as the Grenville Mountains) that was gradually worn down over the following hundreds of millions of years.

Ohio's Precambrian layer is not visible anywhere in the state, lying anywhere between 2,500 and 13,000 feet below the surface. Although it cannot be seen sometimes it can be felt. The relatively minor earthquakes that sometimes occur in Ohio arise from the rifts and faults of its basement layer.

Paleozoic era

At the end of the Precambrian era (about 570 million years ago) the continent that became North America began to separate from the one it had collided with 300 million years earlier. Sitting on the edge of the continent Ohio was engulfed by the body of water geologists call the Iapetus Ocean. For most of the next 300 million years much or all of Ohio lay under water. This era is known as the Paleozoic and it marked by the proliferation of multicellular marine life forms worldwide. This era is the most significant to Ohio geology, not only because of the various resources these life forms left behind, but also because nearly all of the strata that comprise Ohio's current surface were laid down during this time.

Cambrian and Ordovician periods

When the Iapetus Ocean flooded what is now Ohio it brought new geologic processes to bear on the landscape. It deposited layer after layer of silt, sand, mud, as well as shells and skeletons of countless sea creatures over the course of what is known as the Cambrian period. During the early Cambrian period most of Ohio was under a relatively shallow, tropical ocean shelf that left a thick layer (as much as 400 feet in some places) of sandstone. An above-water feature that geologists call the Kerbel Delta formed in north and central Ohio during the middle Cambrian period. At the same time ocean waters began to rise. By the late Cambrian and into the Ordovician period (505–440 million years ago), the entire state was again covered by a warm, shallow sea. Although low muddy islands emerged periodically in the western part of the state the sea eventually reclaimed all of the state by the later Ordovician. At this time, a growing abundance of more complex life forms appeared and flourished.

Sponges, jellyfish, bryozoans (and their coral cousins), brachiopods (clamlike creatures), trilobites (one type of which, *Isoletus*, is Ohio's official state fossil), cephalopods (ancestors of octopi and nautiluses), echinoderms (related to sea stars), snails, and even primitive fish left their traces in the geologic record—not only as fossils, but also as the ever-deepening layers of calcium carbonate from their shells and skeletons. These became the earliest layers of Ohio limestone that were hundreds of feet thick in some places. It is upper Ordovician strata that formed a large island known as the Cincinnati Arch in southwest Ohio. Sitting at the top of the Precambrian superswell these layers are the oldest surface rocks in the state.

Silurian and Devonian periods

At the end of the Ordovician, an ice age in the southern hemisphere (where Ohio was then located) reduced sea levels, making Ohio into dry land by the beginning of the Silurian period (440 million years ago). Warm shallow seas returned and by the middle Silurian they deepened and blanketed all but the most southeastern part of the state. By the late Silurian the seas abated again and had all but dried up by the time the Devonian period began (about 410 million years ago). The retreating Silurian seas left behind vast beds of halite (salt) and gypsum as well as more layers of limestone and shale. By the early Devonian period most of Ohio and parts of Kentucky and Indiana were part of a large island surrounded by tropical waters that lapped the eastern Ohio shore. The first true land plants grew in Ohio at this time. By the middle Devonian period shallow seas once again covered Ohio. The remnants of the shells and large coral reefs of this period became another thick layer of limestone this time with numerous fossils of fish embedded in it. By the late Devonian period, increased volcanic activity from mountain building to the east not only blanketed the area with toxic ash but also created fast-flowing rivers that dumped immense amounts of mud into the increasingly stagnant and lifeless late Devonian sea. These deposits make up the Ohio Shale, which also contains numerous iron concretions and pockets of natural gas (see Figure 1.2 for Ohio's major shale regions). Silurian and Devonian strata make up much of today's surface stone of western Ohio.

Mississippian and Pennsylvanian periods

The ebb and flow of prehistoric seas continued for the rest of the Paleozoic era. The increasingly muddy waters of the late Devonian period continued into the early Mississippian (starting about 360 million years ago) and then eventually gave way to more silt and sand deposits as the period progressed. The early Mississippian mud turned into the Bedford Shale, while the later sandy deposits became the Black Hand and Berea sandstones. A late Mississippian sea laid down more limestone before retreating at the end of the period. Land plants became increasingly abundant during the periods of sea retreat, a trend that continued into the Pennsylvanian period (325–286 million years ago). As the Mississippian sea retreated, much of eastern Ohio became a large delta onto which flowed the pebbly erosion from mountains to the north and east. This eventually created an abundant rock known as the Sharon Conglomerate. In time, a vast tropical swamp forest stretched throughout much of the Pennsylvania, Ohio, West Virginia, Kentucky, and Indiana areas, leaving millions of years of organic deposits. These forested swamps were periodically overtaken by advancing

Figure 1.2   The extent of shales in Ohio.
Source: Courtesy of the State of Ohio Environmental Protection Agency

seas, which buried the plant and animal material under layers of sand and clay, with the cycle repeating many times. The marine-formed strata became new layers of limestone, the silica-rich Middle Pennsylvanian Vanport Limestone in particular, that formed the famous Flint Ridge flint. The Upper Mercer Limestone of the Pottsville formation, which created the prized black flint from Coshocton County, also came from this period. As the layers from the advancing and retreating seas accumulated over the course of the Pennsylvanian period, they created enough pressure on lower strata to convert the trapped swamp forest-life deposits into coal.

Most of the surface rocks seen today in eastern Ohio were created during the Late Pennsylvanian period. Known as "the coal measures," these alternating layers of shales, sandstones, limestones, clays, and coals—up to 2,000 feet thick in some places—suggest numerous episodes of the swamp forest-to-sea cycle. The seas retreated from nearly all of Ohio permanently at the end of the Pennsylvanian and, apart from a narrow band in extreme southeastern Ohio that was a coastal swamp during the Permian period (286–248 million years ago), no further geological strata developed in what became Ohio. However, over the next quarter of a billion years many other processes altered the Ohio landscape significantly.

Topography

Several major factors since the Permian period helped to create Ohio's current landscape. The most significant of these have been orogeny (mountain building) and glaciation (the formation and movement of glaciers) and their effects that include erosion, river and lake formation, and the creation of soil through the deposition of material brought by glaciers (glacial till) and vast amounts of wind-blown silt that accompanied them (loess).

Allegheny uplift

To the east of what is now Ohio the tectonic plate that carried most of North America began to collide with another one as early as the Late Mississippian period to help create the supercontinent of Pangea. Over the next several tens of millions of years these plates ground together, folding and thrusting up the earth at its boundaries to create the Allegheny Mountains. These were originally much higher and rockier. This process continued until the Late Permian period when what is now the North American continent began to move north from its traditionally tropical latitudes on its way to its present location. Although the mountain formation did not occur in what is now Ohio the process significantly altered Ohio's topography. First, the tectonic collision uplifted the entire area, which helped to cause the final retreat of the seas that had periodically flooded Ohio during most of the Paleozoic era. Today, Ohio's mean elevation is 850 feet (259 meters) above sea level. Ohio's lowest point (on the Ohio River where it exits the state) has an elevation of 455 feet (139 meters). Second, over the course of the Mesozoic and Cenozoic eras that followed the Paleozoic, the uplifted plateaus of eastern Ohio began to receive rivers and erosion from the new mountain chain to the east, as well as experience its own weathering and erosion. These forces created the hilly Appalachian Plateau, the characteristic topography of eastern Ohio.

Teays River

At some point during the Tertiary period of the Cenozoic era (roughly 65 to 2 million years ago) a great river rose on the western side of the Appalachians in what is now western North Carolina near Blowing Rock and flowed north and west. Geologists call this river and its tributaries the Teays River system. At one it time drained much of the east-central United States, including Ohio. Entering Ohio in Scioto County and proceeding north, the Teays then proceeded west through the state to Mercer County on the Indiana Border, ultimately flowing into an arm of the Gulf of Mexico that at one time extended up the current Mississippi Valley to southern Illinois (some geologists suggest that the river instead continued to flow north to an extinct river system where Lake Erie is now). As wide as two miles in places, this river cut a broad swath through the Ohio countryside and carved a number of flat-bottomed valleys, some of which are still the beds of contemporary rivers in the southern part of the state. Now buried as much as 500 feet deep in places in northern Ohio, the old Teays riverbed still serves as an aquifer supplying well water to communities living above it.

Glaciation

The reason there is no Teays River today—and indeed the reason why there is an Ohio River instead—can be attributed to the last major event that dramatically affected Ohio's topography: the advance and retreat of glaciers. By the late Cenozoic period the North American continent had more or less arrived at its present latitude, and the climate was considerably cooler than it had been for most of the previous eon. In addition, by the middle of the Pleistocene period (about 1.8 million to 10 thousand years ago) the climate of the entire earth began to cool, and ice caps began to form on earth's polar regions. Around 300,000 years ago, the Laurentide Ice Sheet to the north began a series of glacial advances southward and retreats northward that did not cease in Ohio until about 14,000 years ago. Glaciers are huge juggernauts of ice that move very slowly but scour and rearrange the earth's surface dramatically in their wake. As a result, scientists know relatively little about the specific effects of most early glacial episodes because subsequent glaciers scraped away much of the evidence their predecessors left behind. They do know, however, that these numerous ice sheet advances and retreats significantly altered Ohio's landscape through both erosion and deposition, and the legacy of the glaciers largely explains most of the topography of northern and western Ohio.

Pre-Illinoisan and Illinoisan stages

The first period of glaciation was a series of as many as eleven separate glacial events collectively known as the Pre-Illinoian stage (also known as the Kansan and Nebraskan glaciations) from about 1.8 million to about 300,000 years ago. Although much of the evidence of this event in Ohio became obscured by subsequent episodes, part of Hamilton County in southwest Ohio untouched by other ice sheets reveals evidence of this earliest set of glaciations. This area is marked by ground moraines, which are gently rolling hills of material that were deposited under the moving ice (see Figure 1.3). Similarly, a larger section of southwest Ohio and a ribbon of territory stretching northeast from Ross to Richland counties (see Figure 1.1), as well as another thin sliver in Stark and Columbiana

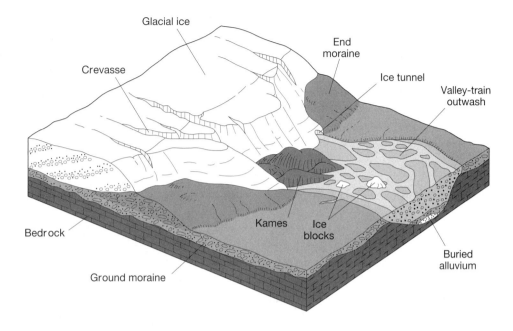

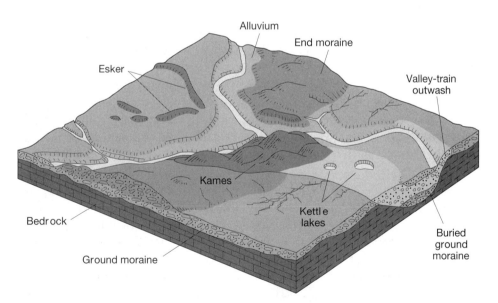

Figure 1.3 Landscape form at the maximum extent and after the retreat of ice.
Source: Ohio Department of Natural Resources, Division of Geological Survey

counties, shows evidence of unsorted rocks, gravel, and other material (till) left over from the Illinoian Stage of glaciation (two periods lasting from 300,000 to 132,000 years ago).

Besides scraping and redepositing material throughout the north and western parts of the state, these early glacial periods also fundamentally changed other aspects of Ohio's landscape. The Pre-Illinoian stage glaciers, for example, destroyed the Teays River system by blocking its path and covering its bed with as much as 500 feet of sediment. Dammed by the glacier, the waters of the Teays created a vast lake in southern Ohio and parts of West Virginia and Kentucky. Called "Lake Tight" by geologists, it was nearly 900 feet deep and up to 7,000 square miles in size (about 70 percent the size of modern Lake Erie). Lasting thousands of years, Lake Tight not only deposited large quantities of clay in central Ohio but it also eventually overcame ancient drainage divides and redirected new drainage channels to the south. This new drainage pattern (known as "Deep Stage") was the beginning of the modern Ohio River.

Wisconsin glaciation
The last major advance of the Laurentide Ice Sheet started about 40,000 years ago and is the most recent stage of the Wisconsin glaciation. Moving about 160–220 feet per year it took the glacier 6,000 years to make its way into Ohio and another 12,000 years to make it to the middle of the state. It advanced irregularly, with major lobes protruding down the Miami and Scioto River valleys, and smaller ones advancing up the Killbuck Creek and Grand River valleys to the east. At its peak, the Wisconsin Glacier was at least a mile thick over modern-day Cleveland and 50 to 200 feet thick at its edge, which stretched from Hamilton County in the southwest to Columbiana County in the northeast. This stage of glaciation ended in Ohio about 14,000 years ago but it continued to have an effect on the state's environment and landscape for thousands of years afterward.

Glaciation fundamentally altered the landscape of much of Ohio. The scraping action of rocks and debris trapped in the glacier scouring the surface below can be seen most dramatically in the deep grooves cut into rocks on Kelleys Island in Lake Erie (see Figure 1.4). However, these same phenomena had a much larger impact, broadening and deepening entire river valleys and eroding hills wherever the glaciers advanced and depositing their collected materials in various ways as they retreated. Apart from spreading vast general deposits of till found throughout the northwestern part of the state, the glaciers also left numerous topographical features. "Terminal" and "recessional moraines" are elongated ridges of till left from the edge of glacial advances that can be as high as 100 feet. The Wabash Moraine, for example, is a glacial ridge that stretches from Celina on the western side of the state all the way to Akron on the east. The Defiance Moraine (Ohio's northernmost) that runs from the south of Cleveland to Defiance, is the reason for the large ridge that runs through the otherwise fairly flat landscape of Seneca and Hancock counties.

Some of the topographical features left by the Wisconsin glaciers were caused by the melting process as a glacier retreated. Kames, for example, are large mounds of material deposited by water melting at the edge of an ice sheet. The highest concentration of kames in Ohio lies in Portage, Stark, Summit and Geauga counties, but they can also be found in dozens of other counties throughout the state. Kames are often accompanied by kettles, small ponds or lakes formed by melting blocks of ice left in depressions among kames by a retreating glacier. The waters from retreating glaciers also left their marks on the landscape, distributing sands, clays, gravels, and other debris in outwash areas of the glacial edge. These waters eventually fed and deepened the new streams and channels that became Ohio's modern river system. The redirection of the old Teays drainage into the more recent Ohio

Figure 1.4   The glacial grooves on Kelleys Island in Lake Erie demonstrate one of the powerful ways in which glaciers could change the landscape. Here, they scoured deep gashes hundreds of feet long into the limestone bedrock of the Island before retreating.
Source: Ohio Department of Natural Resources, Division of Geological Survey

River Valley is just one manifestation of the transformative nature of glaciers on Ohio's natural drainage. Ohio's current "continental divide"—a line that runs across the northern third of the state and marks the boundary between waters that ultimately flow to the Atlantic via Lake Erie and those that end up in the Gulf of Mexico—is a product of glacial action (see dotted line on Figure 1.5).

One of the most significant changes caused by glaciation in Ohio was the effect it had on the formation of the Great Lakes, particularly Lake Erie. By scouring and deepening the lake basin from a previous river valley and filling it with melting water, the Laurentide ice sheet essentially created Ohio's "North Coast." "Lake Maumee," which these melt waters created about 14,000 years ago, was a larger presence in Ohio at one point, keeping much of the northwestern part of the state underwater for thousands of years. Not only did this extension of what became Lake Erie deposit a layer of silt that gave northwest Ohio its distinctive soils, but it also left the Great Black Swamp in its wake, a feature that existed until settlers drained it in the nineteenth century.

Thus, the current topography of Ohio is the product of events stretching from hundreds of millions to just a few thousand years ago. Straddling both the Appalachian and Central Lowlands systems of North America, contemporary Ohio features five distinct landform regions as defined by geologists. The largest of these is the Till Plains, which make up most of the western part of the state (see Figure 1.5). Generally characterized by

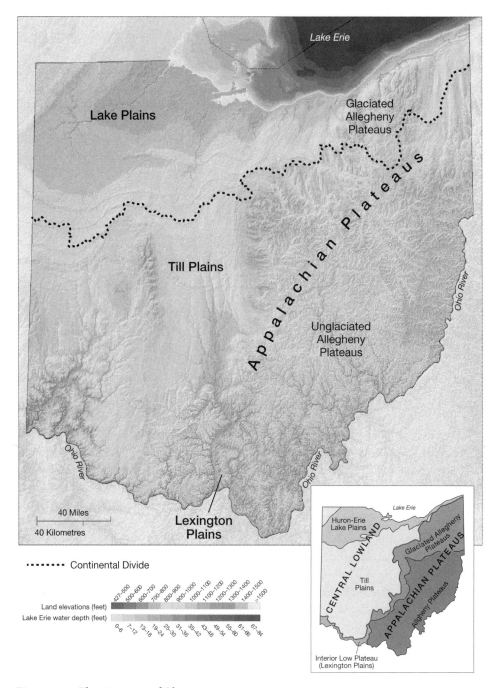

Figure 1.5   Elevation map of Ohio.

flat or rolling landscape, the Till Plains get their name from the vast amounts of till deposited there when the region was glaciated. The Lake Plains stretch from the southern shore of Lake Erie deep into the Maumee Valley of northwest Ohio. Predominantly flat and covered with the sediments of various stages of lake development, the Lake Plains hold many features that reflect their origin including: terraces left by fluctuating lake levels over the years, beach ridge formations, and elevated sand ridges where prehistoric beaches once stood.

The plains of the western part of Ohio give way to the Appalachian Plateau of the east. The Glaciated Plateau, an ever-widening band stretching from Ross County in south-central Ohio to encompass most of the northeastern part of the state, is comprised of the part of the Allegheny Plateau once covered by glaciers. Here, the glaciers leveled the topography by eroding hills and filling valleys. They also created new topographical features by leaving kames, kettles, and new watercourses as well as expanding and deepening other valleys. The Unglaciated Plateau is the most southeastern quarter of the state that remained untouched by the various glacial episodes of the Pleistocene series. As a result it is still a very rugged and hilly remnant of the uplift and erosion of the Appalachians. Soil quality is relatively poor here apart from the river valleys that cut deep into the landscape. The only other general landform represented in Ohio is a finger of land extending from Northern Kentucky into Adams County and parts of Brown and Highland counties. Called the Lexington Plain (or "Bluegrass region"), it is geologically part of an eroded dome called the "Cincinnati Arch"—part of the continent's Interior Low Plateau characterized by flat-topped hills and sinkholes from the erosion of underlying limestone and dolomite layers.

Importance of Ohio Geology and Topography

Although history ultimately concerns itself with the past actions of human beings, it is impossible to understand these fully without a basic knowledge of the land on which they lived. Ohio's topography has always had a significant and varied influence on its inhabitants. Culturally, for example, the kames were some of the earliest known burial locations for Native American groups and many archaeologists believe the kames inspired the mound-building activities of Woodland-period populations. Demographically, the topography of Ohio has deeply influenced population size and settlement patterns throughout the state's history. The best example of this is the fact that the Seven Ranges—the first western public lands opened for sale by the new United States in the 1780s—remain to this day one of the most sparsely-populated areas of the state due in part to its largely unfavorable terrain. Similarly, the swampy areas of northwest Ohio diverted significant U.S. settlement around it to the north and south until the middle of the nineteenth century. What settlement did occur in this area—from prehistoric times until it was largely drained in the late 1800s—was along the elevated glacial moraines and beach ridges left over from glaciers and earlier lakes.

Entire books could be written just about the cultural and demographic significance of Ohio's geology and topography. However, perhaps the most direct and lasting influence these phenomena have had has been the materials they created and the landscape they formed. These minerals and other resources ultimately drew and sustained the millions of people who have lived in what is now Ohio, and have in many ways defined Ohio's historical development.

Minerals

The extraction of minerals has, since prehistoric times, played an important part of the human experience in Ohio. Perhaps the most significant early example of this is the Vanport or "Flint Ridge" variety of flint from Pennsylvanian-period quarries, which was not only highly favored by early Ohio tool makers but was also an important trade item that came to be distributed widely throughout eastern North America. Prehistoric populations also took salt from Ohio's salt springs and turned its clays into ceramics. However, it is the industrial use of minerals that has defined Ohio's development over the past two hundred years. Even though much of Ohio's industrial base had withered by the late twentieth century eighty-six of its eighty-eight counties still extract at least one mineral commercially.

Salt

Salt (or halite) is one of the oldest extracted minerals in the state, most of it being the product of Silurian seas. It was also one of the first minerals to be gathered by humans: archaeologists have discovered that Native Americans made use of Ohio's salt water springs as early as 8,000 years ago. Salt production from boiling the brine from salt licks in large kettles became the first modern industry practiced by European settlers in the late eighteenth and early nineteenth centuries. The resource was considered so important that just weeks after becoming a state the new government passed legislation regulating public salt works and forbidding the state to sell its salt lands in present-day Jackson County. Ohio was the nation's leading salt producer by the time of the Civil War and the discovery of large rock salt deposits near Cleveland in the late 1800s introduced large-scale industrial mining techniques to northeast Ohio. Large underground mines continue to operate near Lake Erie in Lake and Cuyahoga counties, and brining operations (pumping superheated water into underground salt beds and evaporating the resulting brine) take place in Barberton, Rittman, and Newark. Even at the turn of the twentieth century, Ohio still ranked fourth nationally in salt production, with over $100 million in annual sales. Although some of this salt was used as additives for animal feed and water-softening agents, most of Ohio's salt made its way back to the ground in the form of ice control on highways, streets, and sidewalks.

Clay and shale

Clay was another mineral used extensively by prehistoric Native Americans and early U.S. settlers in Ohio. As the next chapter will demonstrate, Native American groups made ceramics from Ohio clays for millennia, and people in the first official U.S. settlement at Marietta made bricks from local clay in the 1780s. Early brickworks and ceramic operations tended to use more recent, glacial-era clay deposits, but as industrial ceramic operations began to grow, the plentiful Mississippian and Pennsylvanian shale strata became increasingly popular raw materials. Eastern Ohio was the primary focus of the ceramic industry, which by the late nineteenth century was one of the state's most important. Brickworks abounded with the demand caused by the rise of industrialization, and they consumed increasing quantities of the clay and shale mined from the Early Mississippian Bedford Shale found in Franklin County. Major stoneware operations developed in New Philadelphia and elsewhere, and businessmen in Akron used the large deposits of native clays found in the region to make the city (for a while) the sewer pipe and toy marble capital of the world. Most of the pipes (agricultural tile) that farmers used to drain the old Black Swamp in Northwest Ohio came from factories processing locally produced clay. Although most of Ohio's ceramic products were utilitarian in nature, the Roseville Pottery Company began producing highly regarded artistic pottery by the start of the twentieth century. Clay and shale continue to make significant contributions to the Ohio economy, with the $15 million worth mined in 2006 ranking seventh nationally. Much of this was destined for use in Ohio industries, including bricks, ceramics, tiles, cement, and landfill covers and linings.

Limestone and dolomite
One of Ohio's most useful and plentiful natural resources comes from the numerous layers of aquatic shells and skeletons that built up from the Ordovician through the Mississippian periods. Limestone (primarily calcium carbonate) and its geological and chemical cousin dolomite (primarily calcium magnesium carbonate) are so versatile that they have been called "the duct tape of geologically derived materials." Major types of limestone found in Ohio come from virtually every period of its geologic past: from the Ordovician Black River group, to the Silurian-derived Brassfield formation of limestone, dolomite, and shale, to Devonian Columbus and Dundee limestones, to the Upper-Mississippian Maxville Limestone, to the Pennsylvanian Putnam Hill and Vanport Limestones. Found in nearly every part of the state, limestone and dolomite have been and continue to be one of the state's most important economic resources. In 2003, 114 mines in 50 counties produced 78.2 million tons.

Early industrial uses for limestone and dolomite in Ohio included the production of lime and building materials, which continue as the primary use of these minerals. First used as the key ingredient of plaster and whitewash, lime soon played a major role in the nascent iron and steel industries of the mid-nineteenth century, as both a flux to remove impurities and as lining for steel furnaces. In the twentieth century, lime's uses expanded to include the chemical industry, notably in the production of rubber. As a building material, Ohio limestone served early settlers of the state as foundation stones, hearth stones, and windowsills. The primary construction use of these materials since the mid-1800s has been as an additive for cement and as aggregate for concrete and asphalt. This continues to be the final destination for most of the limestone and dolomite mined in Ohio. Other uses for these minerals include water purification, sugar refining, glass-making, and the production of heavy chemicals, fertilizers, chalk, paper, plastics, antacids, and porcelain. As a result of its many uses, and because of Ohio's abundant supply, limestone and dolomite have been a rare constant in Ohio's economic profile throughout its industrial history. At the time of Ohio's bicentennial (2003) the state still ranked fourth nationally in the production of lime and fifth in the production of crushed stone (which also includes some sandstone). This resource has an annual value of more than $500 million.

Sandstone and conglomerate

The Paleozoic seas and deltas that laid down layer after layer of sand created the basis of sandstones that have been highly valued for a number of purposes. Although Sharon Conglomerate from the Pennsylvanian period is abundant and has been mined throughout eastern Ohio, the Mississippian-period Berea Sandstone has traditionally been the most highly prized of all Ohio sandstones because of its physical qualities. Pulled from several locations in northern Ohio locations, it derived its name from the Berea quarries, and put Berea on the map as the "Grindstone Capital of the World." At first valued primarily for use as grindstones and millstones, Berea Sandstone reached its highest profile as a building material. Architects used it in the construction of more than twenty Ohio county courthouses and the state capitol building in Ohio during the late nineteenth century. However, its popularity extended far beyond the state. Such land-marks as the Palmer House Hotel in Chicago, the John Hancock Mutual Life Building in Boston, and Denver's Taber Opera House were built with Berea Sandstone, as were prominent buildings at Princeton, Harvard, and Cornell universities. Government buildings ranging from county courthouses to federal post offices, customs houses, or courthouses in at least twenty states are still-standing uses of the stone. The National Parliament building in Ottawa and the Hockey Hall of Fame in Toronto are just two of the scores of buildings in Canada constructed from it.

Although sandstone's popularity as a building stone began to decline in the twentieth century Ohio still ranked third in production of this material in the early twenty-first century. In addition, Ohio sandstone has been put to a number of other traditional uses, including aggregate, filler gravel, glass sand, foundries, filtration, and even pool table surfaces. Newer uses include silica for the computer industry and core samples the petroleum industry, which it uses for testing purposes.

Sand and gravel

The last of Ohio's major minerals to be mined are also among the most widespread. Created by the action of glaciers and bodies of water, sand and gravel have been commercially mined in eighty-four of Ohio's eighty-eight counties in the past fifty years. Whether dredged from Lake Erie or pulled from glacial moraines, kames, and depositional pits, sand and gravel have had a wide range of uses, starting with road paving in the early twen-tieth century and extending to cement and concrete manufacture, road base, fill dirt, ice control, iron molding, glass making, and water filtration. With a value of more than $250 million in 2006 Ohio ranked fifth nationally in the production of construction sand and gravel, and ninth in the production of industrial sand.

Coal

Few minerals have had as profound an influence on the history of Ohio as has coal. In many ways the history of its uses traces that of the state itself. Prehistoric Native American groups used it to make decorative ornaments and pigments, and Europeans first noted outcrops by the mid-1700s. The first reported commercial production of coal in Ohio was in 1800, three years before statehood. Since that time Ohio has produced 3.7 billion tons, primarily from Pennsylvanian-period Allegheny Plateau deposits in its southern and eastern counties. Coal mining began as a relatively minor activity but with the new markets created by the completion of the canal system in the 1820s and 1830s, demand for Ohio coal increased. Coal fueled not only more and more homes, but also the country's rapid industrialization during latter half of the nineteenth century. Railroads, power plants, iron and steel mills, as well as other "smokestack industries" created a nearly insatiable demand for it, and annual production topped 50 million tons by the 1910s. Many of the environmental challenges Ohio faced in the late twentieth century were directly related to the coal industry, not only because the sulfur-heavy nature of the smoke it created polluted the air and returned to earth as acid rain, but also because of the ravaging effects of strip-mining and residual toxins on the countryside. As manufacturing flagged in the late twentieth century, so too did coal production, but it is still an important part of Ohio's everyday life. Although its 22.7 million tons produced in 2006 was only 2 percent of the nation's total and ranked only fourteenth nationwide, its value exceeded $600 million. Furthermore, because Ohio ranked third in the consumption of coal (more than 90 percent of it destined for the electric utility industry), most Ohioans probably were at least indirectly affected by the state's coal industry on any given day.

Other minerals
Over the years, Ohio has excavated commercial quantities of several other materials as well. For example, gypsum—as with halite a Silurian-period evaporite—was mined in Ottawa County for use as plaster and wallboard as recently as 2003. Similarly, peat (a soil-like fibrous material derived from old plant deposits) was extracted from old bogs and glacial kettle lakes in Portage, Champaign, and Williams Counties until the 1990s. Iron ore is perhaps the most historically significant of Ohio's other minerals. Although no longer mined in Ohio, the state exploited its Pennsylvanian-period iron deposits heavily in the 1800s, and this ore—along with domestically produced limestone and coal—enabled Ohio to be one of the largest iron- and steel-producing states in the country until the late twentieth century.

Hydrocarbons

Oil and natural gas are the products of the decay of organic matter laid down throughout the Paleozoic era. As they are in liquid and gaseous form respectively they can migrate through other rock strata until they get trapped by relatively impermeable layers to form pools large enough to be tapped by wells. Most of Ohio's reserves seem to rest in Silurian strata, although deposits can be found from pre-Cambrian through Pennsylvanian layers. In some places, oil seeps to the surface and these areas marked the first places where both Native Americans and early European settlers gathered small quantities to use for lamps and even patent medicines. Ohio actually holds the distinction of the first discovery of oil from a drilled well when early salt-industry drillers looking for saltwater in 1814, in what is now Noble County, discovered oil instead. Residents of Findlay in northwest Ohio discovered and used natural gas as early as 1838, but it was not until the late 1800s that oil and gas became a big industry in Ohio. For a brief time the oil and gas fields of northwest Ohio supplanted those in Pennsylvania to become the most productive in the nation. The industry also created boom towns and new industries like glassworks, which thrived on the cleaner-burning and easier to control natural gas. Although Ohio's hydrocarbon heyday has long since passed, its wells had produced more than one billion barrels of oil and 8.26 trillion cubic feet of gas by 2007. Hundreds of new wells were being drilled each year throughout the late 1990s and early 2000s. Most Ohio counties have productive wells, but the vast majority of the active extraction is in the eastern half of the state. The state produced over 5.5 million barrels of oil in 2007, with a value of almost $369 million. Its gas wells were even more valuable creating $652 million. Although Ohio is not in the top fifteen states in terms of production, the billion dollars' worth of annual production of hydrocarbons make them the state's most valuable extracted resource in the early twenty-first century.

Water

Water was the single most important factor in Ohio's geological development: from the Paleozoic seas that created its landscape to the glaciers that reworked it into its present form. With Lake Erie to the north, a 451-mile stretch of the Ohio river to the south, and more than 25,000 miles of streams and rivers plus countless lakes and ponds in between, Ohio is fortunate to have so many bodies of water (created both through glacial action and water management) as well as the vast aquifers that lie underground. Ohio's plentiful water supply has supported diverse kinds of life and agriculture and long served as vital transportation routes. Ohio's water is also a critical raw material in all sorts of energy and industrial production. Its abundance has also caused some difficulties from time to time, as the frequent flooding in the twentieth century has demonstrated (see, for example, chapter 13).

Soils

Of all the geological activity in Ohio perhaps none have had quite as great an impact on Ohio's history as those forces that created Ohio's soils. Ohio's fertile land and bountiful wildlife attracted its first inhabitants thousands of years ago, and they were the primary factor in drawing its earliest U.S. settlers. For Ohio's entire history as a state, agriculture has played a major role in its economy and although the number of farms and farm acreage has dropped dramatically over the years in the early twenty-first century 55 percent of the state was still farmland, with food production and agriculture creating a $79 billion-a-year industry. One of the main reasons for Ohio's marked agricultural productivity is the quality of its soils. The federal government has designated nearly half of the state's land as "prime farmland" making Ohio one of only five states in the nation to bear that distinction.

Lying at the eastern end of the nation's corn belt, most of Ohio's soils have largely been produced by the same kinds of direct and indirect glacial action that created the rich soils to the west. In addition to the till and water that the glaciers brought to the state they also brought vast amounts of loess, wind-borne dust, and other sediments that swept the face of the ice sheet and blanketed the lands around the glaciers. Although it erodes easily, loess contributes greatly to the fertility of soils and has helped make Ohio's land some of the most agriculturally productive in the United States.

Certainly, there are other aspects of Ohio's geology and topography that have played a role in its historical development, but the examples in this chapter are sufficient to illustrate the point that understanding the formation of Ohio's substructure and topography serves as a good basis for understanding all that came later. Just as Perry County's history—from the Upper Mercer flint that was the state's first processed resource to the gas and oil that continue to be extracted today—was in many ways directed, or at least nudged, by the processes that created its distinctive suite of resources, so too is Ohio's history deeply rooted in the land on which it unfolded. From the tectonic forces that moved and uplifted the very deepest parts of the state, to the seas and plants that deposited millions of years worth of material and converted them into its many layers of bedrock, to the weathering and aging that exposed these layers to the surface, to the vast ice sheets that put much of the state into its current configuration, all of these forces contributed in some way to Ohio's unique history. Yet this chapter's discussion of these contributions has arguably left out the single most important one. The same glacial period that so dramatically altered Ohio's landscape also directly led to something without which our understanding of Ohio history would be impossible: the first Ohioans.

Further Reading

For further information on Ohio Geology, see an excellent collection of pieces on Ohio Geology hosted by The Ohio Department of Natural Resources: *Geofacts*, available at: http://www.dnr. state.oh.us/tabid/7882/default.aspx. Several chapters of Artimus Keefer's edited book *The Geography of Ohio* deal with Ohio geology and geography (2008. 2nd ed. Kent: Kent State University Press). For this and subsequent chapters, George Knepper's *Ohio and Its People* is an invaluable reference work (2003. 3rd ed. Kent: Kent State University Press).

2

The First Ohioans
Prehistoric Ohio

In early 1772, Moravian missionary David Zeisberger made his way through the Ohio wilderness to found the first of three towns for Christianized members of the Lenape (or Delaware) tribe along the Muskingum River. Recording his trip in his daily journal he became the first known person to write an eyewitness account of Ohio's ancient earthworks:

> Long ago, perhaps more than a century ago, Indians must have lived here who fortified themselves against the attacks of their enemies. The ramparts are still plainly to be seen. We found three forts in a distance of a couple of miles. The whole town must have been fortified, but the site is now covered with a thick wood. No one knows to what nation these Indians belonged. It is plain, however, that they were a warlike race.

Zeisberger should be forgiven for misunderstanding the nature and significance of what he saw. After all, no one then alive could have told him that the earthworks he described were at least a thousand years older than he imagined and had not been used as forts. At least he was correct in one important particular: Indians built these earthworks. In the coming generations, various authors would propose more fanciful constructors of these works ranging from an extinct "mound-builder race" through Europeans and Egyptians to the "Ten Lost Tribes" of Israel. More than two centuries of study of these sites has not only proven most of these early conjectures wrong, but also demonstrated that the history of prehistoric Ohio is far more complex than its earliest observers imagined. Nevertheless, these investigations have also shown that, like Zeisberger and his contemporaries, we still have much to learn about the mounds and the people who built them.

Ohio: A History of the Buckeye State, First Edition. Kevin F. Kern and Gregory S. Wilson.
© 2014 John Wiley & Sons, Inc. Published 2014 by John Wiley & Sons, Inc.

If history is ultimately the story of the people who participated in the events of the past, then more than 97 percent of Ohio's history happened before the first European set foot on its soil. Until a few decades ago, historians tended to gloss over or even ignore this vast stretch of time. Although some of this inattention may be attributed to the Eurocentrism once common in most history books, it is probable that the main reason for the omission was a simple lack of information. There are no eyewitness written records for Ohio—the kinds of primary sources on which most historians rely—until the 1600s. The relatively few Ohio historians who sought out the archaeological literature on the topic found that most published information was either generalized assessments of artifacts and earthworks or highly technical accounts by and for archaeologists that were not easily accessible to historians. Furthermore, huge gaps existed even in archaeologists' understanding of Ohio's distant past, making a coherent, meaningful narrative difficult to form.

Although some significant gaps still exist, the last few decades have dramatically changed the picture of Ohio prehistory making it the most dynamic and changing sub-field of Ohio's past. Whereas it is unlikely that any new book will fundamentally change the way historians understand, for example, McKinley's assassination or the process by which Ohio became a state, almost every year there are new archaeological discoveries or articles that significantly enhance the collective understanding of the prehistoric era. While these developments make the field extremely interesting to study they also pose a challenge to authors who wish to keep their work up to date. This chapter provides a summary of the best information available at the time of publication but it is far from the last word on the issue.

Even so, what we know now about the First Ohioans is an increasingly rich and complex story in its own right and one that emphatically illustrates several major points. First, the conception that most people have of "The Ohio Indians" is hopelessly simplistic and does not take into account the complex and often divergent set of cultural and lifeway distinctions that characterized the many people who once occupied what is now Ohio. Second, the sometimes implied or even explicit suggestion in some of the historical literature that succeeding groups of Indians "replaced" each other is largely misleading. While there do seem to be cases of groups of people moving in and out over time, the story of most of Ohio's prehistoric cultural traditions is much more one of continuity and adaptation rather than one of outright replacement. However distinct and remarkable the Adena and Hopewell people may seem, for example, nearly all of the developments that characterize those periods have roots deep in the periods that preceded them. Third, there are several major trends that run through the thousands of years of Ohio prehistory, including movements from nomadic wandering to fixed settlements, from intensive hunting and gathering of wild foods to reliance on true agriculture of domesticated crops, and from cultural uniformity to increasingly complex cultural diversity and long-distance trade with other groups. Last, the prehistory of Ohio dramatically shows that many of the trends that have defined Ohio's traditional history— migration, population increase, resource exploitation, religion, and Ohio's roles as a transportation hub, a regional power, and a contested space—have strong precedents in the prehistoric period. No understanding of Ohio's history is complete without an understanding of its prehistory.

Paleo-Indian Period (c. ?–c. 11,000 years ago)

The same glacial advance that so dramatically reworked Ohio's topography also indirectly introduced humans to that landscape. With so much of the earth's water tied up in vast and deep ice sheets, sea levels dropped greatly, exposing what had been shallow sea floors as dry land. Anatomical and DNA evidence both point to the conclusion that the vast majority of the ancestors of contemporary native populations of North and South America came from northeast Asia, most probably via a land bridge that opened up between what is now Alaska and Siberia. "Beringia," as scientists call this area, probably served as a channel for several different migrations—either following big game on land or skirting the coast in search of aquatic species—until the sea levels rose again at the end of the last ice age. Anatomists have long noted many of the same features between northeast Asians and Native American populations, particularly in the unique dental characteristics that these groups, and no others, share. Furthermore, recent DNA studies seem to confirm this relationship, at least among current Native American groups. While a few new skeletal finds in the western United States and recent discoveries of European-style stoneage tools on the east coast have led scientists to debate whether any other groups might have found their way to the hemisphere at some point, there is to date no conclusive evidence proving that anyone other than Asians were the ancestors of most or all of the prehistoric Ohio populations.

Some considerable debate exists among archaeologists over exactly when the first people set foot in Ohio. Until a few decades ago, the conventional belief was that there were no people anywhere in the hemisphere before about 13,000 years ago. However, several very old radiocarbon dates in both North and South America have challenged this assumption. Radiocarbon (or carbon-14) dating is a method of determining the age of formerly living things by measuring the amount of a naturally occurring carbon isotope that is known to decay at a relatively predictable rate over time.[1] Although the earlier dates have a larger margin of error, some (like those from Buttermilk Creek in Texas or Monte Verde in Chile) seem to have been reliably placed earlier than 15,000 years BP (Before the Present). This has led some archaeologists to posit migrations from Asia as early as 20,000–40,000 BP. What this means for Ohio archaeology is uncertain, because if there were people in the area that early, archaeologists have yet to find any firm artifactual evidence.

The first Ohioans for which direct evidence exists are known as the Paleo-Indians. They were highly nomadic big-game hunters—indeed, with such animals as mammoths and mastodons as their prey, they were among the biggest game hunters ever known. The environment and wildlife of Ohio were notably different at that time. Although the

---

[1]   The further back in time one goes, there is an increasing divergence between "radiocarbon years" and calendar years. This divergence is also relatively predictable based on extensive testing of tree rings, corals, and other things of known ages from those times, and scientists have produced standard conversion charts for these older dates. The dates presented here have been corrected to calendar years, explaining why they may look different from dates published in other books. The divergence in dating largely disappears by about 3,000 years ago.

glaciers had retreated, Ohio had an erratic climate that was still often cold and the land was inhabited by a wide range of plants and animals known to have lived in temperate to colder climates. Spruce and pine forests predominated, but there were also open grasslands and stands of some hardwood trees like willows, poplars, and oaks. A wide array of fauna inhabited the state, including many (like white-tail deer, raccoons, and woodchucks) that still abound in Ohio today. However, the area also hosted "megafauna" such as the mammoth, the giant ground sloth, the giant beaver, the flat-headed peccary (a large wild pig), and the stag moose (a giant deer). With these to hunt, and with nuts, berries, and other plant food to gather, small bands of Paleo-Indians criss-crossed the Ohio landscape in a highly mobile lifestyle for thousands of years.

The nomadic nature of the Paleo-Indians has posed serious problems for archaeologists who wish to know more about their lifestyles. As a result of their brief stays in any one place the Paleo-Indians left relatively little that might have been preserved for study: they made only what they could easily carry with them and they seem to have cremated their dead. Archaeologists have found a number of bone tools and stone scrapers and knives from this period, but the main defining artifacts from the era that have survived to this day are distinctive kinds of spear tips collectively known as Paleo Points. The earliest of these are the Clovis Points: relatively long points knapped from flint with a narrow concavity (or "fluting") extending upward from the base on each side. These were probably attached to the end of a long spear with animal sinew and used to throw or thrust at prey. Collectors and archaeologists have found more than 1,000 Clovis Points in Ohio, from every county, making Ohio second only to Alabama in the number of these artifacts found per square mile. This indicates that Ohio was a popular hunting destination for Paleo-Indian populations.

Despite the relative dearth of Paleo-Indian sites overall, Ohio has several that have proven to be of great importance to archaeologists in understanding this period in eastern North America. Sheridan Cave in northwest Ohio's Wyandot County contains what appears to be a rare, well-preserved short-term camp for Paleo-Indian hunters, with stone and bone tools and a thick layer of wood charcoal. Similarly, the Burning Tree Mastodon site in Licking County has provided archaeologists with a unique record of a mastodon that Paleo-Indian hunters killed, butchered into three large sections, and then dumped in a cold bog in late autumn to preserve the meat for future use. Such direct evidence of a specific Paleo-Indian hunting event is rare, but gives a glimpse into their megafauna hunting practices.

Perhaps the most important Paleo-Indian sites in Ohio, though, are the flint and chert quarries in Licking and Coshocton counties and the Nobles Pond site in Stark County. Flint Ridge is an outcrop of Vanport Flint that for millennia was an easily workable, colorful, and highly prized resource among Native American populations throughout the entire region. One of the earliest Paleo-Indian sites in eastern North America, Meadowcroft Rock Shelter in Western Pennsylvania, contained a number of tools made from this flint. Many other Paleo Points scattered throughout Ohio and neighboring states were also crafted from the flint quarried from Flint Ridge. Similarly, the darker Upper Mercer chert from Coshocton County was a favored raw material of Paleo-Indian hunters and can be found at great distances from its original quarrying site. These sites demonstrate that from the very earliest times central Ohio was a favored destination for human populations and perhaps the source of one of the earliest-known trade items.

Spreading over twenty acres and containing at least ten distinct artifact concentrations, Nobles Pond is one of the largest Paleo-Indian sites excavated in eastern North America. Providing more than 55,000 artifacts—including almost 50 fluted points of various types and more than 6,000 tools—this site also provides a rare insight into Paleo-Indians' way of life. Direct evidence of Paleo-Indian interaction is rare because these people tended to move in small bands. At Nobles Pond, however, evidence points to a larger winter base camp at which several smaller bands came together perhaps to socialize, hunt, work, and trade with each other.

As the Paleo-Indian period wore on, some diversity began to show in their tools with most of the spear points, for example, losing their distinctive fluting. What this means is open for debate but it could reflect both environmental and cultural changes. These changes became increasingly pronounced in the Archaic period.

The Archaic Period (c. 11,000–c. 2,800 years ago)

The Archaic period is the longest period in Ohio prehistory, stretching nearly 10,000 years in length. During this time, Ohio changed dramatically in terms of climate, flora, and fauna. Ohioans, too, changed dramatically. Starting from the intensively nomadic big-game hunting culture of the Paleo-Indian period, the Ohioans of the Archaic period first started to display a number of trends that would characterize the rest of the prehistoric period: decreased ranging; increasing population, trade, communication, and ceremonialism; and diversification of cultural practices and ways of life. Although these trends would become exceptionally pronounced during the later Woodland period, the seeds of all these changes—as well as those of agriculture, which is perhaps the most significant change of all—were first planted in the Archaic period.

As a result of these changes occurring unevenly at different times and places, it is worth noting here that the boundaries between standard period designations (e.g., Early Archaic, Late Woodland) are in some senses arbitrary conveniences created to help provide a "big picture" of the changes that unfolded over vast times and distances. Furthermore, some of these periods may overlap as some traditions continued longer in some places than they did in others. Although potentially confusing, these period names can help form a meaningful understanding of a very long stretch of time.

Early Archaic (c. 11,000–c. 9,000 years ago)

Toward the end of the Paleo-Indian period, the climate began to get more temperate and the kinds of animals available for hunting began to change. Many of the cold-weather megafauna were beginning to disappear, either heading north or toward extinction from the pressures of habitat change and human predation. Faced with an altered set of favored game to hunt, Early Archaic peoples changed their tool-making technologies accordingly. Among the most noticeable of these were an ever-increasing variety of projectile points. Whereas Paleo-Indian spear tips fell along a relatively narrow continuum of types and styles, Early Archaic points (in what is now the Eastern United States) became increasingly diverse. In Ohio, these styles tended to fall into two major complexes: the Kirk/Palmer tradition, which are scattered throughout the state but also to the south and east, and those of the Thebes tradition, which are much rarer but found in a larger area including Indiana and Illinois. Other styles can also be found in Ohio. This diversity, combined with the fact that Early Archaic points are far more plentiful than those that preceded them, indicates that the population of Ohio was getting much larger and more diverse.

The Early Archaic period witnessed another new technological development: ground-stone tools. People at this time began to fashion items out of granite and other hard stones that are more difficult to work than flint. Tools made from these materials included grinding stones, pestles, and woodworking tools like axes and adzes. These tools demonstrate not only more heavy-duty work with wood, such as may have been needed to build shelters or make dugout canoes, but also that the diet of their makers was becoming increasingly reliant on seasonal foods like nuts and seeds that needed to be processed by cracking or grinding. The new tools and new diet also imply that archaic groups, although still nomadic, tended to wander in more restricted areas in which they got to know the specific available resources better, probably leaving the heaviest processing tools behind to come back to when they next returned. Their shelters, intended for relatively short-term use, were caves or simple wooden frames covered with animal hides or woven mats. Ranging in a more restricted area with more limited encounters with other groups would also allow the opportunity for new group-specific tool-making techniques to develop. Although Flint Ridge flint and Coshocton chert remained popular tool-making materials the increased familiarity of their home ranges allowed the people of the Early Archaic period to begin finding and exploiting more local flints and cherts. This also contributed to the increasing variety of points and other chipped-stone tools. These trends would only intensify in the periods that followed.

The introduction of ground-stone tools also made possible a major change in hunting technology. It was during the transition from the Early to the Middle Archaic periods that the spear thrower, or atlatl (pronounced at-l-at-l), became part of the Ohio hunting toolkit. The atlatl is a hooked stick (see Figure 2.1a), often with a weight attached, on to which the end of a spear is placed. Indians crafted the weights (also called bannerstones) from slate, granite, or other hard and heavy rocks. Acting as kind of lever to propel the spear, the atlatl adds greater distance and five times the striking power to that of a hand-thrown spear (see Figure 2.1b). The changing spear point designs between the Early and Middle Archaic periods, including an increasing use of side- and corner-notching, suggests that these tips were attached to the new atlatl-mounted spears in a new way. It was with this new weapon that hunters pursued the somewhat smaller but more plentiful animals of the changing Archaic Era woods.

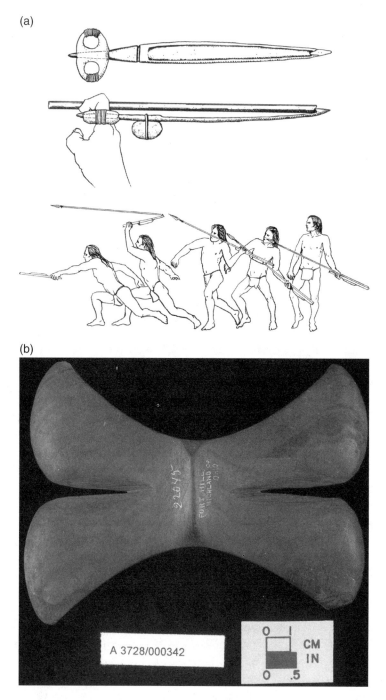

Figure 2.1a, b The introduction of the atlatl (or spear thrower) by the Middle Archaic period gave hunters a powerful tool in hunting the smaller and swifter game that became their primary prey after the extinction of larger mammals like the mammoths. By adding a stone weight (or bannerstone) to the atlatl a hunter could further increase the speed and distance of each throw and the force with which the spear hits its target.

Source: Grant Keddie. 1988. The atlatl or throwing board. *The Midden—The Journal of the Archaeological Society of British Columbia* 20, no. 4 (December); Bannerstone courtesy of the Ohio Historical Society (AL07448)

Middle Archaic (c. 9,000–c. 6,000 years ago)

Archaeologists have found relatively few Middle Archaic sites compared to the periods before and after. Although no one knows why this is, it may have something to do with the warmer and drier climate that prevailed, introducing prairies to western Ohio and perhaps encouraging people accustomed to wetter forested regions to roam elsewhere. Middle Archaic sites from neighboring states indicate that larger, "base" camps appeared with more frequency, exploiting the seasonal nuts and plant foods that were becoming an increasing part of their diet. More aquatic species, such as freshwater mussels and fish, joined the wide variety of animals hunted by people in the Archaic period. Archaeologists suggest that this was the beginning of a "primary forest efficiency" way of life, in which the Archaic people knew the resources of their home range so well that they cyclically moved to various base camps to harvest the best foods in the greatest quantities with the least amount of effort. Evidence of this comes from excavations of their camps and from finds at the earliest known burials of this time. The skeletons from these graves generally indicate that Middle Archaic people were healthy and had good nutrition. Evidence found at burial sites also indicates a change in ceremonial practices when compared with the few cremation sites in earlier periods.

Although Ohio has revealed relatively few habitation sites from the Middle Archaic period it does not mean the state was "empty" during this time. A wide variety of new and different projectile point styles—mostly resembling those found south of the Ohio River—are scattered across the state, often in regional concentrations. These overlapping territories suggest that several different groups exploited a range of favored hunting grounds as part of their foraging strategy. The trends toward reduced wandering in more restricted territories and greater ceremonialism accelerated in the following years.

Late Archaic (c. 5,700–c. 2,800 years ago)

The Late Archaic began with another climate change, one that brought the current temperate conditions to Ohio. The final melting of the ice sheet that still covered part of the upper Saint Lawrence region happened at this time. This raised water levels in Lake Erie and reduced the gradients of streams that fed it. Shellfish ranges expanded northward and beech-maple forests with more nut trees appeared in the now wetter and somewhat cooler climate. These new conditions had a profound influence on Ohio settlement patterns. Whereas Middle Archaic sites are rare in Ohio, Late Archaic sites are more plentiful and show greater population densities than for any preceding period. This is particularly true along Ohio's rivers where the better fishing and more abundant shellfish provided greater quantities of food resources than ever before.

The Late Archaic period brought more food, more people, and more cultural complexity. Archeologists consider Ohio Late Archaic traditions to be part of the more general

"Mast Forest" Archaic period which was characteristic of much of the northeastern part of the continent. However, this period in Ohio saw a proliferation of different local cultural traditions. The Maple Creek Phase and Riverton culture sites found in southwestern Ohio, for example, seem to be related to cultures that can be found further west in Indiana and Illinois. The Glacial Kame and Red Ochre traditions, defined mostly by their burial sites, are parts of larger cultures found in the Great Lakes region. Laurentian Archaic sites seem to be related to a cultural complex found to the north and east along the Saint Lawrence River valley. Each of these different traditions had its own distinctive toolkit, local adaptations, and cultural practices.

In general, though, these cultures exhibited several important trends that would get only more pronounced in the Woodland period that followed. Increased populations and population densities have already been discussed and were tied to a trend toward more intensive use of plant resources, including seeds from sumpweed (or marsh elder), goosefoot, and sunflowers. Although many of these were the products of intensive gathering there was also a trend toward agricultural experimentation. Evidence shows that Late Archaic groups had begun to plant these seeds, as well as squash, while continuing to gather nuts and other resources from their ever-narrowing home ranges. While true agriculture did not arise until later its roots lay in the Late Archaic period.

Associated with this increase in food production was something some archaeologists have called the "container revolution." Late Archaic populations needed a way to store the large amounts of food they were gathering and processing, particularly for the winter and early spring. Storage pits had existed before this time but they became much more numerous in the Late Archaic. Similarly, the fashioning of containers out of a soft mineral called soapstone (or steatite) became more frequent. In addition, the cultivation of squash and other gourds allowed the products of these vines to be hollowed out and used to store or carry things. Perhaps the most significant of these developments, though, was the introduction of a completely new technology: pottery. Developed earlier to the southeast, this invention had made its way to the Ohio Valley by the Late Archaic period. Crude, thick, and tempered with grit these early pots could not have stood the heat of cooking, and were probably used primarily to store seeds, nuts, and other foods.

The introduction of pottery illustrates yet another important trend of the period: long-distance trade and communication networks. Ideas like pottery-making and non-native seeds like squash and sunflower are only some of the things that made their way into Ohio by these means. Late Archaic sites also frequently display exotic materials brought from great distances, including soapstone from Pennsylvania, flint from Indiana, copper from the upper Great Lakes, and shells from the Atlantic and Gulf coasts. Although evidence of long-distance communication had appeared before this time it becomes distinctly more pronounced during the Late Archaic and into the Woodland period.

One of the major eventual destinations of these exotic materials was for burials, pointing toward the trend of increased material ceremonialism and elaboration of mortuary practices. Ceremonialism undoubtedly had existed in some form since the first people had set foot in Ohio, but its material evidence did not begin to appear appreciably in Ohio until the Middle Archaic, when beautifully crafted bannerstones began to appear that seem to be too big or too elaborate for practical use as atlatl weights. However, it was not until the earliest known Ohio burials in the Late Archaic that abundant material evidence of ceremonialism occurs. The groups of northwestern Ohio began to bury bodies in kames and other high grounds and sprinkle them with a mineral powder called red ochre. Glacial Kame burials also include other grave goods including distinctive "bird stones" (bannerstones that look like a stylized bird) and "sandal-sole" gorgets (decorative neck ornaments) made of shell. Red Ochre tradition burials do not have Glacial Kame-type gorgets, but do generally include large, leaf-shaped "turkeytail" points. Although ceremonialism and mortuary practices would become much more widespread and flamboyant during the Early Woodland period, the precedents of this trend were set in the Middle and Late Archaic periods. The variation in mortuary practices also point to increasing cultural diversification among Ohio native groups, a trend that continued throughout the rest of Ohio prehistory.

Agricultural experimentation, the "container revolution," trade and communication networks, and ceremonial burial grounds provide evidence of one of the most important trends of this time: the beginnings of a more settled lifestyle. The trend from the Paleoindian period onward had been toward less nomadism and more concentrated ranging in smaller territories, but developments like agriculture, large-scale storage, the need to overproduce materials for use in trade networks, and communal cemeteries all demanded a more, but not completely, stationary existence (a practice archaeologists refer to as "sedentarism"—this should not be confused with the more contemporary "couch-potato" sense of the word). Excavations of Late Archaic habitation sites demonstrate this trend toward longer settlement, with some exhibiting numerous storage pits and deep refuse features (or "middens") deposited over an extended stay.

Late Archaic sites also reveal several other important insights into the lifeways of these Ohioans. Archaeologists have found evidence of processed fibers that seem to indicate the use of textiles. Tools and artifacts found in graves illustrate clear sexual division of labor and early evidence of minor differences in social status. The bones of Late Archaic people show that they were healthy and well-nourished, but also suggest that the increase in population and decrease in home territories may have produced some conflict. Several individual skeletons from this period have spear points embedded in them, perhaps from violent confrontations with other groups. All of these things proved to be early signs of later developments.

The Woodland Period (c. 3,000–c. 1,000 years ago)

When archaeologists first started categorizing and describing the periods of Ohio prehistory, they generally saw the Woodland period as a sharp break from the past, perhaps even the replacement of previous populations that brought with them agriculture, pottery, and other "new" technologies and practices. Decades of excavation and reinterpretation of evidence proved that this was not really the case, and indeed much of what came to define the Woodland period arose from Archaic precedents. Nevertheless, the Woodland period does mark a clear shift from what came before it in terms of scale and elaboration, as well as a series of major cultural changes that came to define life and interaction between peoples in the Eastern Woodlands for thousands of years.

The Woodland period is probably what most Ohioans think of when considering Ohio's prehistoric Native American populations. After all, it marks the era that produced the mounds and other major earthworks for which Ohio is so famous. It is also the period about which archaeologists know the most because of the wealth of artifacts from it. Despite the fame of Woodland period Ohioans, many common misconceptions about these people exist in the public mind, and even in textbooks on the subject. One—that the Woodland Indians allegedly "replaced" those that came before—has already been addressed. Second—that that there was a monolithic group of "the Ohio Indians" before European contact—is a persistent idea with little basis in fact. Broad continuities and localized diversification continued to characterize Ohio's cultural traditions even at the height of the Woodland period making it far more complex, and far more interesting, than people generally think it is.

Early Woodland (c. 3,000–c. 2,000 years ago)

Some people refer to the Early Woodland period in Ohio as if it were interchangeable with an imagined "Adena Culture." There are two problems with this common belief. First, while the Adena Complex is certainly a significant story of the Ohio Early Woodland period, it is far from the only one. In the northwestern part of the state, for example, the Glacial Kame tradition persisted from its Archaic roots for centuries after the Woodland period started. Similarly, communities in northeast Ohio, although not completely immune from the influences of Adena and Hopewell, would continue to carry on their distinctive cultural traditions for centuries to come. These included the construction of oval earthen enclosures or curved walls on high bluffs or hilltops. Neither of these fit comfortably into the simplistic equation of "Adena" with "Early Woodland" society, thus illustrating the complexity of Ohio's prehistoric traditions during its most celebrated periods of cultural cohesion.

Second, the idea of an "Adena Culture" is a bit too simplistic to describe the tradition that remains the most distinctive Early Woodland cultural complex. Archaeologists prefer to use the term *cultural complex* rather than just *culture* to describe phenomena like Adena and Hopewell because although different sites over a broad area shared many ceremonial traits in common, they often expressed regional variations among other cultural traits. This is analogous to the way that different people in the United States, Ecuador, Nigeria, and South Korea might all participate in Christianity, yet have dramatically different cultural behaviors and everyday lives. Furthermore, "Adena" is just a name that archaeologists have given to this tradition. Like other cultural complexes and phases—Hopewell, for example—Adena derived its name from the earliest-described site of its type: in this case, the mound found on Governor Thomas Worthington's Adena Estate near Chillicothe in south central

Ohio. Archaeologists have no idea what these people called themselves, or even what language they spoke. They do, however, know more than ever about many important aspects of their lives.

One of the most significant aspects of the Adena way of life was a greater degree of sedentarism than ever before. Adena people generally lived in small hamlets of circular houses about ten to fifteen feet in diameter. Sturdier than Late Archaic structures, Adena houses were constructed of log poles probably interlaced with twigs and covered with bark. The amount of time and effort it would have taken to build such shelters indicates that these were more permanent settlements than those of the Late Archaic, a conclusion supported by the numerous storage pits and heavy tools such as grindstones uncovered at these sites. Although these communities would still move from time to time they were beginning to be more settled.

The types of food that the Adena people relied on also promoted greater sedentarism. While they were still hunter-gatherers and relied heavily on game and nuts, they also became increasingly committed to a range of foods that archaeologists refer to as the "Eastern Agricultural Complex" (EAC). This was a group of plants—including various gourds and seed plants such as amaranth, goosefoot, knotweed, maygrass, sumpweed, and sunflowers—that Early Woodland populations domesticated over a period of many years. Although the gathering and processing of these plants and seeds were labor-intensive activities, these foods conferred distinct advantages to the ever-increasing populations of the time. Goosefoot greens and maygrass seeds, for example, are available in the spring, just when winter stores of nuts and other seeds would have been finishing. Selective replanting of these seeds also resulted in succeeding generations producing greater yields going even further toward supporting a growing population. The domestication of cereal crops from native wild species made the eastern woodlands one of only four areas (along with Mexico, Mesopotamia, and East Asia) to accomplish this feat independently. The need to manage, harvest, and store this bounty acted as a powerful incentive for growing populations to stay in a single place for longer periods, further reinforcing a more settled lifestyle.

The gradual cultivation of plants and increasing sedentarism that it entailed allowed for and reinforced the first widespread use of pottery. Although Adena communities stored foods in large pits they also began to use pottery for this purpose. This was probably because the food stored in pottery proved to be more resistant to the ill effects of water and vermin than the food stored in pits. As pottery was fragile and relatively heavy to carry it had not been a practical storage option for the semi-nomadic Archaic people. These concerns were less of an issue with the more settled Adena communities and the people embraced the new technology. Woodland period potters would usually mix clay with some sort of temper (crushed rock, shells, or fibers that served to prevent cracking during the firing process) and then stack coils of this material on top of each other. Using a paddle wrapped in cords made of fibrous material, they would then flatten and smooth the coils together until the pot had reached the desired dimensions. After setting it aside for awhile to dry (heating a pot at this point would make it explode) they would then place the pot in a fire pit to harden it. The resulting pots were not only good for storage and transportation of food, but as the technology was perfected, they could also be used to cook and process food as well. An experiment conducted by archaeologists revealed that boiling hickory nuts—one of the main staples of this period—reduced the time it took to extract the kernels to one-tenth of that needed to do it by cracking the nuts and picking out the pieces. For ever-increasing Early Woodland populations the ability to process ten times as much food in the same amount of time must have been an extremely welcome development.

The adoption of pottery not only proved to be a great boon to the people that made it but it has also proved to be extremely useful to archaeologists. Over time, potters began to adorn their vessels with decorations before placing them in the fire pit to harden. These decorations changed over time and varied between different groups of people. As a result archaeologists can reliably assess the time period and cultural affiliations of different sites based on the ever-evolving shapes, patterns, and composition of pottery found.

Despite the significant changes that the embrace of pottery and the EAC brought, it is the Adena people's mortuary practices that have become best known. Whereas earlier Ohio cultures had placed their dead in natural high spots like glacial kames, the Adena people created hundreds of artificial mounds by piling up dirt, usually (but not always) in a conical shape. Before mound construction started, they would lay the remains (either a body, a bundle of bones, or ashes from cremation) in a bark- or log-lined pit, and at least during the early and middle Adena phases, sprinkle them with a mineral powder like red or yellow ochre. Sometimes they would also build a structure over the burial and then burn it down. They then covered the burial with thousands of basketfuls of earth, and sometimes surrounded the resulting mound with a nearly circular wall, usually with a gap allowing people to enter the enclosure (these circular enclosures also often occur on their own without a mound). Sometimes subsequent burials would be placed at the top of an existing mound, and then covered to make the mound even larger. Miamisburg Mound in Montgomery County, for example, grew to be 68 feet tall and 877 feet in circumference, containing almost 1.5 million cubic feet of earth (see Figure 2.2). Although these earthworks tended to be placed on isolated hilltops during the Early and Middle parts of this period, Late Adena people tended to build them, sometimes in clusters, in valley bottoms. The Wolf Plains group in Athens County is the largest such complex, containing fourteen mounds and ten circular enclosures in a three-square-mile area of glacial outwash plateau.

The major change marked by the rise of Adena Complex extended beyond the mounds to what was inside them. Whereas the rare burials found in Archaic sites had relatively few and largely utilitarian objects associated with them—hunting or sewing tools, for example—Adena burials often had more, and more exotic, grave goods. Some of the most distinctive of these were "cache blades," leaf- or teardrop-shaped chipped knives, often made of flint from Flint Ridge, which seem to have had a ceremonial significance. Characteristic Adena artifacts include tubular pipes made from clay or carved from Ohio pipestone and stone tablets inscribed with artistic designs. Rarer materials found in Adena burials include ceremonial paraphernalia such as ritual masks made of wolf, cougar, and bear skulls. Although the specific beliefs of these people will never be known, their mortuary artifacts suggest that they participated in an animistic type of religion that gave special significance to certain animals and that they had shamans,

Figure 2.2 At nearly 70 feet high and more than 800 feet in circumference, Miamisburg Mound in Miamisburg, Ohio is the largest Adena mound in Ohio and the second-largest cone-shaped mound in North America. Built in stages over several generations using only simple digging tools and baskets the Miamisburg Mound contains the equivalent of 3,400 dump truck loads of soil.
Source: Courtesy of the Ohio Historical Society (AL02905)

or religious specialists, who wore the masks and skins of animals as part of their ceremonial practices. Other rare grave goods—including polished human trophy skulls and bowls, breastplates, and beads made from human skulls and teeth—seem to indicate more human-centered ceremonialism, intergroup conflict, or both.

Some of the most intriguing grave goods found in Adena burials were made from materials not native to Ohio. Adena craftspeople fashioned items from copper brought in from the upper Great Lakes, mica from the Carolinas, and shells from both the Atlantic and Gulf coasts. These items reveal much about Adena culture. Possession of these items, for example, probably denoted the enhanced social status of the person with which they were buried, and perhaps evidence of a kind of social stratification in what seems to be otherwise a fairly egalitarian hunter/gatherer/gardener society. Furthermore, these items also demonstrate quite clearly that the Adena Cultural Complex was not developing in a vacuum, but rather was part of a much larger sphere of interaction. Although the core of the Adena Complex extends from Chillicothe west to southern Indiana, south to Kentucky and West Virginia, and east to western Pennsylvania, it was also an active participant in a trade network that sent out and brought in materials from hundreds of miles away. Similarly, some Adena ideas seem to have been moving beyond its core area,

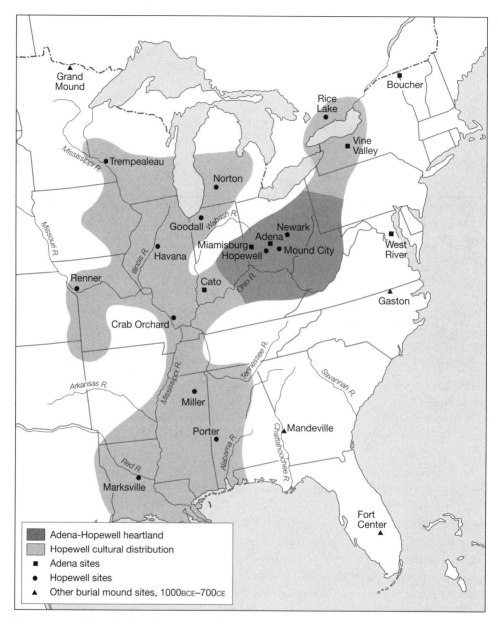

Figure 2.3 Although the Adena Cultural Complex was focused in the Central Ohio River Valley, its influence extended much farther. Adena-style sites have been found as far east as New Jersey and Maryland. The Hopewell Complex was even more influential. At the peak of the Hopewell period, Ohio was the center of a cultural complex that stretched as far west as present-day Texas, up the entire Mississippi River Valley, and extended eastward into present-day New York and Ontario, Canada.

with Adena-style mounds and artifacts appearing in New York, New England, and Canada (see Figure 2.3). Ohio had, by the Early Woodland period, become a key hub of communication and trade.

The myriad changes that the Adena Complex represented led some early observers to suggest that the Adena people moved into Ohio, displacing the Archaic-period populations. As discussed earlier, this interpretation overlooks many of the continuities between the Late Archaic and Early Woodland periods. Recent studies of skeletal and DNA evidence support the idea of continuity, finding little significant difference between the Adena, the Late Archaic peoples who preceded them, and the Hopewell people who arose later in Ohio. Although there was almost certainly some movement and change in territorial boundaries in Ohio populations in the Early and Middle Woodland periods, these changes were probably not wholesale replacements. Knowing this makes the immense changes that happened in the Middle Woodland seem all the more extraordinary.

Middle Woodland (c. 2,100 –c. 1,500 years ago)

In many ways, the Middle Woodland period marked the continuation of several trends that had started in the Archaic period. In most of Ohio, population, trade, communication of ideas, the use of pottery, agriculture, ceremonialism, and sedentarism all steadily increased. Some areas continued to carry on the Adena tradition well into the Middle Woodland, and those populations in the northern part of the state continued and evolved within the contexts of their own traditions, seemingly little affected by the dramatic cultural events taking place farther south. Yet it is for the development of the Hopewell Cultural Complex that the Middle Woodland period is best known. "Like Adena on steroids," as one observer once put it, the Hopewell tradition marked an almost exponential expansion of Adena ceremonialism, both in terms of the nature of artifacts it spawned and its geographic scope.

Although a few Adena-related ceremonial sites can be found far outside its upper Ohio Valley heartland, Hopewell-affiliated sites existed by the hundreds throughout much of what is now the eastern United States, particularly along the Ohio and Mississippi valleys. From Wisconsin south to Louisiana, from Kansas east to New York and Southern Ontario, these Hopewell-influenced sites reflect a ceremonial commonality among sometimes very different local lifeways and cultural traditions. The fullest and most flamboyant form of this ceremonialism, though, was that of the Ohio Hopewell core area found along most of the major rivers of central and southern Ohio.

The everyday life of Ohio Hopewell people showed relatively little difference from that of its Adena ancestors when compared with the dramatic ceremonial changes. They still lived in small hamlets of one or a few houses, although Hopewell structures were squarer in shape and a bit larger (twenty to thirty feet per side). Like Adena houses, they were constructed of wooden posts interlaced with twigs and then covered either with bark or a mud-grass plaster. The Hopewell People lived in clearings, grew gardens of domesticated plants, and hunted and gathered from the surrounding area. Although it is unclear just how long they stayed in any one place on average they seemed to follow the previously mentioned trend toward sedentarism and greater reliance on the EAC. In addition, the first evidence of maize (corn) appears during this period, although this import from the south was not yet a major part of their diet.

Although isolated in terms of everyday life, the Hopewell people were united into much larger groups for the purposes of ceremony and mortuary traditions. Given the dispersed nature of Hopewell settlements and the tremendous amount of labor it took to build the numerous Hopewell ceremonial sites, it is clear that the people must have gathered together in larger groups at certain times and places to accomplish this work. The average Hopewell mound was about thirty feet high and one hundred feet across, containing nearly half a million cubic feet of earth. Built one basketful of earth at a time, a typical mound would have taken 200,000 person-hours to construct according to archaeologists' estimates. To put this into perspective, a class of thirty students working twelve hours a day with no days off would need a year and a half to build just one of these mounds. The ability to organize and direct such vast amounts of labor indicates that there must have been some individuals or groups of people with sufficiently high status and power to make this possible.

That extreme differences in social status existed in Hopewell society is borne out by the kinds of burial traditions they practiced. Whereas many of them followed the same basic model of Adena, including mounds with log-lined pits and burial structures built over them, the Hopewell greatly elaborated this pattern. Some Hopewell burials have large, multiroomed houses built over them, with different furnishings and offerings left in each room. The burial pits could be spread with thick layers of bark, gravel, or stone slabs, sometimes with copper plates directly under the body. The grave goods are also more fantastically lavish than anything found in Adena burials (see Figure 2.4a, 2.4b and 2.4c). For example, two of the hundreds of burials at the Hopewell site (for which the complex is named) were a young adult male and an adult woman accompanied by foot-long copper rods, copper bracelets, fifty copper earspools, a necklace of grizzly bear canines inlaid with pearls, several large copper plates, scores of copper-covered clay, wood, and stone buttons, artificial copper noses, and hundreds of freshwater pearl beads. Hopewell mounds also hold elaborate artwork crafted from stone, copper, ceramic, shell, bone, and teeth. Other distinctive Hopewell artifacts include stone and copper celts (axes), blades made from Flint Ridge flint, and platform pipes made to resemble various animals. The small amounts of nicotine resin, tobacco seeds, and maize (corn) sometimes ceremonially interred with the dead suggests that these were sacred plants in Hopewell custom. That only some of the burials were favored with such sumptuous offerings indicates that some individuals held more status than others.

Of all the many extraordinary features of the Hopewell Complex, though, none is grander or more elaborate than the enormous earthworks. Adena people built impressive mounds and enclosures but the massive mound complexes and geometrical earthworks of the Hopewell are on a much larger scale. For example, the Mound City group in Ross County boasts twenty-three mounds in a fifteen-acre enclosure. The Hopewell Mound group (for which the complex was named) contained 38 mounds in an enclosure covering 110 acres. Seip Mound (also in Ross County) at 250 feet long and 100 feet across contained more than 100 burials, and sat in the middle of a set of conjoined earthworks—a large irregular circle flanked by a regular circle and a square—enclosing more than 120 acres. As impressive as these and the many other Hopewell-era earthworks found throughout the eastern United States may be, none rival the Newark Earthworks in Licking County (see

(a)

(b)

(c)

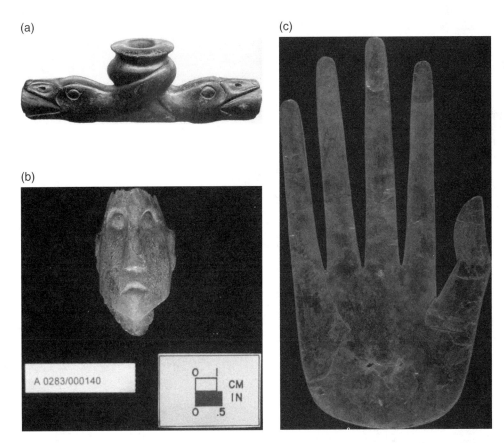

A 0283/000140

0
CM
IN
0   .5

Figure 2.4a, b, c These artifacts from Hopewell mounds demonstrate not only the tremendous variety that the Hopewell craftsman produced but also the wide geographic extent of the Hopewell interaction sphere. Effigy pipes representing dozens of different kinds of animals (like this two-headed snake) have been found in Ohio mounds and are made out of pipestone that originated as far away as northern Illinois and Minnesota. The iconic hand cut from a large sheet of mica from North Carolina shows the delicacy and elegance of Hopewell artists. This carved head not only gives us a rare glimpse into how the Hopewell saw and represented themselves it also boasts a nose made out of copper brought in from the northern Great Lakes.
Source: Courtesy of the Ohio Historical Society (AL00261, AL07210, and AL02821)

Figure 2.5). Sprawling over four square miles, these constructions included giant circles, a square, and a fifty-acre octagon. Paths lined on each side by earthen walls connected different parts of the site, and one enclosed road leading away from the site (known as "The Great Hopewell Road") may have stretched as far as the High Banks works in Chillicothe sixty miles away. Named by noted archeologist Chris Scarre as one of only three North American sites among the top seventy wonders of the ancient world the Newark Earthworks are among the tentative list of sites to be considered for "World Heritage" status by the United Nations as among the most significant cultural treasures on the planet.

As impressive as the Hopewell earthworks were in size, they may be more impressive as an example of the level of Hopewell knowledge. Apart from the massive amounts of

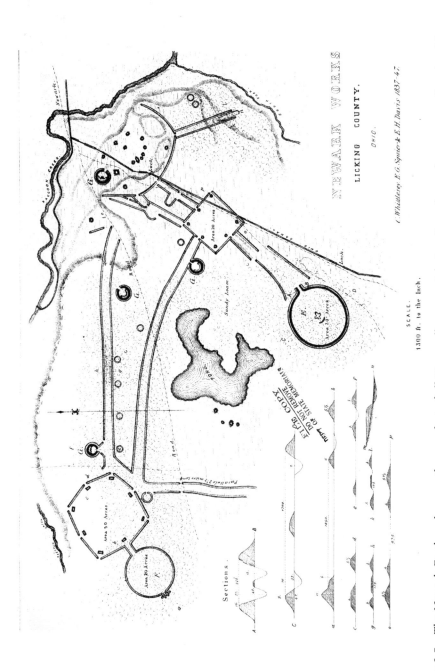

Figure 2.5 The Newark Earthworks were the grandest of all Hopewell ceremonial sites. Spread over four square miles, the elaborate set of large geometric shapes, embankments, and mounds seems to have been a focal point of Hopewell ceremonial life. Recent research indicates that the Octagon may have also been built to align with an 18.6-year cycle of the moon. This map of the Newark site was published by Squire and Davis in the first book published by the Smithsonian Institution in 1848. Unfortunately, the growth of the town of Newark had destroyed nearly all of these structures by the end of the 1800s.

Source: Courtesy of the Ohio Historical Society (AL02754)

labor it took to build them it also took a degree of geometric and astronomical sophistication that has not been recognized until relatively recently. For example, the perimeters of the great circle and the square at the Newark Earthworks are nearly identical, one of only many such similarities found among Hopewell works. Furthermore, not only is the diameter of the Newark Great Circle the same as that of the one at the High Banks works sixty miles away, the two complexes are oriented at exactly ninety degrees to each other. Some of the similarities in size and alignment demonstrate that the Hopewell may have had a common system of measurement and an understanding of some aspects of geometry. The alignments of these and other works also suggest that they possessed significant astronomical prowess as well. In the 1980s Earlham College professors Ray Hively and Robert Horn set out to find whether any alignment with summer or winter solstices of the Octagon at Newark was purely coincidental, and discovered instead that the openings in the octagon at Newark align perfectly with the 18.6-year cycle of maximum and minimum moonrises and moonsets. In the years since investigators have found that other sites have alignments with other astronomical events including solar equinoxes and solstices. Perhaps it should not be surprising that the same people capable of building such enormous earthworks with such precision should have been able to master fundamental astronomical principles, too.

The many magnificent mounds and earthworks of the Ohio Hopewell tradition seem to have lain at the center of what some archaeologists call the "Hopewell Interaction Sphere." Although the Ohio Hopewell were probably the descendents of Adena and Late Archaic peoples of the area, the range of materials the Hopewell people used for their elaborate burials demonstrates that southern Ohio was a major hub of interactions stretching across much of what is now the United States. Using geological and chemical techniques archaeologists have been able to discover that the copper the Hopewell pounded into so many artifacts came from the upper Great Lakes, the mica that they cut into human and animal effigies came from the western Carolinas, and the obsidian (volcanic glass) that they turned into beautiful ceremonial blades and spear points came all the way from the Yellowstone region in the Rocky Mountains. Chalcedony from North Dakota and Manitoba, marine shells from the Florida Atlantic and Gulf coasts, galena from Missouri, quartz from Tennessee, silver from eastern Canada, and even iron from meteorites are among the other exotic materials found in Hopewell mounds. At one time scholars surmised that these materials were received in trade for a commodity produced by the Ohio Hopewell—Flint Ridge flint, perhaps. However, although archaeologists have found bladelets of this kind of flint throughout the Hopewell interaction sphere, the number of these artifacts is a tiny fraction of a huge wealth of exotic materials in Ohio. Thus, although intergroup trade may still have played some role in the transfer of materials, many scholars now believe that nonnative materials also might have come to Ohio either through "extraordinary travels" by Hopewell individuals or as tribute or offerings from pilgrims who came from far away to the see the magnificent earthworks and participate in the ceremonies observed there.

The Hopewell Complex reached its zenith about 1,600 years ago and then went into decline. The influx of exotic materials curtailed dramatically, and mound and earthwork construction slowed down or stopped entirely. Although many unanswered questions about the Ohio Hopewell remain, perhaps the most vexing one since the missionary David Zeisberger first wrote about their works concerns why the Hopewell florescence ended. Theories have abounded for years, but none have been proven conclusively. Nevertheless, recent studies in other fields and with new technologies have provided scholars with new avenues to explore.

For example, paleoclimatologists (scientists who reconstruct ancient climate swings) have discovered that the world started to enter a colder than usual period about 1,600 years ago. Furthermore, studies of tree ring data have shown that the Ohio Hopewell core area underwent a prolonged dry spell at this time. Seventy percent of the years from 396 to 460 were drier than normal, with very dry stretches from 397–98, 405–6, 419–21, 430–31, 435–36, and extremely bad drought years in 398, 420, and 436. Taking these climatic conditions into consideration along with the dramatic population increase during the Hopewell period and the possibility of even more visitors or pilgrims coming to the area for ceremonial reasons, some have suggested that this larger population increasingly taxed the available "home range" territories and may have caused food problems if climatic conditions adversely affected their EAC gardens and traditionally gathered food resources such as hickory nuts. Furthermore, even more severe drought conditions elsewhere on the continent at this time may have pushed populations into migrating, setting off a kind of "domino effect" of moving populations that might have affected the Ohio region at least indirectly.

In conjunction with this evidence, biological anthropologist Lisa Mills's 2003 study of DNA evidence from Late Archaic, Adena, Hopewell, and later Woodland and Mississippian populations showed that although Hopewell DNA is quite similar to that of the populations that preceded it, it is less similar to southern Ohio populations that came afterward. The most closely related known subsequent prehistoric sample to that of the Ohio Hopewell comes not from any site in Ohio but from a burial mound in central Illinois from about 700 years ago. Mills also found that a particularly rare genetic marker found in one of the high-status burials at the Hopewell site also occurred in several elite burials at the Cahokia site in southwestern Illinois several hundred years later. Furthermore, Hopewell DNA shares more similarities with historic tribes farther to the north and west (e.g., Kickapoo and Ojibwa) than that of groups like the Shawnee or Iroquois that occupied Ohio at the cusp of the historic period. Although none of this serves as absolute proof of conflict or displacement, when taken into account with later evidence of conflict in the region, it does suggest that at least some Ohio groups moved or were forced to move at some point after the Hopewell period ended. Whatever their ultimate fate, the legacy that these people left behind marks a period when Ohio became "the heart of it all," long before this became the state slogan.

Late Woodland (c. 1,500–c. 1,100 years ago)

The collapse of the Hopewell Interaction Sphere did not mean the collapse of Ohio Native American populations. On the contrary, by all indications populations increased during the Late Woodland period, although their social organization was different from that of earlier periods. Instead of living in semisedentary small farmsteads or hamlets, Late Woodland people grouped together in larger villages spread more widely across the landscape; and for longer periods of time, from years to decades. These villages, which could be as large as ten acres and could contain more than 100 people, were also increasingly fortified by encircling ditches or stockade walls indicating the need to defend against conflict with other groups. The potential for conflict is borne out by the burials of this time, which show more injuries from flint weapons than those of previous periods.

Although Late Woodland Ohio groups were more sedentary than ever and in general relied more heavily on agriculture, there was still significant variation in their lifeways depending on local conditions. In the southern part of the state villagers cleared much larger areas of land and cultivated larger fields than had their Hopewell predecessors. The EAC crops continued to be very important but as the period wore on increasing quantities of squash and maize appeared. On the other hand, the diet of people around Lake Erie continued to rely more heavily on foraging and fishing. In all areas, though, hunting was still very important, and became particularly intensive. As larger numbers of people were settled in a single place for long periods, Late Woodland hunters had to range further for game. They occupied caves and rock shelters more frequently than any previous cultures—probably as temporary winter hunting camps. Their intensive hunting efforts seem to have stressed the populations of their prey—studies of deer bones have shown that these animals were getting smaller as hunters removed generation after generation of larger and older specimens.

One reason for improved hunting success (as well as more deadly human conflict) was the introduction of a new weapon technology—the bow and arrow. Before about 1,200 years ago all of those points that most people call "arrowheads" were actually tips for spears or throwing darts. True arrowheads made their appearance by the middle of the Late Woodland proving to be a much more efficient hunting tool. Although arrows do not strike with as much force as atlatl-assisted spears, they fly much faster and can be launched in much quicker succession making them more advantageous against swifter prey. Although Adena and Hopewell people would seek out high-quality flint to craft both utilitarian and ceremonial points, Late Woodland hunters seem to have knapped these arrowheads quickly using whatever materials were at hand; and they almost completely ceased making ceremonial points.

In fact, the Late Woodland people curtailed most forms of ceremony that were characteristic of the Hopewell period. Although they sometimes built modest mounds, they built no more geometric earthworks or huge burial mounds. Some exotic items continued to appear in a few burials but the abundant ceremonial use of such materials ceased. The predominance of increasingly inward-centered, fortified villages probably precluded the massive gatherings for ceremonial purposes that made the Hopewell earthworks possible. This is not to say that mortuary ceremonialism disappeared, but it persisted on a much smaller scale and in increasingly diverse forms. Most villages had their own modest cemeteries near the village. Some groups buried their dead under stone-capped mounds, some in stone-lined graves, and some in the tops of preexisting Hopewell and Adena mounds. Some even buried their dead in refuse middens, perhaps the only logical place in winter when frozen ground elsewhere was too hard to dig. This diversification of burial customs is emblematic of an increasing cultural differentiation that becomes even more pronounced in the Late Prehistoric period.

Late Prehistoric Period (c. 1,100–c. 400 years ago)

Archaeologists used to call this period of Ohio prehistory the "Mississippian period," thinking that the seemingly sudden and significant changes that occurred meant Ohio represented an eastward extension of the powerful new cultural complex rising in the Mississippi Valley at this time. Subsequent investigations have shown that although some Ohio populations absorbed Mississippian cultural ideas to a greater or lesser extent, what was going on in the upper Ohio Valley was largely distinct from the cultural complex centered on the site of Cahokia in what is now southwest Illinois. As a result, most archaeologists now generally refer to this period in Ohio prehistory as the Late Prehistoric. Although no longer thought to be the result of Mississippian "invasion" the changes represented by this period were no less real or significant.

Even so, an "invasion" of sorts is not out of the question. The DNA analyses mentioned earlier and anatomical studies of the bones of a number of different burials seem to indicate that at least some Ohio populations were not a direct part of the Late Archaic/Adena/Hopewell continuum. Movement of new people into the area was only one of the major changes happening at this time. Villages became even larger, more fortified, and more socially stratified. Diversification among different populations increased, and ceremonialism made a resurgence. Probably no change was more significant than the reorientation of subsistence away from the EAC and toward a firm embrace of maize.

Maize had been present in Ohio at least since Hopewell times for ceremonial purposes, but the crop had never become a major part of the diet. Archaeologists still do not know the reasons for this. Some have suggested that because it was first domesticated as a semi-tropical plant in the Oaxaca region of Mexico, maize probably took some time to adapt into a reliable crop in more temperate climates (Figure 2.6 shows the development of maize over time). Whatever the reasons for the delay, though, when intensive maize cultivation began in the Late Prehistoric—probably as one of the Mississippian influences that first appeared in the southwestern part of the state—it spread across the state over the next two centuries and unseated the EAC to become the staple part of the diet. There are many reasons why maize became so important. Along with beans and squash it is one of the "three sisters" that form complete proteins in the diet and mutually replenish the soil for each other. Maize is easier to process than the seeds of the EAC, and it stores extremely well. Perhaps most significantly, it provides more calories per acre than any of the EAC plants, which was a crucial factor for the ever-increasing populations of the Late Prehistoric period. With all of these advantages, maize replaced most other previous crops, and came to compose up to 75 percent of the diet of some Late Prehistoric populations.

This proved to be a mixed blessing. Although maize could feed many more people with less relatively less effort, it did not have as much nutrition as the EAC, and as a result

Figure 2.6 Genetics research has shown that the maize (corn) that we eat today started out as a kind of grass called teosinte (left) in Central America more than 7,000 years ago. Although it was present in Ohio by Hopewell times it did not begin to replace the Eastern Agricultural Complex of seed plants until the Late Prehistoric period. The genetically "reconstructed" cob of that era (right) had much larger kernels than its predecessor but is still much smaller than the kind of maize commonly grown today.
Source: Photo by John Doebley, http://teosinte.wisc.edu

people in the Late Prehistoric period were more malnourished than their ancestors. Furthermore, the sugars in maize, along with the grit left in the meal from grinding it with stones, created more wear and cavities in the teeth of its consumers. Additionally, with such a large population so dependent on a single crop, when inevitable crop failures occurred due to droughts, late frosts, or flooding, the chances of widespread malnutrition or starvation increased. Thus, although populations steadily increased during the Late Prehistoric scientific studies of bones from this period show that people in general were shorter, less healthy, had more severe dental problems, suffered higher rates of childhood mortality, and had shorter life spans than previous populations.

Poorer health was not the only thing that Late Prehistoric people in Ohio had in common. The toolkit of this period was more similar from place to place, with simple, often triangular, chipped flint points and knives, hoes made out of shells, and a well-developed bone industry. Fishhooks, awls, needles, pins, beads, beamers (used to scrape hides), picks, and shovels were among the many tools crafted from bones, and hunters fashioned arrowheads out of antler tips. Distinctive artifacts from this period also include "discoidals"—discs fashioned from stone that may have been used for a popular game— and sandstone spools, which were possibly part of the textile-making toolkit. Some exotic materials began to make their way into the Late Prehistoric craft industry via long-distance trade networks as the period wore on, but not approaching the level that had existed in the Middle Woodland.

Despite the similarities in some aspects of Late Prehistoric daily life, the main trend dur- ing this period was toward increasing cultural diversity. Although the Fort Ancient Complex (unfortunately named after a site that was actually built during Hopewell times) has come to represent Ohio's Late Prehistoric period in many books and popular accounts, it was only one of at least five distinct cultural traditions represented in Ohio at that time. In the northwest part of the state, the Western Basin Tradition (a southern extension of an Ontario Iroquoian cultural group that occupied the western shores of Lake Erie) had been present since the Late Woodland. This group appears to have left about 600 years ago, following the spread of groups from a different, "Sandusky tradition" into the area. In the northeast part of the state, the Whittlesey people built impressively-fortified villages on raised bluffs overlooking river valleys, and they seemed to have been influenced by cultural develop- ments to the east. In the east and southeast part of the state, villages of the Monongahela Woodland Complex predominate, part of a larger tradition that occupied parts of western Pennsylvania and West Virginia. Even the Fort Ancient-dominated central and southern parts of the state display considerable diversity with subgroupings like the Anderson, Baum, and Feurt Phases showing differences in village layout, architecture, and pottery, and inter- spersed Madisonville-type settlements that seemed to reflect different cultural influences from the south. Contrary to some historical accounts, the Late Prehistoric period marked a high point in the population and cultural diversity of Ohio Native American peoples.

The bewildering array of cultural traditions and influences present in Ohio at this time also manifested itself in the types of ceremonialism expressed throughout the land. Southwestern Ohio saw a renewal in astronomical ceremonialism, with the Sunwatch Site in Montgomery County, for example, boasting a Mississippian-influenced "calendar post" of cedar in the middle of the village that cast its shadow on the hearth of the "big house" at the time of the equinox. Burial ceremonialism took on a number of different forms, from simple interments in pits, to slab-covered graves in town sites, to new mounds of earth or earth and stone, again often built near or in the villages themselves. The most extravagant expression of Late Prehistoric ceremonialism, though, was the construction of effigy mounds. Once attributed to Early or Middle Woodland groups, the "Alligator" and "Serpent" Mounds in southern Ohio, as shown in Figure 2.7, are a unique pair in Ohio's rich earth- work heritage in that they are representations of animals rather than just mounds or geometrical designs. Although the cultural significance of these works to the people that built them remains unknown, they obviously must have been quite meaningful and reflect the ability of some groups to mobilize large amounts of labor for ceremonial purposes.

The concentration of larger numbers of people and the ability to coordinate them to a common purpose represents another hallmark of the Late Prehistoric. Villages of this period were larger than ever—sometimes containing hundreds of people—and were increasingly heavily fortified with ramparts and/or palisade walls of posts, probably interlaced with

Figure 2.7 Perhaps the most famous effigy earthwork in the world, Serpent Mound near Peebles, Ohio is almost 1,350 feet long. Experts long thought it to be a relic of the Adena Complex, but recent research seems to indicate rather that it was built during the Late Prehistoric period. Archaeologists still debate the figure's meaning and significance.
Source: Aerial view of Serpent Mound State Memorial, Ohio. © Tom Till/SuperStock/Corbis

branches and sticks. Based on differences in house sizes and positions in these villages, as well as relative differentials in health and grave goods of high status individuals, it seems that some social inequality was also evident at this time. Leaders probably determined where a group was to move and settle, coordinated defenses, or led raids on other groups. The potential of conflict must have been very real among these larger and more diverse Ohio populations, as the heavily-fortified villages and numerous burials showing signs of violence. Long before the interactions of Europeans and Native American groups that characterized Ohio's early historical period, Ohio was a highly contested space.

For all the many different and complex changes represented in the artifacts of the Late Prehistoric period, portents of greater changes still appear in the relatively humble glass beads and scraps of copper and brass that crop up in the terminal phases of Late Prehistoric sites. These European-made trade goods, probably received third- or fourth-hand through the long-distance trade networks that stretched across the continent, mark the beginning of the end of Ohio as any of its natives knew it at the time. Over the next couple of hundred years, prehistoric Ohio would become historic Ohio, and the descendents of the first Ohioans would be anywhere but Ohio. Although archaeologists and anthropologists surmise that the Sandusky culture became part of the Kickapoo and Mascouten tradition, and that some of the Fort Ancient groups may have become part of the group known today as the Shawnee, scientists and archaeologists still do not know the ultimate fate of the complex set of peoples that made up Ohio prehistory. With the advent of DNA analysis and other new archaeological techniques, maybe some of these questions will be answered in the future. For now they remain, like so many other aspects of life in Ohio before written records, frustratingly out of reach.

For all the complexity and confusion evident in the prehistoric era, what scholars do know about it is instructive. Indeed, the confusion and complexity itself may be one of the most valuable object lessons derived from Ohio's prehistory. All too often the prehistoric period of Ohio—when historians address it at all—is presented in oversimplified fashion, with requisite mentions of Adena and Hopewell as phases of the now extinct "Ohio Indians." Some books all but dismiss these people entirely, saying that these people "sparsely populated" the area and "left the land unchanged." The picture of prehistoric Ohio that has developed over the past few decades of archaeological and anthropological research is much more textured and nuanced, revealing a dynamic and sometimes violent interaction of numerous cultures that became the first clearers of the land, tillers of the soil, exploiters of the resources, and architects of the landscape of what became Ohio. Knowing the events of the prehistoric period is crucial to understanding those of the early historic period. Although now dispersed in time and space, the First Ohioans left an indelible imprint on Ohio's history and Ohio itself.

Further Reading

Bradley Lepper's *Ohio Archaeology: An Illustrated Chronicle of Ohio's Ancient American Indian Culture* is an excellent survey of American Indian culture (2005. Wilmington, OH: Orange Frazer Press). Olaf Prufer, Sara Pedde, and Richard Meindl's edited volume *Archaic Transitions in Ohio and Kentucky Prehistory* studies the Archaic-Woodland transition (2002. Kent: Kent State University Press), while Darlene Applegate and Robert Mainfort Jr., eds., *Woodland Period Systematics in the Middle Ohio* Valley (eds. 2005. Tuscaloosa: University of Alabama Press), provides a comprehensive collection of articles on the Woodland period. William Dancey and Paul Pacheco, *Ohio Hopewell: Community Organization*, synthesizes studies of Ohio Hopewell society(eds. 1997. Kent: Kent State University Press). Robert Cook's *SunWatch: Fort Ancient Development in the Mississippian World* uses a site in southwest Ohio to examine culture and society during the Late Prehistoric period (2007, Tuscaloosa: University of Alabama Press).

3

The Middle Ground

European and Native American Interaction in Ohio

On May 4, 1789, King Louis XVI of France appeared in public with Queen Marie Antoinette to take part in the procession to Versailles for the first meeting of the Estates General (France's traditional legislative body) in 175 years. There was no way he could have known it at the time, but this day started a chain of events culminating in the loss of his head, which on this spring day sported a fine beaver hat with white plumes and a diamond pin. Although this was a momentous event in European history, the circumstances that brought Louis to his unfortunate end stretched far beyond Paris, even to Ohio. King Louis had called this meeting of the Estates General because his government had run out of money. This was in large part a result of the debts amassed supporting the American Revolution. France's participation in that war—some of the most violent fighting of which took place on the Ohio frontier—was partially motivated by its humiliating defeat at the hands of the British twenty years earlier in the Seven Year's War. France's loss in this conflict resulted largely from the defection of some of its long-time Indian allies because of changing trade and social relationships and the issue of land claims in the Ohio region. The Seven Years' War itself, though, was only the last of a series of colonial wars waged over the previous seventy years. During this time the French and British struggled for imperial mastery over the North American continent while its native peoples sought to protect their own interests through judicious use of their support or neutrality. The fault lines of this bloody struggle ran through the Ohio Valley and had begun decades earlier among the Native people surrounding Lake Erie, well before the first Europeans had set foot in the area. These brutal Indian conflicts of the 1640s and 1650s—which fundamentally changed thousands of years of Ohio population and settlement trends—were largely the result of European demand for beaver skins that Native Americans sought throughout the Great Lakes region, including the prime hunting grounds of Ohio. It seems that

Ohio: A History of the Buckeye State, First Edition. Kevin F. Kern and Gregory S. Wilson.
© 2014 John Wiley & Sons, Inc. Published 2014 by John Wiley & Sons, Inc.

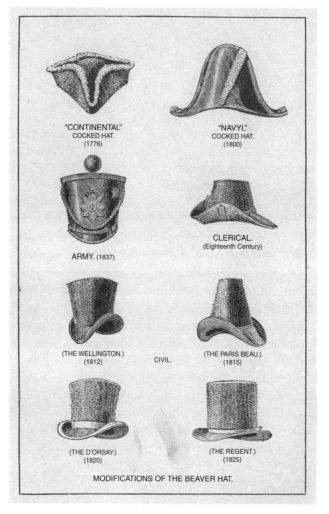

"CONTINENTAL"
COCKED HAT.
(1776)

"NAVYL"
COCKED HAT.
(1800)

ARMY. (1837)

CLERICAL.
(Eighteenth Century)

(THE WELLINGTON.)
(1812)

CIVIL.

(THE PARIS BEAU.)
(1815)

(THE D'ORSAY.)
(1820)

(THE REGENT.)
(1825)

MODIFICATIONS OF THE BEAVER HAT.

Figure 3.1   Beaver fur was a highly-prized commodity in Europe from the 1600s to the early 1800s. Although sometimes used for coats and fur trimmings it became the preferred material for hat making because it was easy to form into a number of different shapes. The resulting hats were sturdy and easy to maintain.

Source: "Modifications of the Beaver Hat," Freshwater and Marine Image Bank, University of Washington Libraries

fashionable gentlemen in England and France, including the nobility, increasingly wanted beaver hats to wear when they appeared in public (see Figure 3.1).

This particular web of connections—one of many—illustrates several important concepts for the understanding of Ohio history. First, Ohio has been involved in the world system of politics and economics since at least the mid-1600s. Although its role was at times peripheral or tangential, the area, its people, and its resources increasingly came to be integrated into this system and sometimes played a key role in the events that shaped it. Second, Ohio during the 1600s and 1700s was what historian Richard White has called "The Middle Ground": a place not only physically in the middle of imperial conflict, but also where social and cultural ideas met and influenced each other. Neither Native Americans nor Europeans could dictate conditions to the other here, and thus both groups fell into a mutually-changing set of relationships in which each one adopted ideas from the other in an attempt to seek the best advantage. Third, the arrival of Europeans on the North American continent began a series of events that culminated in an unprecedented and catastrophic reorganization of Native American life in what is now Ohio. For better or worse, Ohio would become significantly intertwined in the world system, and this would have dramatic effects on all parties concerned.

Early Effects of European Contact

From the late 1400s on, Spain, France, and England would all eventually make claims on what is now Ohio, but only France and England would ever have a significant presence in the area. European countries at this time were expanding overseas and setting up colonies for political and economic reasons. The French crown had dispatched mariners like Giovanni de Verrazano and Jacques Cartier in the early 1500s to explore the eastern coast of North America, finally setting up its first permanent colony in Quebec in 1608. This became the nucleus of what would become a French colonial empire stretching like a crescent from eastern Canada through the Great Lakes and down the Mississippi to the Gulf of Mexico. Meant to rival the English and Spanish presence in North America, "New France" was primarily a trading empire built on the sale of furs rather than on large French settlements.

England's King Henry VII sent John Cabot to explore and claim the North American coast earlier than France did (1497) but the country was unable to establish permanent colonies on the east coast until the early 1600s. England's *First Charter of Virginia* gave it claim to lands westward to the Pacific Coast, and other British colonial charters also made claims on western territories. British colonies were more settlement-oriented than those in New France, but with most of British North America's settlements hugging the Atlantic coast and oriented toward trading locally produced commodities with Europe, colonial expansion west into the interior lagged well behind colonial land claims.

Nevertheless, France and England soon came into conflict over western lands and control of the fur trade. Some of this conflict was a continuation of long-standing antipathies between the two nations, which had been at war with each other on and off for hundreds of years. Their colonial rivalry in North America took on a life of its own, however, incorporating as it did the long-standing rivalries and trade relationships among the many Native American groups that also claimed the disputed lands. Although what was essentially an invasion of North America by competing groups of Europeans at first only affected regions near the east coast and the Saint Lawrence River, it soon grew to encompass areas hundreds of miles inland.

Ohio's native peoples felt the presence of Europeans long before they first saw them. The European trade items found in Late Prehistoric archaeological sites are only the most tangible and benign testimony to the far-reaching impact the presence of Europeans in North America had on Ohio natives of the 1600s. The most dramatic of these changes at first were biological and political. Either one of these factors by itself would have put Ohio Native groups under some duress, but the combination of the two brought what is likely the most devastating period ever suffered by residents of the area.

Accompanying the glass beads and metal utensils making their way from across the Atlantic into the interior of the continent during the Late Prehistoric period were viruses and bacteria that caused epidemic diseases. Native Ohioans were unusually susceptible to these germs for a couple of reasons. First, they belonged to an ancestral population that had come to North America before most of these diseases had become endemic in the populations that they left behind. Scientists attribute the rise of epidemic disease to a combination of animal domestication and urbanization that combined to build up a critical mass of pathogens and people in the same place—a process that began five to seven thousand years ago in Africa, Europe, and Asia. For the next several thousand years, the people on those continents suffered numerous epidemic diseases and began building resistance to them. Meanwhile the North American populations, separated from these diseases by the Atlantic and Pacific oceans, were remarkably free from the majority of them. Thus, when the Europeans introduced these diseases to Native Americans in the 1500s and 1600s they represented what scientists call a "virgin soil population" (a group with no previous exposure).

Furthermore, as discussed in chapter 2, most Ohio Native populations had been suffering from the health-weakening effects of hundreds of years of maize monoculture. The nutritional deficiencies that had already shortened lifespan, raised infant mortality rates, and affected other health aspects that left these people even more prone to infection than an otherwise healthy population. As virgin-soil epidemics usually kill off 30–40 percent of affected populations, the compound effect of several different virgin-soil diseases appearing in succession plus the lowered resistance caused by nutritional issues brought about untold destruction of Native Ohioan populations. Although the exact scale of this biological cataclysm will never be known, based on estimates of other areas for which records are available and epidemiological studies, it is possible that it reduced the populations of Ohio and surrounding areas by more than 80 percent over the course of just a few generations. Compounding this tragedy was the loss of culture continuity, leadership, and traditional knowledge that further destabilized Ohio's Native cultures and left their people more prone to cultural, political, and social disruption.

As destructive as these biological challenges would have been by themselves, they were worsened by the political events that accompanied them. Since Late Woodland times, the Ohio area experienced a trend toward larger and more heavily fortified villages, suggesting intensified intergroup conflict among populations in the area. Farther to the east, there is clear evidence that by the Late Prehistoric period people had begun to form larger alliances and confederations. The most famous of these is the Iroquois Confederacy, a powerful alliance of Iroquois-language-group villages of the Mohawk, Oneida, Onondaga, Cayuga, and Seneca nations that formed by the late 1500s. However, the

Iroquois (who called themselves "Haudenosaunee" or "People of the Long House) were just one of several such organizations that occupied the Great Lakes region at this time. The people who the French called Hurons and Petuns (also known as Wendats or Wyandots, whose alliance predated and perhaps inspired the Iroquois Confederacy), the Neutral Nation (which had villages in southern Ontario and Eastern Michigan and may have included descendants of the Western Basin tradition people), and the Eries (which the French called the "Cat Nation" and which occupied the eastern Lake Erie region) were other Iroquois-language-group alliances of villages that formed to the north and west of the Iroquois Confederacy and were often at odds with it. Further to the west were a number of Algonquian-language-speaking groups, including the "Fire Nation," which occupied the western Lake Erie basin and seem to have included the descendants of the Late Prehistoric Sandusky people. Relations between these alliances of villages seem to have been intricate and ever-changing, with conflicts sometimes altering the balance of power and creating new alliances throughout the area.

The introduction of European-manufactured iron and steel weapons as well as firearms into this complex political system radically altered it and shifted the balance of power decisively in favor of those groups that had acquired these armaments. More lethal than the stone, wood, and bone weapons that preceded them, these powerful new weapons meant that traditional warfare among Native American groups would inflict untraditionally-high fatality rates on populations already reeling from newly introduced diseases. Although some of the conflicts settled by these arms were doubtless continuations of long-standing grievances among the various groups, at stake was a potent new element that Europeans had introduced: the fur trade. The French, English, and Dutch (who had established a colony in what is now New York in the early 1600s) all offered excellent trading opportunities to any Native group that could bring them pelts, particularly the highly-valued beaver skins. Rivalries over access to these trading partnerships and to prime hunting grounds combined with traditional conflicts and rivalries to explode into a series of devastating conflicts collectively known as "The Beaver Wars." Although broadly encompassing the last seventy years of the seventeenth century, the most intense period of this conflict—from the 1640s to the 1650s—resulted in the almost complete depopulation of Ohio.

The origins of the Beaver Wars stem from the early 1600s, when the new French colony in Quebec decided to ally with the Huron-Petuns for the purpose of expanding the fur trade through their trade connections with western groups. Supplying their new allies with firearms and sometimes fighting by their side against their traditional Iroquois enemies, the French help soon gave the Huron-Petuns the upper hand in this conflict. In response, the Iroquois sought weapons from the Dutch (and later, the British) in New York, and succeeded in shifting the balance of power again by mid-century. The Iroquois finished off significant Huron-Petun resistance by 1649, and then turned on and defeated the Neutrals (whose name derived from their traditional neutrality in the Huron/Iroquois rivalry) by 1651.

Unfortunately, historians have relatively little direct knowledge of how exactly this conflict played out in what is now Ohio. Secondhand accounts related to the French by the Huron-Petuns indicate that the Fire Nation defeated a Neutral-allied group south of Lake

Erie in the 1630s, only to be decisively beaten and driven from the area by the Neutrals in 1641. After defeat at the hands of the Iroquois ten years later, a significant number of Neutrals sought refuge with the Eries who lived south and east of Lake Erie. The latter held out until 1656, when the Iroquois overran the last Erie village and ended its existence as a separate nation in the area (a fragment of these people moved south to become the Westo Indians of South Carolina and Virginia). Those members of the Erie and other defeated groups that the Iroquois did not kill or scatter they adopted into Iroquois villages, further increasing their size and power. With superiority in both numbers and weapons, the Iroquois waged an aggressive war throughout the Ohio Valley and Great Lakes, ranging as far west as Illinois and Wisconsin in a deliberate attempt to clear out all occupation of the upper Ohio Valley and destroy any lingering resistance.

The twin forces of disease and war—both ultimately the result of European contact, but also spread by Native Americans themselves—essentially destroyed the continuity of the human record south of Lake Erie and north of the Ohio River. Ohio, which had been continually occupied for thousands of years, became virtually devoid of human settlement as members of the Iroquois Confederacy—particularly the Seneca—policed the region, maintaining it as a sort of hunting reserve and warpath to their western enemies. The Iroquois remaking of the territory extended to its very name. Although the long-time residents of the area had many names for it, it was the Iroquois designation "O-Y-O" or "O-He-Yo" meaning "Great River," that with some alteration became the common name for the region. Many of Ohio's native refugees fled west and joined with other displaced populations that flooded into the area around western Lake Michigan and southern Lake Superior. There they blended with other displaced peoples to form new villages and tribes that often masked their earlier Ohio affiliations. Although some of their descendants would eventually filter back into Ohio decades later, it often would be in the form of groups and villages of more diverse origins and different names than the ones that had preceded them in the area. Culturally, therefore, the first Ohio as represented by its archaeological and proto-historical record more or less ended in the 1650s.

It just so happened to be at this unprecedented time in Ohio history that the first known European explorers ventured into the area after being dissuaded for years by the Iroquois presence. Starting in 1669 after the French and Iroquois agreed to a peace, several groups of Frenchmen, including parties led by explorers Adrien Joliet and Jean Peré, missionaries Francois Dollier de Casson and Rene de Bréhant de Galinée, and René Robert Cavalier Sieur de La Salle, passed by or through the Ohio region, claiming it for France and noting its relative lack of habitation. This idea that Ohio was nearly "empty" unfortunately led some people in later years to believe that there had been relatively little human activity in Ohio in the prehistoric period.

Ohio as "The Middle Ground"

The new Ohio that arose in the wake of the Beaver Wars was a joint creation of numerous Native and European groups under the complete control of none of them after Iroquois influence began to wane toward the end of the 1600s. It serves as a prime example of what historian Richard White describes as a cultural and political "Middle Ground" in which various groups took cues from other cultures and invented new ways of living and relating to each other. For example, French officials soon realized that they could not impose their own system on the lands they claimed. In fact they found that they could do little at all without active cooperation of Native American groups, and that such cooperation could not be compelled, only cultivated. Adopting traditional Native American cultural mores of gift exchanges and inserting themselves into long recognized tribal hierarchies as a "father" nation, the French found that they could convert their relatively small numbers of soldiers, settlers, traders, trappers, and missionaries to tremendous influence by acting as mediators in disputes among their "children" nations and generously supplying their leaders with gifts and trade opportunities. Many Frenchmen—including independent *coureurs de bois* and officially-licensed *voyageurs* who travelled and lived among Native peoples cultivating and maintaining trade and political relationships—took Native American wives or partners, placing themselves and their *Métis* children squarely in a middle status that was neither wholly Indian or French. For their part, the British also found that they could not force western natives to do their bidding, and worked to insert themselves into existing trade and alliance relationships to gain influence. Both French and English residents living in the Middle Ground adopted or adapted traditional Native American ways of life (e.g., grow crops like maize, wear similar clothes such as buckskins and moccasins), models of warfare, and other conflict resolution techniques. In addition to councils and the calumet or "peace pipe," Native Americans used wampum belts—usually made of beads from shells—to communicate messages and ideas.

The Native Americans who created many of the cultural cues and drove a number of the changes of the Middle Ground were also changed by it in fundamental ways. For example, in one sense the trade for European goods was little different from the long-standing trend of seeking out large quantities of exotic goods that was present in the Adena and Hopewell periods. Although materials like cloth, copper kettles, and knives met utilitarian needs, they also served important cultural and ceremonial purposes among the people who traded for them, entering into previously-existing social exchange patterns and status displays. Europeans like the trader depicted in Figure 3.2 often catered to these needs, for example, by making brass gorgets that came to replace the shell and stone ones that had been in use for thousands of years. Nevertheless, generations of this trade increasingly drew the Native American participants of this trade into a reliance on and then a dependence on these goods— particularly items like guns, powder, and shot. In addition, new items like liquor, which had been unknown before the Europeans came, proved to have a destructive influence on groups that were already weakened by disease and war. In order to obtain these goods, Native peoples gradually changed their traditional ways of subsistence hunting to accommodate these perceived needs, with overhunting for pelts reducing game populations, leading to periods of hunger and exacerbating intergroup conflicts.

The result of these various forces and constant cultural improvisation on the Middle Ground was something that was neither entirely Indian nor European but a new invention that affected Europeans and Native Americans mutually. It had social, cultural, economic, and political correlates that historians are still exploring. It also had dramatic, often violent, effects on the peoples who met on Ohio's Middle Ground.

Figure 3.2 Traders were among the first Europeans to venture into the Ohio country. Native groups greeted them with ambivalence. While they desired the goods the traders offered, they also realized that some did not bargain in good faith. Others had ulterior motives, including George Croghan, who was not only a well-respected trader but also an agent of the British Empire who used his trade relationships to advance imperial aims.
Source: With permission of the Royal Ontario Museum © ROM

Colonial Wars and Life in Middle Ground Ohio

Most U.S. history books that deal with late seventeenth- and early eighteenth-century North America tend to define the era by the colonial wars that corresponded to broader conflicts happening in Europe at the same time. For example, the conflict that British colonists called "King William's War" was a colonial ancillary to the Nine Years War (or War of the League of Augsburg, 1688–97), "Queen Anne's War" was part of the broader War of the Spanish Succession (1701–14) and "King George's War" played out as an off-shoot of the War of the Austrian Succession (1740–48). While it is important to keep in mind that these conflicts were part of a world system of interaction, this traditional kind of categorization can hamper an understanding of the full picture of events in Ohio. First, the naming of these wars after British monarchs is a colloquialism only used by English colonists in North America, who were only one of many parties to these conflicts. Second, and more significantly with regard to Ohio history, even these colonial designations are problematic in reflecting the true nature of conflict and interaction in the Great Lakes region. The official dates assigned to these conflicts often do not correspond to the relative levels of peace and violence evident in the Ohio Valley, nor do they take into account other major developments among various groups that had profound effects on the region. Thus, although it is important to know the greater contexts of these conflicts, a full understanding of events in Ohio during this period must also rely on the idiosyncrasies of the region that in many cases were independent of these larger events.

Resettlement and conflict

Iroquois hegemony over the lands south of the Great Lakes lasted for several decades. The French made peace with the Iroquois in the 1660s while at the same time carefully cultivating individual relationships—through mediation and gifts of highly desired European-made goods—with a growing family of primarily Algonquian-language groups to the west (including Mississaugas, Potawatomis, Ottawas, Kickapoos, Illinois, Miamis, Chippewas, and others). This set of western allies, along with their traditional Huron-Petun friends became, by the late seventeenth century, an impressive coalition that could stand up to Iroquois pressure. Turning back an Iroquois attack on the Illinois in 1684 this new grand alliance went on the offensive starting in 1687. Over the next few years the French staged devastating raids against Iroquois Confederacy members—particularly against the Mohawks in the winter of 1693 and the Onondaga and Oneida the summer of 1696 in which they destroyed both villages and food supplies—effectively checking Iroquois power. These military setbacks, along with hunger and outbreaks of disease that attended them, led the Iroquois to agree to the Peace of Montreal (or "Grand Settlement") in 1701. In it, they agreed to remain neutral in future French/English conflicts and to let New France mediate future conflicts between its allies and the Iroquois. Although the Iroquois would still be a potent force in the region and still claimed nominal authority over the Ohio Country their power over the area diminished and opened the door for Ohio's resettlement. It also brought the Ohio region closer to the center of imperial disputes between England and France.

Having been more or less unoccupied for close to fifty years, the Ohio territory was particularly inviting to those refugees of the Beaver Wars who had often struggled to make their way in the overtaxed lands and crowded villages of the frequently cold and inhospitable upper Great Lakes. Ohio's fields had been fallow, its game had not been overhunted, its climate was more temperate, and it was closer to English traders from the east. Furthermore, a new set of conflicts among Algonquian groups and including the French began to flare up in Michigan and points west starting in 1706 and continued with sporadic intensity for decades, putting those areas to the north and west of Ohio in the path of the violence. Thus, as the upper Great Lakes refugee villages began to disperse in the decades after 1701, a number of groups of people chose to relocate to the relatively more fertile and peaceful Ohio territory. Miami, Kickapoo, Mascouten, and Ottawa villages all moved in from the north and west, and an independent group of Huron-Petuns who became known as Wyandots moved in from the northeast. Joining these in subsequent years were other disaffected groups from other areas, often escaping the encroachments of European settlement. These included splinter groups

Figure 3.3   Contest for control in the Ohio Country, 1741–63.

of Iroquois—perhaps disproportionately made up of adopted captives from the Beaver Wars and their descendants—who began to move in from the northeast and became known as "Mingo," as well as Lenape (Delaware) and Shawnee from the east and even some Cherokee from the south (see Figure 3.3).

The nature of settlement that characterized Ohio after 1701 differed in significant ways from the order of things before the Beaver Wars. Although some groups like the Miami, Kickapoo, and Mascouten may well have returned with organizational structures more or less similar to those that they had before the 1650s, a number of these new settlements in Ohio were villages comprised of Native Americans from numerous tribal affiliations and claiming allegiance to no single external group. This gave these mixed settlements some protection from attack from outside groups because so many villagers had come from those groups originally and could dissuade violence from those with whom they shared a cultural and linguistic connection. Multiethnic, unallied, and with no clear territorial claims, these villages disturbed the French authorities, who referred to them disdainfully as "Indian republics." Two main concentrations of these "republics" had developed by the 1740s and 1750s. One, located in the east from the Cuyahoga River down to the upper Muskingum River, contained elements from all of the Iroquois nations (particularly Seneca and Onandaga) as well as scatterings of other groups including Lenape, Mohican, Ottawa, Abenaki, and Chippewa. These people collectively came to be known as the "White River Indians," after the French name for the Cuyahoga River. Another set of villages located nearer the Ohio River contained a mixture of people of Mingo, Shawnee, Lenape, Miami, Munsee, and several other heritages. Chiningué (Logstown), a few miles downstream from the forks of the Ohio, and Sonnontio, near the mouth of the Scioto River, were the major villages of this grouping, but they were only two of several in the area. More ethnically uniform, but equally independent, was the Wyandot settlement on the Sandusky River led by Angouriot and Orontony (also known as Nicholas). The Wyandot had broken with their Huron-Petun brethren over political issues including French desires to control their actions and movements. This Iroquois-language group was the one that the Iroquois Confederacy officially designated as a kind of viceroy to the region, but it actuality had little more control than any other group in the area, and perhaps less than the Shawnee Confederation to the south that was increasingly active in efforts to broker peace in the region independent of the French.

Although many of these Native American groups came to Ohio in the early eighteenth century to seek a better life, the continuing imperial rivalry between England and France and changing relationships among Indian groups throughout the region increasingly placed these newcomers in the middle of conflicts over trade, allegiance, and lands. Trade with the British was one of the major factors that spurred Native resettlement of the Ohio region. Throughout the early 1700s, a number of Native groups began to express increasing dissatisfaction with the quality, quantity, and price of French trade goods, finding that those offered by the British were superior in most of these respects. The Native Americans of eastern North America had grown increasingly reliant on European goods, particularly cloth and firearms (including powder and shot) for both utilitarian and cultural purposes, just as the French had cut back on supplies of such materials for budgetary and logistical reasons. British traders, on the other hand, actively sought out new trading relationships with western Indian groups from their bases in western New York and Pennsylvania, and some of them had entered Ohio Territory by the 1720s and 1730s. The British were also much more interested than the French in the many deerskins that the Indians brought to trade, providing Native groups with even more trading leverage. The French viewed these developments with alarm, fearing that the lure of British goods might draw increasing numbers of Native groups out of the carefully crafted alliance that had helped maintain French hegemony over the trans-Appalachian region.

These French fears were not unfounded. The independent Indian republics along the Cuyahoga and Ohio rivers served as prime examples of groups leaving the orbit of the French-Algonquian Alliance. In addition, the Wyandot had already broken with the

French when they moved to the Ohio from Detroit, subsequently inviting British traders to set up a trading post in their village on the Sandusky River (near present-day Castalia) as early as 1745. Many other erstwhile French allies made their way to English traders to the east of Ohio, particularly at the British outpost in Oswego, New York. Here British traders offered friendship with British authorities along with their abundant and relatively less expensive trade goods. Some enterprising British traders, the most notable being the redoubtable Scots-Irish agent of Pennsylvania commercial interests George Croghan, risked French wrath by repeatedly going deep into the Ohio Territory to make contact and set up trading relationships with the new Ohio communities. In the process he also endeavored to cultivate pro-British sympathies among his Indian trading partners.

Shifting allegiances within the Native American and British communities themselves also played a role in the escalating conflict of the mid-1700s. Certain Lenape, Shawnee, and Mingo groups had begun to chafe under the Iroquois Confederacy's nominal authority over them and at times stood in open defiance of their traditionally subordinate roles. Other groups alternately supported or opposed Native leaders like Orontony as a function of their own interests. Furthermore, there was in no real sense a unified "British" position regarding Ohio and its residents. British traders—the main contact points of most Ohio Indians—were primarily promoting their own interests and occasionally acted in violation of official British policy. However, even the idea of "British policy" itself is problematical. Although the British imperial government in London did have official strategies and guide-lines regarding relations with the French and Indians in North America, several different and often competing entities vied with each other over access and control of the region. The governments and groups of private citizens in New York, Pennsylvania, and Virginia all had interests in the Ohio area that were often at odds with each other. No better example of this exists than the Ohio Company of Virginia. A private land speculation company chartered by King George II and composed of such influential men as Virginia's Governor Dinwiddie and two of George Washington's brothers, the Virginia Company received a grant of 200,000 acres of the upper Ohio Valley from the crown. This action not only upset France, which claimed the area, but also the colonial governments of Pennsylvania and New York, which had their own claims on the region, as well other influential Virginians who had set up the competing Loyal Company. Naturally, the tens of thousands of Native Americans who were the actual residents of the lands in question were probably the people most distressed by the news. The Ohio Company, the ever-increasing numbers of English settlers, and the 1744 Treaty of Lancaster in which the Iroquois granted lands west of the Appalachians to the British colonists without the consent of the groups that lived there all exemplified a fundamental threat to their homeland in the Ohio Country. The one-time refuge was now being drawn into another set of conflicts.

Anglo-French-Indian wars

All of the competing interests of dozens of British, French, and Native American groups came to a head in a series of conflicts that proved to be decisive in the larger imperial rivalry that had been affecting Ohio for more than a century. Although France joined a powerful alliance with Prussia during the War of the Austrian Succession overseas, its Great Lakes alliance seemed to fall apart as the war progressed. At the start of the colonial offshoot of this war in 1744, the French courted the Ohio Indian republics to join with them, and met with some initial success. Some of the White River republics on the Cuyahoga and some Shawnee in the south pledged to plunder British traders, and some of the Miamis and Wyandots threw their support to the French. Yet the system began to disintegrate almost immediately. As a budgetary move, the French government had begun cutting back on gifts of European goods to their Indian allies and leased out western trade franchises to private traders who raised prices to make a profit. This, combined with a British blockade of Canada, made these highly prized goods more difficult to obtain and much more expensive. That these shortages came at a time when France was asking warriors to risk their lives in a war against England struck many Native groups as unfair and a failure of the French to uphold their end of the alliance. Feeling exploited, several Native leaders warned the French of their discontent with the status quo.

By 1747 this discontent had blossomed into open rebellion in several places. A combination of Wyandot and "White River" Indians from northern Ohio attacked and killed a party of five French traders in their territory, stealing their furs in the process. An informant foiled the Wyandots' subsequent plan to attack Detroit; and either fearing French wrath, wishing to be closer to the British, or both, the Wyandots burned their village on the Sandusky River and moved further east to the mouth of the Cuyahoga. Before they left, though, they had called for aid from Pennsylvania, which after some lobbying by George Croghan they received, officially allying their group with the British. Also in 1747 Memeskia (or "Dragonfly"), who despite being of Piankashaw extraction, rose quickly to become a leader in the large western Miami Confederation in what is now northern Indiana and staged the war's most brazen Native-American attack against French hegemony. He sacked the French Fort Miami in Kekionga (near present-day Fort Wayne) and went with a number of his Miami followers to a new village called Pickawillany on the upper Great Miami River (near present-day Piqua). By 1750 this settlement had grown into a multiethnic, British-aligned settlement of more than 400 families and several British traders. In pursuing this course, Memeskia was not only providing greater independence from the French for the people who chose to live with him, he was also seeking to enhance his personal political prestige and influence in the increasingly turbulent world of Native American intergroup politics of the Great Lakes region. Memeskia's representativeness of the swaying allegiances of Ohio groups extends right down to his very name. The French called him "La Demoiselle," which although a literal translation of "dragonfly," also means "young lady" and seems to have served as a play on words referring to what the French saw as his capriciousness. The traders from Pennsylvania who set up a post at his village referred to him as "Old Briton" due to his steadfast attachment to the British.

The official end of hostilities between England and France on the European continent in 1748 hardly quelled the potential for turmoil in Ohio. In fact, if anything, tensions continued to rise. Instead of relying on their traditional attitude of mediation and gift giving, the French government decided to pursue a policy of asserting their authority over the Native groups around the Great Lakes. Having been of the opinion that they were allies with the French, and not subjects to be commanded, many Native Americans refused to abide by the new French policy, particularly in Ohio. In 1749, intent on gaining control of the Indians to the south, the Governor of New France stationed in Quebec dispatched Captain Pierre-Joseph Céloron de Blainville to the Ohio Country with a force of 200 French and 30 Native allies of various groups. His mission was to force the Wyandot back to Detroit, scatter the large Indian republic at Sonnontio, expel British traders, and plant a series of lead plates at major confluences to mark New France's claims on the Ohio territory (see Figure 3.4). Instead of the show of power it was intended to be, Céloron's expedition instead proved just how tenuous France's claim on Ohio had become. Warned of the mission and encouraged to resist by the British in New York, the Ohio Indian groups hugely outnumbered Céloron's band of potential warriors, forcing Céloron to plead for, rather than demand, cooperation and increasingly fear that his expedition would come under attack. In the end, Céloron could not banish the British traders nor keep Ohio Indians from traveling to Pennsylvania or New York to trade with the British. As if to prove the point, the Wyandot under Orontony soon moved to the new village of Conchake on the Muskingum River (near present-day Coshocton), where they would be both farther from the French (who built Fort Sandoské near their old village on the Sandusky) and nearer to the British. Subsequent missions under Sieur Chabert de Joncaire in 1750 and 1751 to pull the Ohio republican villages closer back into the French domain also failed.

By 1752, both the French and the British authorities had begun to feel that fate of the Ohio republics would be crucial to their imperial control of the continent. A British official called the Ohio villages "the only Body of Indians now upon the Continent whose Friendship or alliance is most worthy of courting or continuing," and speculated that if they fell back under French influence, the Iroquois would follow. Similarly, the governor of New France wrote a memo stating his fear that if Ohio fell to the British, it would eventually cause the French to lose Canada, Louisiana, and their holdings in the Caribbean. Feeling that a show of force was necessary to bring the Ohio groups in line, the governor of New France ordered Céloron, now commanding the post at Detroit, to organize the Detroit Indians to attack Memeskia (who had become the primary voice of resistance in Ohio with the death of Orontony in 1750). Although Céloron was unable to convince enough allies to form a major expedition, a small group led by Marie François Picote, Sieur de Bellestre, ventured to Pickawillany, capturing two British traders and killing two villagers. This resulted in reprisals from Memeskia and his allies, who killed several French people throughout the region before a smallpox epidemic ravaged the Great Lakes and weakened resistance. Seizing this opportunity, a force of 250 Ottawa and Chippewa warriors under Charles Langlade, a *Métis* fur-trader and nephew of an Ottawa war chief, descended on Pickawillany in June 1752. In the brief fight and siege that ensued, they forced the surrender of the village and its resident traders. After killing a wounded trader and eating his heart, Langlade and company killed, boiled, and ate Memeskia as the villagers looked on, and took their British prisoners up to Detroit. The remaining villagers professed their allegiance to the French, who told them to move back to the banks of the Maumee. They soon abandoned Pickawillany and returned to what is now Indiana.

(a)

(b)

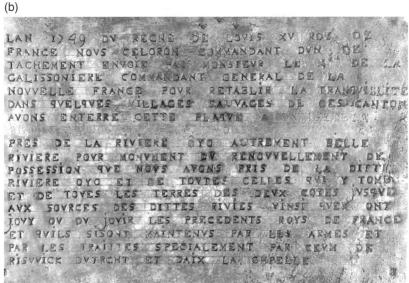

Figure 3.4 Captain Pierre-Joseph Céloron de Blainville had the unenviable task of bringing the independent-minded "republics" of Native Americans in the Ohio Country back firmly into the French sphere of influence alongside asserting French claims to the land in the face of British encroachment. The fact that Native groups there increasingly resisted his demands and that he could only reinforce French claims by burying inscribed lead plates (including the one below) at the mouths of rivers demonstrates how weak French hold on the territory had become.

Source: Courtesy of the Ohio Historical Society (AL04622 and AL04493)

The attack on Pickawillany signaled a change in dynamics in the Ohio Country. The French show of force combined with the failure of the Iroquois or the British colonial governments to aid the Ohio republics when they called for help afterward effectively ended Native Ohioan resistance to the French. The Ohio Indians generally returned to the French orbit and the French came to the conclusion that a show of force would help secure the area. New France Governor Ange de Menneville, Marquis de Duquesne, sent an army under Pierre-Paul de la Malgue de Marin to make a permanent French presence on the upper Ohio River in 1753. Although Marin died en route, his party met no resistance and founded posts at the major eastern portages between Lake Erie and the Ohio River: Presque Isle and Fort Le Boeuf. The following year, an expedition under Claude-Pierre Pecaudy de Contrecoeur established Fort Machault at Venango and Fort Duquesne at the forks of the Ohio, effectively making a cordon of French forts to protect the Ohio Territory.

At the same time, the British colonists were insisting that the Treaty of Lancaster nego-tiated with the Iroquois in 1744 gave them claim to the Ohio Valley. At a council held at Chiningué (Logstown) in the fall of 1753, the Virginians asserted these claims through their representatives—including the Ohio Company of Virginia's official explorer and mapper Christopher Gist, and a twenty-one-year-old George Washington who was a major in the Virginia colonial militia. Washington and Gist proceeded up to Fort Le Boeuf with a letter from Governor Dinwiddie demanding that the French leave the area, a demand that the French firmly repudiated. Washington returned in early 1754 at the head of a military expedition to claim the forks of the Ohio. The Ohio Country, which only fifty years earlier had become a refuge from conflict, was now squarely in the middle of a new one, one that would dramatically alter the political dynamics of North America.

The End of French North America

The ensuing imperial conflict (called by several names, including the Seven Years' War and the French and Indian War) differed from the ones that preceded it in both its course and its outcome. However, in Ohio it manifested itself as a continuation of a struggle that had been in progress for years. While some historians have argued that the attack on Pickawillany was actually the first battle of the French and Indian War, for the residents of Ohio the larger war was more of a parallel conflict through which the Ohio republics continued to pursue a path toward independence from France, England, and the Iroquois. Several Native groups attempted to remain neutral with varying degrees of success. Other Ohio groups did align themselves with the French but it was an attachment of expediency rather than devotion. In both word and action the British colonists (with the complicity of the Iroquois) seemed more intent on physically taking parts of the Ohio territory and mistreating Indian prisoners, which made them a more immediate threat. Thus, the war was actually more of a multi-sided affair in the Ohio Country, a war for Ohio Native independence in the midst of a larger imperial conflict.

The first major direct clash between France and England in what would eventually become a world war happened near the forks of the Ohio River. Virginia's governor had dispatched George Washington with a force of nearly 400 Virginia militiamen and South Carolina regulars to man a fort that a previous party was supposed to have built at the strategic location. Finding that the French had driven off the earlier expedition and built Fort Duquesne there instead, Washington built a stockade called Fort Necessity in a meadow to the southeast. In the process, Washington's command skirmished with a French party sent to warn them off, killing its leader, Joseph Coulon de Villiers de Jumonville, as a spy. His brother, Louis Coulon de Villiers, commanded Fort Duquesne and responded by leading a large expedition that forced George Washington to sign a humiliating surrender at Fort Necessity on July 4, 1754.

This setback made Great Britain take notice, and in 1755 it escalated the conflict by planning multiple attacks in North America and sending Major General Edward Braddock as commander-in-chief of all British forces in North America. He personally led a force of 2,400 men—including Washington, who volunteered as an aide—to take Fort Duquesne. The campaign was a disaster. Braddock spurned help offered by several groups of Lenapes, Shawnees, and Mingos, contemptuously assuring them that "no savage should inherit the land." This turned whatever positive sentiment that might have remained among these groups against the British, as well as lost them the chance to have experienced warriors, scouts, guides in the Ohio wilderness. They could have used them. On July 9, almost exactly a year after Washington's defeat nearby, French and Indian forces surprised Braddock's advanced force, causing them to fall back on the rear guard. Adding to the confusion, most of the officers were killed or disabled and the battle turned into a rout. The British suffered 900 casualties out of 1,400 engaged, including Braddock himself, who was buried in the road during the retreat (see Figure 3.5).

The defeats of the British in the Ohio region convinced many Ohio Native groups that the French were the militarily superior power, and many—particularly parties of Shawnee and Delaware—joined in raids against British colonial settlements in Pennsylvania. Shingas, a Western Lenape military leader whose aid Braddock had refused, became one of the most feared figures on the Pennsylvania and Virginia Middle Ground, and repeated military expeditions against him and his warriors proved ineffective. Western residents of these colonies increasingly demanded that their governments do something to quell the violence, as did General John Forbes, who was to lead the next British campaign against Fort Duquesne and wanted to fight only the French. Many Native leaders, including Shingas's brother Tamaqua, also desired peace. The war had also been difficult for many Native groups and the British blockade of French North America had resulted in a situation in which Ohio Indians could not get trade items from the French but were forbidden to trade with the British. In 1758 colonial authorities negotiated the Iroquois-brokered Treaty of Easton with Lenape diplomats, sending Moravian missionary Christian Frederick Post as their representative to seek Lenape neutrality. In exchange, they promised not to build any new forts in the Ohio Country and that colonists would drop all claims to the upper Ohio region. Post and the diplomats were able to get Lenape and other military leaders of other groups to agree, although one Lenape diplomat warned the British that if they did try to settle in the Ohio lands, "all the nations would be against them; and ... it would be a great war and never come to a peace again." These words would prove to be prophetic.

Figure 3.5   "No savage should inherit the land," General Braddock asserted to Native American leaders when they offered military help against the French in exchange for being able to continue to live in the Ohio Country. Braddock's lack of understanding of Middle Ground dynamics drove Ohio groups back into the arms of the French and ultimately contributed to his disastrous defeat and death at the Battle of Monongahela on July 9, 1755.
Source: Library of Congress Prints and Photographs Division (LC-USZ62-51691)

Without the crucial support of the Upper Ohio Native groups, the situation of the outnumbered and undersupplied French forces in the area became untenable and they abandoned their posts in the region. The French at the same time began to lose many of their Middle Ground Native allies through a paucity of trade goods and an increasingly authoritarian attitude that seemed to reduce Indian groups from allies to mere soldiers under their direct command. As the residents of the Middle Ground sought neither British nor French domination, many began to fall away from the French and a few actually began to attack French soldiers. Without the strong backing of their Native allies the French became a paper tiger. Abandoning Fort Duquesne, they soon lost Fort Niagara, causing them to abandon Forts Machault and Presque Isle. The British decisively defeated a major French army at Quebec in 1759, and the French governor surrendered the colony at Montreal the following year. Although the European phase of the war would continue until 1763, the military threat of the French empire in North America had been essentially extinguished by 1760.

Thinking that they had finally won a modicum of independence for themselves, the Ohio republics grew alarmed at their treatment by the British once the French were no longer a threat. Repeating the mistakes the French had made during the late stages of the war, the British under General Jeffrey Amherst (shown in Figure 3.6) believed that they

Figure 3.6 General Jeffrey Amherst was another British general who refused to acknowledge the compromises that were fundamental to Middle Ground politics. His disdainful and imperious treatment of Native American groups contributed to the Resistance of 1763, during which he infamously made the first recorded attempt of biological warfare in North America by giving smallpox-infested blankets to Indians at Fort Pitt.
Source: Library of Congress Prints and Photographs Division (LC-USZ62-45182)

could treat the Indians as conquered subjects. Amherst did not believe in the Middle Ground tradition of giving presents to build relationships, believing that it only encouraged laziness among a group of people he already thought to be savages. Instead, he directed that all exchanges of goods should be done through regulated trade. Already upset by this sudden change, Indians became even more galled by his seemingly contradictory policy of specifically restricting the amount of powder and shot sold to Indians. Unable to get European goods without furs to trade, yet unable to get the shot and powder with which to get the furs, Native groups were caught in a double bind. These and other policies that Ohio natives viewed as arbitrary and humiliating left some wishing for the return of the French, and they continued to hold out hopes that the peace settlement ending the war might bring their old ally back. When it became clear that this would not happen, three years of resentment over British policies would boil over into a violent attempt by Natives on the Great Lakes to seize back the Middle Ground.

Further Reading

The standard text for this period is Richard White's *The Middle Ground: Indians, Empires, and Republics in the Great Lakes Region 1650–1815* (1991. Cambridge: Cambridge University Press). A general survey of this era can be found in R. Douglas Hurt's *The Ohio Frontier: Crucible of the Old Northwest, 1720–1830* (1998. Bloomington: Indiana University Press), while Michael McConnell's *A Country Between: The Upper Ohio Valley and its Peoples, 1724–1774* is a more targeted study of the middle part of the century (1997. Lincoln: University of Nebraska Press). For a collection of essays dealing with topics during the latter part of this period see *The Boundaries between Us: Natives and Newcomers along the Frontiers of the Old Northwest Territory, 1750–1850* edited by Daniel Barr (2006. Kent: Kent State University Press).

4

War and Peace

The End of "Middle Ground" Ohio

On the morning of March 7, 1782 a group of at least 160 Pennsylvania militiamen under the command of Lieutenant Colonel David Williamson marched up the Tuscarawas River toward Gnadenhutten, a mission settlement of Lenape (Delaware) Indians who had converted to the pacifist Moravian Protestant denomination. A detachment of Williamson's force met a few residents along the way, whom they killed and scalped. As the militia drew near the town, they found the main body of villagers working in the fields. The Lenapes greeted the soldiers with friendship—they had been sympathetic with the American cause during the Revolution that had been ravaging the Ohio frontier for the previous few years, and their pacifist stance had angered other Indian groups who demanded they make war on the Americans or face retribution. Williamson announced that his men had come to escort them and others from the similar settlement in nearby Salem to the protection of Fort Pitt, and requested that the people turn in their arms to the soldiers for safe-keeping and gather in Gnadenhutten for their own safety. The Moravian Indians, as they were commonly called, had just spent a winter starving in the captivity of British-allied Wyandot and Lenape to the north, and they generally welcomed the prospect of being protected and fed. Once the residents of both towns had assembled there, Williamson accused them of raiding Pennsylvania settlements and had them bound and placed in two houses, men in one, women and children in the other. Once their prisoners were secured, the militia voted—with only eighteen objecting—to kill them. Advised of their fate, the villagers requested that they have some time to prepare for death, and they spent the night praying and singing hymns. Early the next morning soldiers led the Indians in groups of two or three to the cabins designated for the executions. The first group was met by a militiaman who picked up a cooper's mallet, stated that it would be a perfect tool for "the business," and proceeded to bludgeon fourteen people to death before declaring "My arm fails me; go on in the same way. I think I have done pretty well." By the end of the morning,

Ohio: A History of the Buckeye State, First Edition. Kevin F. Kern and Gregory S. Wilson.
© 2014 John Wiley & Sons, Inc. Published 2014 by John Wiley & Sons, Inc.

Figure 4.1   Almost ninety years after the massacre, the Gnadenhutten Historical Society raised this 35-foot high limestone monument to its victims at the site of the original Moravian Indian village. The town has also reconstructed some of the original buildings and currently maintains the site, including the mound covering the remains of the dead.
Source: http://en.wikipedia.org/wiki/File:Gnadenhutten_Massacre_Site.jpg

with hammers, tomahawks, and the butts of guns, the militiamen had killed ninety-six Lenape, including at least thirty-four children. Of the entire group, only two teenage boys escaped from the massacre: one had hidden under a trap door in the floor of a cabin, the other had been stunned by the blow to the head, scalped, and left for dead. After scalping the bodies, the soldiers burned down the entire town of Gnadenhutten, a name that translates from German as "cabins of grace" (see Figure 4.1).

Although perhaps unique in the nature of its brutality, the Gnadenhutten Massacre was unfortunately far from unique in exemplifying the violence that beset Ohio in the late eighteenth century. The period between 1763 and 1795 in Ohio was perhaps the most turbulent and contentious in its history, marked by upheaval, resistance, revolution, and increasing migration and movement of both Native American and white settlers (or "Long Knives," as the Indians sometimes referred to them). Nominal authority over the area changed as well, from French to British, and then from British to American, although it was only in the final years that the new United States government was able to assert its control—not only over the Native Americans, but also over its own citizens who populated the area. Only then did nearly a century of Ohio as a "Middle Ground" come to an end.

The Resistance of 1763

The signing of the Treaty of Paris in 1763 officially ended the Seven Years' (or French and Indian) War that had already largely ceased in North America in 1760. The "peace" achieved by this treaty was deceptive in the Middle Ground of the Ohio region, and for many reasons. First, the sudden British change of policy after dismissing the French—retreating from the practice of gift-giving, raising trading rates for scarcer and scarcer amounts of goods, limiting trade to certain locations, and restricting trade of shot, powder, and anything else that might be used as a weapon—struck many Native Americans as unfair and a shocking change from the relatively generous terms they had received from the British while the war was raging. Many Indians also viewed British demands for the return of captives—a number of whom had been adopted into Indian families and integrated into village life—as unreasonable and mean-spirited. These policies led many Native American leaders to doubt the sincerity and trustworthiness of the British. In addition to these suspicions, other actions of the British seemed overtly threatening. Not only did the British expand the defenses and settlement at Fort Pitt (after promising only to construct a small post to protect trade there), but they also reoccupied a number of smaller French forts in the Ohio country, establishing a larger military presence in the area than the French had ever boasted. At the same time, more British colonial hunters and settlers began flocking into the Ohio country than ever before, in seeming violation of the Treaty of Easton. Although British Colonel Henry Bouquet at Fort Pitt made a show of good faith by forcibly evicting squatters in the Monongahela and Youghiogheny valleys in the autumn of 1761, the effect on Native Americans in the area was undermined by General Amherst's decision to encourage white settlement around frontier forts to provide the materials needed to sustain the posts. For the many groups of Native Americans who felt they had won a peace with the British on their own terms during the war, all of these events seemed to indicate that the British had further territorial ambitions and were planning on treating them like conquered peoples. Native American chiefs who had advocated peace and friendly relationships with the British began to lose influence with the change in British policy. War belts of wampum had begun to circulate in the region as early as the summer of 1761, with the Senecas in particular urging unified Native resistance.

It was about this time that the Lenape Prophet Neolin began preaching that the Master of Life had told him that the Lenape should return to traditional ways, refusing alcohol, removing dependence on European goods, and resisting British encroachment on their lands. Despite his appeals to return to ancient Lenape custom and beliefs Neolin's revelations reflected a decided Christian influence—not only was returning to ancestral ways the path that Lenape should take to "purify themselves of sin," but that in so doing they could make for themselves a good afterlife in heaven. He insisted that the British were evil and needed to be driven out of the land, and warned that the Master of Life would no longer favor the Lenape if they continued to trade and cooperate with the British. As if to fulfill this prophecy, the years of 1761 and 1762 brought poor harvests, poor hunting, famine, and widespread disease throughout the trans-Appalachian area. Tamaqua, the moderate, accommodationist Lenape leader, began to lose influence to a faction led by Netawatwees (Newcomer), who stated that he thought the British had grown so powerful that they "seemed as if they would be too strong for God himself" and became an advocate of Neolin's path. Although initially intended specifically for the Lenape, Neolin's message began to find converts among other Native groups throughout the Ohio region, most notably including the Ottawa Chief Pontiac. Things were thus already at an edge by late 1762/early 1763 when news of the terms of the Treaty of Paris began to filter into the Ohio Country. Many groups in the area had endured the resentments and reversals of the previous few years in the hopes that the final treaty might restore some semblance of the *status quo ante bellum*, as had been the case in previous wars. When it became clear this would not be the case, and that their long-time allies the French had given their territory away to the British, sentiment throughout the trans-Appalachian swung heavily toward war.

The resulting conflict has been known by many names over the years, "Pontiac's War," "Pontiac's Uprising," "Pontiac's Conspiracy," and "Pontiac's Rebellion" being perhaps the most common. There are several problems with all of these designations, not the least of which is the fact that they seem to exaggerate Pontiac's control and influence in a conflict that was actually a much more widespread resistance. "Uprising," "conspiracy," and "rebellion" do not seem to capture the nature of the conflict, either, as the Native Americans who participated in it had not been militarily conquered by the British and did not consider themselves to be under British rule. Indeed, to the Native Americans involved, the war was a resistance against what they suspected was a British conspiracy to feign acceptance of Indian independence while secretly pursuing a policy of subjugation and territorial encroachment. This has led several historians in recent years to suggest other names—including "The Resistance of 1763," which will be used here—as being a more accurate description of the conflict. Whatever one chooses to call it, though, the war and its aftermath had significant effects on the Ohio country.

Pontiac and his Ojibwa and Potawatomi allies struck first, on May 7. Pontiac had intended to take Fort Detroit by surprise by entering it with a number of warriors under the pretense of wishing to have a council with the British, after which they would take out their concealed weaponry. The British had learned of his plans, however, and greeted them heavily armed. Instead, the Indian alliance laid siege to the fort with the tacit support of the French inhabitants nearby, who also had cause to resent the British. News of the attack spread quickly among Native American groups throughout the trans-Appalachian region, inspiring other groups to engage in similar attacks across the British frontier. The first fort to fall in the Resistance of 1763 was Fort Sandusky, on the Sandusky River near present-day Venice, Ohio.

Fort Sandusky was an ill-fated experiment, starting as a treaty violation, built and occupied only with great hardship, and ending as the only fort in Ohio history to be successfully attacked. With the military defeat of the French in 1760 the British acquired all French outposts in the Great Lakes region and moved to restaff them with British troops, as well as to build new forts in strategic areas, even after hostilities had ceased. This latter move seemed to be in violation of treaty arrangements the British had made with the Indians, and the Wyandots in particular resented the construction of the new Fort Sandusky near Sandusky Bay along the main path from Fort Pitt to Fort Detroit. (The French had built a different outpost called Fort Sandoské in 1751, but it was located near the Marblehead Peninsula and had been abandoned by 1754.) Fort Pitt's commander, Henry Bouquet, sent Lieutenant Elias Meyer and thirty-eight men from the Royal American Regiment to build the blockhouse and palisade in the autumn of 1761. However, his men were hampered by a lack of food and supplies as well as poor weather, illness, worn-out horses, and the presence of resentful Wyandots who threatened violence against them. When asked about his progress, Meyer wrote to Bouquet "rest assured, Sir, that I shall neglect nothing to finish it as soon as possible, so as to be delivered from this purgatory." Meyer finally finished the task in November, and happily turned the post over to a small garrison of fifteen men under twenty-four-year-old Ensign H. C. Pauli in early 1762. The local Wyandots greeted Pauli by warning him that the fort represented a treaty violation and that they would burn it down by the following spring. Nevertheless, an uneasy relationship developed between the command at Fort Sandusky and its Wyandot neighbors. Perpetually poorly supplied, the garrison came to rely on the Indians for food, and the British traders stationed there provided trade goods the Wyandot wanted in exchange for food and skins. A couple of the soldiers, seemingly unhappy with conditions in the fort, deserted to live among the Indians later that same year. On May 16, 1763, a group of Wyandots who had been frequent trading visitors to the fort asked for a council with Pauli. Unaware that this was the same tactic that Pontiac had tried unsuccessfully a little more than a week before in Detroit, Pauli let them in. Just after smoking the pipe that was a ritual in such meetings, the Wyandot leader gave a signal and the warriors seized Pauli and systematically killed all of his men plus the dozen traders assembled there. They bound Pauli, carried him off, and—just as they had promised the year before—burned down the fort. They took Pauli to Detroit, where he was made to run the gauntlet, a tradition practiced by some Native American groups in which captives were forced to run between two rows of people who would strike at them with sticks or clubs as they passed. Having survived the ordeal, Pauli was then adopted by an Ottawa woman who had lost her husband. Pretending to fight with the besieging forces, he escaped to the fort that July. Weeks later a relief force under Captain Dalyell stopped by the ruins of Fort Sandusky, and seeing the grisly remains, burned a nearby Wyandot village and its surrounding fields in retribution.

Fort Sandusky was the first, but not the last, British fort to fall in the Resistance of 1763. Throughout the spring and summer various groups of Native Americans took seven other forts throughout the Great Lakes region often by similar methods. They attacked others, too, and Forts Pitt and Detroit lay under siege for months. It was during this time that one of the most infamous events in the conflict took place: General Amherst and Colonel Bouquet arranged to give smallpox-infected blankets to the besieging Indians at Fort Pitt in what was the first recorded attempt of biological warfare in North America. Colonel Bouquet broke the siege at Fort Pitt after his relief column took heavy casualties in defeating Indian forces at the Battle of Bushy Run on August 5. A British attempt to break the siege at Detroit led to decisive defeat by Pontiac's forces at the Battle of Bloody Run on July 31, prolonging the siege several more months. As autumn approached, many of Pontiac's warriors were anxious to get back to their villages to help with the harvest and in September they began to melt away. By late October, Pontiac told Detroit's commander, Major Henry Gladwin, that he was ready to negotiate peace.

Although the siege of Forts Pitt and Detroit had ended, the resistance had not. Raids on British settlements throughout the Appalachian regions of Pennsylvania and Virginia would continue through 1763 and into 1764, with Ohio Indians taking a leading role. Fighting for what they saw as their independence from British control and British settlers, these groups faced the most direct threat from the increased British presence in the area. But even as the "Five Nations of the Scioto Plains" (including the elements of the Shawnee, Wyandot, and Lenape) pursued continued resistance, circumstances had tipped the scales against them. Never a unified resistance in the first place, cracks began to show in the confederacies that had formed at the beginning of the conflict. General Amherst returned to England in November, replaced by General Thomas Gage, who was more amenable to negotiating with the Indians. After some diplomatic missteps, the British secured preliminary peace agreements with some of the Iroquois and Hurons at Fort Niagara in August of 1764. They also dispatched twin military missions into the Ohio country with the discretion of making war or peace as they saw fit. One, a force of 1,200 men led by Colonel John Bradstreet, marched along Lake Erie and made peace arrangements with representatives of some Mingo, Lenape, Ottawa, Chippewa, Shawnee, and Wyandot groups. Although the council he held at Detroit not a complete success—Pontiac and a number of other major chiefs did not attend, and the Shawnee and Lenape failed to meet Bradstreet at the site of a planned prisoner exchange on the Sandusky River—it was clear that many of the Great Lakes groups were ready for peace. Now increasingly isolated, the Ohio Indian Republics faced a second military expedition of 1,500 men down the Ohio Valley led by Colonel Bouquet. Meeting with Lenape, Mingo, and Shawnee representatives in the Scioto Plains near present-day Coshocton, Bouquet managed, through threat of force, not only to negotiate a preliminary armistice but also to succeed in pressuring these groups to return more than 200 captives (see Figure 4.2). Although the issue of peace deeply divided pro- and antiwar factions within the Ohio Indian groups, over the next two years the British were able to negotiate formal treaties with most major parties, including Pontiac and his strong supporters among the Ottawa villages on the Maumee River. This officially brought an end to hostilities.

Nevertheless, one should not view the end of the Resistance of 1763 as a victory by the British or a defeat by Native American groups, but rather a reaffirmation of the Middle Ground in the Great Lakes region. Although the Native American groups made some concessions to the British in the treaties that followed the conflict, the British made some concessions, too, by backing away from Amherst's more forceful policies and giving up claims of subjugation of the Indians. Not only did gift-giving resume, but the British also vowed to respect Native American land claims both by treaty and by King George III's Proclamation of 1763, which set the crest of the Appalachian Mountains as the westernmost limit of English settlement. In many ways, then, the end of the conflict restored the *status quo antebellum*, only with the British standing in place of the French as the "father" and mediator of an alliance of Great Lakes Indians. Yet the lack of a state of open war did not mean there was complete peace. Symbolic of this was the fate of Pontiac, who had tried to turn his status as a new ally of the British into a position of leadership among all western Indians. Most groups in the Great Lakes did not wish to see an Indian overlord any more than a British one, and in April of 1769 a Peoria Indian of the Illinois confederation clubbed and stabbed Pontiac from behind as he came out of a trader's shop in the village of Cahokia on the Mississippi River. Maintaining a stable alliance in the face of divisions among the various groups in the region would have been difficult enough for the British, but the situation came to be

Figure 4.2   This depiction of the return of captives to Colonel Henry Bouquet after the Resistance of 1763 is by Benjamin West, an American painter who achieved great fame and fortune in England by painting scenes from the Seven Years' War. Although it was common for European artists of this time to present Native Americans as bloodthirsty savages, this work portrays them more sympathetically, highlighting the great sorrow that many captives and their adoptive Indian families alike felt regarding the forced return.
Source: Library of Congress Prints and Photographs Division (LC-USZC2-1595)

further destabilized by the addition of new and growing sets of groups into the area: traders, soldiers, missionaries, and especially settlers.

Ohio Native Americans had long experience with traders and generally welcomed them. Traders supplied goods—particularly metal pots and knives, guns and powder, and especially European fabrics—that the Native Americans desired and could not make on their own. Yet Indian relations with English traders were not devoid of tensions. One of the commodities that traders brought to Indians in ever-increasing quantities was alcohol, with all its attendant problems. In addition, the scale of trade was greater than ever before, with the Philadelphia firm of Baynton, Wharton, and Morgan employing more than 300 boatmen and 600 pack animals to transport the contemporary equivalent of millions of dollars worth of goods down the Ohio River by the mid-1760s. Unscrupulous practices and rivalries among certain traders kept many Native Americans on their guard, and a number of these traders ended up being killed during this time.

Still, because of the potential profits, there were always plenty of Englishmen willing to take the risks as well as villages of Indians willing to invite them in.

Although the presence of British soldiers has sometimes been pointed to as a cause of Native American resentment, the real nature of the relationship was more complex. Native Americans certainly had cause to fear troops of soldiers when they marched into Indian territory but many times Ohio Valley Indians viewed them as a welcome sign of authority and protection. British soldiers were usually the ones who enforced government policies against colonial settlers encroaching on Indian lands and treaty rights. In the relative safety of British forts and nearby settlements, Indians could also call upon soldiers as a kind of police force when individual settlers cheated or otherwise abused a Native American. However, the ever-increasing presence of British soldiers in the trans-Appalachian area was a cause for alarm in many Native American villages, as the Resistance of 1763 amply illustrates.

Native American residents of Ohio also greeted Christian missionaries with mixed feelings. The most significant members of this group were Moravian Protestant missionaries (from a Bohemian evangelical denomination now known as the Church of the Brethren) who had converted several hundred Lenape Indians to their pacifistic sect in villages they built near the east coast, particularly eastern Pennsylvania. Although they were devoutly Christian and did not believe in using violence, the Indians in these villages increasingly faced the general anti-Indian wrath that many colonists held in the wake of the French and Indian War and the Resistance of 1763. Christian Frederick Post had conducted mission work among the Ohio Lenape in the 1760s, and in the early 1770s these Moravian Indians decided to avoid further conflict by accepting the invitation of Lenape Chief Netawatwees (Newcomer) to move nearer to their non-Christian Lenape brethren in Eastern Ohio. The main figures in this move were the tireless missionaries David Zeisberger and John Heckewelder, who founded Schoenbrunn ("beautiful spring," near present-day New Philadelphia) and Gnadenhutten in 1772, and Lichtenau ("meadows of light," near present-day Coshocton) in 1776. Although most Ohio Natives generally did not perceive these missionaries as a threat—they practiced pacifism and did not seem to be after Indian land—others viewed them quite rightly as people intent on challenging traditional beliefs and leading Natives away from long-established tribal relationships. These "praying Indians" would increasingly prove to be a thorn in the side of more militant Ohio Native groups when conflict erupted.

The least welcome, and by far the most destabilizing, new presence in the Ohio Valley were the ever-increasing numbers of colonial settlers who began moving into the trans-Appalachian region in the 1760s. In many ways the British and colonial governments had more control over their Indian allies than they had over the individualistic people who chose to violate the Proclamation of 1763 and settle in lands long claimed by Indians. Official correspondence between British government officials often commented on the problems these settlers caused, dismissing them as "the very dregs of the people," and "lawless banditti." Although this reflects a certain amount of class-based prejudice against people of the lowest socioeconomic status in the colonies, many of these settlers had little regard for the laws of the British government or their native colonies when the rules conflicted with their desire to seek out land that they wanted and could not have acquired by conventional means back east. Unlike the French, who had centuries of close contact with the Indians and were better attuned to their customs and ways, most settlers of British descent had for generations lived apart from their Native American neighbors and often had starkly simple and bigoted views of Indians and their customs. Many (but not all) of these British settlers were "Indian haters" who viewed all Native Americans as interchangeable savages who ought to be wiped from the land as soon as possible. Some of this hatred stemmed from personal experience, as many had known friends or family members who had died at the hands of Indians. Some of it was the product of a cultural distrust handed down through generations of family and community beliefs. Whatever the cause, the vastly-increasing numbers of these settlers and the hatred many of them shared toward all Indians came to be the greatest source of instability and conflict that beset Ohio for most of the rest of the eighteenth century.

Lord Dunmore's War

Eventually the issues that arose from the actions of illegal settlers shattered the tenuous peace achieved after the Resistance of 1763. In the spring of 1774, Daniel Greathouse and Joshua Baker led a group of settlers in the northern Virginia panhandle that lured two men and a woman from the Mingo village of Yellow Creek (near present-day Steubenville) across the Ohio River to come to drink with them at Baker's cabin. As the Mingos of Yellow Creek had often crossed the river to meet and trade with the Virginians, the Indians did not suspect foul play. As soon as the visitors were drunk, the Virginians murdered them in cold blood, and then murdered two more who had followed them. When even more Mingos came over to investigate what had happened, they too fell prey to the same group. In all, the Virginians killed and scalped eight to ten Mingos that day, and a few others in the days that followed. Many of the dead were relatives of the Mingo war leader known as Logan (scholars disagree on what his given name may have been), including his brother and his pregnant sister, who had already borne one child to a white Virginia trader named John Gibson. The massacre disturbed both British and moderate Indian leaders alike. Experienced British agents and traders George Croghan and Alexander McKee attempted conciliatory efforts with Shawnee chief Hokolesqua (Cornstalk), and Lenape chiefs Quequedegatha (George White Eyes) and Netawatwees (Newcomer). They hoped that they might be able to convince Logan to accept ceremonial restitution for his losses and keep the peace—after all, both Logan and his father (who had been an important Cayuga diplomat) had maintained lifelong friendly relations with whites on the frontier. Logan refused to be placated, however, and committed himself to gaining vengeance on the Virginians, scalp for scalp. He recruited a party of thirteen warriors from the Mingo/Shawnee village of Old Wakatomika (on the Muskingum River near present-day Dresden), a village that had tended to oppose peace with the British. Together, they raided the Virginia backcountry, killing and scalping thirteen people including a husband, wife, and three children at Muddy Creek. Although Logan restricted his raids to the areas of Virginia west of the Monongahela (a concession he granted to the chiefs who had tried to make peace) and said he had satisfied his vengeance when the number of white scalps matched the number of those of his dead kinsmen, the entire Pennsylvania and Virginia borderlands went into a panic, with hundreds fleeing the area entirely and thousands seeking the security of fortified locations. A group of militia marched into Ohio and destroyed the already-abandoned village of Old Wakatomika as well as several other surrounding settlements. The Shawnee in turn said they would take up arms to avenge these new attacks.

The ensuing conflict came to be known as "Lord Dunmore's War," after the Royal Governor of Virginia who presided over and personally led part of the military campaign. The name is apt, for it reflects the fact that it was a conflict the governor sought even after it looked like peace might have been arranged—perhaps in order to strengthen Virginian claims to territories disputed by neighboring Pennsylvania (not to mention the speculative land claims that he and other investors had in the area). Lord Dunmore sent a force of Virginians to seize Fort Pitt as a preliminary move, and by early June the Shawnee had ceased retaliatory raids and several Lenape and Shawnee leaders of the peace faction had sought (with the aid of some Pennsylvanian leaders) to negotiate an end of hostilities with Dunmore. Nevertheless, his lieutenants continued to foster a warlike sentiment among the local Pennsylvanians, who obligingly launched new attacks against Shawnees that were accompanying a colonial trading party. This reignited the conflict, and Dunmore began to plan a campaign that went deep into Shawnee territory. When the Shawnee send out war belts of wampum requesting aid, other groups in the region opted to remain neutral. Thus isolated, the Shawnee found the odds heavily stacked against them, with only a few hundred men to face the more than 2,000 Virginia militiamen who had set out to invade Ohio. Lord Dunmore planned a two-pronged attack: Colonel Andrew Lewis (a veteran of the French and Indian war and a Virginia militia leader) was to lead about 1,100 men north up the Kanawha River from Virginia; Dunmore himself was to lead a similar number of men west from Fort Pitt to meet up on the Ohio River and turn north toward the major Shawnee villages of the Scioto Plains (see Figure 4.3). He dispatched Major William Crawford (a childhood friend of another Virginian military leader named George Washington) in advance to build Fort Gower at the mouth of the Hocking River to support the expedition. Knowing they were greatly outnumbered and without hope of help from other Native groups, Hokolesqua (Cornstalk) decided that his only reasonable chance lay in attacking Lewis's group before it met up with Dunmore's. Accordingly, on October 10, his 300–500 warriors surprised the much larger force of Virginians near the mouth of the Kanawha River at a place near modern-day Point Pleasant, West Virginia. The battle took much of the day and exacted heavy casualties from the Virginians, but by nightfall Hokolesqua ultimately decided he could not win and withdrew to the other side of the Ohio River. Apart from being the only major battle of Lord Dunmore's War, Point Pleasant is significant for the way it shaped the future of Ohio as represented in the fates of some of its major leaders. One, Hokolesqua, resigned himself and his people thereafter to peace with the Long Knives. He became an outspoken voice against further conflict, even though it eventually resulted in his own death at the hands of the colonists. In contrast, Weyapiersenwah (Blue Jacket) remained an intractable foe of the American colonists, and devoted the next twenty years of his life to fighting them. Puckeshinwa was another major voice against giving any more ground to the Long Knives, and although he

Figure 4.3   The Ohio Country during the revolutionary era, 1774–83.

was killed at Point Pleasant, his death reinforced the resolute opposition to white encroachment in his son, the future Shawnee leader Tecumseh.

After the battle, Lewis crossed the Ohio River and burned several Shawnee villages before attempting to meet up with Dunmore on the Pickaway Plains where the governor had already forced the Shawnee and Mingo into a peace signed at Camp Charlotte (on Sippo Creek near present-day Circleville). The Shawnee agreed to return captives and give up their hunting claims south of the Ohio River, finally affirming the provisions of the Treaty of Fort Stanwix that they had earlier rejected. There was, however, one notable absence from the negotiations ultimately prompted by Logan's raids of vengeance: Logan himself. Although he was nearby and had pledged not to engage in any more attacks against the Long Knives, he refused to be a party to the treaty, even after Dunmore sent John Gibson to invite him to the talks. If anyone might have convinced Logan to attend, it would have been his brother-in-law Gibson. Gibson's pregnant Indian wife was Logan's sister who Greathouse and his men had killed in the massacre at Baker's cabin the previous spring. Logan, however, would not be persuaded, and instead reportedly gave the following speech that Thomas Jefferson later compared to those of the best classical orators, and that generations of school children in Ohio's one-room schoolhouses would have to memorize:

> I appeal to any white man to say, if ever he entered Logan's cabin hungry, and he gave him not meat; if ever he came cold and naked, and he clothed him not. During the course of the last long and bloody war, Logan remained idle in his cabin, an advocate for peace. Such was my love for the whites, that my countrymen pointed as they passed, and said, Logan is the friend of the white men. I have even thought to live with you but for the injuries of one man[, who], the last spring, in cold blood, and unprovoked, murdered all the relations of Logan, not sparing even my women and children. There runs not a drop of my blood in the veins of any living creature. This has called on me for revenge. I have sought it: I have killed many: I have fully glutted my vengeance. For my country, I rejoice at the beams of peace. But do not harbor a thought that mine is the joy of fear. Logan never felt fear. He will not turn on his heel to save his life. Who is there to mourn for Logan? Not one.

Logan's reluctance to negotiate was matched by that of some of his Mingo brethren, and a detachment of 240 men under Crawford marched up the Scioto to Seekunk (Salt Lick Town) and destroyed and plundered the Mingo village there. With this, Lord Dunmore's War ended.

This was far from the end of conflict, though, and Dunmore's War served as a portent of things to come in Ohio history. Although Ohio had long been a metaphorical Middle Ground of Indian/white relations it was now becoming a literal battleground over those relationships. Dunmore's War was the first conflict between whites and Ohio Natives in which the majority of conflict took place on Ohio soil, and it also brought about the first surrendering of Ohio Territory lands by the resident Natives. In neither instance would it be the last. From this point on, Ohio Native American groups would be fighting a defensive struggle to preserve their claims to the land, but these would systematically be removed by both military and diplomatic action. Furthermore, Dunmore's War bore harbingers of a much larger conflict that would follow. Both British military and governmental officials sternly chastised the Pennsylvanian and Virginian colonists for their actions surrounding the war, highlighting the increasing distance between imperial and colonial interests at the time. In addition, when Dunmore's men returned to Fort Gower on their way home, they first learned of the actions of the First Continental Congress that had been meeting since September. On November 5, the officers met and passed a set of resolutions that on the one hand commended Lord Dunmore and expressed their allegiance to the King, yet on the other warned:

> But as the love of Liberty, and attachment to the real interests and just rights of America outweigh every other consideration, we resolve that we will exert every power within us for

the defense of American liberty, and for the support of her just rights and privileges; not in any precipitate, riotous, or tumultuous manner, but when regularly called forth by the unanimous voice of our countrymen.

These resolves were eventually printed and reprinted in Virginia and beyond. While numerous other bodies throughout the colonies passed similar memorials in support of the ideals represented by the First Continental Congress, the Fort Gower Resolves were the only ones adopted by an army in the field. Although in the past some people (including the U.S. Senate in 1908) have erroneously referred to Point Pleasant as "the first battle of the American Revolution" both it and Lord Dunmore's War did foreshadow the nature of the American Revolution as it would be fought in Ohio soon after.

The American Revolution

The Fort Gower Resolves demonstrated that events pertaining to Ohio were part of the background that eventually led to the conflict that started at Lexington and Concord in Massachusetts in 1775. Indeed, one of the earliest British governmental acts that most U.S. history textbooks point to as a precipitating cause of the Revolution dealt squarely with Ohio. The Proclamation of 1763—described earlier as a reasoned measure to put a boundary between white and Indian lands in the wake of the Resistance of 1763—had the side-effect of causing intense resentment from those colonists. This was particularly true in Virginia, which had colonial charter claims to the territory and was home to early spec-ulators in Ohio lands (including those of the Ohio Company of Virginia discussed in chapter 3). Similarly, the Quebec Act of 1774 was another Parliamentary act dealing with Ohio that historians credit as one of the final precipitating causes of the Revolution. By its terms, Parliament sought to give the Roman Catholic French Canadians greater religious and civil liberties and expand the boundaries of Quebec to encompass nearly all of the Great Lakes region, including Ohio. While giving French-Canadians more rights was an enlightened move, and while it might have made some sense administratively to have all the major Indian groups in the area in the same colony, the Quebec Act had the unin-tended consequence of fanning the flames of suspicion among American colonists. Not only did it further jeopardize colonial claims and speculations in the Ohio Valley, it also stirred up anti-Catholic sentiment in some quarters, leading some colonists to believe the British government intended to use the French Canadians and Indians to control or sub-jugate the American colonies. Although it was a completely different measure from the Coercive Acts (meant to punish Boston and Massachusetts for the Boston Tea Party) that Parliament passed at about the same time, colonists lumped the Quebec Act and Coercive Acts into a group which they called "The Intolerable Acts," a kind of "final straw" that led to the formation of the First Continental Congress. Thus, while Ohio was certainly not right at the front among the causes of the American Revolution it was nevertheless part of the background to it and would soon emerge as an important aspect of the war.

It is sometimes tempting to view the Revolutionary War in Ohio as basically a contest between Americans and the British and their respective Indian allies for control over the west, but this is far too simple a picture. By the time war officially broke out in the spring of 1775, fighting had already flared up on and off in Ohio and neighboring areas for a dozen years and for several reasons; in many ways the war was as much a continuation or evolution of those conflicts as it was a new struggle between the British and American governments. Furthermore, the British/Indian alliance was complex, and deep divisions between and among the Native American groups of the region further complicated the situation. Although the British did indeed have a number of Indian allies in Ohio, many of them were using the British Alliance for their own ends, which included preserving their land and relative independence. In addition, there was no unanimity among Indians regarding what to do regarding the war, and the conflict often turned on the politics between and within Native American groups and villages in Ohio. Peace factions and peace chiefs sought neutrality and sometimes even cooperated with the Americans to try to preserve their way of life in Ohio. Others decided that the conflict was too much for them and chose to leave Ohio forever. In the end, while the war ultimately preserved the Middle Ground for the time being, it also set the circumstances by which it would come to an end.

At the start of the war in 1775 the British found themselves in a weakened position in the Ohio Valley. They had no more than 500 soldiers at their headquarters in Detroit, far too small a number to secure such a vast expanse of territory. In addition, with the upheavals of Lord Dunmore's War fresh in the minds of many, most Native groups and villages—especially in the Ohio region—chose at first to remain neutral. Certainly, some Shawnee (primarily led by Chief Cottawamago [Blackfish]) and some Mingo (primarily led by Plukkemehnotee [Pluggy]) were interested in actively helping the British, but this seems to have been motivated more from settling old scores and resisting the encroachment of American settlers than out of any loyalty to King George and his cause. The Americans sought to turn this situation to their advantage by holding a grand conference at Fort Pitt in the fall of 1775 where they secured assurances of neutrality and peace from the Lenape, Mingo, Potawatomi, Seneca, Shawnee, and Wyandot representatives gathered there. While the Native American groups pledged to uphold the terms of the Treaty of Fort Stanwix, the Americans promised not to cross the Ohio River. Among the strongest voices for peace were the Shawnee Chief Hokolesqua (Cornstalk) and the Lenape leader Quequedegatha (George White Eyes). Hokolesqua's experiences in Lord Dunmore's War had convinced him that peace was the best course for his people to follow, and he was outspoken in countering the calls to war from other leaders of the deeply divided Shawnee. Quequedegatha had been a relatively successful tavern-keeper and trader in the frontier between the American colonists and the Ohio Indians before Lord Dunmore's War, and he was, perhaps, better acquainted than most Lenape with the ways and attitudes of the Americans who were now fighting for independence. He had not succeeded in keeping the Lenape out of Lord Dunmore's War, but he had, at some peril to his own life, worked as a go-between in negotiating an end to that conflict. He now believed that the best chance for his people would be to join the Americans in return for which he hoped the Continental Congress would grant the Lenape their own state in the new nation. Another major force for peace was Congress's official representative in the area, George Morgan, a successful trader who was well-versed in Native

American traditions and understanding of their desires. He had the respect and loyalty of many chiefs in Ohio, with Lenape Chief Gelelemend (John Killbuck Jr. or Killbuck) calling him "The wisest, faithfullest and best man I ever had anything to do with." With all these circumstances working in its favor, the new American nation had a very strong hand at the beginning of the war. It might have used this strength to forge a relatively peaceful western front and good relations with many of the Native Americans in the region. Unfortunately for all parties concerned the subsequent actions of some Americans—both soldiers and civilians—undermined this early advantage and helped turn Ohio into one of the most brutal and bloody fronts of the war.

This is not to say that the British and some Native Americans played no part in this. In 1777, Lieutenant Governor Henry Hamilton, the British Commander at Detroit, called together representatives from the various Native American groups in the region, urging them to raid American settlements in Virginia and Kentucky. He is alleged to have offered bounties for American scalps and as a result the frightened American settlers hated him, calling him "Hair-Buyer Hamilton." Some Wyandots, Lenapes, and Iroquois joined the Shawnee and Mingo groups that had already been striking Kentucky settlements, and these raids from Ohio into Kentucky killed hundreds and concentrated the increasingly terrified white population there into a few fortified towns. Virginia Governor Patrick Henry at first considered a military expedition into Ohio to strike at the Mingo settlement known as Pluggy's Town (near present-day Delaware, Ohio) but decided against it because he feared it might turn neutral Shawnee and Lenape groups into active belligerents. Henry's fears were well-grounded. The neutrality that the Americans had negotiated in 1775 had begun to unravel, not only through the actions of the British and Indian war parties, but also through tragic missteps by Americans. For example, a peace conference with major Indian groups planned for July of 1777 fell apart when Pennsylvania frontiersmen murdered a group of Senecas who had come to negotiate. Similarly, in September Hokolesqua (Cornstalk) crossed the Ohio River to warn the Americans at Fort Randolph (at the mouth of the Kanawha River) that the joint pressures of the British and the Shawnee war factions might soon force neutral Shawnee to go on the warpath, and that he would be unable to stop this. Hokolesqua had been one of the most conspicuous Native American advocates of peace and, over the previous couple of years, he had passed important information about the situation in Ohio to the Americans. However, Fort Randolph's commander Captain Matthew Arbuckle seemed to misjudge Hokolesqua's intentions and instead of trying to placate him he took him and his companion Red Hawk hostage to try to force his people to remain neutral. When Hokolesqua's son Elinipsico arrived a week later, Arbuckle took him hostage as well. A few days later, some Virginia militiamen, who had been attacked when they crossed into Ohio to hunt, decided to take revenge on the hostages. Storming the cabin where Hokolesqua, Red Hawk, and Elinipsico were held, they shot all three of them and mutilated their bodies. The news of Hokolesqua's murder, at American hands, (and Arbuckle's refusal to punish the culprits) quickly spread throughout the region largely ending any hopes for maintaining peace. The rest of the Shawnee as well as other groups broke their neutrality, and new Indian retaliatory raids began to occur along the Virginia and Pennsylvania frontiers.

By the end of 1777 about the only major Native groups in Ohio who were still friendly to the American cause were elements of the Lenape, including the residents of the Moravian villages and those under the leadership of Quequedegetha (White Eyes), Hopocan (Captain Pipe) and Gelelemend (Killbuck). However, their loyalty became severely tested by the events of 1778. The year started badly for the Americans, and then got worse. In early February, prompted by the increased raids in response to Hokolesqua's death and the news that the British had deposited military supplies for their Native American allies at the mouth of the Cuyahoga River, the American Commander of Fort Pitt, General Edward Hand, took 500 militiamen on a retaliatory raid into Ohio to engage the Native Americans war parties there. They found none before the brutal winter weather forced them to return. On the way back they came across a village of peaceful Lenape, relatives of Chief Hopocan (Captain Pipe) who was a friend to the Americans. The unruly militiamen wounded Hopocan's mother and killed his brother and another woman, whom they shot repeatedly and scalped. A foray into a neighboring Lenape village resulted in the murder of three more women and a boy. Upon returning to Fort Pitt, news of what came to be known derisively as the "Squaw Campaign" spread, resulting in further outrage among Native Americans and General Hand's request to be transferred. At about the same time, Shawnee leader Cottawamago (Blackfish) was leading a devastating raid into Kentucky that also resulted in the capture of famed frontiersman Daniel Boone. Taken back as a prisoner, Boone was adopted into Cottawamago's village of Old Chillicothe (near present day Xenia) and lived there until June before escaping to warn the people of Boonesboro of another impending raid.

The capture of someone who was already a famous frontiersman along with the ignominious "Squaw Campaign" were more evidence for many—both Indian and American alike—that the American cause was no longer worth supporting. Among these were American Indian agent Alexander McKee and the talented scout and translator Simon Girty at Fort Pitt. Both had close ties to Native American groups (McKee's mother had been a Shawnee captive who had taught him Indian traditions, Girty had been a captive himself of the Seneca for several years during the Seven Year's War), and both of them had become increasingly disenchanted with the American dealings with the Native Americans and with their own perceived ill-treatment. (Girty in particular had been jailed and kicked out of the militia for unruly behavior the previous year, although he accompanied General Hand in his campaign on a freelance basis.) In March, McKee and Girty escaped Fort Pitt and made their way to Detroit, where they offered their services to the British. They became invaluable to the British cause, McKee as an Indian agent and Girty as a translator, scout, and leader of Indian military raids in Ohio and Kentucky. Known infamously as "The Great Renegade" and "Dirty Girty," Simon Girty was not only reviled as a traitor, but feared among American settlers throughout the region—so much so that frontier parents would threaten their children that "Girty would get them" if they did not behave.

In light of all the reverses the Americans were suffering, the new Commander at Fort Pitt, Lachlan McIntosh, decided the best course of action would be to go on the offensive, a move supported by General George Washington himself. It was this decision that led to the extremely ill-fated experiment that was Fort Laurens, the only Revolutionary-era fort to be built in Ohio. McIntosh rather optimistically believed that he could launch an attack on Fort Detroit from Fort Pitt if he could get the men and supplies and a promise of safe passage through Ohio. As only a couple of Lenape groups were still on speaking terms with the Americans, Quequedegatha (White Eyes) saw this as an opportunity to advance the goals of his people by helping the Americans. Not only did he still cherish a desire to have a Lenape state in the new nation at some point in the future, but he also wanted some immediate protection for Lenape villages. British-allied Mingo, Wyandot, and Shawnee territories surrounded the neutral Lenape settlements, and they were unhappy about the Lenape cooperating with the Americans, threatening them with destruction if they continued to do so. At a conference at Fort Pitt attended by McIntosh and Dunmore's War veterans Andrew Lewis and William Crawford, Quequedegatha, Hopocan (Captain Pipe), and Gelelemend (Killbuck) agreed to continue to cooperate with the Americans if they would press Congress for the Lenape state and build a fort in the heart of Lenape territory (preferably near their main village of Goshachgunk [Coshocton]), which would serve to protect the Lenape as well as serving as a staging point for further military expeditions.

For all the sound military and diplomatic reasoning that might have inspired the idea to build the fort, in practice it was a nearly disastrous expedition, one that served as prime example of nearly all the difficulties the United States faced in prosecuting the Revolutionary War in the west. Delays in gathering men and supplies pushed the starting date of the expedition from spring to autumn, ensuring unfavorable weather and difficult construction conditions. Then, just as the expedition was getting underway, frontiersmen murdered Quequedegatha. Although the Americans successfully covered up the circumstances of his death when giving the news to the Lenape (they attributed it instead to a smallpox outbreak near Fort Pitt) the loss of a person who was perhaps their most ardent high-ranking Native American ally was a terrible blow to the American cause. The expedition moved slowly, only a few miles a day, in part because of the dreadful state of the pack animals they were forced to use. They did not reach the banks of the Tuscarawas River (near present-day Bolivar) until mid-November and, with the weather already turning against them, they decided to build the fort on the spot, too far away from Goshachgunk to be of much protection to the Lenape there and too far away from Fort Pitt to be easily resupplied.

Named after the current president of the Continental Congress (a friend of McIntosh's) Fort Laurens was a step above the simple log palisade and blockhouse construction that typified most frontier forts of the time. Designed by a French military engineer, its walls were well-defended by excellent sight-lines from protruding battlements, but its interior buildings had not yet been finished when the main portion of McIntosh's expedition returned to Fort Pitt in early December. The garrison left behind under the command of Colonel John Gibson had to face the beginning of an Ohio winter with inadequate clothing and supplies, sleeping either in tents or in the buildings that were left window-less and doorless due to a lack of building materials. Gibson had already quelled a near-mutiny by late December, and he sent a series of dispatches to Fort Pitt communicating his problems and begging for some material support. Sensing the desperate nature of the outpost, the British and their Native American allies harassed the fort periodically throughout the winter. In January Simon Girty and a small group of Mingos captured, tortured, and killed a courier carrying Gibson's pleas for supplies and reinforcements that revealed the sorry state of the fort. This inspired the British to send Girty with a much larger force of 180 Wyandot, Shawnee, and Mingo warriors there to try to take it by force. Arriving undetected on February 22, they killed and scalped almost all of a wood-gathering detail of eighteen men just out of American rifle range, before laying siege to the fort. Indians also turned back a relief column from Fort Pitt in March, and sickness and malnutrition set in at the place the men dubbed "Fort Nonsense." Men cleaned, boiled, and ate the leather of their footwear to have something in their stomachs, and two men died from consuming poisonous roots gathered nearby. When two brave soldiers chanced a hunting expedition and brought back a deer, the men consumed it in minutes, many not even bothering to cook their portions. When a reinforcement/resupply mission finally reached the fort in late March, they found the siege had been lifted, and the expedition's commanding officer still had plans to use the fort to launch an attack against the Wyandots to the north. But when the men inside fired their guns in joy to greet their rescuers, the noise scared off the pack animals, with most of the supplies still strapped to their backs. Any hope of an offensive campaign had run off with the pack animals, and for the next few months Fort Laurens limped along as little more than a decoy to distract British attention from the main campaign the Americans eventually launched that summer against the New York Iroquois. The Americans finally abandoned Fort Laurens in August of 1779, with Fort Pitt's new commander, Daniel Brodhead, calling it "a slaughter-pen, impossible to maintain." It would be the last attempt by the Americans to build anything in the Ohio Territory until after the war had ended.

As bad as things were at Fort Laurens, they could have been even worse. American General George Rogers Clark's Virginians had taken Cahokia, Kaskaskia, and Vincennes in the Illinois country in late 1778 and early 1779, capturing "Hair-Buyer" Hamilton in the process. The loss of Detroit's commander and his army forestalled concerted British action against Fort Laurens during the crucial early months of 1779. Then, when the British and their Indian allies had finally regrouped and planned a major attack with 200 men and artillery on the weakened fort in June, the assembled Wyandot, Mingo, and Shawnee instead moved south to meet the threat posed by Colonel John Bowman and his 300 Kentucky militiamen who invaded Ohio and went up the Little Miami River Valley to burn the Shawnee town of Old Chillicothe on the Mad River (near present-day Xenia) and other nearby villages. Although the Bowman raid had the unintended consequence of perhaps saving Fort Laurens, its long-term consequences were far more dire to the American cause. The Shawnees, who had still been somewhat divided regarding the war, now became literally split, with many leaving Ohio entirely for the more peaceful West. Those that remained became implacable foes of the Americans, intensifying the conflict and engaging in numerous raids on Kentucky settlements, including a major one under the Command of British General Henry Bird in the summer of 1780. These remaining Shawnee were also able to help convince other Native groups to come to fight the Americans, including many of the formerly-neutral Lenape.

In response to this latest defection, Brodhead led an expedition from Fort Pitt and destroyed the main Lenape town of Goshachgunk (Coshocton) in April 1781. Despite meeting little resistance, and indeed having many Lenape surrender without a fight, the Americans murdered fifteen of their Lenape prisoners in cold blood. This act caused most of the remaining neutral Lenape to move up to the Sandusky River and join the Wyandot and their other Lenape brethren there to fight the Americans. Rather than pacify Ohio, Brodhead's expedition instead further inflamed Native resentments to the point where it had become almost wholly a British-friendly staging ground for attacks on the American backcountry. As a result, this made it impossible for even the otherwise successful George Rogers Clark to achieve his key objective of seizing Detroit. Although the fort was vulnerable in 1781, Clark's intended expedition against it disintegrated on August 24. The formidable Mohawk war chief Thayendanegea (Joseph Brant), using Ohio as a staging ground to foil the campaign, ambushed and destroyed Pennsylvania militia Colonel Archibald Lochry's supporting detachment that day when it stopped on its rendezvousing trip down the Ohio River to get food for its men and horses. All of Lochry's force—about a hundred in number—were killed or captured, and Clark reluctantly called off his planned campaign.

Although in most history books British Lieutenant General Cornwallis's surrender of his army at Yorktown in 1781 traditionally marks the end of the fighting in the American Revolution, hostilities in the Western Theater were actually intensifying. Nearly all major Native American groups had allied with the British, and the few remaining Indians in Ohio with any kind of pro-American sympathies, namely the Moravian Lenape, found themselves in an increasingly untenable situation. Early in the war, Zeisberger and Heckewelder had moved their converts from Gnadenhutten and Schoenbrunn to Lichtenau near Goshachgunk for protection from other Ohio Indian groups who had sided with the British. When it became clear in 1780 that sentiment there was turning more belligerent against the Americans, the nearly 400 Moravians abandoned Lichtenau to avoid getting caught in the potential conflict. They moved back up the Tuscarawas, reoccupying Gnadenhutten and building the new communities of Salem and New Schoenbrunn. At first it appeared to be a wise move, as Brodhead's expedition in 1781 burned Lichtenau to the ground. Soon thereafter, though, Fort Detroit commandant Major Arent De Peyster ordered the Wyandot under Tanacharison (Half-King) and allied Lenape under Hopocan (Captain Pipe) to remove the Moravians to Wyandot territory near Lake Erie because of their past record of passing information to the Americans at Fort Pitt. Forced to march to "Captive Town" on the Sandusky River in early September, the Moravians had not had time to harvest their crops before departing and suffered all winter from terrible hunger. Some Moravians left the group and went back to their traditional ways with their Lenape brethren. In early spring, in an attempt to offset starvation, Zeisberger sent a large party of his remaining flock back to Gnadenhutten and Salem to glean what they could from the fields. It was this group that Colonel Williamson's force of Pennsylvania militia slaughtered on the morning of March 8, 1782. On their return to Fort Pitt, and unprovoked, a smaller party of the Williamson's expedition killed several Lenape living near the Fort, including two who were commissioned as captains in the American army.

The massacre of the Lenape at Gnadenhutten eliminated any degree of remaining neutrality among Ohio natives, and the outrage over this act inflamed the Ohio Country even further. Even those few Lenape who were still favorably disposed to American individuals let them know that they could no longer intercede on behalf of American prisoners. Now, nervous western Pennsylvanians and Virginians called upon Fort Pitt's Commander William Irvine to mount an expedition against the hotbed of Indian resistance on the Sandusky River. While Irvine refused to spare any Continental soldiers for the campaign he authorized the formation of a volunteer force to go as long as they could get enough men, did not expand American settlements, followed military discipline, and paid for the expedition themselves. When the volunteers pressed him for officers, Irvine sent a surgeon as well as his aide-de-camp Lieutenant John Rose (the *nom de guerre* of Gustave Rosenthal, a Russo-German baron) to join the group. Although militia at this time usually elected their leaders, Irvine also convinced Colonel William Crawford to come out of retirement to join the expedition and worked to get him chosen to lead it. Colonel Crawford was a childhood friend of (and fellow speculator in Ohio lands with) George Washington and had led regiments under Washington at Long Island and Trenton. He was no stranger to warfare in Ohio having served in Dunmore's War and helped with the construction of Forts McIntosh and Laurens. His second in command was David Williamson, fresh from his Gnadenhutten campaign. On May 25, close to 500 men rendezvoused at Mingo Bottom on the Ohio River (in present day Jefferson County Ohio), the same spot from which Williamson had departed for Gnadenhutten and near the place that Logan had called home before Lord Dunmore's War. The militia reached the Sandusky plains on June 3. The Wyandot and Lenape forces assembled nearby attacked them the next day at a stand of trees called "Battle Island" (between present-day Carey and Upper Sandusky). Although the militia held its own the first day, a British Loyalist ranger unit and more than 100 Shawnee warriors under Shemenetoo (Blacksnake) recruited by Alexander McKee reinforced the already considerable Wyandot and Lenape force on June 5, virtually surrounding the Americans. What followed was a confusing night-time retreat by Crawford's forces in which the expedition broke into pieces, while Indian warriors harried groups of the escapees in the dark. Rose and Williamson led a major body of the survivors back to Fort Pitt, while others straggled back in the following days. Colonel Crawford was not so lucky. Taken captive with several others, Hopocan himself marked Crawford for death by painting his face black.

Although Crawford was not involved with the Gnadenhutten massacre, he led Williamson and others who had, and he himself had taken part in the "Squaw Campaign." Through these associations and the still-fervent Lenape outrage over Gnadenhutten, Crawford's death was an elaborate, hours-long act of torture. Stripped naked with his hands bound behind his back, various Lenape beat him and cut off his ears, nose, and scalp, and tied him by a short tether to a post surrounded by a ring of fire. Someone poured hot coals on his exposed skull, while others discharged shots of powder from their guns at his body from point-blank range. As he bled and slowly roasted from the coals he could hardly avoid walking on, he begged Simon Girty, who had been observing the proceedings, to put a bullet in his head. Girty refused, perhaps in part because he knew that to try to deprive the Lenape of their revenge would threaten his own life as well. Crawford's slow and painful death took as long as two hours to perform, and he was not the only one who met a similar fate. The Shawnee tortured their own prisoners to death at New Wakatomika, including Crawford's son-in-law and nephew. The rest of the year continued to see violence in and around Ohio, with a British and Indian force gathering on the Mad River in August to deal a devastating blow to the Kentuckians at the Battle of Blue Licks, and George Rogers Clark retaliating with a major invasion of Shawnee territory in November. With more than 1,000 men under his command, Clark burned five villages including Old Chillicothe, although most had been abandoned before he arrived. Despite Yorktown ending the war in the east in 1781, 1782 proved to be the bloodiest year of the war in Ohio.

Even as Clark was preparing to invade Ohio for the last time, the end of the war had already been negotiated. Nearly half a world away in France on September 3, 1782, British and American diplomats signed an agreement to end the war, which became known as the Treaty of Paris. Although the primary provision of the treaty in American eyes was its acknowledgment of American Independence, another major concession of great import was its granting of the entire trans-Appalachian west to the Mississippi River—including the Ohio Territory—to the new United States. When news of the January 1783 treaty ratification spread through the west, Native Americans were shocked to hear of yet another treaty in Paris, almost twenty years to the month from the one that ended the Seven Years' War, that had dealt away Indian lands to another nation without their representation or consent. Many Native people felt grossly betrayed by the British, who had vowed to protect them and their interests. While, unlike the French of twenty years earlier, the British would continue to occupy forts in the Great Lakes, it was clear that they could no longer be the same kind of ally they had been. Given the violence and bitter feelings that had marked the years of struggle on all sides, it was probably inevitable that, as was true in 1763, peace on paper signed far to the east did not translate into peace in Ohio.

The Western Confederacy and the End of the Middle Ground

Although the new American government claimed the land west of the Appalachians it had very little control over the area or its people. This is not to say that it did not try to exert its authority. At the Second Treaty of Fort Stanwix in 1784 the U.S. government got the Iroquois to cede their claims to the Ohio Territory once and for all. Then, with the Treaty of Fort McIntosh in 1785, American commissioners (including George Rogers Clark) signed an agreement with Lenape, Ojibwa, Ottawa, and Wyandot representatives that, at least on paper, ceded most of the southern part of Ohio and put the signers under U.S. government protection. The treaty was of little practical effect though, considering that many villages among those groups had not been consulted or represented, and two of the most important presences in that area—the Shawnee and the Miami—refused to attend the conference or abide by its terms. In response to this, the government tried to make a separate treaty with these groups at Fort Finney (at the mouth of the Great Miami River) in January 1786. They met with only limited success: the Miami and most of the Shawnee refused to attend the negotiations. Those that did found themselves intimidated, by threat of war, into signing a document that recognized American authority over them and ceded most of their Ohio lands without compensation.

Intended to create peace, this and the other new treaties only exacerbated tensions. The Americans based their demands on their supposed conquest of the Ohio Indians in the Revolutionary War, the same mistake the British had made twenty years earlier. Most Native residents of Ohio—particularly the northern confederacies of villages that had formed in the years after the end of the Revolution—did not acknowledge military defeat and refused to recognize treaties that they did not sign. White settlers took these same treaties as proof that the Indians were occupying most of Ohio illegally. Combined with the bitterness and mutual hatred that had developed on both sides during the course of the Revolution, these agreements were a recipe for even more violence, as Long Knives and Indians alike sought to punish each other for breeching what they thought were their legitimate territorial claims. In the middle was the U.S. government. Although it posed as a mighty power in its treaty negotiations, it proved itself instead to be only a paper tiger, unable to control either the Indians or its own citizens. For all of these reasons, the year after the Treaty of Fort Finney was the most violent since the war began. Indians from the Wabash region in particular staged attacks south into Kentucky, and the Kentuckians in retaliation sent a two-pronged expedition into the Wabash and Miami valleys in the autumn. George Rogers Clark led the Wabash campaign, but he had to turn back when a large number of his men mutinied and departed. The other group, led by General Benjamin Logan (and including the famous frontiersmen Daniel Boone and Simon Kenton) crossed the Ohio River in August to attack Shawnee villages in the Miami Valley region. The first town at which they arrived was Mequachaka on the Mad River (see Figure 4.4). The village chief, Moluntha, was one of the few Shawnee who had signed the Treaty of Fort Finney, and he flew an American flag over his village as a symbol of the U.S. government's protection promised in the treaty. Logan's men attacked the village, even though its residents put up no resistance, and Moluntha carried his copy of the treaty as he peacefully surrendered to the militiamen. Nevertheless, Major Hugh McGary sought him out among the prisoners and buried an axe in the chief's head in revenge for the Kentuckians' defeat at Blue Licks four years earlier. At another village, Logan's men burned a prisoner at the stake with a bag of gunpowder tied around his waist, which they knew would explode once the fire got hot enough. In all, Logan's men killed dozens of Shawnee men, women, and children and burned eight Shawnee villages and fifteen thousand bushels of corn before they returned to Kentucky. Rather than "pacifying" the Indians, though, Logan's Raid only further enraged and unified the Shawnee—who pushed for a broader Indian confederacy and British help at Detroit just weeks later—and ignited the Northwest Indian War that would rage for another eight years. By flagrantly defying the goals and treaties of the U.S. government, Logan's Raid also proved the impotence of the Continental Congress in administering Ohio Country. Further illustrating the government's tenuous control of Ohio was the fact that it could not prevent white settlement, even though it officially deemed such "squatting" as illegal and posted warnings for squatters to stay out of Ohio. Unauthorized settlement continued through the 1780s causing increasing friction and helping to inspire unified Native resistance.

The new Western Confederacy of Native American villages had been developing since the end of the Revolution. In some ways this Indian Confederation bore a striking resemblance to the American Confederation. It was a loose organization of representatives

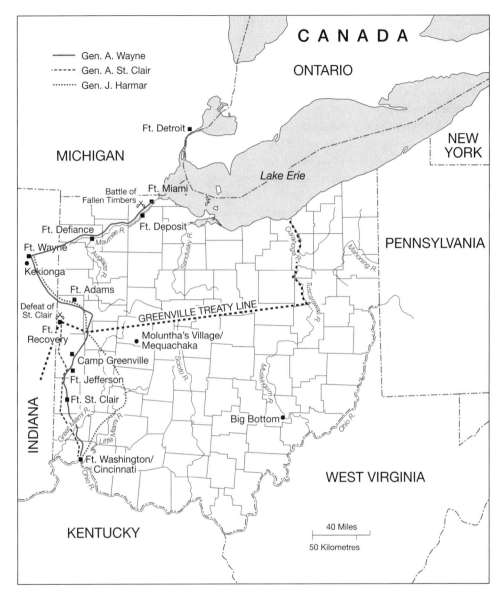

Figure 4.4 Early national conflict with Native Americans, 1785–95.

from autonomous political units that pronounced sweeping and unifying objectives but had difficulties in controlling its members or enforcing its decisions. It tried to take as its model the Iroquois Confederacy, and it invited representatives from that venerable alliance to their meetings. At a grand Confederation council at Brownstown (near Detroit) in November of 1786, Thayendanegea (Joseph Brant), the formidable Mohawk leader who had played a key role in the formation of the Western Confederacy three years earlier, exhorted the Great Lakes villages to band together in the face of American encroachment. Using the Algonquian Indian metaphor of the "common dish," which traditionally represented peace and alliance, Brant pleaded that all the Great Lakes tribes should use a single spoon: act as one bargaining unit in dealing with American demands for land. The council asked Congress to invalidate its previous controversial and poorly representative treaties in favor of negotiating a new one that would deal with the Confederacy as a whole. But in the meantime the Western Confederacy, like its Continental Congress counterpart, found itself unable to control its own people. Border raiding continued despite the various chiefs' attempts to rein it in, and future councils devolved into fractious bickering among members. A major treaty negotiation scheduled for the summer of 1788 was delayed when a freelance band of Ottawas and Ojibwas attacked a detachment of American soldiers as they prepared the site for the talks at the falls of the Muskingum, at which point Northwest Territory governor Arthur St. Clair cancelled the meeting. This and other undiplomatic pronouncements by St. Clair in turn provoked the many members of the Confederacy to forego negotiations entirely, and any appearance of unity began to unravel. The relatively small group of Indians that affirmed earlier land cessions at the subsequent Fort Harmar Treaty negotiations of 1789 were not representative of most of the Confederacy, and it included few major leaders of any group. Even an American observer, Major Ebenezer Denny, regarded the treaty negotiations as a farce, and both Indians and Americans broadly ignored it. The Western Confederacy, now led by such strident voices as Shawnee War Chief Weyapiersenwah (Blue Jacket), counseled resistance against any further American encroachment and cultivated stronger ties with the British in Detroit. Indian raiding increased, bringing the toll of killed and captured American settlers in the Ohio Valley in the years 1783 to 1790 to around 1,500. Both sides expected war.

By 1790, however, there was one crucial difference between the United States and the Western Confederacy. In 1789, the United States adopted the Constitution, a stronger form of government with greater military and enforcement provisions than the Articles of Confederation that had preceded it. The first major test of these powers came in 1790, when Congress authorized President Washington to call the militias of Virginia, Kentucky, and Western Pennsylvania to mount an organized expedition against the Indians, particularly targeting the heart of the Confederacy at Kekionga (present-day Fort Wayne, Indiana; see Figure 4.4). Washington's choice of General Josiah Harmar to lead the campaign seemed to be a good one. He had served under Washington in the Revolution and, at the time of his appointment, had been the senior officer of the U.S. Army for six years. Furthermore, he had acquired a great deal of first-hand experience on the ground in Ohio, from leading the efforts to expel squatters to helping negotiate the Treaty of Fort McIntosh. Despite his obvious strengths, though, several factors conspired to put him at a disadvantage. Although he had more than 1,400 men under his command, more than three-quarters of them were militiamen who for the most part exhibited poor training and poor discipline. Even the 320 U.S. Army regulars the War Department granted him suffered from poor morale, as their pay had just been cut and some had resorted to selling their shoes just to get money. Beyond footwear, the entire expedition was not particularly well-supplied in general with either provisions or pack animals. For all of his abilities, Harmar also made a key strategic blunder before he left. Knowing that the British still occupied Fort Detroit, and fearing that they may think the campaign was

Figure 4.5   Miami Chief Mishikinakwa was among the most fearsome and talented adversaries of the early U.S. military. When finally defeated at the Battle of Fallen Timbers, he became an advocate of peace with the Americans. "I am the last to sign this treaty," he is reported to have said when agreeing to the Treaty of Greenville, "I will be the last to break it." He later met with several U.S. presidents, and died quietly near Fort Wayne, Indiana in 1812.
Source: Courtesy of the Ohio Historical Society (AL02985)

directed at them and send troops to resist, Harmar alerted the British there of the purposes and general plan of his expedition, information that the British happily passed along to their Indian allies. Having full knowledge of American plans would have been a great advantage to the Indian Confederacy all by itself, but this combined with the fact that the brilliant Miami War Chief Mishikinakwa (Little Turtle; see Figure 4.5) was coordinating the Confederacy's response almost guaranteed Harmar's failure. Under Mishikinakwa's direction Indians along the path of the invasion burned their own villages, and when a detachment of 400 of Harmar's men plundered what was left of one of them on the Eel River (in present-day Northeastern Indiana) on September 19, the chief dispatched a decoy warrior to lure the Americans to pursue him into an ambush. His plan worked. As Indians rained fire on a surprised militia, 90 percent of them immediately fled, some flinging away their guns without having fired a shot. The remaining regular army soldiers (under Captain John Armstrong) took heavy casualties before they could get back to the main body. Retreating, the expedition conducted two more reconnoiterings-in-force, both of which Mishikinakwa's men similarly defeated, with more heavy casualties and desertions resulting. Harmar came back to Fort Washington declaring victory, but 183 of his men had been killed, close to 100 more wounded, and the Native Americans were not inclined to be any more peaceful. If anything, victory emboldened them, and they stepped up their raids on American settlements, including an attack on a blockhouse at Big Bottom (on the Muskingum north of Marietta) in January 1791 that killed thirteen settlers. Harmar's expedition was the worst defeat Native Americans had yet inflicted on an American army, and there were rumors that Harmer had been drunk and failed to send reinforcements when he should have. He eventually survived the court-martial that followed, but the experience ended his military career and he retired to Philadelphia.

Washington's famous temper flared when he heard about Harmar's defeat. He had his secretary of war Henry Knox appoint General Arthur St. Clair as commander of the next attempt. On paper, this seemed to be another good choice. Not only had St. Clair served in the French and Indian War and the American Revolution, but he was also the governor of the Northwest Territory. He was supposed to have twice as many men as Harmar and was to build a chain of forts along the way to pose a stronger presence in the area. However, St. Clair was plagued with many of the same problems Harmar faced. Although he eventually mustered about 2,000 men, most were not real professional soldiers—about 70 percent were either militia or unemployed civilians from eastern cities who had been recruited for enlistments as short as six months and were little better than militiamen in terms of training or discipline. Supplies were again insufficient and of poor quality, as were the pack animals to carry them. Originally planned as a summer campaign, it took until October to gather all the necessary men and supplies. In addition, St. Clair had little experience with frontier warfare, and he was almost too ill to mount his horse when the expedition started. Furthermore, Mishikinakwa (Little Turtle), Weyapiersenwah (Blue Jacket), and the Lenape Chief Buckongahelas benefitted from St. Clair's delays. They used the time to put together a force of a little more than 1,000 men from a number of different tribes, including Miami, Shawnee, Mingo, Lenape, Wyandot, Ojibwa, Ottawa, Potawatomi, and even a few Cherokee. Simon Girty was also among them to provide his expertise and leadership. Not aware of any of this, St. Clair assembled his force of about 1,500 (there had been many desertions even before the campaign began) at Fort Washington and then made his way north toward the Wabash villages, building Forts Hamilton and Jefferson along the way. The going was slow—sometimes only five miles a day—and the forts were not particularly imposing at first. They also took time to build, and St. Clair had to leave men behind at the nascent forts to garrison them. Desertion was common and some deserters captured by the Indians revealed details about the whereabouts, size, strength, and morale of American forces. Disease and terrible weather took their toll on his army, too, to the point that St. Clair actually had fewer than 1,000 men ready for duty (plus a couple of hundred civilian camp followers) when they stopped near the headwaters of the Wabash River (near present-day Fort Recovery) on November 3.

At dawn the next morning, the Native American army sprang on the camp it had surrounded the night before, catching it completely by surprise. Mishikinakwa had scouted St. Clair's forces over the course of the night, and the chief deliberately chose to attack a portion dominated by militiamen first. As he correctly surmised, they put up only token resistance before fleeing and throwing the rest of the camp into disorder, impeding the more disciplined soldiers from putting up an organized defense. Indian sharpshooters targeted artillerymen—keeping the cannons out of play—as well as officers, creating even more confusion and disorder in the ranks. American attempts at bayonet charges on the Indian lines seemed to force them back, but the soldiers found that these retreats were only a tactic to draw American forces out in order to destroy them. Completely surrounding the American army, the Native American forces tightened the noose for the next three hours, pouring fire into the camp until St. Clair decided to focus his remaining forces for a desperate bayonet charge to break through the lines and escape with his remaining men. St. Clair was quite brave during the encounter—he had three horses shot out from under him and he emerged from battle with eight bullet holes in his clothes—but in leaving he pretty much abandoned all of the civilians and wounded and all of his supplies, including his entire store of food and 1,200 muskets. The Indian warriors killed almost everyone who remained behind, including a number of civilian contractors and nearly all of the hundreds of camp followers. Some also stuffed the mouths of the American dead with dirt, a symbolic statement on the American hunger for Indian land that underlay the conflict.

If the Harmar campaign had been a disaster for the Americans, the St. Clair expedition was a catastrophe, and the broadside in Figure 4.6 helped spread the news. The Indians had succeeded in killing 56 percent of his officers and nearly 70 percent of his men overall (and this does not include any civilian deaths). Only a couple of dozen servicemen returned uninjured. With a casualty rate of about 97 percent (in comparison, Indian losses stood at about 20 killed and another 40 wounded) it was, by far, the worst defeat Indians ever inflicted on the U.S. military, as it destroyed nearly a quarter of the small U.S. Army in a single day. It was the greatest military defeat by an American army ever in terms of losses in proportion to numbers engaged. Although St. Clair asked for a court martial to exonerate himself, a now furious George Washington demanded his immediate resignation, ending his military career. In contrast, it was also the greatest success the Northwest Indian Confederacy would ever have, and the victory further emboldened Indians to launch attacks throughout western Ohio, including Fort Jefferson in 1792, just outside Cincinnati in 1793, and near Fort Jefferson and Fort Hamilton in 1794. The British increased their support of the Confederacy, new white settlement in Ohio reached a standstill, and the "single spoon" of the Northwest Confederacy seemed to be succeeding in preventing further American encroachment. Like the British in the 1760s, the United States was forced to give up its claim to Indian lands by right of conquest, saying from now on they would only acquire further lands by treaty and purchase.

Ironically, at this moment of its greatest success the Confederacy was beginning to unravel. General Rufus Putnam, a leader of the tiny American settlement at Marietta, was able to negotiate a treaty that peeled away most of the Wabash Villages in 1792, and moderates like the Mohican Aupaumut and Lenape Chief Hopocan (Captain Pipe) counseled further negotiations consistent with the new U.S. policy. Thayendanegea (Joseph Brant) thought Aupaumut too accommodating, while at the same time suggesting that the Confederacy should consider a Muskingum River boundary for American

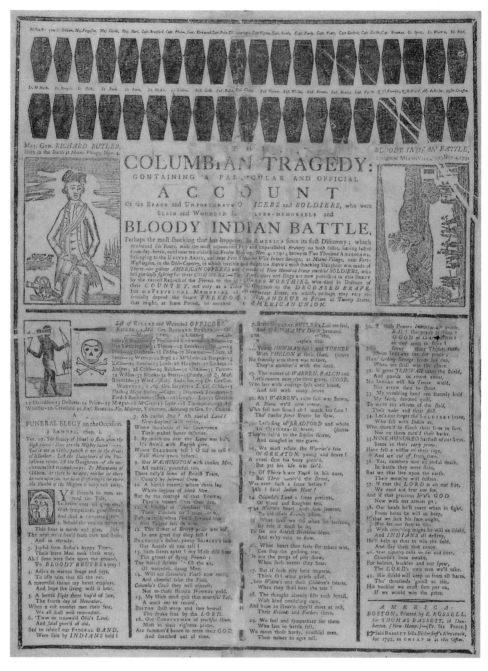

Figure 4.6 Broadsides were large, poster-like publications that were a common way of relaying information and opinion in the seventeenth century. This broadside from 1791 reflects the way that news of St. Clair's disastrous defeat that year reached many Americans of the time.
Source: Courtesy of the Ohio Historical Society (OVS2500)

settlement. Others, particularly the Miami and Shawnee, had little interest in negotiation, and both Buckongahelas and Weyapiersenwah refused to accept any boundary north of the Ohio River. Shawnee Indians murdered two American envoys on their way to the Wabash to try to make peace in the spring of 1792, a planned peace council on the Lower Sandusky in 1793 never took place because neither side would compromise on the issue of the Ohio River boundary and Indian and Kentuckian raiding parties stepped up attacks. A shadow of its earlier self, the Western Confederacy was then forced to meet its greatest challenge in General "Mad" Anthony Wayne's Legion of the United States.

Washington had chosen Wayne to take over after St. Clair's defeat, and in him Washington finally found a commander up to the task. As a highly distinguished officer of the Revolutionary Army whose bravery in battle and legendary temper earned him the nickname "Mad Anthony," Wayne was determined to avoid the mistakes of his predecessors. Despite Washington's preference to get the army on its feet and into the field as fast as possible, Wayne realized that lack of preparation and proper training had been key factors in the previous defeats. He thus took the time necessary to properly equip and train a much larger force—around 5,000 at its peak—of mostly professional soldiers, and he encamped his men away from Cincinnati and its distractions to ensure better discipline. An experienced Indian-fighter himself, Wayne took great pains to train the men in frontier tactics. He also cultivated a much more sophisticated intelligence network, with the use of Indian scouts and the extraordinary services of William Wells. Wells was a Kentuckian who had been captured at the age of twelve and adopted by the Miami, eventually becoming Mishikinakwa's son-in-law and a trusted scout and battlefield leader in the Confederacy victories against Harmar and St. Clair. Reunited with his Anglo-American family in 1793, he served as a captain and valuable source of information to Wayne as the expedition proceeded into the country Wells knew so well. By October 1793, almost two years from St. Clair's defeat, and despite some problems with disease and supplies, Wayne finally believed his legion was ready to engage the Confederacy.

Moving carefully yet decisively, Wayne took roughly the same route as St. Clair, planting well-garrisoned forts along the way and making a point of constructing one on the grounds of St. Clair's defeat, which he symbolically named Fort Recovery. The men constructing the fort faced the grisly reminders of that battle, as they had to sweep the grounds of human bones before they could pitch their tents for the first time. It was here on June 30, 1794 that the Confederacy first attacked the Legion of the United States. A war party led by Weyapiersenwah (and including a young Tecumseh) fell on a major supply train, killing more than thirty, but a subsequent general attack on the fort led by Mishikinakwa, Weyapiersenwah, and Simon Girty failed. This loss and the greater awareness of the nature of the forces they were facing took its toll on the Indian army, as did the departure of many warriors who felt that they had met their battle obligations to the Confederacy with this encounter. The reduced Indian forces were unable to stop Wayne in early August from building Fort Defiance at "The Glaize," the confluence of the Auglaize and Maumee rivers. It was one of the valley's most important Native American settlements, with a trading post run by Alexander McKee and Simon Girty at the confluence and the homes of Mishikinakwa, Weyapiersenwah, and Buckongahelas nearby. From there Wayne offered the Confederacy, now concentrated on the lower

Maumee, one last chance at a negotiated settlement. Mishikinakwa urged his colleagues to take Wayne up on his offer. He knew that this force was different from the ones they had been able to surprise and defeat before, telling his peers that Wayne "never sleeps." In addition, in the days after the defeat at Fort Recovery he had pleaded with the British in Detroit to send military aid, but they had refused—the British government was in preliminary negotiations with the United States in what would become the Jay Treaty, and they did not want to take the chance of provoking a war. Thinking military victory impossible without British help, Mishikinakwa advocated negotiation with Wayne, but when Weyapiersenwah and Buckongahelas refused, he ceded overall command of the forces to them (although he retained command of his Miami warriors). Many of the Confederacy's warriors apparently believed that the construction of Fort Miamis (a British fort on the lower Maumee River officially in support of the fur trade) just months earlier proved that the British would indeed come to their Indian allies' aid once fighting began. It was no coincidence that the Confederacy forces chose to make their stand at a spot not too far from this well-armed fort.

The resulting Battle of Fallen Timbers (see Figure 4.7) was in some ways anticlimactic. Wayne's legion reached the rapids of the Maumee on August 18, where it stopped to build Fort Deposit to guard their supplies. The Native American army expected Wayne to advance the next day, and as was their tradition before battles, they began a fast that they ordinarily did not end until after the fighting. Wayne, on the other hand, gave his men a couple of days to finish Fort Deposit before marching on the Confederacy Army on August 20, at which point the Indian warriors were weakened from days without food, and a large number of them had gone back several miles to Fort Miamis to get provisions. The resulting battle was almost a foregone conclusion. Outnumbered more than two-to-one, the Confederacy forces (including a few Canadian militiamen) fortified themselves among a natural breastwork of trees knocked down earlier by a tornado. Some Ottawa and Potawatomi warriors moved out to attack an advanced unit of Kentucky militia, perhaps hoping to create the same kind of confusion that this tactic had spread among St. Clair's men. Although the militia did run, this was a ploy to lure the pursuing Indian warriors into a much sturdier line of regular army legionnaires that stopped the advance and pushed them back to their defensive position. Wayne ordered a bayonet attack against the Indians among the trees, with a simultaneous sweep of his mounted dragoons. Outflanked by the swift-moving cavalry, badly outnumbered, and stung by the deaths of several Huron chiefs and the wounding of the main Ottawa leaders Agushiway and Nekeik (Little Otter) the Indian army was forced to flee after only about an hour of fighting. A determined rear-guard action by Wyandot and Canadian militia soldiers prevented the retreat from becoming a rout, but perhaps the most painful blow came when the retreating warriors ran to Fort Miamis for protection only to find the gates closed to them. When they beseeched the post's commander Major William Campbell for sanctuary, he reportedly shouted back down to them "You are painted [for war] too much, my children, and I cannot let you in." Perhaps as much as Wayne's decisive military victory, this rebuff by the British in the Confederacy's hour of greatest need crushed any lingering hopes that they could stand against the United States.

Figure 4.7   Some U.S. military historians have called the Battle of Fallen Timbers one of the three most important battles ever fought on American soil because of its significant long-term effects. By breaking the back of Native American resistance east of the Mississippi, the clash (and the Treaty of Greenville it spawned) ended the long "Middle Ground" era of the region and helped initiate a massive migration of settlers from the east into western lands. For Native Americans, it represented the beginnings of a long retreat across the continent and an early chapter of the U.S. reservation system.
Source: Courtesy of the Ohio Historical Society (AL00232)

Wayne augmented his victory in the following days by burning all the villages and crops in a fifty-mile swath on either side of the Maumee, and as added emphasis, building Fort Wayne squarely in the middle of what used to be the Western Confederacy capital at Kekionga, near where Harmar's men had been routed. Thoroughly defeated and without the hope of British aid, most Native American groups in the area began to answer Wayne's call to meet with him at the formidable military city of Camp Greene Ville (usually now written as Greenville) to negotiate peace. Throughout the winter of 1795 Wayne reached preliminary agreements with each of the main groups of the Confederacy, building up to the Treaty of Greenville negotiated in June and August of that year that ceded all but the swampy northwestern portion of what is now Ohio to the United States in exchange for gifts, annuities, return of prisoners, and protection from white settlers—many of whom still bore violent grudges against any Indian they saw (see Figure 4.8). Still couched in the language and guise of an agreement between diplomatic equals, these and other such treaties nevertheless reflected the U.S. government's ability to dictate terms by implicit threat of force. The following several years would see some violence, but much less than that which had characterized the 1780s and early 1790s.

Figure 4.8   This 1945 painting is currently hanging in the rotunda of the Ohio Statehouse. It depicts the signing of the Treaty of Greenville. In it, Mishikinakwa (Little Turtle) presents a wampum belt of peace to Anthony Wayne. Standing on the far right is William Henry Harrison, while on the far left Weaypiersenwah (Blue Jacket) talks with Tarhe (The Crane). Symbolically standing in between the Americans and the Native Americans—as he did in life—is Mishikinakwa's son-in-law and Anthony Wayne's scout, William Wells.
Source: Courtesy of the Ohio Historical Society (AL04501)

The Battle of Fallen Timbers and the Treaty of Greenville ended Middle Ground Ohio forever. The United States had broken the back of Indian resistance east of the Mississippi and, as a result, settlers began to pour into the territory in greater numbers than ever before. These events deeply influenced the course and momentum of American expansion into the West, and it is for this reason that some military historians have called the Battle of Fallen Timbers one of the three most important battles ever fought on American soil. In subsequent treaties, the remaining Native American groups soon began to give away even the little land that remained to them in Ohio. Yet the death of the Middle Ground did not mean the end of conflict in Ohio. A few Indian chiefs participated in the negotiations but refused to sign the treaty. Others decried the negotiations and any kind of cessions to the Americans, including the young Shawnee firebrand Tecumseh, who had fought at Fallen Timbers. Pitted against him at that battle and serving by Wayne's side at Greenville was twenty-one-year-old William Henry Harrison. These men were only two of the many participants in these events who seventeen years later would find themselves engaging in yet another major conflict focused in Ohio.

Three years after the signing of the Treaty of Greenville, John Heckewelder returned to the Tuscarawas Valley accompanied by Rufus Putnam and his son. They came to survey 12,000 acres of land that the Continental Congress had granted to the Moravians in 1787 in recompense for the lands they had lost in the war, as well as the lives they had lost at American hands. Heckewelder and Zeisberger intended to replant the Moravian villages with the handful of their remaining converts who would follow them there. While platting the new town of Gnadenhutten, he encountered the bones of the victims of the massacre sixteen years earlier. Gathering up as many as he could find, he laid them to rest in a common grave with a mound raised over it. It is product of nearly all the forces that shaped Ohio during the late eighteenth century: Native American villages; European-Indian cultural interaction; U.S., Indian, and British military conflict; and the eventual territorial control of the U.S. government. It still stands in a quiet village of about 1,200 people, none of whom are Native American. In some ways emblematic of the fate of Native American Ohio, it is the last Indian burial mound ever constructed in the state.

Further Reading

Good resources for this period are: Richard White's *The Middle Ground: Indians, Empires, and Republics in the Great Lakes Region 1650–1815* (1991. Cambridge: Cambridge University Press); R. Douglas Hurt's *The Ohio Frontier: Crucible of the Old Northwest, 1720–1830* (1998. Bloomington: Indiana University Press); Michael McConnell's *A Country Between: The Upper Ohio Valley and its Peoples, 1724–1774* (1997. Lincoln: University of Nebraska Press; and Daniel Barr's edited volume *The Boundaries between Us: Natives and Newcomers along the Frontiers of the Old Northwest Territory, 1750–1850* (2006. Kent: Kent State University Press). Additionally, Elizabeth Perkins's *Border Life: Experience and Memory in the Revolutionary Ohio Valley* deals with culture and society during the war (1998. Chapel Hill: University of North Carolina Press) while Thomas Pieper and James Gidney's *Fort Laurens, 1778–1779: The Revolutionary War in Ohio* focuses more specifically on military aspects of the war in Ohio (1980. Kent: Kent State University Press). David Skaggs and Larry Nelson's *The Sixty Years' War for the Great Lakes, 1754–1815* deals broadly with the series of conflicts during this period (eds. 2001. Baltimore: Johns Hopkins University Press, 2001).

5

The Ohio Experiment

*Formation of the Northwest Territory, Early
American Settlements, and Statehood*

When viewed from above Ohio's most characteristic landscape feature is its wide expanse of farmland, in most places boxed in by a regular grid of perpendicular county roads. In 2007, Ohio's abundant farmland hosted more than 75,000 farms. Families ran most of these, partnerships and corporations ran the bulk of those remaining, and agricultural science institutions most of the rest. Finally, a few thousand acres of farms and smaller plots across the state—from Hardin County in the northwest to Marietta in the southeast and from Columbiana County in the northeast to Hamilton County in the southwest—were not leased out by any person or company, but by the state government. The proceeds of these leases, some of them made out for 99 years renewable in perpetuity, went to support education, although until 1968 some of the money had gone to support local religious institutions. These "school lands," the revenue they raise, and even the placement of the county roads that surround them, are the twenty-first century remnants of laws passed in the 1780s—before the United States had officially organized Ohio as a U.S. territory, and even before the nation had organized itself under a federal government. To this day Ohio's lands represent one of the state's most unique contributions to the development and history of the United States.

In a very real sense Ohio was a testing ground the fledgling United States used to develop its public land system through a process of trial and error. Starting with Ohio the new country had to solve a number of problems for which there was no precedent: How should the United States establish national control of these lands? How should they be integrated politically into the nation? How should they be distributed for settlement? In trying to resolve these issues, the government tried some experiments in Ohio and did not repeat them elsewhere. Others it tried for the first time in Ohio, refined, and then used as a model for the rest of the United States. This status of Ohio as a public lands "guinea pig" makes the story of its formative years of great significance to the history of

Ohio: A History of the Buckeye State, First Edition. Kevin F. Kern and Gregory S. Wilson.
© 2014 John Wiley & Sons, Inc. Published 2014 by John Wiley & Sons, Inc.

the United States. It also makes this chapter of Ohio's history a bit complicated. Several distinct public and corporate entities produced nine different major land surveys of the state and forty-six subsurveys. In addition, those authorities used several different surveying standards and made at least one major resurvey. As a result, Ohio's original survey map resembles a patchwork quilt when compared with the more regularized maps of most of the states to its west. Its early political development was also patchy as the United States implemented and refined a system of policies designed to help the area make the transition from an unorganized territory, to an organized one, to a state on equal footing with the others in the nation. Although the process was at times rocky and complex, the results of the "Ohio Experiment" helped shape the course of nearly every state that followed it into the Union.

Clearing Title and Related Problems

In the Treaty of Paris (1783) that ended the American Revolution, Britain gave the new United States official possession of Ohio along with nearly all the land lying between the original thirteen states and the Mississippi River. However, the matter of who actually controlled Ohio had long been under dispute, and would continue to be so for some time. Although Congress had agreed on October 19, 1780 that any western lands the United States might acquire would become public domain out of which the national government would carve free and equal states, several states had already laid claim to all or part of Ohio, and these claims were the cause of considerable contention. Conflicting claims between Virginia and Pennsylvania had contributed to Lord Dunmore's War in 1774, and the ratification of the Articles of Confederation had been held up for several years in part because of disputes among the various new states over the issue of western land claims. The problem was that colonial charters, which had been issued at various times over the course of more than 100 years, sometimes granted overlapping claims to western lands (see Figure 5.1). In Ohio's case, both Virginia and Connecticut laid claim to parts of Ohio based on these documents and as new states they had already promised some of these lands as payment to individuals, particularly veterans. In addition, New York claimed Ohio by virtue of having won Iroquois claims to the territory during the Revolution. Eventually the Continental Congress resolved these conflicting claims by convincing New York to surrender its claim, and by granting both Virginia (1784) and Connecticut (1786) portions of the Ohio territory to satisfy their previous obligations in exchange for those states surrendering the rest of Ohio to the government.

As difficult and time-consuming as settling these competing state claims was, it proved to be relatively easy in comparison with settling Native American claims to the land. The various treaties and conflicts described in the previous chapter were a constant backdrop to the territorial organization process until the Treaty of Greenville in 1795 removed Indian claims to most of the state. The fact that the government remained determined to press on in organizing its western lands despite the volatility of conditions in Ohio says much about how important Congress believed the process to be.

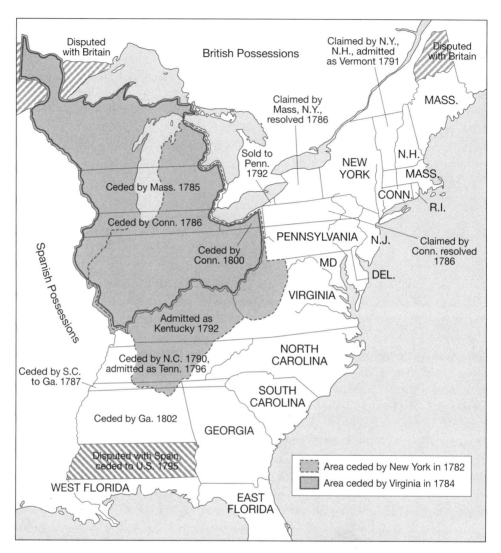

Figure 5.1   State land claims and cessions to the federal government, 1782–1802.
Source: Created by Karl Musser, fantasymaps.com (CC BY-SA 2.5)

Organizing Ohio and the Birth of the Public Land System

Congressional ordinances

Two main motivations drove the congressional imperative to organize the west. One was the issue of defense. Although the United States officially received the western lands in the Treaty of Paris, these lands were bounded by Spain (which had received the Louisiana Territory from France at the end of the Seven Years' War) and Britain, which not only held Canada but also still had several military posts on U.S. soil, including Fort Detroit. Some Americans feared that either of these nations could ally with Natives in the Great

Lakes to seize part or all of the western territories if there were no significant American presence there. Congress's primary motivation for developing these lands, though, was financial. Although the United States had won its independence it had done so by taking on an extraordinary amount of debt. The Articles of Confederation that governed the new nation were relatively weak and did not allow Congress to levy taxes, and as a result about the only avenue available for raising large amounts of money was the sale of western lands. Thus, congressional leaders believed that the sooner they could sell land and settle people in places like Ohio, the more secure their frontiers would be against the threat of Indian attack or foreign invasion, and the higher subsequent land prices would be after having made the land safer and more developed.

Congress first addressed this problem by adopting a plan drafted by Thomas Jefferson (with the help of Geographer of the United States Thomas Hutchins) that originally would have divided the western territories into as many as seventeen future states, including ten that would lie entirely or partially north of the Ohio River. Inspired by the rationalist ideas of the enlightenment to which Jefferson and other leaders of the young nation subscribed, the Ordinance of 1784 would have drawn the lines of these territories not along geographical features (as had usually been the case previously) but primarily by lines of latitude and longitude, in roughly two-degree increments. The law also provided for the organization of these proposed territories by allowing the settlers therein to form their own temporary territorial government, and then to draw up a constitution when its population reached 20,000. Once the territory had a constitution, it would then be eligible to join the United States on an equal footing with the other states when its population reached that of one of the current states. Jefferson's original draft of the plan went so far as to assign names to the new proto-states, including Assenisippia, Cherronesus, Illinoia, Michigania, Polypotamia, and Sylvania (present-day Ohio occupies what would have been the state of Washington plus parts of the states of Metropotamia, Saratoga, and Pelisipia). These names—perhaps thankfully—did not survive into later drafts of the bill. Another provision that did not survive banned slavery in the Northwest Territory, having failed to pass Congress by a single vote. (This led Jefferson to remark, "Thus we see the fate of millions unborn hanging on the tongue of one man, and Heaven was silent in that awful moment.") Although the Ordinance of 1784 is largely forgotten today because subsequent laws have superseded it, this neglect is unfortunate. Key provisions first envisioned by this original ordinance—including a process for developing territorial government, the ability to join the United States on an equal basis, and the failed provision banning slavery—later became parts of the major acts that replaced it: the Land Ordinance of 1785 and the Northwest Ordinance of 1787.

The Land Ordinance of 1785 addressed in a more detailed way the surveying and sale of western lands, and it did so in a completely new way. Whereas surveying at this time was usually done by the traditional "metes and bounds" method—marking out irregularly-shaped parcels using natural landmarks such as trees, rocks, and streams—the Land Ordinance created a regularized and systematic gridwork from a set baseline that largely ignored natural features. The basic unit was a one-square mile "section." There were thirty-six such sections in each of the six-by-six-mile square "townships," which were in turn units of the larger north-to-south running "ranges." Sales of these lands were to be

(a)

36	30	24	18	12	6
35	29	23	17	11	5
34	28	22	16	10	4
33	27	21	15	9	3
32	26	20	14	8	2
31	25	19	13	7	1

(b)

6	5	4	3	2	1
7	8	9	10	11	12
18	17	16	15	14	13
19	20	21	22	23	24
30	29	28	27	26	25
31	32	33	34	35	36

Figure 5.2 Numbering under the Land Ordinance of 1785 (a, left). Numbering under the Land Ordinance of 1796 (b, right).

in units no smaller than a section and in cash for no less than a dollar an acre. Until 1796, the surveyors numbered sections from south to north, starting in the southeast corner and returning to the southern baseline every six miles (see Figure 5.2a). In 1796, the law was amended to start numbering in the northeast corner, moving back and forth in a serpentine fashion from east to west and west to east (see Figure 5.2b).

The rectangular survey style was not the only innovative aspect of the 1785 law. One seventh of all lands surveyed were to be set aside to compensate veterans of the Continental Army, and sections 8, 11, 26, and 29 of each township were to be withheld for future sale in the hope that the sections developed around them would increase the price of these lands (in 1796, Congress changed these reservations to the four central sections of 15, 16, 21, and 22). The ordinance's most far-sighted innovation, however, was the reservation of section 16 of each township for the support of education. These lands were to be rented or otherwise used to ensure a steady income to create public schools throughout the territory at a time when public schools were rare and mostly confined to parts of New England and New York. Although the funds raised by section 16 later proved to be largely insufficient for the purpose, Ohio became the first experimental testing ground of the national government's commitment to a widespread expansion of public education.

The effects of the Land Ordinance of 1785 are hard to overestimate. The free and general public education system that it attempted to establish was not only more ambitious than any school system then in operation in the United States, but it was the first of its kind in the history of the world. The school reservation in each township served as a precedent that eventually resulted in 80 million acres of the public domain being set aside for the purposes of education. Furthermore, the Land Ordinance of 1785 became the basis of the U.S. public land system that was to survey most of the United States from the Appalachian Mountains to the Pacific Ocean, and the terms it defined (range, township, section) became the standard legal property designations for most of the land the United States surveyed thereafter. Even more than 225 years after Congress passed the Ordinance, travelers flying over the Midwest can still see the gridwork pattern it laid on the landscape by looking down at the county road systems. In fact, the Land Ordinance of 1785 would probably have no rival for the distinction of being the most important act ever passed by the Continental Congress under the Articles of Confederation were it not for the Northwest Ordinance passed two years later.

The Northwest Ordinance was a sweeping law that attempted to regularize the settlement, government, and eventual admission of territories in the Northwest Territory (those lands north of the Ohio River and east of the Mississippi River) as states. This law set up an orderly process for dividing the territory and providing stages of government for each division. In the first stage, Congress would appoint a governor, a secretary, and three judges to administer the territory by choosing and implementing civil and criminal laws from existing states. The governor had a great deal of power during this stage, with the ability to make most local government appointments, create new counties and townships, and serve as commander-in-chief of the militia. After the territory reached a population of 5,000 free males, a second stage would begin in which the population could elect a representative assembly. This was a sort of "training wheels" stage of self-government, one in which the assembly could initiate and pass legislation but had only limited powers otherwise. For example, while the assembly could nominate a slate of candidates for the upper house or "legislative council," Congress would choose which nominees would serve. The assembly and legislative council could also elect a congressional representative, but he would be a nonvoting member. Furthermore, even if the assembly and legislative council passed a bill, the governor could still veto it with no provision for override. The governor also held the power to convene and dissolve the assembly at his own discretion. Finally, when the territory reached a population of 60,000 free residents, it could become a state on equal footing with all the other states as long as its constitution and government was republican (representative) in nature. Although the initial experiment of this plan in Ohio made for rocky going at times (particularly regarding the governor and his powers) this three-stage path to statehood became (with modifications) the model for the territorial organization and admission of most subsequent states.

As important as its governmental plan was, the Northwest Ordinance also boasted several other provisions of significance. The first paragraph contained a detailed guarantee of property rights, something that proved to be an important issue as claims to these territories started to be filed. Other articles guaranteed such due process rights as habeus corpus and preservation of private contracts, as well as several freedoms that later became enshrined in the U.S Bill of Rights, including freedom of religion, trial by jury, and the banning of excessive fines and cruel and unusual punishment. The Ordinance's idealistic Article Three famously stated that "Religion, morality, and knowledge, being necessary to good government and the happiness of mankind, schools and the means of education shall forever be encouraged." It also—perhaps infamously—asserted that "the utmost good faith shall always be observed towards the Indians; their lands and property shall never be taken from them without their consent... ." While the document proved to have little power to achieve these goals, it was successful in implementing another idealistic provision that loomed large over the subsequent history of the United States. Article Six banned slavery from the Northwest Territory, a resurrection of Jefferson's ban that Congress struck from the Ordinance of 1784. Historians have cited this clause as a major factor in making slavery a regional, rather than a national, institution. Had the Virginians and Kentuckians, who were some of the earliest settlers of Ohio, been able to take their slaves with them the history of Ohio and the United States might have been very different indeed.

Early surveys and settlement

Eager to start the process of getting land ready for sale, Congress dispatched Thomas Hutchins as the head of a group of surveyors, with members representing every state of the new country, to begin the initial survey of Ohio lands. Hutchins had led an adventurous life to that point, having fought with the British in the Seven Years' War and the Revolutionary War before being charged with treason for refusing to bear arms against the Americans and switching sides in 1780. None of this, though, fully prepared him for this adventure. On September 30, 1785—just four months and ten days after Congress had passed its Land Ordinance—Hutchins and his team began to lay the geographer's baseline that became the starting point for the "Seven Ranges" (see Figure 5.3). As historic as this first official rectangular survey was to the history of Ohio and the United States it was fraught with difficulty and disappointment throughout. Starting at the intersection of the Ohio River and the Pennsylvania state line (present-day East Liverpool) Hutchins had only surveyed four miles of the baseline before the threat of an Iroquois attack sent him and his party fleeing back to Pittsburgh, where he remained until he felt conditions were safer. By August 1786, the United States had negotiated the Treaty of Fort Finney with the Shawnee and fully established Fort Harmar on the mouth of the Muskingum to provide military support and a place for surveyors to seek protection in case of trouble. Thus, Hutchins and his team began the survey again, only to break it off on more than one occasion thereafter for various reasons, including fear of Indian attacks, foul weather, and lack of supplies. Also slowing the survey was the hilly and heavily forested land itself, as well as mosquitoes and the malaria they carried. By February 1787, Hutchins and his team had finished the plats of only four ranges.

Congress was displeased with the survey's slow progress, its cost overruns, and its increasingly evident inaccuracies (it turned out that Hutchins had miscalculated the latitude of the baseline by half a mile, and the surveying party did not correct their lines to allow for the curvature of the earth, therefore leaving the far end of the line 1,500 feet further south than at its beginning). Nevertheless, the desperately cash-poor government decided to put the first four ranges up for sale. Running advertisements in every state throughout the summer, Congress ran an auction for these lands from September 21 to October 9. Even this proved to be a disappointment. Of the approximately 800,000 acres available, only 108,431 drew bids, and buyers soon defaulted on about a third of that acreage, leaving only about 73,000 acres—about 9 percent—sold. The roughly $100,000 net profit from the first sale of the Seven Ranges in depreciated American currency was substantially less than Congress had hoped for, but they were at least partially to blame for the result. Although the land near the river sold well, most of the rest of the area was unsuitable for farming and drew little interest from the largely agrarian population of the country. Even if the land had been better, though, Congress's own rules for the land sale

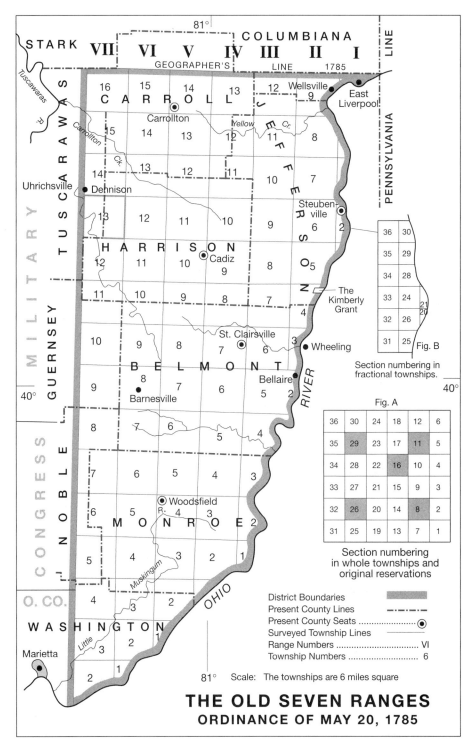

Figure 5.3 This diagram of the Seven Ranges—the first government survey in Ohio—highlights several of the 1785 Land Ordinance's innovative aspects. The square survey units had never been attempted before on such a large scale anywhere in the world. Furthermore, the setting aside of sections 8, 11, 26, and 29 for future sale and section 16 for support of public education demonstrated the far-sighted nature of the law.

were prohibitive. The smallest unit a buyer could purchase was an entire section at no less than a dollar an acre ($640), with one-third of the money down and the rest to be paid in three months. As this figure was more than most Americans could expect to make in a year (and roughly four to five times the annual wage of an unskilled worker) it is small wonder that so few of them chose to spend so much on land of such little promise. Furthermore, 640 acres was about fifteen times more than an average farmer could expect to clear and cultivate, meaning that most of those bidding were probably land speculators hoping to carve up the sections and sell them at a profit. Although it eventually finished the survey of the Seven Ranges in the early 1800s, Congress in the meantime discovered different, and more profitable, models for selling its Ohio lands.

One of Hutchins's surveyors inspired one of these new ideas. Winthrop Sargent—who had done some exploring on his own—sent encouraging reports about lands to the south and west of the Seven Ranges back to some friends in Massachusetts. These speculators formed the Ohio Company of Associates at the Bunch of Grapes Tavern in Boston on March 1, 1786. With Winthrop Sargent serving as its secretary, the Ohio Company's membership boasted many other prominent men of the area, including the Reverend Manasseh Cutler, and distinguished Revolutionary War generals Rufus Putnam and Benjamin Tupper. Investors could buy up to five shares at $125 in gold (or $1,000 in devalued Continental paper dollars). Their plan was to buy 1.5 million acres of Ohio lands for the equivalent of $1 million in cash and securities. Cutler may be considered one of the first successful corporate lobbyists in U.S. history. Replacing an earlier ineffective company representative in Philadelphia, Reverend Cutler set to work convincing individual members of Congress that the Ohio Company's plan was in the national interest. Touting the high character, industriousness, and virtue of the prospective settlers, the order and military protection that these men—most of whom were Revolutionary War veterans—would bring to the frontier, and the money they would bring to Congress's coffers, Cutler won over most of the Continental Congress, including its president, Arthur St. Clair. With the disappointing experience of the Seven Ranges sale unfolding as Cutler lobbied and the prospect of ten times as much profit from the Ohio Company's plan, Congress approved the sale on October 27, 1787, demanding $500,000 down and the rest upon completion of a survey. With a discount of 1/3 for "bad lands" and Congressional acceptance of depreciated currency and pre-existing land warrants for veterans in payment, the Ohio Company's purchase amounted to about eight and a half cents per acre. Although the Ohio Company was unable to come up with the second half of its million-dollar payment, it took the 750,000 acres acquired from its first purchase and added more than 200,000 acres in a smaller second purchase to make a total land claim of 965,285 acres.

The relatively successful model set by the Ohio Company Purchase inspired another, more troubled purchase farther west. John Cleves Symmes, a former New Jersey Supreme Court judge and member of the Continental Congress who held certificates of indebtedness for helping Washington's army in its retreat through his state in 1776, applied for up to 2 million acres between the Great and Little Miami rivers a month after the Ohio Company presented its claim. With a similar one-third discount for "bad lands" and the use of land warrants and securities for payment, the deal worked out to about sixty-seven cents an acre. The Symmes Purchase, however, was plagued with problems from the start. First, he had overestimated the amount of land available, which turned out to be less than 600,000 acres. Second, he was only able to raise enough money to pay for about half of that amount. Third, the original surveys of the area were largely left to individual buyers, and as a result were poorly-run, idiosyncratically numbered, and often overlapped each other, resulting in litigation, resurveys, and irregularly shaped quadrilaterals throughout. Last, Symmes mistakenly sold some lands twice, and sold others that lay outside his jurisdiction to sell. These mistakes resulted in more litigation and appeals to Congress for decades afterward. Hoping to make a fortune as a land proprietor, Symmes instead had much of his property seized to settle lawsuits and died in poverty in 1814. Despite all the difficulties that accompanied the Symmes Purchase, however, it soon grew into a thriving center of American settlement in Ohio, focused in particular on the area surrounding the military post of Fort Washington and the city that eventually became Cincinnati.

Both the Symmes and Ohio Company purchases shared important aspects that illustrated both successful (in other words, copied later elsewhere) and unsuccessful (never tried again) experiments on the Ohio "guinea pig." These lands were, for example, the last major surveys conducted under the first version of the rectangular survey system before its 1796 revision. In addition, not only did they have the usual sections set aside for the support of public schools, they also had reservations of land to support colleges and religion, presumably in accordance with Article 3 of the Northwest Ordinance. The college lands—two entire townships in the Ohio Company purchase and one associated with the Symmes purchase—ultimately resulted in the formation of Ohio and Miami Universities, respectively (as Symmes had already sold the college township in his purchase, Miami University ended up being located on government lands farther to the west). These became the models and first examples of what would be many "land grant" universities in the United States. The income from the more than 43,000 acres of "ministerial lands" (section 29 of each township) was to provide support for organized religion there, in proportion to its representation among the population. Passed by the Continental Congress before the adoption of the U.S. Constitution and its prohibition against the establishment of religion, this experiment was never repeated. Most of the ministerial lands ended up being sold in the 1830s with the proceeds invested to support the churches of the township. Even at the beginning of the twenty-first century, Ohio still takes in a small amount of money from these investments each year, all of which since 1968 has gone to the support of education.

Although the Seven Ranges, Ohio Company Lands, and Symmes Purchase provided the basis of the U.S. public land system, the overall initial survey of Ohio looks much more like a mismatched patchwork quilt than the more uniform surveys of the states that followed (see Figure 5.4). This is because a number of other surveys, grants, and other reservations characterized the Ohio experiment in its early years. The most significant of these idiosyncratic surveys took place in the south central and northeastern parts of the state: The Virginia Military District and the Connecticut Western Reserve and "Firelands."

The Virginia Military District originated in a deal that Virginia struck with Congress when it agreed to cede its western land claims to the United States. Virginia had already

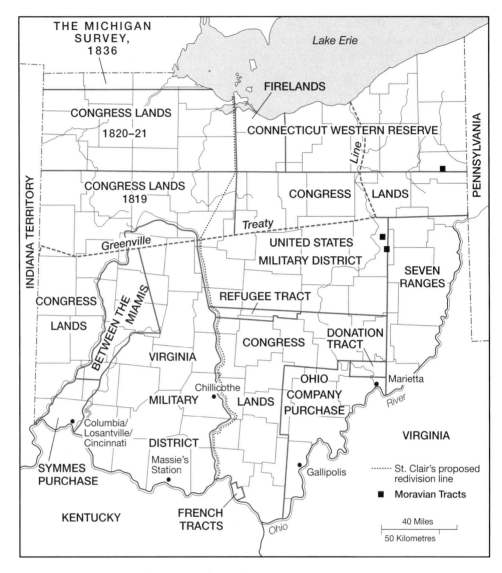

Figure 5.4   Ohio during the territorial period, 1788–1803.
Source: Adapted from Knepper, G.W. 2003. *Ohio and Its People* (Kent, OH: Kent State University, p. 55).
Copyright © by The Kent State University

promised generous land grants to its Revolutionary War veterans, and Congress agreed
to allow Virginia to distribute as much land in Ohio as it needed to meet these obligations. Located mostly between the Little Miami and Scioto rivers this tract is unique in
that it was surveyed by the old "indiscriminant" or "metes and bounds" system resulting
in extremely irregularly shaped townships and parcels of land compared with those in
the rest of the state (see Figure 5.5). In addition, because surveyors used natural land-
marks such as marked trees and rocks that could easily be forged, moved, or destroyed,

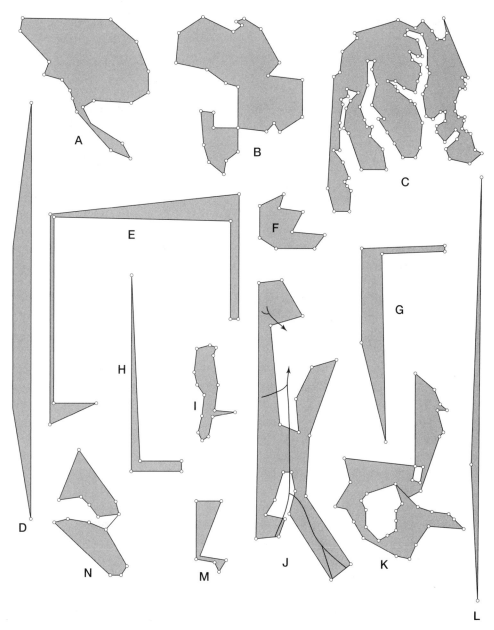

The above figures, selected at random from the Records, merely
suggest the great variety of shapes of surveys that were made in the District.

Figure 5.5 The Virginia Military District (VMD) stood in sharp contrast to the other major
Ohio surveys that used regular, square-shaped units. As it was surveyed by the traditional "metes
and bounds" system, the land claims there could take wildly different shapes and sizes, as these
random examples of VMD surveys show. The boundaries were irregular and based on land-
marks that were impermanent, and as a result legal disputes over holdings in this area continued
for more than a century afterward.

conflicting and overlapping surveys were rife throughout the district and resulted in lit-igation that in some cases extended into the early 1900s. Despite these problems, the Virginia Military District drew a number of settlers from an early stage, and by 1803 it boasted the state capital in Chillicothe.

Like the Virginia Military District, the Connecticut Western Reserve was a tract of land held by an eastern state in exchange for ceding all other western land claims to the United States. This strip of land, between 41 and 42 degrees north latitude and extending 120 miles west of the Pennsylvania border, included on its far end lands set aside to com-pensate victims of Benedict Arnold's Revolutionary War raids that burned large sections of several Connecticut towns, including New Haven, Greenwich, Norwalk, and New London. It is no coincidence, then, that the "Firelands" (or "Sufferer's Lands") hosts towns bearing all those names (Fairfield, another major victim of the raids, was a name already claimed by a town near Dayton by the time Indian claims were extinguished and settlers started to arrive. The "Firelands" instead has a "North Fairfield"). To raise money for education, Connecticut sold the rest of the Western Reserve to the Connecticut Land Company in 1795, and this group of speculators dispatched a team under the leadership of Moses Cleaveland to survey the area. Using a modified rectangular survey of five-square-mile townships (later subdivided into quarter townships in the "Firelands") this surveying party also platted the town of Cleaveland (later shortened to "Cleveland") before returning to Connecticut.

Congress made a number of other grants, surveys, and reservations of Ohio lands in subsequent years. The United States Military District in central Ohio, like the Virginia Military District, compensated veterans of the Continental Army during the Revolution. The "Donation Tract" to the north of the Ohio Company lands presaged the later Homestead Act by giving away parcels of land to settlers who promised to live on and develop them (and also to protect established settlements to the south from Indian attacks). Congress set aside the Refugee Tract to give to American sympathizers in Canada who lost their property there as a result of the American Revolution. Ohio also had some of the first western Indian Reservations, including three "Moravian Tracts" given to Moravian and Lenape families at Gnadenhutten, Schoenbrunn, and Salem. Among the most interesting stories behind the disposition of Ohio lands concerns what are known as the French Grants. The Scioto Company, a group of speculators that had no title to Ohio lands but hoped to make a purchase like the Ohio Company, hired as a European agent perhaps the most inappropriately named person in Ohio history: William Playfair. An unscrupulous Englishman with a gift for persuasion, Playfair con-vinced hundreds of well-to-do refugees from the French Revolution that Ohio was an Edenic paradise where they would be able to live off the abundance of nature with very little effort, and he took their money in exchange for fraudulent land claims. Upon arriving in the United States, these émigrés were chagrined to find they had been duped. However, they found hospitality from the Ohio Company, which let them buy a tract of land and live there, until Congress voted to give them 25,200 acres on the Ohio River to compensate them for the swindle. Almost thirty years after the English took Ohio from French control, Gallipolis ("City of the Gauls") became one of its first officially-recognized settlements.

Early Ohio Settlements

Settlers: Old versus new

Even as the United States was surveying and selling Ohio lands, it faced the uncomfortable reality that a number of people already called these lands home. A series of treaties and military campaigns (discussed in the previous chapter) extinguished most Indian claims to the state, but another group proved to be almost as difficult for the new government to control. As early as the 1770s, Moravian missionaries noted the presence of white settlers along the Muskingum Valley, and Fort Pitt's commander Daniel Brodhead wrote in 1779 that whites had settled on the north side of the Ohio and thirty miles up some of its tributaries. By 1785 more than 2,200 families were illegally living north of the Ohio River. An army officer reported that along the Ohio from Wheeling to the Miami River there was "scarcely one Bottom on the river but has one or more families, living thereon" and more were constantly moving in "by forties and fifties." Many of these people were poor families who had moved to Kentucky only to find that the land there had already been snatched up by politically favored speculators and was too expensive for them to purchase. Having little allegiance to the states they had left or to the fledgling American government whose capital was remote and power questionable, a number of these illegal settlers believed that their labors and risks in settling the land superseded any putative national control, and sought to form a new political unit on the western frontier that would be under their own direction. For their part, American military and political officials held these people in the lowest regard, referring to them variously as "indigent and ignorant," "shiftless fellows," "vagabonds," "white savages," "bandits whose actions are a disgrace to human nature," or, as Ohio land speculator George Washington himself put it, "a parcel of banditti, who will bid defiance to all authority." These leaders feared that the illegal settlers posed a real threat not just to the peace in the region but also to American authority itself, believing the "squatters" might listen to inducements from agents from Spain or England to separate western lands from the United States. In addition, the cash-strapped Continental Congress wished to place Ohio lands on sale at the earliest possible date, but feared the presence of large numbers of squatters would dampen the enthusiasm of potential buyers. For all these reasons, the Continental Congress attempted to remove them by force. In addition to official surveyors, they dispatched the military under General Josiah Harmar to build forts (Fort Harmar at the mouth of the Muskingum and Fort Steuben in present-day Steubenville) as bases from which to support surveying teams and mount expeditions against illegal settlers. In the spring of 1785 Harmar sent a detachment of twenty men under the command of Ensign John Armstrong on a mission to seek out illegal settlers, make them leave, and to destroy their buildings. Faced with the threat of armed soldiers many either agreed to leave immediately or asked for a little time to vacate the premises. However, the near futility of this task was exemplified on the fourth day of their mission, when they attempted to evict Joseph Ross, his family, and his neighbors from Mingo Bottom. Despite Armstrong's presentation of his written orders, Ross replied, "I don't care where you come from, I'm going to keep my home, and if you burn it down I'll build six more in a week." After a shouting match, Armstrong arrested him and sent him under guard to Wheeling. Yet, when an Indian commissioner came through Mingo Bottom in October of that year, he found Ross and his family still living there. Ross, like many other settlers, had grasped the basic fact that even with the six hundred men under his command Harmar could not conceivably evict the thousands of squatters and police the entire Ohio Territory in such a way as to prevent determined settlers from simply moving a few miles upstream or returning to their earlier settlement. Harmer himself admitted as much to Secretary of War, saying that under the given circumstances, it would be "impossible to prevent the lands being settled." The government had to postpone dealing with the problem of squatters until a later time, after the Northwest Ordinance had set up a legal system in the territory. In keeping with its "guinea pig" status, though, Forts Steuben and Harmar remain the only ones ever built by the United States primarily to curb unlawful settlement.

The first official settlements

Despite the constant threat of conflict with squatters and Indians new settlers began to move into the Ohio territory soon after land sales began in earnest. While land sales in the Seven Ranges languished, early settlement focused on the Ohio Company lands, Symmes Purchase, and Virginia Military District because of the generally better quality of these lands for farming and the ability of settlers to buy in smaller-sized parcels from land companies and speculators. The model of settlement in each of these areas was unique, however, representing the different origins of their settlers and the different conditions of land availability.

Despite the presence of thousands of Native Americans and thousands more white squatters at the time of its founding, Marietta has traditionally held the distinction of being the first official American settlement in Ohio. On April 7, 1788, the initial boatload of Ohio Company settlers disembarked near Fort Harmar (see Figure 5.6) on the mouth of the Muskingum and immediately set to work building their new village. Designed by military engineer and Ohio Company director General Rufus Putnam, the original settlement resembled an elaborate fort, with the outer wall of each house serving as part of a continuous wall around the settlement. The community ran itself as if it were a military outpost, too. Putnam named the structure Campus Martius (after ancient Rome's "Field of Mars" where the military trained) and the mostly war-veteran men of Marietta had regular patrol and militia duties. The settlers originally called the town that they platted outside the Campus Martius Adelphia (from the Greek word for brotherhood), but soon renamed it after Queen Marie Antoinette in recognition of French aid to the United States in the Revolutionary War.

The use of classical Greek and Roman references, as well as the layout of the town—with "in lots" (for homes) and "out lots" (for agriculture) all surrounding a town square—were tangible evidence of the relatively educated nature, and New England heritage, of the men who planned it. The Ohio Company of Associates represented an attempt to settle the

Figure 5.6 Fort Harmar, at the mouth of the Muskingum River, served as the first official presence of the national government in the Ohio Territory. This installation and Fort Steuben (built a year later) were the only forts ever built by the U.S. government primarily to curb unlawful settlement. Although they failed at that task, they also functioned as bases for surveying teams and American troops protecting the region.
Source: Courtesy of the Ohio Historical Society (AL02986)

country's western frontier in a distinctly orderly and systematic way, and to serve as an example for future settlement. It was applauded by the same people in the East who had feared what unregulated settlement might bring, with George Washington remarking, "No colony in America was ever settled under such favorable auspices as that which has just commenced at the Muskingum. … If I was a young man, just preparing to begin the world, or if advanced in life and had a family to make provision for, I know of no country where I should rather fix my habitation." Hoping not only to escape turmoil in the East and provide a buffer against Native Americans and foreign powers in the west, the Ohio Company settlers also brought with them the "City on a Hill" ethic that had characterized their New England ancestors. Almost as if to put the seal of law and order represented by Marietta on the Ohio frontier, newly minted Governor of the Northwest Territory Arthur St. Clair arrived there on July 15 and made it his capital.

At the other extreme from the Ohio Company's attempt at highly ordered and systematic community settlement was the often haphazard and individualized settlement that characterized the Virginia Military District. These lands, already deeded to individuals in irregularly sized plots, were endlessly sold, resold, and subdivided. Many of the biggest landowners were absentee landlords or speculators who rarely or never set foot in Ohio (to be discussed more fully in chapter 6). However, this was not completely the case, as successful surveyor and land speculator Nathaniel Massie chose to live there, bringing nineteen men to whom he had given some of his land to start a base known as Massie's Station on the Ohio River in 1791. Later renamed Manchester, this became the first official town in the district. At the other end of the land-ownership spectrum were people like those who Massie brought with him—small farmers who acquired modest-sized plots from the larger landholders, usually at prices lower than those offered by the government. As a result, settlement tended to be more diffuse, although until the end of the Indian Wars in the mid-1790s, settlers would often cluster around temporary settlements (often called "stations") for the purposes of mutual defense. Despite the hazards, the easy availability of land led to an influx of settlement, and by the time Massie formed the town of Chillicothe in 1796 the Virginia Military District's population of settlers—primarily from Virginia and Kentucky—had swollen to become a force to be reckoned with in territorial politics. The local orientation shared by most of these people soon became a counterweight to the national orientation of the territorial government.

Although positioned at the far southwestern end of the state, the Symmes Purchase actually lay between the Ohio Company lands and the Virginia Military District in terms of the way its settlement proceeded. Like the Ohio Company lands to the east, the tract was centrally directed, rectangularly surveyed, and had lands set aside for support of religion, public schools, and a college. Similarly, a disproportionate number of its early investors and town planners were Revolutionary War officers who came from the East Coast. Fort Washington, established in 1789, offered the same kind of national military presence and defense as Fort Harmar served at Marietta. Also like Marietta (and founded late in the same year), both Columbia (the first new town settled in the Symmes purchase), and Losantiville (founded not far away just a few weeks later) were regularly platted towns with in lots and out lots. Even the educational attainments of these towns' founders were similar, as exemplified by the names chosen for the second settlement. Both Losantiville's name (a combination of "L" for the Licking River, "os" the Latin word for mouth, "anti" the Latin word for opposite, and "ville" for town, all suggesting a town opposite the mouth of Kentucky's Licking River) and Cincinnati, the name that replaced it, bore the stamp of people familiar with a classical education.

Despite these similarities to the Ohio Company settlement, the Symmes Purchase in practice often more strongly resembled the Virginia Military District. Although supposedly centrally-directed through Symmes, his administrative weaknesses (some might say chicanery) made the settlement of these lands much more haphazard than those of the Ohio Company, and the botched rectangular surveys created some disorder and conflict that stretched on for years. Similarly, while the founders and many early settlers may have come from the east coast, many more of the people who came to settle there had either migrated from western Pennsylvania or crossed the Ohio River from Kentucky and Virginia. Furthermore, although the towns of Losantiville and Columbia may have been regularly platted, by 1790 several temporary "stations" (Dunlap's, Ludlow's, and Covalt's) had sprung up farther north in the manner of those in the Virginia Military District. And, unlike life in Marietta, life in Cincinnati was so legendarily rowdy and turbulent that General Wayne chose to encamp his army as far away from the city as possible to avoid the problems such distractions might cause.

In truth, though, none of these three main early centers of settlement were quite as easily definable as their stereotypes in the historical literature would make them seem. The supposed orderliness and New England propriety of the Ohio Company lands was belied by the conflicts that arose both among Ohio Company members and between them and the influx of settlers from Kentucky and Virginia who acquired lands in the area. Although perhaps less ordered to begin with, the Virginia Military District began to have regularly-platted towns by the mid-1790s, including the town that became the territorial capital. The Symmes Purchase, for all of its similarities to the other two centers and difficulties of its initial settlement, quickly became something unique to the new territory: an economic powerhouse and center of trade to the entire Ohio Valley due to its strategic location. Nevertheless, the different origins and orientations of the residents of these areas and the different nature of their development (to be discussed more fully in chapter 6) continued to affect Ohio life and politics for generations after.

From Territory to State

The early administration of Ohio reflected Congress's desire to establish there an orderly and virtuous society oriented to the national government. Thus it was no coincidence that the judges Congress appointed to the territory included New England Revolutionary War generals Samuel Holden Parsons and James Mitchell Varnum, as well as Rufus Putnam, who replaced Parsons when he died in 1789. Another New England Revolutionary War officer, Ohio Company Secretary Winthrop Sargent, served as territorial secretary and *de facto* governor during St. Clair's frequent absences on territorial business. To bring government to a more centrally located position in the vast Northwest Territory, St. Clair moved his capital from Marietta to Losantiville in January of 1790, renaming it Cincinnati in honor of the society of Revolutionary War officers named after the legendary Roman citizen-general Cincinnatus. Like George Washington Cincinnatus had given up the offer of great political power to return to his farm after saving his country from crisis. People had begun to refer to Washington as the "American Cincinnatus." Although an indirect homage to the sitting president, St. Clair's selection of this name was also appropriate in perhaps an unintended way. Cincinnatus was a patrician who steadfastly opposed the political designs of the small landholding Roman plebeians, and from the seat of Cincinnati St. Clair, Sargent and the judges, sought to impose order and obedience to the national government upon a territorial population that they generally felt lacked both qualities.

The difficulties of administering so large a territory with so few administrators were exacerbated by absenteeism and conflicts among the territorial officers, as well as friction between these men and the people they governed. Governor St. Clair (see Figure 5.7) and Judges Symmes and George Turner (who replaced Varnum upon his death in 1789) were frequently absent during their tenure, often on personal business. Sargent estimated that St. Clair was away for five and a half years of the first ten years of his tenure, and Turner's frequent trips back east resulted in legal papers being drawn up to order him back to Ohio several times. The governor and his judges quarreled over which laws to select for the territory, whether they could legislate new ones, and over how their

Figure 5.7   Governor Arthur St. Clair's imperious nature and administrative style led some early Ohio leaders to refer to him as "King Arthur." Disdainful of many of Ohio's early settlers and their Republican philosophy of government, he used the power of his office to thwart his political opponents and impede the statehood process.
Source: Courtesy of the Ohio Historical Society (AL06998)

rulings affected the territory and the personal interests of each other (St. Clair and Symmes in particular jousted over Symmes's administration of his lands). Furthermore, neither St. Clair nor his stand-in Sargent had much respect for the majority of the settlers in the territory, Sargent at one time described the people who surrounded him as "licentious and too great a portion indolent and extremely debauched." Although St. Clair often would take local opinions into consideration regarding local matters, he generally did not believe that most of the population of Ohio was fit to make important decisions, and he freely used his executive power to make appointments, create counties, and move county seats as he saw fit.

Ohio's small population generally tolerated the strong hand and national orientation of the territorial government as long as it felt they needed it to deal with Indian affairs. However, after the Treaty of Greeneville the territory experienced a massive influx of new settlers who increasingly began to chafe under St. Clair's and Sargent's authoritarian style. In this, they were reflecting the basic positions of the national parties that had begun to coalesce at the same time. The Federalists, defenders of a strong national government over state and local interests, were in ascendancy in the nation's capital, and thus made the major

Figure 5.8   Thomas Worthington, one of the largest landholders in Ohio, rose in political prominence during the late territorial period as one of the "Chillicothe Faction" who opposed St. Clair and pushed the statehood movement. For his efforts, he became known as "The Father of Ohio Statehood."
Source: Courtesy of the Ohio Historical Society (AL04648)

territorial appointments. This party was particularly strong among New Englanders. As a result, St. Clair and the territorial administration, in addition to most of the population of the Ohio Company Lands and the Connecticut Western Reserve (which began to be settled in earnest starting around 1800), tended to share this party's expansive nationalistic views and distrust of "mob rule" (i.e., democracy). The Republicans, exemplified on the national level by Thomas Jefferson and particularly strong in Virginia other southern states, tended to be suspicious of a strong central government and trusted the voice of the people as represented by state and local governments more. Those settlers from Virginia and Kentucky who populated the Virginia Military district tended to bring these beliefs with them.

These broad parameters of debate increasingly came to define the political discourse in Ohio, although it was also colored and swayed by local issues and personalities. While St. Clair and his judges implemented a new code of laws for the territory using pre-existing laws (primarily from St. Clair's home state of Pennsylvania, but also drawing on those of several other states), a faction of prominent men centered in Chillicothe, including large landholders Thomas Worthington (see Figure 5.8), his brother-in-law Edward Tiffin, and Nathaniel Massie, began to agitate to form an assembly so that the people could draw up their own laws favoring more local control. St. Clair resisted this movement for as long as he could as he thought the people were unready to govern themselves. Nevertheless, by late 1798 the governor could not deny that the Northwest Territory had reached the population of 5,000 "free male inhabitants of full age," the benchmark stipulated in the Northwest Ordinance for the next stage of government to begin. Not even waiting for the results of the census he had ordered, St. Clair declared that there would be an election for a territorial assembly on December 17. This precedent-setting body would be the first of many territorial assemblies that would define the westward expansion of the United States. Of the twenty-two men elected to the lower house of the assembly, fifteen came from what is now Ohio (including Worthington, Tiffin, and Massie) and this group tended to steer legislation. Despite the property requirements for both voting and serving, the lower house generally favored measures supported by the public at large. St. Clair freely used his absolute veto power to thwart such challenges to his vision of strong central authority. Although the issues in dispute—including the jurisdiction of local judges and the location of county seats—may seem trivial today, they reflected larger competing philosophies of centralized and nationally oriented authority versus local autonomy and the preservation of personal liberties. St. Clair and his opponents could find common ground at first, but the governor's frequent vetoes served to radicalize the Republican faction, which increasingly began to refer to St. Clair's government as tyrannical. In 1800 they moved the territorial capital to Chillicothe, in part to take it out of St. Clair's sphere of influence. For their part, St. Clair, Sargent, and their political allies in Cincinnati and the Ohio Company lands viewed Worthington and his friends as self-promoting and insubordinate threats to governmental authority. It was through this that the national political tensions between the nascent Federalist and Republican parties manifested themselves in the Ohio Territory.

A major turning point of this political battle came with one of the earliest decisions the territorial assembly had to make. Allowed to select a nonvoting representative to Congress, the assembly chose William Henry Harrison over St. Clair's son, Arthur Jr. Harrison, representing the interests of smaller landholders, proposed a land act passed by Congress in 1800 that made public lands much easier for regular small farmers to buy. The minimum amount one could buy was cut in half to 320 acres, and although the minimum price remained at $2 an acre, it could be paid partially on credit by putting half down and paying the rest in four equal installments. With public lands now within the reach of more individuals or small groups of farmers, Ohio felt the effects of the Harrison Land Act almost immediately. Within months new buyers had snapped up nearly a half-million dollars worth of land, and by 1803 the government had sold close to a million acres. The Land Act of 1804 passed the next year made things even easier by reducing the minimum purchase acreage to 160 acres. The tens of thousands of people who came to occupy these lands tended to ally themselves with Republican policies, thereby shifting power decidedly to the Chillicothe faction of territorial government.

Just weeks after the passage of his Land Act, Harrison also dealt another blow to St. Clair's political fortunes. Knowing that statehood for Ohio could be imminent, St. Clair sought to divide the territory in such a way that would delay it for as long as possible while at the same time preserving the political power of his faction. By dividing the Northwest Territory into three parts, with capitals at nationalistic strongholds of Marietta, Cincinnati, and Vincennes, St. Clair hoped also to divide the power of his political opponents on the Scioto and make it harder for any of these territories to meet the 60,000 population limit for statehood. Harrison instead pushed for a new Ohio Territory to be carved out of the Northwest Territory encompassing most of its eastern portion, with a boundary at statehood to be drawn north from the mouth of the Great Miami River (as stipulated in the Northwest Ordinance). Congress agreed to Harrison's plan, and then appointed him governor of the new Indiana Territory to the west. With Jefferson's election as president the same year portending a Republican-oriented national government the odds seemed to be stacked against the agenda of St. Clair and his faction.

St. Clair, however, was not yet defeated. After regular elections, the new territorial assembly that met in November of 1800 returned a bare majority in St. Clair's favor, largely on the strength of support from the area around Cincinnati, the Ohio Company lands, and some far-flung outposts in areas beyond what would become the state of Ohio. Precedent-setting in its own right, this version of the assembly incorporated the St. Clair-supporting town of Marietta and allowed its inhabitants to hold elections to select local leaders, as well as the ability to levy taxes and enact local laws. In this way Marietta became a model of local self-government emulated countless times as the United States expanded westward. The assembly also increased the jurisdiction of local judges and regularized local election laws. Despite these bows to greater local control, the assembly ran afoul of the Chillicothe Republicans by passing a law that would have recommended the Ohio Territory to be divided into two states, one east of the Scioto with a capital at Marietta, and one to the west with a capital at Cincinnati. Residents of both Marietta and Cincinnati feared that the growing influence of Chillicothe might come at their expense, and they worked together to divide the Scioto Valley's power base in this way. Knowing they could not influence either St. Clair (whom President John Adams had reappointed while a lame duck) or the state assembly in this matter, Massie and other Chillicothe Republicans appealed directly to the nation's capital, lobbying both Jefferson and the Republican-majority Congress to adhere to the boundary lines for Ohio as designated by the Northwest Ordinance. The assembly also voted to remove the territorial capital back to Cincinnati, causing riots in Chillicothe with an effigy of St. Clair burned in front of his boarding house.

The Chillicothe Republicans again decided to go over the heads of the assembly and St. Clair by dispatching Worthington and his erstwhile opponent in local politics, Michael Baldwin, to go straight to Washington with armloads of petitions gathered from Ohio citizens. He was to lobby on behalf of immediate statehood using the boundaries Congress had already agreed to under Harrison's territorial plan. Their lobbying was effective, and over the objections of Ohio's Federalist House representative, Paul Fearing, the largely sympathetic Republican Congress rejected the division of Ohio and sent an Enabling Act to Jefferson, which he signed on April 30, 1802. The Enabling Act set the western boundary of the new state as a line drawn northward from the mouth of the Great Miami and the northern boundary as a line drawn eastward from the southern tip of Lake Michigan to the international boundary in Lake Erie (little remarked on at the time, this boundary would later be the cause of some dispute and the "Toledo War" of the 1830s). It also set the rules for a constitutional convention, authorizing it to draft a constitution and select a name for the state. Once these things were accomplished and Congress had approved the constitution, Ohio would become a state on equal footing with all the others.

Of the thirty-five delegates that convened on November 1, 1802, to write the Ohio Constitution, twenty-six were Republicans, and the final document reflected both their core values and their antipathy toward St. Clair. Inspired by Jeffersonian principles, it was perhaps the most democratic state constitution to date, with nearly all power residing in the legislative branch. Annual election of house members and biennial elections of senators were meant to keep the state assembly responsive to the people. One notable exception to the generally broad democratic principles of the document, however, was the way it dealt with African Americans. Many of the convention delegates were of southern extraction, and some had chafed at the Northwest Ordinance's ban of the institution. Although the convention ultimately voted to ban slavery, the document they drafted allowed a form of indentured servitude that some slaveholders would later use to keep their slaves in bondage in the state. Furthermore, the vote on a measure to give African Americans the right to vote tied at 17-17, with convention president Edward Tiffin casting the deciding vote against the measure. This would be only the beginning of Ohio's prolonged legal debate over the status of its African American residents.

Also notable in the finished document was its unequivocal attitude toward the executive branch of government. General Republican attitudes toward local control and against a strong executive had become magnified in Ohio through its experience with St. Clair. Accordingly, although the convention made the governorship popularly elected, the office had little real power. Probably in reaction to how St. Clair had wielded the power of his office, the constitution denied the veto to the governor's office, and gave the assembly the right to make most major appointments to state offices, including judges.

Predictably, St. Clair vehemently opposed the convention and its work, trying in vain to insinuate himself into the proceedings and influence them to decide against statehood. Allowed to address the convention, he seemed to lose his erstwhile nationalistic bearings, saying that Congress did not have the right to pass the Enabling Act, that the territory was "no more bound by an act of Congress than . . . by an edict of the first consul of France," and that Ohio ought to use its means to "bring Congress to reason," presumably by running its own affairs beyond Congress's control. Not only did his speech fail to sway the convention, which voted 32-1 to proceed with drafting the constitution, but it also got St. Clair fired. Although Worthington and his allies earlier had unsuccessfully tried to get Jefferson to remove St. Clair soon after the new president took office, he had demurred. Upon hearing of St. Clair's "intemperate and indecorous" speech, however, Jefferson dispatched one of St. Clair's staunchest critics, Charles Willing Byrd, to tell him that he was replacing him as governor.

In the meantime, the convention finished the constitution on November 29 and decided to forego public ratification so that Ohio might become a state as soon as possible, setting the first Tuesday in March as the date the new state government would convene. Wasting no time, Thomas Worthington personally rode his horse over the Appalachian Mountains to Washington DC to deliver the document to Congress, arriving on December 19. After the House and Senate approved the Ohio Constitution as a bill, Jefferson signed it into law on February 19, 1803. As this fulfilled the Enabling Act of the previous year, Ohio officially became a state on that day. This is worthy of note, for it is yet another example of an experiment in Ohio that was never repeated. Later states carved out of the public domain had separate resolutions passed by Congress declaring them a state, and because Ohio's idiosyncratic admission did not include one of these separate resolutions, it has led some people over the years to the erroneous conclusion that Ohio was never officially admitted. Although one may argue the technicalities of whether February 19 or "the first Tuesday in March" of 1803 was *the* day on which Ohio became a state, there is no legitimate argument over *if* it became a state that year. (Just to be on the safe side, President Dwight Eisenhower actually signed a Congressional resolution in 1953 retroactively affirming March 1, 1803 as the official date of Ohio's statehood.)

Ohio's admittance into the United States was a triumph for those who had struggled for years against St. Clair's centralized and at times autocratic control over the people of the territory. At the same time, though, it is ironic that these passionate advocates of local control in opposition to St. Clair's more nationally-oriented vision ultimately found themselves using the national government to advance their ends over the opposition of both St. Clair and even the locally elected territorial legislature. In going to Congress and Jefferson to reverse the redivision of the Ohio territory, in refusing to submit the new constitution to popular approval, and in appealing to Jefferson to remove St. Clair from power, the Ohio Republicans demonstrated that their commitment to the principles of local control was limited by expediency. In so doing, they exhibited similar changes to those soon to come in the Republican Party at the national level as it began to wield the reins of power as well as presage and future debates on the limits of state governmental power that would define the early nineteenth century.

On a larger scale, the admission of Ohio also served as yet another example of Ohio's unique status as a "guinea pig" for public policy in the still-young United States. From the experiments that succeeded and continued to influence U.S. history for years to come (for example, the development of the public land system, land grants to support education, systematically directed territorial government, giving free homesteads to settlers, carving new states out of the public domain) to those that were tried in Ohio but never repeated (for example, forts for the suppression of illegal settlements, ministerial lands, becoming a state exclusively through an Enabling Act) Ohio served as a test case for the rest of the nation. Although it would continue to play this role in some ways afterward, Ohio's tremendous influence in this regard during this relatively brief fifteen-year territorial period *en route* to statehood was extraordinary and never really duplicated by it or any other state in the years that followed. The "Ohio Experiment" of the late eighteenth century has proven to have a legacy enduring into the early twenty-first.

Further Reading

The standard volume on Ohio's original surveys is C.E. Sherman's *Original Ohio Land Subdivisions: Volume III of the Final Report* (1952. Columbus: State of Ohio Geological Survey). Peter S. Onuf's *Statehood and Union: History of the Northwest Ordinance* examines the critical role that document played in the development of the Northwest Territory and the United States (1992. Bloomington: Indiana University Press). Discussion of the politics of Ohio's territorial period can be found in Donald J. Ratcliffe's *Party Spirit in a Frontier Republic: Democratic Politics in Ohio, 1793–1821* (1998. Columbus: Ohio State University Press) and Andrew Cayton's *Frontier Republic: Ideology and Politics in the Ohio Country, 1780–1825* (1989. Kent: Kent State University Press). Although originally written in the 1950s, Alfred Byron Sears's *Thomas Worthington: Father of Ohio Statehood* (1998. Columbus: Ohio State University Press) is still the standard Worthington biography.

6

A Community of Communities
Early Ohio Society

On July 19, 1843, the residents of Cincinnati crowded its streets to witness an unusual and historic sight. Between 600 and 800 Wyandots, the remnants of the last Native American tribe still living in Ohio, made their way through the city with all of their belongings on more than one hundred wagons along with hundreds of their horses. Their destination was the pair of steamboats *Nodaway* and *Republic* on the Ohio River that had been hired to take them to their new home in Indian Territory (present-day Kansas). It had already been an eventful month for the Queen City. Portending an even greater population shift, over the first few days of July the city had hosted a convention of expansionists from Ohio, Kentucky, Indiana, Louisiana, Tennessee, and Iowa who demanded that the United States assert its claims to the Oregon Territory. Also, in that month's session of the U.S. Circuit Court held in Cincinnati, former Cornish, New Hampshire resident Salmon P. Chase argued what became the landmark case of *Jones v. Van Zandt*, one of the first major legal challenges to the constitutionality of slavery. Chase would later claim that Harriet Beecher Stowe based the character of abolitionist John Van Trompe in *Uncle Tom's Cabin* on John Van Zandt, a former Kentucky slaveholder who lost the case but drew great public attention to his cause. Stowe, a Cincinnati minister's wife originally from Litchfield, Connecticut, published the first installment of that book almost exactly eight years later in the *National Era*, a paper edited by New Jersey native Gamaliel Bailey.

In July of 1843 Bailey was covering the Wyandot removal, the Oregon Convention, Van Zandt, and other stories as editor of *The Philanthropist*, an abolitionist newspaper that—despite twice having its press destroyed by anti-abolitionist mobs—had been publishing in Cincinnati for seven years. *The Philanthropist* was only one of several newspapers catering to different audiences in the increasingly cosmopolitan city. Not only did it boast the *Enquirer*, the *Commercial*, the *Daily Gazette*, and the *Spirit of the Times*; it was also home to the *Catholic*

Ohio: A History of the Buckeye State, First Edition. Kevin F. Kern and Gregory S. Wilson.
© 2014 John Wiley & Sons, Inc. Published 2014 by John Wiley & Sons, Inc.

Telegraph and the relatively new *Occident and American Jewish Advocate.* The city had become the fourth-largest publishing center in the country, in part because it hosted the home press for extremely popular McGuffey's *Readers.* Originally from Pennsylvania, William Holmes McGuffey was, at the time, in the process of moving to Cincinnati to take a position at Woodward High School (soon to be Woodward College) after serving as president of Ohio's first state college, Ohio University in Athens.

Cincinnati presses also specialized in religious publications, including the sermons and writings of famed local minister Lyman Beecher, who had come to Ohio from Connecticut. Early that same July one of the city's presses published a major history of German Methodism by Reverend Adam Miller. Miller was born to Amish parents in Maryland but moved with them in infancy to Ohio, where the family converted to Methodism. Two years earlier, he led the building of the first German Methodist Church in Cincinnati. Yet his book probably did not resonate with many local Germans, most of whom populated the Over-the-Rhine neighborhood in town. Although about 30 percent of Cincinnati's population was German-speaking, two-thirds of them were Catholic. Some were undoubtedly among the many city residents crowding the path so closely that the long train of Indians could barely get through on July 19. They, along with the slaves Van Zandt had helped to escape, the readers of the *Catholic Telegraph* and the *Occident and American Jewish Advocate,* Chase, Stowe, Bailey, McGuffey, Beecher, and Miller were all part of the flood of people who had come to Ohio from elsewhere in the previous decades and had pushed the Wyandot and the rest of Ohio's first population out.

These disparate events in a single month of 1843 reflect numerous aspects of Ohio's tumultuous social development in the early statehood period. Ohio's new population came from every region of the country as well as overseas, often grouping together along the lines of origin, tradition, ethnicity, and religion. In the early days, Ohio was not so much a society as a community of communities—sometimes in conflict with each other—that bore a much closer resemblance socially to the collection of independent Ohio Indian "republics" of the 1700s than anything like a unified state. Yet even amid the extraordinary diversity and clannishness of the state were elements that were already beginning to serve as larger unifying forces: national politics, standardized education, the popular media, and religious and social reform movements led by a dedicated group of mostly middle-class residents who had a vision of a prosperous, unified, and respectable Ohio culture.

Demographics

Population

In assessing Ohio society in the late territorial and early statehood period, the single factor that seems to stand out most is the state's truly phenomenal growth in population. From just a few thousand American settlers scattered mostly across the southern fringes of the Ohio Territory in 1790, Ohio's population multiplied more than fifteen-fold by 1800 to 45,365. The population more than quadrupled to 230,760 by 1810, and then increased another 150 percent to 581,434 by 1820. Each of the next two decades witnessed greater than 60 percent growth, with 937,903 by 1830 and 1,519,467 by 1840. Despite an economic depression and the virtual absence of any more federal land to sell in the state after 1840, the state still swelled another 30 percent to 1,980,329 in 1850. Overall, Ohio's population from 1800 to 1850 increased by 4,265 percent. Similarly, Ohio's population density per square mile of land grew from 1.1 to 47.9 people during that period. This not only made it more densely populated than any other western state, but also more crowded than half of the states to its east, most of which boasted more than a hundred years of settlement. In comparison, neighboring Kentucky—which had started its American settlement period earlier and was of comparable size—already lagged behind Ohio in population by 1820 and had almost a million fewer residents by 1850.

Land ownership trends

Ohio's incredible growth caused considerable comment across the United States. Early nineteenth-century New Englanders openly worried about depopulation of their communities to the fertile lands of Ohio. Other observers noted that while Ohio lands were indeed more amenable to farming than the more mountainous areas of Kentucky or Tennessee, the rich land was only one important factor. Kentucky had slavery while Ohio did not, and this funneled independent farmers—who did not care to compete with slave-owning farmers—north of the Ohio River. In addition, wealthy patricians from Virginia snapped up much of Kentucky's best lands as soon as they were available. Wishing to exert economic and political control over the public, they traded their land at as much as four to five times the cost of Ohio lands. As such, there was relatively little chance for large numbers of small farmers in Kentucky to acquire farms easily. In contrast, Ohio witnessed a different set of land-ownership trends: from non-resident to resident owners, and from large to small holders.

Ohio was the first territory cut out of the public land system, and partially because of this its earliest large landholders initially did not choose to live there. A number of Ohio Company of Associates shareholders chose to redeem their near-worthless promissory notes for Ohio land with the intention of selling it at a profit. Similarly, many original Virginia Military District landowners never set foot there. Virginia military veterans acquired vast tracts of Ohio lands because of the state's extremely liberal land bounty policies. A major general could make claims of up to 15,000 acres, or even more with six years of service (George Washington was entitled to more than 23,000, but eventually only claimed a more modest amount and never finished his claim nor moved to the state). Other officers could receive grants in the hundreds and thousands of acres, and even a private could claim 100 acres. Congress also gave substantial (but not quite as generous) claims to former continental soldiers in the United States Military District it created north of the Ohio Company lands in 1796. Yet most of these veterans or their heirs never intended to move to Ohio, choosing to instead to cash in their claims to willing buyers or speculators, often at a great discount. Speculators acquiring these lands had little trouble selling most of them after 1800, and by 1815, three-quarters of Ohio lands had resident owners.

Those owners held increasingly more manageable plots of land. Initially, much of the privately owned land was in the hands of a handful of people. Speculators purchased huge quantities of land for as little as twenty cents an acre from their Eastern owners. More than half the lands in the United States Military District—569,542 acres—found their way into the hands of just twenty-two people (an average of more than 25,800 acres each). Just twenty-five people held the patents on more a million acres of the Virginia Military District for an average of more than 41,400 acres per person. Surveyors could also acquire a huge amount of land by taking from a quarter to a half of the lands they surveyed for non-resident owners as in-kind fees in lieu of cash. Surveyor and speculator Nathaniel Massie owned 75,000 acres at one point, and his former assistant Duncan McArthur amassed 91,000 in this way. As such, people often moved to Ohio knowing the many of the best areas belonged to these large landholders, hoping to make enough through share and tenant farming to eventually purchase their own plots of land. In 1810, only 45 percent of Ohio households owned land, which was not much higher than some places in Western New York and Pennsylvania. Nevertheless, the trend was toward the small farmer, particularly as the Land Acts of 1800, 1804, and 1820 made it easier for men of smaller means to acquire lands. By 1821 the government had sold two-thirds of all federal lands, and most of the rest was in private hands by 1840. Although there would continue to be large landowners for some time (including such noted political leaders as Thomas Worthington and Edward Tiffin), they and their heirs had already begun to sell off much of their vast holdings by the 1820s as the rush of settlers made it increasingly profitable to do so. By mid-century, small family farms predominated throughout the Ohio countryside.

Urbanization

While most of Ohio's residents were rural small farmers, larger settlements began to form from the very beginning. Towns could spring up for numerous reasons. Many towns such as Wooster, Conneaut, and Defiance grew on the location of previous Indian settlements or trails. Others developed along the major waterways, especially on high river terraces inside river bends for maximum easy access to the river. Cincinnati was a prime example of this, but so were Steubenville, East Liverpool, and Portsmouth. Portsmouth was also the terminus of the Ohio and Erie Canal, and many other towns developed because they were located astride canal (or later, railroad) routes. Akron, Massillon, and Willard are only a few of these transportation-linked towns. Some settlements developed at the falls of rivers, which not only brought traffic to the head of navigation of those rivers but also supplied waterpower for mills. Elyria, Piqua, Fremont, Zanesville and others developed this way. Zanesville is also an example of another prime town location: at the confluence of two (or more) rivers. Franklintown (now Columbus), Coshocton, Newark, and Dayton are all representative of this phenomenon, the last being at the confluence of four rivers. River mouths also were magnets for settlement. On just a one hundred mile stretch of Lake Erie alone, Toledo, Port Clinton, Huron, Vermillion, Lorain, and Cleveland sprang up at the at the terminus of the Maumee, Portage, Huron, Vermillion, Black, and Cuyahoga Rivers, respectively. In the particularly swampy areas of the Lake Plains, some settlers developed towns on the higher and drier glacial moraines or glacial lake beach ridges (see chapter 1), especially where these intersected with each other or with rivers. Bowling Green, Norwalk, Painesville, and Findlay are just a few towns in debt to Ohio's glacial period. Yet many, many other towns originated primarily as speculative ventures in which landowners bought land and platted a town in hopes of drawing settlement. Some of these, like Lima, Troy, Washington Court House, and Ravenna were at the center of newly-formed counties and thus designed as county seats. A number of others, like Canton, Mansfield, Marion, and Xenia, had no special advantage in location, but grew because their organizers and residents successfully sold them to other settlers. "Boosterism" was a common part of civic life in the 1800s, and town boosters would try to lure settlers or lobby businesses and railroads to locate in their municipality, often by offering incentives in the form of land or money. These boosters met with varying degrees of success, and for every town mentioned above, there are countless examples of speculator-planned settlements that either never materialized or eventually became ghost towns. Those that succeeded in the early 1800s generally did so because they met the needs of the surrounding agricultural population.

Marietta may have been the first of Ohio's official towns, but Cincinnati soon outstripped it, boasting 750 residents by 1800. Thanks to its key location near three tributaries of the Ohio River and surrounded by fertile farmland, by 1840 it had a population of 46,000, which made it the sixth-largest city in the United States. By that year the state claimed six of the country's 100 largest cities, Cleveland, Dayton, Columbus, Zanesville, and Steubenville all ranking considerably behind Cincinnati and ranging in population from 4,200 to 6,000. Yet despite its phenomenal growth and its status as the third largest state, Ohio was predominantly rural throughout its early period. Less than 2 percent of its population lived in urban areas as late as 1820, and even with the growth fostered by the canal system, that number rose only to 3.9 percent in 1830 and 5.5 percent by 1840. Perhaps not coincidentally, it was only after all federal land had been sold in the 1840s that the urban share of the state's population jumped to double digits (12.2 percent) in 1850. Whereas in 1830 only 7.6 percent and in 1840 8.1 percent of Ohio's incoming population had moved into its cities, in 1850 that number had shot up to 34.5 percent. Although these figures reflect a national population that was also still largely rural, Ohio remained more rural than the United States as a whole until after the Civil War.

Pioneer life

Ohio's population may have been a dispersed set of numerous different communities but this is not to say that Ohioans had nothing in common. On the contrary, they shared quite a lot on a basic level. Nearly all came to Ohio not only to make better lives for themselves, but also to secure a livelihood for their descendants. Some were merchants or artisans, but most came to work the land as independent farmers. Such a lifestyle was increasingly beyond the reach of most farmers in other parts of the country. The lands in the East had been spoken for long ago, and some had begun to lose their fertility. Ironically, as Ohio lands began filling up, many of its farmers chose to sell their improved

Ohio lands at a profit and purchase even larger and cheaper tracts of land that were just beginning to open up in the Indiana, Illinois, and Iowa territories. While this created a tremendous amount of change in Ohio's population, such decisions were rooted in the same principle that brought people to Ohio in the first place.

Another similarity uniting Ohioans was the fundamentally local level of life and work. As was the case elsewhere in rural United States household production was the basic unit of the economy but opportunities for cooperation and a rural labor market quickly arose. Farmers often needed help clearing land or building barns, and when labor for hire was scarce, they might be able to count on reciprocal exchanges of labor from surrounding farmers. While the earliest settlers in any area needed to be largely self-sufficient, these networks of labor interactions worked as an integrating mechanism and created close-knit local community sufficiency. This model persists to the present in Ohio's Amish country.

Beyond this there was a basic vision that also united most early settlers. Rufus Putnam and the Ohio Company leadership believed that it was their mission to impose order on the wilderness, making the way clear for orderly expansion of the American nation in the West. While others who came to settle other parts of the state did not necessarily subscribe to such specifically-defined or nationalistic views, most new Ohioans probably shared in general a philosophy that they were expanding civilization by "taming" the land, and that this was as it should be. In practice, "taming" the land meant clearing it of impediments to "civilization" and building well-tended farms and towns in their places. The first order of business in clearing the land had been removing its Native inhabitants, whom of most settlers viewed as being little better than savages incapable of civilization. The federal government had accomplished most of this through wars and treaties by the time Ohio had become a state, although this continued to be an issue in the early statehood era (see chapter 8).

The next item settlers cleared from the land was the forest that carpeted most of Ohio. It was no small task to fell the many trees that greeted a new settler upon his arrival at his wilderness farm. Those that had the means to do so might hire men to saw or chop down the trees, but most farmers had to deal with the trees themselves or hope for help from neighbors. For some this meant starting immediately in cutting down the trees, using some of the lumber for building a house and fences and storing more for firewood. Most of the remaining trees were burned, either letting the ash fertilize the ground or collecting it and selling it as potash. The stumps that remained could take years to remove. Other farmers chose instead to "girdle" the trees by cutting through the bark to the wood completely around the trunk. This essentially starved the tree by preventing it from sending leaf-produced sugars down to the roots. The tree eventually died, and the farmer could deal with its trunk later. Despite the immense amount of work tree-clearing entailed, Ohio's settlers were all too successful in accomplishing it: Ohio was a vast forest at the beginning of the territorial period, but by 1900 only 10 percent of the state remained forested.

While they were clearing the land of trees, early Ohioans were also intent on clearing it of wild animals. Ohio was still very much a wild country, with copious numbers of timber rattlesnakes that threatened humans; bears, wolves, and wildcats that threatened livestock; and deer, raccoons, squirrels, and other herbivores that threatened crops. Early

Ohio residents considered it a public service to kill as many of these animals as possible, and the state and local governments passed laws encouraging them to do so. One early law required all men eighteen to forty-five years old to present township officials with proof of one hundred dead squirrels each year. Despite being almost perpetually cash-strapped, state and local governments also paid bounties in reward for killing wolves and other predators. Perhaps the most notable (and by contemporary standards, notorious) event characterizing this single-minded desire to extinguish local fauna was the Great Hinckley Hunt in present-day Medina County. On the morning of Christmas Eve 1818, more than 500 settlers gathered at regular intervals around the perimeter of Hinckley Township. At a given signal, they began moving toward the center of the township, shooting everything that moved and driving panicked animals into a smaller and smaller area as the hunters continued to tighten the noose. Converging in the middle, the marksmen participated in a general slaughter. At the end of the day, they counted seventeen wolves, twenty-one bears, and over three hundred deer, with heaps of dead rabbits, squirrels, raccoons, and other forest creatures too numerous to be counted. A large feast celebrated the end of the hunt, but the settlers could not possibly eat or store all the meat they had created that day, and turkey buzzards were still picking at the numerous leftover animal carcasses well into spring. Although perhaps not as famous as Capistrano and its swallows, Hinckley is best known today for the annual March 15 return of the buzzards that acts as a harbinger of spring. Local legend still holds that the aftermath of 1818's great hunt is what established the buzzards' migration pattern. Although many contemporary Americans would be appalled at such indiscriminate extermination of wildlife, the event illustrates in a vivid manner the worldview shared by most early farmers about Ohio's wildlife.

As farmers cleared the land they also had to get their crops in as early as they could. Moving to his new land in the late winter and early spring to minimize the time his family had to live on stored supplies, the typical new settler immediately got to work building a lean-to or simple house and clearing away enough trees to start planting crops among the girdled trunks or tree stumps. Fences came next, both to keep livestock in and predatory and herbivorous animals out. Home improvements and outbuildings such as barns could begin when there was time and ability, and any other thing the farmer needed had to be improvised on the spot. From sunup to sundown, there was always something for the pioneer farmer to do.

Perhaps the only person who worked harder than the pioneer farmer was the pioneer farmer's wife. If the farmer worked from sunup to sundown, the wife usually worked from before sunrise until well after sunset. Most work inside the home was traditionally gendered so that the females took care of cooking, cleaning, hauling water in from the well or the nearby stream, bringing wood for the cooking and heating fires, tending the garden, churning butter, preserving food, spinning yarn, sewing, knitting, and repairing all the clothing for the family, making candles and soap, and taking care of the children who could often number ten to fifteen per household. Large families were common, and the more children a family had, the more work those children could do around the farm. Still, even with the help of children when they got old enough, it was an exhausting and often isolated life, one that many women would not have chosen for themselves before their husband decided that the family would be moving to the wilderness. Letters and journal entries from pioneer women often express the stresses of daily life and the sadness at separation from family and friends in their native communities. The stresses, sadness, hard work, sometimes poor nutrition, frequent and/or difficult childbirth, and lack of access to medical care common on the frontier often led to early death for pioneer women. Given her many important roles, the death of a farmer's wife often created massive disruptions in the home, and widowers often sought to marry again as soon as a decent period of mourning allowed.

As Ohio grew and became more densely settled, the style of life described above became more the exception than the norm. Stump- and trunk-strewn fields became rolling farmland, wild fauna died off, log cabins with dirt floors became comfortable clapboard homes, farm machinery made toil easier and more productive, towns and stores offered basic needs and manufactured goods, and growing communities increased social support and reduced isolation. The transportation networks that had grown with the state made farming more profitable than ever before, and many Ohio farmers became quite prosperous. Farm life was still hard work by contemporary standards, but by 1850 the large numbers of independent Ohio farms were much like those long-established farms that the farmers or their ancestors had left back East. In a very real sense, Ohio had become more of an Eastern than a Western state.

Migration

For all the similarities that characterized pioneer Ohio life, it also harbored a number of significant differences. The challenges and lifestyles that Ohio newcomers faced may have been comparable, but the settlers themselves were extremely diverse and brought with them disparate and sometimes conflicting traditions. Ohio attracted people in significant numbers from multiple sections of the country and from overseas, making it in its early years the most diverse state in the Republic and more a microcosm of the country as a whole than any other state (see Figure 6.1). This remarkable diversity helps to explain a number of social and cultural developments that defined Ohio during the early statehood period and beyond.

New Englanders populated the Ohio Company Lands around Marietta, but they dominated the northern part of the state as well, due to the fact that much of that section was the Connecticut Western Reserve and the Firelands (see chapter 5). New England's struggling agricultural economy and growing population prompted many natives to leave, and significant portions of entire towns occasionally moved to Ohio. While most of them chose the Western Reserve or Ohio Company Lands, they created other islands of New England in Ohio, including places like Granville. People in the neighboring towns of Granville, Massachusetts and Granby, Connecticut purchased more than 29,000 acres of the United States Military District, and in late 1805, 150 residents moved *en masse* to the area, which originally had been populated predominantly by Welsh immigrants. Granby, Connecticut had also been where Colonel James Kilbourne formed the Scioto Company in 1801, and he brought another group of New Englanders to settle what is now Worthington near present-day Columbus. New Yorkers from the

Figure 6.1 More than any other state, Ohio's population became a microcosm of the whole country due to migration patterns in the early statehood period. Northeasterners dominated among settlers of the northern part of the state while migrants mostly from Virginia, Maryland, and Kentucky provided the bulk of the population in the southern part. The middle filled primarily with settlers from the Mid-Atlantic states.

Source: Adapted from Keiffer, A. ed. 2008. *The Geography of Ohio* (Kent, OH: Kent State University, p. 72). Copyright © 2008 by The Kent State University Press. Reprinted with permission

upstate region and the area neighboring New England also increasingly joined their fellow Northeasterners in northern Ohio.

In contrast, residents of Virginia, Maryland, and Kentucky disproportionately populated the southern part of Ohio, particularly the Virginia Military District. Even the Ohio

Company lands relatively quickly (and to the chagrin of some of its New Englander settlers) hosted a large contingent of southern settlers spilling over the Ohio River from Appalachia. The rest of Ohio—including most of the central portion and the area around the Symmes Purchase in the Southwestern part of the state—became home to the largest single contingent of regional settlers, those from the Mid-Atlantic region. Although most of these settlers came from Pennsylvania, healthy numbers of former New York and New Jersey residents also made up the population of this region.

One subset of primarily Southern migrants deserves special note given the significantly different experience they faced. African Americans had been in Ohio from the earliest days of the Ohio Company settlements and in the decades after statehood more began to trickle in. Their numbers were never large during the early period but did grow steadily: only 337 appear in the 1800 census, but by 1850 that number had grown to 25,279. Even then, though, African Americans only represented 1.3 percent of Ohio's rapidly-swelling population. Black communities tended to cluster in the Scioto River Valley, but Cincinnati and Hamilton County claimed 10 percent of the state's black population, and hundreds of emancipated slaves from the estate of Virginia planter Samuel Gist settled in Brown County in 1819. Gallia, Muskingum, Belmont, and Jefferson Counties also contained notable concentrations of black settlers. The earliest African American Ohioans were either free blacks or newly-emancipated slaves from the South. The Northwest Ordinance had banned slavery and the State Constitution had upheld that ban, but that did not prevent some southerners from bringing their slaves as "indentured servants," a ruse that worked for a while. Some did not even maintain this pretense—as late as the 1840 census, three of Ohio's residents appear in the enumeration as slaves.

Effects of regional origins of settlers

The regional origin of Ohio migrants cast a long shadow on Ohio's social and political life for years and the effects of it can still be seen today. The landscape itself changes from place to place depending on its earliest settlers. As mentioned in chapter 5, surveyors laid out most of Ohio in six-by-six square mile grids, and the Western Reserve townships are five-by-five miles square. Township and county roads often eventually ran along these lines and, as a result, traveling along country roads has a certain level of straight-line, right-angle predictability. The same cannot be said of the Virginia Military District. Surveyed by the old metes and bounds system used by its Southern settlers, it has no real grid system and the shapes of townships and country roads can be quite irregular. Visitors who meet with a roadblock while driving along country roads laid out by the original Virginia settlers are well-advised not to divert without a map.

The towns that sprang up along these roads also sometimes reflect the regional origins of their original inhabitants. New Englanders who moved into the Western Reserve and Ohio Company lands tended to plat out towns the way they were in New England, with a square or rectangular village green standing in the middle surrounded by the settlement's major buildings. Town planners also often arranged the area around the outside of town into larger "out lots." Examples of this kind of design are scattered particularly throughout the northern part of the state, including Hudson, Twinsburg, and the little town of Merry's Mill that became Milan. Other parts of the state have town layouts that are more typical of other areas, from simple crossroads to a gridwork pattern of streets. Pennsylvanian-settled towns like Cambridge or Somerset occasionally have a central diamond or square assembled out of blocks from the street grid. Southerners in particular liked to put the county courthouse in the middle of a central town square. The names these towns received also occasionally reflect the origins of their original settlers. New Haven, New London, Norwalk, and Greenwich in the Firelands are all names of Connecticut towns burned by the British. Leesburg, Lynchburg, and Williamsburg can all be found both in Virginia and in the Virginia Military District; and central Ohio's Pennsylvania/New Jersey heritage shows in the names of Lancaster, Newark, and New Philadelphia.

The architecture in these different areas had regional flavors as well. New Englanders typically built the traditional English Three-Bay Barn with a threshing floor in the middle flanked on either side by storage space or stables. As farms outgrew these smaller barns, "Raised" or "Basement" Barns placed on a stone foundation became more common, with a lower level set aside for livestock. The most popular style of houses in Northern Ohio were the New England "One-and-a-Half Cottage," the "Gable-Front House," and the "Upright and Wing," which shared the Greek Revival stylistic elements popular in the Northeast. The New England "Saltbox" house was more common to the Ohio Company lands to the south. The Pennsylvanians who tended to settle the middle portion of the state built the distinctive Pennsylvania-Dutch or "Bank" Barn—so called because it was built into a bank of a hill that provided a ramp for easy access to the upper level. True log cabins were more typical residences of the central part of the state early on, after which the "I-house"—so named because it came to be associated with the "I" states of Indian, Illinois, and Iowa—came to predominate in this area. Barns in southern Ohio were more likely to be the Transverse Frame Barn (which unlike the others mentioned had their main doors under the gable at the end), and a few traditional elongated tobacco barns still dot the landscape in this area. Typical homes there include a regional variant of the "I-house," with a double porch and a roof that was not as steeply-gabled as the ones further north. Other houses common to the southern part of the state were the so-called "Saddlebag" and "Double-Pen" houses, which were the modest two-room, single story abodes of less-affluent families. One can still see examples of all of these types of buildings in Ohio's small towns and countryside.

Ohio speech patterns, too, came to be affected by early migration patterns. Early on, numerous linguistic indicators instantly distinguished a speaker's origins: while a northern Ohio farmer might have said that he closed the shades at 3:45 and took a pail of swill out to the pigs, his southern Ohio counterpart might have said that he closed the blinds and took the bucket of slop out to the hogs at a quarter till three. Pennsylvania-Dutchisms such as "school leaves out," "make the door to" (close the door), and "red up" (clean) characterized the speech of ethnic Germans in the middle part of the state. While time has faded many of these tell-tale indicators, the broader impact of these speech patterns has left Ohio as one of the few states that is home to three major American regional dialects. Although the terminology linguists use for these categories varies, it is not surprising that the boundaries they draw roughly correspond to Ohio's settlement patterns. The northern part of the state shares speech characteristics with states areas around the Great Lakes. The middle of the state participates in a "North Midland" dialect that stretches to the Great Plains and is closest to what most people think as "general American English." Southern Ohioans are more prone to speak Southern- or Appalachian-inflected English. Most Ohioans are not aware of the more subtle distinctions that differentiate these speech patterns, but some are obvious enough to create an instant recognition the speaker's region. To this day, for example, many Southeastern Ohioans will "warsh" the dishes or their car.

The regional origins of early Ohio settlers also had long-term economic and political effects that chapters 7, 8, and 9 will discuss more extensively. It is worth noting here, however, that particular farm products also had a strong regional basis: early dairy farming took place mostly in northern Ohio and Ohio Company lands, while tobacco cultivation was more prevalent in the south-settled areas. Similarly, the staunchly anti-slavery-extension Free Soil Party that began the state's major political realignment in the 1840s and 1850s was primarily a Northern Ohio phenomenon, while the Butternut region that largely opposed Lincoln and the Civil War took in much of southern Ohio, Indiana, and Illinois.

Religious diversity was another aspect of Ohio life resulting from settlers' regional origins. New Englanders were most likely than others to bring Congregationalism and Unitarianism with them, and a number of New England Presbyterians also settled in the Western Reserve. Presbyterianism was also quite common among the Scots-Irish Appalachian settlers in the south, as was the Disciples of Christ denomination that arose out of it in Western Pennsylvania and Kentucky in the early 1800s. Most Ohio Episcopalians came from Virginia, where that denomination had been the established church and tended to be the denomination of wealthy and powerful people. A denomination that arose from the Anglican/Episcopalian Church, the Methodists, also first came to Ohio from the south in the late 1700s. The first Ohio Friends (commonly known as Quakers) came from Virginia, and more followed from even further South, especially North Carolina. Although the Baptists were not as influential as other denominations, they were also a Southern import to the state as early as 1790 in the Symmes Purchase. Moravians (now the Brethren) occupied the middle part of Ohio as early as the Lenape mission towns of the 1770s, and other like-minded Anabaptist sects like the Mennonites and the Amish joined them there, working their way west from Pennsylvania soon after statehood. German Reformed followers and Pennsylvania Friends (Quakers) also moved into the same eastern and southwestern portions of the state that Mid-Atlantic migrants tended to settle. Most Evangelical United Brethren would also come from that area, although generally later in the century. Ohio's pattern of denominational diversity continued to have regional correlates on into the twentieth century, with other newcomers adding to the state's already rich religious landscape.

Immigration

Overlaying the regional origins of Ohio's settlers were other sets of migrants who ultimately came from much farther away than Connecticut, Pennsylvania, or Virginia. Beginning in the early nineteenth century, Ohio increasingly became a destination for immigrants from overseas. Germans were the earliest major national group to settle in the state, either indirectly through Pennsylvania, or often directly from Europe. More than 70,000 inhabited Ohio by 1850, comprising almost half of all foreign-born residents. Although many of them were farmers, a relatively large German population came to characterize cities like Cincinnati (particularly the "Over-The-Rhine" neighborhood) and Columbus (especially in "German Village"), where they grew to be close to a third of the population. The Irish—almost 33,000 by 1850—were the other early major immigrant group, many of them originally coming via New York to help build the canals in the 1820s and 1830s.

The large numbers of Germans and Irish had a profound impact on Ohio's culture. Whereas most non-Indian Ohio residents had been English-speaking, the state now for the first time had entire German-speaking communities, both urban and rural. The Germans also brought religious traditions with them that were new to Ohio. Although individual Jews (mostly from England) had made their way to Ohio earlier, Ohio's earliest Jewish communities mostly arose from Germans who began to arrive in the 1830s. By 1850, Ohio had four established Jewish communities in Cincinnati, Dayton, Columbus, and Cleveland. Among Protestant denominations, the new German immigrants brought large numbers of Lutherans for the first time, but also smaller numbers of other sects like the German Baptists ("Dunkers"). More influential than any of these, though, was introduction of a major Catholic population that came with the increased Irish and German immigration. Small numbers of primarily Pennsylvania Catholics had made their way to Ohio even before statehood, and settlers near Somerset in Perry County established the first Catholic Church in 1818. Yet the number of Catholics in the entire Northwest was still relatively small. When the Catholic Church established the Cincinnati Diocese in 1821, the boundaries of the new bishopric stretched up to Green Bay, Wisconsin. It was not until Irish canal workers began to move to the state in large numbers in the 1820s followed by German immigrants starting in the 1830s that Ohio could claim a significant Catholic presence.

Other nationalities were less frequent overall but could still make up significant pockets of habitation as immigrants often chose to group together in communities. The French around Gallipolis and the French Grants are the earliest examples of this, and by 1850 they were still the fourth largest immigrant group. In third place with about 13 percent of the foreign-born population were the English, who tended to concentrate in the counties near Lake Erie and Cincinnati. Ohio's 5,000 Welsh settled mostly in south-central and central Ohio—particularly Jackson, Gallia, Meigs, Licking, Delaware, and Franklin Counties—although Portage and Hamilton Counties also had significant concentrations. Of Ohio's 4,000 Scots in 1850, most had settled in just four counties: Hamilton, Cuyahoga, Columbiana and Washington. While the French, Welsh, and Scots were no more 3–4 percent each of Ohio's immigrant population, their concentration in certain areas helped to preserve ethnic and religious customs and gave them a disproportionate influence over local affairs. In this way they, along with the larger Irish, German, and English immigrant groups, African Americans, and the even larger numbers of Northeastern, Mid-Atlantic, and Southern migrants contributed to the sometimes fractious community of communities that characterized the state by 1850.

Social Conflict

As discussed above, Ohioans in the early period tended to live in small communities that shared similar backgrounds, languages, and traditions. Most farmers and their families routinely ventured no further than a few dozen miles of their homesteads. Disparate groups had relatively little opportunity for broader contact with each other, especially in the days before the canals and railroads. However, as the state became more crowded and transportation threw these groups into closer proximity, some conflict was perhaps inevitable. One of the earliest examples of this was the relationship between white settlers and Native Americans.

It would be too easy to characterize the relationship between white Ohioans and Native-American Ohioans during the late territorial and early statehood period as unremittingly and mutually hostile. Certainly, in the time before the Treaty of Greenville, and even excluding the major military campaigns against the Indians (see chapter 5), a *de facto* state of war often existed between these groups. Perhaps the most famous example of this was the "Big-Bottom Massacre" in 1791, when a party of Lenape and Wyandots attacked a poorly-defended settler outpost about thirty miles up the Muskingum River from the Marietta settlement, killing more than a dozen. White settlers also frequently killed Indians with impunity, especially the farther away they were from the already tenuous reach of the territorial government. Many settlers also often revered men like Captain Samuel Brady, a famed frontiersman who professed an implacable hatred for the Indians and liked to brag about how many he had killed. In early county histories there are too many stories to count of individuals like Brady and his Indian counterparts—each type of which had no interest in sharing Ohio with the other.

Yet to paint the relationship between Ohio whites and Indians as one of constant conflict would be overly simplistic. The Ohio Company leadership tried to establish good relations with local Native groups, and one of the tensions between New England settlers around Marietta and the Appalachian southerners they viewed as interlopers was the concern that the newcomers would mistreat the Native Americans. Early Ohio merchants often sought out trade with Native Americans, and many set up amicable working relationships. Even at times of violence on the frontier it would often be the case that Native American raiders chose to bypass nearby white communities with which they had established good relations and attack further off in Virginia or Kentucky. After the Treaty of Greenville the chance for direct interaction between most whites and Natives dissipated as many Indians left and others withdrew to the Northwest corner that the treaty allotted them. Relations were generally more peaceful among those Indians and the American settlers on their borders. For example, in Stow Township on the upper Cuyahoga River in the early 1800s Judge William Wetmore lived near both a Seneca village and a Lenape village on the other side of the river. People from both villages often visited his cabin and his four sons played with the Indian boys. Wetmore's wife set up what may have been the first sewing circle in the Western Reserve with the Indian girls and women. Beyond individual relationships like these, certain larger groups of settlers cultivated mutually-friendly relations with Ohio's Native Americans. Adherents of the Society of

Friends (Quakers) in particular—whose pacifism and belief in the inner light of all humans made them think of all people as friends—grew to be allies and defenders of the Native Americans, sometimes interceding on their behalf when they appeared to be cheated or abused by unscrupulous traders or government Indian Agents. Although a certain kind of patronizing attitude and desire to "civilize" the Natives often drove their efforts, the Friends in general seemed to be sincerely interested in helping the Ohio Indians. Missionary William Kirk in particular labored hard for a number of years from 1807 to provide up-to-date agricultural expertise to the Shawnee at Wapakoneta, setting up a model farming community with a blacksmith and mills to aid their self-sufficiency.

The Kirk mission was part of a larger trend that was quickly becoming a no-win situation for Ohio's last Native populations. The Indians who remained in Ohio by the 1830s had often assimilated to the point where their villages were practically indistinguishable from white settlements. For years government agents and missionaries had implored them to become "civilized" by settling down in towns and emulating the rest of the farmers who were "taming" the wilderness. Some Native Americans had hoped that by doing this, they would be able to remain on their land, and the Wyandots in particular built a thriving village on their reservation near present-day Upper Sandusky, with mills, businesses, and an educated population including their own trained lawyer, John Armstrong. By the late 1830s, though, it became clear that no amount of assimilation would alter the fact that white settlers and the government were determined to take their land. It is perhaps a testament to how well the Wyandots had assimilated that John Armstrong used his legal skills to negotiate a much better deal for their lands than the last Lenape and Shawnee groups had achieved. Although the United States government had budgeted about $20,000 to pay for the reservation, the government's own appraisal of the property revealed that it owed its residents more than six times that amount. The Wyandots who boarded the steamships on that Cincinnati wharf in July 1843 were the last official tribe to leave Ohio, but in another sense tribal Ohio had ended long beforehand.

Ohioans also tended to greet African Americans with hostility even before statehood. The 1802 Ohio Constitution deprived African Americans of the right to vote, and subsequent "Black Laws" of 1804 and 1807 rendered them legally second-class citizens (see chapter 8). Never great in number before the Civil War, African Americans found that even their relatively tiny presence often elicited alarmist rhetoric from the lowest to the highest levels of Ohio society. In 1827 Governor Allen Trimble ended his address to the Ohio Senate noting that the "rapid increase" of African Americans had caused consternation among many citizens, ominously warning that, "it will be a question of grave and solemn inquiry how long Ohio will continue to tolerate the emigration … of this unfortunate and degraded race." As if to fulfill his prophecy, in July and August of 1829, hundreds of mostly Irish workers in Cincinnati rioted against the neighborhoods of "Bucktown" and "Little Africa." They believed that black residents were driving down wages and decreasing job opportunities. Hundreds of black Cincinnatians chose to flee the country and set up the Wilberforce Colony (named after the famed British abolitionist) north of present-day London, Ontario. Subsequent race riots rocked the city in 1836—in response to the abolitionist *Philanthropist* newspaper beginning to publish there—and in August 1841, when a severe drought stopped Ohio River traffic, causing a number of mostly Irish river workers to lose their jobs. Kentuckians from across the river joined in the violence in September, at which point the police arrested as many African Americans as they could and threw them in jail. Although this was allegedly for their own protection whites continued to beat them while they were in custody and also attacked their homes, causing $150,000 worth of damage. Other cities also witnessed white-on-black violence, most notably Portsmouth, whose citizens drove out eighty black families in 1830.

Violence against African Americans was not just restricted to Ohio's cities, either. In 1833, the famous Virginia politician John Randolph of Roanoke died, his will stipulating that his slaves should be freed and given land in Ohio. After a lengthy court battle, Randolph's estate purchased land for them near the thriving Quaker-established black community of Carthagena in Mercer County, and in 1846 the 518 emancipated slaves attempted to settle there. The mostly German farmers in the surrounding area attacked the new settlers and chased them away. Scattered, most eventually found more hospitable places to settle in Rossville (near Piqua), Marshall Town (near Troy), and Hanktown (near West Milton), and Rumley (near Sidney). White rural Scioto Valley residents also drove some black farmers from their land during this period.

Native Americans and African Americans were not the only flashpoints of conflict in early Ohio. Anti-Catholic, anti-German, and anti-Irish sentiments rose with the appearance of these groups in Ohio and all of them faced some discrimination in the state as a result. By the 1840s and 1850s the larger Nativist movement that had swept the country pervaded the state. On top of a basic distrust of anyone who was not a white Anglo Saxon Protestant, Nativists also suspected that American Catholics owed primary allegiance to the Vatican rather than to the U.S. government. Cincinnati Nativists in particular resented Bishop John Baptist Purcell's outspoken lobbying against Catholic citizens having to pay taxes to support public schools while most of them were also paying for parochial education. On election day in 1855 these tensions spilled over into a full-scale riot, which targeted the Over-the-Rhine neighborhood. Germans set up barricades to protect themselves, and even fired a canon over the heads of their attackers. Several men died before the authorities restored order.

Conflict also frequently occurred within and among immigrant groups. German Catholics and Irish Catholics shared little in common other than their religion, and often sought to have separate churches. Even within the German community there were significant splits, not just between Protestants and Catholics but also between earlier and later comers. A large number of liberal Germans who had left Germany after the failed Revolutions of 1848 were incensed when Papal Emissary Cardinal Bedini came to visit Bishop Purcell in 1853. Bedini had supported the successful crushing of the revolutions, an act that had pushed many of Cincinnati's "Forty-Eighter" Germans out of Europe. A crowd of more than 500 marched on Purcell's home to protest, carrying signs and hanging effigies of Bedini. There they met one hundred policemen sent to protect Bedini and Purcell. When one of the marchers fired a shot, a general brawl ensued injuring nearly twenty and killing one. Tensions within and among Ohio's many groups of migrants would continue throughout the century.

Class

Although race and religion provided the most overt examples of conflict during the early statehood period, some of the discontent in the state revolved around issues of class. Disputes of this nature extended back to the territorial period, when squatters and poor farmers resented what they perceived as land-grabs by wealthy speculators. These resentments extended to the bankers whom small farmers blamed for the Panic of 1819 (see chapters 7 and 8). Yet with the vast majority of Ohio's population living in rural areas, recognizable class conflict, in its more modern sense, could not really develop until Ohio began to urbanize. Labor was relatively scarce in the state during the early period, and Cincinnati businesses paid workers nearly twice the average wage of laborers back east. After 1830, the growing influx of black, Irish, and German immigrants created more competition for work and kept wages lower. This created increasing discontent (as exemplified by the Cincinnati Riots of 1829 and 1841), as did the introduction of mass-production techniques that threatened the work of skilled craftsmen. Labor groups began to form as early as 1813 when workers in Dayton created a Mechanic's Association. By the 1830s, most trades had formed their own organizations, and they began to call strikes to protect jobs, wages, and working conditions. Although Cincinnati was first, other cities like Cleveland, Columbus, and Dayton followed suit as they acquired a critical mass of laborers.

One class that witnessed the growing conflict and disorder with dismay was Ohio's growing nucleus of a true middle class. Made up mostly of merchants, artisans, and professional people, a subset of this group longed to form what historian Andrew Cayton has called a "culture of respectability" in the state. They believed that their material success depended on the success of the state as a whole, and wanted to improve and unite the state for the benefit not just of themselves, but for all. As the first half of the century unfolded, more and more of these mostly middle-class Protestant believers sought to remake the state in a number of ways: religiously, educationally, morally, and even aesthetically. In these efforts they mirrored the efforts of people like them across the country who were making the early 1800s the country's first great era of reform.

Reform

Religion

During early U.S. history organized religion was only a minor factor in most people's lives. In 1800, only 5–10 percent of people in the United States were members of any church. This number was often even lower out west, where isolation and work prevented even those settlers who might have been inclined to join from forming active congregations. Missionaries to Ohio despaired of the population, most of whom were not only unchurched but seemingly happy to remain so. Starting on the Kentucky frontier in 1800 and 1801, however, a new religious reform movement began to spread that fundamentally changed not only American religious patterns but also society at large. Like the First Great Awakening that

Figure 6.2	Called "The Father of Modern Revivalism," Charles Grandison Finney was one of the best-known evangelists of the Second Great Awakening. Originally from Connecticut, he moved to Ohio in 1835 to teach at Oberlin College. From his position there, he became a vocal proponent of the abolitionist movement.
Source: Courtesy of the Ohio Historical Society (AL00616)

preceded it in the mid-eighteenth century, the Second Great Awakening stressed revivalistic and emotional calls for personal salvation that contrasted sharply from more staid, traditional church services. Days-long camp meetings brought residents from miles around to listen to preaching, hear music, witness the emotional response of the audience, and often get swept up in the movement themselves. These camp meetings reformed the church experience for most Americans, not only tripling church membership by the 1840s, but also often changing the ways people responded to society around them. Over the next few decades the movement accelerated and spread throughout the frontier and eventually to the East Coast. It found a special home in Upstate New York in the 1820s and 1830s, which hosted so many revivals that that area became known as the "burned-over district."

The Second Great Awakening took hold in Ohio around that time and the state not only hosted a number of revival meetings but also drew some of the biggest names in the movement. Charles Grandison Finney (see Figure 6.2), sometimes called "The Father of Modern Revivalism," came to Ohio from the Northeast in 1835 to become a professor at Oberlin College. Famed preacher Lyman Beecher moved to Cincinnati from Connecticut in 1832 to become the first president of Lane Theological Seminary and pastor of the

Second Presbyterian Church. Once an opponent of the "new measures" Finney advocated, he caused a sensation (and turmoil within the Presbyterian Church) when he switched positions to support Finney's work. Methodism—which had long emphasized informal and emotional (sometimes boisterous) worship and itinerant circuit-riding preachers—was a natural vehicle for the movement, and the denomination found Ohio to be a particularly fertile ground for converts. By 1850 one-third of all church members in the U.S. were Methodists and the percentage seems to have been even higher in Ohio. By 1870 the sect had 3.4 times as many church buildings as its nearest rival (the Presbyterians), and by 1890 the Methodists claimed more members than the Presbyterian, Baptist, Episcopalian, Lutheran, and Congregationalist denominations combined.

For all the expansion the Second Great Awakening brought to religion, it also caused further divisions among adherents. Religious traditionalists—sometimes referred to as "old lights"—did not care for the more enthusiastic expressions of faith of the "new lights," and often fought to keep things the way they had been before. This resulted in the fracture of congregations as one or the other group withdrew to practice their religion in the way they thought best. Furthermore, when some of the "new lights" also became very active in social reform movements—particularly abolition—they increasingly chafed against denominational establishments that often refused to take a definitive stand on these issues. If the situation got too intolerable, they were prone to split from the congregation to form a new one, becoming known as "come-outers." In this way Ohio's already denominationally diverse religious atmosphere became even more complex in the years before the Civil War.

Social reform

The "come-outers" reflect one of the main effects the Second Great Awakening had on American (and Ohio) society. Religious people predisposed to reform the church and bring about personal salvation needed to make only a small step to want to bring the same kind of perfection to society as a whole. Throughout the early 1800s, numerous people gathered in groups to try to improve a society that they viewed as immoral or chaotic. Ohio, which was in an almost constant state of flux and movement at this time, was a particularly fertile field for what would become one of the most vibrant reform periods in United States history.

The most radical of these reformers saw the surrounding society as hopelessly corrupt and sought to rebuild it almost from scratch. They usually organized around religious principles, but sometimes relied instead on secular communitarian ideals. Moving away from the baneful influence of the contemporary world, these reformers formed separate communities according to their new model. Known generally as "utopian societies," these settlements sprang up across the United States especially in the early 1800s. Some of the best known were Brook Farm in Massachusetts, Oneida in New York, and New Harmony in Indiana. However, perhaps because of its plentiful fertile land and isolation from the East Coast, Ohio became a prime location for erstwhile utopias. Arthur Bestor's *Backwoods Utopias*, a classic study of these groups, identified at least one hundred. Ohio topped the list with twenty-one, far more than Indiana's second-place eleven.

Figure 6.3 The Zoar community was one of the most successful of all religious communes in U.S. history. Moving to Tuscarawas County from Germany in 1817, Zoarites owned and worked all of their land in common until the late 1890s. Although financially stressed in its early years, the Zoar Community got on a firmer financial footing by contracting to dig the section of the Ohio and Erie Canal that went through the area.
Source: Courtesy of the Ohio Historical Society (AL05975)

Perhaps the most famous of these religious idealists were the Shakers (The United Society of Believers in Christ's Second Appearing), a millennialist group which otherwise shared some of the same basic ideas of the Society of Friends. One of their most important leaders, "Mother" Ann Lee, came to America in the late 1700s with seven of her followers and established the movement in New York. Shakers practiced an active form of worship involving singing and dancing, but were even more unusual for the time in their beliefs in the equality of the sexes and communalism in living and property. Believing in simplicity and industry, they were noted craftspeople and cultivators who built productive workshops and farms. The Shakers established five communities in Ohio, the most successful of which were Watervliet (present-day Kettering), Union Village (near present-day Lebanon), and North Union (present-day Shaker Heights). Thousands of people lived in Ohio Shaker communities over the course of the nineteenth century but because the group also firmly believed in complete celibacy, their numbers dwindled dramatically by the early 1900s. Another important religious commune in Ohio was the German Society of Separatists who created the Zoar settlement in 1817 (see Figure 6.3). Breaking with the Lutheran Church in the Kingdom of Württemburg (in present-day Germany) and seeking a place to practice their simpler form of worship, about 300 Separatists under the leadership of Joseph Bäumeler (often written "Bimeler") planted their communal, religion-centered settlement on 5,500 acres in northern Tuscarawas County. Although there were lean times in the early years, the group's collective farming efforts and their work in building the Ohio and Erie Canal nearby helped the community thrive, and by 1852 it controlled more than a million dollars in assets. Bäumeler, however, died the next year, and the settlement began a long decline that ended in 1898 when the remaining members divided the assets and disbanded.

Even though they all eventually disbanded, the Zoar and Shaker communities in Ohio were some of the longest-lived utopian communities of the period. Other attempts at religious communities relatively soon became more standard towns, including the Congregationalist-planned settlements of Oberlin and Tallmadge, and the Community of United Christians settlement at Berea. The Latter Day Saints (Mormons) followed a somewhat different model. Moving from Palmyra, New York in the heart of the "Burned-Over District," Joseph Smith and his followers planted a community at the pre-existing town of Kirtland in Lake County from 1831–38. It was here that they constructed their first temple and most of their canonical book the *Doctrine and Covenants* took form before Smith and most of his followers moved further west after tensions rose with the non-Mormon residents of the area. Several attempts at secular socialist utopian communities, including settlements at Kendal (Massillon), Yellow Springs, and Phalanx Mills (near Warren in Trumbull County) had only short existences.

Although not quite utopian communities, Society of Friends' (Quaker) settlements in Ohio deserve special note. A denomination of pacifists who advocated simplicity, humility, consensus, and the awareness of the "inner light" in all people, Friends often chose to move into areas with other Friends, particularly in the Eastern and Southwestern parts of the state (although the first known settlement was at Quaker Bottom in Lawrence County at the Southern tip of Ohio in 1799). Belmont County across the Ohio River from Wheeling saw the first formal organization of Friends in the territory, and by 1826, more than 8,000 Quakers lived in Eastern Ohio. Another nucleus of Friends settled in the Miami Valley, many of its members coming from North Carolina to get away from the slave society of the South. Together, these groupings represented a distinct and relatively close-knit religious community, one that disproportionately affected and participated in reform movements statewide—particularly education, women's rights, and abolition.

Most reform-minded people in Ohio and elsewhere did not view separate communities as a practical way to bring about the changes they desired to see. Instead, these overlapping groups of mostly Protestant, middle-class reformers sought to engage society's problems head-on, not only by trying to mitigate the problems of certain groups, but also by using moral arguments to exhort the public at large to advance these reforms. Rising at about the same time as the Second Great Awakening (and including many of its adherents) numerous reform movements grew in Ohio tying like-minded people together in state and national organizations. These organizations—which served purposes coinciding with what American culture assumed were innate feminine nurturing capabilities—were also notable for their relatively large female participation in a culture that afforded women few opportunities to be active in the public sphere.

The religious zeal that permeated Ohio's reform movements of the early 1800s sometimes found practical expression in biblical admonitions to help the unfortunate. These included a focus on Ohioans with special needs for which contemporary institutions either did not exist or were dreadful. Mentally ill people, for example, often found themselves languishing and even abused in local jails for the lack of any other place to hold them. In 1821 the General Assembly contributed to the construction and maintenance of the Commercial Hospital and Lunatic Asylum for the State of Ohio in Cincinnati (later Longview State Hospital), but this was primarily a county hospital (see Figure 6.4). Devout Presbyterian William Awl, a Pennsylvania native who was not only the physician of the State Penitentiary but also in the state legislature, saw the need for a separate place to take care of the mentally ill. In 1835 he successfully lobbied his fellow State Assemblymen to create what became Ohio's first State Mental Hospital, and served as its head from the time it opened in 1838 until 1850. Awl also lobbied the General Assembly to found The Ohio Institution for the Education of the Blind (now the Ohio State School for the Blind) in 1837, making it the first public school for the blind in the country. Similarly, the Ohio School for the Deaf established in 1829 was one of the earliest, and is the fifth oldest residential school of its kind in the country.

Figure 6.4   The Commercial Hospital and Lunatic Asylum for the State of Ohio, chartered in 1821, was the earliest example of the Ohio state government creating an institution for people with special needs. Later known as Longview State Hospital in Cincinnati, it gave rise to several other important local facilities, including an orphanage, the City Infirmary, and the Cincinnati Hospital. Moved and enlarged several times over the years, the complex is currently known as the Pauline Warfield Lewis Center.

Source: From the Collection of the Public Library of Cincinnati and Hamilton County

Women's rights

Other reformers sought to redress the problems of larger societal groups. The first Women's Rights Convention famously occurred in Seneca Falls, New York in 1848, but soon thereafter Ohio became a focal point of the movement. The first Women's Rights Convention to be held outside New York convened in Salem, Ohio in April of 1850, and several other smaller ones happened over the course of the year. At these conventions women collected signatures on petitions that demanded delegates to the soon-to-be-held state Constitutional Convention grant women the right to vote. One of these conferences took place in McConnelsville, led by one of the rising figures of the movement, Frances Dana Gage (see Figure 6.5). A native of Marietta, Gage had earlier won some regional fame as a writer for various journals under the name "Aunt Fanny," but had become increasingly active in reform causes. Although the Constitutional Convention defeated a women's suffrage provision by a wide margin Gage was undaunted and led another women's rights convention in Akron, Ohio in May 1851. It was here that tradition holds that Sojourner Truth gave her famous

Figure 6.5   Frances Dana Gage was emblematic of the reform impulse that followed in the wake of the Second Great Awakening. A writer of children's literature, she also was active in the abolition, temperance, and women's rights movements. She lectured widely, advocating the then-radical ideas of giving women and African Americans the right to vote.
Source: Courtesy of the Ohio Historical Society (AL04122)

"Ain't I a Woman?" speech. Unpublished at the time, this oration's only record is Gage's printed remembrance of it years later. Gage also presided over 1,500 participants of the 1853 National Women's Rights Convention held in Cleveland. Like-minded women founded the Ohio Women's Rights Association in Massillon that same year, and Cincinnati held another national convention in 1855, but despite all of this activity the legal status of women changed little before the Civil War. The General Assembly passed the nation's first law intended to protect women in the workplace in 1852, but little came of it. In 1861 the state made a law allowing women limited property ownership and contract rights, but Ohio women would have to wait quite a while for major advances in their legal status.

Education

One area in which Ohio women saw advancement during this period was education. Oberlin College, shown in Figure 6.6, became the first co-educational college in the nation when it opened in 1833, admitting women first as secondary students and then in 1837 as college students on an equal footing with males. Only a few other colleges nation-wide had followed Oberlin's lead before Antioch and Urbana admitted women in the 1850s. Oberlin was also a pioneer educational institution regarding race, being among the first to admit African American students regularly, and graduating the first African American female B.A. in 1862.

Figure 6.6   Presbyterian ministers John J. Shipherd and Philo P. Stewart planned Oberlin as a joint community and college in which "town and gown" would function together. Tuition was free when the school opened in 1833, but students were expected to work in the community, hence the school motto: "Learning and Labor." As the first college in the United States to admit women and African Americans on an equal basis, Oberlin quickly became a hotbed of the abolition movement.
Source: Courtesy of the Ohio Historical Society (AL04148)

Oberlin, Antioch, and Urbana also exemplify another trend in Ohio education. One effect of having such rich denominational diversity in the state and people wishing to create a culture of respectability was the unusual variety of small liberal arts colleges that characterize Ohio's educational landscape. Most denominations wanted to have institutions in which they could train ministers in approved doctrine and offer higher education to its adherents. As a result, over the course of the nineteenth century, Ohio became the home of dozens of small liberal arts and normal (teacher training) colleges. Kenyon was the earliest, founded by Episcopalians in 1824. The Methodists were the most prolific denomination in this regard, creating Ohio Wesleyan, Mount Union, Ohio Northern, and both Baldwin College and German Wallace College (which merged to become Baldwin Wallace in 1913). They also founded Wilberforce with the African Methodist Episcopal Church in 1856, making it the oldest African American owned and operated college in the United States. Other Protestant denominations claimed multiple college affiliations, too. What became Western Reserve (later Case-Western Reserve) University, Muskingum, Wooster, and Cedarville were Presbyterian-affiliated, Lutherans founded Wittenberg and Capital, Baptists built Denison and Rio Grande, and Quakers started Malone and Wilmington. Many other colleges arose from smaller denominations, including Antioch (Christian Connection and Unitarian), Ashland (Brethren), Bluffton (Mennonite), Buchtel, later the University of Akron (Universalist), Findlay (Church of God), Heidelberg (German Reformed), Hiram (Disciples of Christ), Otterbein (United Brethren), and Urbana (Swedenborgian). By the turn of the twentieth century Catholics had also started Dayton, Ursuline, John Carroll, Xavier, and the Pontifical College Josephinium, a seminary in Columbus. These are just the ones that survived to the present—for every existing private college in Ohio today, there were roughly two others that existed but failed to survive. Most of these were also church-affiliated: Ohio Presbyterians alone founded antislavery-oriented Franklin and Providence Colleges in New Athens and Iberia College in Iberia in the 1840s, ran Richmond College in Jefferson County for a while in the 1850s, and created McCorkle College in Bloomfield in the 1870s. Some of these colleges serve as prime examples of the reformist zeal that characterized the early 1800s. Franklin College had the distinction of being the first private college in Ohio to graduate an African American student, and noted abolitionist John Rankin founded Ripley College in Ripley in 1830. Others were among the most successful of their day: Scio College in Scio admitted more than 20,000 students in its roughly fifty years, and Hopedale Normal School in Hopedale trained 18,000 students over the course of 43 years.

For all of Ohio's wealth of private liberal arts colleges its very first colleges were public institutions and among the earliest state universities in the country. A condition of both the Ohio Company and Symmes Purchases was that land therein be set aside for the construction of colleges. Just one year after statehood, the Ohio General Assembly chartered Ohio University in Athens, making it the oldest college in the Northwest Territory and the fourth-oldest continually-operating state university in the United States. Ohio University proved to be precedent-setting in other ways, too: in 1828 OU's John Newton Templeton was one of the first African Americans to earn a college degree. One of the many problems that plagued the Symmes Purchase was the fact that Symmes neglected to set aside the land promised for the college there. In response, the Ohio General Assembly instead located Miami University in what is now the northwestern Butler County town of Oxford in 1809. Various difficulties, including the War of 1812, postponed its construction, but the school accepted its first college students until 1824.

Educational reform also marked the American professions during the early eighteenth century as the long-established apprenticeship tradition gave way to a new model of professional schools. Ohio quickly became home to a number of these new institutions. Cincinnati had a medical college by 1819, and Willoughby College near Lake Erie spawned both the Cleveland Medical College in 1843 and the Starling Medical College in Columbus in 1847. Law schools were quite uncommon in the nineteenth century, with most lawyers continuing to "read law" under the tutelage of an established lawyer. Nevertheless, distinguished Massachusetts lawyer Timothy Walker helped set the precedent for a new method of instruction when he founded the Cincinnati Law School in 1833—the first Law School west of the Appalachians and the fourth oldest continually operating law school in the country. Walker's *Introduction to American Law* became the standard text of its kind for the rest of the century. Another precedent-setting educational professional was New York native Dr. John Harris of Bainbridge in Ross County. A doctor who specialized in dental work, in 1827 he began training students in the dental arts from his office, the first person in the country to do so. Viewed by the profession as "The Father of Dental Education in the United States," Harris's students would go on to found the first formal schools of dentistry in the world: his brother Chapin created the Baltimore College of Dental Surgery (and the D.D.S. degree) in 1840, and John Allen founded the Ohio College of Dental Surgery in Cincinnati in 1845.

Yet in the 1800s most Ohioans did not go to high school, much less college or professional school. The only contact the average Ohio resident had with education—if any—was the local public common school. Public education had deep roots in the state. The Land Ordinance of 1785 had set aside one square mile in every township for support of public education: a far-sighted measure in a country that had few public schools even in the East. Furthermore, the Northwest Ordinance stated that "schools and the means of education shall forever be encouraged" in the territory. Despite the ordinances' lofty intentions, it became quite clear by the early nineteenth century that their provisions were inadequate in practice. The revenues from the sixteenth section of each township rarely provided enough money to support schools (often due to mismanagement by township trustees), and many townships in sparsely-populated areas often did not contain a sufficient concentration of children or transportation infrastructure needed to make schools practicable. As a result, only the most populated regions with the most motivated residents had schools in the state's early days. Most other children had no formal school training, and the average educational level of Ohio's population actually declined during the first couple of decades of statehood.

This state of affairs distressed an increasing number of reformers, who thought that an uneducated public would jeopardize Ohio's future. Some did what they could to promote learning in their localities given the resources available. Residents of Ames in the Ohio Company Lands, for instance, created the "Coonskin Library" in 1804, naming Ephraim Cutler (a Massachusetts-born resident of Marietta who was a son of Ohio Company founder and lobbyist Manasseh Cutler) as its first librarian. With money scarce, the town collected furs (mostly raccoon) and sold them in the east to raise money for books in one of the state's first libraries. Such creative initiatives did not solve the statewide problem, though, and reformers began to push for better school funding. This proved to be a difficult sell to an Ohio General Assembly that tended to be tight with its money and not convinced of the need for a public system. A compromise measure passed in 1821 allowed localities to levy taxes to support schools, but few of them did because such taxes remained optional. A commission headed by former Massachusetts native and New York schoolmaster Caleb Atwater of Circleville the following year judged that the law was still insufficient, and instead recommended in pamphlets (published mostly at Atwater's expense) that the state create a public school system modeled on New York's, paid for by the sale of school lands. Commission member Nathan Guilford of Cincinnati suggested that property taxes ought to be used instead, and when he and fellow Commissioner Ephraim Cutler won election to the Ohio Senate in 1824, they set to work writing a new school law in 1825 that would require property taxes in each county to pay for public schools and create a system of certifying teachers. Despite strong opposition, they strategically exchanged votes with an overlapping constituency of transportation reformers who wanted to build the Ohio and Erie Canal in order to get the new tax passed. Illustrating the theme of the significance of regional origins of Ohioans, it is per-haps not a coincidence that Atwater, Guilford, and Cutler all had roots in the Northeast, which had the strongest educational system in the country at the time.

New Englanders also played an active part in further public school reforms. Although the new law provided a steady income for schools for the first time, it did not do as much as its supporters hoped. In 1838, Massachusetts native Samuel Lewis travelled 1,200 miles on horseback visiting 300 schools across the state in his capacity as the newly-created Superintendent of Common Schools, and issued a report stating that Ohio's schools were still woefully underserving the state's nearly half a million school-age children. The money allocated by the state amounted to less than fourteen cents per child, and 3,000 of the 8,000 school districts in the state still did not have schools. Lewis recommended a major increase in funding and the hiring of thousands of new teachers. Although the state did nothing with this report (and abolished Lewis's position when he stepped down the next year due to poor health), other New Englanders in Akron, Ohio took matters into their own hands. Massachusetts native Henry W. King led several other like-minded reformers in a movement to create a new model for public education (see Figure 6.7). The new plan turned the entire town into a single school district, which had several elementary schools, each subdivided into different grades (first, second, etc.) based on the students' achieve-ment. When conditions and numbers of students allowed, the town could build a public high school. Local property taxes paid for the system, which an elected board of education would oversee and hire professionals to administrate. In its first year it was such a success that the state legislature recommended it to all other Ohio districts and in 1849 the General Assembly passed the Ohio School Law based on the Akron experiment. If this plan sounds familiar, it should: it is the model on which most public schools across the United States eventually based their own school systems. Yet as progressive and reformist as the Ohio School Law was it coexisted with some less reformist tendencies of the Ohio public. Early Ohio state law forbade African Americans from attending public schools with white children. Although the more socially egalitarian Northeasterners who settled Toledo and Cleveland in the northern part of the state allowed the few African American

Figure 6.7 The 1847 Akron School Law reforming public education in the city later became a model for the Ohio School Law two years later. The "Old Stone School" in Akron is characteristic of the one-room schoolhouses that defined the public school experience in nineteenth-century Ohio. *Source*: Photo, courtesy Thomas Fritsch; Eric Milasck, Waymarking.com

children there to attend in violation of the law, the only way most African American families could get instruction for their children was through private schools. In 1848 the Ohio Assembly relented a little, allowing segregated black schools in places where there were at least twenty black children. If there were fewer than twenty, the children could attend the local public school, but only if local custom allowed it. Unfortunately, local custom often did not favor the black children, and by the late 1850s less than 40 percent of Ohio's African American children attended school. Those that did often found themselves in classes held in sheds or basement rooms with little furniture and poorly-trained teachers. Ohio's black school children continued to deal with these adverse conditions until the Ohio Assembly repealed the segregation law in 1876.

By the 1850s, one-room schoolhouses dotted most of the state, from dirt-floored, sparsely-furnished log cabins in poorer areas to tidy clapboard buildings with central cast-iron stoves in more affluent communities. The heat the stoves provided was necessary, because school terms were usually only a few months during the coldest weather when children's labor was not as necessary on the farm. Children usually learned by rote memorization, with all different grades working simultaneously on their own work. Aiding teachers with their work by mid-century were a series of graded works in mathematics and reading penned by two Ohio educators. Virginia-born Joseph Ray came to Ohio to attend Franklin College, and after a failed attempt at a medical career found himself teaching math

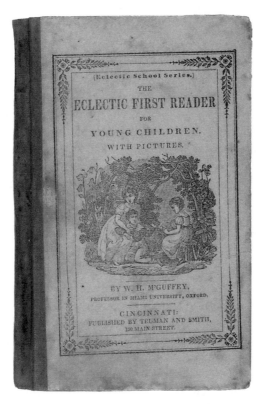

Figure 6.8 Building on the success of Joseph Ray's math textbooks, the Truman and Smith Publishing Company hired Ray's colleague William Holmes McGuffey to write elementary school primers. Countless American schoolchildren throughout the 1800s and early 1900s used Ray's and McGuffey's textbooks, which went through multiple editions and sold more than 100 million copies. *Source*: From the Walter Havighurst Special Collections, Miami University Libraries, Oxford, Ohio

at Woodward High School in Cincinnati. While there he wrote a series of basic arithmetic texts starting in 1834. These were published by Truman and Smith, one of the city's several publishing houses. These books were immediately successful, and Truman and Smith the next year sought out someone to write a similar set of texts for reading. They offered the job to the Reverend Lyman Beecher's daughter Harriet, but she declined, suggesting instead her friend William Holmes McGuffey (Harriet married Calvin Stowe in 1836, and later wrote her own best-selling book, *Uncle Tom's Cabin*). McGuffey was a Pennsylvania native and staunch Presbyterian who spent most of his career teaching in Ohio at Ohio University, Woodward and Cincinnati Colleges in Cincinnati, and Miami University. He was also Joseph Ray's friend and colleague from the Western Literary Institute and College of Professional Teachers, an educational reform organization. McGuffey produced series of graded *Readers* that revolutionized the school textbook, blending reading, history, literature, and moral lessons in increasingly more challenging volumes (see Figure 6.8). Just as Ohio's School Law became standard across the country, Ray's mathematic books and McGuffey's *Readers* became the standard texts in the new systems the law inspired across the country, each series of texts eventually selling more than 120 million copies.

Temperance

Education in a broader moral sense was one of McGuffey's goals, and among the final lessons of his first *Reader* were "Don't Take Strong Drink" and "The Whisky Boy." The latter lesson told the tale of a boy named John who became a drunkard by age eight and died in a poorhouse. In writing these, McGuffey reflected one of the biggest reform issues of the day: temperance. To modern eyes, temperance advocates may seem stern and prudish, and while many of them were, the truth is that they had serious reasons for concern. Alcohol permeated American society in the 1820s, particularly out west where turning corn into liquor was one of the most economical and convenient ways for a farmer to get money for his crops. The rate of alcohol consumption in the United States was both statistically and literally staggering. Historians have estimated liquor consumption in the United States during this period to be as high as seven gallons per person per year, with even higher average rates for adults and people living in western regions. While not everyone who consumed alcohol did so to excess, its deleterious effects were hard to ignore in most communities. Public drunkenness was a common sight, and alcohol often contributed to tavern fights, domestic violence, chronic illness, farm or workplace accidents, and financial ruin. "Drinking away the farm" came to be a standard expression acknowledging how many unfortunate families ultimately lost everything as a result of this addiction.

The temperance movement arose in the 1820s and 1830s, the highest point in average liquor consumption in United States history. Copley Township (now in Summit County) founded the first known local temperance society in the state in 1829, but by the next year neighboring Portage County had sixteen. These local groups often came to be affiliated with larger state and national organizations that sometimes specialized in certain constituencies, including the Washingtonians (a group of reformed alcoholics which filled a niche similar to the twentieth-century Alcoholics Anonymous), the Sons of Temperance (a more class-oriented society catering to artisans, merchants, and professionals), and the Father Mathew Temperance Society (an exception to the mostly Protestant-oriented movement in its primarily Irish Catholic focus). One of the most important of these, though, was the American Temperance Society, co-founded in 1826 by Reverend Lyman Beecher in Boston, Massachusetts. When Beecher moved to Cincinnati in the 1830s he brought his temperance zeal with him: the national organization claimed more than 8,000 local chapters and 1.5 million members.

In one sense the popularity of the temperance movement served as a unifying force in the still socially-fractured state, bringing together people from different localities and backgrounds in a common purpose. Yet in another way it exacerbated more general rips in Ohio's social fabric. Much of the impetus for temperance and other reforms like education came from either implicit or explicit fear of and/or hostility toward immigrants and Catholics. Some temperance advocates were also highly critical of these groups and mixed their anti-alcohol rhetoric with anti-Irish, anti-German, and anti-Catholic overtones. Lyman Beecher was among the most prominent of these and also used the perceived threat from these groups as justifications for educational reform. In his famous tract *A Plea for the West*—published by Truman and Smith along with Ray's and McGuffey's texts in 1835—Beecher warned,

If we do not provide the schools which are requisite for the cheap and effectual education of the children of the nation, it is perfectly certain that the Catholic powers of Europe intend to make up our deficiency ... they are doing it, and they will do it, unless as a nation of republicans, jealous of our liberties, and prompt to sustain them by a thorough intellectual and religious culture as well as by the sword, we arise, all denominations and all political parties to the work of national education.

Not all Ohio reformers, of course, were similarly bigoted, nor were the state's reform movements devoid of German, Irish, and Catholic participation. Yet Beecher's *Plea* illustrates how Ohio's otherwise laudable reform efforts could be tempered by local conditions and prejudices; and how they could also be as divisive as they were unifying.

Abolition

Perhaps no early nineteenth-century reform movement was as divisive as the effort to abolish slavery in the United States. While many people may have moved to Ohio at least in part because it did not have slavery, this does not mean that most Ohioans favored the abolition of the institution. Some had no moral qualms with slavery, others had moral qualms but did not believe there was any constitutional way to abolish it, and still others feared that abolition would bring tens of thousands of former slaves flocking into Ohio. As a result, early abolitionist efforts often met with hostility. The movement had roots in the eighteenth century on the East Coast, but Benjamin Lundy, a Friend (Quaker) originally from New Jersey, founded the first antislavery society west of the Appalachians in St. Clairsville in 1815. A few years later he began publishing an antislavery newspaper called *The Genius of Universal Emancipation* in Steubenville. After moving back to the East Coast, he convinced William Lloyd Garrison to devote his life to abolition, and Garrison served as an assistant editor for Lundy's paper before establishing his own more influential paper *The Liberator*. Charles Osborn, another Ohio Friend, actually published the first abolitionist newspaper in the United States. Originally from North Carolina and Tennessee, Osborn moved to Mount Pleasant in 1816 and began publishing *The Philanthropist* the following year (Figure 6.9). Achieving a small regional circulation, the paper was notable for its relatively radical stance. Whereas most abolitionists of the time favored gradual emancipation with the freed slaves to be sent "back" to Africa (where most had never been), Osborn and *The Philanthropist* advocated the immediate abolition of slavery without required African colonization.

The issue of gradual emancipation versus immediate abolition split the movement nationally and caused considerable disruption in Ohio. Perhaps the most notable example of this happened at Cincinnati's Lane Seminary in 1834. Lane Seminary was a Presbyterian school funded by wealthy New York merchants Arthur and Lewis Tappan. These brothers were active reformers and helped found the American Anti-Slavery Society in 1833 with a persuasive young abolitionist from Connecticut named Theodore Dwight Weld. Weld enrolled at Lane and eventually became a professor. There he was one of the leaders of the "Lane Rebels" who engaged their fellow classmen in eighteen days of debate over the

Figure 6.9 Although organized abolition began in the east, Ohio quickly became one of the leading centers of the movement and pioneered the use of popular media in the cause. Charles Osborn's *The Philanthropist* and Benjamin Lundy's *The Genius of Universal Emancipation* were among the earliest abolitionist newspapers published in the United States, and William Lloyd Garrison's work under Lundy launched his career as one of the most important leaders of the abolitionist movement.

issue that divided the school and community until the Lane trustees and President Lyman Beecher ordered them to desist. They left the school in protest, many of them enrolling at Oberlin after that school had agreed to accept African American students and give positions to some of the dissenting Lane faculty, including Weld. Although Weld declined the appointment, he helped to bring Charles Grandison Finney there instead. Weld became one of the foremost abolitionist organizers and pamphleteers in the country, co-publishing *Slavery As It Is: Testimony of a Thousand Witnesses*, an extremely influential abolitionist text that provided inspiration to Harriet Beecher Stowe in writing *Uncle Tom's Cabin*. Former Kentucky and Alabama slave owner James G. Birney further inflamed the Cincinnati community when he moved the latest version of *The Philanthropist* newspaper there in 1836. After increasing protest, angry mobs twice attacked and destroyed his printing press in mid- and late July. Undaunted, he continued to publish it until he turned it over to Gamaliel Bailey in 1837 so Birney could move to New York and become Secretary of the American Anti-Slavery Society. He later ran twice as the abolitionist Liberty Party candidate for president. The mob that destroyed Birney's press shocked Salmon P. Chase, a local lawyer originally from Cornish, New Hampshire. Until that time he had not taken strong views on abolition, but this event inspired Chase to come to Birney's defense and become a powerful voice for abolition in the coming years, eventually becoming a senator and Lincoln's Secretary of the Treasury. Other Ohio politicians, including Democratic Senator Thomas Morris of Clermont County (Birney's running mate in 1840) and Whig Representative Joshua Giddings of Ashtabula County, were some of the most outspoken antislavery Congressmen of the period.

Abolitionism grew in the state through the 1830s, although it could never claim anything approaching a majority of the state's population before the Civil War. The Ohio Anti-Slavery Society—an affiliate of the national organization—began operating in 1835, and within a few years the state had more than 200 local antislavery societies. Portage County's American Anti-Slavery Society chapter alone numbered over 900 members, and claimed to be the country's largest. The Western Reserve—with its Northeastern heritage—was a particularly fertile ground for the movement, and the southern part of the state—with its large "butternut" population from the Upper South—often expressed the greatest hostility to it, however, such generalizations do not represent the complex nature of abolitionism in the state as a whole. Antislavery meetings in the Western Reserve sometimes drew attacks from local residents, and anti-antislavery societies organized to resist the reformers. Conversely, Lundy, Osborne, Birney, Bailey, and several Friends groups all operated in southern Ohio, as did many others who had been swept up in the Second Great Awakening's reformist impulse. Indeed, the southern part of the state provided some of the most daring examples of devotion to the antislavery cause.

The Underground Railroad, a secret and loosely-organized system of people dedicated to helping slaves escape to freedom, had deep roots in Ohio's history. As early as 1815 Ohioans were actively aiding runaways but, by the time abolitionist sentiment became more prevalent in the 1830s and 1840s, the number of people participating increased immensely. Ohio served as the main trunk of the Underground Railroad: in part because it bordered both the South and Canada and was the shortest distance for many slaves, but also because it had a dedicated group of residents committed to aiding escaped slaves. Some were surprisingly open about their role in the endeavor. Levi Coffin—a Society of Friends businessman originally from North Carolina—settled in Cincinnati and in 1847 immediately began helping slaves escape. He was perhaps the Railroad's most prolific "conductor," helping as many as 3,000 slaves journey to freedom. Fellow abolitionists admiringly referred to him as "The President of the Underground Railroad." John Rankin, a Presbyterian minister originally from Tennessee and a founder of the Ohio Anti-Slavery Society, hosted one of the best-known "stations" on the Railroad. His house was on a bluff high above the Ohio River at Ripley. He built one hundred wooden steps down to the river and hung a lantern outside his house as a beacon for escaping slaves. In the years before the Civil War he aided as many as 2,000 slaves escaping from the South. Yet for every Coffin and Rankin there were hundreds of other men and women throughout Ohio who worked at the same task in anonymity. In his attempt to construct a comprehensive directory of known "conductors," historian Wilbur Siebert in the late 1890s listed 3,210 names, of which 1,540 (48 percent) were from Ohio (in comparison, second-place Pennsylvania claims 348 [11 percent]). Yet these are just the names that are known, and Siebert's directory probably seriously undercounts contributions of many others, especially women and African Americans. Even though their work with the escaped slaves was illegal they continued to do it, often out of religious conviction. Friends, Methodists, Presbyterians, and Congregationalists were most active denominations in the effort, but nearly every religious persuasion had adherents who also helped. It sometimes became a family tradition. Stern Congregationalist Owen Brown moved to Hudson, Ohio with his family in 1805. He became active in the Underground Railroad, and his house had a secret trap door to a completely walled-off section of his basement that was an ideal place for hiding runaways from slave hunters. He eventually involved his young son John in leading slaves under cover of night from Wellsville to Hudson. It was in Hudson's Congregationalist Church that the adult John Brown stood in 1837 to give his first public speech vowing to destroy slavery. After bouncing around for more than twenty years from Hudson to Franklin Mills (Kent) to Akron, as well as to New York and Kansas, he made national headlines in a spectacularly unsuccessful attempt to do exactly what he had vowed.

As divisive a figure as exists in U.S. history, John Brown is in many ways an apt representative of the various forces that shaped Ohio society in its early years. He was a product of the swirling patterns of migration, religious enthusiasm, ethnic diversity, reformism, and conflict that defined the state in his lifetime. Although Ohio was still a community of communities at mid-century, that was beginning to change. By the time of the Civil War, most Ohioans had been born and raised in the state. They were going to public schools that were becoming more systematic in instruction and learning using the same McGuffey's *Readers* and Ray's mathematics texts. Ohioans across numerous different communities had been swept up in the religious fervor of the Second Great Awakening, and many of these people and others joined common organizations to reform the larger society. As Andrew Cayton has argued, these Ohioans had already "constructed the framework of a public culture that would dominate the state well into the twentieth century."

Tied together by larger social and cultural bonds, Ohioans at the same time were finding themselves bound closer by significant economic and transportation trends exemplified by other developments in Cincinnati's eventful month of July, 1843. Even as the boats bearing the last Ohio Wyandots were steaming down the Ohio River, workers were finishing construction of Cincinnati and Whitewater Canal, and in Cincinnati's Pendleton neighborhood the Little Miami Railroad—the state's second railway—was building its first depot.

Further Reading

For this and all subsequent chapters, Andrew Cayton's *Ohio: The History of A People* is an invaluable reference work (2002. Athens: Ohio State University Press). Phillp R. Shriver and Clarence Wunderlin's edited *The Documentary Heritage of* Ohio is an excellent set of primary sources for this and all other periods (2010. Athens: Ohio University Press). Also Cayton and Stuart Hobbs, eds., *The Center of a Great Empire: The Ohio Country in the Early Republic* is a fine collection of essays on early Ohio society (2005. Athens: Ohio State University Press). Several chapters of Artimus Keefer, ed., *The Geography of Ohio* deal with Ohio demographics and the effects of migration patterns (2008. 2d ed. Kent: Kent State University Press). Many, many works exist on The Second Great Awakening, social reform, and education in the early part of the 1800s, including: Nathan O. Hatch's *The Democratization of American* Christianity (1991. New Haven: Yale University Press); Catherine Rokicky's, *Creating a Perfect World: Religious and Secular Utopias in Nineteenth-Century* Ohio (2002. Athens: Ohio University Press); Keith P. Griffler's, *Front Line of Freedom: African Americans and the Forging of the Underground Railroad in the Ohio* Valley (2010. Lexington: University Press of Kentucky); Stacey M. Robertson's, *Hearts Beating for Liberty: Women Abolitionists in the Old Northwest* (2010. Chapel Hill: University of North Carolina Press); Scott Martin's, *Devil of the Domestic Sphere: Temperance, Gender, and Middle-class Ideology, 1800–1860* (2010. DeKalb: Northern Illinois Press); and James A. Hodges, James H. O'Donnell, and John William Oliver's edited volume *Cradles of Conscience: Ohio's Independent Colleges and Universities* (2003. Kent: Kent State University Press).

7

Revolutions

Early Ohio Economic Developments

In 1847 a list of the most prolific grain-exporting cities in the United States included not only such major cities as Buffalo, New York (population c. 40,000) and Chicago, Illinois (population c. 20,000), but also Milan, Ohio (population c. 3,000). Sitting near the southern border of Erie County about twelve miles southeast of Sandusky, Milan traces its history as a community back to the earliest days of Ohio's territorial status, when subsistence-farming Moravian Lenapes formed the settlements of Petquotting and New Salem in the vicinity. An influx of white settlers caused them to move away in 1809, and the new residents laid out the town of Beatty there in 1814. A few years later, Ebenezer Merry began construction of a dam and a millrace that ran a sawmill (for cutting lumber) and a gristmill (for grinding flour). These businesses drew numerous farmers in from the surrounding area and the community became known as Merry's Mill before finally being renamed Milan. Other businesses developed near the mills, and the population grew to 675 in 1827. By 1832, Merry and a group of 116 other investors formed the Milan Canal Company to construct a three-mile waterway big enough to accommodate lake-going ships connecting the town to the head of navigation on the Huron River. Finished in 1839, this canal suddenly opened up many nearby counties in the interior to national markets and a great economic boom hit the burgeoning town as farmers came from as far as 150 miles away to sell their grain. In its first five years, the canal not only paid off its construction costs of $23,392, it also earned its investors $20,000 in dividends. At times there were not enough boats to handle the increased traffic, and local shipbuilders constructed as many as 75 lake schooners to handle the cargoes. In the peak year of 1847, hundreds of wagons were backed up as far as three miles to unload their grain. The town's fourteen warehouses were insufficient to handle the supply with more than a million bushels of wheat and corn being shipped from Milan's wharves. Even as Milan was reaching its peak, though, other investors were already building railroads connecting

Ohio: A History of the Buckeye State, First Edition. Kevin F. Kern and Gregory S. Wilson.
© 2014 John Wiley & Sons, Inc. Published 2014 by John Wiley & Sons, Inc.

interior towns like Mansfield and Norwalk with the Lake Erie ports of Sandusky and Cleveland. By 1851 wheat exports from Milan had dropped to little more than a quarter of their high point four years earlier, and by 1853 the Mansfield, Sandusky, and Newark Railroad had swallowed up most of the grain trade of north central Ohio. Within a few years business in Milan had diminished considerably. The canal transported its last vessel in 1864 and the town sank into obscurity in the shadow of industrializing cities like Toledo and Cleveland.

Although not as well known as Ohio's major cities, Milan is emblematic of early Ohio's economic development as a whole. Just like Milan, the state started with a population of mostly subsistence farmers, but its economy grew quickly as an expansion in agriculture, investments of entrepreneurs, and innovations in transportation fostered a market revolution that made the state a vital part of regional and national trade. Industries developed, most of which at first arose to serve agricultural demands. Yet as technology changed, so did the focus of the economy. By 1860, heavy industry had begun to rival Ohio's agriculture sector, drawing ever more people and business from the country not only to Ohio's cities, but also to an expanding West. While there are countless charts, graphs, and tables that could describe this phenomenon, perhaps nothing frames the rise and fall of Milan's fortunes and the forces driving the early Ohio economy as well as the experiences of one of the town's families. Samuel and Nancy Edison moved to Milan from Canada in 1839 as the canal was turning it into a boomtown. Riding the tide of prosperity, Samuel served the busy town as a shopkeeper and shingle-maker, and in that busy year of 1847 the Edisons welcomed the arrival of their seventh and final child, Thomas Alva. As exports slowed in the years following, business dried up, and the Edisons left Milan for Port Huron, Michigan in 1854. The man who helped shape the world economy of the late 1800s was himself both a product, and a reflection, of Ohio's boisterous economic development in the early 1800s.

Early Ohio's Economy

Agriculture

From prehistoric times, Ohio's economy had focused primarily on subsistence agriculture, and this did not change much even after it became a territory of the United States. The Native Americans and European squatters who populated the area before the Northwest Ordinance certainly bartered in commodities like furs and liquor, but most trade was local and small-scale. Even after government-authorized settlement began in 1788, most of Ohio's newcomers sought little more at first than farms of their own to support themselves and provide some surpluses to exchange locally for goods and services. They had little choice in the matter: even if they had wanted to sell their crops to the country's major cities of Philadelphia or New York, there was no effective way to transport them. Overland transport across the Appalachians was so prohibitively expensive that it cost less to ship a ton of cargo the 3,000 miles from London to Philadelphia than it did to ship it the 300 miles from Philadelphia to Pittsburgh. Population was sparse, and as most families were farmers, there were relatively few local buyers for agricultural surpluses. As a result, many farmers used their grain either to fatten livestock or to convert into whiskey. In a good year, a pig might bring a better price than the grain used to feed it. A jug of whiskey was much easier to transport than the bushels of corn used to make it, and had the added benefit that it could always find a buyer on the frontier. Indeed, whiskey was a kind of currency in the traditionally cash-strapped western region of the country, with standard exchange rates (the equivalent of about fifty cents a gallon) for various necessary commodities. Farming mainly for their families' subsistence and some local trade, these self-provisioning farmers were the major portion of Ohio's settlers well into the early statehood period.

Early commerce

Yet from Ohio's earliest days as a territory, some Ohio entrepreneurs sought to push commerce into the frontier, especially the founders of the Ohio Company settlements. Their goal was to impose a diversified economy on the wilderness, often by planting towns deep inland to attract business from farmers. For their part, many Ohio farmers welcomed these settlements as an opportunity to acquire trade goods and to sell their surplus grain and other farm products for better prices to markets farther away. To do this, both the businessmen and farmers needed to use the region's natural transportation system: the Ohio River and its tributaries. Far from dividing Ohio from Virginia and Kentucky, in many ways the Ohio River unified the region as a vehicle of commerce: the river and its tributaries were the superhighways of their time. An active trade existed along the Ohio between settlements like Pittsburgh, Wheeling, Marietta, Cincinnati, Maysville, and especially Louisville. Located on the Falls of the Ohio—an area of rapids that are the only natural navigation barrier along the length of the Ohio River—Louisville served as a natural stopping place for river travel and the most important downriver trading center in the region in the early years of American settlement. When the United States signed Pinckney's Treaty with Spain in 1795, free navigation of the Mississippi became possible, opening up new opportunities. A farmer who was willing to make the trip could float his produce on a barge, flatboat, or keelboat all the way down the Ohio River (with a stop at Louisville to cart the goods to the river's lower level if he did not want to risk "shooting the rapids") to the Mississippi and thence down to New Orleans. Being an international port, prices for grain and other farm products were considerably higher than they were in Cincinnati or Louisville, and a person willing to make the trip could turn a tidy profit. As it was exceedingly difficult to move a boat upriver against the current (in 1807, for example, only eleven boats departed upriver from New Orleans) the enterprising farmer would usually sell the craft as lumber and take his profits home by walking or riding up from New Orleans along the old Natchez Trace or other wilderness paths. The arduous and sometimes dangerous nature of the trip to New Orleans and back prompted many farmers to sell their goods at lower prices to trading companies in Cincinnati, which would then assume the risk of the trip. The Ohio River already hosted active flatboat traffic by the early 1800s, with 85,000 barrels of flour passing through Louisville in the first six months of 1802 alone, about a third of which was from Western

Pennsylvania and Ohio. By 1816, more than 1,200 flatboats were making the trip down to New Orleans annually. However, many Ohio farmers found that there were not enough buyers or trading companies to deal with the volume of grain Ohio was producing, and there was no guarantee that even if they got their crops to New Orleans that they would be able to get a good price for it. If a farmer departed at the wrong time of the season or during a year of bumper crops, he could find himself leaving his cargo rotting on the docks for the lack of a buyer.

Things began to change in the second decade of the 1800s. The War of 1812, for all of its disruptions and threat of invasion (see chapter 8) paid Ohio enormous economic dividends, mostly thanks to the federal and state governments. Military contracts and the necessity to feed, clothe, and outfit soldiers created more demand for Ohio goods and caused a boom in certain sectors of the new state's economy. The defeat of the Indian Confederacy and the subsequent removal of Native Americans from Ohio encouraged even more settlers to come from the east. Aiding these new immigrants were the military roads built to move soldiers and supplies during the war, which later served as vital paths to the interior. Ohio had few long-distance roads during its first decades as a state, the main exception being Zane's Trace, a trail blazed by Ebenezer Zane starting in 1796. Zane was a land speculator and businessman who convinced Congress of the benefits of having a finished road into the interior. With government financing (and land concessions to Zane at river crossings where he could set up ferries to profit from the traffic) Zane created a trail from Wheeling, Virginia (much of which he owned) through the southern part of Ohio to the bank of the Ohio River opposite Maysville, Kentucky. The road was little better than a wilderness path along much of its length, though, with much of its route following pre-existing Indian trails. Congress's Enabling Act for Ohio in 1802 also gave Ohio a grant of 3 percent of all land sales to use for roads, and soon after the state allocated money to improve Zane's road so that it could accommodate wagons along its entire length. Not long after this, the U.S. Congress voted to construct what became known as the National Road, a macadam-paved thoroughfare intended to be a major overland route connecting the East Coast with the new states west of the Alleghenies. Starting in Cumberland, Maryland, the road had reached Wheeling in 1818, and then continued across Ohio to Indiana through St. Clairsville, Zanesville, Columbus, and Springfield by 1838 (present-day U.S. Route 40 follows much of its length). Along with the transportation routes provided by the state's river systems and Lake Erie, these government-financed roads made the interior of Ohio more accessible than ever. This increased accessibility along with government changes in land policy (see chapter 8) created a huge demand for Ohio lands and caused a speculative boom.

Early financial issues

Helping fuel the boom was an abundance of paper money that became increasingly common after the War of 1812. Hard currency had always been scarce on the frontier, a reality that forced early Ohioans to have a barter-heavy economy and inhibited business growth in many places. In response, one of the earliest acts of the Ohio General Assembly was to grant the Miami Exporting Company of Cincinnati the right to issue paper notes

Figure 7.1 With a dearth of hard currency in the Ohio frontier, a number of companies and banks began to issue the paper money that became an important mode of exchange in the early statehood period. Although many of these bills were backed by reputable institutions, many others became known as worthless "shinplasters," especially after the Panics of 1819 and 1837 caused even formerly reputable banks and companies to fail.
Source: Courtesy of the Ohio Historical Society (SA1039AV_B12F02_016_001)

in April 1803, and between 1808–18 the Assembly chartered more than twenty-five local banks, most of which were spread across the southern part of the state. Although the state had some control over these banks, the same could not be said for the numerous "wildcat" banks that sprang up in the post-war period. New banks, businesses, and even individuals started to issue paper money in unprecedented amounts. Some were reputable, but others were fly-by-night operations (see Figure 7.1). Illustrative are a couple of banks in Jefferson County, one of which lured investors by showing them a keg apparently brimming with gold and silver coin, but which was actually mostly filled with nails. At least that bank had a few coins unlike a nearby bank in Salem whose only asset, when it failed, appeared to be a table. With a riot of various kinds of paper notes in circulation—not to mention the counterfeit bills that also flooded the system—it was difficult to know what any of them were actually worth. Despite the confusion, many Ohioans welcomed the new economic landscape, which enabled them to have easier access to money and credit than ever before. With hundreds of thousands of dollars of paper notes circulating but probably less than $50,000 of actual hard currency in the state, the speculative boom of the immediate post-war period was turning into a speculative bubble. Helping to burst the bubble was the soundest financial institution in the state: the Bank of the United States.

Although the depression that would grip the country at the end of the 1810s is known as the Panic of 1819, the first harbingers of the crisis arose in Cincinnati the year before.

The charter of the first Bank of the United States had expired in 1811, but Congress created a new version in 1816, and Ohio gained branches of it in Cincinnati and Chillicothe. State-chartered banks borrowed money from these "safe" institutions and loaned these moneys out in their local areas. Seeking to rein in inflation, the Bank of the United States started calling in notes and contracting its credit in the summer of 1818, and ordered its branch in Cincinnati to collect its outstanding balances of its loans to the local state banks at a rate of 20 percent a month. This started a chain reaction that had disastrous effects on the economy of the area. The state banks in turn began to call in their loans at a time when hard currency was hard to come by and many people had borrowed money to pay installments on their new land claims. Since the banks would refuse to redeem paper for specie (gold and silver) and paper notes were all many people had, numerous people and businesses lost the unpaid portions of their land to foreclosure. Depending on the issuing bank, notes that had just the year before traded at face value were exchanged for pennies on the dollar, and even some of Ohio's wealthiest individuals found themselves financially embarrassed. The depression dragged on for years and hit Ohioans very hard. In 1817, wheat was at $1 a bushel. By October 1819, it had fallen to 62½ cents, and by 1821, it dropped as low as 20 cents. In the meantime, the Bank of the United States came to own a great deal of land as a result of the payment of debts and foreclosures. This land later appreciated as Cincinnati grew, not only making the bank richer but also giving it possession of a large part of Cincinnati. These events generated immense resentment toward the Bank and it is little wonder that where people stood regarding the Bank of the United States became one of the most important defining issues of Ohio politics in the 1820s and 1830s (see chapter 8).

If there was a silver lining to the Panic of 1819, it was that the crisis served to motivate two important policy changes on the national and state levels that were to have a tremendous impact on Ohio's future. In response to the numerous defaults on land purchases in the wake of the Panic, Congress passed the Land Act of 1820, which significantly revised the Land Act of 1804. According to the new law, the government would no longer sell land on credit: buyers had to purchase with cash in full at the time of sale. Although this change sounds like it might have inhibited sales, the act had other provisions that in some ways made it easier. Under the 1804 law, the smallest amount a person could purchase was a quarter section (160 acres) for a minimum of $2 an acre, forcing a farmer to come up with $320. The new law reduced the minimum amount of land to 80 acres and the minimum price to $1.25 an acre. This meant that with just $100 cash and a little luck a farmer could purchase a small farm in the West. Combined with the Relief Act of 1821 (which allowed indebted farmers to return unpaid-for land to the government as credit toward their debt) this encouraged new purchases and eased the financial burdens of those who had already purchased farms.

The Panic of 1819 also inspired an important shift in state policy, pushed over a period of years by a coalition of businessmen, entrepreneurs, and local boosters who sought to integrate Ohio more fully into the national economy. These people called for the construction of a canal, at state expense, between the Ohio River and Lake Erie. It took years of political maneuvering (see chapter 8) but the pro-canal forces eventually prevailed and construction of the Ohio and Erie Canal began in 1825. The significance of this development to the future of Ohio is difficult to overestimate, as it contributed to three interrelated "revolutions" that fundamentally changed life in Ohio and the United States: The Market Revolution, the Transportation Revolution, and the Industrial Revolution.

Economic Revolutions

The Market Revolution

Even as Marietta and Cincinnati were becoming the first small footholds of American presence in Ohio, another trend was gaining a foothold in the country at large. The 1790s is a period that many historians mark as the beginning of the Market Revolution—a fundamental transformation of the national economy into regional and national markets through both mechanical and transportation innovations. More than just an economic event, the Market Revolution also marked major changes in behavior and social relationships. Farmers increasingly thought in terms of producing for markets rather than for home consumption, the bond between master and apprentice increasingly dissolved into the more distant relationship of employer and day laborer, and traditional, personal modes of trade turned increasingly to impersonal cash exchanges. These changes could be unsettling and disconcerting to the people experiencing them, particularly those at the lower end of the socioeconomic ladder. The Market Revolution greatly increased the number of opportunities for personal profit, but it came at a price that disproportionately affected the lower classes, particularly in times of economic stress. The speculative booms of the 1810s and 1830s described above—fueled by the economic forces of the Market Revolution—resulted in severe depressions that wiped out small business owners, forced small farmers off their land, and threw laborers out of work and often into destitution. While it is important to understand the larger contours of the set of immense economic changes described below, it is also important to remember both the optimism and anxieties that the Market Revolution fostered in the lives of everyday people.

Although a national phenomenon, the Market Revolution meant different things in different places. In the South, it refers to the rise of cotton agriculture stemming from the invention of the laborsaving cotton gin. In the Northeast, it refers to the rise in manufacturing, especially textiles. For the West, including Ohio, the Market Revolution first manifested itself as a rise in commercial agriculture. As the cotton gin fueled the revolution in the South, the innovation that caused the Western Market Revolution to accelerate was the advent of steamships in the Ohio and Mississippi rivers (see Figure 7.2). Robert Fulton ran the first commercially-successful steamboat along the Hudson River in 1807, and by 1811 the first steamboat on the Ohio River departed downriver from Pittsburgh. Steamboats had two great advantages over the river crafts that preceded them: speed and countercurrent navigation. Not only could a steamboat make the trip to New Orleans much faster than a barge or a flatboat, it could also move easily both upstream and downstream, making an effective two-way trade along the Ohio and Mississippi rivers possible. As the number of steamboats multiplied in the early decades of the nineteenth century, shipping costs dropped dramatically, and Ohio farmers could profit even more from serving the rapidly expanding American West. The largest and most profitable markets, though, remained on the East Coast, and even with steamships, the cost of sending goods to and from places like

Figure 7.2 Steamships were the first major innovation of the Transportation Revolution, not only speeding traffic down rivers, but also making it easy for the first time to travel rapidly upriver, too. Although superseded in significance by railroads in the late 1800s, they continued to ply the waters of the Ohio River and Lake Erie until the twentieth century. This image was taken of a steamboat race down the Ohio River in 1929.
Source: Courtesy of the Ohio Historical Society (SA1039AV_B12F02_016_001)

New York or Philadelphia was still very high, involving either a month-long overland trip in large wagons across the mountains; or a roundabout voyage down to New Orleans, through the Gulf of Mexico, and up the Atlantic coast. Another new transportation innovation would soon open Ohio to these markets and the rest of the world.

The Transportation Revolution: Canal Era

What made the Market Revolution possible was a series of innovations in transportation that historians sometimes call the Transportation Revolution. Steamboats were the first major development in this process, but because they were limited to the natural, navigable waterways of the country, many interior portions of the country could not fully benefit from them. This began to change in 1817, when New York began construction on the most ambitious transportation project yet attempted in the United States: The Erie Canal. Its advocates, among the most vocal of which was New York Governor DeWitt Clinton, proposed that an artificial waterway connecting the Hudson River in Albany to

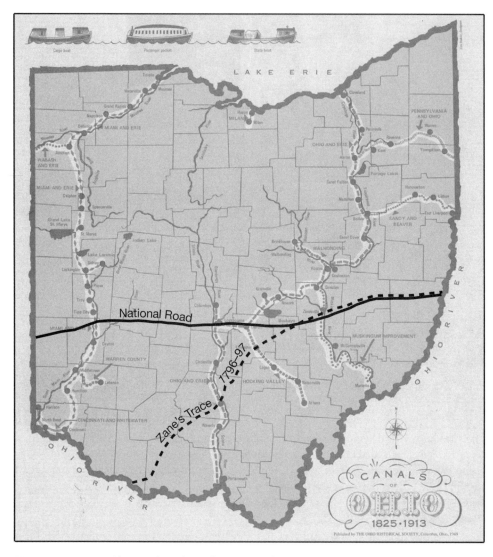

Figure 7.3　Major Ohio roads and canals, 1850, in the Transportation Revolution's Canal Era.
Source: Courtesy of the Ohio Historical Society (AL07264); adapted to include Zane's Trace and National Road

the Great Lakes in Buffalo would greatly expand trade by creating new markets for agricultural produce and raw materials in the East, and for manufactured goods in the West. An extremely expensive and time-intensive initiative, the canal took eight years to complete and cost the then-outrageous figure of about $7 million. Its opponents dismissed it as "Clinton's Folly" or "Clinton's Ditch," but the canal soon proved its worth by reducing shipping prices through the state by 90 percent and recouping some of its construction costs through tolls. Some Ohioans and boosters in other states began to see the benefit of building canals out West, especially now that being able to get goods to Buffalo on Lake Erie meant relatively quick and cheap access to the profitable market of New York City (see Figure 7.3).

The fight to get a canal for Ohio was intense. Some Ohioans balked at the price, which was in the millions and much more than the entire state budget in an average year. While those counties likely to be in the path of the new canal tended to support it, those that the prospective path bypassed did not like the idea of committing state resources for the benefit of others. Nevertheless, by 1822 the newly formed Ohio Board of Canal Commissioners undertook a study of three potential canal routes: one each in the western, central, and eastern portions of the state. James Geddes, the Erie Canal engineer hired to do the survey, found that there was insufficient water in the central Scioto/Sandusky river watersheds to create a central route, but that either an eastern or a western canal would be possible. Eventually, the Board decided on a main route that would run from Portsmouth on the Ohio River up the Scioto Valley almost to Columbus, then northeast through Newark to the Muskingum Valley. From there it would proceed north up the Muskingum and Tuscarawas Valleys, across the old Native American portage between the Tuscarawas and Cuyahoga Rivers, then down the Cuyahoga Valley to Cleveland. Bowing to powerful political and business interests elsewhere, they also agreed to "canalize" the southern Muskingum River (making it navigable year-round) and approved smaller canals from Dayton to Cincinnati (with a promise to extend it to Lake Erie later) and from Columbus to the main trunk of the canal. With the route set, the state legislature formed a Canal Fund Commission and began construction on the Ohio and Erie Canal on July 4, 1825 (see Figure 7.4). At the groundbreaking ceremony near present-day Heath, Ohio Governor Jeremiah Morrow and honored guest DeWitt Clinton turned the first shovelfuls of earth.

For the next seven years, work proceeded on what was a daunting, labor-intensive, and sometimes dangerous task. State engineers and inspectors supervised the work, but the state contracted out the job of canal construction to any group that won the bidding process for each small increment (usually a half-mile or a single lock). Although local entrepreneurs or farmers would often win bids and hire hands to do the work, the state awarded a large amount of work to contractors with experience on the Erie Canal who enticed mostly-Irish work gangs to follow them to Ohio. To meet specifications, workers had to fashion a four-feet-deep ditch that was forty feet wide at the top (wide enough so that two canal boats could pass each other), twenty-six feet wide at the bottom, and as close to level as possible. They also had to clear the land for twenty feet on each side of the canal and build a ten-foot wide towpath alongside. Every rise or drop of six feet in the terrain required a lock installation. Locks were the ninety-foot long and fifteen-foot wide stone and timber "elevators" of the canal, raising or lowering the boat for the next leg of the journey by pumping in or releasing water to put the boat at the right water level. Forty-four of these were needed in just the last thirty-eight miles to Lake Erie, including twenty-one in a very steep descending stretch north from the canal's highest point in Akron. To ensure proper water supply where it was needed, the canal system also included several reservoirs and twenty-three aqueducts. In all, the canal stretched 309 miles when it was completed in 1832, but the northern branch from Akron to Cleveland opened with much fanfare on July 3, 1827, with Governor Allen Trimble and canal officials riding the canal boat *State of Ohio* north from Akron to arrive in Cleveland on Independence Day. Work on the state's other canals (including short links and "feeder" canals to other areas) also proceeded simultaneously. When the 245-mile Miami and

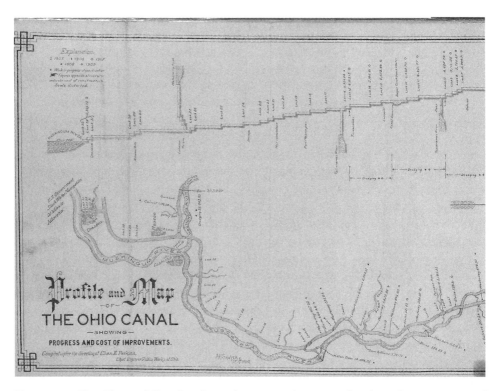

Figure 7.4 The Ohio and Erie Canal was the most ambitious undertaking the young state of Ohio had embarked upon. It stretched more than 300 miles and rose and descended hundreds of feet of elevation through the use of more than 70 locks. The Miami and Erie Canal soon followed, tracing a 245-mile course from Cincinnati to Toledo. Factoring in all expenses, it eventually cost $41 million, the equivalent of more than a $800 million in 2011.

Source: Canal Society of Ohio Collection at The University of Akron Archival Services

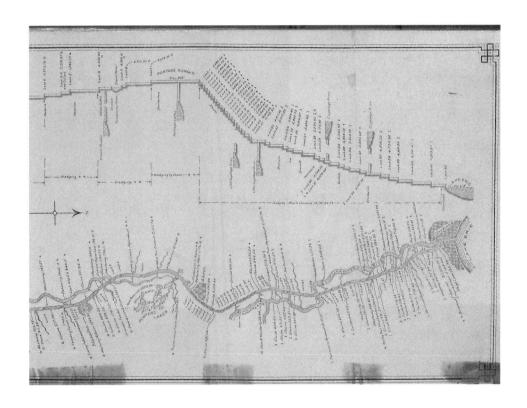

Erie Canal from Cincinnati to Toledo reached completion in 1845, the state could boast more than six hundred miles of canals running through about 40 percent of its counties. Most of the commerce on these canals never went more than halfway along their length, usually from southern Ohio to the Ohio River or from northern Ohio to Lake Erie. Yet, these waterways made Ohio a crucial link in a transportation system that stretched from the Gulf of Mexico up the Mississippi and Ohio Rivers, through the canals to Lake Erie, and from there to New York City and even Europe. As Ohio goods made their way to New York, New Orleans, and even the wider world, the goods of the wider world similarly made their way to Ohio quicker and more inexpensively than ever before.

Work on the canal was backbreaking, involving heavy work from sunrise to sunset, twenty-six days a month. Using only basic tools, laborers not only had to dig and remove earth, but also build embankments, clear growth, fell trees, remove stumps, clear out muck, dig drainage ditches in swampy areas, and lift heavy stones and timbers. For this they routinely earned 30 cents plus a jigger of whiskey a day in the early years of construction. Later, for more difficult sections toward the end, the rate could be double that amount. Apart from the ever-present danger of injuries at the work site, laborers also had to worry about diseases that plagued the workforce with some regularity. Malaria was particularly a risk in swampy areas, but epidemics of smallpox and typhoid fever were common, too. A particularly virulent cholera epidemic hit in 1832, which slowed construction as many opted to skip work to avoid exposure to the disease. Those that died were often interred near the canal bed as work continued. Neither contractors nor the state usually kept mortality records of common laborers in those days, so no one knows just how many workers died on the canals as a result of injury or disease. It was said at the time, though, that there was "a dead Irishman for every mile of the canal." While canal histories often focus on the names of the politicians and engineers who planned the Ohio canals, more recent historians have begun to pay greater attention to the nameless workers who actually built them.

Life on the canal

Once the canal was in operation, an ever-multiplying fleet of vessels began to glide through its waters. Canal boats had to be no more than 14½ feet wide and 85 feet long so they could easily fit in the locks, although early ones tended to be smaller to make pulling them easier. Drivers coaxed mules or horses to pull the boat by a towline while walking on the towpath that ran alongside the canal. The driver was only one of seven to nine crewmen needed to run a boat, the others tending to loading and unloading cargo, cooking, or tending to passengers. Traffic ran day and night, especially passenger packet boats that sold their customers on quick transport across the state. Most boats could carry both passengers and freight, but freight was the lifeblood of the canal system. A boat could carry between thirty and fifty tons, and often also carried extra draft animals to change to as the towing animals tired. The entire system was thoroughly organized, with toll offices making careful records of all the boats and cargoes that passed. Well-defined rules existed to regulate how boats were to pass each other, which boat had right-of-way, and which boat would be first through a lock. Despite the rules, it was not unusual for arguments to break out between canal men and one of the crewmen on board often was the designated physical enforcer of the boat's privilege when arguments failed. The canals gave employment to thousands of Ohioans of all ages, including a sixteen-year-old canal driver named James Abram Garfield. His humble service on the Ohio and Erie Canal became part of his campaign electioneering during his successful run for the presidency thirty-three years later.

Paying for such a monumental feat of engineering was beyond the immediate resources of such a relatively cash-poor state. The Canal Fund Commission thus decided to follow New York's lead and sell bonds backed by the state to raise capital. The early issues sold well, eventually raising about $13.2 million toward the construction and maintenance of all state canals. In addition, Congress granted Ohio more than a million acres of federal land (primarily in the northwestern part of the state), the sale of which was to help finance the Miami and Erie Canal. The state also tried to encourage even more canals through the Ohio Loan Law of 1837 that staked state money to help private businesses build internal improvements. The fact that many of these businesses either did not fare well or went bankrupt left the state holding even more debt, which led critics to call the act "The Plunder Law." By the early 1840s, with Ohio's debt increasing, it became much more difficult to sell Ohio bonds, and the state came close to defaulting. Nevertheless, Ohio fared much better in this regard than many of it its neighboring states. Whereas Ohio's total debt in 1841 was almost $11 million (or about $7.19 per capita), New York's was close to $22 million ($8.97 per capita). Indiana and Michigan, which saw New York and Ohio's success and overbuilt canals in response, fell $12.8 million into debt ($18.59 per capita) and $5.6 million ($26.47 per capita) respectively. Both states ended up defaulting on their loans. Although Ohio faced some difficult days financially and did not end up retiring its canal debt until 1903, it was actually one of the more successful states in the region in managing its canal finances.

On the ledger-sheet, the canals appeared to be a money-losing proposition for the state: tolls and grants never covered the cost of construction and maintenance, and the government eventually had to use public money to bail out the system. However, most historians believe the benefits the canals brought to the state more than justified their expense, and not just in terms of increased trade: they also fundamentally altered Ohio in a number of ways. Even before the first boat carried its first load, the canals gave a tremendous boost to the state economy. As a multi-million-dollar public works project, canal construction infused the state with tremendous amounts of cash, which created numerous employment and business opportunities. The market for raw materials like timber and stone fed local economies, as did the demand for food and goods that canal workers created as they worked through an area.

When the workers moved on they left localities with economic opportunities where few had existed before. New communities quickly sprang up to serve the needs of the canal traffic, often named for the entity that brought them into existence. A quick look at an Ohio map shows places like Portsmouth, Lockbourne, Canal Winchester, Canal Dover, Canal Fulton, and perhaps the most forthright of them all, the Tuscarawas County village of Lock Seventeen. Perhaps the biggest success story of them all was Akron, a town that had not existed before the canals. Local landowner Simon Perkins donated prime land along what was thought to be the best path for the canal in the (correct) assumption that the Canal Commissioners would choose to route it through there (and

Figure 7.5 The canals created some towns almost overnight, and greatly expanded the population and businesses of others. Created from nearly vacant land at the highest point of the Ohio and Erie Canal route, Akron was an early product of the canal. From a township population of 325 in 1825, the city had burgeoned to nearly 10,000 by the late 1860s, when this picture was taken.
Source: Courtesy of the Ohio Historical Society (SA1039AV_B08F01_27_001)

thus make his other land holdings in the area more valuable). Drawing its name from the Greek root meaning "high," it marked the highest elevation along the entire path of the canal. The time it took to pass through the many locks needed to raise and lower the boats over this point meant that farmers, canal men, and passengers alike could stop for food, supplies, or services at the stores and other businesses that grew to serve the needs of the people using the canal (see Figure 7.5). Gristmills also began to spring up all along the paths of the canals, often powering their waterwheels with the excess water from the system. New distilleries provided a similar service, and not only sent Ohio liquor to other states but also helped stock the shelves of the many taverns that lubricated canal patrons. Of course pre-existing communities lying on the canal's path also benefitted from the traffic, none more so than Cleveland. In 1820, Cleveland was a small town of 606 people, but by 1840 it had experienced a nearly ten-fold increase to 6,071, and by 1850 nearly tripled in size again to 17,034. In addition to the trade the canals brought to the burgeoning city, it also became a major shipbuilding center. Sandusky, Lorain, Ashtabula, and of course Milan were other Ohio towns that supplied ships for Lake Erie's rapidly-expanding commercial traffic.

Populating these new and growing communities were new immigrants, drawn to the area by canal construction and the businesses the canals fostered. Construction of The Ohio and Erie Canal started as the Erie Canal in New York reached completion. Thousands of canal workers, most of them Irish-Catholic immigrants, poured into the state altering Ohio's ethnic and religious make-up. In 1820, Ohio's population was 581,434. By 1840, after most of the canals were completed, it had nearly tripled to 1,519,467, making Ohio the third largest state in the Union. By 1850, it had nearly quadrupled its pre-canal population with 1,980,329 residents. While not all of the increase was the direct result of the canals, the economic and social environment the canals brought about, both directly and indirectly, was a magnet for most of the people who chose to move to the state during this period.

On a more basic level, the canals integrated Ohio both economically and socially in a way it had never been before. The continental divide that ran through the northern part of the state had inhibited the shipment of large loads and as a result northern Ohio was effectively economically distinct from the southern part of the state, oriented more toward Lake Erie and the Northeast than the Ohio River and the Southwest. With the advent of the canals, farmers and businessmen in the Western Reserve could now trade more easily with the southern part of the state and vice-versa, leaving the state with a more unified economic profile than had been possible before. To send a wagonload of forty bushels of wheat one hundred miles on Ohio's roads cost a farmer about $18 and took several days, but sending the same load the same distance on the canal cost only $1.68 and could take as little as twenty-six hours. The canals also drew Ohioans closer than they had been. Even at the standard speed of just under four miles per hour, it was possible to travel from one end of the state to the other in 80 hours, and in greater relative comfort than was the case in stagecoaches that jostled riders over the often-questionable roads.

The canals also integrated Ohio into the larger regional and national economies more fully than had been possible earlier. Other states' canal systems began to link with Ohio's, including the Penn–Ohio Canal that connected the Western Reserve with Pennsylvania and the Cincinnati and Whitewater Canal that tied Cincinnati with Indiana. Having more goods to carry, ship traffic on Lake Erie increased immensely, with many more sailing and steam vessels taking Ohio goods to the Erie Canal's terminus in Buffalo and bringing back manufactured goods more quickly and cheaply. Whereas it used to take a month to get freight from Northeast Ohio to New York City, shippers could now make the trip in ten days. With both costs and travel times down considerably, Ohio quickly became an important participant in the national economy; and the formerly cash-poor state for the first time witnessed a significant and prolonged inward flow of hard money. In the first year after the Ohio and Erie Canal's opening, Buffalo merchants increased their purchase of wheat from Cleveland wharves from about 1,000 bushels annually to more than a quarter of a million. The increased demand significantly raised wholesale prices in the state. Before the canal era, a bushel of wheat that used to fetch a Massillon-area farmer perhaps 25 cents in kind—and even less if the farmer wanted cash—could now bring him 75 cents cash from a buyer on the canal who could sell it in New York City for a dollar. From its modest beginnings of flatboat cargoes floating down to New Orleans in the 1790s, the Market Revolution had, by the 1850s, finally swept through Ohio.

Ohio was uniquely situated to profit from its new status as a participant in the growing U.S. economy. Sitting astride a crucial link between east and west as well as north and south, Ohio goods could not only find a ready market on the east coast, but its products and its transportation network could also help supply a rapidly expanding West with seemingly insatiable material demands. Ohio's economy both boomed and diversified as it strove to make the most of the Market Revolution.

Crops

From the earliest times, the main crop of Ohio farmers was corn (maize), a versatile grain that produced a good return for each seed planted. The region had been fertile ground for maize agriculture since the late prehistoric period, and the first American settlers in the new Ohio territory continued this tradition. The growth in Ohio agriculture in an expanding west meant that for a few years after 1848 it grew more corn than any other state—almost 60 million bushels in 1850. Although Ohioans did eat various foods made of corn meal, about half of the crops produced became either animal feed or whiskey. Ohio farmers also grew large quantities of wheat—a profitable cash crop—especially along waterways that could whisk it to market. The state also briefly ranked first in wheat production in 1839, before falling behind newer states further west. Other crops Ohio farmers produced for market included tobacco, hemp (primarily among farmers of southern extraction), and flax, the fiber of which was used to make linen and the seed to produce linseed oil. The timber found on most Ohio farms also found increasingly ready markets, either as raw materials for construction or furniture-making, or burned and processed into potash or pearl ash that was a raw material for several industrial purposes, including soap-making.

Even before statehood, some Ohio farmers were also very active in orchard culture, particularly the cultivation of apple trees. Brothers Israel and Aaron Putnam of the Ohio Company Lands brought a number of tree saplings from Connecticut in 1796, setting up Ohio's first major nursery near Marietta. This orchard was the most significant in the Ohio Valley for a generation, providing the parent grafts for orchards in southern Ohio, southern Indiana, Northern Virginia, and northern Kentucky. Yankee settlers in the Western Reserve also brought their favorite varieties of apple trees with them, too, setting up significant orchards there from the time of its earliest settlement. One unforeseen effect of transplanting eastern varieties to the different soil and climate in Ohio was the origin of new, well-regarded local varieties of apples including the Northern Spy, the Early Joe, the Cooper, and the Putnam Russet. By the 1810s apple trees could be found in most parts of the state, many of them the result of the efforts of another New Englander, apple (and Swedenborgian faith) apostle John Chapman. More popularly known as "Johnny Appleseed," Chapman was an itinerant seller of apple trees and missionary of "The New Church," who planted nurseries and distributed religious tracts across central and northwest Ohio. Most of the fruit grown from Ohio apple trees initially became cider for local consumption, but by the time steam power and the Market Revolution had begun to take hold, Ohio apple-growers were loading thousands of barrels of both apples and cider onto boats to sell to increasingly far-away markets.

Nicholas Longworth of Cincinnati was responsible for introducing another fruit crop that became increasingly important: the Catawba grape. First cultivating Catawba vines by the mid-1820s, Longworth found initial success catering to the city's burgeoning German population. When he started producing a sparkling Catawba wine in the 1840s, it was an immediate national success and soon Cincinnati was the major wine-making city of the American West, producing tens of thousands of gallons a year. Prominent American poet Henry Wadsworth Longfellow was inspired enough by Ohio's signature wine to write:

> While pure as a spring
> Is the wine I sing,
> And to praise it, one needs but name it;
> For Catawba wine
> Has need of no sign,
> No tavern-bush to proclaim it.
> And this Song of the Vine,
> This greeting of mine,
> The winds and the birds shall deliver
> To the Queen of the West,
> In her garlands dressed,
> On the banks of the Beautiful River.

Although the vines on the banks of the Ohio eventually fell victim to a virulent blight and root rot, the Lake Erie Islands near Sandusky (particularly Kelleys Island) had already begun to produce significant amounts, and became Ohio's leading wine region until the time of Prohibition in the 1920s.

Livestock

Another way a farmer could get his corn to market would be to convert it to meat on the hoof by feeding it to pigs or cattle. Pigs were by far the most important farm animals on the frontier, and for good reason. They were relatively low-maintenance animals that could be fed with leftover food or left to forage for themselves in the forest. Whether by smoking or salting, their meat was the easiest to preserve, and could either be used to feed the family over the winter or to sell to others. Keeping track of the large numbers of free-roaming hogs was not easy, so farmers came up with a system of notching their ears in identifiable patterns—these "earmarks" worked much in the same way as branding cattle. When it was time to take pigs to market, they had the added advantage of being able to walk there themselves under the watch of the farmer or a paid drover, rooting around the ground along the way to feed. While in the early years Ohioans drove tens of thousands of hogs over the Appalachians to eastern markets or up to the long-established settlement at Detroit, by the 1810s more began to drive their swine to meatpacking houses in Chillicothe, Hamilton, and especially Cincinnati, which was processing tens of thousands of pigs annually by the 1820s.

Although pigs were of primary importance in the early days, they were not the only animals found on Ohio pioneer farms. Cattle had come with the earliest settlers, and grazing herds of beef cattle could be found across the state, particularly in the Virginia Military District and westward, where Kentucky cattlemen immigrants were most likely to move. After fattening the cattle on grass and corn, cattlemen could either sell them or pay a drover to herd them to Baltimore, Philadelphia, or New York where they brought much better prices than they could in the cash-strapped frontier. In 1817 it cost one cattleman an average of $56 per head to raise, feed, and drive his herd to Philadelphia, where it sold for $133 per head. Another way to make a profit from cattle was to start a dairy farm, but large-scale dairy farming occurred in limited areas, mostly among the New England Yankees of the Ohio Company lands and especially the Western Reserve.

Other livestock also played an important role in Ohio's economy. Although Kentucky was better-known for its horses, Ohio ranked first in the nation as a horse market by mid-century, and an 1850 agricultural census counted over 463,000 in the state. Sheep also proved to be of increasing importance, especially after Quaker businessman Thomas Rotch brought a flock of 410 Spanish Merino sheep—which grew highly-prized fleeces—to his settlement at Kendal (later Massillon). This marked the beginning of Ohio's woolen industry. By the 1850s Ohio had the largest sheep population in the country with nearly 4 million head, and antislavery firebrand John Brown spent years working in the wool business before his later fame (or infamy) at Pottawatomie Creek and Harpers Ferry.

Industry

Historians and economists often discuss agriculture and industry almost as if they are diametrically-opposed sectors of the economy. Although these scholars usually make this categorization for the sake of convenience, it gives an impression that does not reflect the situation in the early Ohio economy well. Most of early Ohio's industry grew from, or allied itself with, Ohio's agricultural economy, which in turn grew in response to these industrial developments. Ebenezer Merry's mills of the 1810s were businesses that served the needs of the area's farmers, and although Milan's later shipbuilders in the 1840s and 1850s were certainly in the ship-construction industry, most of the lake schooners they built were explicitly intended for grain transportation. Similarly, Cincinnati—Ohio's first major industrial city—built its industries squarely on the needs and products of Ohio farmers. The first big industry Cincinnati hosted was meat-packing. Thousands of farmers and drovers with their hundreds of thousands of pigs descended on Cincinnati to have their hogs processed into hams, sausages and other pork products in the numerous slaughterhouses and packing plants that sprung up in the city (see Figure 7.6). So important was this business to the city's economy that Ohioans informally began to refer to the city as "Porkopolis" (a designation that city fathers were happy to substitute with the more poetic "Queen City" nickname later popularized by Longfellow). As a result of the sheer volume of the pork they had to process (400,000 hogs per year by the 1850s), Cincinnati pork-processing plants began to use innovative methods to increase efficiency, dividing the labor into a series of steps. Some workers killed the pigs, sending the carcasses by hook on a conveyer to another set of workers that would gut them and send them off to be cut by another set of workers, and so on through the plant until the finished products appeared at the other end of the factory. Chicago stockyards later emulated the techniques developed in Cincinnati, and it was this process that inspired Henry Ford in the early twentieth century to apply the same principle to the manufacture of automobiles. Thus, a fundamental component

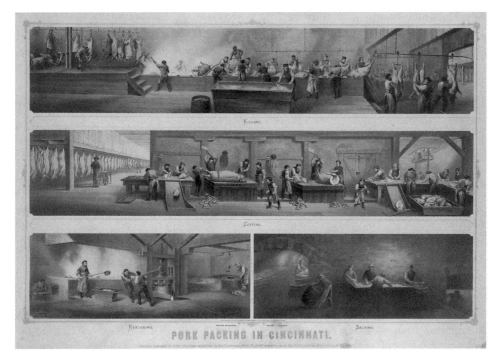

Figure 7.6 The meatpacking plants of Cincinnati sometimes processed hundreds of thousands of hogs in a year. To meet the demand, they created the antecedent of the assembly lines that were later adopted by American heavy industry of the early twentieth century. This image shows the process from the beginning to the end of the line in one "Porkopolis" meatpacking facility.
Source: Library of Congress Prints and Photographs Division (LC-DIG-pga03169)

of the modern industrial economy—the assembly line—ultimately arose from the "disassembly lines" perfected in the Cincinnati meatpacking plants.

Yet meatpacking was not the only major industry Cincinnati built on Ohio's agricultural sector. Despite the old joke that sausages in the 1800s contained "everything but the squeal," pork processing actually left large quantities of by-products, including bones, hooves, fat, and oil. A candle maker from England and a soap maker's apprentice from Ireland began using these cast-off materials to manufacture their wares, and when they both married daughters of a prominent candle maker in the city, their new father-in-law encouraged them to pool their resources and go into business together. In this way did William Procter and James Gamble found a company that in time became the country's largest producer of household consumer goods. In 2007, Procter and Gamble observed its 170th year in Cincinnati, a still-vibrant legacy of Ohio's early agricultural and industrial past.

Other industries tied to Ohio's burgeoning agricultural sector included over a thousand flourmills by 1850, as well as 130 woolen factories producing over a million square yards of cloth. There were also a number of breweries, wineries, and distilleries that filled the glasses not only of Ohioans but also the many communities downriver in the expanding west.

Other agriculturally-related industries included boat makers (for sending Ohio produce to market) and tanneries (that processed the hides of Ohio cattle). Ohio factories also began to produce farm machinery by mid century, including iron plows in Canton and mowers and reapers in Cincinnati and Akron, not only aiding local farmers but helping provide the tools that farmers were using to bring vast new western lands under cultivation.

Although businesses that derived either directly or indirectly from agriculture provided the lion's share of early Ohio's industry, from its earliest days Ohio was laying the groundwork for its heavy industrial future as well. Mineral extraction had a 13,000-year history in Ohio, especially in the commodities of flint, salt, and clay. Although early settlers consumed only small quantities of flint, both salt and clay became the basis of early Ohio industries. Early settlers were already aware of several salt springs or "licks" that ultimately derived from Silurian seas (see chapter 1). As early as 1795, early settler Joseph Conklin was boiling salt from the Scioto Salt Licks in Jackson County, and one of the first acts of the new State Government in March of 1803 was to regulate the salt works there. By the mid-1810s, entrepreneurs had begun larger-scale commercial salt operations, including a well near Zanesville that was hundreds of feet deep. Some of these wells turned up unexpected results. When Silas Thorla and Robert McKee were drilling for salt along Duck Creek in Noble County in 1814, crude oil came up with the brine. Not ones to waste an opportunity, Thorla and McKee bottled and sold the petroleum as "Seneca Oil," a topical treatment for rheumatism, sprains, and bruises. The first oil-producing well in North America was thus more of a salt-and-patent-medicine well, but subsequent Ohioans found different uses for the substance later in the century. Valuable clay deposits from Mississippian- and Pennsylvanian-Era strata formed the basis of an early and extremely competitive ceramic industry, particularly in the eastern part of the state and the Tuscarawas and Muskingum River Valleys. Focusing mostly on simple and cheap utilitarian pottery at first, these ceramic makers would later become the basis of a much more varied industry in the late 1800s. Coal was another mineral that early settlers mined—primarily in the Southern and Eastern parts of the state—but it was not until the advent of steam engines that Ohio had a steady market for it (see Figure 7.7). Only a year after the northern branch of the Ohio and Erie Canal opened, coalmines in Portage County were already sending boatloads up to Cleveland to help power the yearly-multiplying steamships plying Lake Erie.

Another mineral—iron ore—early settlers exploited became the basis of Ohio's first true heavy industry. In 1803, the same year Ohio achieved statehood, brothers Dan and James Heaton build the Hopewell Furnace on the banks of Yellow Creek in Northeast Ohio (near modern-day Struthers). This was the state's first iron-producing blast furnace, and although it would be years until iron production became one of Ohio's biggest economic engines, the Heatons were pioneering the iron-making process in the United States. Their furnaces were among the first in the country to use coal instead of wood charcoal for fuel, an innovation that made the iron cheaper to produce by replacing the small forest's worth of timber that early blast furnaces originally consumed. Within a few years blast furnaces had spread to numerous locations in eastern and southern Ohio that had the requisite amount of iron ore, limestone (used as a purifying agent), and timber or coal. By mid-century Cleveland, Canton/Massillon, and the Mahoning Valley in the northeast, and

Figure 7.7 The coal created from the Carboniferous period forests more than 300 million years ago began to be extracted in large amounts in the 1800s. Mines operated throughout the eastern part of the state, tapping the rich "coal measures" found in the Appalachian Plateau. The mines employed boys as young as ten, who might make 50 or 75 cents a day for a ten-hour working day. *Source*: Courtesy of the Ohio Historical Society (AL05155)

Zanesville, Portsmouth, and the appropriately-named Ironton in the south had established themselves as Ohio's major iron-producing areas. By 1850 Ohio was producing over 50,000 tons of pig iron, 38,000 tons of iron castings, and 14,000 tons of wrought iron.

Transportation Revolution: Railroads

Although Ohio's nascent iron industry was an important patron of the Ohio canal system, it also contributed to its demise. Only one year to the day after Governor Trimble triumphantly arrived in Cleveland on the *State of Ohio* to celebrate the opening of the Ohio and Erie Canal, construction began on the Baltimore and Ohio Railroad, one of the first and most successful early railroads in the United States. Commercial railroads had not been economically feasible before this because of technological limitations of the early engines, but by the 1820s new innovations made lighter and more powerful engines possible just as increased iron production was making the large amounts of iron necessary to construct a railroad much cheaper to acquire. Despite its commitment to canals, Ohio was not averse to railroad transport, and the state had its first few miles of operating track by 1836 when the Erie and Kalamazoo Railroad opened between Toledo and Adrian, Michigan. Originally a set of carriages pulled by horses over wooden rails, the railroad laid iron strips over the rails and acquired a steam locomotive the following year. In 1838, the Mad River and Lake Erie Railroad opened between Sandusky and Bellevue, making it the first railroad to operate entirely within the state. These were the exceptions, though. Numerous other railroad companies received charters from the state government in subsequent years, but most never became operational. Although many (perhaps over-)eager private investors and the state's "Plunder Law" provided some initial capital, poor planning and a lack of expertise among many operators left most of these companies unable accomplish the myriad tasks necessary to buy the land, survey and engineer the route, contract the workers, buy the supplies, lay the track, acquire the rolling stock, and construct the necessary buildings with the money available. The state chartered 216 railroads between 1840 and 1859, but only a few dozen ever went into operation. Despite the fact that a lot of investors lost a lot of money, some of these efforts were successful, and by 1850 Ohio had almost 300 miles of railroad track.

For all the early success of Ohio's canals, and for all the problems with the state's early railroads, the heyday of the canal era was remarkably short—about twenty years. As a form of transportation, railroads had several advantages over the canals. While canals could only run where there was sufficient water to operate them, railroads could be built between any two points. Railroads were also faster, even the earliest, slowest ones easily outpacing the approximately four-mile-per-hour speed of a canal boat. Furthermore, they could run in any season year round, while canals had to cease operations in the winter when the water froze. The linking of different railroad systems made continuous transport over great distances possible without the loading and unloading of canal boats necessary to get a cargo from the canal to the next mode of transportation. Despite the poor track record of early railroad construction efforts, railroads always seemed to find investors because they provided the same kinds of local benefits that the canals had promised. This time, though, these benefits could be spread across the entire state as the town leaders in each locality—particularly those bypassed by the canals—sought to bring a railroad through their town. As Ohio's railroad network slowly began to develop at the same time as the canal system was reaching its zenith, more and more of the Market Revolution freight traffic began move on the rails rather than the canals. In the 1850s Ohio's railroad mileage increased tenfold, its 2,974 miles ranking it first in the country. Although Ohio's canals continued to operate until 1913, railroads had already eclipsed them in significance before the Civil War, marking the culmination of the Market Revolution.

Financial reform

For all the tremendous successes of the Ohio economy during the canal era, it was still hampered at times by some of the same financial issues that had plagued its earlier development. The aftermath of the Panic of 1819 left many people distrustful of banks in general and the Bank of the United States in particular. Many in Ohio wished the National Bank good riddance when President Andrew Jackson succeeded in killing it, but its absence left little to rein in a new round of over-speculation in western lands in the mid-1830s. Most of Ohio's land was spoken for by that point, but the new land bubble, along with Jackson's Specie Circular of 1836 (which required all land payments to be in gold or silver) helped bring about the Panic of 1837. Coupled with the banking upheaval earlier, the depression caused the ruin of most Ohio banks. The banks that struggled to stay afloat found their notes trading for fractions of their face value, and wildcat banks made another appearance, circulating nearly worthless "shinplaster" notes (see Figure 7.1). Hard money became extremely tight, and a pre-canal-era barter economy returned in many places, including Ohio's largest city Cincinnati. Grinding on for years, this depression caused grave economic strains, throwing thousands out of work and causing many to lose their homes, farms, and businesses. Yet there seemed to be no consensus on how Ohio ought to deal with the crisis. Democrats who were generally hostile to banks prevented much reform on the state level, and the one reform that did pass—a state banking commission created in 1839—did not succeed in preventing abuses. Finally, with Whigs in control of both houses of the Assembly and the Governor's office in 1845, they were able to pass a banking reform bill sponsored by respected banker, canal commissioner, and state senator Alfred Kelley. The Kelley Bank Act created the State Bank of Ohio, which was actually a consortium of member banks under the direction of a Board of Control comprised of representatives from each bank. The state capitalized the bank at more than $6 million and made strict regulations on the minimum amount of capital that each member bank had to hold. The Board of Control issued the bank notes to each branch in proportion to the amount of collateral it could deposit with the Board. These securities were a "safety fund" against the possible default of any bank. This fund turned out to be a wise provision. Of the forty-one branches in the State Bank of Ohio system, five failed: one in Cincinnati, one in Akron, one in Newark, and two in Toledo. As a result of the safety fund, though, when these banks failed, their notes still passed at face value and were just as redeemable in specie as the notes from any other branch. This instilled—perhaps for the first time in Ohio history—some genuine confidence in the Ohio banking system, and the State Bank of Ohio remained an important stabilizing force in the Ohio economy until the National Banking Act of 1863 superseded it. This, along with continually expanding trade, manufacturing, and transportation had, by the 1850s, made Ohio a national economic powerhouse.

The birth of industrial Ohio

Ohio's fortunate collection of natural resources, agriculture, and nascent industries relatively quickly established it as a major manufacturing center. By 1820, Ohio's manufactured products ranked third in the country in total value, and the advent of the canal system only expanded and solidified its place. By the 1850s, Ohio was not only the third largest state in population, but also the third largest manufacturing state by most measures, behind only New York and Pennsylvania. Whereas Ohio had started its path to the Market Revolution by following the phenomenon's Western, agricultural model, within just a few decades it had also grown into a representative of the Revolution's eastern, manufacturing model thanks in part to its simultaneous participation the Transportation Revolution. By the time of the Civil War, these two revolutions had placed Ohio squarely in the middle of a third that overlapped the other two: the Industrial Revolution. This was a fundamental change in production methods and division of labor that had started in Europe in the late 1700 s and moved to the United States by the early 1800s. Industrialization produced the most sweeping changes in human society since the introduction of agriculture, and it would fundamentally alter Ohio in the coming years, bringing with it dramatic social and economic changes. By the early 1800 s the groundwork for these changes was already in place in Ohio and the state would have ample opportunity to flex its industrial muscle in the decades to come.

An old proverb of the real estate business states that the three most important factors in determining the value of a property are "location, location, and location." In evaluating Ohio's economy of the early statehood era, it is difficult to avoid coming to a similar conclusion. The story of Ohio's phenomenal growth in the early nineteenth century was deeply rooted in its unique location. Home of the first areas made available in the U.S. Public Land System, a multitude of farmers descended on its fertile lands, firmly establishing the agricultural base that drove its early economy. As the first western state with an improved transportation system and a state that linked eastern, western, northern, and southern markets, Ohio parlayed its prime location into tremendous economic success nationally. However, this success is not the entire significance of Ohio's economic development during this time. As historian Kim Gruenwald has persuasively argued, Ohio's early merchants and businessmen acted as an integrating force from the earliest days of Ohio's American settlements, tying outlying communities together in a network of interaction that in some ways systematized the seemingly haphazard nature of American settlement in the area. Between Ohio's favored location and the economic framework imposed on it by interactions between its early merchants, businessmen, and farmers, Ohio was ripe for the economic revolutions of the early 1800s.

Further Reading

The standard work on this era is Charles Sellers, *The Market Revolution: Jacksonian America, 1815–1846* (1994. Oxford: Oxford University Press) while Daniel Walker Howe's *What Hath God Wrought: The Transformation of America, 1815–1848* deals more specifically with the effects of the transportation and communication revolutions (Oxford: Oxford University Press, 2009). Merritt Roe Smith and Robert Martello's "Taking Stock of the Industrial Revolution in America," is a recent reappraisal of this phenomenon (pp. 169–200 in Jeff Horn, Leonard N. Rosenband, and Merritt Roe Smith, eds., 2010. *Reconceptualizing the Industrial Revolution.* Cambridge, MA: MIT Press). In addition a few of the many works that deal with these topics in an Ohio context are: Kim Gruenwald, *River of Enterprise: The Commercial Origins of Regional Identity in the Ohio Valley, 1790–1850* (2002. Bloomington: Indiana University Press); Lynn Metzger and Peg Bobel, eds., *Canal Fever: The Ohio & Erie Canal from Waterway to Canalway* (2009. Kent: Kent State University Press); and Terry Woods, *Ohio's Grand Canal: A Brief History of the Ohio & Erie Canal* (2008. Kent: Kent State University Press, 2008).

8

From Periphery to Center
Early Statehood and National Politics

One of the tools geographers use to describe the distribution of the population of a country is the concept of the "mean center of population." If one imagines the map of the United States to be flat and rigid with equal weights placed on it to represent the location of every living person in the country, the mean center of population would be the point at which that map would balance on the tip of an imaginary pole. In 1790, just two years after the founding of Marietta, that point was about twenty miles east of Baltimore, Maryland, reflecting both the concentration of population on the East Coast and the relatively equal division of the population between north and south. By the eve of the U.S. Civil War in 1860, that point had moved to Pike County, Ohio, just twenty miles southeast of Chillicothe. Only a few decades after it had joined the Union as a small state on the country's western fringes, Ohio had literally become the center of the nation, and not merely as a geographer's statistic. Its demographic rise helped bring about a rise in political prominence and prestige of unprecedented magnitude and quickness. When Jeremiah Morrow became Ohio's first (and for nearly ten years, only) United States congressman in 1803, Ohio was one of the least populous states and represented only seven-tenths of 1 percent of the total votes in the U.S. House of Representatives. By the time of Morrow's death in 1853, Ohio's population had increased to become the country's third largest, and its congressional delegation of twenty-one seats represented 9 percent of that body. It had already sent one of its residents to the White House, the first of eight U.S. presidents to call Ohio home. Thus, Ohio had not just become the center of American population, it had also become central to American politics.

The story of Ohio's rise to political prominence is one deeply rooted in the state's economic and demographic trends. It is also a complex story involving intensely local and personal issues as well as the reflection of national political trends. It even took on international characteristics during the War of 1812, when Ohioans had to respond to military disaster and foreign invasion. Despite the sometimes bewildering complexity of

Ohio: A History of the Buckeye State, First Edition. Kevin F. Kern and Gregory S. Wilson.

Ohio's early politics there are however, several overarching trends that mark this turbulent period. These include: (1) an ever-expanding electorate characterized by political pluralism; (2) a volatile political landscape featuring issues concerning race, the administration of justice, the locus of power, the role of government, and the rise of political parties; and (3) a dramatically increasing stature in national affairs. The last of these phenomena also brought an increasing internal sectionalism that began to destroy the political status quo in the state years before it would do the same to the nation as a whole.

Early Statehood Politics

The high hopes and celebrations of the successful statehood groundswell almost immediately evaporated when the first General Assembly met in the Ross County Courthouse in March of 1803 (see Figure 8.1). With no common opponent like St. Clair against which they could unify, those who had composed the statehood consensus began to

Figure 8.1   The Ross County Courthouse, built in 1801, was perhaps the most important building in the early political history of the state. It was the site of the final session territorial assembly, and Ohio's first Constitution was drafted there in 1802. It became the first Ohio Statehouse in 1803, and served in that capacity until 1810, and then again from 1812 to 1816 when the capital moved to Columbus. The county razed the building in 1852 to make room for a new, larger county courthouse.
Source: Courtesy of the Ohio Historical Society (SA1039AV_B02F02_016)

bicker and splintered into pieces. The majority, although still nominally Republican in national politics, differed with each other over a host of local, economic, class, and personal issues. Such state fathers as Thomas Worthington and Ohio's first governor, Edward Tiffin, found themselves challenged not only by their traditional Federalist-leaning foes in Marietta and Cincinnati, but also both more radical and more conservative people in their own party, sometimes from their own local area. Michael Baldwin, for example, was a populist Chillicothe lawyer and the first Speaker of the Ohio House who had led "The Bloodhounds," a group composed mostly of artisans and laborers, during the late territorial period. A rough-and-tumble subset of this group had burned a St. Clair effigy during the 1801 debates over the division of the state and threatened physical violence to certain of their opponents. Baldwin, Chillicothe state representative Elias Langham, and others in this faction were aggressively democratic in outlook, fully trusting the people to govern themselves and increasingly suspicious of what they viewed as the elitist tendencies of so-called "Regular Republicans" like Worthington and Tiffin. On the other end of the Republican Party spectrum were more conservative voices, largely represented by professional and business interests in urban areas and many others on the periphery of the state's main locus of power in the Scioto Valley. These people viewed the Baldwins and Langhams of Ohio politics as dangerously individualistic demagogues whose policies bordered on anarchy, and they also resented the Scioto Valley "Regular Republican" control of state power. Although these conservative Republicans favored an open society to a point, they wanted legislation favorable to their economic interests and a strong and independent judiciary to act as a counterweight to the possible excesses of the state legislature. Positioned in the political center of Ohio Republicanism were Worthington, Tiffin and the other Regular Republicans. They shared most of the conservatives' qualms about the more radically democratic faction, as well as the threat that the group posed to the nascent political structure the Regular Republicans had constructed, yet they still trusted the legislature to act as the voice of the people. They sought to steer a course by which the people would have local control, but in a systematic way and under the guidance and leadership of the most talented and accomplished of their number—persons much like themselves. This three-way split in the Republican Party meant that the remnants of the Federalist Party, focused primarily in Marietta, areas in and around Cincinnati, and the growing Western Reserve, sometimes found themselves in the unaccustomed role of power-brokers, able to throw their support behind whichever candidates or policies they felt most closely represented their interests.

Although these political divisions reflected those beginning to beset the national party system—the Jeffersonian Republicans also faced the divisiveness and internal ideological debates that came with being in power—they took on a particularly local flavor as they played out in Ohio state politics. No national presidential election drew more than 20 percent of Ohio's electorate until 1824, and early gubernatorial and congressional elections often turned as much on the perceived class and personality of the candidates as they did on ideology. The Regular Republicans like Worthington sought to bring some order and control to the process by using county nominating conventions and caucuses of their members in the state legislature to nominate candidates for elective offices. Both the more conservative and more democratic fringes of the party criticized these tactics as being exclusionary or even aristocratic in nature. By the early 1810s Thomas Worthington, only a few years removed from being the "Father of Ohio Statehood," found himself rejected by Republicans and Federalists alike as being part of what they perceived as a self-serving Scioto Valley oligarchy whose power needed containing.

Perhaps Worthington, knowing the turbulence of early statehood Ohio politics as well as he did, should not have been surprised. The rapidly-expanding population and accompanying proliferation of counties and county offices, when combined with the frequent elections mandated by the Constitution and the lack of any real party unity, resulted in an abundance of candidates for offices and extraordinary amount of turnover. For example, between 1805 and 1815, no fewer than eighteen different men held the three state legislative seats from the Steubenville area, and only one of those men served for as long as four years. Steubenville was hardly exceptional in this regard. Despite the fact that the State House of Representatives grew from twenty-eight to forty-eight seats in the two years after 1807, only five of those original twenty-eight representatives were still serving after the 1809 election. Although this high rate of turnover made politics confusing and lacking in continuity many Ohioans believed that this was exactly what had been promised by the State Constitution: frequent elections among increasingly localized political units was the very ideal of the democratic principles espoused by opponents of St. Clair and the Federalists during the territorial period.

Ironically, for all the burgeoning electorate's talk of expanding Ohio's democracy, some of the earliest and least publicly debated acts of the Ohio legislature were designed to restrict the rights of certain Ohioans. On March 1, 1803, the very first day of the first session of the new Ohio government, the General Assembly codified the Constitution's exclusion of African Americans from enumeration and soon after restricted military service to white men. By December 15 of that year it had organized a committee to draft the first of its "Black Laws." The finished bill passed the House on December 31, and with the Senate's approval in early January 1804, "An Act to Regulate Black and Mulatto Persons" became law. The law required all African American residents of the state to register (after having paid a twelve-and-a-half cent fee) with their county clerk of courts and that all new African American immigrants had to prove their freedom immediately and register with the county within two years of moving to the state. The law further levied a fine of $10 to $50 dollars on anyone hiring an undocumented African American, with a further fifty cents per day paid to the owner if the worker was an escaped slave. Harboring an escaped slave could also draw a $10 to $50 dollar fine and the law required the local judiciary and sheriff to aid in recapture of such runaways. Nevertheless, slave hunters were not given *carte blanche*—should they try to capture an African American who was not the slave for whom they were looking they were to be fined $1,000 and liable for further damages.

Ohio's 1804 Black Law seems to have been addressing several audiences. It reassured slaveholders in bordering Kentucky and Virginia—in many cases kindred to the large number of southern-born residents of Ohio—that Ohio would be no safe haven for runaway slaves. It also reassured the many Ohioans who feared an increase in the state's African American population that their presence (and also their competition to white labor) in the state would be kept to a minimum. On the other hand, it also issued a warning to people who wished to help escaped slaves that such actions would not be tolerated. To Ohio's relatively few African Americans, though, the intent of the law was somewhat ambiguous. While it certainly was meant to discourage African American settlement in the state and hardly made African Americans who were already there feel welcome, the law was not as harsh as its counterparts in other states. The twelve-and-a-half cent fee was not prohibitive (a similar fee in neighboring Pennsylvania at that time was $2) and the two-year window for registration was generous, especially considering that there was no penalty for failing to register. Furthermore, the fine for hiring an escaped slave paled in comparison to the twenty to one hundred times greater fine for capturing a free black, who was also entitled to sue for damages. While Ohio's African Americans may have been second-class citizens, the 1804 law offered some protection of what rights they did have.

In contrast, there was far less ambiguity in the version of the Black Law passed three years later. Fairfield County representative Philemon Beecher had proposed the 1804 law but he claimed that it had failed to satisfy southern slave owners who were convinced that an increasing numbers of slaves were seeking safe haven in Ohio's northwestern Indian reservation. With alarmist rhetoric of a possible armed invasion of southerners or even a more general civil war, Beecher urged the assembly to pass a more stringent statute immediately in the name of a state emergency. Proposed in late 1806 and enacted in January 1807, the new Black Law significantly amended the earlier statute. Not only did it raise the county registration fee to $1, but all African Americans who wished to immigrate to Ohio also had to, within twenty days, get two or more property holders in the state to give a surety bond of $500 to be paid if the immigrant became a burden to the state or failed to meet "good behavior" standards. The penalty for failing to comply with the law was the physical removal of the unfortunate immigrant. In addition, the new law doubled the maximum fine for harboring an unregistered African American and made the violator financially responsible for that person. Furthermore, and perhaps most significantly, the 1807 law repealed all protections of free African Americans given in the 1804 version and stripped them of the right to testify in court against a white person. Already unable to serve in the militia, be counted in the census, vote, or serve on juries, Ohio's African Americans saw the 1807 Black Law complete the process of turning them into second-class citizens (see Figure 8.2). Although Ohio's Black Laws were rarely enforced and failed to keep African Americans from entering the state (Ohio's black population increased more than thirteen-fold during the four decades following the passage of the 1807 law) they stood in stark contrast to Ohio's erstwhile democratized political culture, and as such would become the subject of increasing scrutiny and political attention by the 1840s. Yet at the time they were passed, these laws drew relatively little public debate, perhaps reflecting a general antiblack consensus among the state's population. Ohio's voters and politicians were instead focused on another aspect of the state's legal system.

Perhaps no issue serves as a better example of the many forces shaping early Ohio politics than the one that was the most contentious of all: the debate over the tenure and jurisdiction of judges. In reaction to perceived excesses of territorial judges, the Ohio Constitutional Convention had stripped the judicial branch of government of many of its accustomed powers. State and county judges had set terms of seven years and had to

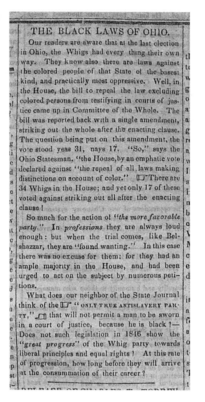

THE BLACK LAWS OF OHIO.

Our readers are aware that at the last election in Ohio, the Whigs had every thing their own way. They know also there are laws against the colored people of that State of the basest kind, and practically most oppressive. Well, in the House, the bill to repeal the law excluding colored persons from testifying in courts of justice came up in Committee of the Whole. The bill was reported back with a single amendment, striking out the whole after the enacting clause. The question being put on this amendment, the vote stood yeas 31, nays 17. "So," says the Ohio Statesman, "the House, by an emphatic vote declared against "the repeal of all laws making distinctions on account of color." There are 34 Whigs in the House; and yet only 17 of these voted against striking out all after the enacting clause!

So much for the action of "the more favorable party." In professions they are always loud enough: but when the trial comes, like Belshazzar, they are "found wanting." In this case there was no excuse for them: for they had an ample majority in the House, and had been urged to act on the subject by numerous petitions.

What does our neighbor of the State Journal think of the ONLY TRUE ANTISLAVERY PARTY, that will not permit a man to be sworn in a court of justice, because he is black?—Does not such legislation in 1846 show the "great progress" of the Whig party towards liberal principles and equal rights? At this rate of progression, how long before they will arrive at the consummation of their career?

Figure 8.2   The Black Laws passed in the first decade of the 1800s turned African-Americans legally into second-class citizens and demonstrated the antipathy many early Ohioans held toward Black migration into the state. They increasingly became a political issue in the 1840s, particularly among many Whigs and later Free-Soil party members who worked for their repeal.
Source: Courtesy of the Ann Arbor District Library and the Bentley Historical Library, http://signalofliberty. aadl.org/

be appointed and renewed by vote of the Ohio Assembly. Once statehood had been achieved, the General Assembly sought to limit the judiciary even further by repealing the application of the common law (thus making all law dependent on the General Assembly rather than the discretion and tradition of the judiciary), and increasing the power of local Justices of the Peace by increasing their jurisdiction to all cases concerning matters up to $50 in value (this was close to $1,000 in contemporary terms). Judges Calvin Pease, Samuel Huntington, and George Tod all found this last law unconstitutional because the Ohio Constitution set the jurisdiction for a jury trial at twenty dollars. The principle of judicial review was still a relatively new one, with a only a few precedents in state courts before the famous *Marbury v. Madison* Supreme Court ruling the year Ohio became a state. Worthington, already stung by being labeled an aristocrat because of his support of caucuses and county nominating conventions, sought to renew his democratic credentials and political fortunes by running for governor on the issue of "judicial encroachment" against Judge Huntington. Muddying the electoral waters was

THE SIGNAL OF LIBERTY.

ANN ARBOR, MONDAY, MARCH 16, 1846.

ANTISLAVERY.

SIGNAL OF LIBERTY.

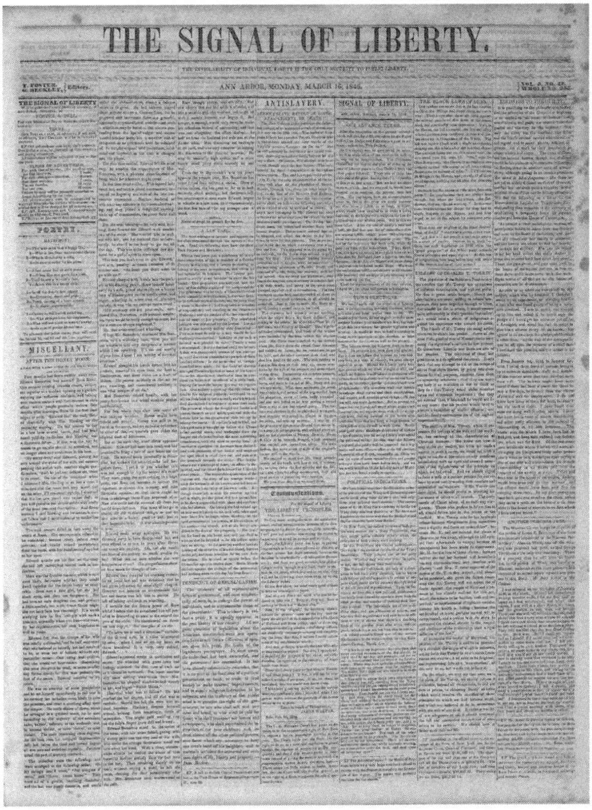

Figure 8.2 (*continued*)

Thomas Kirker, another Regular Republican and Speaker of the Senate who had ascended to the governorship when the General Assembly elected Governor Edward Tiffin to the U.S. Senate in 1807. Kirker also stood for election and drew enough support from "Regular Republicans" who were tired of Worthington's political hegemony to split the Republican vote and give Huntington the governorship with less than a majority.

Undeterred by this setback, Worthington and other opponents of an independent judiciary spent the next few years seeking to curb its powers, almost at the cost of destroying the state Republican Party. Soon after the election the Ohio House impeached Tod and Pease, who survived their trials in the State Senate by only a single vote. Undeterred, the anticourt forces passed the "Sweeping Resolution" that removed all incumbent judges from their seats in 1810. So important did they view this piece of legislation that they agreed to move the state capital to Zanesville in exchange for enough votes to pass the bill. Worthington, Tiffin, and other Regular Republicans also actively founded "wigwams" (or local chapters) of the secret national Tammany Society to help organize their faction on the local level. Despite their success in restricting the Ohio judiciary, Regular Republicans faced a popular backlash against the secretive, exclusive, and seemingly antidemocratic nature of the Tammany Societies, and Worthington lost the 1810 gubernatorial election to anti-Tammany Moderate Republican and former U.S. Senator Return Jonathan Meigs, Jr. Although Worthington's Tammany power base in the General Assembly was strong enough to get him elected to the U.S. Senate in 1810 and to fend off a repeal of the Sweeping Resolution in 1811, Tammany power had peaked, and the General Assembly finally repealed the Sweeping Resolution in 1812. By this time, the judicial issue that had once seemed so important had largely run its course, and Republicans of all stripes had begun to reunify for both external and internal political reasons. The threat of impending war against the Indians and the British seemed to dwarf the issues dividing the party, pushing Republicans to work together to meet this external threat. In addition, the party's division over the judicial issue raised the possibility that their common opponents, the Federalists, might take political advantage of the split to win some of the five new congressional seats the state received after the Census of 1810. The reunited Republican Party voted to move the capital back to Chillicothe in 1812, and then closer to the geographical center of the state in the new city of Columbus in 1816. This move, the last of seven shifts the capital had made since 1788, proved to be lasting and helped reduce regional rivalries that had been lingering since territorial times.

Despite the fractiousness and heated differences that characterized early Ohio state politics, Ohioans of all persuasions could come together when faced with an emergency. For example, when Aaron Burr used Blennerhasset Island in the Ohio River as a staging ground for his still-murky filibustering conspiracy, Governor Tiffin sought and received special emergency powers from the legislature to send the militia there to seize the expedition's boats and supplies. The action brought the conspiracy to an abrupt end while at the same time serving as the first major political act of national significance in Ohio's history as a state. Although Burr turned out to have a higher level of sympathy among some segments of Ohio's population than the Federalists and "Regular Republicans" would have liked, Ohio politicians used this event to demonstrate the new state's allegiance to the federal government.

The War of 1812

Similarly, the very real threat of invasion during the War of 1812 allowed Ohioans to pull together in the face of an external threat while at the same time demonstrating that Ohio was part—and at times at the center—of national and international events. Violence had actually started earlier, the product of heightened tensions between the ever-increasing volume of white settlers and the rise of a powerful Indian Confederacy developed around the Shawnee Prophet (see Figure 8.3) and his brother Tecumseh. Born Lalawethika ("The Noise Maker") "The Prophet" had led a relatively undistinguished (and often self-indulgent) life until a night in April 1805 when he fell into a trance and saw the first of a series of visions that would define his movement. In them, the Master of Life advised all Native Americans to work together, to return to traditional ways, and to forsake the goods and practices of the white Americans, whom he said were the offspring of the evil Great Serpent. If the Native Americans followed these practices, the Master of Life would then sweep the non-Indian peoples from the land, ushering in peace and happiness for

Figure 8.3 Tenskwatawa, also known as Lalawethika or The Prophet, went from obscurity among his own group of Shawnees to one of the most powerful religious leaders of Native Americans in the Great Lakes region. It was from the strong following that Tenskwatawa amassed that his brother Tecumseh was able to form a Pan-Indian military confederation to oppose U.S. encroachment into the area.
Source: Courtesy of the Ohio Historical Society (AL04623)

Native Americans. Changing his name to Tenskwatawa ("The Open Door") The Prophet soon gained followers, not only among the Shawnee but also from numerous other groups who had been demoralized after Fallen Timbers and the Treaty of Greenville. The messages of self-sufficiency, traditional values, and a world without the Long Knives appealed greatly to Indians who had seen little hope of restoring the Middle Ground, much less a world without Americans. Much as Anthony Wayne had built Fort Recovery on the site of St. Clair's defeat, Tenskwatawa founded a village for his followers near Greenville, and over the next few years his fame and following grew so much that it began to alarm the American authorities, including former St. Clair aide and Indiana governor William Henry Harrison. When pressure from the accommodationist Shawnee Chief Black Hoof and his followers nearby caused Tenskwatawa to move his village to Tippecanoe (or "Prophetstown") on the Wabash River (near present-day Lafayette, Indiana) in 1808, a large multiethnic assemblage of representatives from nearly all the major Great Lakes groups descended there, living with The Prophet, receiving his teachings, and sending missionaries out to spread them further. By 1810, the movement had grown so large that Harrison was predicting conflict would ensue.

Harrison had good reason to be concerned. Just as Pontiac had built his Northwest Confederacy on the foundation of similar teachings by the Lenape (Delaware) prophet Neolin, Tecumseh had been hard at work building a new pan-Indian confederacy to resist further American encroachment by using his brother's movement as a unifying force. Tecumseh had spent nearly his entire life at odds with the Americans. His father Puckeshinwa was a Shawnee chief who Virginian soldiers had killed at the Battle of Point Pleasant during Lord Dunmore's War. His mother, a Creek woman with no family roots in Ohio, then moved from the strife-torn region further west, leaving Tecumseh in the care of his older brother, a famed war leader named Chiksika (or sometimes "Cheeseekau"), and his sister Tecumpease. By the time Chiksika died battling American settlers in Tennessee in the early 1790s Tecumseh had acquired an implacable opposition to the Americans and advocated a policy of not giving any more land to the United States. A participant at the Battle of Fallen Timbers and an opponent of the ensuing Treaty of Greenville, Tecumseh envisioned an alliance of tribes from the Great Lakes south to the Gulf of Mexico that would halt American expansion along its entire frontier. When his brother's religious movement began to gain followers from numerous Indian groups and to gather momentum, Tecumseh saw an opportunity to build the alliance he desired.

Like Tecumseh, Harrison had come from a prominent family and rose to become both a war and political leader. The youngest of seven children of a wealthy Virginia planter and politician who had signed the Declaration of Independence, Harrison embarked on a military career in the west at the age of eighteen. He served as a lieutenant with Anthony Wayne's Legion of the United States against the Western Confederacy and signed the Treaty of Greenville in 1795. That year he married the daughter of John Cleves Symmes and left the army two years later in 1797, settling on some of the Symmes Purchase lands at North Bend. With political connections both in Cincinnati and in the east he quickly rose to political prominence, serving as Secretary of the Northwest Territory before being elected as a territorial representative to Congress and proposing the Harrison Land Act of 1800. President John Adams appointed him Governor of the new Indiana Territory (which included all of the old Northwest Territory except Ohio, which was on the track to statehood). One of his main goals as governor was to acquire large quantities of Indian lands for settlement, and he was quite successful, negotiating numerous treaties that purchased huge swaths of Indian territory. The 1809 Treaty of Fort Wayne in particular was the last straw for Tecumseh. Outraged that some Indian groups had given up 3 million acres along the Wabash River without the consent of the Native people who lived there, Tecumseh threatened the accommodationist Indian leaders that had signed it and confronted Harrison in person for perpetrating what Tecumseh viewed as an illegitimate swindle. When Harrison refused to repudiate the treaty Tecumseh's actions to form a confederacy took on new urgency and he began to seek help beyond the Indian groups around the Great Lakes.

Forging an alliance with the British in Canada, Tecumseh also intended to use his Creek ancestry as a way by which he could bring the southern tribes into the new confederacy. Before he left on a trip to the south to accomplish this mission he told Tenskwatawa to avoid confronting the Americans until he returned. Harrison forced the issue, however, by marching more than 1,000 soldiers to Prophetstown in November 1811 to strike at the Confederacy he already viewed as a threat. Rather than heed his brother's warning, Tenskwatawa had his warriors encircle and attack Harrison's camp near the confluence of the Wabash and Tippecanoe Rivers early on the morning of November 7 in what became known as the Battle of Tippecanoe. Although Harrison's forces took heavy casualties in the two-hour battle that followed, the fact that they had camped in battle array on a strong hilltop position helped them hold their ground and repulse the attack. Harrison had lost more men than Tenskwatawa, but it was a crushing defeat for the Indians, who believed that their faith in Tenskwatawa's religion would protect them and allow them to prevail. Harrison's men regrouped and scalped the corpses of a number of the fallen Indians as Tenskwatawa ordered Prophetstown abandoned, and the next day the American soldiers burned the settlement to the ground. The defeat caused Tenskwatawa's appeal to wane among those who had expected his power to be greater, and Tecumseh's hopes for a massive pan-Indian alliance largely died at Tippecanoe. Nevertheless, Tecumseh continued to rally sympathetic Native groups to his cause and cast his lot in with the British as the last, best hope to stop further American encroachment.

Events like the Battle of Tippecanoe and the supposed British aid to, and incitement of, the Indians of the Northwest contributed significantly to public sentiment in the west in favor of war with Britain. Within months, these and other issues Americans had with the British led the Congress to declare war. A major player in the origins of this international conflict, Ohio would soon be on its front lines.

Ohioans largely approved Congress's declaration of war on June 18, 1812, although support was not unanimous. With its heavy New England Federalist and Quaker representation, the southeastern portion of the state in particular opposed the war and some of its consequences, such as tax and militia levies. Ohio's congressional delegation was split on the issue, with Congressman Morrow voting for the war and Senator Worthington voting against it—mostly because the latter felt the nation was unprepared for it (Ohio's other senator was absent for the vote). Enthusiasm turned to fear for many Ohioans, though, when the early stages of what became known as the War of 1812 (1812–15) did not go well for the United States (see Figure 8.4). General William Hull, a Revolutionary War veteran and governor of the Michigan territory, received orders even before the war began to gather militia in Ohio and march them to Detroit, where they would be stationed to launch an anticipated invasion of Canada. The expedition turned out to be a disaster. Gathering more than 2,000 men at Urbana, Hull faced repeated insubordination, supply problems, and difficult conditions as he attempted to make a way through the swampy northwest part of the state. Not knowing Congress had declared war, he sent his plans by boat to Detroit. The better-informed British intercepted the boat and used the captured plans to their advantage. After he finally arrived in Detroit, Hull attempted a push into Canada but retreated after meeting with spirited resistance led by Tecumseh and British general Isaac Brock. In the meantime another British and Indian force took the northern Michigan Fort Mackinac without a shot being fired. This shook Hull, who expected that it would lead to further Indian reinforcements to flood south in aid of the British. The General seemed to lose his nerve, having to be talked out of withdrawing all the way back to Ohio by his subordinates and withstanding a near mutiny of his men. Although Hull

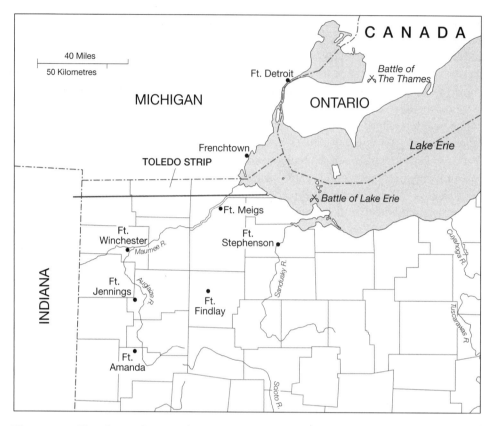

Figure 8.4   Ohio during the War of 1812.

held a significant numerical advantage over the joint British-Indian force, Brock staged an elaborate ruse convincing Hull he was badly outnumbered and suggested that he should surrender the fort to prevent a massacre. Despite vigorous opposition from his regimental leaders, Lewis Cass, James Findlay, and Duncan McArthur, Hull surrendered Detroit, his entire force, and all of its armaments on August 16. The British and Indians used these to build a formidable presence and military threat to Ohio. Court-martialed and sentenced to be shot for the fiasco, General Hull received a commutation of his death sentence by President Madison in recognition of his Revolutionary War service.

The rather ignominious start and very real danger that Hull's surrender represented threw many in Ohio into a panic, one not mitigated by subsequent events. After the fall of Detroit, the ranking American commanders in the area were William Henry Harrison and James Winchester. As Winchester (another aging Revolutionary War veteran) had seniority, he initially assumed overall command. Harrison accepted a commission of Major General of Kentucky militia rather than take a federal commission subordinate to Winchester's, and distinguished himself in lifting a siege at Fort Wayne. This impressed President Madison enough to hand supreme command over northwest forces to him. Now Harrison ordered Winchester to build a fort at the rapids of the Maumee, hoping to use it as a base to launch an assault on Detroit by Christmas. His slow-moving rival eventually began to fortify a camp on the Maumee River in January 1813, but then exceeded his orders by leading his men into Michigan to take Frenchtown on the River Raisin (now Monroe). Initially meeting with success, Winchester failed to prepare his overextended forces for the overwhelming British counterattack that followed, and he soon found himself surrendering to Colonel Henry Proctor on the condition that the British would protect the prisoners from the Indians. Although Proctor guarded the men who could walk he left the wounded behind to be killed and maimed by his Indian allies. Winchester's defeat once again left Ohio vulnerable and scrapped Harrison's plans to attack Detroit, but "Remember the Raisin" became a battle cry for American troops in the confrontations that followed.

For most of 1813, Ohio lay under direct threat of British invasion. Fortifications sprang up throughout the state in anticipation of the threat, but only two of them saw any military action. The most important and largest was Fort Meigs on the Maumee River (in present-day Perrysburg), which Harrison built after Winchester's defeat and named after Ohio's governor. Proctor and Tecumseh led a joint British/Indian expedition of 2,200 against Harrison in the first of two sieges that spring and summer, firing as many as 1,700 cannonballs at the fort over a four-day period in May. Harrison's men took significant losses in an engagement designed to disable the British cannons, but thanks to the fort's skillful design by military engineer Eleazor Wood and the timely arrival of reinforcements from a troop of Kentucky militia, Harrison held the fort and Proctor broke the siege. As of May 1813 the American forces around Lake Erie had not won a single battle in the war. After that, they never lost one.

In July Tecumseh and Proctor launched a second siege of Fort Meigs with more than 3,000 Indians and 350 British, but as the British were using most of their large artillery to outfit their naval fleet, this expedition stood even less chance of success than the first one. Instead, the British broke the siege to attack Fort Stephenson on the Sandusky River in present-day Fremont. Harrison had viewed the post as undefendable and ordered its commander, twenty-one-year-old George Croghan, to abandon it in the face of the British/Indian advance. Croghan received the orders too late for his 160 men to make a safe retreat and instead prepared for the assault. Despite being outnumbered more than ten-to-one and being pounded by small artillery and gunboats that had sailed up the Sandusky, Croghan staged an admirable resistance, moving his only cannon, "Old Betsy," to different spots to make the enemy think he had several artillery pieces. A British direct assault on the afternoon of August 2 resulted in 100 British casualties, including most participating officers, in comparison to one man killed and seven wounded in the fort. Exactly fifty years earlier and only a few miles away during the Resistance of 1763, Fort Sandusky became the first fort ever to be attacked in Ohio, ushering in a prolonged period of European/Indian conflict on Ohio soil. Although no one knew it at the time, when Proctor and Tecumseh retreated with their men that night, Fort Stephenson had become the last Ohio fort to come under attack, thus marking the state's last pitched battle between whites and Indians, as well as its last foreign invasion.

Meanwhile, on Lake Erie, Oliver Hazard Perry had been hard at work on Presque Isle (near present-day Erie, Pennsylvania) constructing a fleet of ships to take on the British for mastery of the Great Lakes. The task before him was daunting. Not only were the British the world's unquestioned naval power but Perry had to use largely uncured wood and unskilled labor to build his ships, and then man them with mostly inexperienced militiamen and free blacks. Nevertheless, once the ships were built and after only two weeks' training for the men, Perry set off to engage the British fleet that was under the command of Captain Robert Barclay. The adversaries met near Perry's South Bass Island anchorage of Put-in-Bay on September 10, 1813. Although roughly comparable in tonnage and armaments, Perry's fleet held a slight advantage in both categories (Barclay had had experienced his own troubles equipping and manning his ships). In the three-hour battle that followed, Perry's flagship, the *Lawrence*, took such a heavy beating that four-fifths of its crew and all its guns fell out of service. Perry ordered his men to row him under heavy fire to the *Niagara* to continue the battle from it. He took with him the blue and white flag bearing the phrase "Don't Give Up the Ship"—the dying words of his old ship's namesake, Captain James Lawrence, during his battle with the British off the coast of Boston earlier that summer—and ran it up the mast of his new ship. A shift of wind in Perry's favor, an accidental collision between two British ships, the deaths or severe injury of most British officers, and skillful maneuvering and firing from the remaining American ships all contributed to the surrender of the British fleet, giving the British Navy one of the worst defeats it had ever suffered. Perry's succinct report announcing his victory, "We have met the enemy and they are ours; two ships, two brigs, one schooner and one sloop" is one of the most celebrated official dispatches in American military history (see Figure 8.5).

Perry's decisive victory in the Battle of Lake Erie was of almost incalculable value to the American war effort, and not just by providing a much-needed boost to American morale after such a lackluster start to the war. With no ships to guard it and its artillery removed to arm the lost fleet, the British position in Detroit was untenable, and Major General Henry Proctor ordered his men to abandon it and retreat up the Ontario peninsula. Within days of the battle, Perry's ships were taking Harrison's troops to Canada to confront Proctor, and less than a month after Perry's victory, William Henry Harrison's forces decisively defeated the badly outnumbered British and Indian army at the Battle of the Thames. Although the war would continue for more than another year, this battle marked the end of any serious military threat to Ohio.

The Battle of the Thames also marked another kind of end for Ohio, one that drew a full circle to a conflict that had continued for decades. The clash is also known as the Battle of Moraviantown because it took place near the settlement where David Zeisberger led the remaining Christian Lenapes after the Gnadenhutten Massacre. Just as Colonel Williamson had done almost thirty years before, American cavalry burned the entire settlement to the ground before leaving the area. The destruction of Moraviantown is symbolic of the destruction of Indian Ohio that the Battle of the Thames represented. Tecumseh was among the dead at the battle, and his goal of creating an effective pan-Indian alliance died with him. Although The Prophet still had his adherents, and Indians would still continue to aid the British in Canada and skirmish with settlers in the Northwest until the end of the war, it was clear to the remaining Ohio Native American groups that there was no chance of forestalling American encroachment. In a series of treaties including Maumee Rapids (1817), St. Mary's (1818), Sandusky River (1825), Pleasant Plains (1831), Wapakoneta (1831), and Upper Sandusky (1842), the remaining Native American groups ceded all their

Figure 8.5   One of the most iconic images inspired by the War of 1812 is this painting by William Henry Powell of Cincinnati portraying the key moment in the Battle when Perry has himself rowed under heavy fire from his disabled flagship *Lawrence* to the *Niagara* to continue the fight. The original currently hangs in the rotunda of the Ohio Statehouse.
Source: Courtesy of the Ohio Historical Society (AL00195)

claims to Ohio lands and moved from their traditional center to the American periphery west of the Mississippi River. The Wyandot—the first group officially to move back to Ohio after Iroquois hegemony over the region waned in the early 1700s—were the last to leave in 1843, although they had already left their traditional way of life behind years before. Removed to a portion of the Lenape reservation in Kansas, within a few years a majority of the group voted to give up their tribal status and become American citizens. In this way did more than 10,000 years of Native American history in Ohio come to an end.

Although the War of 1812 had a number of economic and social effects (discussed in Chapters Six and Seven), it is the political effects that have traditionally drawn the most attention from historians. Often called "The Second War for American Independence," the war served to establish the United States as an independent power on the world stage and promoted a feeling of nationalism exemplified by its lore (including the poem that eventually became the National Anthem) and leaders (including Andrew Jackson). Similarly, Ohio participation in the war paid several political dividends to the state and some of its leaders. On the local level the conflict served to dampen some of the political divisions that had marked the state's early history, as exemplified by Thomas Worthington finally winning the governorship on his third try in 1814. Ohio's key role in fending off British invasion reaffirmed its national profile as well. Its political stature on the national level increased when President Madison in 1814 named Governor Meigs Postmaster General, making him the first Ohioan to hold a high-level post in the executive branch. Other military leaders parlayed their wartime military service into notable political careers. Hull's regimental commanders Duncan McArthur and Lewis Cass, for example, each served as governors (of Ohio and the Michigan Territory, respectively), and Cass became the Democratic nominee for president in 1848. Most notable of all, of course, was William Henry Harrison, "Old Tippecanoe," who became the first Ohio favorite son to serve as president. The war that had started so disastrously for Ohio turned out to pay large dividends in political capital and continued to influence Ohio's political life for many years to come.

State and National Politics, 1815–36

The years after the War of 1812 were a boom and bust period for Ohio economically, and the state's politics reflected these changes, as well as those on the national level and the continuing legacy of its early settlement patterns. The population of the state increased dramatically as land sales spiked after the war and one of the constant tasks of state government was creating new counties to keep up with the expanding population. Ohio had nine counties at the time of statehood, and in spite of the bickering over other issues, the General Assembly managed to add another thirty-five between 1803 and 1813. The decade after the war saw the creation of another twenty-eight counties, including a record number of fifteen between March 1 and April 1, 1820. These new counties, carved out of old ones as population warranted, were a natural product of Ohio's political consensus toward keeping political power as local as possible, with small counties and nearby county seats. Successful in creating an expansion of local government, this proliferation of counties also created a headache for the state judicial system, one that would take a generation to resolve.

For a while after the war, the hyper-partisanship of the prewar period waned as the nation entered what historians used to call "The Era of Good Feelings." A largely-discredited concept on the national level (the Missouri Crisis, among other things, had already begun to tear at the national fabric during this time) the label applies better to this relatively less-turbulent interlude in Ohio politics. The caucuses and nominating conventions that had drawn such vocal opposition largely ceased to operate, old-time party animosities seemed to dim, and even the occasional old Federalist could get elected to statewide office, as happened when Allen Trimble won gubernatorial elections in 1826 and 1828. The boom-time political landscape largely revolved around economic concerns, particularly issues regarding money and banking. The flood of paper money issued by wildcat institutions that was democratizing the economy caused some concern among Ohio politicians, and at the urging of Governor Worthington the General Assembly made some attempts to regulate the banks between 1815 and 1818. It limited the amount of paper currency banks could circulate, chartered new state banks with stricter regulations, and solicited new branches of the Bank of the United States, which generally had a sounder financial footing. These measures, however, did little to restrain the abundance of paper money in circulation and the rampant speculation it allowed. Not only were the laws passed inadequate to stop these things entirely, but many of the lawmakers and other political leaders in the states were also deeply involved financially in the booming economy and its institutions. Furthermore, a vocal segment of the population wanted even more easy money and credit, and these people denounced the Bank of the United States and the state banks as elitist institutions unresponsive to the needs of most of the population.

These feelings only intensified as the financial bubble began to burst in 1818. Antibank sentiment was extremely widespread and passionate, and the Ohio legislature responded by voting in February 1819—with only three dissenting votes in the House—to tax the Bank of the United States at a rate of $50,000 per branch. Although just weeks later the Supreme Court handed down the *McCullough v. Maryland* decision declaring such acts unconstitutional, in September, State Auditor Ralph Osborn moved to enforce the "Crowbar Law" deputizing a sheriff (John L. Harper) to demand payment at the U.S. Bank's Chillicothe branch. Showing up with a wagon and other officers, the sheriff demanded payment. When the bank manager refused, the sheriff and his assistants essentially robbed the bank of $100,000 ($50,000 for each of the U.S. Bank branches in Ohio). Although Governor Ethan Allen Brown tried to get the money back to the National Bank, Ohio's Constitution gave him little power to do so and the state treasurer's office kept the money (minus the $2000 Harper had kept for his fee) until a Federal Circuit Court ordered the arrest of State Treasurer Samuel Sullivan when he refused to return it. Federal agents seized Sullivan's keys and returned the remaining $98,000 to the U.S. Bank. Despite strong Democratic-Republican qualms over the Supreme Court's jurisdiction and right of judicial review, the case made it to the Supreme Court, which ruled that in the case of *Osborn v. Bank of the United States* (1824) the seizure was illegal, and that the state must return the additional $2,000 to the Bank. Although the case has an important place in U.S. constitutional law, for the people of Ohio it had serious political ramifications. Lead counsel for the Bank was Henry Clay, an erstwhile political hero to many in the West. His association with the unpopular side of this dispute would have immediate political consequences in Southwest Ohio. In addition to the great unpopularity it engendered from this case, the U.S. Bank came to own a great deal of land through the payment of debts and foreclosures in Cincinnati. These lands later appreciated as the city grew, not only making the Bank richer but also giving it posses-sion of a large part of the city. As a result immense resentment built against the National Bank and any politician who had been affiliated with or supported the bank (including Clay and William Henry Harrison) found himself in the political wilderness there throughout the 1820s.

The banking issue was only one of several that determined political allegiance in 1820s Ohio. Sometimes national issues intruded in state political debates, as happened during the Missouri Crisis of 1820–21. Clay's compromise unleashed a passionate response among large sections of the Ohio populace that felt that the compromise marked the growing power of the southern slave-owning elite, which further alienated Clay from voters in some areas. This was mitigated somewhat by Clay's staunch support for higher tariffs and federal money to make internal transportation improvements, both of which many Ohioans favored because they thought such policies would be good for the state's economic development. The state's representation in Congress was set to double as a result of the 1820 census, and considerable debate ensued over how the new congressional districts would be apportioned. On the whole, though, personalities, ethnicity, regional origins of Ohio settlers, and local issues tended to predominate over national parties or issues, much as they had since Ohio's birth.

All of these things came to bear on perhaps the major state issues of the 1820s: the debates over how best to deal with improvements to Ohio's educational and transportation systems. Territories to the west began to organize and become states (Indiana joined the Union in 1816, Illinois in 1818, and Missouri in 1821), and many Ohio boosters began to fear that the westward movement that was gaining strength at the time might pass Ohio by unless the state could be made more attractive to settlers by improving internal infrastructure. Others believed Ohio's status and prestige were being hobbled by a hopelessly inadequate school system. Although the interests both groups of these boosters pursued were very different (and discussed in more detail in chapters 6 and 7) they turned out to coincide politically in 1825.

Ethan Allen Brown, a popular and forceful personality in state politics, had been a tireless advocate of building canals in Ohio while serving as governor from 1818–22 and convinced the Ohio General Assembly to form the Ohio Board of Canal Commissioners just before he resigned to take a U.S. Senate seat. (For his efforts, Brown is often referred to as the "Father of Ohio Canals.") Also during Brown's term in office, Ephraim Cutler, Caleb Atwater, and Nathan Guilford were launching their efforts to push the General Assembly for a mandatory property tax to support public education.

Both the canal initiative and the proposed public school law faced fierce opposition. Although counties through which the proposed canal would go tended to be enthusiastic about it, others—particularly those in central and western Ohio, where other possible routes to the canal were considered—were more likely to oppose the vast expenditures such a project would inevitably entail. Similarly, many Ohio residents believed that one needed only a rudimentary education to lead the agrarian life that prevailed in the state, and that the responsibility of attaining such knowledge ought to lay with the individual. In addition, a number of property-owners across the state—both large and small—balked at the idea of any kind of mandated property tax to support education. In what was a textbook case of the nineteenth-century political practice of "log-rolling" (legislators supporting different laws exchanging votes to ensure passage of both), the public education advocates and canal advocates agreed to support each other's bills, and both the canal and the school tax passed on February 4 and 5, 1825 respectively. These bills marked an important departure from Ohio's generally Jeffersonian, small-government past, and introduced improvements that would greatly change the state economically and socially.

Also changing the state politically was the continued flow of immigrants from all parts of the country. Whereas southerners had predominated in the early years of Ohio statehood and would continue to be a major force for years to come, their numbers began to be matched by settlers from the Mid-Atlantic states in Ohio's central region, and increased immigration from New England to the Western Reserve and other northern parts of the state (see chapter 6). Along with the social, ethnic, and religious diversity these new Ohioans brought, they also brought more political diversity. This was particularly true of erstwhile New Englanders in the Western Reserve. As became clear in the votes over canals and schools, these immigrants tended to be more likely to favor internal improvements and educational reform. They also tended to be more strongly opposed to slavery and the Black Laws and to favor social reform movements. When added in rising numbers to Ohio's already diverse population, they proved to be an increasingly important constituency of Ohio's body politic.

No election better exemplified the pluralistic nature of Ohio's population and the complexity of its political landscape than the 1824 presidential race. With no competing parties or incumbents on the ballot the race was one of the most wide-open in American history, and three different candidates received greater than 20 percent of Ohio's popular vote. Despite the relatively even split, the vote was not very evenly distributed. Four-fifths of Ohio counties gave one of the candidates an absolute majority over both of the others. The Western Reserve and the areas in the Southeast that also had significant New England representation went strongly for the New Englander John Quincy Adams. Those areas along the path of the proposed Ohio and Erie Canal and the National Road, as well as most areas settled predominantly by Virginians and Kentuckians, went for Henry Clay, a Kentuckian himself and vocal advocate of internal improvements. Those counties settled predominantly by Scots-Irish (Jackson's heritage) and those with a heavy Pennsylvania "Dutch" population tended to support Jackson, perhaps because he was seen to champion the economic interests and mirror the anti-British and anti-Yankee sentiments of these groups. In addition, the areas around Cincinnati—which might have been expected to favor Clay's policies on internal improvements—instead went with Jackson (who had not yet revealed his strong attitudes against internal improvements). Clay had been an outspoken advocate of the National Bank and Cincinnati still had much lingering resentment over the Bank of the United States' role in the aftermath of the Panic of 1819. In the end, a plurality of Ohioans voted for Clay, who in turn threw his support behind Adams when the House of Representatives decided the election. Voting on this was by state, and with ten of Ohio's fourteen congressmen casting their votes for Adams, Ohio's vote in the House went to the candidate who came in third there. Such irregularities as this, and Adams's subsequent appointment of Clay as Secretary of State in his new cabinet, led Jackson supporters to claim a "corrupt bargain" had been made, and they spent the next four years working to get their candidate elected in 1828.

Despite all the turmoil surrounding the election of 1824, only about a third of eligible Ohioans voted in this contest. Even so, change was occurring. Over the next few years the number of political meetings and conventions—from the ward to the state level—increased dramatically, particularly among Jacksonian Democratic-Republicans. Politicians increasingly began to see that in a population as pluralistic as Ohio's, organization and alliance building among disparate groups was the key to electoral success. The realignment that had begun during the election of 1824 continued as the often-Balkanized parts of the Ohio electorate began to coalesce into two major groups with national correlates: the generally strict-constructionist, limited-government, state's rights partisans of Andrew Jackson (the Democratic-Republicans), and the broad-constructionist, strong government, more nationally-oriented supporters of Henry Clay and his "American System" of economic development (the National-Republicans). By this time, the Democratic-Republican Party had begun to drop the "Republican" from its name and became simply the "Democratic Party" on the national level, while its supporters in the state referred to it as "The Democracy of Ohio." It boasted a multilevel organization from local clubs up to state conventions, and built on the gains it had made during the Election of 1824 among Ohio's rural base and Scots-Irish and German ethnic groups. The National-Republican Party that coalesced nationally around Henry Clay and John Quincy Adams was not as well organized on the state level in Ohio, but held its own local and state meetings and claimed significant numbers of adherents in the Western Reserve and along Ohio's canal corridors.

The Election of 1828 turned out to be a significant one for Ohio politics for several reasons. With a record 82.6 percent of Ohio's electorate turning out at the polls, it demonstrated the vastly increased interest and position that Ohio was taking in national political affairs. The fact that these voters had unified into two generally-well-defined political camps was an indication that the state's pluralistic population had been harnessed into a larger political division that would hold for a generation despite future massive additions to Ohio's population. Furthermore, although Jackson won the state, he did so with a bare majority of 51.6 percent of the vote, significantly less than his national majority, and would receive only 51.3 percent of the Ohio electorate in his re-election four years later. The closely divided nature of Ohio's political landscape and its beginnings as a crucial "swing-state" in national politics can be traced to the campaign of 1828. Although most Ohioans still may have had more interest in state and local politics they were starting to become a force to be reckoned with on the national level.

The "Toledo War"

One state issue that took on regional and even national implications was a boundary dispute with Michigan that resulted in the almost comical "Toledo War" of 1835–36. The Northwest Ordinance had drawn a line from the southern tip of Lake Michigan to Lake Erie as a northern boundary for its southern tier of prospective states. While faulty maps of the time seemed to indicate that this would give Ohio a boundary north of present-day Toledo, a trapper told the Constitutional Convention of 1802 that Lake Michigan projected farther south than generally thought. As this would deprive the new state of the potentially important transportation hub represented by the mouth of the Maumee River, the convention passed a proviso stating that—with Congressional approval—Ohio's northern boundary would run along a line from Lake Michigan's tip to the northernmost cape of Maumee Bay. Although Congress took no action at the time, Ohio political leaders considered the matter settled, and in December 1816 Ohio Surveyor-General Edward Tiffin commissioned William Harris to survey a line accordingly. Michigan Territorial leaders instead relied on a line run by John A. Fulton in 1818 that went according to the Northwest Ordinance. The area between the "Harris Line" and the "Fulton Line," also known as "The Toledo Strip," (see Figure 8.4) was about five miles wide to the west and eight miles wide on the east and amounted to 468 square miles. Both sides claimed the territory, and when Michigan began the process of applying for statehood in 1833, the issue flared up into a nearly three-year conflict.

At first, the "war" was fought mostly on paper, with both the Ohio Assembly and the Michigan Territorial legislature passing competing acts affirming their control over the contested strip and pressing legal challenges against the acts of the other. By early 1835, however, residents on both sides began harassing the others, and both Ohio governor Robert Lucas and acting Michigan territorial governor Stevens Mason had called out their militias and dispatched them to the area. Although the militias never clashed with each other, a few shots were fired at the rather grandly named "Battle of Phillips Corners" on April 26, 1835 (near the present-day Fulton County community of Lyons), by a posse of Michigan partisans over the heads of an Ohio surveying party before arresting several of them. The only bloodshed of the war came in July when a Michigan deputy sheriff attempted to arrest outspoken Ohio partisan Major Benjamin Stickney. In addition to being a fierce advocate of Ohio's claim in the matter, Stickney was fiercely straightforward in naming his children, calling his sons "One," "Two," and "Three" (and his daughters "First," "Second," etc.). As the deputy sheriff moved against his father, Two Stickney stabbed him in the leg with a penknife and then escaped back to Ohio in the ensuing brawl.

Even before these events had happened, though, the conflict had begun to draw unfavorable national attention and President Andrew Jackson decided to intervene. Although the opinion of his own attorney general was that the strip belonged to Michigan until Congress acted otherwise, this was apparently not what the president wanted to hear. With a national election only one year away, Jackson seemed to want to resolve the situation in such a way that would not antagonize Ohioans and make it easier for his vice president and hand-picked successor, Martin Van Buren, to win the toss-up state. Thus, he dispatched arbitrators to Toledo to present a compromise forbidding Michigan from interfering with Ohio surveying parties and allowing the residents of the area to choose their allegiance until Congress made a final decision on the matter. Although Governor Lucas complied, the sometimes-hotheaded "Boy Governor" Mason (who was twenty-one when the conflict started) refused, and the saber rattling continued from both sides.

By August a fed up Jackson removed the recalcitrant Mason, installing in his place as governor the more amenable John S. Horner. While this served to reduce tensions along the border, Horner was wildly unpopular and only two months later Michigan residents responded by drafting a constitution and electing Mason as governor of the new state. Congress refused to seat Michigan's representatives and in June of 1836 it passed a law allowing Michigan to become a state only if they ceded the Toledo Strip. In exchange for this loss Michigan would receive instead what is now the Upper Peninsula. A territorial convention initially rejected the offer, but the expenses from the "war" had left the territory nearly bankrupt and political leaders realized that

Michigan would fail to collect a large sum of money that Jackson was going to distribute from the dismantled Bank of the United States if they were not officially a state. A second convention at Ann Arbor (known as the "Frostbitten Convention" because of the disagreeable weather at the time) reluctantly accepted the deal, losing Toledo, but gaining what would turn out to be more than 16,000 square miles of extremely mineral-rich territory in exchange.

Political Ascendance and its Problems

Although on its surface the "Toledo War" seems to be at best an amusing footnote of little lasting historical consequence, it is in fact a telling example of Ohio's growing political stature. "Never in the course of my life," stated congressman and former president John Quincy Adams early in the affair, "have I known a controversy of which all the right was so clearly on one side and all the power so overwhelmingly on the other." To the frustration of Adams and those people from Michigan who felt that they had a better case, political considerations seemed to be more important than strength of reason in the halls of power. Not only were congressmen from Illinois and Indiana—newer states whose boundaries lay even farther north than the Harris line and might have come into question if Michigan prevailed—on Ohio's side in the matter, but Ohio's two senators and nineteen congressional representatives had considerably more political clout in Washington than Michigan's lone non-voting delegate. These numbers would only increase after 1840, when the census of that year counted Ohio's population at more than 1.5 million: a whopping 62 percent increase from 1830 that garnered Ohio two more congressmen and gave Ohio's delegation nearly 9.5 percent of the total House membership, its highest proportion either before or since except for the South-boycotted congresses of the Civil War. (By way of comparison, in 2010 Texas's 32 congressmen made up 7.4 percent of the House, and New York's 29 made up 6.7 percent).

As if to drive the point home, the same year that the "Toledo War" ended, Ohio played its most significant role to date in an American presidential race. Fearing that no single candidate would be able to compete with Andrew Jackson's hand-picked successor Van Buren running for the well-organized and established Democratic Party, the new Whig Party decided to try several "favorite son" candidates to win enough electoral votes regionally to deprive Van Buren of a majority and throw the election into the House of Representatives. This strategy was not as big of a gamble as it might appear in retrospect: after all, a similar outcome had occurred just a dozen years earlier when John Quincy Adams and Henry Clay had become president and secretary of state, respectively. Although early electioneering focused on Massachusetts senator Daniel Webster in the North and Tennessee senator Hugh Lawson White in the South, by the middle of 1836 a groundswell of support rallied around Ohio's favorite son: William Henry Harrison. Harrison ended up with the support of most northern state nominating conventions as well as those of three border states. Although the Whig strategy failed and Van Buren won the election, Harrison was by far the most successful Whig

Figure 8.6 The election of William Henry Harrison in 1840 demonstrated just how far Ohio had come politically in just a few decades. Not just a resident of Ohio, Harrison achieved his fame in the state as a Major General during the War of 1812. This campaign ribbon touts his military credentials as the "Hero of Tippecanoe, Fort Meigs, and Thames."
Source: Courtesy of the Ohio Historical Society (Om1427_1534367_001)

candidate, taking nearly 37 percent of the popular vote and 75 percent of the votes cast for Whig candidates.

When the election of 1840 approached the Whigs closed ranks around Harrison (see Figure 8.6) at their first national convention in 1839. With the country in the grips of a depression and Van Buren highly unpopular, the Whigs felt they had a good chance to seize the presidency, and they took a page out of the Jacksonian playbook by touting Harrison ("Old Tippecanoe") as a humble frontiersman and hero of the War of 1812. Harrison actually came from a distinguished Virginia family, but his supporters took what was supposed to be a Democratic attack on Harrison's supposed provincial uncouthness and turned it into the centerpiece of the famous "Log Cabin and Hard Cider" campaign, one that took American presidential electioneering to new (albeit low) levels. Contrasting Harrison's putative everyman status with Van Buren's alleged luxurious lifestyle, Whig supporters would chant such rhymes as "Old Tip he wore a homespun coat, he had no ruffled shirt-wirt-wirt, But Matt he has the golden plate, and he's a little squirt-wirt-wirt!" The song "Tippecanoe and Tyler too," written by Zanesville Whig

Alexander Coffman Ross and sung at Whig events all across the country, became one of the most famous in American electoral history. When election day finally arrived, a record turnout gave Harrison a solid six-point margin of victory and an electoral landslide. His inaugural speech in March 1841 was the longest in history, delivered by the hatless and coatless sixty-eight year old during a winter storm. The stress this caused to his system probably contributed to the pneumonia that killed him only a month into office. Although serving the shortest and most undistinguished tenure of any president, Harrison's election was an example of just how much Ohio had become central to American politics—the state had sent its adopted son to the White House, the first of eight presidents (to date) to call Ohio home.

Harrison's electoral success also reflected the growing power of his Whig Party in the state. A strong anti-Jackson faction had not kept Old Hickory from posting narrow wins in the state in 1828 and 1832, but the National-Republican faction had elected Allen Trimble to the governorship in 1826 and 1828, and War of 1812 hero Duncan McArthur in 1830. It was from this base that the new Whig Party not only delivered the state for presidential candidate Harrison in both 1836 and 1840, but also elected Joseph Vance as the first Whig governor in 1836. By the 1840s the Whigs had taken a slight edge in Ohio's closely contested political landscape, taking all but one of the five gubernatorial elections of the decade and pushing through a set of legislation that that reflected the national party's pro-business, pro-internal improvement ethos, particularly after taking both houses of the General Assembly in 1845. One major item on the Whig agenda was to bring order to the disruptions in the banking system came into being when Andrew Jackson killed the Second Bank of the United States in the 1830s. They achieved victory in this area with the Kelley Bank Law of 1845 (see chapter 7). Similarly, the Whigs sought to improve Ohio's educational system by passing the Ohio School Law of 1848, expanding statewide Akron's successful reform of their public schools the year before (see chapter 6). Although the Whig Party had made some poor choices—particularly regarding unwise loans of public money in unsuccessful private transportation projects (see the "Plunder Law" discussed in chapter 7) and an 1848 gerrymandering apportionment scheme that for the first time attempted to divide counties—it was generally successful both at the ballot-box and in implementing major points of its agenda of improvement and reform. At the time, Whig supporters may have been forgiven for thinking that theirs was the party of Ohio's future.

Sectional Politics and the End of the Second Party System

Somewhat lost in the rousing songs and parades of the log cabin and hard cider campaign that launched a decade of Whig success was another important change that the election of 1840 represented. Former Cincinnati resident James Birney, candidate of the relatively obscure abolitionist Liberty Party, polled a mere 6,737 votes, or three-tenths of 1 percent of the country's overall total. Yet in this moment of the Whig Party's ascendance, Birney's very place on the ballot represented the beginning of a change that would ultimately shake the American political system to its foundation and destroy Ohio's Whig Party.

The Liberty Party chose him as its nominee again in 1844, picking former Ohio Senator Thomas Morris from Clermont County as his vice-presidential running mate. The party showed a nine-fold improvement on its 1840 results, and although the 62,103 votes it received were only 2.3 percent of the total, the Birney-Morris ticket took enough of New York's vote that many at the time felt it threw the state and the closely-contested national election to Democrat James K. Polk, an ardent advocate for territorial expansion and the extension of slavery.

The effects of the Liberty Party on Ohio politics were far out of proportion to its relatively paltry numbers and represented the beginnings of a seismic shift in state and national politics. Although the Whigs may have held a slight advantage, the state was nearly evenly split between Democrats and Whigs. The four gubernatorial elections between 1842 and 1848, for example, were decided by an average margin of less than sixth-tenths of 1 percent (the 1848 election was so close the General Assembly had to examine the returns, Whig candidate Seabury Ford was declared the winner by 311 votes out of the nearly 300,000 cast). Thus, both parties believed the relatively small abolitionist vote held the balance of power in the state. In the presidential election of 1844 Ohio Democrats suffered because their national nominee, James K. Polk, favored the extension of slavery. As a result of this, and because the Whig Party took an uncompromising stand against extending slavery, Clay narrowly took the state but lost the election. The Ohio Whig Party at least thought it had successfully brought the antislavery vote to its side, but 1844 would be the last year in which a Whig presidential candidate would win the state of Ohio. Young Whig political activist John Sherman, just starting out on what would be a remarkable political career, remarked in 1847 that "[t]he question of slavery in the newly conquered territory, the relative influences of the North and South ... will, in my opinion, break down the old parties and build up new ones, divided by different principles and led by different men." Sherman proved to be prescient. Polk's policies and their repercussions made Ohio one of the first states to suffer the disruption to the party system that would soon engulf the nation.

The admission of Texas in the waning days of the Tyler administration and the Polk administration's pursuit of war with Mexico to gain land in the southwest set off a national debate over the extension of slavery. Although 7,000 Ohioans volunteered to serve in the Mexican-American War (nearly 10 percent of the total number of U.S. volunteers, most of whom ended up in Zachary Taylor's command) the state was split over the war, with many especially in the northern part of the state tending to oppose "Mr. Polk's War." The Wilmot Proviso, a congressional proposal to ban slavery from any new lands acquired from Mexico, divided the country and both of its national parties. Ohio Democrats and Whigs alike tended to oppose the extension of slavery, with Ohio's Whig congressional delegation voting unanimously for the proposal (which some scholarship indicates was originally a proposal by Ohio Democrat Jacob Brinkerhoff). Any antislavery credibility that might have accrued to Ohio Whigs on this issue, though, was dispelled by the national Whig Party's selection of the southerner and large slaveholder Zachary Taylor as its candidate for president in 1848. Ohio Whigs watched in dismay as abolitionist and antiextension forces in the state started to coalesce under the banner of the new Free Soil Party. Although a fair number of Democrats and most Liberty Party followers would join this party on principle, the Free Soilers got their biggest boost from disaffected Whigs disgusted by Taylor's selection. Free Soilers instead backed former president Martin Van Buren in the election, and the party ran its own slate of state and local candidates as well under the slogan "Free Soil, Free Speech, Free Labor, and Free Men." As the Whigs had a larger share of the abolitionist and reformist-minded populace, they suffered more crippling defections to the new party than the Democrats, and the almost 11 percent of Ohio's vote that went to Van Buren was enough to swing the state to Democrat Lewis Cass and his 47 percent of the vote. Particularly telling was the vote in the heavily New England-influenced Western Reserve, an area key to Whig strength in the state. Van Buren actually outpolled Taylor there 15,869 to 14,528, allowing Cass to take the area with only 18,829 (38 percent of the vote). Whig loyalists were furious at the Free Soil defections, and although closely aligned ideologically with the new party, Whigs became openly hostile to it and adamantly refused to cooperate with it legislatively. This proved to be the undoing of the Whig Party in Ohio, and it presented an unlikely opportunity for the Free Soilers in the General Assembly.

Salmon P. Chase, James Birney's one time collaborator in Cincinnati, had been active in state's Liberty Party earlier in the decade, and became a major force among the Free Soilers by 1848. It was under his skillful political maneuvering that the new party managed to wield political clout out of proportion to its relatively small numbers. Neither the Whigs nor the Democrats had a majority in the General Assembly, which gave the handful of Free Soil representatives there the balance of power. They soon became experts at log-rolling to get key parts of their party agenda passed. With the Whig Party steadfastly hostile to the Free Soilers, Chase struck up an alliance with the Democratic Party to advance party objectives. These included not only getting Chase elected to the U.S. Senate, but also its most cherished goal on the state level: the repeal of many of the infamous Black Laws from the early statehood period. Given the deep and abiding ties between the Democratic Party and the Black Laws, this represented a major political coup for the new party. A bill pushed through in January 1849 repealed the immigration and testimony provisions of the 1807 law, as well as a later one that banned African Americans from public schools. (Other restrictions remained, however, including segregation provisions and prohibitions from voting and serving on juries. The last of these would not be rolled back until the 1880s). In return for these things, the Free Soilers agreed to support several Democratic objectives including patronage and apportionment measures. The most significant of these *quid pro quos*, though, was a move to revise the Ohio Constitution.

The Constitution of 1851

Critics had noted problems with Ohio's Constitution almost since its ratification, and several early governors had called for revisions—particularly to its judicial provisions. According to the first State Constitution, the Ohio Supreme Court had to convene at least once in every county every year. While this may have seemed like a minor inconvenience when the document was drafted in 1802 and Ohio had only nine counties, the state doubled that number in its first year of existence, and the court's docket became increasingly difficult to maintain. Unfortunately, the original constitution allowed only one method of amendment: rewriting the document at a state constitutional convention called by two-thirds of the legislature and approved by the people, which was an extremely difficult thing to achieve in such a politically fractious state. By 1818, with fifty-three counties already formed and more due to come, the legislature initiated a referendum on holding a constitutional convention, but the electorate voted it down by a five-to-one margin. Despite repeated calls from governors and judges, the issue remained on the back burner for another generation.

By 1848 the situation had become increasingly untenable. One observer called the court a "flying express running a tilt against the wind on a trial of speed" in its effort to meet in all of the then eighty-five counties every year. In addition to these issues with the judiciary, other perceived constitutional deficiencies drew increasing fire. The ultimate legislative supremacy, which may have seemed like a good idea in 1802 to Ohioans with fresh memories of Governor St. Clair's use of executive power, had lost some of its luster in the years that followed. In an effort to expand transportation in the state, the General Assembly had contracted massive amounts of debt in aiding private railroad and turnpike enterprises, many of which had since gone bankrupt. Furthermore, as the body in charge of most appointive offices and apportionment, the General Assembly had made many state offices spoils-system rewards and was constantly gerrymandering legislative districts to favor whichever party held power. In 1848 for the first time it split counties in the process. For all of these reasons, popular sentiment increasingly called for a constitutional convention. Whereas Whig legislators had been able to block earlier attempts, the Free Soil power brokers in the House voted with the Democratic plurality to put the issue on the ballot, and almost three-quarters of Ohio's voters approved the measure in the state elections of October 1849.

The convention convened in Columbus in May 1850 and deliberated there until a cholera outbreak in July prompted it to reconvene in Cincinnati that December. The convention had a solid Democratic majority, but this seeming dominance was deceptive given the often class-based divisions within the party. Minority Whigs and Free Soilers were able to work with these Democratic factions to achieve some of their ends, including a mandate for state-supported and efficient public schools. Farmers and lawyers led the list of occupations of delegates, with a scattering of other professions but few from the artisan class. In a telling example of Ohio's relative youth as a state and explosive growth over previous years, fewer than 30 percent of the delegates had been born in the state.

The document created by the convention significantly restructured the Ohio judicial system. It added a new justice to the Supreme Court and dropped the requirement that it meet in every county annually. To help with the ever-increasing caseload of the growing state, it added a new system of district courts of appeal between the Supreme Court and the Common Pleas Courts, and it restored an earlier system of county probate courts. Many of the reforms in the new constitution reined in the powers of the legislature from its previous, near-total control of state government. To the delight of Jacksonian Democrats, who had long been suspicious of public debt and government funding for internal improvements, the new constitution greatly curtailed the state's powers in these areas. It set the state's debt ceiling at $750,000, and forbade it to incur any debt for internal improvements, to lend its credit to any company, to become a stockholder or part owner of any business, or to make any special laws of incorporation. The Constitutional Convention sought to limit the legislative branch in other ways, too. It circumscribed the General Assembly's power to divide and create counties and confer banking powers, requiring the approval of the people for these acts (as a result, Ohio made no new counties after the addition of Noble, its eighty-eighth and last, in 1851). It also required the legislature to tax all property at the same rate. The legislature also lost many of its appointive powers, with all major state and county offices and judgeships thereafter to be elected by the people, including the new offices of attorney general and lieutenant governor. In hopes of limiting legislation, the convention moved from annual to biennial elections, with the thought that the General Assembly would meet only once every two years as well.

Although it stripped the legislative branch of some of its power, the new constitution did not radically change the balance of power between the branches of government. It reapportioned most of the powers taken from the legislature to the people, not to the executive or judicial branches. The governor no longer faced term limits and did acquire some important appointment and pardoning abilities, but the chief executive still had considerably less power than counterparts in most other states—despite heated debate on the subject, the constitution still failed to provide the governor with a veto. Similarly, the people now elected Supreme Court justices, and to shorter five-year terms. While the final document moved the state in a more democratic direction, two provisions that might have radically widened suffrage were soundly defeated. A motion to allow African Americans to vote ultimately failed in the convention by a vote of 13 to 75, and a clause allowing women's suffrage suffered an even greater (7 to 72) defeat. In contrast, delegates also debated two measures to ban further African American immigration to the state and deport all current black residents in Ohio to Africa at state expense, both of which received considerably more votes than the suffrage provisions before they, too, failed. James Loudon, delegate from Brown County, speaking in defense of one of these measures, said that his constituents "believe[d] with the fathers of this State—the pioneers of 1802, when they drew up the constitutions under which we are now assembled, that this should be a State for the white man, and the white man only." Clearly, despite the repeal of the Black Laws and the general sentiment of Ohioans against the extension of slavery, the new Constitution and the debates over it showed that the state continued to be unwelcoming of African Americans in many places.

Although born in part from political and economic issues that were quite contemporary, the Constitution of 1851 was in many ways still a backward-looking document. It made little provision for, and in some ways actually hindered, the new economic order that was already in evidence from the market and transportation revolutions. It maintained a predominantly Jeffersonian-Jacksonian agrarian outlook politically, socially, and economically; as such it became the subject of vigorous debate almost from the moment it was adopted. Unlike the Constitution it replaced, however, the new document provided not only an amendment process but also the ability to call a constitutional convention every twenty years. These gave Ohioans much greater flexibility to deal with emergent issues over time, and they have played a large role in Ohio's political history ever since. Although amended more than 150 times since its approval, the Constitution of 1851 is still the fundamental law of the state.

The process of negotiating and adopting the Constitution of 1851 highlighted the many transitions Ohio faced at the time. Economically, the debates over funding of internal improvements and government's role in business reflect that fact that Ohio was poised to become one of the largest manufacturing states in the Union as well as one of its most important transportation hubs. Politically, the breakdown of the party system that allowed the constitutional convention to occur in the first place was an early sign of a more general political crisis and disintegration of the two-party system that would soon shake, and even tear apart, the nation. Socially, Ohio's ascendance to the third largest state in the country brought with it continuing debates over how it would integrate its burgeoning and still-pluralistic population. As the incipient geographic center of the United States, Ohio would soon also be at the center of the upheavals the nation would confront in the 1850s and 1860s.

Further Reading

There is an abundance of works on Ohio Politics in the early nineteenth century including: *Lest We Be Marshall'd: Judicial Powers and Politics in Ohio, 1806–1812* by Donald Melhorn Jr. (2003. Akron: University of Akron Press); Daniel J. Ratcliffe's *Party Spirit in a Frontier Republic: Democratic Politics in Ohio, 1793–1821* (1998. Columbus: Ohio State University Press) and *The Politics of Long Division: The Birth of the Second Party System in Ohio, 1818–1828* (2000. Columbus: Ohio State University Press); Stephen Middleton's *The Black Laws: Race and the Legal Process in Early Ohio* (2005. Athens: Ohio University Press); and *The Triumph of Sectionalism: The Transformation of Ohio Politics, 1844–1856* by Stephen E. Maizlish (1983. Kent: Kent State University Press). For an overview of Ohio politics in general Michael F. Curtin's *The Ohio Politics Almanac* provides a helpful reference (2006. 2d ed. Kent State University Press). There are also many books that discuss Ohio and the War of 1812, including: Donald R. Hickey's Bicentennial Edition of *The War of 1812: A Forgotten Conflict* (2012. Champaign: University of Illinois Press), David Edmunds's *The Shawnee* Prophet (1985. Lincoln: University of Nebraska Press, 1985), and *Tecumseh and the Quest for Indian Leadership* also by David Edmunds (2006. 2d ed. New York: Pearson Longman).

9

Ohio Must Lead!

The Civil War and Reconstruction

Historians of the American Civil War often point to July 1863 as the major military turning point. Over the first three days of the month, the largest battle of the war ended in victory for the Union cause at Gettysburg. Helping seal the victory was the defeat of a major Confederate assault against the center of the Union lines on July 3, when a devastating rain of artillery weakened the right flank and the 8th Ohio Infantry jumped from concealed picket positions hundreds of yards in front of Union lines and collapsed the Confederate left end with a withering line of fire and a flanking maneuver. Elsewhere that day, George Armstrong Custer neutralized a threat to the rear of Union lines when he led a mounted charge of the 1st Michigan Cavalry against the Confederate Army's most celebrated cavalry unit. His brigade lost 257 men—the most of any Union cavalry brigade at the battle—but it broke the Confederate assault. That same day almost 700 miles away near Tullahoma, Tennessee, Gen. William Rosecrans completed his masterful campaign that drove the Confederates from central Tennessee with a minimal number of casualties. The turning point of this campaign had been a few days earlier when Union Gen. August Willich and Gen. Alexander McCook took and held Liberty Gap and other Union forces including the 9th Ohio Infantry—Ohio's first regiment of three-year enlistees and among the first primarily German units mustered into service—held nearby Hoover's Gap against an assault by Confederate Gen. Bushrod Rust Johnson's men. The day after Rosecrans's victory, the city of Vicksburg, Mississippi surrendered to Ulysses S. Grant after a prolonged siege executed by his trusted corps commanders, Maj. Gen. William T. Sherman and Maj. Gen. James B. McPherson and supported by ironclad gunboats on the river including the *Benton*, commanded by James Greer. When Port Hudson surrendered four days later to Union forces led in part by Division Commanders Godfrey Weizel and Halbert Paine, the Union controlled the entire Mississippi River, effectively cutting the Confederacy in half. On July 11, the Union struck at the very heart

Ohio: A History of the Buckeye State, First Edition. Kevin F. Kern and Gregory S. Wilson.
© 2014 John Wiley & Sons, Inc. Published 2014 by John Wiley & Sons, Inc.

of the secession itself, making an unsuccessful assault against the Charleston Harbor fortifications commanded by Confederate Gen. Roswell Ripley. A week later, in a move symbolic of the larger issues that surrounded the war, the Union attacked again, led by the 54th Massachusetts, one of the first African American regiments mustered in the Civil War. There would still be nearly two years of hard fighting ahead, but in July 1863 the Confederacy had received a series of blows from which it would never recover.

July 1863 was also a significant month in the war for Ohio. Although Pickett's famous charge on the third day of Gettysburg has often been called the "High Water Mark of the Confederacy," the real one—at least geographically speaking—was in Ohio. John Hunt Morgan—in part to show Confederate resolve in the face of the losses at Gettysburg, Vicksburg, and Tullahoma—crossed the Ohio River into Indiana, and then commenced to lead a prolonged raid, entering Ohio on July 13 and tearing through the southern part of the state for almost two weeks. He lost most of his force at the Battle of Buffington Island on the Ohio River (against forces that included future presidents Rutherford Hayes and William McKinley) before turning north with the remnants of his force. He finally surrendered after one last skirmish near Salineville in Columbiana County on July 26. Apart from setting the Ohio countryside into an uproar, it was the northernmost engagement by a regular Confederate unit in the entire war. While this was happening, Clement Vallandigham, the outspoken leader of Ohio's antiwar Peace Democrats ("Copperheads" to their enemies), made his way to Canada, just months after President Lincoln had ordered him exiled to the Confederacy. Arriving at the Clifton House of Niagara Falls on July 15, he formally accepted "The Ohio Democracy's" nomination to run *in absentia* as the official Democratic candidate for governor. Ohioans were far from united around the cause of the Civil War, and less than a week after Vallandigham made his announcement the Cincinnati Chamber of Commerce expelled thirty-three members for refusing to take an oath of allegiance to the United States. Elsewhere in the state, noted African American abolitionist and Oberlin graduate John Mercer Langston was recruiting soldiers for the 127th Ohio Volunteer Infantry, Ohio's first official African American unit. Langston was a talented recruiter, having gathered 158 Ohio soldiers for the 54th Massachusetts unit that was fighting in South Carolina, and 222 Ohioans for the 55th, its sister regiment. Governor David Tod had authorized the creation of the 127th (later designated the 5th U.S. Colored Troops, see Figure 9.1) in mid-June, and by July they were beginning to muster at their camp in Delaware. In Cleveland, the women of the Soldier's Aid Society of Northern Ohio organized a benefit dinner for nearly 400 soldiers at Camp Cleveland Military Hospital on July 4, and collected hundred of boxes of food, bedding, clothes, washing supplies, books and other goods for distribution to soldiers over the next few weeks. At the end of the month, the brig *J. H. Harmon* was loading oil in what the *Daily Cleveland Herald* was calling the beginning of an "oil line" directly between Cleveland and Europe. "The oil trade of Cleveland has already attained great importance," stated the *Herald*, no doubt referring in part to the new business of Andrews, Clark & Co. that had already become the largest oil refiner in the city. The "& Co." in the name of the business referred to their third partner, a man named John Davison Rockefeller who had just turned twenty-four.

This sample of activities during one month illustrates Ohio's deep involvement in the Civil War and how thoroughly the war affected Ohio society. Ohio proved to be critical to

Figure 9.1   When the government allowed African Americans to serve in uniform in early 1863, Ohio initially hesitated recruiting its own black units. Through the efforts of noted African American abolitionist and Oberlin graduate John Mercer Langston, more than 150 black Ohioans (including some who had served in the "Black Brigade" in 1862) joined the first black regiments: the 54th and 55th Massachusetts. Finally, in the summer of 1863 Governor Tod authorized the creation of the 127th Ohio Volunteer Infantry (later designated the 5th U.S. Colored Troops). This photo shows the unit at its training base in Delaware, Ohio.
Source: Courtesy of the Ohio Historical Society (Om1277_781147_123)

the Union's success. Every person mentioned by name in the first paragraph of this chapter—including the Confederate generals Johnson and Ripley—came from Ohio, as of course did the men of the 8th and 9th Ohio Volunteer Infantry and many of the men of the 54th Massachusetts. In all, Ohio sent nearly 347,000 troops to the Union, the third highest of any state, and nearly 35,000 died from battle wounds or disease. Back in Ohio, the war came home in a very literal sense with Morgan's raid, but the conflict had already made a significant impact upon Ohio, sweeping before it Ohio's politics, economy, and society and leaving the lives of all Ohioans forever changed. Through Grant, Hayes, Garfield, McKinley, and Rockefeller it also set the stage for Ohio's future political and economic dominance.

Ohio and Sectional Conflict

The Compromise of 1850 temporarily resolved the issue of the expansion of slavery that had been lingering since the end of the Mexican-American War. By granting concessions to both Northern and Southern sides, Henry Clay and his supporters hoped to defuse sectional tensions that threatened to tear the country apart. However, any hope that Clay's effort would succeed soon dimmed. The most unpopular provision of the Compromise in the North was the enhanced Fugitive Slave Law that required citizens to help federal authorities apprehend runaway slaves and harshly penalized those that aided them. Abolitionists in Ohio and elsewhere were incensed at what they called the "Kidnap Law," and vowed to defy it. The act moved abolitionist Harriet Beecher Stowe—whose seventeen years in Cincinnati as a Lane Seminary professor's wife had provided her with ample first-hand experience with the plight of escaped slaves—to write the novel *Uncle Tom's Cabin* as a series of installments for former Ohio abolitionist editor Gamaliel Bailey's *National Era*. When she published it in book form in 1852 it became an immediate hit, selling 300,000 copies in its first year and was on its way to becoming the best-selling American novel of the nineteenth century. Some of the most dramatic action in the book takes place in Ohio, especially Eliza's escape with her child across the ice floes on the Ohio River and her subsequent near-capture by a slave hunter near a Quaker settlement in Ohio. Frankly melodramatic and intended to stir an emotional chord with Americans, the book and the numerous theatrical productions it inspired helped sway the opinion of many Northerners who had never before had strong feelings against slavery. To respond to critics who suggested she fabricated incidents in the book for dramatic effect, Stowe the next year published *Key to Uncle Tom's Cabin*, which listed the sources she used. Abraham Lincoln checked this book out of the Library of Congress just weeks before he decided to issue the Emancipation Proclamation. According to the later remembrance of one of Stowe's daughters, when Abraham Lincoln met Stowe in December 1862, he greeted her by asking, "Is this the little woman who made this great war?" Although the quote may be apocryphal and is obviously an overstatement, contemporary observers in both the North and the South and later historians have agreed that the book had a powerful impact in shaping public sentiment regarding slavery in the decade before the Civil War.

Although the Compromise of 1850 and *Uncle Tom's Cabin* stirred up segments of the population in the early 1850s, it was the Kansas–Nebraska Act of 1854 that shattered the American political system. Illinois Senator Stephen Douglas, a leader in the Democratic Party, wanted to clear the way to build the Transcontinental Railroad through the central part of the continent, but that would mean organizing new territories in an already highly-charged political climate. Douglas's solution was to organize the Kansas and Nebraska Territories using the principle of "popular sovereignty" on the slavery issue—in other words, letting the residents of the territory decide whether they would allow slavery or not. The act infuriated many northerners because it repealed the Missouri Compromise of 1820 by potentially allowing the expansion of slavery above a line that extended from the southern border of Missouri. Almost immediately proslavery and antislavery immigrants descended on Kansas with the intention of swaying the territory in their direction, igniting a years-long conflict that came to be known as "Bleeding Kansas." Among the most notorious participants of the conflict was former Hudson, Akron, and Kent resident John Brown who had moved to Kansas to join five of his sons in their struggle to make Kansas a free territory. Enraged by the "Sack of Lawrence" by proslavery forces and fearing an attack by some of them, on the night of May 24, 1856 Brown took a group of men along Pottawatomie Creek on a pre-emptive strike. The band stopped at the cabins of militant proslavery sympathizers, dragging five men out into the darkness to hack them to death with broadswords. A retaliatory raid against Brown's nearby antislavery settlement of Osawatomie killed his son Frederick, but Brown's spirited defense earned him the nickname "Osawatomie Brown" and even inspired a Broadway play by that name. The Kansas–Nebraska Act and the violence it inspired inflamed national passions and effectively destroyed the national party system. The Whig Party shattered over the issue, and many antislavery Northern Democrats left their party in protest.

When the Kansas–Nebraska Act shook the country's political foundations in 1854, Ohio had already developed an active alternative to the old party system. Ohio had been a harbinger of these events, its political system rocked in the late 1840s and early 1850s by the emergence of the Free Soil Party. Ohio voters favoring reform and opposing slavery initially split their votes between Free Soilers and Whigs, but the Free Soil Party had the momentum. Despite their ascendancy over much of the previous decade, by the late 1840s Whigs found themselves increasingly irrelevant in state politics and when they fielded their last gubernatorial candidate in 1853 he only received 30 percent of the vote. Adding to the chaos, the virulently anti-Immigrant and anti-Catholic American (or "Know Nothing") Party had emerged in the late 1840s and early 1850s. The party drew strength from residents where there had been considerable (and generally Democratic-leaning) immigration. The Free Soilers, antislavery "Conscience" Whigs, most Know-Nothings, and some anti-Kansas–Nebraska Act Democrats joined together at a convention on July 13, 1854 to form a new opposition to the state Democratic Party. Derisively (yet appropriately) named the "Fusionists" by its opponents, the new party immediately beat the Democrats with a landslide victory, sweeping Ohio's Congressional delegation with thirteen former Whigs, five anti-Nebraska Democrats, two former Free Soilers, and one professed Abolitionist. At a convention the following year, the Fusionists officially renamed themselves the Republican Party, bringing it in line with similar parties that had formed in other states. The Republicans nominated Salmon P. Chase for governor, and he and the other Republicans swept the statewide offices in 1855. Once in power, Chase and the Republicans passed antislavery legislation and improved education. Even the Panic of 1857 (discussed later) and a scandal at the state Treasury could not prevent Chase's re-election, although these did cause the Republicans to lose control of the General Assembly. Republican Treasurer William H. Gibson announced that summer that the treasury was missing $550,000 and could not make interest payments on state bonds. Further investigation revealed that his predecessor and brother-in-law Democrat John G. Breslin had embezzled the money and Gibson had given him time to try to repay it. The new Democratic-controlled Assembly established an independent State Treasury in response to the scandal. It was the last major victory Democrats would have in the state for a while.

Outside the state, Ohio became a foundation of the new national Republican Party. At its first national convention in 1856, it chose John C. Fremont as its presidential candidate over runner-up John McLean, a U.S. Supreme Court justice from Cincinnati who had also been a congressman and Postmaster General. In the general election, only New York gave Fremont more popular votes than Ohio, and Ohio provided Fremont with 20 percent of his electoral votes in his losing campaign against Democrat James Buchanan (Know-Nothing candidate Millard Fillmore ran a distant third and, after unsuccessfully running a candidate for the governorship the next year, the American Party in Ohio folded). This would start a string of fourteen straight presidential contests in which Ohio would vote for the Republican candidate. This also signaled the beginning of Ohio's importance to the Republican Party. As of 2012, no Republican had ever won the presidency without taking Ohio, and many of the party's most important leaders hailed from the state, especially in the 1800s.

Although the unraveling of the United States that culminated in the Civil War arose from many factors, Buchanan's decisions as president contributed materially to the crisis. Not without reason, Republicans (and some Democrats) called him a "doughface," a derisive term that by the late 1850s meant a Northern Democrat who bowed to the will of the Southern proslavery wing of the party. Before he took office on March 4, 1857, Buchanan had pushed for a broad decision in the extremely controversial Dred Scott Case that was before the Supreme Court and disingenuously said he would support the decision "whatever this may be." Dred Scott was a slave who had accompanied his owner, Maj. John Emerson, to U.S. Army posts in Illinois and the Wisconsin Territory. When Emerson died, Scott sued for his freedom arguing that his residence in free territories made him free. Two days after Buchanan's inauguration, the Supreme Court ruled against Scott in a 7–2 decision that held, among other things, that Scott as a slave and an African American had no legal right to bring a case to court or any rights "which the white man was bound to respect;" and that the Missouri Compromise was illegal because banning slavery from the territories violated Fifth Amendment property rights of slave owners. One of the two dissenting Justices was Ohioan John McLean, who strongly questioned Chief Justice Taney's reasoning, ultimately calling it "more a matter of taste than of law." Most Northerners were appalled at the implications of the decision: that slavery was by law a national institution and could be extended into all territories and perhaps even the free states. The decision also had negative economic consequences. Markets were already jittery as the end of the Crimean War overseas led to a sharp decline in the demand for American agricultural goods, which in turn lowered the value of land in the Western territories. The Dred Scott decision further lowered the value as concerns grew that the decision might lead to another round of "Bleeding Kansas"-type conflict in the territories. Finally, the last straw came when the Cincinnati-based Ohio Life Insurance and Trust Company went bankrupt in late August, leading to the Panic of 1857, a two-year depression that disproportionately affected the industrializing North. As if all this was not bad enough for the nation and Buchanan, the president then decided to flout the advice of his own territorial governor of Kansas and back the proposed state constitution drafted by proslavery Kansans at Lecompton over the free-state constitution created by the antislavery majority at Topeka two years earlier. Many Democrats in the north opposed the Lecompton Constitution and it went down to defeat, critically splitting the Democratic Party even further in the process.

These national events hardened the resolve of many in Ohio against federal laws regarding slavery. Activity on the Underground Railroad increased, and several escaped slave incidents became the subject of public note, none more heartbreaking than the case of Margaret Garner. Having escaped Kentucky to Cincinnati over the Ohio River, slave catchers caught up with her and her daughter at Mill Creek. Rather than return her daughter to slavery, she killed her with a butcher's knife (Toni Morrison used the case as inspiration for her 1988 Pulitzer-Prize winning novel *Beloved*). Perhaps the most celebrated event in the country during this period, though, was the Oberlin–Wellington Rescue and trials of 1858–59. John Price, an escaped slave from Kentucky, made his way up to the abolitionist college community of Oberlin, which welcomed him as an equal. Price felt relatively safe there and decided to stay for a while. In September 1858 a slave catcher identified him to a federal marshal who seized him and spirited him away to a hotel in the town of Wellington a few miles to the south with the intent of sending him back to his owner the next day. When the Oberlin community heard about the capture, a crowd of them—Oberlin students, professors, residents, and free blacks—dashed to Wellington, where they eventually fought their way into the hotel past Price's outnumbered captors and took Price back to Oberlin. Oberlin Professor of Moral Philosophy James Fairchild harbored Price until others took him to Canada a few days later. The flagrant violation of the Fugitive Slave Law resulted in 37 arrests on federal warrants, and in retaliation state authorities (then under the control of a Republican state government) arrested Price's captors—including the federal marshal—on charges of kidnapping. A jury of Democrats convicted two in April 1859: Simeon Bushnell (a white clerk and printer) and Charles Langston (a black schoolteacher, brother of abolitionist John Mercer Langston, and grandfather of famed poet Langston Hughes). Sentenced to sixty and twenty days in jail respectively and assessed fines and court costs, the two appealed to the Ohio Supreme Court on the grounds that the Fugitive Slave Law unconstitutionally restricted state's rights. Showing just how bitterly divided even Ohio's legal system was, the court ruled 3-2 against the suit on May 30. Justice Joseph Swan, personally opposed to slavery and a beneficiary of the Fusion Party sweep of 1854, cast the deciding vote on the grounds that to do otherwise would violate the supremacy clause of the Constitution. The decision cost him his political career. The Republicans refused to renominate him and he never served in elective office again. After negotiations among all parties, the federal government eventually dropped charges against the other unrepentant 35 rescuers (see Figure 9.2). Ohio similarly dropped the kidnapping charges against the captors. The local community greeted the rescuers as heroes upon their release from prison. Supporters of the rescue got a call to repeal of the Fugitive Slave Law into the Ohio Republican Party platform that Fall, much to the consternation of more moderate national Republican leaders like Abraham Lincoln. The case drew national attention and heightened tensions both north and south. Another event a few months later increased these tensions to a breaking point.

A few months after the Oberlin rescuers' release, John Brown, Jr. approached several of them about participating in his father's scheme to end slavery in the south once and for all. Two of them, Lewis Sheridan Leary and John A. Copeland, Jr. agreed, as did Shields Green, a runaway slave who was a newcomer to Oberlin. Brown intended his raid on the Federal Arsenal at Harpers Ferry, Virginia in October 1859 to lead to a slave revolt, local slaves rallying to collect arms and then spreading out to free surrounding slaves by force.

Figure 9.2 "Oberlin commenst this war, Oberlin wuz the prime cause uv all the trubble" wrote satirical writer David Ross Locke in the persona of Copperhead Petroleum V. Nasby. Oberlin had long been a hotbed of antislavery activism, but its involvement in the Oberlin–Wellington Rescue case drew even greater national attention, its participants lauded by sympathizers throughout the north and reviled by opponents of abolition throughout the south. Here the unrepentant rescuers pose at the Cuyahoga County Jail where they were held.
Source: Courtesy of the Ohio Historical Society (AL03156)

Instead, Brown and his men succeeded only in killing a few residents including the town mayor and a free black railroad worker before being cornered and eventually captured after a fight that killed Brown's son Oliver. The courts quickly convicted and hanged Brown, Leary, Copeland, and Green and the other surviving raiders. The event convinced many white Southerners that Northern abolitionism represented a dire threat, and contributed to the militarization of the South as state militias began to train in earnest to meet any future similar raids. In the North, both Democrats and Republicans alike criticized Brown's use of violence, but some Ohio radicals, particularly free blacks and the passionately antislavery communities of the Western Reserve, treated Brown and his men as martyrs to a higher cause. A sentence from Brown's final written statement—"I, John Brown, am now quite certain that the crimes of this guilty land will never be purged away; but with Blood"—served as a call to arms for both Southern secessionists and Northern abolitionists alike.

It was in this volatile atmosphere that the election of 1860 unfolded. The Republican Convention had no shortage of contenders, including Ohioans Salmon Chase and John

McLean. Nonetheless, Abraham Lincoln's national ascendancy since his 1858 debates with Stephen Douglas and the location of the convention in Chicago, Illinois, gave him the nomination on the third ballot, some of Ohio's Chase delegates switching their votes to help put him over the top. The Democrats were hopelessly split. When the convention in Charleston, South Carolina, refused to adopt an explicitly pro-slavery platform, the Deep South delegates walked out and the convention disintegrated. Another attempt in Baltimore resulted in the party officially splitting in two, with the Northern Democrats nominating Stephen Douglas and the Southern Democrats nominating John C. Breckinridge of Kentucky. Some remnant Southern Whigs and former Know-Nothings who felt they could support none of the candidates nominated John Bell of Tennessee for the Constitutional Union Party. Given the deep division in the Democratic Party, the result of the election was almost a foregone conclusion. Despite taking only 40 percent of the vote Lincoln won a majority in the Electoral College and the presidency. Ohio again was key to Republican chances: it gave Lincoln a clear majority among the four candidates, the third highest number of popular votes behind New York and Pennsylvania, and more votes than seven of the remaining fourteen states he took combined. For southerners, the election of a man who was not even on the ballot in most southern states was the final straw. Starting with South Carolina on December 20, one by one southern states began to secede from the Union. Buchanan, who believed secession was unconstitutional and also believed trying to stop it by force was unconstitutional, did nothing. Lincoln was determined to keep the country together, but by the time he took office in March 1861 eleven states had declared themselves a Confederacy independent of the United States. Then, at 4:30 in the morning on April 12, Confederate batteries opened fire on the Federal position at Fort Sumter in Charleston Harbor, starting what would be the four bloodiest years in U.S. history.

Ohio and the Civil War

The early war

Historians have called the Civil War "the first modern war" as this conflict, for the first time, pitted not just one army against another, but instead two societies against each other. Each society had massive numbers of soldiers that were supported by advances in telecommunications and also the infrastructure, weapons, and material improvements of the transportation and industrial revolutions. Hence, for the Union and the Confederacy, success demanded not only having enough soldiers who were well-trained, supplied, and ably led, but also high-quality political leadership, the ability to generate and mobilize economic resources, and citizens' willingness to support the war beyond the initial wave of enthusiasm.

Ohio was well-placed to contribute to the Union cause in such an endeavor. On the eve of war, Ohio ranked third in population, with 2,339,511 people, trailing only New York and Pennsylvania. More than 98 percent of Ohioans were white, but about 1.6 percent (36,673) were African American; the third largest black population of any northern state. Its economy was vibrant and diverse, yet it remained a state of small towns and farms. Over 82 percent of all Ohioans lived in rural areas, contributing to Ohio's leadership in the production of crops and livestock. The state ranked highest in horses, sheep, and wool, and second in corn, cheese, flax, milk cows, and total value of livestock. Ohio's industrial base had been growing and the war accelerated this trend. With over 3,000 miles of railroad track, Ohio led the nation. Railroads, which had supplanted the canals, prompted further industrial development and urbanization, especially at terminus points for shipping. These included Cincinnati, the largest of the western cities and the third most industrialized in the nation behind New York and Philadelphia, as well as fast growing Cleveland and Toledo. Railroads also helped to reorient trade out of Ohio. Before 1850, most of Cincinnati's shipments of flour went south down the Ohio River. However, by 1860 almost all of it went east, at a fraction of the cost. Ohio's economic role in linking the old Northwest to the Northeast enabled the political unification in the North around the Republican Party.

Yet as the crisis leading to the Civil War made clear, Ohio remained a divided state in several ways. Not only was it split along northern and southern regional lines, but also socially between immigrants and natives and blacks and whites. Women had been pushing for their own measure of equality, further adding to the complex situation. The divisions and tensions present in Ohio society could be seen in politics: as the Whigs faded Republicans emerged, and the Democrats split into proslavery and antislavery factions, which in turn became antiwar and prowar respectively.

All of this meant that despite the tremendous potential Ohio possessed for the Union cause, it would take a significant amount of work to keep the state on a war footing. The first governor to whom this task fell was Republican William Dennison, who had taken office in 1860. On the day after Fort Sumter fell, President Lincoln called for 75,000 volunteers for a three-month enlistment, 13,000 of them to come from Ohio. Cincinnati alone could have raised that number, and from all corners of the state more than 30,000 men offered themselves for service. Ohio's state militia had fewer men and armaments than any other in the North and Dennison had to scramble to arrange for lodging, uniforms, weapons, and other supplies for the eleven new military camps that sprang up virtually overnight. Enthusiasm turned to frustration for many of these men as days dragged into weeks with little activity. Adding to the chaos was the fact that men in volunteer units generally got to choose their own immediate officers and that the governor appointed higher-level officers, often more out of political rather than military considerations. To lead all of Ohio's units, Dennison's first choice was Irvin McDowell, but powerful political interests in Cincinnati prevailed upon him to choose Democrat George McClellan, a Pennsylvanian native working in the city as an executive for the Ohio and Mississippi Railroad. Although the appointment was politically motivated, McClellan had at least graduated near the top of his class at West Point, as had Delaware County native William Rosecrans who soon rose to Brigadier General under him.

Despite the early difficulties, Dennison displayed great ability in imposing order on the chaos and getting Ohio ready to fight. Only four days after Lincoln's call, the 1st and 2nd Ohio Volunteer Infantry regiments had already organized themselves in Columbus and Dennison immediately dispatched them to help defend Washington. Frustrated at the impediments and inefficiencies that hampered mobilization, Dennison took control of the railroads and express shipping companies to smooth military supply problems and commandeered the telegraph companies to aid in military communication and control the information leaving the state. In May 1861, on learning that the government was planning new, three-year enlistments that would become the bulk of the army, Dennison immediately telegraphed a request to fellow Ohioan and new Secretary of the Treasury Salmon Chase to get McClellan a three-year commission immediately "so as to make him rank over all others ... Ohio must lead throughout the war." Within days Chase wired back that they had made McClellan a Major General—ranking second only to army head Winfield Scott. At Dennison's urging, McClellan ordered troops across the Ohio River into western Virginia to aid the loyalists there, to secure Ohio's river border with the state, and to control important railway lines. It was in this way that Ohio's soldiers came to participate in the war's first planned land engagement, the Battle of Philippi, easily chasing Confederate forces twenty-five miles south in what the Northern press called "The Philippi Races." With 20,000 men in western Virginia by the end of June, McClellan had secured the border and the railroads. His units under Rosecrans then decisively defeated the Confederates at Rich Mountain and Corrick's Ford, and secured the Kanawha Valley by November, clearing the entire western region of Virginia and allowing these counties to secede from the state in the process of becoming the new state of West Virginia, officially admitted to the Union in 1863. This campaign proved to be one of the few bright spots for the Union early in the war, as the Confederates defeated Union armies at Bull Run in northern Virginia in July. Looking for success, Lincoln called McClellan up to be the top commander of Union armies in the east. After Bull Run, Lincoln called for 500,000 more volunteers, and Ohio once again oversubscribed the state's quota: the government asked for 67,000 and 77,000 Ohioans answered the call. Dennison had proved to be prophetic: Ohio was indeed leading.

For all his success, Dennison had made some powerful enemies in getting Ohio on a war footing. People he had passed over for political appointments held grudges, and others considered his taking over of the railroads and telegraphs as tantamount to dictatorship. He also angered many Democrats with his outspoken opposition to the Fugitive Slave Law and his loud denunciations of Peace Democrats. Popular calls to support the Union regardless of party grew louder. Thus, when the 1861 gubernatorial election approached the Ohio Republican Party abandoned Dennison and cut a deal with prowar Democrats to nominate Youngstown-area industrialist Democrat David Tod on a new Union Party ticket. Tod received almost 58 percent of the vote in the fall election, and set to work in 1862 continuing Dennison's efforts to keep Ohio mobilized.

These endeavors went into high gear when Confederate Gen. Kirby Smith invaded Kentucky in September and dispatched Gen. Henry Heth to menace Cincinnati. The Union army sent Gen. Lewis Wallace to defend the city, where he declared martial law and asked for help. Governor Tod put out the call for able-bodied men to come to aid in Cincinnati's defense immediately and at the expense of the state government. The response was overwhelming, and the thousands of these civilian-clad "squirrel hunters" soon outnumbered the soldiers, forcing Tod to put a halt to his call. The volunteers built fortifications and batteries around the city, some of which still exist. Among the builders

Figure 9.3 When Confederate General Kirby Smith's forces threatened Cincinnati in September 1862, Governor Tod called for all available men to help defend the city; and thousands of "squirrel hunters" flocked there from throughout the state. Cincinnati's African American men were unable to join the militia or the army because of their race, but local police rounded up 700 of them and pressed them into service as a quasi-military unit building fortifications. This "Black Brigade," as it became known, was among the earliest organized groups of African Americans in the Union war effort.
Source: Courtesy of the Ohio Historical Society (SA 4605 E2)

of these works were the men of the "Black Brigade" of local African Americans organized into a quasi-military unit (see Figure 9.3). Although they were not yet allowed to bear arms, this unit marked one of the first organized uses of African Americans for the war effort. When Smith's Army left Kentucky in mid-September, the state sent the squirrel hunters home with certificates honoring their service.

The enthusiasm of the squirrel hunters and the over-subscription of Ohio's military quotas points to the general support that most Ohioans had for the war. However, opposition grew as the war progressed in 1862, with casualties growing, the Confederacy intact, and the fate of the Union hanging in the balance. Through early 1862 Ohioans had suffered relatively few casualties. That changed as action heated up in the western theater where most Ohio troops had been sent. The Union Army of the Tennessee under the command of Maj. Gen. Ulysses S. Grant of Point Pleasant, Ohio, and the Army of the Ohio, led by Maj. Gen. Don Carlos Buell of Lowell, Ohio, had been making progress south through Kentucky and Tennessee. On April 6 and 7, though, Confederates mounted a surprise attack on Grant's forces at Shiloh, Tennessee, with those under the command of Lancaster's William Tecumseh Sherman bearing the brunt of the initial assault. Grant and Sherman, aided by Buell's army, repulsed the attack, but not before sustaining 13,047 casualties, some 2,000 of whom were Ohioans. It had been the first major combat experience for Ohio's soldiers and the costliest battle thus far. Newspapers in Ohio reported that many Ohio soldiers fled at the first sign of battle (many had), and criticized Grant, spreading rumors that he was drunk in battle, and calling on Lincoln to fire him. In response, Lincoln is said to have claimed, "I can't spare this man; he fights!" Governor Tod organized a relief expedition to aid the soldiers at Shiloh, with eleven steamboats sending doctors, nurses, and supplies, paid for mainly by state finances, with additional money coming from private donations and the forerunner to the Red Cross, the U.S. Sanitary Commission (a relief organization created in 1861 to coordinate the volunteer efforts of women who wished to contribute the war effort). Ohio's first branch organized in Cleveland in April 1861 and the one in Cincinnati was among the most active in the North. Among those nurses at Shiloh was Mary Bickerdyke of Knox County, who spent the war traveling with various Union armies, often risking her life to search for wounded soldiers and provide them aid. She established more than 300 field hospitals throughout the war and earned the nickname "Mother Bickerdyke" for her care and concern. After the war, she fought for pensions for male veterans and female nurses, not earning her own until the 1880s. Among the thousands of female nurses was Lucy Webb Hayes, wife of Rutherford B. Hayes, who traveled three times to the battlefield to tend to her husband and also help other wounded soldiers.

After Shiloh, the remainder of 1862 saw progress for the Union in the western theater, but more frustration in Virginia. There McClellan launched a campaign up the peninsula between the James and York Rivers towards the Confederate capital of Richmond. However, Confederate forces under Robert E. Lee halted the Union advance, and later in August Lee and his Army of Northern Virginia defeated the Yankees at the Second Battle of Bull Run (Second Manassas). Lee then made an advance north into Maryland and McClellan shadowed him, keeping the Army of the Potomac between Lee and Washington, D.C. McClellan finally met Lee in Maryland at Antietam (Sharpsburg), September 16–18. It proved to be the bloodiest single day battle in American history, with some 23,000 casualties. It ended in a tactical draw, as McClellan had defended Washington but Lee escaped back into Virginia. It was enough, though, to give President Lincoln the confidence to issue the Emancipation Proclamation to become effective January 1, 1863. The Proclamation declared slaves in areas still in rebellion free. It did not apply to border states or areas controlled by Union troops.

With the Emancipation Proclamation, the Union army became the "agent of emancipation" and linked the Union with abolition. It was a major transformation. Initially a war solely to preserve the Union, the Civil War now became one that would alter Southern society—and thereby the whole nation—and broaden the concept of liberty and freedom to include African Americans. During 1862 the issue of race and the war had become more pronounced. Initially, Lincoln appealed to the North's free labor beliefs as he worked to gather support for the war, but he steered clear of making the war one to end slavery. By the summer of 1862 Lincoln's views and those of many of his military commanders had shifted. In military terms, Lincoln and others understood that the South possessed some 4 million slaves that contributed to the Confederate cause; hence removing these laborers would deprive the enemy of substantial resources. There were political risks to making the war about freeing the slaves, which threatened unity on the home front and perhaps Republican chances for re-election, including Lincoln's in 1864. Blacks, meanwhile, had already been calling the Civil War the "freedom war" and as Union armies moved into the South, slaves by the thousands had come over to Union lines. Northern whites, however, remained divided over the war's progress, and the conscious injection of ending slavery into the war's purpose threatened to fracture Northern white support. Slowly, though, the war's purpose in the North shifted. The announcement of the Emancipation Proclamation followed a speech by Lincoln earlier in the year in which he urged Congress to support gradual, compensated emancipation in the border states. In July 1862, Congress approved the Second Confiscation Act, which allowed for the confiscation of Confederate property, and declared slaves who crossed into Union lines "captives of war" and forever free. When Lincoln signed the Proclamation on January 1, 1863, it allowed for the systematic recruiting of black soldiers who had previously been denied service in the military. By the war's end, some 5,000 black Ohioans had served for the Union. Also in 1863, the initial surge of volunteers had ebbed, and so Congress approved a national draft law in March. Lincoln also called state militias into service for one hundred days in April 1864—a plan created by Ohio's governor, John Brough. There were further calls for troops later that year.

As some had feared, these developments prompted sharp and sometimes violent reactions among Ohioans and altered the political landscape there. As Congress debated the Second Confiscation Act in 1862 the *Urbana Union*, a Democratic Party newspaper, called the emancipation of slaves "a thing beyond the power of Congress" for slaves were property and any such forfeiture must "be declared and fixed" by the courts. On the other hand, the *Gallipolis Journal*, a Republican newspaper, saw the emancipation of slaves as a military necessity as warfare "justifies armies in supporting themselves from resources of the enemy." Meanwhile, rumors of blacks migrating into Ohio and "taking white laborers jobs" spread throughout the state. On July 8, 1862 a riot broke out on the Toledo docks between black and white laborers. Democratic newspapers were quick to blame the riot on black laborers; the *Defiance Democrat* published a letter to the editor that the riot's causes came from the "flood of Negroes" pouring into the city, "all of them idle, indolent, and following no regular avocation but theft and plunder." One of the most famous of the war's propagandists was David Ross Locke, an editor of the *Findlay Jeffersonian* at the beginning of the war. Just a week after Fort Sumter surrendered Locke began to write satirical letters under the pseudonym of Petroleum Vesuvius Nasby, a lazy, semi-literate, bigoted Peace Democrat with an implacable contempt for Lincoln and the Ohio citizens who supported him. The Nasby letters soon became published widely throughout the North, and one of their biggest fans was Abraham Lincoln, who quoted them frequently and read them to his cabinet members. Nasby left little doubt who he blamed for the war:

Oberlin commenst this war, Oberlin wuz the prime cause uv all the trubble. . . . Our Suthrin brethrin wantid the territories—Oberlin objected. They wantid Kansas fer ther blessed instooshn. Oberlin agin objecks. They sent colonies with muskits and sich, to hold the territory—Oberlin sent 2 thowsand armed with Bibles and Sharp's rifles—two instooshns Dimocrisy cood never stand afore—and druv em out. They wantid Breckinridge fer President—Oberlin refused and elektid Linkin … Our Suthern brethren wuz reasonable. So long ez the dimocrisy controld things, and they got all the wanted, they wuz peaceable. Oberlin ariz—the dimocrisy wuz beet down, and they riz up agin it.

Figure 9.4   Clement Laird Vallandigham was a Dayton lawyer and Democratic Congressman who rose to become one of the foremost leaders of the Copperhead movement. Exiled by Lincoln to the Confederacy in 1863, Ohio's Democratic Party nominated him for the governor's race that year, and he ran in absentia from a hotel in Canada. After losing the election, he eventually moved back to Ohio in defiance of his exile, and remained active in Democratic Party activities during and after the war. In 1871, while defending a client accused of murder by re-enacting the event in the courtroom, he accidentally shot himself to death with a pistol. Few Union sympathizers mourned his passing, the *New York Times* obituary calling him "one of [the country's] most active and influential enemies."
Source: Courtesy of the Ohio Historical Society (AL02843)

Although Locke intended his letters originally to criticize the southern slaveholding states and their supporters, his attention increasingly focused on Ohio's antiwar Democrats, also known as Peace Democrats or "Copperheads" to their foes, especially Clement Laird Vallandigham.

Vallandigham, shown in Figure 9.4, was a Dayton lawyer widely acknowledged as the foremost figure in the Copperhead movement, and he reveled in being a thorn in Lincoln's side. He believed the war and the war powers Lincoln had assumed to be unconstitutional. As the congressional elections of 1862 approached, he and other Democrats felt empowered as opposition to Lincoln and the Republican Congress grew. The Ohio legislature remained in the hands of the Republican/Unionists and had redistricted in the hopes of enhancing their party's chances in November. The effort largely failed, however, as Democrats captured fourteen of Ohio's nineteen U.S. congressional seats. There was one bright spot for the Republicans and Unionists, though: Vallandigham lost.

However, the loss did not stop Vallandigham and it soon landed him in trouble. After his defeat at Fredericksburg in December 1862, Maj. Gen. Ambrose Burnside assumed command of the Department of Ohio, headquartered in Cincinnati. Hoping to quell and intimidate antiwar sentiment, and with an eye toward Vallandigham, in April 1863 Burnside issued General Order No. 38, which punished those "declaring sympathy for the enemy" with arrest and possible shipment into the Confederacy. Extreme cases of disloyalty, Burnside declared, could result in death. Vallandigham and other Peace Democrats took the bait and organized a rally in Mount Vernon on May 1. The speeches were typical for Vallandigham, who called Lincoln a despot, and claimed that the war was "for the liberation of blacks, and the enslavement of the whites." Burnside sent soldiers to record the speeches, and when he read the reports he ordered Vallandigham's arrest while the others escaped punishment. He was tried and convicted in a military court and sentenced to confinement. (Although it came too late for Vallandigham, in 1866 the Supreme Court ruled in the case of *ex parte Milligan* that civilians could not be tried in military courts when civil courts were functioning.) Lincoln commuted Vallandigham's sentence to exile and banished the Democrat to the Confederacy. From there he escaped to Bermuda and then to Canada, where in 1863 he ran as an antiwar candidate for Ohio's governor, drawing national headlines in the process. The conviction and banishment led to a severe reaction, with mobs attacking Republican newspapers in Dayton. Clearly, Vallandigham was not alone in his opposition. Reflecting Ohio's deeply-conflicted nature, the state also claimed some of the most influential critics of Lincoln and the war, particularly from its southern, "butternut" region. Representative George Pendleton of Cincinnati was an outspoken Peace Democrat who was McClellan's Democratic vice presidential running mate against Lincoln in 1864. Zanesville's Samuel Cox was one of the most active race-baiting Democrats in Congress, and Alexander Long of the Second Congressional District along the Ohio River north of Kentucky openly advocated independence for the Confederacy and received official censure from the House.

An estimated 18,000 Ohioans deserted the Union Army, and most returned home where fellow community members protected them. Across the state, people aided men evading the draft, including helping some move to Canada. Perhaps the most virulent objection to the war arose in protest to the institution of conscription in 1863. Although, in that year, Ohio did not have draft riots to match New York's it did have the "Holmes County War." In June a group of 900 men in heavily-Democratic Holmes County constructed "Fort Fizzle" to protect against forces sent there to enforce the draft. More than 400 Union troops faced them in a brief skirmish in which two were wounded before most of the protesters escaped into the woods. Resistance to the draft would continue for the rest of the war, although not in quite so flamboyant a fashion.

There was more than simply racism at work among the "Copperheads" and those who opposed the war. As they had since the days of Andrew Jackson, antiwar Democrats defended individualism and local autonomy against the rise of a powerful federal government that had, in their eyes, run roughshod over the Constitution by suspending the writ of habeas corpus, enforcing the draft, and denying free speech and freedom of the press. Moreover, objection to the war did not always derive from political or racial motivations. Ohio had numerous residents who belonged to traditional "peace" denominations— Quakers, Moravians, Mennonites, and others—that objected to war in all of its forms. Generally not as outspoken as the Copperheads, members of these sects privately objected to the war, although because some of these denominations were also passionately antislavery, a surprising number of these men ended up joining the Union army.

1863 to the war's close

Opposition to Lincoln and the war continued even as fortunes for the Union forces improved in the summer of 1863. In the western theater Grant continued to prove his mettle by laying siege to the city of Vicksburg. After six weeks of pounding from Union artillery, the city's Confederate defenders gave in and surrendered on July 4. When Port Hudson in Louisiana surrendered on July 8, the Union gained control of the Mississippi River, having already captured New Orleans in 1862.

Meanwhile, in Virginia, it initially seemed that Lee's Army of Northern Virginia, with some 60,000 soldiers, would at last defeat Union forces for good and force the North to sue for peace. In May, Lee obtained a victory at Chancellorsville, defeating the Army of the Potomac. This army was more than twice the size of Lee's forces and was under the command of Maj. Gen. Joseph "Fighting Joe" Hooker. Lee's confidence grew and he followed his brilliant victory with an invasion into Pennsylvania. The Army of the Potomac, which after June 28 came under the command of Maj. Gen. George G. Meade, again shadowed Lee to the east, protecting Washington. The two armies—Lee's at roughly 75,000 and Meade's more than 90,000—met again, this time at Gettysburg. For three days (July 1–3) the forces clashed in the most celebrated battle of the war. Ultimately, Meade prevailed, but only after both sides had sustained some 51,000 casualties between them. As he had after Antietam Lee moved back into Virginia. At least 4,300 Ohioans fought in the battle, and as Lincoln so eloquently phrased it in his Gettysburg Address that November, those that perished "gave the last full measure of devotion" to give the nation a "new birth of freedom." These men included those of the 4th and 8th Ohio Volunteer Infantry who formed part of the "Gibraltar Brigade" that helped repulse Pickett's Charge against the Union center along Cemetery Ridge.

In the same month as these Union victories, Ohio itself was invaded. Morgan's raiders entered Ohio from Indiana on July 13 and terrorized southern Ohio before being stopped on July 26 near Salineville. Among the Union casualties was Maj. Daniel McCook, the sixty-five-year-old father of eight of the "Fighting McCooks." Brothers Daniel and John McCook (from Carrollton and Steubenville, respectively) went to war with at least thirteen of their sons. Four of the McCooks, including Daniel, died during the war. Nearly all became officers, six became generals, and two were major generals by the end of the war. Morgan and his surviving officers were sent to the Ohio Penitentiary from where they made a daring escape in November. Only two were recaptured while the rest returned to the South. Morgan was later killed in Tennessee.

A gubernatorial election again arrived in the wake of the battles and tensions in 1863. Vallandigham, spurred on by Samuel Medary (noted editor of the *Columbus Crisis*) and other passionate supporters, secured the Democratic nomination over more moderate voices. The Democrat's platform included opposition to emancipation and martial law. Meanwhile Unionists were growing more radical in their war support and they dumped incumbent governor Tod (who was soft on emancipation) in favor of War Democrat John Brough. After an active campaign the Ohioans sided with Brough, giving him 288,374 votes to Vallandigham's 187,492. Unionists still controlled the Ohio legislature and had approved legislation to allow soldiers in the field to vote; they supported Brough by a nearly 19-to-1 margin. Lincoln himself expressed elation at the result, congratulating Brough with a telegram saying, "Glory to God in the highest: Ohio has saved the Union!" No doubt the Union victories in July and Morgan's invasion persuaded many voters to support the Republican/Unionist platform. Still, the sizable vote for Vallandigham showed the deep antiwar sentiment in Ohio.

One of Brough's first acts was to get approval in the legislature for an increase in the tax that provided support for soldiers' families and military hospitals. The money was sorely needed as the war entered its third year. Casualties continued to come home and many families struggled to cope as they endured the instability, uncertainty, and heartbreak of war. As Mary Searles wrote in September 1861 when her husband Alfred enlisted: "Oh, how hard it was to let him go and how uneasy I feel not knowing one minit from another if I have a husband or my children have a father." She remained on the farm with her daughters. She faced economic difficulty within a month of her husband leaving; Alfred did not return from the war. Women were far from passive as they managed farms and businesses, worked as nurses, worked in factories, searched for soldiers, and tended to the dead. Women aided the U.S. Sanitary Commission by raising money and donating food items—much of which they grew or raised, such as fruits and vegetables. They also became active politically, supporting the war or resisting it, and this activism would help inspire the revival of several antebellum causes including temperance and suffrage once the war had concluded. Indeed, Ohio's women were as divided as the men. Lincoln's election in 1860 prompted a Belmont County woman to comment to her nephew that she was "a secessionist" and that she hoped Ohio would join the South and "let the 'Almighty Niggers' and Abolitionists take the North." Whereas in Cincinnati, Amanda Wilson went to see Lincoln as he passed through the city on his way to his inaugural, exclaiming in her diary "God Bless him! God bless our country!" During the 1863 gubernatorial campaign a group of Republican women in Liverpool tarred and feathered several Democratic women, and in Portsmouth, after a Democratic mass meeting, a number of Republican women "throwing aside all modesty, unsexed themselves and appeared upon the streets with brazen faces to shout their insulting words at passers-by." They also "threw tomatoes, potatoes," and "rotten eggs." In a letter to the editor, a woman of the Salt Creek Aid Society in Wayne County called the Democrats "traitors" and "mean, low, contemptible wretches." She reported on one encounter with a female Copperhead storeowner, who, upon being asked for a donation for soldiers, said she would "rather give her stores to the dogs than give to a Union soldier."

Among Republicans, many were becoming radicalized as the war continued. White soldiers in the field had also shifted their views, at least when it came to ending slavery and accepting blacks as soldiers. Seeing the South had convinced them of the superiority of Ohio society. As one historian noted "[to] be from Ohio meant to stand up for the Union, for labor, for education, for progress, for liberty." Lt. Col. Alvin C. Vorhis of Akron wrote in 1864: "I am glad the Union Party put the emancipation doctrine directly in issue." He noted "that in the army the prejudice heretofore existing against the negro has almost entirely died out." Vorhis qualified his assessment and thereby delineated the lines of white sentiment. "I do not mean by this that they make them their social associates, but they are not ashamed to recognize them as fellow soldiers." For blacks there was of course no doubt as to the war's purpose. John H. B. Payne of Logan County joined the 55th Regiment of Massachusetts in 1863. "Give me my rights," he wrote, "the rights that this Government owes me, the same rights that the white man has."

The excitement after Vicksburg and Gettysburg faded as the war continued. Following these battles, in September the Army of the Cumberland (formerly the Army of the Ohio) under the command of Maj. Gen. William Rosecrans of Delaware County suffered a major defeat at Chickamauga, in northwest Georgia, in which a number of Ohioans served. The army had fallen back to nearby Chattanooga, Tennessee and remained besieged there. Rosecrans had been admired, but the defeat effectively ended his military career. Grant moved in, assumed command, and pushed the Confederate forces out by November. Afterwards, in March 1864 Lincoln promoted Grant to Lieutenant General and named him General-in-Chief. Sherman then assumed command of the western army. Grant took command of the Army of the Potomac and began grinding against Lee's Army of Northern Virginia, using the North's superior manpower and equipment in a deadly war of attrition. Unfriendly newspapers called Grant "Butcher," and by the summer of 1864 Grant's forces lay outside Petersburg, closing in on Richmond. Meanwhile, Sherman launched an offensive towards Atlanta. Ohioans felt again the weariness of war, with the conflict entering its fourth summer in a stalemate as Petersburg, Richmond, and Atlanta remained in Confederate hands.

In the campaigns of 1864 politics and battlefield were again drawn together. Governor Brough crafted a plan that called for new state militia, the 100-day men, to serve on a temporary basis, which then freed up experienced veterans for the fight in the east. In addition, Lincoln issued more calls for regular troops, either by volunteer or draft, and again Ohio met its share with 148,979 men. As these tensions grew there was an unsuccessful effort by Confederates to free officers held at the prison camp on Johnson's Island in Sandusky Bay (see Figure 9.5). As many as 10,000 Confederate soldiers stayed there over the course of the war and because it was surrounded by water the rate of escape was extremely low. This was despite an elaborate plan in 1864 in which Confederate soldiers planned to steal a steamboat, use it to capture a federal gunboat, and then use that gunboat to force the freedom of the Confederate prisoners on the island. Once free, they were to move to Columbus to free the prisoners at Camp Chase and together stage raids throughout the state. They only got as far as stealing the steamboat before being arrested. In addition, Camp Dennison (Figure 9.5) north of Cincinnati was a major army training

Figure 9.5 Ohio during the Civil War.
Source: Courtesy of the Ohio Historical Society (AL04263) with the addition of camps and islands

center started by George McClellan and laid out by William Rosecrans early in the war. More than 50,000 soldiers passed through the camp, as well as several thousand patients in the military hospital established there. Camp Chase in Columbus was not only a major mustering and training center, it also served as a major prisoner of war camp. As many as 8,000 Confederate prisoners lived there at one time, thousands of whom died of disease. As a result, Columbus has one of the largest Confederate cemeteries north of the Mason–Dixon Line.

With war at a stalemate and new debates over the call for troops, the presidential and congressional elections of 1864 went ahead. In the summer, Lincoln faced a challenge for the Republican nomination from Salmon Chase, now Lincoln's treasury secretary. Urging Chase on were fellow Ohioans—U.S. Senator John Sherman and financier

Jay Cooke. However, Lincoln secured the nomination and at the end of June accepted Chase's fourth offer to resign. Meanwhile, the Democrats faced their own internal struggles between prowar and antiwar factions. In the end, former Union commander Maj. Gen. George McClellan secured the nomination, with "Gentleman George" Pendleton as his running mate. Lincoln looked in trouble until September when a series of dramatic Union military victories saved him. That month Atlanta fell as did the port of Mobile, Alabama. Sherman then began his "March to the Sea" campaign to the coast of Georgia. In Virginia, Union cavalry units led by Maj. Gen. Philip Sheridan of Somerset and served by another Ohioan, George Custer, secured control of the Shenandoah Valley. In November, Lincoln won Ohio by more than 60,000 votes on his way to re-election with a 400,000 vote margin nationally over McClellan. Soldiers again widely supported Lincoln. Voters also gave the Republicans firm control of Ohio's Congressional delegation, with control of seventeen of the nineteen seats. In the U.S. Senate, Benjamin Wade had been elected in 1863, a Radical Republican voice alongside the more moderate Republican John Sherman.

By spring 1865 it was clear that the Confederacy was on its last legs. After his devastating march through Georgia, Sherman had turned north into South Carolina then North Carolina, laying waste as he went. As this happened, Congress approved the Thirteenth Amendment that ended slavery once and for all. Ohio's legislature approved the measure by wide margins. Meanwhile, Petersburg and then Richmond fell and Grant pursued Lee until April 9 when Lee surrendered to Grant at McLean's Appomattox Court House. The war was finally over and spontaneous celebrations sprang up throughout Ohio and the North. Jubilation turned quickly to sorrow with Lincoln's assassination by John Wilkes Booth. The news stunned Ohio and the nation. Crowds by the thousands turned out to pay respects to the slain president as his funeral train passed through Ohio. In Columbus, Lincoln's body lay in state at the statehouse for almost seven hours as thousands of mourners filed past the coffin.

Ohio's Civil War Contribution: A Summary

Ohioans had certainly given much to support the war effort. As many contemporary observers up to and including Abraham Lincoln knew, Ohio was crucial to the success of the Union cause. In fact, some historians have argued that no state was more important to the outcome of the war when taking the state's total contribution in terms of leadership, men, supplies and transportation into account.

Political leadership

When the war started, the absence of southern Congressmen meant that Ohio's already considerable congressional power increased. Ohio's delegation in the House of Representatives was almost an eighth of both the Republican caucus and the entire body. As such it was influential not only in pushing through war measures, but also in helping the Republicans pass measures that Southern Democrats had traditionally blocked. The Morrill Tariff of 1861 benefitted American industry and began a more than fifty-year period of protectionism in U.S. tax and trade policy. The Homestead Act of 1862 gave federal land to settlers virtually free and played a large part in the rapid expansion of American settlers into the West. The Pacific Railroad Act of 1862 made possible the Transcontinental Railroad that by the end of the decade had tied the nation together with railroad and telegraph lines. The Morrill Land Grant Act of 1862 in some ways built on the much earlier precedent of Ohio University and Miami University by providing states with federal land to use for the creation and support of agricultural and mechanical colleges. Many of the nation's most prominent colleges, including the University of California, the University of Illinois, Pennsylvania State University, and Ohio State University were products of the Morrill Land Grant. Ohio's Republican senators were among the most influential in that body. Lancaster native and Cleveland resident John Sherman was already the powerful Chairman of the House Ways and Means Committee when he replaced Salmon P. Chase in the Senate in 1861. There he served as the Chairman of both the Committee on Finance and the Committee on Agriculture in what was only the beginning of a long and distinguished political career. Benjamin Wade of Ashtabula County was a leader of the Radical Republican caucus and chairman of the powerful Joint Committee on the Conduct of the War. He also chaired the Committee on Territories, being influential in the abolition of slavery there. Although the Election of 1862 thinned Republican ranks in the House, Ohio's Congressional leadership—particularly in the Senate—materially aided in the legislative prosecution of the war.

Ohio's leadership also extended to the executive branch. Two of Lincoln's most important cabinet officials came from Ohio. Steubenville native and former Democrat Edwin Stanton served as Lincoln's Secretary of War for most of the war, replacing the incompetent and possibly corrupt political appointee Simon Cameron. Prickly, abrasive, and even vengeful at times, Stanton was nevertheless a model of effectiveness, energy, and incorruptibility in turning the unwieldy War Department into an efficient administrator of the largest endeavor the federal government had ever attempted. Despite the fact that Stanton held a dim view of Lincoln and personally often overrode the president's decisions, Lincoln continued to support him, saying that he was "the rock on the beach of our national ocean against which the breakers dash and roar, dash and roar, without ceasing … Without him I should be destroyed. He performs his task superhumanly." Stanton's opinion of Lincoln steadily improved over the course of the war, and it was he who first eulogized Lincoln at his deathbed with "Now he belongs to the angels" (the last word of which he later altered to the more poetic "ages"). Stanton was among the strongest forces in Lincoln's cabinet pushing for emancipation, along with Salmon Chase, who as Secretary of the Treasury held the second most important cabinet post during the Civil War. The U.S. government had never taken on such an extravagantly expensive task before and the Buchanan Administration had left the Treasury in a desperate condition. Despite not having a background in high finance Chase quickly learned what he needed to know and promptly instituted measures that helped the Union make it through the early years of the war. He introduced paper currency, "greenbacks"

Figure 9.6   Salmon Chase was a man not only of immense talent, but also immense ambition. His stint as Secretary of the Treasury reflected both characteristics. Chase's innovative measures at the Treasury Department and his choice of Jay Cooke to sell government bonds not only kept the government afloat financially during and after the war, but set the precedent for future government policies in these areas. As praiseworthy as these efforts were, they also show that he was not above self-promotion: he chose to feature his own portrait prominently on this "greenback" issued at a time when he was considering running against Lincoln in the Election of 1864.
Source: Denver Public Archives

as shown in Figure 9.6, which not only gave the government much needed financial flexibility but also served as the precedent for today's paper money. Chase also helped see through the National Banking Act that gave the country a more uniform and stable banking system. He could also be self-serving and petulant. He put his own face on the greenbacks and secretly sought to unseat Lincoln as the Republican nominee in 1864. He threatened to resign several times to try to force the president's hand in various matters, but Lincoln kept him on in part because of the important work he was doing at the Treasury. Upon finally accepting his last resignation Lincoln named him Chief Justice of the United States.

Economic leadership

Working hand-in-glove with Chase was Sandusky native Jay Cooke. A successful banker with important connections in the financial community, Cooke helped Chase to get loans from major bankers to keep the country afloat in the early stages of the war. When Chase found himself unable to sell half a billion dollars worth of desperately needed bonds authorized by Congress, he engaged Cooke to sell as many of them as possible. Cooke hired thousands of subagents across the country to sell the bonds in every locality, and engaged in a public relations campaign to sell ads to local media extolling the bonds as a source of both patriotism and profit. He proved to be too successful by selling millions of dollars more bonds than Congress had authorized. His subsequent efforts were similarly successful and in all he raised three billion dollars for the government (and quite a lot for himself through commissions), justly earning himself the unofficial title "Financier of the Union."

Supplies and transportation

Ohio's economic leadership extended to a less splashy an often-overlooked area of the war: supplies. If, as Napoleon is supposed to have said, "an army marches on its stomach," then much of the Union army marched on Ohio produce. Ohio possessed one of the nation's largest and perhaps most diverse agricultural bases. This was a result of the large and diverse population that brought their agricultural traditions with them to the state. Although western states had long surpassed Ohio and "Porkopolis" in hog production, Ohio still ranked fifth in this statistic in 1860, and third among free states. The most notable thing about Ohio's prewar fourth place ranking in wheat production (behind the growing western states of Illinois, Indiana, and Wisconsin) is that this was the lowest the state ranked among Union states in most major remaining categories of agricultural production. Ohio's third place ranking among Union states in cattle is a bit misleading as distant California was in second place and not in a position to compete economically. Although most army personnel did not have regular beef rations, the army created a tremendous demand for cowhide for belts, straps, cartridge boxes, shoes, and boots. While all of these commodities were of greater or lesser importance in supporting the Northern population and the Union Army during the war, Ohio's most important contributions came in items of direct military support. In 1860 Ohio ranked first in the nation in wool and produced more than a fifth of the supply in Union states. An army may march on its stomach, but it will not go far if it has nothing to wear. Deprived of southern cotton for most of the war, the contractors for the Union Army made most uniforms and blankets out of wool. Prosecuting a nineteenth-century war was also impossible without a large supply of horses, and Ohio again ranked first in this category. Not only did the army need replacements for horses killed or wounded in battle, they also pressed countless numbers into service as draft animals for transportation. Taken as a whole, few states could boast as great and varied agricultural contribution to the Union as Ohio. Adding to this Ohio's significant timber resources, its pig iron and coal production that in the 1850s ranked second only to Pennsylvania's, and its manufacturing sector that was third-largest before the war and grew 122 percent over the 1860s, few can argue that Ohio was a leader in providing the Union the resources for war.

The most ample amount of supplies is useless without the ability to transport it to where it is needed, and this fact illustrates perhaps Ohio's most overlooked contribution to the Union war effort. The state was the most vital link in the Union transportation network, especially early in the war when Kentucky was neutral and Ohio was the sole conduit between the eastern and western sections of the country. With Lake Erie to its north, the Ohio River to its south, an elaborate canal system, and more railroad mileage than any other state in the Union, Ohio literally stood at the crossroads of the nation and was crucial in the movement of men and supplies throughout the war.

Military leadership

It is in military terms, though, that most people think of leadership during times of war, and this is where Ohio made its clearest case for living up to Governor Dennison's prediction. Although New York and Pennsylvania had larger populations and provided more men to the Union cause, no state provided more men per capita than Ohio. While many states had difficulty fulfilling enlistment requirements, Ohio ended the war thousands of men over its total quota. Almost 30 percent of Ohio's male population served the Union, and when males younger than 18 and older than 50 are excluded, the percentage is even higher. This also does not count the hundreds or even thousands of men mostly from butternut areas of southern Ohio who decided to join the Confederacy, seven of whom served as generals. As one of the most enthusiastic antislavery states before the war, it is perhaps no coincidence that Ohio was also the most enthusiastic state in providing soldiers for the fight against the Confederacy.

Beyond its clear leadership in *per capita* enlistment, Ohio also produced a disproportionate number of the men who became the most important leaders of the war. The six McCook generals were only a fraction of the more than 200 Ohioans who achieved that rank. Ohio claimed nearly twenty Major Generals, some of whom are quite familiar to even casual students of the Civil War. These included: George Armstrong Custer, who at 23 was one of the youngest men in U.S. history ever to achieve the rank of general; Irvin McDowell, who commanded the Union troops at First Bull Run; Don Carlos Buell, whose timely reinforcements helped win the Battle of Shiloh; William Rosecrans, whose brilliant Tullahoma Campaign was overshadowed by Gettysburg, Vicksburg, and his later defeat at Chickamauga; and James McPherson, who was the highest-ranking Union officer to be killed in action. Ohio's greatest contribution in this area, though, was a triumvirate of generals that many historians consider to be the three most important on the Union side. Philip Sheridan was a cavalry officer who grew up in Somerset, Perry County. An indefatigable fighter, he served with distinction at Stone's River, Tullahoma, and Missionary Ridge, before moving to Northern Virginia to help defeat Robert E. Lee. It was Sheridan's forces who ultimately trapped Lee at Appomattox Courthouse and forced his surrender. William Tecumseh Sherman from Lancaster (Senator John Sherman's brother) was one of the few generals who at the outset of the war knew it would be a long and bloody conflict. He served with distinction at Shiloh, and soon became General Grant's most trusted subordinate.

Yet Ohio's—and the Union's—most important military leader of the war was Gen. Ulysses S. Grant. Born Hiram Ulysses Grant in Point Pleasant, he moved with his family at a young age to Georgetown in Brown County. A West Point graduate, he served as an officer in the Mexican-American War (even though he personally disagreed with it). Stationed in western posts away from his family, he became depressed and began to drink, eventually resigning his commission. When the war started he was a clerk in his father's leather shop in Galena, Illinois. He soon found himself leading Illinois troops to early successes at Forts Henry and Donelson near the Tennessee/Kentucky border. His terms for surrender of the Confederate forces there earned him the sobriquet "Unconditional Surrender" Grant. His victory at the Battle of Shiloh got him moved to an unimportant

Honor to the Brave.

Figure 9.7   This lithograph exemplifies the immense contribution Ohio made to the Union's military leadership during the Civil War. Issued near the war's end in 1865, it depicts Lady Liberty holding laurels of honor over the men thought by many in the country as the Union's most important Army (left) and Navy (right) officers. The trio of U.S. Army generals—Sherman, Grant, and Sheridan—all hailed from Ohio.
Source: Library of Congress Prints and Photographs Division (LC-USZ62-115110)

command because of the heavy casualties incurred, but few other generals seemed to have his resolve, and it was Grant who finally succeeded in doing what no other Union General came close to: forcing Robert E. Lee to surrender. By the end of the war, Grant had risen to lieutenant general—a rank only George Washington had received before him.

In examining Ohio's place in the Civil War it is important to guard against a temptation to go too far. New York and Illinois could draw up similar lists showing that the Union cause would have been difficult without them, so Ohio was not solely indispensable. Also, simply naming every person with an Ohio connection introduces "Ohioans" who really more appropriately belong elsewhere. Some might even question claiming Stanton or Grant, who left the state in young adulthood, or Chase or Sheridan, who moved to the state as youngsters (see Figure 9.7). Yet the Ohio experience shaped all of these men and their views. It was the Cincinnati race riot of 1836 and being at the crossroads of the Underground Railroad, for example, that radicalized Chase on the issue of abolition. Grant's father spent his formative years in the Western Reserve and for a while lived in the same house as Owen and John Brown. Grant himself went to school for a while in the abolitionist haven of Ripley. It would be difficult to argue that these experiences had no influence on Grant's upbringing and personality. Thus, considering all of Ohio's contributions together—political, economic, material, and military—Ohio proved Governor Dennison right. Ohio DID lead in the Civil War and it is difficult to imagine what the war might have been like without its contributions. It would soon parlay its wartime experience into economic and political prominence.

The Reconstruction Period, 1865–77

Ohio's leadership during the war, and the tensions and divisions, continued in the postwar period known as Reconstruction. The question became how to unify North and South after four years of bloody conflict. The answers hinged on policies towards former Confederates and the 4 million former slaves. The political struggle in Ohio as seen through elections and referenda served as a microcosm of the national one. Andrew Johnson, who came into the presidency with Lincoln's assassination, favored a lenient policy towards former Confederates that also left the fate of former slaves largely in the hands of their former masters. In a dramatic fashion, so-called Radical Republicans in Congress, led by men such as Ohioans Benjamin Wade and John Bingham, gained the upper hand and pushed to impeach Johnson as Ohioans and most white northerners initially seemed to favor a stronger policy against former Confederates and greater federal protection for former slaves. Wade, Bingham and others joined free blacks and former slaves to expand the meaning of freedom to include African Americans. However, the widespread support for Radical Reconstruction lasted a short time. By 1867 and 1868 white Ohioans showed their ambivalence towards black equality, and moderate Republicans and Democrats opposed to the Radical agenda gained power. Reconstruction ended officially when Ohioan Rutherford B. Hayes became President in 1877. While black freedom remained uneven in Ohio and elsewhere across the nation, Reconstruction saw national laws and the U.S. Constitution rewritten to recognize the equality of blacks (or at least black men) before the law, laying the groundwork for later developments associated with the civil rights movement.

The Radical moment, 1865–68

Radicals in Congress gained influence at the expense of Andrew Johnson. Johnson had been governor of Tennessee but remained loyal to the Union. In 1862 Lincoln had made him military governor of Tennessee when Union troops occupied the state and then in 1864 Republicans nominated Johnson—a Southerner and Democrat—as vice-president, hoping to extend their influence into the South and to show that the Union was for all loyal men. Johnson was no Lincoln. He was stubborn, unable to handle criticism, and lacked political acumen. He also believed strongly in state's rights and held deeply racist views of African Americans. Beginning in 1865, while

Congress was not in session, Johnson issued a series of proclamations as he set about taking charge of reconstructing the former Confederate states. He pardoned all those who took an oath of allegiance to the United States, but those of wealth had to apply for individual pardons from the President. Johnson allowed new state governments to convene, elected by whites alone, but as long as they formally abolished slavery and denounced secession, the new governments were free to manage their own affairs. Soon, these all-white governments were dominated by former Confederates and began to establish all-white control, including creating "black codes" to regulate the behavior of former slaves.

Moderate Republicans initially hoped to work with Johnson, but Radicals in Congress pushed to create their own plan. Led by men including Senators Benjamin Wade of Ohio and Charles Sumner of Massachusetts and Representatives John Bingham of Cadiz, Ohio and Thaddeus Stevens of Pennsylvania, Radicals saw the South as akin to conquered territory, fully under the power of the federal government that had the responsibility for ensuring equal rights for all Americans regardless of race. Moderate Republicans in Congress sided with the Radicals after Johnson vetoed a bill to extend the Freedmen's Bureau beyond one year and vetoed a civil rights bill. Congress failed to override the veto of the Freedmen's Bureau (although Congress later extended it to 1870) but in April 1866 Congress overrode the Civil Rights Bill veto and approved a new law that provided equality before the law regardless of race. In June, Congress approved (with no Democrats supporting it) the Fourteenth Amendment. Authored primarily by John Bingham, who had been one of the judges on the Lincoln assassination trials, the Fourteenth Amendment established the principle that blacks were citizens, but did not provide blacks with the right to vote. In Ohio, Republicans held the governor's office under former Union General Jacob D. Cox of Warren. Showing the level of ambivalence among whites in Ohio over black equality, during the 1865 campaign, Cox published an open letter to Radical Republicans in Oberlin, in which he argued against black suffrage and favored the "peaceable separation of the races," going on to propose giving Southern blacks their own territory, much like those in the West. During Cox's one term and with his approval the General Assembly approved the Fourteenth Amendment in January 1867. As the election season opened in the fall of 1866, Johnson campaigned in the North on a blatantly racist message, hoping to use white opposition to Radical Republicans to forge a new coalition of Democrats and moderate Republicans. It backfired horribly for the President as Republicans fared well in Ohio and the nation, giving the Radicals the upper hand in dictating Reconstruction, at least for a short time.

Now emboldened, the Republican Congress pursued a more aggressive plan for Reconstruction that included passage over Johnson's veto of the first Reconstruction Act in March 1867. This act, authored by Ohio Senator John Sherman, abolished the state governments organized under Johnson's plan, divided the South into five military districts (excluding Tennessee, which had been readmitted), required the creation of new state constitutions that allowed black men the right to vote, and demanded that the remaining Confederate states ratify the Fourteenth Amendment prior to readmission. It was a bold move that altered not only national politics but also those in Ohio. Republicans in Ohio placed before voters in the state a resolution to remove the word "white" from the state constitution—in the thinking of Republicans, if Congress was going to enforce black voting rights in the South, then Ohio should also follow suit. White Ohioans rejected such reasoning. In the 1867 state elections, Democrats nominated Allen Thurman of Chillicothe on a platform opposed to black suffrage and Congressional Reconstruction. Republicans nominated Rutherford B. Hayes, the war hero and U.S. Representative who had sided with the Radicals. Hayes won the governor's race by only 2,983 votes, and the black suffrage measure failed by some 50,000 votes. It would not be until the twentieth century that Ohio would amend the language of the state constitution. Although voters gave Hayes the victory, they also gave Democrats control of the Ohio General Assembly. In the wake of the election, the Democratic assembly nominated Thurman to replace Radical Republican Benjamin Wade in the U.S. Senate and attempted to repeal Ohio's approval of the Fourteenth Amendment. Congress continued to count Ohio as favoring it as it went into effect in July 1868. Ohio ratified the Fourteenth Amendment again in 2003. The assembly also approved a law to remove voting rights from anyone of black ancestry; only the Ohio Supreme Court prevented this law from going into effect.

Meanwhile, Congress and President Johnson continued their feud. Three separate amendments to the first Reconstruction Act each met with a Johnson veto that Congress overrode. In 1868, the fight between Congress and Johnson led to the impeachment of the President and Ohioans were deeply involved the events. What precipitated this was the Tenure of Office Act, which Congress had approved over Johnson's veto in March 1867, barring the President from removing cabinet members and other officeholders without the approval of Congress. Congress had in mind Edwin Stanton, the secretary of war who sided with the Radicals. Johnson considered this an unconstitutional abridgment of his power and in February 1868 he removed Stanton. Introducing the impeachment resolution in the House was Toledo Republican James Ashley, who had been the first U.S. representative to call for a constitutional amendment ending slavery. The House voted to impeach Johnson, which meant a House committee led by John Bingham presented charges against the president to the Senate. The Senate then had to decide whether or not to remove him from office. Presiding over the trial was Chief Justice of the United States, Salmon Chase, whom Lincoln had appointed in 1864 following Chase's resignation as secretary of the treasury. When the vote came in May, both Ohio senators, John Sherman and Benjamin Wade, voted to impeach the president, but seven Republicans joined all Democrats and impeachment failed by only one vote, meaning that Wade, as president pro tempore of the Senate, had been so close to being president of the United States. Johnson was now finished as a political force but, as the elections in Ohio had shown, the fate of Reconstruction and black equality remained in doubt.

Decline and end of reconstruction, 1868–77

Ohio-born Ulysses S. Grant (see Figure 9.8) emerged from the war as a national hero. As head of the army he had supported the work of Congressional reconstruction and deplored the racial violence that had sprung up in the South. After Johnson had tried to involve Grant in a plan to thwart Congress over the removal of Stanton, Grant publicly broke with Johnson and supported impeachment, calling Johnson an "infernal liar."

Figure 9.8 Ulysses S. Grant emerged from the Civil War as perhaps the most popular man in the country. A war hero for the Union, he also won some grudging respect from some former Confederates who appreciated the generous peace terms he offered to Robert E. Lee upon his surrender. He parlayed this popularity into two terms as president, the beginning of the "Ohio Dynasty" in the White House. With a conciliatory campaign slogan of "Let us have peace," he intended to appeal to many in the country who wished to hasten the national postwar healing process.
Source: Courtesy of the Ohio Historical Society (AL03869)

Grant also read Ohio's refusal to support black voting rights at the state level as a sign that radicals like Wade would lose a general election should they secure the presidential nomination in 1868. At the same time, he could not stomach a Democratic victory, which he equated with white supremacy and rebellion. Although he had no strong desire to be president these developments convinced Grant that he should allow his name to be entered as a nominee at the Republican Party convention in Chicago. He won on the first ballot, despite the tawdry efforts of Chase and Wade to gain the nomination, with Chase—the nation's Chief Justice—going so far as to try to gain the Democratic nomination once he failed against Grant. In accepting the nomination, Grant appealed for national unity. "Let us have peace," he remarked. His running mate was Indiana Republican and Speaker of the House Schuyler Colfax. The Democrats nominated former New York governor Horatio Seymour and Frank Blair of Missouri. Both men had been virulent critics of Lincoln and vowed to undo Republican reconstruction if elected. Grant won by 300,000 votes, with his popular majority owing much to the votes of newly enfranchised blacks in the South, who were able to vote under Republican reconstruction.

As Grant entered office in March 1869, Congress had just sent to the states the Fifteenth Amendment, which prohibited disenfranchisement based on race, color, or previous condition of servitude. However, passage of the amendment remained in doubt, with Ohio continuing to play a central part in the drama. Although Grant and Governor Hayes supported the amendment, Democrats controlled the Ohio legislature and refused to approve it. With success now in doubt across the nation, Congress mandated that all remaining Southern states that had yet to be readmitted must approve not only the Fourteenth but also the Fifteenth Amendment. In the fall of 1869, Hayes won a narrow re-election as governor and Republicans took a slim majority in the Ohio General Assembly. In 1870 Ohio approved the Fifteenth Amendment—by one vote in the Senate, and two votes in the House. With remaining Southern states also approving, the amendment became part of the U.S. Constitution in March 1870.

Support for Reconstruction in Ohio and other northern states had faded by this time. It became part of a growing dissatisfaction with Grant and the Republicans that would see Democrats gain more power during the early 1870s. One major contributing factor was a series of scandals in the Grant administration, calling into question Grant's reputation for sound judgment that he had earned on the battlefield. Grant's brother-in-law, Abel Corbin, introduced Grant to Jay Gould and Jim Fisk, two New York speculators, who, as one historian noted, had "more than a whiff of the unsavory about them." Gould and Fisk tried to involve Grant in their plan to corner the gold market. Rather than refuse to be seen with them, Grant met with them several times, although he refused to divulge any information that would help the two men. When Grant heard about the plot, he ordered the government to sell millions of dollars in government gold, thereby lowering the price and foiling the plans of Gould and Fisk. While Grant was not personally implicated in the plot, Corbin and several office-holders did face charges and Grant showed poor judgment even meeting with Gould and Fisk. Despite the scandal, Grant won re-election in the 1872 campaign, but soon another one emerged. Several Republican Party leaders, including Grant's outgoing Vice President Schuyler Colfax and Ohio Representative James Garfield, were named in a bribery scheme associated with the Credit Mobilier construction company and the building of the transcontinental railroad. Although the activities associated with the scheme occurred largely under Johnson's presidency, the events tarnished Grant and the Republicans. So, too did a third scandal, the Whiskey Ring, which involved mostly Republican politicians and various liquor industry employees in a scheme to defraud the federal government of millions of dollars in taxes. Indicted in the probe was Grant's personal secretary, Gen. Orville Babcock, who was later acquitted. Beyond the scandals, Grant gave in to pressure to open lands in South Dakota after the discovery of gold there. He had in his first term attempted a somewhat more pacific approach to Native Americans in the West, but he abandoned hopes of a more peaceful resolution of the conflict. He ordered a massive assault against Sioux lands that culminated in the

Battle of Little Big Horn on June 25, 1876 in which Ohioan George Custer and his 7th Cavalry met with ignominious defeat. Adding to voter frustration with Grant and the Republicans was a severe economic depression that began in 1873 and lasted four years. Agricultural prices dropped, jobs disappeared, and Grant had no solution to the nation's economic woes.

Ohio's seesaw political culture continued that year. As discussed in chapter 10, Hayes held the governorship for two terms, and the Republicans kept control with the election in 1871 of Maj. Edward Noyes of Cincinnati, who beat Gen. George McCook, one of the fighting McCooks. The depression of 1873 hurt the Republicans. They lost control of the General Assembly again and Noyes lost his re-election bid to septuagenarian Democrat William Allen, former representative and U.S. senator. During the Civil War, Allen had declared himself a Peace Democrat and had been one of Lincoln's sharpest critics. Allen served one term as governor and died in 1879, and his statue sat among those from all fifty states in the National Statuary Hall in the U.S. Capitol until recently, when he was replaced with Thomas A. Edison.

In assessing his presidency and the fate of black equality and Reconstruction, Grant acknowledged that he had fallen short of expectations. As a result of his own views and actions, as well as a set of events beyond his control, Grant's time in office inaugurated a series of presidencies by Ohioans that have suffered at the judgment of historians. Buffeted with corruption and a faltering economy, as well as shifting white Northern opinion on Reconstruction, the forces playing upon Grant certainly would have baffled even the best political leaders. As one observer noted upon visiting Ohio's Western Reserve, "the abolition element" had "almost died out in that old stronghold of radicalism." The same was true across the North. Many whites had come to the conclusion that Republican rule in the South had been a disaster and the African Americans were simply unfit to govern. Grant, too felt less and less compunction to increase federal power in the South. He also faced a series of Supreme Court decisions that hemmed in his presidential authority. The most famous of these were the Slaughterhouse Cases in which the Court severely limited the application of the Fourteenth Amendment, ruling in 1873 that most rights of citizens remained in the hands of states, not the federal government. Worried more about economic issues, whites in the North drifted away from enforcing black rights in the South. Moreover, the effects of rapid industrialization were already becoming apparent, with immigration, the spread of wage labor, and the growing power of corporations all becoming more important issues. Grant himself grew frustrated at the reconstruction governments in the South. "I am done with them," he wrote in 1874. That year, Democrats took the U.S. House, signaling a major turning point in the process of Reconstruction, which would officially end in 1877 with the election of Rutherford B. Hayes.

Reconstruction, like the war that preceded it, had been a significant episode in Ohio and national history. In an 1874 speech given at a celebration of the Fifteenth Amendment in Oberlin, John Mercer Langston, one of Ohio's most revered black leaders, remarked that, "within the last fifteen years" the "Slave Oligarchy of the land" had been "overthrown, and the nation itself emancipated from its barbarous rule." In the wake of war, the nation now possessed "a purified constitution and legislation no longer construed and enforced to sanction and support inhumanity and crime, but to sustain and perpetuate the freedom and rights of us all." But blacks, Langston reminded his audience, still had not "been given the full exercise and enjoyment of all the rights which appertain by law to American citizenship." Indeed, it would take a second reconstruction almost a century later to fully realize those rights. In the meantime, Ohioans and the nation turned their attention to the massive transformations underway as the world shifted from its rural, agricultural past to its urban, industrial future.

Further Reading

There is an abundance of reading on Ohio and the Civil War that includes: Jim Bissland, *Blood, Tears, and Glory: How Ohioans Won the Civil War* (2008. Wilmington, OH: Orange Frazer Press); Frederick J. Blue, *Salmon P. Chase: A Life in Politics* (1987. Kent: Kent State University Press); Gerald J. Prokopowicz, *All for the Regiment: The Army of the Ohio, 1861–1862* (2000. Chapel Hill: University of North Carolina Press); Susan G. Hall, *Appalachian Ohio and the Civil War, 1862–1863* (2008. Jefferson, NC: McFarland Publishing); Christine Dee, ed., *Ohio's War: The Civil War in Documents* (2006. Athens: Ohio University Press); Noel Fisher, "Groping Toward Victory: Ohio's Administration of the Civil War," *Ohio History* 105 (1996. Winter–Spring, pp. 25–450); Frank L. Klement, *The Limits of Dissent: Clement L. Vallandigham and the Civil War* (1998. New York: Fordham University Press); George H. Porter, *Ohio Politics during the Civil War Period* (1911. New York: Columbia University Press); and Internet Archive, accessed March 18, 2013 at: http://archive.org/details/ohiopolitics00portrich. David Ross Locke's *The Struggles: Social, Financial and Political , of Petroleum V. Nasby; Embracing his Trials and Troubles, Likewise his Views of Men and Things* is a recent reissue of a large collection of David Ross Locke's satirical articles, with illustrations by Thomas Nast (2008. Whitefish, MT: Kessinger Publishing). On the Reconstruction period, see Eric Foner's *Reconstruction: America's Unfinished Revolution, 1863–1877* (1988. New York: Harper & Row), and Brooks Simpson's *The Reconstruction Presidents* (2d ed. 2009. Lawrence: University Press of Kansas).

10

Why Ohio?

Late Nineteenth-Century Politics and Presidents

In the late nineteenth century, Ohio sent more men to the presidency than any other state. While William Henry Harrison was the first of eight Ohioans to become president, the other seven were elected within sixty years following the Civil War, beginning with Ulysses S. Grant in 1868 and ending with Warren G. Harding in 1920. Only Virginia can claim as many presidents. What made each of these men—Ulysses Grant, Rutherford B. Hayes, James A. Garfield, Benjamin Harrison, William McKinley, William Howard Taft and Warren G. Harding—a popular and successful choice for a presidential candidate, especially in the late nineteenth century? Why were all of the men elected in this roughly sixty-year period Republican? This chapter considers these questions by examining Ohio's presidents in the late nineteenth century, from Hayes to McKinley, as well as state politics in the period after Reconstruction. This run of presidents from Ohio was a result of Ohio's central place in the Civil War, Reconstruction, and the nation's shift from a mainly rural, agrarian society to an urban industrial one with a growing significance in world affairs.

Why Ohio?

Without question, from the founding of the current two-party system in the mid-nineteenth century to the present, Ohio has remained central to American politics, rightfully earning a reputation as a "battleground" state. Indeed, even before the Civil War Ohio had a reputation as a "swing state." In choosing presidential candidates in the decades after the Civil War, both major parties took an avid interest in leaders from the Buckeye State. Ohio has been particularly important for Republicans—no GOP candidate has won the presidency

Ohio: A History of the Buckeye State, First Edition. Kevin F. Kern and Gregory S. Wilson.
© 2014 John Wiley & Sons, Inc. Published 2014 by John Wiley & Sons, Inc.

without having carried Ohio and all seven of the Ohio-born men who became president were Republicans.

There were several reasons why political parties after the Civil War looked to Ohio when selecting presidential candidates. As we have seen, over the first half of the nineteenth century, Ohio moved from the periphery to the center of the nation in terms of economic growth, population, and politics. The experience of the Civil War reinforced these developments as Ohio played a critical role in the conflict, particularly in providing military leaders including Grant and Sherman and political leaders including Chase, John Sherman, and Wade. Afterwards, military service in the war proved beneficial to men aspiring to elected office. Five of Ohio's presidents served ably in the victorious Union Army. At the same time, the war solidified the Republican Party's reputation as the party of Lincoln, emancipation, and saving the Union.

Ohio and its people became essential to the industrial revolution of the late nineteenth century while at the same time maintaining their place as leaders in agriculture. Ohioans were involved in all major industrial innovations and developments as both big business and big labor found Ohio fertile ground for growth. The state remained the nation's third most populous until 1900 when it fell to fourth, which among other things gave Ohio the third or fourth largest delegation in Congress. Moreover, its people grew increasingly diverse in the decades after the Civil War, representing a cross-section of America. Flocking to work in Ohio's burgeoning cities and factories were more and more migrants from southern and eastern Europe as well as an increasing number of African Americans from the South. Alongside urbanization, industrialization, and immigration, Ohio solidified its role as a leading farming state. Ohio's rural counties maintained their largely native-born white majorities and agricultural focus. These whites were diverse as well, having roots in the Northeast, the Mid Atlantic and the Upper South. Hence, for political leaders in Ohio, garnering enough votes to secure office often meant appealing to broad and diverse constituencies, from workers and farmers to merchants and big business leaders. In short, as one historian has noted, Ohio "was as near a microcosm of America as one could find in the late nineteenth century." A politician who could succeed in Ohio held great potential for holding national office.

The political situation between the two major parties also aided Ohio's status as a critical state. In the late nineteenth century, sixteen states, mainly in the North, were reliably Republican and fourteen, mostly Southern, voted Democratic. That left a few states, Connecticut, New Jersey, New York, Indiana, Illinois and Ohio, as "swing" states that could decide elections. Party loyalty remained strong, with the Civil War only reinforcing this. Turnout was high among those who could vote (mainly white males) and elections were close. For example, in the presidential elections between 1876 and 1892 an average difference of only 1.4 percent separated the Republican and Democratic candidates. With elections so close, neither major party took chances; they looked for "safe" candidates that could unite various factions and get party loyalists to the polls. Each of Ohio's presidents from Hayes to McKinley met these requirements.

In the late nineteenth century, the Republican Party tended to promote what its leaders saw as both "material and moral progress." The GOP generally drew support from native-born whites, Protestants, skilled workers, and middle-class voters. German immigrants also tended to vote Republican, although the temperance issue divided this group. Even as the Republican Party shifted away from vigorous enforcement of civil rights, African Americans supported the party of Lincoln until the New Deal of Franklin D. Roosevelt shifted their allegiance to the Democrats. Indeed, as the party of reform in the 1850s, Republicans represented the status quo by the 1880s. Republicans came to identify themselves as the party of big business, their leaders favoring low or no corporate taxes and high tariffs on foreign goods as a way to protect American industry. They also opted for a tight money supply, wishing to keep the value of paper currency based on gold. Republicans sympathized with social legislation such as temperance and public education, but were generally uneasy about the influx of new immigrants from southern and eastern Europe.

For their part, Democrats gained greater support from non-Protestant immigrants in urban areas. Those who swelled the ranks of the unskilled industrial workforce became a key constituency for the Democratic Party. Outside the cities, Democrats maintained strength among small farmers, particularly those in the southern part of Ohio whose roots lay below the Mason–Dixon Line. Representing unskilled workers led Democrats to favor legislation to support higher wages, safer working conditions and the regulation of large businesses. Since temperance meant changing immigrant social customs, Democrats opposed it and other Republican efforts at government intervention in the lives of citizens. Their base of rural whites of southern heritage also led Democrats to resist Republican sympathies for civil rights. Representing workers and farmers led Democrats to favor easing credit and an inflationary monetary policy that would expand the money supply (called "greenbackism"). This also led them to support "bimetallism"— using both silver and gold as foundations for paper currency.

Although both parties were competitive in the years after the Civil War, Republicans dominated Ohio's governorship and legislature. Between 1865 and 1900 the Republicans controlled the governorship for twenty-seven years compared with the Democrats' eight. Republicans controlled the state legislature more than twice as often as Democrats. Additionally as mentioned, the only Ohioans to reach the White House were Republicans. Examining the political situation in Ohio in the late nineteenth century provides further insight into how Ohio became the "Mother of Presidents."

State Politics

Ohio's presidents emerged out of the tussle of state politics that involved not just local concerns but also those of national significance. After grappling largely with issues related to Reconstruction and black equality, temperance came to occupy the political stage. It had been of national significance before the Civil War and had re-emerged in the 1870s with Ohio taking a central part in the debate.

As in its earlier variation, women became the driving force behind the post-Civil War temperance movement. For many temperance advocates, the problems associated with Ohio's move towards industrialization and urbanization, such as crime, unemployment, and corruption, emanated from the use of alcohol. Women also decried the role alcohol played in domestic violence and in the temptation saloons gave to male breadwinners for spending their weekly pay on drink. There were also ethnic and religious aspects, too. Those persons favoring temperance tended to be native-born Ohioans of British ancestry, and came mainly from Protestant churches, especially Methodism. Opposing them were those involved in the business of manufacturing, transporting, or selling liquor as well as other European immigrants, especially the sizable population of Germans and Irish whose social customs involved alcohol. The temperance movement gained more ground in rural areas than in cities. All of this fed politics, with the Republican Party generally supporting temperance and the Democrats opposing it. Again, those were the trends, albeit with plenty of variation within them.

Temperance reached the state government during the Reconstruction period when voters authorized a state constitutional convention in 1871, with the delegates elected in 1873 and finishing their work of drafting changes to the state constitution in May 1874. Voters elected 105 delegates to the convention: fifty Republicans, forty-six Democrats, and nine Liberals or Independents. After deliberation, the proposed constitution the delegates presented to the voters included annual sessions of the legislature, a veto for the governor that could be overwritten by a three-fifths vote of each house, the creation of state circuit courts, the eligibility of women for election to school boards, and restrictions on municipal debt. Delegates also made approval for licensing in intoxicating liquors a separate issue; since 1851 the state constitution prohibited licensing in intoxicating liquors. Some temperance advocates saw regulation as the best method to control liquor, while others continued to push for an outright ban. After three years of debate, the public's interest and enthusiasm had waned. With various groups opposed to parts of the new proposed constitution—and temperance advocates urging voters to reject the entire document and not just the licensing issue—voters rejected the 1874 amended version, 102,885 to 250,169 as well as the licensing law. The next time delegates came to revise Ohio's constitution they would offer each item separately and find much greater success.

As the work on the new state constitution proceeded, an organized temperance movement began in Ohio in December 1873, at the beginning of a national depression that would last until 1877. The spark was a visit from the influential doctor, philosopher, and activist Diocletian Lewis. Lewis had promoted antislavery and women's rights, along with health and physical fitness. For many years he had given his speech, "The Duty of Christian Women," on temperance but, in the winter of 1873, it set off a movement in Ohio and across the nation. On December 24, two days after hearing Lewis's speech, seventy-five women in Hillsboro, near Cincinnati, marched through town and from three drugstores gained pledges to stop selling liquor. Leading the group was Eliza Jane Trimble Thompson (see Figure 10.1) daughter of the former governor and wife of a local judge. On Christmas Day Lewis spoke in Washington Court House. The next day, forty-two women began a campaign that at the end of eight days had succeeded in closing all of the town's saloons and halting the sale of liquor. By February 1874, some forty-one similar events had occurred in towns across Ohio, with varying degrees of success.

The women used direct-action tactics. Marchers either moved silently or sang hymns as they filed down the main street in a town, and then stopped at the targeted business and asked permission to enter. If granted, they filed inside and began pleading with the owner, praying and singing. If refused entry, they knelt in prayer

Figure 10.1 Eliza Jane Trimble Thompson (1816–1905), also known as "Mother Thompson," pictured here in around 1900. At the age of twenty, she accompanied her father, former governor of Ohio, Allen Trimble to the National Temperance Convention where she is said to have been the first woman to have ever entered this annual convention. As Thompson later told her story of the Hillsboro crusade in 1873–74, she did not attend the lecture given by Diocletian Lewis in Hillsboro, but her sixteen-year-old son did and he came back to let his mother know that several other women of the Presbyterian church had elected her as their leader to follow Lewis's advice and protest against the sale of alcohol. As she prayed for guidance on whether to accept the leadership position, her youngest daughter handed her the Bible with the page open to the 146th Psalm, the "Crusade Psalm," and that convinced Thompson to join.
Source: Courtesy of the Ohio Historical Society (AL00007)

outside the establishment (see Figure 10.2). The women could be persuasive. As one crusader noted, "I employ my sweetest accents; I exhaust all the argument I am possessed of; I look into their eyes and grow pathetic; I shed tears and I joke with them— but all in terrible earnest. And they surrender." By the end of 1874, the crusades in Ohio involved over 32,000 women.

The same year a group of churchwomen met in Cleveland to form the national Women's Christian Temperance Union (WCTU), which became the largest women's organization in the 1880s. The WCTU continued the direct-action tactics of the crusades. Under the national leadership of Frances Willard, the WCTU expanded its interests to include those associated with labor and poverty. In addition to the WCTU, Ohio also witnessed the

Figure 10.2   Here, a group of women kneel in front of J. C. Mader's Saloon in Bucyrus, during the temperance crusade of 1873–74.
Source: Courtesy of the Ohio Historical Society (AL01173)

creation of the Ohio Anti-Saloon League. Formed in 1893 in Oberlin and headquartered in Westerville near Columbus, the Ohio League joined with one formed in Washington, D.C., to create the National Anti-Saloon League in 1895, which later became the Anti-Saloon League of America. Its early motto was "The saloon must go." Unlike the WCTU, the League organized itself in a more bureaucratic fashion, with men dominating the League's leadership. Leading the group was Oberlin educated Rev. Howard Hyde Russell and assisting him was the powerful and persuasive Wayne Wheeler (see Figure 10.3). While a student at Oberlin he had been among the first to sign up as a member of the League after hearing Russell deliver a temperance speech there. Indeed, Wheeler, who had been born on a farm near Youngstown in 1869, would become one of the most powerful figures in the United States for his political lobbying in state houses and in the halls of Congress.

In between the formation of these two national groups, temperance was foremost on Ohio legislators' agendas. March 1882 saw passage of the Pond Bill that inaugurated efforts to tax saloons. Saloons were required to obtain a license, for which a saloon had to pay between $100 and $300 depending on the size of the community's population. In addition, the saloon had to pay a bond of $1,000 to guarantee payment of the tax. Some owners of larger saloons with more revenue favored the bill, so as to remove competition. Smaller saloons, which primarily served the less well off and sold mostly beer, fought the tax with help from Ohio's brewers. The law was challenged and in May the Ohio Supreme Court declared it unconstitutional, since, in the Court's view, the law amounted to a licensing provision. As one reporter put it, the "Germans have received the news with the most marked evidences of approval. With the law and order class, the news is depressing."

Figure 10.3   Wayne Wheeler became one of the strongest advocates for prohibition, developing what is now known as "pressure politics" on a single issue. His hatred of alcohol stemmed from his boyhood, where a drunken pitchfork-wielding hired hand injured Wheeler's leg as they worked on the family farm. Wheeler graduated from Oberlin in 1894 and in law from Western Reserve University in 1898. He worked tirelessly on behalf of prohibition in Ohio and nationally serving as principle lawyer and then president of the League. His work resulted in the 1920 passage of the Eighteenth Amendment and the Volstead Act to enforce prohibition.
Source: Courtesy of the Ohio Historical Society (AL03900)

In response, the legislature in 1883 approved the Scott Law, which taxed retail sales of liquor and banned Sunday sales. This, too the Ohio Supreme Court eventually judged unconstitutional in 1884. Meanwhile, the governor, Republican Charles Foster, strongly favored controlling the liquor trade and supported the legislature as they approved two constitutional amendments in April 1883 that proposed creating a local option for alcohol regulation, the taxation of liquor, and opened the possibility of statewide prohibition.

If Republicans and temperance advocates expected a resounding victory in the fall elections of 1883, they were disappointed. Voters rejected the amendments and elected as governor Democrat George Hoadly over the thirty-seven-year-old Republican Joseph Benson Foraker by 359,793 votes to 347,164. Voters also gave the Democrats a two-to-one edge in the Senate and a four-to-three edge in the House. These results presaged the 1884 presidential election, in which Grover Cleveland became the first Democrat to capture the White House since 1856. Temperance advocates also suffered a blow when in October 1884 the Ohio Supreme Court declared the Scott Law unconstitutional.

Hoadly only served one term as governor, bested in 1885 by Foraker, who went on to win again in 1887. In what was a typical biographical trope for successful Ohio politicians, Foraker parlayed military experience and law into political success. Foraker had risen to the rank of captain during the Civil War, riding with Sherman in the "March to the Sea." He then became a lawyer and judge in Cincinnati. Foraker was a tough political fighter, and he earned the nickname "Fire Alarm" for his incendiary rhetoric as he "waved the bloody shirt" against Democrats as the party of disunion and slavery. He boasted a record of accomplishment, supporting a successful 1886 law (the Dow Law) that finally secured the power of the state government to tax the liquor businesses, and another that created a state board of health. Unfortunately, he also embodied the corruption that would soon become a major issue of reform. Foraker had deep connections to various businesses and accepted their money in exchange for favorable votes. He represented the Cincinnati wing of the Republican Party, led by George "Boss" Cox. Based in Cincinnati, Cox owned a saloon, briefly held a city council seat, and then became head of the Hamilton County Republican Committee. His power lay in his control over patronage. Like other city bosses, he distributed favors and delivered the votes (which were often illegal), demanding loyalty, favors, and money in return. While many reformers despised him and his system, he remained popular with constituents because he responded to the needs of city residents. His political machine gave Cincinnati professional fire and police forces, modernized the schools, and dealt successfully with the delivery of city services such as water, electricity, and transportation. His influence finally withered in the early 1900s with the onslaught of reformers.

Within the state Republican Party the rivalry between factions grew intense with Cox and Marcus Hanna regularly at odds over appointments, patronage, and which candidates to support for office. In 1895, the Cox faction won the governorship with their candidate, the wealthy manufacturer Asa Bushnell of Springfield. When a U.S. Senate seat opened in 1896, Bushnell appointed Foraker, but Hanna was not to be outdone. He had supported William McKinley of Canton, who would go on to become governor of Ohio and then be elected president in 1896 and 1900. With McKinley winning the presidency, he appointed Senator John Sherman as secretary of state. This opened the second Ohio Senate seat and Bushnell, acceding to pressure, appointed Hanna. Now both wings of the Ohio GOP had a seat in the Senate, but Hanna also had McKinley as president. Hanna served until his death in 1904, succeeded by his loyal protégé, U.S. Representative Charles Dick of Akron. As senator, Foraker was an active supporter of McKinley's decision to go to war with Spain, wrote the first organic law of Puerto Rico, and played an active role in the negotiations that led to approval for building the Panama Canal. As a leader of the conservative wing of the Republican Party, however, Foraker often stood at odds with Presidents Teddy Roosevelt and Taft as they pursued their reformist agenda. Foraker served until 1909 when he resigned after publication of letters showing that while in the Senate he received direct payment from Standard Oil. Like Boss Cox, Foraker could not withstand the reformist wave.

As they fought each other and attempted to address internal rivalries, Ohio's two major parties faced the challenge of the Populist or People's Party. Despite the growing

Figure 10.4 This portrait of Jacob Coxey (1854–1951) was taken about the time he led his march to Washington D.C. in 1894. Coxey was born in Pennsylvania and settled in Massillon in 1881 where he owned a farm and operated a sandstone quarry and crushing mill. He educated himself on many key political issues of the time, including banking, interest rates, and money. After the march, Coxey returned to Massillon where he devoted his life to politics and business. He ran unsuccessfully for several offices, including Ohio governor in 1895 and 1897, Senate in 1916, and Congress in 1928 and 1930. In 1931, at the age of 77, voters elected him mayor of Massillon. During the Great Depression, President Franklin Roosevelt brought Coxey to Washington, D.C. to discuss the WPA program, based on many of Coxey's ideas from 1894. In 1944, on the steps of the Capitol, Coxey finally delivered the speech he had planned to fifty years earlier.
Source: Courtesy of the Ohio Historical Society (AL01140)

concerns of Ohio's farmers and workers, the Populist Party initially gained little traction as a third party in the Buckeye State. Their first candidate for governor, John Seitz, only managed 23,472 votes in the 1891 election. In 1892, the Populist candidate for president, James B. Weaver, garnered only 10,000 votes in Ohio. Held in the midst of the 1890s depression, the 1895 governor's race drew national attention with the candidate of the People's Party, Jacob Sechler Coxey (see Figure 10.4). Coxey was a successful Massillon businessman who had developed a plan to return the nation to prosperity. He argued that the federal government should develop public works projects to solve unemployment and pay for those projects with bonds. To publicize his plan, in 1894 Coxey organized a march from Massillon to Washington, D.C. Calling themselves the "Commonweal in

Figure 10.5　A group of followers of Jacob Coxey, known as Coxey's Army, in Hagerstown, Maryland on their way to Washington D.C. to protest the lack of response by the federal government to the depression of 1890s. The "army" marched on foot while the Coxey family (including his second wife and his youngest son named Legal Tender) traveled in a horse drawn open carriage.
Source: Courtesy of the Ohio Historical Society (AL01139)

Christ," but popularly known as "Coxey's Army," the group of 100 men left on Easter Sunday, March 25 and were joined by hundreds more as they made their way East.

As it turned out, Coxey's was one of several industrial "armies" headed for the capitol to demand government action in the midst of the depression. To handle the suspected onslaught authorities stationed 1,500 soldiers in Washington. Although he expected thousands to join him, Coxey arrived on May 1 with only 500 men. He demanded to speak to Congress about his plan, but U.S. Capitol police arrested him for trespassing on the grass. His army (see Figure 10.5) and the others that had arrived dispersed over the next several weeks as did the crowds who had been paying to see them in their encampments. Like the Populists he represented, Coxey's ideas were viewed as too radical for the times. It so happened, however, that when the next major depression hit the nation in 1930s, the federal government did exactly as Coxey had hoped.

Ohio's Presidents from Hayes to McKinley

Backgrounds: Early lives, civil war, and politics

Ohio's late nineteenth-century presidents emerged from this milieu of issues and developments at the state level. Drawing on this experience, as well as their records of service in the military and politics, they took advantage of Ohio's centrality to national developments and its political power to reach the nation's highest office. Voters and the Republican Party saw them as moderates, able to bring together various factions, and as offering modest domestic reforms while supporting the rise of big business. Clouds of corruption surrounded Grant and continued with Hayes's victory in the disputed election of 1876. Tragedy surrounds the group as well, as both Garfield and McKinley were assassinated. Until McKinley, each president won in an era of razor thin margins that decided elections. McKinley broke with these trends in two key ways, as discussed below. He won in 1896 in what many call a "realigning election" and by even wider margins in 1900. In 1898 he led the United States to war against Spain, the first against a European power since 1812. The results of the war helped launch the United States as a global power.

Beginning with their lives prior to becoming president, Hayes, Garfield, Harrison and McKinley all had varied backgrounds, but within them were key similarities that prepared each for the presidency. Hayes was born in Delaware, Ohio in 1822. His father ran a successful distillery and farm, but died ten weeks before little "Rud" was born. His mother, Sophia ran the farm with the help of her younger brother, Sardis, who served as a surrogate father to Rud and his older sister, Fanny.

After these tragic early years, Rutherford and Fanny experienced a comfortable childhood. Both were active and eager to learn, but as they grew older, Fanny pushed Rutherford to achieve the prominent career denied to her because of her sex. Rutherford studied hard and with Sardis's financial help managed to attend Kenyon College in Gambier, where he graduated valedictorian in 1842. The honor surprised him, because it was one usually reserved for a church member, which he was not, nor would he ever be. Rutherford then graduated Harvard Law School in 1845 and after beginning work in Lower Sandusky (later renamed Fremont) he moved in 1849 to Cincinnati, where he settled into a successful career a criminal defense lawyer.

In these years, Cincinnati billed itself as the "Queen City of the West," and Rutherford took advantage of the social life and opportunities for success the city offered to someone of his charm, intelligence, and standing. Amid his courting of female socialites, Hayes fell in love with a young woman from his hometown, Lucy Webb, who had been attending the Wesleyan Female College in Cincinnati. They were married in December 1852. Lucy would eventually give birth to eight children (all but one of them boys), three of whom died in infancy.

The couple possessed the strong sense of self-improvement and reform typical of those of similar backgrounds who came to dominate Ohio's public culture during the last half of the nineteenth century. Rutherford and Lucy maintained a lifelong concern for respectability, for the betterment of themselves as well as society. Along these lines, Lucy developed a strong stance for temperance and against slavery, and strengthened Rutherford's views on these issues. As the slavery issue heated up, Rutherford joined with others in 1855 to form the Republican Party in Ohio. Hayes's entry into politics came in 1858 when leaders selected him to fill out the remaining term of the city solicitor for Cincinnati. He was re-elected to that post in 1859. At this point in his career, Hayes had already established himself as a likable and kind man, a person of integrity and fairness, and as one who avoided taking extreme positions. All of this made him appealing to a broad range of people, an aspect of Hayes's personality that would help him as a leader in politics but also in the coming Civil War.

James Abram Garfield too suffered the loss of his father in childhood, but unlike Hayes Garfield faced poverty. Garfield was born in Orange Township, Cuyahoga County in 1831 and was the last president to be born in a log cabin. Garfield's father died when James was two, leaving the family to struggle economically. As soon as he was old enough James worked to support his widowed mother, including a brief stint as a mule driver on the Ohio and Erie Canal at the age of sixteen. As an adult, Garfield would make political capital from his rags-to-riches background, and his was literally a Horatio Alger story, for none other than Alger penned Garfield's campaign biography, *From Canal Boy to President*.

At the age of seventeen Garfield enrolled in the Western Reserve Eclectic Institute (later Hiram College), run by the Disciples of Christ, who claimed his allegiance. Garfield was an intelligent, hard-working student, and after two years at the Institute he began teaching his fellow students, chiefly in the area of classical studies. At twenty-three he gained admission to Williams College in Massachusetts, where he again excelled. After graduating he returned home to become an educator.

After one year teaching at the Eclectic Institute, Garfield became the school's president. Finding the bickering among faculty intolerable, he decided to enter politics. He established himself as a skilled orator and a staunch Unionist, and the Republican Party chose him to run for the state senate in 1859. Garfield emerged from the election victorious and became the youngest member of the legislature when he began his term in 1860.

Unlike Hayes and Garfield, Benjamin Harrison came from a distinguished political family. Born near Cincinnati on August 20, 1833, Benjamin was the grandson of William Henry Harrison, the ninth President of the United States and the great-grandson of Colonel Benjamin Harrison of Virginia, who signed the Declaration of Independence. He was educated at first on his father's farm, along with his eight siblings, and later attended Farmer's College, near Cincinnati. There he exhibited his lifelong qualities of personal resolve, intelligence, seriousness, and hard work. During these years he also acquired his strong Presbyterian faith, often giving speeches on temperance and regularly discussing his spiritual beliefs. His hard work paid off, for in 1850, at the age of seventeen, he entered Miami University as a junior. He graduated third in his class two years later. He began reading law in Cincinnati and in 1853 married Caroline Scott, one year his senior and daughter of Presbyterian minister and Farmer's College professor Rev. John W. Scott. In 1854 Harrison was admitted to the bar and moved to Indianapolis to practice law. A great achievement given that he was not yet twenty-one years old.

Harrison began building a successful law practice through skill, hard work, and good connections. He also gravitated toward politics, and as the sectional crisis grew he aligned himself with the newly formed Republican Party. He ran successfully for Indianapolis city attorney in 1858 and for Indiana's Supreme Court Reporter in 1860.

Hayes, Garfield and Harrison grew up with farming as the mainstay of the family livelihood. McKinley though reflected the growing industrial makeup of Ohio. He was born in Niles, Ohio on January 29, 1843, the seventh of eight children born to William McKinley, Sr., and Nancy Allison McKinley. The family moved to nearby Poland, Ohio, when William was ten. His father worked in iron foundries and then ran a small business while his mother ran the household. McKinley was educated at local schools and then attended Allegheny College in Meadville Pennsylvania for one term in 1860.

Although emerging from varied backgrounds, as it was for Grant, the Civil War would become the defining experience for Hayes, Garfield, Harrison, and McKinley. When the Confederate assault on Fort Sumter in April 1861 signaled the beginning of the Civil War, Rutherford Hayes was nearly forty years old, with three children at home and his wife, Lucy, expecting their fourth. He did not volunteer for military service immediately, but after a month his desire to serve won out. "I would prefer to go into it if I knew I was to die or be killed in the course of it, than to live through and after it without taking any part in it." Like the other Ohio presidents who served in the Civil War, Hayes's personal life and his political career were shaped by the experience.

Hayes was among the first three-year volunteers, and like other men of his social standing, he used his political connections to gain an appointment as an officer, in his case as a major with the 23rd Ohio Volunteer Infantry (OVI). Though he lacked military experience, Hayes learned quickly, fought bravely, and soon earned the respect of the enlisted soldiers as well as his officers, one of whom was fellow Ohioan and future president, William McKinley. Wounded five times, Hayes ended the war as a brevetted major general. Throughout the conflict, Hayes strengthened his love of Ohio and his bias towards western soldiers and people generally. He lauded his own 23rd OVI as the "crack regiment," idolized fellow Ohioan General William Tecumseh Sherman, and regularly criticized easterners and the Army of the Potomac as being weak willed. Meanwhile, Lucy served as a nurse, aiding Rutherford and other soldiers in Middletown, Maryland, in 1862 following the battle of Antietam.

James Garfield had been serving in the state legislature since 1860, but resigned his seat to organize the 42nd OVI. Fighting at Middle Creek, Shiloh, and Chickamauga he rose quickly from the rank of lieutenant colonel to major general. His last assignment was as chief of staff to General William S. Rosecrans in the Army of the Cumberland.

From Indiana, Benjamin Harrison raised his own regiment, the 70th Indiana, and was appointed colonel. Through 1864, he and his men saw only a brief skirmish in Kentucky, spending most of the time protecting fortifications and rail lines there and in Tennessee. Then, in May 1864 at Resaca, Georgia, Harrison's regiment saw its first taste of battle as part of Sherman's Atlanta campaign. Harrison led assaults near the city and again at New Hope Church and Golgotha Church. His courage and skill won him command of a brigade of which the 70th was a part. At Peach Tree Creek, in July, he exhibited great decisiveness that would lead to his promotion to brevet brigadier general in February 1865. He saw action in December 1864 defending Nashville and finished the war with Sherman in South Carolina.

At the age of eighteen, McKinley had been in college and when war broke out he joined the 23rd OVI serving to the end of the war and acquiring the rank of brevet major. The 23rd OVI was, as mentioned, commanded for a time by Rutherford Hayes, and McKinley considered Hayes his friend and mentor.

In addition to the common experience of the Civil War each of these men served some kind of political apprenticeship prior to becoming president, with Hayes and McKinley each serving as Ohio's governor before becoming president. While Hayes and his men were still in the Shenandoah Valley in 1864, Republicans in Cincinnati nominated him to run for the U.S. House of Representatives. Hayes refused to leave the battlefield to campaign, shrewdly proclaiming in a letter that "an officer fit for duty who at this crisis would abandon his post to electioneer for a seat in Congress ought to be scalped." That, as it turned out, was all the campaigning he needed to do. Hayes won the election and the war ended before he took his seat in December 1865. Hayes won re-election in 1866 and during his terms in Congress he supported the radical Republicans' program to use the federal government to secure equal rights for African Americans in the South.

Hayes did not enjoy being a congressman and he prepared to give up politics altogether after his second term. Then, in 1867, Ohio Republicans asked him to run for governor. Hayes accepted the offer, resigned from Congress, and threw himself into the gubernatorial campaign. Beginning in August, Hayes spoke nearly every day. He supported free public schools as a way to secure economic and intellectual progress and to heal the racial divide. That same year, the Ohio legislature also placed on the ballot a constitutional amendment granting voting rights for African American men, and Hayes spoke vigorously for its passage. His Democratic opponent was Allen G. Thurman, former congressman and chief justice of the Ohio Supreme Court. Overall, 1867 was a bad year for the Republicans. Democrats, who had appealed to racial prejudice, captured the state legislature and saw the voting rights amendment fail. Hayes, though, ran ahead of his party, managing to secure a narrow victory of 2,983 votes out of 484,603 cast.

By design, the office of governor had little power. The biggest influence the state's chief executive had was his ability to make appointments. Other than that, he could only suggest legislation and try to influence the legislature. The situation was made worse for Hayes who, in his first term as governor, faced a Democratic-controlled legislature. In 1869 the legislature did approve one of Hayes's ideas, a state geological survey. Hayes ran for re-election that year, facing George H. Pendleton of Cincinnati. Hayes again pushed the issue of suffrage for African American men and also attacked Democrats for supporting "greenbackism" instead of the conservative orthodoxy of paying off the war debt with gold-backed notes. This time, Hayes won by 7,500 votes and Republicans would gain and manage to hold a slim margin in the upcoming legislature.

Now Hayes urged the legislature to consider several issues. His first priority was securing Ohio's approval of the Fifteenth Amendment to the U.S. Constitution. This would protect the voting rights of adult men regardless of "race, color or previous condition of servitude." With a Republican majority, and Hayes promising federal patronage for some fellow Republicans, Ohio approved the amendment, 57 to 55 in the Ohio house and 19 to 18 in the Ohio senate. Hayes also pushed the legislature to decide on a location for a land grant college. The Morrill Land Grant Act had passed in 1862 granting states money to construct public colleges to provide primarily agricultural and mechanical training. Ohio's lawmakers could never agree on a location. Finally, in 1870, they chose Columbus where they founded the Agricultural and Mechanical College that would become the Ohio State University.

Hayes advocated for a civil service system to appointments, as opposed to the "spoils" system that meant quality civil servants were thrown out of office whenever their party lost power. Hayes also hoped to make the judiciary more independent. In Hayes's era, justices were elected and poorly paid. Hayes believed this combination made them more susceptible to the influence of wealthy individuals and corporations. Therefore he urged the legislature to increase the pay for justices and have them appointed by the governor and confirmed by the state senate. He also advocated for reform of the state's penal system.

Hayes was the first Ohio governor to serve three terms. After his second he retired to his beloved Fremont estate, Spiegel Grove, only to be called upon by his party in 1875 to run again for governor. At this time, the Republicans were in disarray. The depression that had begun in 1873 under Republican leadership was in its second year. Democrats controlled the U.S. House of Representatives in 1875 and in Ohio, Democrats controlled the state. Party leaders turned to Hayes as their best chance to regain power. Hayes accepted, facing another tough fight against his earlier foe, Allen Thurman.

Once again, Hayes beat Thurman. As many other Republicans did in these years, throughout the campaign Hayes "waved the bloody shirt," attacking the Democrats for having supported slavery, rebellion, and the denial of black rights. In his third run, Hayes also exploited anti-Catholic sentiment, especially over the issue of using public money to support parochial schools. The Ohio Supreme Court had recently upheld the Cincinnati school board's decision to ban hymns and prayers in schools. Meanwhile, Democrats supported the Geghan Bill, which mandated equal facilities for worship by all denominations in state custodial institutions. During the campaign, Hayes maintained he was simply supporting secular public schooling, but he was playing upon Protestant fears and prejudice in order to win election. The Geghan Bill was repealed during Hayes's brief third term.

In the meantime, Garfield, Harrison, and McKinley were developing their own political careers. In 1862 as the Civil War continued (Hayes continued fighting for two more years) Garfield ran for the U.S. Congress and won. Aged 32 when he entered the House in December 1863, he was the youngest member. While there, he supported the Radical Republicans, agitating for civil rights, the creation of the Freedmen's Bureau, and supporting the impeachment of President Andrew Johnson. In time, Garfield's major interest became finances, and he was one of the most forceful and intelligent advocates of hard money. He also served on the commission to determine the winner of the 1876 presidential election.

Through the early 1860s Garfield's personal life was in distress. Although he would fall deeply in love with his wife, Lucretia ("Crete" as he called her), this was not so early in their marriage. Although he had already promised himself to Crete, Garfield had developed strong feelings for another woman, Rebecca Selleck, whom he had met in Massachusetts. During his first term in Congress, Garfield drifted away from Crete and had an affair with a twenty-year-old widow named Lucia Calhoun. He broke off the affair in June 1864 and from that point his marriage strengthened. There is reason to believe that Garfield sought a way to avoid his domestic life through political life and then through fighting in the war. Dissatisfied with teaching at Hiram and his marriage, Garfield's actions were as much principled and ambitious as they were personal.

At the war's end Harrison returned to his position as clerk for the Supreme Court and his law practice. He became part of two prominent legal events, those stemming from the Supreme Court's 1866 *Ex parte Milligan* case and the Whiskey Ring surrounding President Grant. Once the Supreme Court had invalidated Indianan Lambdin Milligan's conviction for conspiracy during the Civil War, Milligan sued in Indiana state court for damages. The case went to federal court, and President Grant asked Harrison to argue for the U.S. government against Milligan, who was represented by Democratic attorneys.

Both sides claimed victory, since the jury ruled for Milligan but limited his damages to five dollars. Then, as part of the Whiskey Ring scandal whereby federal agents took bribes from distillers to avoid paying taxes, Harrison successfully defended one of the accused agents, a fellow Hoosier from a prominent family.

Politics again called to Harrison, and he ran unsuccessfully for governor in 1876. At the 1880 Republican convention, Harrison led the Indiana delegation. At first he supported James Blaine, but he was among those who led their supporters over to Garfield, allowing the Ohioan to gain the nomination. Republicans captured the legislature in Indiana as well and awarded Harrison by appointing him to the U.S. Senate.

Harrison served one term in the upper house and while there he supported the Republican platform on high tariffs, though he was willing to support adjustments. He also voted for the Civil Service Act in 1883, while maintaining that one ought not to be disqualified based on political commitments. Harrison favored railroad regulation, settlement of western states through federal assistance, internal improvements, and veterans' benefits. He argued for full rights for African Americans and supported federal aid to education.

As others had done, when the war ended, McKinley opted for law, although he had a strong desire to enter politics. He settled in Canton and ran successfully for Stark County prosecutor in 1869. He held the post for two years and then resumed his law practice. In 1871 he married Ida Saxton, granddaughter of the founder and editor of the *Canton Repository*.

Through 1873 all seemed well, as family and William's law practice reflected happiness and success. Then tragedy struck. Ida, the couple's second daughter, died at the age of six months. Two years later their remaining child, Katie, died of typhoid fever at the age of three. The events left both William and Ida devastated, but Ida never fully recovered, remaining virtually an invalid and clinging to William for support. McKinley remained a devoted companion, caring for and nursing his wife for the remainder of their lives together.

In the face of these hardships, the McKinleys maintained an active public life as William pursued a political career. In 1875 he campaigned for his old commander Rutherford Hayes, helping Hayes to win a third term as governor. The next year, McKinley ran for Congress and won, serving from 1877 to 1891 with only one two-year interruption. In 1890, McKinley lost his seat, but the next year he ran successfully for governor. After serving two terms he left the governorship as a leading contender for the Republican presidential nomination in 1896. He received 661 votes on the first ballot at the GOP convention in St. Louis, easily winning the nomination.

Remembered as having many friends, McKinley listened more than he talked and remained patient and steady in his dealings with other political leaders. He was charming, tactful, and thoughtful, but he grew into a respected orator. In the Congress, McKinley developed a reputation as a moderate. As a representative of industrial Canton and the surrounding hinterland, he won support from workers as well as business owners and farmers. While he supported the expansion of business he was also sympathetic to labor unions. He also managed to remain above the ethnic and religious divisions of the day, expressing tolerance and inclusiveness and preferring to emphasize better jobs and a higher standard of living. He gained a powerful role as chair of the

House Ways and Means Committee, which allowed him to exert control over legislation. While his name is on the tariff of 1890, he remained open to compromise. For McKinley, the tariff was a means to provide a stable, growing economy that would help both producers and consumers, and he became one of the leading spokesmen on the issue.

After his congressional defeat in 1890, attributed to opposition to rising prices the public blamed on his Tariff Act, McKinley ran for governor of Ohio in 1891. He drew huge crowds as he campaigned across the state against his opponent, sitting governor James Campbell. The main issues were the coinage of silver and the tariff. Come November, McKinley won a close contest, with a margin of 21,511 votes out of the 795,629 cast. Republicans also captured the legislature. During McKinley's first term, he supported the legislature as it moved toward moderate reforms, approving laws to increase safety regulations for workers on railroads and a voluntary arbitration system for labor disputes. The legislature also had to address a continuing budget deficit and did so with a corporate franchise tax. They also had time to prohibit barbering on Sunday.

Although he won his second term by a wider margin, some 80,000 votes, it would be much different than the first. A severe economic depression hit the nation in the spring of 1893, and within a year 15,000 businesses had failed and some 4 million Americans were out of work. In Ohio, the ranks of the unemployed swelled to hundreds of thousands. Strikes and riots broke out across the state, and mobs attacked or threatened courthouses and other public buildings in several locations. McKinley responded by sending out the National Guard to keep order. He would often stay late in his office monitoring various incidents, reading and sending telegrams directing Guard troops throughout Ohio. While he used the Guard to keep order, he also expressed sympathy for the unemployed. In January 1895 after an appeal for help from unemployed miners in the Hocking Valley and the mayor of Nelsonville, McKinley personally led a relief drive that managed to send food and supplies to the area. His sentiments kept him popular among workers even as the depression deepened, while his commitment to law and order pleased business owners and professionals. While dealing with the chaos and calamity of the depression, McKinley and the legislature managed to secure laws granting limited suffrage to women and allowing married women to act as executors of estates. They also approved a law requiring railroad companies to disclose all names and addresses of stockholders.

When it came time for each of these men to decide whether to accept the nomination for president, they all possessed a good deal of experience addressing key issues of the day and had developed a positive reputation for leadership. They also had respect within the Republican Party. Yet while as a group their presidencies were filled with some success, controversy and tragedy marked them as well.

Hayes's presidency

Not long after his third victory for governor, Hayes drew a great deal of interest from Republicans in Ohio and from voters across the nation who hoped to maintain the GOP's hold on the presidency in the election of 1876 (see Figure 10.6). As a candidate with broad

Figure 10.6   This is a campaign banner for the 1876 Republican presidential ticket of Ohio governor Rutherford B. Hayes and New York Representative William A. Wheeler. Hayes and Wheeler had both earned reputations for honesty, which the Republicans needed after the scandals of the Grant administration, and all factions of the Republican Party were able to unite behind them.
Source: Library of Congress Prints and Photographs Division (LC-DIG-ppmsca-07604)

appeal, Hayes held the potential to unite the fractious party and repair the damage caused by the corruption associated with Grant. As he often had in his political career, Hayes did not actively campaign for the nomination but did nothing to dissuade his supporters. With his strong record as governor, war-hero status, and ability to appeal to various factions within the Republican Party, Hayes earned the presidential nomination at the national convention held that year in Cincinnati.

His Democratic opponent was Samuel Tilden, the popular reformist governor of New York. The year 1876 marked the nation's centennial but the country lay mired in an economic depression; still faced the thorny question of reconstructing the South; and found itself reeling from the dramatic effects of rapid industrialization, urbanization, and foreign immigration. The corruption and scandals associated with the Grant administration did not make Hayes's quest for the White House any easier. Hayes himself believed he would lose. On the day of the election Tilden carried the popular vote, but with the totals from Oregon and the three southern states of Florida, Louisiana, and South Carolina in dispute, the New Yorker remained one electoral vote short of victory. When in December electors met to vote for president, both Republican and Democratic electors cast conflicting votes in Oregon, Florida, Louisiana, and South Carolina. All hinged on a special commission appointed by Congress in January 1877 to decide the winner.

Until *Bush v. Gore* in 2000, the 1876 election proved to be the nation's closest, most hostile and most controversial presidential election. Initially the commission comprised five congressional Republicans (including James Garfield) five congressional Democrats (including Allen Thurman) and five Supreme Court justices, two Republican, two Democrat and one independent, David Davis. However, just before the commission was to meet, the Illinois senate, controlled by Democrats, voted to appoint Davis to the U.S. Senate. Democrats believed that the appointment would persuade Davis to vote for Tilden but, rather than stay on the commission, Davis promptly resigned. The remaining justices available to serve on the commission were all Republicans. Davis's successor, Joseph P. Bradley, ultimately had the deciding vote in giving the presidency to Hayes, with 185 electoral votes to Tilden's 184.

It remained for the electoral votes to be officially counted in Congress. With Hayes's opponents calling him "Rutherfraud" and "His Fraudulency," Democrats filibustered the vote count to delay the result and try to extract concessions from Republicans. Talks began among Hayes's supporters and southern Democrats, out of which supposedly came a bargain or the "Compromise of 1877." In exchange for acquiescing in Hayes's election and promising to respect black civil rights in the South, Democrats received assurances that upon becoming president, Hayes would remove the remaining federal troops who were protecting the capitals in Louisiana and South Carolina, recognize Democratic "home rule" in the South, promote federal support for a transcontinental railroad through the South, and appoint a southerner to the cabinet. With a deal in place, the story goes, the official vote count ended. At 4:10 a.m. on March 2, 1877, with four guards armed with revolvers surrounding him, the presiding officer of the Senate, Republican Thomas Ferry of Michigan, announced Hayes the winner. Hayes took the oath of office on Saturday, March 3.

While leaders of both sides did meet, it remains uncertain whether they struck an official bargain to give Hayes the election. Hayes had already announced his intention to appoint a Southerner to the cabinet, and Tennessean David M. Key became postmaster general. Support for the transcontinental railroad never materialized. However, the key item in the "corrupt bargain" scenario was Hayes's order to have the remaining federal troops protecting the statehouses in Louisiana and South Carolina return to their barracks, thereby ending Reconstruction. In the campaign Hayes had already made assurances to support "home rule" in the South, which included the removal of troops. So-called Democratic "Redeemer" governments had taken back power in all other Southern states by then. Entering the presidency after such drama and without a mandate from the voters Hayes adopted a conciliatory tone on this issue in his inaugural address. While he called on the South to respect the rights of both races, he ended his address with an appeal for a "union depending not upon the constraint of force, but upon the loving devotion of a free people."

Moreover, Democrats controlled the House and refused to appropriate funds to pay the Army if troops remained in New Orleans and Charleston. Already reduced to a force of 25,000, the focus of the Army had shifted to battling Native Americans in the West, not protecting the rights of former slaves in the South. White northerners and the Republican Party had grown weary of trying to remake the South and under the Grant administration had been turning their attention to issues surrounding industrialization, urbanization, and immigration. Native-born whites were uneasy over southern and eastern Europeans beginning to enter the United States, and those in California clamored for an end to Chinese immigration. Thus, it was easier for them to identify with whites in the South who called for "home rule" and an end to what they claimed were the corrupt governments supported by African Americans. Furthermore, in the midst of a depression that began in 1873, Northerners were worried more about their own security than that of blacks in the South.

Before ordering the troops back to their barracks, Hayes demanded and received assurances from Democratic leaders in Louisiana and South Carolina that in taking power for the first time since the Civil War they would respect black rights. Hayes was cautiously optimistic that race relations would improve; he had supported radical Republicans while in Congress and as governor of Ohio pushed the state legislature to approve the Fifteenth Amendment. By the time he took the presidential oath, Hayes had moderated his views, believing that the military presence in the South had made race relations worse, not better, and that reform would come with time and patience through education and development. Of course, Hayes was wrong. Relations only worsened as lynching spread and all white governments in the South began to enact the foundation of the Jim Crow system of laws and customs that repressed African Americans for at least another century until the civil rights movement of the 1960s. Bargain or no bargain, sadly, as one scholar concluded, on civil rights Hayes "chose to avert his eyes from the painful sights around him."

Hayes has also drawn attention for his role in the Great Railroad Strike of 1877, the first nationwide labor upheaval in the United States. Early in July, several railroads notified their employees that wages would be cut 10 percent for the second time since 1873. With the news coming in the midst of a depression, brakemen and firemen in West Virginia employed by the Baltimore & Ohio Railroad refused to let the trains run. The governor sent state militia to get the trains moving, but the militiamen ended up fraternizing with the disgruntled workers. The governor of West Virginia requested and received federal troops from Hayes, whose order came just less than three months after Hayes's order ending Reconstruction. Workers in Martinsburg set up barricades, but the troops succeeded in getting some trains moving. Meanwhile, violence erupted in Baltimore, Maryland, and Pittsburgh, Pennsylvania. In city after city, citizen militias composed mainly of veterans groups and members of the middle and upper classes battled crowds comprised of strikers as well as sympathetic members of the working class, men and women. In many locations National Guardsmen dispatched by governors entered the fray in order to quell the violence. In Indianapolis, Indiana, future president Benjamin Harrison donned his Civil War uniform and marched down the streets of the city. General strikes occurred in Chicago and St. Louis and sympathy strikes broke out among workers in other industries. In San Francisco the violence was directed as much against Chinese workers as it was the management of the railroads.

Ohio was spared the worst of the violence, but mobs did attack property in Columbus and protests shut down rail service in several cities, including Zanesville, Lancaster, and

Steubenville. In Newark, a major depot for the Baltimore & Ohio, militiamen managed to get trains moving after challenging strikers to a game of baseball, reflecting a great deal of mutual respect and sympathy among the guard and strikers.

Hayes moved cautiously in dispatching federal troops to the strike scenes, only doing so when it was clear to him that local and state authorities had exhausted all efforts. Hayes also refused to have troops run trains or otherwise be involved in breaking strikes. He believed in protecting property, especially federal installations, and keeping peace. By late August the strike had ended. Over the next three years, wages and conditions improved. In the wake of the strike, Hayes received acclamation from many for his calm response and for refusing to listen to those such as former president Grant who wanted Hayes to call up reserves and crush the strikes. However, Hayes did support antilabor federal judges who ruled for railroad companies by effectively outlawing strikes against bankrupt railroads. Despite his sympathies for workers, Hayes offered them nothing concrete.

The violence of the 1877 strike had come six years after the Paris Commune, the much publicized effort by workers in France to seize power and create a workers' republic. Many Americans associated violence and upheaval with labor unions, immigrants, and "foreign" ideas such as communism and socialism, and the 1877 episode struck fear into the hearts of many middle- and upper-class Americans that the United States was headed for revolution. The Great Strike and subsequent strikes led cities and towns in Ohio and across the country to expand their police forces, states to professionalize their National Guard, and the federal government to support the construction of armories throughout the North.

In other matters of his presidency, Hayes continued to advocate for civil service reform and an end to patronage in government offices. His most famous act came when he succeeded in removing future president Chester A. Arthur from his post as Collector of the Port of New York. Hayes had appointed a commission to investigate corruption in the nation's largest and most important customs house; not surprisingly, the commission found evidence of bribes, kickbacks, and other forms of favoritism. Arthur routinely accepted a portion of all fines levied against imports and funneled salary kickbacks from port employees to support the New York Republican political machine headed by Senator Roscoe Conkling. Hayes succeeded in using this as a showcase for reform, thereby helping to build support for the eventual passage of the Pendleton Civil Service Reform Act of 1883, written by Ohio Senator George Pendleton (Hayes's onetime foe) and signed by none other than Chester Arthur.

Hayes had pledged to serve just one term and in 1881 he, Lucy, and five of their children retired to Spiegel Grove in Fremont. Lucy died in 1889 and Rutherford in 1893. Both are buried there. The estate remained in family hands until eventually becoming part of the Rutherford B. Hayes Presidential Center.

With Hayes vowing to leave after one term the presidential nomination for the GOP was thrown open. By the time the 1880 Republican national convention arrived Garfield had developed a reputation as a strong leader. Although his name had been mentioned as a possible presidential candidate, Garfield attended the convention to plead the case for fellow Ohioan John Sherman. When the convention deadlocked, it was Garfield who emerged as the candidate who could best satisfy the warring factions. To please the more conservative "stalwarts," the delegates nominated Chester A. Arthur of New York for Vice President, the same person who Hayes had dismissed from the New York customs house for lax administration. In the 1880 election, Garfield narrowly defeated his Democratic opponent (and fellow veteran) Winfield Scott Hancock of Pennsylvania by less than 10,000 votes.

Garfield's presidency

Garfield's tenure as president was too short to evaluate meaningfully. In Congress and as president he allied himself with the hard-money and low-tariff wing of his party and opposed labor unions. He also sided with those pushing expansion of trade and maintaining the influence of the United States in Latin America and Hawaii. Garfield generally believed that the industrial revolution was beneficial to society, not something to oppose or reform. Though he believed that business should have access to the cheapest labor it could obtain, Garfield remained uneasy about foreign immigration, supporting the restriction of immigrant Chinese laborers.

Although allied with the conservative position, there remained, in James Garfield, some youthful radicalism. He maintained his suspicion of cooperative farm programs supported by the Grange, a powerful organization of farmers that he called "communism in disguise." He attacked corporate monopoly and in Congress he supported railroad regulation. Garfield supported issues such as the creation of a federal department of education, the Smithsonian, and federal support for coastal and geologic surveys. Garfield spoke strongly in favor of increased federal aid for education of African Americans in the South. He continued to voice his frustration over corruption and the spoils system, something his predecessor had also done. Garfield despised having to fill his days by meeting with office seekers. While one might view civil service reform as a challenge to conservative leadership, in reality it was designed and led by elites. Beholden neither to politicians nor the masses, this group of well-educated, upper-class men feared that in the wake of industrialization, society no longer adhered to their values and worldview. Civil service reform could help ensure that only the "best" men, ones like themselves, would be in positions of influence within government. At times Garfield seemed to support this view, at other times he remained quite partisan. In any event, the main issue for Garfield was preserving the power of the president to make appointments. Controversy erupted within GOP ranks over Garfield's appointments, with neither the reformers nor the stalwarts satisfied.

In May 1881, Lucretia contracted what was probably malaria and went to Elberon, a popular village on the New Jersey shore, to recuperate. On the morning of July 2, Garfield entered Washington's Baltimore and Potomac Station to begin his summer vacation. He planned to meet his wife and attend a reunion at his alma mater, Williams College. As he walked through the station with two of his sons and Secretary of State James Blaine, a deranged office seeker, Charles Julius Guiteau, shot Garfield twice in the back at point-blank-range. Guiteau had been stalking the president and planning the assassination for months after failing in his attempts to gain an ambassadorship. One bullet grazed Garfield's arm, the other lodged in his spine. The president lingered on through the

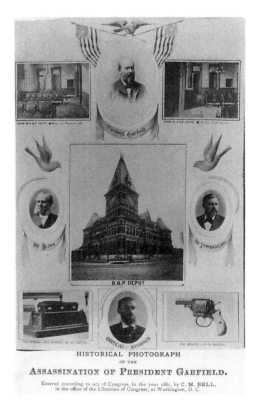

HISTORICAL PHOTOGRAPH
OF THE
ASSASSINATION OF PRESIDENT GARFIELD.
Entered according to act of Congress, in the year 1881, by C. M. BELL,
in the office of the Librarian of Congress, at Washington, D. C.

Figure 10.7 Photographer C.M. (Charles Milton) Bell operated a studio in Washington, D.C. that became a favored business for official photographs. Pictured in this set are portraits of Garfield, two doctors who worked on Garfield, D. Willard Bliss (who earlier attended to Lincoln after the president was shot), Smith Townsend, and Charles Guiteau. During Guiteau's imprisonment, Bell was the only photographer permitted to visit him and Bell took pictures of Guiteau who then sold the signed pictures to generate publicity and support for himself. Bell also benefited from the work. Also shown is the exterior and interior of the B&P Depot where Garfield was shot, the coffin lying in State at the Capitol, and the gun used.
Source: Library of Congress Prints and Photographs Division (LC-USZ62-80339)

summer, but he continued to weaken. At times doctors inserted unsterilized instruments and their fingers into the president's wound in a failed attempt to find the bullet. Even Alexander Graham Bell could not locate it with a special metal detection device he invented to try to save the president. In early September, Garfield was moved to Elberon in one last hope the beach air might save him. Garfield died there on September 19, 1881 (see Figure 10.7). The assassin, Guiteau, went to the gallows in June 1882 convinced he had done God's will.

Garfield's body was placed in the Capitol Rotunda for two days while between 70,000 and 100,000 mourners filed past the fallen president. Then Garfield's body, aboard a long train draped in black, traveled from the nation's capital to Cleveland's Public Square. Along the route, silent crowds watched the train roll by as bells tolled in the towns and cities. In Cleveland, Garfield's body lay atop a 100-foot pavilion, where some 150,000 mourners paid their respects. He was then buried in Cleveland's Lakeview Cemetery. Garfield's assassination by a deranged office seeker helped push forward the Civil Service Act of 1883, an act signed into law by Garfield's successor, Chester Arthur.

Harrison's presidency

As noted earlier, Democrats gained the presidency in 1884 with the election of New York's Grover Cleveland. He then lost his re-election bid in 1888 against the Ohio-born Benjamin Harrison. As was often the case in these years, Harrison was the best available candidate who, while not strongly favored by any one faction of the Republican Party, did not anger any of them either. It also helped that Blaine, the favorite and 1884 candidate, declined to run again. So at the GOP's 1888 national convention in Chicago "Little Ben" (he was barely 5'7") managed to secure the nomination over Ohioan John Sherman, who once again failed to capture the nomination he had sought for many years.

In the general election Harrison faced incumbent Grover Cleveland and like most elections in these years it proved to be a close one. The tariff issue remained the major one for both candidates and Harrison pulled no punches on the question. The "protective tariff," he insisted, was "wholesome and necessary" to "preserve the American market for American producers, and to maintain the American scale of wages." In typical fashion, neither Harrison nor Cleveland undertook campaign tours. Harrison stood on his front porch in Indianapolis and gave speeches to visiting delegations. Incredibly, some 300,000 people stopped by his house to hear Harrison speak. Meanwhile, the state party organizations carried the weight of generating even more enthusiasm with parades, rallies, bands, and producing various political ephemera such as posters and buttons. As was the case in 1876, the Democratic candidate won the popular vote but lost the electoral vote to the Republican. Harrison carried all of the West and most of the North, including Cleveland's New York. Republicans also gained control of both houses of Congress.

With the White House and Congress in Republican hands, Harrison's first two years in office were among the most active for any president. Harrison signed the McKinley Tariff Act in October 1890. The new law, named for Ohio Congressman and future president William McKinley, raised rates on many imported goods, pushing the average rate to its highest in U.S. history, some 48 percent. The law did, however, add some goods, notably sugar, to the "duty free" list. It also gave greater power to Harrison by granting authority to the president to negotiate reciprocity agreements with other nations. Public perception (shaped in part by skillful Democrats) was that Republicans had managed to increase prices on almost everything, and thus not long after Harrison signed the law, Democrats carried the mid-term elections in the House. The new law also led to retaliation by a number of nations as they raised their own tariff rates or imposed restrictions on U.S. imports, mostly agricultural and food products. All of this would add to tensions within the Republican Party and contributed to Harrison's defeat in 1892.

While the tariff was a deeply partisan issue, there was greater agreement on antitrust legislation. By the time Harrison took office, the public had become concerned over the concentration of power by large corporations to dominate industries, especially through the use of trusts. An example is John D. Rockefeller's Standard Oil Trust. Rockefeller had formed the company in Cleveland in 1870, and created the Standard Oil Trust in 1882 that controlled some 90 percent of all refining in the United States. In December 1889, Ohio's John Sherman, Chair of the Senate Finance Committee was the first member of the Senate to propose a federal law aimed at curbing the power of big business, and his name became attached to the legislation that moved through Congress. The measure passed 51-1 in the Senate in April and 242-0 in the House in June. On July 2, 1890, Harrison signed the Sherman Antitrust Act, the first federal law to forbid monopolistic business practices. Although Harrison did not use the law, his successors, including Theodore Roosevelt and William Howard Taft, would do so. It represented a major milestone in federal regulation and has remained a vital law ever since.

Twelve days later, Harrison signed the Sherman Silver Purchase Act on July 14. The Act represented a compromise plan among those wanting to adhere strictly to the gold standard and those pushing for the free coinage of silver. It also was part of a deal to gain support from Westerners for the McKinley Tariff. The Silver Purchase Act required the federal government to buy greater amounts of silver and to issue new paper notes redeemable in either gold or silver. Farmers hoped issuing notes would lead to inflation, which would help reduce their debt burden. Western mining interests hoped the act would increase the price of silver. What happened was that rather than exchange the new notes for silver, investors demanded gold, nearly depleting the nation of its gold reserves. Nor did inflation materialize; in fact, prices dropped as a severe depression began in 1893. This prompted Congress to repeal the Silver Purchase Act that same year.

Harrison also dealt with the continued growth and expansion of the United States in the West. He signed the Land Revision Act of 1891, which among other things established the national forests. Harrison moved fairly vigorously in adding some 22 million acres during his presidency. He authorized statehood for North and South Dakota, Washington, Montana, Wyoming and Idaho and he kept California's leaders happy by pledging his support to restrict Chinese immigration.

Western expansion increased pressure on Native Americans and it was Harrison who was in office when the tragic massacre at Wounded Knee took place in December 1890. The incident marked the end of nearly 400 years of armed conflict between Native peoples and European settlers and their descendents. In response to the pressure and conflict, some Indians followed the "Ghost Dance," a revivalist campaign centered in South Dakota similar to those conducted earlier by leaders such as Neolin and Tenskwatawa. Federal authorities, worried the revival might lead to further armed conflict, dispatched about 600 Army troops to Pine Ridge and Rosebud reservations of the Sioux. On December 29, at the Wounded Knee Creek, soldiers opened fire on a large group of Indians, killing at least 150 and possibly as many as 350 men, women, and children. With that act, the Sioux had been beaten and with them the Indian wars of the West came to an end. Harrison was shocked by what happened but was satisfied with the explanation offered by his commanders, commenting that it "is a great gratification to know that it has been closed so speedily."

Harrison ran for re-election in 1892, but his heart was not in the race and he did little campaigning. His wife had become gravely ill again and died in October. He lost the election one month later to his 1888 opponent, Grover Cleveland. Harrison returned to Indianapolis, where he practiced law and wrote two books. In 1896 at the age of sixty-two he was remarried, this time to Mary Lord Dimmick, the thirty-seven-year-old widowed niece of his first wife. Mary gave birth to a daughter, Elizabeth, the next year. In March 1901 Harrison fell ill and died of pneumonia. He was buried next to his first wife in the Crown Hill Cemetery in Indianapolis.

McKinley's presidency

As the 1892 campaign between Cleveland and Harrison moved forward, William McKinley wrote: "I shall in 1896 be nominated and elected to the presidency of the United States." This was not as arrogant and farfetched as it may sound, for as a popular governor of a major state, he enjoyed a growing national reputation. In a short space of time McKinley emerged as the leading contender for his party's presidential nomination. Republican leaders begged him to help restore their power in Congress, and during the campaign season of 1894, McKinley gave some 400 speeches to more than 2 million people across the country, with a concentration in the upper Midwest. His efforts played a major role in the GOP's success that year as they took control of the House.

McKinley's success came from a combination of personality, political acumen, and an ability to surround himself with capable and influential associates. The most notable of these was Marcus Alonzo Hanna of Cleveland. Hanna had made his fortune in Great Lakes shipping, iron, and other ventures. He had been loyal to Ohio's leading political figure, John Sherman, but during the 1880s Hanna began to work with McKinley. Hanna initially did not desire political office, but worked behind the scenes and he saw McKinley as the future of the Republican Party. At the time, newspaper cartoons, political writers, and Democratic opponents characterized McKinley as Hanna's puppet on a string, but Hanna was always the subordinate. He carried out McKinley's wishes and let McKinley bask in the public eye. Hanna was invaluable to McKinley as a fundraiser and organizer and together they brought about the emergence of the modern campaign and the modern presidency.

Hanna and McKinley began working on securing delegates as early as 1894 while McKinley stumped for Republicans. By the time delegates arrived in St. Louis in June 1896 McKinley had emerged as the clear nominee, so the convention was more coronation than contest. In addition to a strong statement on returning to the gold standard to restore prosperity, the 1896 platform also called for "acquisition of Hawaii, the construction of a canal across Central America, expansion of the Navy, restrictions on the acceptance of illiterate immigrants into the country, equal pay for equal work for women, and a national board of arbitration to settle labor disputes." Republicans were confident going into the election, for McKinley seemed new and invigorating, a candidate who had broad popular appeal and was an effective speaker and campaigner.

The Democrats equaled the GOP in nominating a fresh face with perhaps even better oratorical skills: Nebraskan William Jennings Bryan. Dubbed the "boy orator of the Platte," Bryan's "Cross of Gold" speech electrified the Democratic convention and has since become a hallmark of political oratory. He defended his party as the best representative of the people. The "Democratic idea has been that if you legislate to make the masses prosperous their prosperity will find its way up and through every class that rests upon it." After attacking the gold standard, the thirty-six year old closed his speech with the famous line: "You shall not press down upon the brow of labor this crown of thorns. You shall not crucify mankind upon a cross of gold."

Bryan had also received the endorsement of the insurgent Populist or People's Party that had gained political momentum since the 1870s and now was poised to have its candidate elected president, albeit one shared with the Democrats. The Populist base came from farmers in the South and trans-Mississippi West. Just as industrialization in the late nineteenth century had created a great deal of insecurity among workers, farmers were also vulnerable as a result of falling agricultural prices and increasing debt. Many believed that expanding the money supply through silver would cause inflation and help reduce their debts, lowering tariffs would help increase trade for the agricultural goods they produced, and that stronger regulation or outright government ownership of railroads would ensure fair prices for the shipping of those goods. Farmers also wanted a larger voice for the people in government affairs. The Populist platform of 1892 (called the Omaha Platform) summarized these concerns and added others, many of which would become federal policy in the decades ahead: the direct election of U.S. Senators; federal control of the currency; federally subsidized agriculture; a graduated income tax; and recognition of the rights of workers to form unions.

Scholars consider the election of 1896 as a watershed in terms of the money raised during the campaign, the organizational machinery deployed, and the decision by Bryan to break tradition and crisscross the country himself. Hanna urged McKinley to do so as well, but McKinley refused to break tradition. He also felt it would put him in a defensive posture, always responding to Bryan rather than being his own man. So McKinley stayed at home, speaking to groups from his front porch on North Market Street in Canton. But this was no ordinary campaign. Hanna's legendary organizational skills came into full force as he directed every aspect of McKinley's run. Hanna established campaign headquarters in New York City and Chicago, directed the hiring of campaign staff, secured Republicans to give speeches as often as possible to promote the message that Republicans represented the change needed to end the economic crisis, and authorized millions of pamphlets printed in every language spoken in the United States that extolled McKinley's virtues. By going back to the gold standard, the campaign line promised, McKinley would restore the "full dinner pail" for every American as the "Advance Agent of Prosperity."

Meanwhile, back in Canton, the campaign reached an even greater level of organization. Delegations who wished to see McKinley had to first have their leader arrange a meeting with him, who would go over the leader's speech, recommend changes, and urge the leader not to divert from the edited script. The delegation received train tickets to Canton, with a precise schedule and instructions on what to do and say while there. At the appointed time, the group disembarked at the station, unfurled their banner for McKinley, and proceeded to march up North Market Street. At McKinley's house, McKinley emerged on to the porch, listened to the speaker (feigning surprise at the words) who invariably pledged to work tirelessly for McKinley back home. McKinley then mounted a box or chair and gave a short speech on a few key issues such as the fallacy of silver and the necessity of protectionism to restore prosperity. Afterwards the group walked onto the porch for handshakes before being ushered politely through the house and back to the train station so the next group could begin. Meanwhile, McKinley's words were printed, collected, and sent to voters. On any given day, McKinley could address twelve or more such groups and from September to November some 500,000 people came to his home, destroying his lawn in the process. Running such a system required money, and Hanna and his lieutenants raised the then staggering sum of $4 million, most of it coming from businesses favoring the high tariff.

Bryan was not to be outdone. As the first presidential candidate to make a systematic tour of the states he needed for victory, he traveled by train across the country, from small towns to large cities, giving some 500 speeches. Like McKinley he used a few simple ideas and sought to distribute these to as many voters as possible. In the end, Bryan's efforts were not enough. McKinley became the first presidential candidate since Grant to receive a majority (not simply a plurality) of the popular vote. The results also revealed a nation yet divided along sectional lines. Bryan carried the South and trans-Mississippi West, receiving 6.5 million votes. McKinley carried the more populous industrial states of the Northeast and upper Midwest, with 7.1 million votes. Despite the conflict among labor and business, both groups voted solidly Republican, a loyalty reinforced when prosperity returned in 1897. McKinley and Hanna had succeeded in strengthening the winning coalition of "urban residents in the North, prosperous Midwestern farmers, industrial workers, ethnic voters (with the exception of the Irish), and reform-minded professionals." The victory set the stage for Republican victories through the 1920s and made the Democratic Party weaker outside the South.

When McKinley took the nation's highest office in March 1897, he called a special session of Congress to begin enacting the Republican economic program. The first result was the Dingley Tariff, which raised rates again and continued to allow the president authority to negotiate reciprocal agreements. After failing to achieve international agreements allowing for bimetallism in currencies, in 1900 he signed the Gold Standard Act, which formally placed U.S. currency on the gold standard.

In other economic matters, McKinley did not use the Sherman Act to attack trusts and he supported the Supreme Court decision in *E.C. Knight* (1895) that limited the effectiveness of the act in prosecuting trusts. Business remained friendly to the McKinley administration as did most organized labor. McKinley, like other Ohio presidents, towed a moderate line on labor issues, but it was enough to keep many workers in the GOP column. He invited Samuel Gompers, head of the American Federation of Labor and the nation's most powerful and recognized union leader to the White House for meetings and appointed a number of labor leaders to federal posts, including Terence V. Powderly, former head of the Knights of Labor, as Commissioner General of Immigration.

He also favored the continued exclusion of Chinese laborers. McKinley endorsed the Erdman Act of 1898, which allowed for mediation of wage disputes on interstate railroads.

Race relations, especially in the South, grew worse in the 1890s, especially after the Supreme Court ruled in *Plessy v. Ferguson* (1896) that separate facilities for blacks and whites did not violate the Constitution. McKinley made weak gestures towards securing equal rights for African Americans, further eroding a once potent commitment by the Republican Party. He did appoint blacks to federal posts and during the Spanish American War he countermanded army orders preventing the recruitment of blacks. He also condemned lynching, which by the 1890s had grown into a terrifying and all-too-frequent phenomenon in the South, but did nothing to stop it.

Foreign affairs would come to dominate McKinley's presidency, and here he made a sharp break with the previous Ohio presidents through the Spanish-American War. The late nineteenth century was the age of imperialism, during which European powers actively carved up significant parts of Asia and Africa. To demonstrate leadership in world affairs, many influential writers and political leaders argued that the United States also needed to adopt a more assertive, expansionist role beyond its borders. For example, Admiral Alfred Thayer Mahan wrote numerous books and articles on the necessity of a strong navy, overseas trade and colonies if the United States was to maintain prosperity and achieve great-nation status. His work and that of others influenced McKinley and a rising Republican star named Theodore Roosevelt.

A sizable and vocal number of Americans stood firmly against such a policy, including notables such as Bryan, Mark Twain, and former president Benjamin Harrison. These "anti-imperialists," as they have been called, came from different perspectives. Some thought expansionism too expensive, others that it would bring too many non-whites into U.S. territory. Labor leaders feared an influx of foreign workers who would push wages down. Sugar growers in the South feared competition from areas in the Caribbean such as Cuba and Puerto Rico should the United States take them from Spain. Despite their different perspectives they all agreed to oppose any effort by the United States to acquire overseas territory.

Within this context came the situation in Cuba, one of the last vestiges of the once powerful Spanish empire, which eventually led McKinley to declare war on Spain. In 1868, Cuban nationals began a ten-year guerilla war to try to free the island from Spanish rule, only to see the Spanish brutally crush their struggle. Fighting broke out once again in 1895 and the Spanish responded again with oppressive measures, which this time included herding some 300,000 Cubans into camps in order to stop the insurgency. Spanish actions outraged most Americans with some of them even traveling to Cuba to fight alongside the rebels. American businesses with interests in Cuba also grew alarmed and urged McKinley and other politicians to settle the issue. Newspapers, particularly William Randolph Hearst's *New York Journal* and Joseph Pulitzer's *New York World*, ran sensationalized stories (dubbed "yellow journalism" because of the "Yellow Kid," a character in a popular Hearst comic strip) that demonized the Spanish and heroicized the rebels.

Throughout 1897 McKinley pressured Spain to act humanely and settle the conflict in a way that respected the insurgents. Spain refused. Two events forced the issue. First, in early

1898 Hearst published an intercepted letter from the Spanish minister to the United States in which the Spaniard called McKinley "weak" and admitted that Spain had not been negotiating in good faith. Public anger swelled to outrage after the battleship U.S.S. *Maine* exploded and sunk in Havana harbor on February 15, killing nearly 270 Americans. McKinley ordered an investigation, but the yellow press had already blamed Spain. What further enhanced the blame was the Navy investigation that concluded it was an external explosion that had sunk the ship. By then, McKinley felt he could no longer rely on diplomacy to end the situation. In mid-April he asked Congress for, and received, the right to intervene in Cuba. After the Unites States blockaded Cuba's ports, on April 23, Spain declared war on the Unites States and two days later the Unites States reciprocated.

The war lasted four months, a "splendid little war" as Secretary of State John Hay called it. It took longer to amass and ship armed soldiers to Cuba than for them to fight. Ohio, under the leadership of Governor Asa Bushnell, claimed to be the first state to organize and send soldiers to the war. The state sent three regiments to the fighting, but the men saw virtually no action. Of the 15,345 militia and volunteers, 230 died, mainly by disease. Teddy Roosevelt resigned his post as assistant secretary of the navy and organized his own unit, the "Rough Riders," to fight in Cuba. His well-publicized charge up San Juan Hill made him widely popular back home. The fighting there and in Puerto Rico ceased in July. Meanwhile, in the Pacific, the taking of the Philippines became a bonus trophy for the United States. With war declared, Commodore George Dewey defeated the Spanish navy in Manila Bay on May 1, 1898. Soldiers soon went ashore, becoming the first U.S. soldiers to engage in combat outside the Western Hemisphere.

With the fighting ended, but before a formal peace treaty had been signed, Congress approved U.S. occupation of Cuba but had not acted on the more distant Philippines. This opened a window during the fall of 1898 for a vigorous public discussion over the fate of the Philippines. The anti-imperialists mounted a spirited campaign against annexation, with those who favored acquisition responding in kind. In October McKinley himself undertook a speaking tour of the Midwest to gauge public opinion. While the anti-imperialists remained potent, the President came away convinced that the Unites States had no alterative but annexation. The treaty with Spain (negotiated in Paris without representatives from Cuba or the Philippines present) signed by McKinley on December 10, 1898, granted the Unites States control over Cuba, the Philippines, Guam, and Puerto Rico. With the Unites States approving annexation of Hawaii in July 1898, the nation now possessed a small overseas empire. The treaty now had to go to the Senate, which, after a heated debate approved it on February 6, 1899, 57 to 27, one more vote than the two-thirds required.

Tensions in the Philippines had been building and fighting broke out even as the Senate debate went forward. The violence intensified in the days after the vote, and it was not long before the U.S. found itself battling Filipinos, just as the Spanish had. For three years a brutal guerilla war engulfed the archipelago, costing the lives of some 4,300 Americans, 20,000 Filipino soldiers, and nearly 250,000 Filipino civilians. As the war was winding down, McKinley appointed fellow Ohioan, future president, and chief justice of the United States, William Howard Taft as chief civil administrator for the islands.

Figure 10.8 This is a campaign poster from 1900 supporting the re-election of William McKinley with new vice presidential candidate Theodore Roosevelt. The poster contrasts economic conditions in the United States in 1896 when McKinley took office at the end of a major depression with the return of economic growth by 1900. The poster also references the beneficial effects of U.S. involvement with Cuba as part of the Spanish-American War.
Source: Courtesy of the Ohio Historical Society (AL07001)

McKinley ran for re-election in 1900. The death of his vice president, Garret Hobart provided the opportunity to pair McKinley with Teddy Roosevelt, the war hero and then popular governor of New York (see Figure 10.8). In the general election, McKinley again faced Bryan, but this time McKinley could build upon the successes of the past four years. McKinley's status as a successful commander in chief and the general prosperity saw him increase his popular and electoral vote margin from that of 1896. Republicans came to dominate the House and Senate, solidifying their power at the national level.

Six months into his second term, in September of 1901, McKinley agreed to greet well-wishers while attending the Pan American Exposition in Buffalo. In line was twenty-eight-year-old Leon Czolgosz, a dedicated anarchist. In his hand, Czolgosz held a pistol concealed with a handkerchief. As McKinley reached out to shake his hand, Czolgosz fired twice into the president's midsection. McKinley fell to the ground. After eight days, McKinley succumbed to his wounds and died on September 14, vaulting Teddy Roosevelt into the presidency. Czolgosz was tried and executed.

Once again Ohioans and the nation faced the assassination of their president. McKinley's body lay in state in Buffalo, then Washington, D.C., and finally Canton, where he was initially buried in Westlawn Cemetery. Pennies from schoolchildren helped build the mausoleum, dedicated in 1907, where he, his wife Ida and their two children are now interred.

Summary

After McKinley's death, Ohio would send two more native sons to the White House in the twentieth century, William Howard Taft and Warren Harding. In the 1920 election, Harding defeated fellow Ohioan James Cox, showing further how central the Buckeye State remained in American politics. Yet while Ohio has remained a battleground state, Harding would be the last Ohioan to win the presidency.

In addition to presidents Ohio produced many other notable national political and military leaders in the decades following the Civil War. Five men either representing or born in Ohio served on the Supreme Court: Salmon P. Chase, Noah H. Swayne, Morrison R. Waite, William B. Woods, and Stanley Matthews. Chase served as chief justice until his death in 1873, followed by Waite who served another fourteen years. There were notable cabinet members as well. John Sherman served as secretary of the Treasury under Hayes and briefly as McKinley's secretary of state. Following Sherman as secretary of state under McKinley were William R. Day and John Hay. Serving as secretaries of war were Edwin Stanton, Alphonso Taft, and Ohio-born Russell Alger. William T. Sherman also served briefly as secretary of war, but his major service was as commanding general of the army from 1869 to his death in 1883. Succeeding him was Philip Sheridan.

Despite equaling Virginia in numbers, overall Ohio's nineteenth-century presidents appear to be a bland lot and their rather negative reputations are, to some degree, deserved. Although they are examined elsewhere, extensive corruption marred both the Grant and Harding administrations. While the presidents from Hayes to McKinley spoke of equal rights for African Americans, and appointed many blacks to office, it is also true that as a group they abandoned aggressive efforts to disrupt the advent of the Jim Crow South. They remained either opposed or indifferent to suffrage. On labor and industry, Ohio's presidents offered some help to workers and some modification to the traditional laissez-faire approach to corporate affairs, while maintaining a commitment to high tariffs and the general expansion of big business. They pursued with aggression the wars in the West to conquer Native American land. Tragedy befell them as well. Garfield and McKinley were both assassinated. One earlier and one later Ohio president died in office, William Henry Harrison and Warren Harding.

Yet any assessment of Ohio's late nineteenth-century presidents should consider other items as well. Certainly few presidents can compare with Virginia's list that includes such notables as Washington and Jefferson. Ohio's late-nineteenth-century presidents were not assertive reformers, although they did pursue civil service reform and some pushed for greater protection of black civil rights. They were thoughtful men and each Ohio president entered the Oval Office with significant experience. Hayes and McKinley had both been governor of Ohio and had served in U.S. Congress. Garfield and Harrison had been in Congress as well. They all served in the Union Army; Hayes, Garfield and Harrison were generals, while McKinley was a major. Perhaps it is best to see Hayes, Garfield, Harrison and McKinley not as presidents who rose above the times, but who fully embodied what party leaders and politics allowed and desired. They occupied the White House in an age when Ohio and the nation moved from a rural, agricultural society to an urban, industrial one.

In the midst of this transition, these men faced serious issues: the tariff; depressions; the growth of industry and labor; temperance; as well as wars in the West and U.S. expansion overseas. In facing these questions, each steered the nation on a moderate course. It was a political era of razor-thin margins and diversity of interests, such that each major party looked to safe candidates that could unite the factions and draw party loyalists to the polls. For the GOP, its hold on the South diminished as Democratic redeemers gained power. Considering all of this, Ohio represented a critical state with its cross-section of interests that mirrored the larger political landscape. Finally, under McKinley especially, these presidents expanded American power overseas, and—rightly or wrongly—helped to establish the United States as a global power.

Further Reading

The Miller Center at the University of Virginia (http://millercenter.org/) contains a wealth of information on the presidency, including scholarly articles on each president. In addition to this, a good starting place on Ohio's presidents is the American Presidency Series by the University Press of Kansas, including: Justus Doenecke, *The Presidencies of James A. Garfield and Chester A. Arthur* (1981); Lewis L. Gould, *The Presidency of William A. McKinley* (1981); Ari Hoogenboom, *The Presidency of Rutherford B. Hayes* (1988); and Homer E. Socolofsky and Allan B. Spetter, *The Presidency of Benjamin Harrison* (1987). See also Philip Weeks, *Buckeye Presidents: Ohioans in the White House* (2003. Kent: The Kent State University Press). On the temperance crusade see Jack S. Blocker, Jr., *"Give to the Winds Thy Fears": The Women's Temperance Crusade, 1873–1874* (1985. New York: Praeger) and K. Austin Kerr, *Organized for Prohibition: A New History of the Anti-Saloon League* (1985. New Haven: Yale University Press). On Coxey and Populism see Michael Pierce, "Farmers and the Failure of Populism in Ohio, 1890–1891," *Agricultural History*, Vol. 74, No. 1 (2000. Winter, pp. 58–85) and Carlos A. *Schwantes, Coxey's Army: An American Odyssey* (1985. Lincoln: University of Nebraska Press).

11

The Making of an Industrial State
1865–1920

In an address to the Ohio Society of New York in 1910, Wilbur Wright observed: "Ohio stands at the gateway between the East and West and her sons possess the boundless energy and enthusiasm of the West, and combine it with the salt of conservatism of the East. The result is a combination that carries Ohio men to victory everywhere. If I were giving a young man advice as to how he might succeed in life, I would say to him, pick out a good father and mother, and begin life in Ohio."

That there was an Ohio Society in New York City reinforces Ohio's central place in American life at the turn of the twentieth century. Leadership in national politics went hand-in-hand with the state's industrial, urban, and population growth. Founded in 1885, the Society soon included the Vice President of the United States (Thomas Hendricks born near Zanesville), Chief Justice of the United States Morrison Waite, other political leaders including John Sherman and Benjamin Harrison, as well as leaders from newspapers, finance, railroads, and other industries. With Ohio among the leaders of the industrial revolution of the late nineteenth century, it is easy to understand Wilbur Wright's optimism. Between the end of Civil War and the beginning of World War I, Ohio moved quickly into the modern age, with an emphasis on "the machine and money culture." What had been a state of small towns and farms seemed overnight to transform into one of large cities and factories. Many Ohioans at the time found the transformation exciting, seeing it as being filled with possibilities that might lead to great fame and fortune. For thousands of others, however, the transformation seemed unnerving and unjust.

Whatever the view, the changes took Ohio by storm. Businesses became conglomerates, mere villages became cities, and cities became metropolises. Railroads and then the automobile replaced the horse and buggy and the mule-drawn barges of the canal. Shipping along the Ohio River and Lake Erie grew apace. Communications accelerated with the telegraph and telephone. Finding Ohio fertile ground for their work, entrepreneurs and

Ohio: A History of the Buckeye State, First Edition. Kevin F. Kern and Gregory S. Wilson.
© 2014 John Wiley & Sons, Inc. Published 2014 by John Wiley & Sons, Inc.

inventors such as the Wright Brothers and John D. Rockefeller attracted the world's attention. Indeed, Ohioans took leading positions in the wave of innovations, inventions, and patents that emerged after the Civil War. Meanwhile, immigrants from all over the world flocked to the mines and factories of Ohio for the chance of a better life, swelling Ohio's population and transforming its culture and urban landscapes in the process. Agriculture remained important to Ohio, but it became more mechanized, requiring fewer hands for work. Farmers also faced greater global competition. All this, combined with the pull of cities and factories, led millions to leave rural Ohio for urban areas.

Industrialization

At the turn of the twentieth century, the United States would become the world leader in many industries. This meant Ohio played both a national and a global role in the industrial revolution. A brief overview shows this. In 1900, Ohio produced nearly 2.5 million tons of coal, coke, and pig iron, second only to Pennsylvania. Ohio was fourth in bituminous coal in 1900, with nearly 17 million tons. The state also ranked fourth in the number of manufacturing establishments with 13,868 and fifth in capital invested at over $570 million and in wage earners at just over 308,000. During Ohio's oil boom that began in the late nineteenth century it moved from 38,940 barrels per year in 1880 to over 16 million in 1890, peaking above 22 million in 1900, leading the nation. In 1890, it was second to the pig and bar iron industry in terms of capital invested. Agriculture as a whole also remained critical.

At this time, Ohio's two leading centers of industrial production were Cincinnati and Cleveland. Cincinnati maintained a diverse industrial base, as it had before the Civil War, which included Procter and Gamble a world leader in the production and sale of soaps and other consumer goods. In the 1880s, Cincinnati led the nation in producing "carriages, furniture, glycerin, coffins, plug tobacco, wine, whiskey, and safes." It came in second in boot and shoes, and clothing. Cincinnati's population rose from just over 161,000 in 1860 to 401,000 by 1920, which ranked it sixteenth in the United States. The Queen City maintained its lead as Ohio's largest city until 1900, when the Forest City took over. Cleveland became widely known for its oil refineries, dominated by John D. Rockefeller's Standard Oil Company, first organized there in 1870. Cleveland also solidified its role as a port city in these years and along with oil witnessed the growth of its steel, chemical, and machine-tool industries. The area known as the "Flats," a low lying floodplain along the Cuyahoga River became an industrial center with railroads feeding the iron furnaces, factories, and various mills that had developed there. Cleveland's population grew dramatically, from around 43,000 in 1860 to over 796,000 by 1920, making it the fifth largest city in the United States.

Other cities either emerged or expanded their roles as industrial centers. Lying in the southwest portion of the state about fifty miles north of Cincinnati, Dayton at the turn of the twentieth century represented the practical, problem-solving approach to life that characterized Ohio. In or around Dayton, home of the Wright Brothers, were James Patterson's National Cash Register Corporation (NCR) and Charles Kettering's DELCO.

All of these men, their inventions, and their companies attracted global attention. These and other industrial developments led Dayton's population to expand from 38,678 in 1880 to 152,559 by 1920.

The northeast section of Ohio acquired its reputation as the most industrialized in the state with urban centers including Cleveland, Akron, Canton, and Youngstown. Akron became the nation's fastest growing city between 1910 and 1920, its population soaring from 69,000 to over 208,000. The increase came mainly from the rapid expansion of the tire industry, with four major world rubber corporations located in Akron: Goodrich, Goodyear, Firestone, and General Tire. Akron also maintained its leadership in the production of agricultural implements, milling, matches (O. C. Barber's Diamond Match Company), and sewer pipe. Canton, home of William McKinley, grew from a population of over 4,000 in 1860 to over 87,000 by 1920. The industries that emerged there included iron and steel, watches, and bearings, the latter when in 1901 Henry Timken relocated his plant from St. Louis to Canton, later renamed the Timken Roller Bearing Axle Company. Youngstown's population expanded from 15,435 in 1880 to 132,358 in 1920. First iron and then steel production became concentrated in northeast Ohio, and no city in Ohio is more associated with steel than Youngstown. Located amid coal and iron ore deposits along the Mahoning River, Youngstown emerged as a center for mining and iron manufacturing during the first half of the nineteenth century. With the advent of steel in the late nineteenth century, Youngstown secured its place as gritty, industrial hub, a reputation it carried until the 1980s.

In central Ohio, the state capital of Columbus grew from 51,647 residents in 1880 to 237,031 by 1920. Already the seat of government and higher education, Columbus developed its industrial elements during and after the Civil War. The city boasted industries that included printing and binding, wagon and carriage, foundries, and agricultural implements. The large German population spurred the brewing industry there as well.

In the northwest, Toledo embodied the changes at work in Ohio. In the 1880s, the discovery of oil and natural gas near Lima and Findlay led to the expansion of refineries in northwest Ohio and helped the port city of Toledo to expand. The promise of free natural gas convinced Libbey Glass Works to relocate to the city in the 1890s, earning Toledo its nickname, "city of glass." Not long after this, when the automobile industry began to take off, Toledo emerged as a leader in that industry as well. The Willys-Overland Company in Toledo was the nation's second largest producer of automobiles from 1912–18, and it would later become famous for producing Jeeps. Its subsidiary, Electric Auto-Lite, also flourished and in 1922 it became a separate company that manufactured starting and lighting equipment for automobiles. Toledo grew from a population of 50,137 in 1880 to 243,164 in 1920.

Ohio's smaller cities also expanded in these decades. Zanesville, once the state capital, had 10,011 residents in 1870. By 1900 it had more than doubled to 23,538. Rich deposits of clay in the region made pottery the major industry there and among the most important was the factory of Samuel Weller, which produced three boxcars full of pottery each day to make it the largest in the world by the 1910s. Pottery shaped the history of East Liverpool, which earned the nickname "Crockery City." Its population nearly quadrupled, from 5,568 in 1880 to over 21,000 by 1920. Glassmaking, spurred by discoveries of natural gas and coal, helped Cambridge in Guernsey County grow from 2,883 people in 1880 to 8,241 in 1900 and to 13,104 by 1920.

Such growth transformed the political climate. Although both major parties remained competitive, the Republicans still won more elections. By the late nineteenth century their ties to big business had solidified. In addition, the Republicans exemplified a belief in the sanctity and power of the market. They followed the principles of laissez-faire derived from a French term literally meaning let it be. This indicated that government should avoid involvement in economic affairs as much as possible. Business leaders like Rockefeller also supported a popular philosophy of the time, Social Darwinism, which loosely applied Charles Darwin's theories of evolution to human society. Great wealth and success, the argument went, came about solely from pure individual effort, through ingenuity, hard work, and thrift. Anyone who developed the right character could succeed, no matter what the circumstances of one's birth. These were the traditional values of Protestant America. Moreover, the argument went, those individuals or businesses that succeeded must be the fittest, and society benefited from the survival of the strongest and talented, and the relegation or elimination of the weakest. Supporters of Social Darwinism believed that the system was natural, if not ordained by God, and any effort to reform or alter it was useless if not dangerous. As Rockefeller is said to have remarked, "God gave me my money."

Along with the theory of Social Darwinism came a transformation in how Ohioans began to measure progress. Before the industrialization of the late nineteenth century, moral and material advancement were usually associated with individuals, often mechanics or artisans. Increasingly, however, the message became that technology, and the industries and inventions associated with it, was the new engine of advancement. Many Ohioans now lauded machines, buildings, and technological innovations as measures of greatness.

Location and Transportation

Ohio benefited from several factors that came together to make it an industrial society. Among these was Ohio's geography as it related to transportation networks. As Wilbur Wright noted, Ohio had been recognized as the westernmost eastern state, and the easternmost western state. Ohio's very location, therefore, enabled the early-nineteenth-century developments in places like Cincinnati. These accelerated after the Civil War. Situated between the Great Lakes and the Ohio River, Ohio lay at the nexus of migrations between the crowded East and the expanding West, as well as for those leaving the South for opportunities and greater freedom, especially African Americans. Transportation networks followed these migrations, as roads, canals, trains, and eventually paved roads designed for automobiles all crisscrossed through Ohio.

Among the transportation developments, in the late nineteenth century nothing was more central to industrial growth in Ohio than the railroads. The railroad companies were America's first big business, and all of the major east-west rail lines came through the Buckeye State. In time they stretched across the entire continent, shrinking space and even reorganizing time by creating the time zones still in use today. Before the railroads, people in Ohio and elsewhere across the country set their own "local" time by the location of the sun in their community. Once railroads joined factories, as exemplars of the new modern age, time became regulated and centralized. Railroads, and the telegraph lines that often ran alongside them, also linked smaller, rural places with larger, urban ones, integrating more Ohioans into the national economy, building mass consumption and production, and speeding communication. The large and complex operations of the railroads also required new systems of management and capital, with large labor forces from white-collar office workers, to skilled and unskilled laborers. The railroad boom spurred growth in related industries that built, supplied, and maintained them. The rail lines became central to Ohio's leadership in steel production. Iron ore and coke was shipped from Lake Superior to Cleveland and other ports along Lake Erie. Coal from Ohio or nearby Pennsylvania and West Virginia could easily be brought into the steel mills that sprouted up throughout northeast Ohio. Railroads shipped these materials through Ohio and outward to other destinations. Of course, iron and steel were used to build the railroads themselves. Along with national carriers, intrastate rail lines emerged. Products of the industrial revolution such as coal, coke, and iron ore formed the foundation of lines such as the Wheeling & Lake Erie as well as the Hocking Valley, which stretched from Pomeroy to Toledo with branches to the coal mines of the valley.

Passenger service also expanded, tripling in the United States between 1896 and 1916, with the peak in 1920 seeing 1.2 billion passengers. Railroads first added Pullman cars, which offered berths or small beds, dining cars and other amenities. Competing with steam railroads were the electric interurban trains that increased rapidly in the late nineteenth century. Cheaper to build than steam railroads, interurban trains carried mostly passengers, but some also hauled farm and industrial products. These lines expanded across Ohio, linking all major cities and most of the smaller ones. The first interurban line in the United States connected Newark and Granville and by World War I, Ohio's 2,798 miles of interurban track exceeded that of all other states.

The benefits of railroads to Ohio's economic growth were tangible. So, too, were the negative consequences. As railroads rose, practical use of Ohio's canal system faded. Certain sections of the canals were still used by "state boats" to haul bulk items short distances and there were pleasure rides as well. Nonetheless, both state and privately-owned canals started to disappear, often being filled in to make way for various projects. The flood of 1913 destroyed the remaining utility of the canals for transportation, their main function turning to the management of industrial water.

Even more serious was the railroad companies' corruption, greed, and abuse of power, which drew the ire of farmers, small business owners, and political reformers. Railroads were often undercapitalized and the victims or cause of the economic panics that hit Ohio and the entire nation in the late nineteenth century. The chaotic process of failure, reorganization, and consolidation pushed out smaller railroad companies and led to fewer but larger firms whose ownership and control often came from New York City, as opposed to Ohio. This process made many people wealthy, but it also devastated investors, those employees who lost jobs, and cities and small towns who had made concessions in land and money to attract the railroad only to see the scheme fall apart as the railroad collapsed. Railroad companies also formed a strong lobby in Columbus and in Washington, D.C., offering various kickbacks, sweetheart stock deals, and outright bribes to politicians and government officials. Rail lines also discriminated on rates by charging big customers less than smaller ones, and formed pools and trusts to limit competition. This earned the indignation of many, especially Ohio's farmers, whether as part of the Grange or as Populists, who pressured political leaders for change. For their part, workers on the railroads began forming unions and also pushed for reforms, especially in the area of worker safety. It is no wonder these workers were worried; more than 500 railway workers died and some seven thousand others were injured on the job in 1900 alone, even as railroads were beginning to adopt various procedures and technologies designed to improve safety.

Despite the corruption, enough legislators in Ohio and Washington D.C. heard those pushing for change and made railroads one their primary targets for reform. In 1872, under pressure from the Grange and other farm groups, the Ohio legislature mandated that railroads charge the same freight rate for all shippers. By 1881 Ohio had enacted various schedules for freight and that same year Republican Attorney General George K. Nash (who would serve two terms as governor, 1900–4) filed a suit in the Ohio Supreme Court to prevent William Vanderbilt and associates from consolidating two rail lines into one. Nash won the case but railroads continued to ignore regulations. Eventually, pressure built for a federal response, one that culminated in the creation of the Interstate Commerce Commission in 1887 that was charged with overseeing railroads.

While railroads dominated transportation, travel along the Ohio River and across Lake Erie continued to be vital into the twentieth century. During World War I the Ohio River served as an important transportation route for freight. After the war, the Army Corps of Engineers began constructing a series of dams and locks to "canalize" the river to improve and regulate navigation on it. Lake Erie increased in importance, especially for moving coal and iron ore associated with railroads and steel. As the demands for iron ore increased, the shipping industry responded with two developments. First, the Hulett Automatic Ore Unloader, as shown in Figure 11.1, debuted in the port of Conneaut in 1899. Designed by George Hulett of Cleveland and built by the Webster, Camp & Lane Company of Akron, these 100-feet tall, 800 ton machines used cantilevered arms and shovels to unload up to 17 tons of material in a single sweep. In response, shipbuilders began to construct larger vessels. For example, in 1904 the American Shipbuilding Company launched the *Augustus B. Wolvin* at its Lorain yard. The vessel measured 560 feet long, with thirty-three hatches and a hold designed to maximize and simplify the amount of ore unloaded by the new machines. On her maiden voyage, the *Wolvin* hauled 10,694 tons of iron ore from Two Harbors, Minnesota, to Conneaut. The Huletts reduced the time needed to unload such freighters from one week to half a day. Passenger sailing on Lake Erie also developed during the late nineteenth century, chiefly between Cleveland and Buffalo or Detroit. The latter declined rapidly from the combined effects of the automobile and the Great Depression.

As it would with other forms of transportation, Ohio would become central to road and highway construction. Outside cities, roads remained gravel or dirt. First the bicycle craze of the 1890s, then the increased use of cars and trucks, led to the formation of the Ohio Good Roads Federation in 1909. The state was already a leader in cement and brick paving blocks, and the manufacturing of automobiles, trucks, and parts became key

Figure 11.1 George Hulett (1846–1923) was born in Conneaut and became a self-trained inventor after spending the first part of his adult career as a merchant and in the produce and commission business. At the age of 52 he became an engineer of construction and while working for the McMyler Manufacturing Company of Cleveland he invented the ore unloading machine that bears his name. The Hulett not only saved time, but also lowered the cost of unloading ore by more than two-thirds. At their height, as many as seventy-seven of these giant machines operated along the Great Lakes. Their use ended in the 1990s when self-unloading ships became standard. All but two of the Huletts were demolished; the remaining pair remains dismantled in storage awaiting a possible place in Chicago as part of a steel heritage site.

Source: Western Reserve Historical Society. Wellman-Seaver-Morgan Company photographs

aspects of Ohio's economy. For example, Akron's major tire companies were central to the Good Roads movement and the new transportation revolution that would dominate the twentieth century. The Good Roads movement also led, in 1913, to the creation of the Lincoln Highway, the first road across the nation, a portion of which today runs through Ohio as Route 30.

With Dayton being home to the Wright Brothers Ohio earned a critical place in the development of powered flight as well. In 1910, Ohio was the site of America's first air freight shipment, from Dayton to Columbus and beginning in the early 1920s, Ohio stood at the forefront of commercial air passenger service. At the same time airplanes were emerging, Ohio forged ahead in the development of dirigibles. The rubber companies of Akron were uniquely positioned to become pioneers in the construction of lighter-than-air ships. World War I led the U.S. military to demand dirigibles and Goodyear stepped in to fill the need, building observation balloons and blimps and running an airship training school at Wingfoot Lake near Akron. After the war Goodyear partnered with leading German businessmen and engineers to form the Goodyear-Zeppelin Corporation to continue both military and commercial applications of airship technology.

Disaster marred early airships associated with Goodyear and Ohio. In September 1925, the United States Navy's first rigid airship, the 680-foot long *Shenandoah*, built in the Navy's Lakehurst Naval Air Station in New Jersey, went down in pieces over Noble County, Ohio, after being caught in a violent storm. Fourteen crew members perished in the accident. The two other American built airships of the era, the U.S.S. *Akron* and the U.S.S. *Macon*, met similar fates. The 785-foot long *Akron* and the 784-foot long *Macon* were built at the Goodyear Airdock near Akron and were among the largest flying objects in the world. Each was designed as an early version of the aircraft carrier, meant to hold and launch airplanes. The *Akron* went down off the coast of New Jersey in April 1933, with seventy-three of the seventy-six crew members lost. Then, in February 1935 the *Macon* went down off the coast of California; luckily only two of its crew perished since they had life vests and rafts, added after the *Akron* crash. Further interest in commercial airship travel faded when the German-made *Hindenburg*, the largest airship ever built, crashed in flames at Lakehurst in 1937. Today, "blimps" are used as marketing tools for Goodyear and the military continues to experiment with the technology.

Natural Resources

The products of nature continued as vital resources for Ohio's industrial growth, and their extraction became businesses in and of themselves. The rich clays of Ohio continued to support the manufacture of pottery, bricks, tiles, and sewer pipe. Ohio became second only to Michigan in the extraction of salt. Ohio's limestone, sandstone and gypsum were quarried as well.

For the new industrial age, the more important resources were coal, oil, and natural gas. Bituminous coal fueled the industrial revolution of the late nineteenth century in Ohio and elsewhere, with coal mining becoming a major source of employment. By 1900, Ohio was fourth among states in bituminous coal mined, with nearly 17 million tons. No fewer than thirty Ohio counties mined coal at that time with the most active in the late nineteenth century in southern and eastern Ohio. By 1900, more than 90 percent of Ohio's factories ran on coal-produced steam power and coal fueled the railroad locomotives and generated the electricity for the interurban lines and many other machines. Coal remains the main source of electric power in Ohio today. Ohio experienced an oil and gas boom in the area around Lima and Findlay, which became the nation's second major commercial field after the first in Titusville, Pennsylvania. Oil surged from 38,940 barrels per year to over 16 million in 1890, peaking at almost 24 million in 1896, leading the nation until 1903 when Texas and Oklahoma surpassed it.

Finances, Entrepreneurs, and Innovation

At first, Ohio's industrial growth fed off of local capital. For example, Rockefeller began his rise to power by saving money from his job as a bookkeeper in Cleveland. He combined this with money from a partner and loans from banks to enter the fledgling oil refining business. In 1870, after eleven years, Rockefeller and his three partners formed Standard Oil, capitalized at $1 million. That same year, local business leaders in Akron raised $13,600 to entice B. F. Goodrich to locate the first rubber factory west of the Appalachians there. In 1898, Frank Seiberling used his local connections to borrow $43,000 to start the Goodyear Tire and Rubber Company. Other successful businesses began in a similar fashion. As they expanded, however, these businesses sought capital and connections outside Ohio, usually from Chicago or New York City. Railroads were already leading the way in this endeavor.

Rockefeller and others represented Ohio's leadership in producing the entrepreneurs and innovators necessary for the industrial revolution. They represented not only hard work and raw ambition, but also ruthlessness. Rockefeller drove out rival firms through cut-throat competition, secret deals with railroads, fixed prices, and production quotas. Like other big business leaders, to expand his holdings Rockefeller used horizontal integration—buying up competing refineries—as well as vertical integration—controlling the entire process of refining, from drilling through to distribution. By the 1880s, Standard Oil controlled 90 percent of the nation's oil business. In building the National Cash Register Company (NCR), John Patterson (Figure 11.2) introduced new, aggressive sales techniques that saw the company expand quickly after its founding it 1884. Patterson also created a special Competition Department that used a number of predatory techniques to destroy competitors, including injuring their salesmen, bribing shippers to delay their shipments, and pouring sand in their machines. In this sense, Patterson almost literally followed the company motto: "We do not buy out, we knock out." Such actions helped NCR gain about 95 percent of the U.S. market in cash registers by 1911. They also nearly landed Patterson and other executives of the company, including Charles Kettering, in jail. These men were all convicted of violating the Sherman Antitrust Act and sentenced to one year in prison. The case was appealed and the convictions were overturned in 1915.

Leaders like Rockefeller and Patterson inspired both admiration and condemnation. Detractors called them "robber barons" who flaunted their wealth and threatened democracy. Supporters preferred to call them "captains of industry," guiding the chaotic transition of industrialism while generating growth and prosperity. Many leaders, including Rockefeller donated millions to charity. Yet the era has been popularized as the Gilded Age. The name derives from the title of an 1873 novel by Mark Twain and Charles Dudley Warner. The word "gilded" refers to gilding, a technique of covering an object in a thin layer of gold. Twain and Warner suggested that America's new wealth masked a society filled with political corruption and large disparities of wealth and power. The many scandals associated with political and business leaders, including those involving Ohioans such as Grant and Harding, contributed to the popular view of the era developed by Twain and Warner.

Figure 11.2 John Henry Patterson (1844–1922) was born on the family farm near Dayton. He served 100 days at the end of the Civil War and graduated from Dartmouth in 1867. He entered the coal business, wherein he discovered that clerks at his mining supply store were consistently shortchanging the till. He came across an advertisement for James Ritty's primitive cash register, the "Incorruptible Cashier" in 1879 and bought two—perhaps the largest sale Ritty ever made for his invention. Patterson's store soon made a profit, but his coal dealing business went under. Patterson then turned his attention to the cash register and he became partial owner of the National Manufacturing Company in 1883. The next year he bought out the other investors and formed the National Cash Register Company. Through the ingenuity and ruthlessness of Patterson, by 1910 the cash register, something no one wanted, had become an essential tool of retailing.
Source: Courtesy of the Ohio Historical Society (SA1039AV_B07F10_009_1)

Other contradictions emerged in Ohio's Gilded Age as well. Patterson and other industrial leaders celebrated the individual but their work succeeded in creating the modern world whose major characteristic was the growing power of institutions over individual lives. Ohio's industrial achievements were eminently practical, full of ambition tied to the ordinary, creating the radical transformations associated with the modern but representing something conservative. As one scholar has remarked, men like the Wright Brothers or Charles Kettering "sustained the power of the middle-class vision of Ohio's progress in an era that saw the triumph of the corporations and consumerism."

Alongside Rockefeller and Patterson, Ohio can claim a number of influential entrepreneurs and innovators. Others followed Goodrich into the rubber business located in

Akron. Frank Seiberling, who started in his father's business, the Empire Mower and Reaper Works, formed Goodyear in 1898. Harvey Firestone, born on a farm in Columbiana, Ohio, sold his first tire company in Chicago and moved to Akron in 1900, opening the Firestone Tire and Rubber Company. In 1905, he had secured his first order for tires from Henry Ford. This eventually led to an exclusive deal between Firestone and Ford Motor Company. Ford and Firestone became friends and would often go camping together along with another Ohioan and even more influential inventor, innovator, and entrepreneur Thomas Alva Edison.

Born on February 11, 1847, on a farm in Milan, Ohio, Edison received only three months of formal education. He moved to Michigan when he was seven and did most of his pioneering work in the field of electricity and communications at Menlo Park, New Jersey. He returned to Ohio to marry Mina Miller, daughter of Lewis Miller, one of Akron's industrialists in the farm machinery business. Edison received his first patent in 1869 for an electric vote recorder and went on to become the world's most famous inventor, helping to create much of the world as we know it.

Other Ohioans were at work in the emerging field of electricity as well. Charles Brush of Cleveland earned fame with improvements in the dynamo for producing electric power more efficiently and improvement to the arc light. Brush demonstrated his improved lighting and dynamo system in Cleveland in 1879, and soon other cities including New York, Boston, and San Francisco were using his designs for lighting public streets. Benjamin Lamme of Springfield graduated from Ohio State University in 1888 and went to work with Westinghouse, becoming chief engineer there from 1903 to his death in 1924. He created more than 160 patents, mainly in the area of electrical power design. His work included the hydroelectric power plant at Niagara Falls and most of the apparatus for the Westinghouse exhibit at the 1893 Columbian Exposition in Chicago.

His sister, Bertha worked directly with him for a number of years. She was the first woman in the nation to earn a degree in electrical engineering, from Ohio State University in 1893. As was common for women, her professional career ended in 1905 when she married, in her case a fellow engineer and Ohio State University graduate, Russell Feicht.

Along with electricity, the automobile transformed life in significant ways, and Ohio was again at the center of that shift. The Winton Motor Carriage Company incorporated in 1897 in Cleveland. Under the leadership of Alexander Winton, a Scottish immigrant, it was, in 1900, the largest manufacturer of gas-powered automobiles in the world, selling over 100 that year. Winton ceased automobile production in 1924, but continued to make engines. The Packard brothers, James and William, began building automobiles in their hometown of Warren in 1899. Perhaps no Ohioan was more critical in the development of the automobile than Charles Kettering of Dayton (Figure 11.3). He is second to Edison in holding the most significant patents, involving automotive technology, air conditioning, and the diesel locomotive. Kettering's first job as an electrical engineer was for Patterson's NCR where he invented the electric cash register. Kettering left NCR to form DELCO (Dayton Engineering Laboratories Company) in 1909. Kettering, along with Clyde Coleman, invented the electric starter motor for automobiles in 1911. Kettering's

Figure 11.3   Charles Kettering (1876–1958) was born on a farm near Loudonville, Ohio. Poor eyesight hindered his studies and after two attempts he finished college on his third, graduating in 1904 with a BS in Electrical Engineering from Ohio State University. Kettering holds some 180 patents, including one for an aerial torpedo in 1918, nicknamed the "Kettering Bug," which helped lead to the later development of guided missiles. Working with Kettering on the project was Orville Wright.
Source: General Motors Archive Photo (121305)

work attracted the attention of General Motors (GM), which purchased DELCO in 1920 and made Kettering head of GM research. At GM he acquired the nickname "Boss Ket" and went on to oversee numerous developments. One of the researchers working in his lab, Charles Midgely, discovered that adding lead to gasoline prevented engine knock. Midgely and Kettering also invented Freon in 1928. Kettering invented many other items as well, including solar energy apparatus, an incubator for premature infants, and proto-types for magnetic diagnostic devices. After his wife died of cancer, Kettering joined with GM President Alfred Sloan to create the Memorial Sloan-Kettering Cancer Center, a world leader in cancer research. For all his achievements, Kettering made the cover of *Time* Magazine in January 1933.

   Also making Dayton home were the pioneers of powered flight and the aerial age, Orville and Wilbur Wright. They are credited with inventing the first practical airplane and the first controlled, sustained powered flight, at Kitty Hawk, North Carolina on

December 17, 1903. Wilbur was born in Indiana in 1867 before the family moved to Dayton, where Orville was born in 1871. The brothers were members of a large family that included two older brothers, Loren and Reuchlin, and a younger sister, Katherine. Neither Wilbur nor Orville married and both of them continued to live at the family home on the west side of Dayton; Wilbur until he died of typhoid fever in 1912 and Orville until 1914, when he built a family mansion, Hawthorn Hill, near Dayton in Oakwood. Orville died in 1948. The brothers first capitalized on the bicycle craze of the 1890s by forming the Wright Cycle Company in 1892. The money and experience they gained working there enabled them to begin their experiments in flight. They traveled to Kitty Hawk each year from 1900 to 1903 to test their work. After their first successful flight of 12 seconds with Orville at the controls, they continued to improve their designs, producing the world's first practical airplane in 1905. They patented their design, the key to which was lateral control, and formed airplane companies in Europe and the United States. The public did not witness the early flights, prompting skepticism (particularly from European developers) that the Wright Brothers could claim their patents and their place as the first in flight. In 1908 they demonstrated their plane for the U.S. military and Wilbur traveled to France to make the first public flights. The brothers and their plane became instant celebrities and in 1909 returned to the United States as heroes (see Figure 11.4).

This, however, did not stop the challenges to the Wright's claims. Many individuals in the United States and Europe had been working on the problem of sustainable flight, including Samuel Pierpont Langley, Glenn Curtiss, Octave Chanute, and Germany's Otto Lilienthal (who died while flying one of his gliders in 1896). With success being so spectacular and the potential for commercial rewards huge, the effort by the Wright's to claim royalties from their design led to nasty legal and public relations battles. Langley in particular was angry, since he had been given a contract from the War Department to develop a manned airplane, only to have his piloted "Aerodrome" models crash into Potomac River just weeks before the Wright's 1903 flight in Kitty Hawk. Langley even had the Smithsonian involved in supporting his claim to have made the first successful manned, powered, heavier-than-air flight. Others have pointed to Gustave Whitehead, a German immigrant living in Connecticut, who is said to have built and flown a powered aircraft in 1901. Controversy continues, and the battles damaged the Wright's reputation at the time, but today they are acknowledged as the men who opened the world to aviation.

Finally, Ohio is also home to two African American innovators who have gained notoriety in recent years. The most famous is Granville Woods, popularly known as the "black Thomas Edison." His early life is fairly murky, but it seems that Woods was born in Australia and moved to Columbus as a small child. He holds more than fifty patents for inventions that include his 1887 contribution of the multiplex telegraph system, which allowed dispatchers to know the locations of all trains at all times so as to avoid accidents. Woods also invented an overhead conducting system for electric railways and something he called "telegraphony," which allowed one to send voice and telegraph messages over a single wire. Like the Wrights, Woods was also involved in several patent disputes. Edison claimed he had invented the multiplex first and twice sued Woods, with Woods winning both cases. Never one to quit, Edison then offered Woods a job with his company, Edison Electric. Woods declined the offer and continued working in New York to pursue various

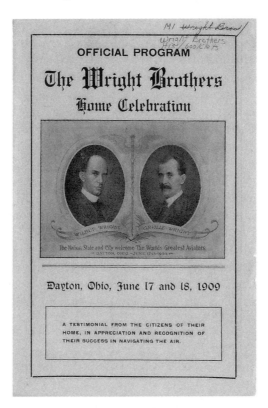

Figure 11.4   Neither Orville nor Wilbur graduated from high school or college, yet their family environment encouraged curiosity and intellectual development. The brothers read widely from the large family library in the home and thus were well educated. Before turning to bicycles, the brothers operated a print shop and published a newspaper in Dayton on a printing press they designed and built. One of the clients with whom they worked was fellow Daytonian and high school classmate of Orville, poet Paul Laurence Dunbar. The brothers printed the *Dayton Tattler*, a newspaper Dunbar briefly edited. Bicycle manufacturing and repair followed printing and by the 1890s the Wright brothers were deeply involved in researching flight.
Source: The National Museum of the U.S. Air Force

improvements centered on railways and communications. Unlike his white contemporaries such as Edison and the Wrights, Woods had to fight racial discrimination to achieve his success, and in many ways the racism drove him harder towards his goals. Despite his greatness, Woods died destitute in a New York hospital in 1910.

Another African American innovator was Garrett Morgan. He has been credited with inventing the modern-day traffic light and the prototype of the gas mask. Born to former slaves in Kentucky in 1877 at the age of fourteen Morgan migrated first to Cincinnati and then Cleveland where he went into business for himself in 1907 by opening a shop to sell and repair sewing machines. In 1909 he opened a tailor's shop and then started the G. A. Morgan Hair Refining Company to manufacture and market a hair-straightening solution he had invented by accident in 1905. Morgan has two major patents to his credit, both in safety. His first was the safety hood, granted in 1914. He and his device received national and international attention when he and two others donned masks to rescue workers and retrieve bodies after a tunnel explosion occurred under Lake Erie in July 1916 during the construction of a new water intake system for Cleveland. While his hood and its later adaptations sold mostly to fire departments, it does not appear that Morgan's hood was the same one used later by the Army as a gas mask.

Morgan's second patent came for his T-shaped traffic signal in 1923. General Electric may have purchased his patent, but by this time, the modern three-light automated one was in use in a number of places. A two-color (red and green) design by an Ohioan, James Hoge of Cleveland, served as the basis for the first traffic signal system, installed in 1914 in the city at the corner of East 105th Street and Euclid Avenue. In addition to his business activities, Morgan remained active in Cleveland. He was a model of self-discipline and hard work and a representative of the African American professional class that espoused the belief that by demonstrating upward mobility one could end discrimination. Morgan also believed in pressuring whites to acknowledge the injustice of racism through investigations and publicity of cases of discrimination. To this end he was one of the founders of the Cleveland Association of Colored Men in 1908, which later merged with the NAACP. In 1920 Morgan also started the *Cleveland Call*, a prominent African American newspaper.

People

The rise of large industries, especially manufacturing, generated a seemingly insatiable demand for labor, which in turn prompted a significant shift in the social makeup of the working class and led to rapid urban growth in Ohio. Indeed, Ohio became mostly an urban state as its population grew dramatically after the Civil War. There were 2,665,260 people in Ohio in 1870, 4,157,545 in 1900 and 5,759,000 by 1920 (see also Table 11.1).

Between 1820 and 1924 the largest wave of migration in U.S. history occurred, as more than 33 million foreign born individuals entered the United States. Indeed, by 1910 about one-seventh of the nation's population was foreign born. Some 13 million immigrants arrived between 1900 and the outbreak of World War I in 1914. In the United States and Ohio, before 1880, the majority of these immigrants came from northwest Europe or Canada. After 1880, Central, Eastern, and Southern Europeans dominated. There were also Asians and Mexicans entering, mainly in the West and Southwest. African Americans joined the industrial workforce, usually migrating from the rural South to cities such as Cincinnati and Cleveland. Their numbers began to swell with the industrial boom brought about by World War I. These were all part

Table 11.1   Urban and rural population in Ohio, 1860–1910

	1860	*1880*	*1910*
Urban	400,000	1,031,000	2,665,000
Rural	1,939,000	2,167,000	2,102,000

of a massive global migration set in motion by the expansion of industry and the decline of traditional agriculture, as well as political turmoil. In addition to the millions leaving Europe for the United States, millions more moved from India and China across Asia and the South Pacific, or from Russia to Manchuria, Siberia and Central Asia.

In looking at Ohio's immigration experience, by 1920 Ohio had 11.8 percent foreign-born white and 21.3 percent native white of foreign or mixed parentage. This was about average for the nation (13 and 21.5 percent respectively). This was still less than all states in New England and Mid-Atlantic, and other than Indiana, lowest among those surrounding the Great Lakes. Meanwhile, Ohio's native white population of 63.7 percent was higher than the national average of 55.3 percent. Regardless of the statistics, the immigration experience profoundly altered Ohio.

For many immigrants, the move was organized through networks of family and friends. Businesses, shipping companies, and agents also worked to bring immigrants to Ohio. These new arrivals, most of whom did not speak English and were Catholic or Jewish, tended to concentrate in the state's urban areas. In general, immigrant men found work in the expanding industrial areas of Ohio's cities. Most of them were unskilled, but some possessed enough skill to carve out a more prosperous life. Others entered business and contributed to Ohio's industrial expansion. Many of the male immigrants were "birds of passage," persons who came to the United States to earn money with the intention of returning home to pay off debts or perhaps acquire land. Immigrant women usually worked at home, but many of them earned money by taking care of boarders or earning wages in domestic service or urban enterprises like the garment industry. Over time families settled permanently in Ohio developing a sense of ethnic identity, both as it was understood in Europe and as it was created and recreated in Ohio.

The new immigrants settled by ethnicity into the same neighborhoods, generally near the factories or shops in which they worked. Although different groups did congregate together, many ethnic neighborhoods were heterogeneous. Adults interacted on the porches of their wooden frame houses, in the streets, shops, or (for men) the saloon. Children played together in lots, gardens, and yards. Over time, immigrants created various institutions such as newspapers and benefit societies designed to serve their particular group and promote a shared identity. The center of cultural life for many new arrivals became the church or the synagogue. In addition to spiritual needs, these institutions housed schools, social clubs, even orphanages, and performed a host of other activities. The churches and synagogues also became significant institutions for both maintaining ethnic identity and assimilation into the larger, Anglo-dominated American culture. Like other Ohioans, new immigrants were active agents in shaping their lives and that of Ohio more broadly.

From the 1870s and into twentieth century, Ohio and its communities became theaters "for debates about national identity, about the civil obligations of religious commitment, about socialism, about race, about economic and social opportunity." These issues are illustrated below in examining some of the major groups that came to Ohio and reshaped the state during the age of industrialization.

Germans

Among the many groups that came to Ohio, Germans were the most important prior to the 1880s. As late as 1870, half of all foreign-born Ohioans were German and they could be found in all parts of the state, rural and urban. The German influence was perhaps greatest in Cincinnati, where, in 1890, over 57 percent of the population was German. Some were Catholic, some Protestant, some Jewish. They represented all classes and varied in their political outlook, although most voted Republican and worked hard to assimilate and support the efforts of native white Ohioans to create a public culture built on respectability, industry, and improvement.

In addition to business and industry, Germans also contributed well to the music and arts. Germans organized the Saengerfest in 1870 that occupied a newly built, two-story music hall near Over-the-Rhine. Later, Germans helped organize the opera house and the permanent orchestra that came in 1895. Prussian Adolph Strauch designed the city's first public park, Eden Park; August von Kreling designed the Tyler Davidson fountain now at the city's Fountain Square, and it was cast in Ferdinand von Mueller's foundry. German language was offered widely in public and parochial schools in Cincinnati. Some schools offered students the chance to alternate their days between English and German-speaking teachers. German could be heard throughout the city; by the time World War I began, some 34 percent of residents spoke German.

However, the deep German presence in Cincinnati made native white Ohioans uneasy; and the focus of much attention centered on the Over-the-Rhine district along Vine Street. With lax enforcement of ordinances, the area was home to a thriving community, one filled with restaurants, shops, and beer gardens, but also less reputable saloons, dance halls, and gambling houses. While Germans saw the saloons, music festivals, and coffeehouses as a central part of living, in Cincinnati and other urban areas, native Anglos associated Germans with crime and vice. Such tensions already infused the temperance issue and would explode once the United States entered World War I against Germany.

Snapshot Cleveland: Poles, Czechs, Hungarians, and Italians

In 1900, Cleveland became the state's largest and most diverse city; with its 381,768 people it outpaced Cincinnati's 325,902 residents. What made these twin developments possible was the influx of new immigrants. In 1900, 75 percent of Cleveland's people were non-native born. There were forty separate languages spoken in the city, and newspapers were published in many of them. Here we examine four of the major groups involved: Poles and Czechs, Hungarians, and Italians.

Among the many groups arriving in Cleveland, Slavs outnumbered all others. And within this group, Poles and Czechs were the most numerous. "Slavic" was a general term that included at least a dozen different nationalities with distinct cultural practices. East Slavs (Great Russians, Carpatho-Russians, Byelorussians, Ukrainians) adhered to the

Orthodox Church and used the Cyrillic alphabet. West Slavs (Poles, Czechs, Moravians, Slovaks, Lusatian Sorbs) and South Slavs (Bulgarians, Serbs, Slovenes, Croatians, Macedonians, Montenegrins) were mostly Roman Catholic and used the Latin alphabet. A 1918 survey of Cleveland showed 49,000 Poles, 46,296 Czechs, 19,000 Slovenes, 18,977 Slovaks, and 6,000 Croatians. The survey did not include other nationalities, and even accounting for estimates in some areas, the 139,273 Slavs shown in Cleveland here outnumbered the 31,628 Hungarians, 30,000 Russian Jews, and 23,000 Italians in the city.

With the highest number of residents among the new immigrants, Poles became a prominent part of Cleveland and Ohio history. Indeed, most Poles in Ohio lived in the city. By 1800, the lands that made up Poland had been partitioned among Russia, Austria, and Prussia. During the nineteenth century each government exerted its control over Poles, which included emancipation of peasants. The push of disruption combined with the pull of excitement, interest, and opportunity led many Poles to seek new lives elsewhere. In Cleveland, Poles congregated in three major neighborhoods whose location was largely determined by the availability of work from a nearby industry. With some 15,000 residents by 1900, the largest was the Warszawa neighborhood, at the center of the Cleveland Rolling Mills complex. Another was Poznan near industries around East 79th Street and Superior Avenue. The third, Kantowo, arose as steel mills expanded in the near West Side of the city along the Cuyahoga River.

In this era, Poles were largely part of the industrial working class, although there were some, such as Michael Kniola, who assimilated into the business class. Kniola came to Cleveland in 1880 and worked for the Cleveland Rolling Mills. He went to night school, became a foreman, and then opened a grocery store from which he began offering assistance not only to other Poles but also Czechs and Hungarians newly arrived or already established in Cleveland. This included advancing credit, insurance, and finding jobs. He also arranged steamship passage for those coming from Europe, which led to formation of his Kniola Travel Bureau business. He helped organize Cleveland's first Polish newspaper, *Polonia w Ameryce*, began the Polish Republican Club, and directed the Polish-American Chamber of Commerce.

Most Polish women remained at home, and those working for wages were mainly single women contributing to the family income. Over time, they became more organized and involved in civic affairs. In 1912 Polish women in Cleveland organized their own benefit society, the Association of Polish Women in the U.S.A. In the 1990s the Association merged with the Polish National Alliance, the nation's largest ethnically-based benefit society. Immigrant women used such organizations, as well as Catholic schools and hospitals, as ways to participate in public society. Increasingly, they would find expression through union activity and the suffrage movement.

Cleveland had the second largest population of Czechs (which included Bohemians, Moravians, and Silesians) in the United States, behind Chicago, and the fourth largest in the world. The Broadway area from East 37th Street to Union Avenue, known as "Little Bohemia," contained the largest and most prosperous Czech settlement in Cleveland from the late 1870s to the end of World War I. The first major migration began when political persecution by the Austrian government forced many well-educated Czechs to flee their homeland. Some had participated in an unsuccessful revolt against the Austrian government in 1848. Political factors continued to fuel migration, but the largest wave of Czech immigrants arrived between 1870 and World War I, prompted primarily by economic conditions. The literacy rate of Czechs was the highest of all ethnic groups migrating out of the Austro-Hungarian Empire in the late nineteenth and early twentieth centuries. Czech newspapers in Cleveland presented the views of three different segments of Czech society: freethinkers, socialists, and religious. While the Catholic groups maintained a strong influence, freethinking lodges, schools, and other organizations gained a greater influence in the 1890s as did socialists. As with other groups, Czech women sought greater influence and expression though their own lodges and institutions, which in their case included such groups as the Union of Czech Women, a national benefit society founded in Cleveland in 1870. Another significant cultural institution among Czechs was the Sokols, gymnastic organizations that combined physical fitness with nationalism and education. The first Czech Sokol in the United States was organized in Cleveland in 1870. These were not original to Czechs, as German *Turnverein* gymnastic groups predated those of the Czechs in the United States by about forty years.

The 1920 Census showed 43,134 Hungarians living in Cleveland, second only to New York City. Like other such ethnic terms, "Hungarian" was a broad one that encompassed not only ethnic Hungarians, Magyars, (the focus of this section) but also Jews, Germans, and Slovaks. More than half of the Hungarian immigrants to the United States between 1908 and 1914 went back home with their earnings making the Hungarian neighborhoods in Cleveland and elsewhere transient places, at least until World War I.

Nevertheless, a distinct Hungarian presence emerged in Cleveland. The city's first Hungarian residents were Jews, an example being David and Morris Black, who went on to become successful in the clothing industry by founding H. Black & Company. Another prominent Hungarian, Theodor Kundtz, who came to Cleveland in 1873, was of German-Hungarian background. He established the Kundtz Sewing Machine Cabinet Company on the city's West Side that employed some 2,500 workers, mostly Hungarians. His company became the largest employer in Cleveland in the early 1900s, with five factories in Cleveland's Flats making not only sewing machine cabinets but also bicycle wheels, furniture, and automobile and truck bodies. Cleveland's National Malleable Castings Company opened a new foundry in the Birmingham neighborhood in Toledo in 1890, transferring 200 Hungarian workers there, which increased the presence of Hungarians in Toledo.

Hungarian men living on Cleveland's West Side were mainly skilled workers, while those who settled on the East Side were unskilled laborers in heavy industry. There the Buckeye Road neighborhood developed, eventually becoming Cleveland's largest Hungarian community. Hungarian women worked outside the home as well; 71 percent of married Hungarian women earned wages or kept boarders, the largest of any nationality in Cleveland. At least five Hungarian newspapers circulated in Cleveland. One daily, the *Szabadsag*, was the largest Hungarian newspaper in the United States. At the same time, the first Roman Catholic Hungarian church in the United States, St. Elizabeth's, was built in Cleveland in 1893.

Next in numbers to Slavs and Hungarians were Italians. Most of the Italians who immigrated to Cleveland at this time originated in two regions, Sicily and Abruzzi.

Even more astounding is that half of Cleveland's Italians had come from just ten villages in southern Italy. Most of the newcomers were *contadini* (peasants) who left poverty and the lack of arable land in the Old World for opportunities in the United States. These families had no national identity as such, instead they identified with their village and their fellow villagers. Village identity remained strong through World War I as most Italian benefit societies limited their membership to persons from a particular village and most sponsored a festival in honor of a village patron saint. These societies connected new immigrants in an immediate way to the traditional world of rural Italy.

By choice, Italians remained the most segregated group in the city, including African Americans. As one resident noted, "We Italians like to live with people from our own province who speak our own dialect and will help us if we get into trouble." The largest of the Italian neighborhoods in Cleveland was Big Italy, an area along Woodland and Orange avenues near the city's markets. Sicilian born Italians made up 90 percent of the residents. The area now known as Little Italy (where most residents were Neapolitan at the time) became more prominent after World War I.

Most Italian men entered Cleveland as blue-collar workers, laboring mainly in construction and factories, with more skilled men and women finding work in the garment industry. Italians also came to hold a dominant place in the fruit industry. Frank Catalano came to Ohio from northern Sicily and started a wholesale fruit business expanding to include olive oil and other items. He and other Italians in this line of work helped make Cleveland the state's produce distribution center. Italians also became central to stonework. Joseph Carabelli, a Protestant from northern Italy, founded the Lakeview Granite and Monumental Works in 1880, hiring other Italian stonemasons to produce works for the Lakeview Cemetery among others. Working with Italian women, Carabelli used his money and that of John D. Rockefeller to found Alta House, a social settlement that provided a kindergarten, nursery, and other social welfare services. In 1908 Carabelli was elected to the Ohio House of Representatives as a Republican and is best known for securing Columbus Day as an official state holiday in 1910.

While these men were gaining notoriety in business and public life, the neighborhood remained the central focus for most Italians. The first Italian newspaper in Ohio, *La Voce del Popolo Italiano* began publication in 1903. As was common for many immigrant groups, other means of securing community life came from benefit societies and the church. In May 1887 St. Anthony's became the first Italian nationality church in Ohio, serving the Big Italy neighborhood.

Jews

Jews formed part of the larger immigrant population entering Ohio. Prior to the influx of Southern and Eastern Europeans, most Jews who came to Ohio were from Germany. Like most urban Ohioans before the Civil War, they concentrated in Cincinnati and they looked to assimilate, to become part of the vision of Ohio being created by the Protestant

Figure 11.5 Parts of Isaac Meyer Wise's experience show some of the larger issues associated with immigration. Wise left his native Bohemia because of continued restrictions on Jews there and found greater religious freedom in New York and then Ohio. He also changed the spelling of this last name, from Weiss to Wise. Finally, his founding of Reform Judaism was itself a way of adopting his native culture and faith to new surroundings in the United States and Ohio.
Source: Courtesy of the Jacon Rader Marcus Center of the American Jewish Archives, Cincinnati, Ohio. http://americanjewisharchives.org/

middle and upper classes. Thus, unlike many Jews who would come from Eastern and Southern Europe, German Jews did not look favorably upon Zionism, for the Jews of Cincinnati already saw their new community in the United States as a haven. Believing in civic betterment, they desired to "settle as citizens, succeed economically, practice their religion freely and coexist happily and on equal terms with their Christian neighbors." Perhaps the desire these Jewish newcomers expressed led to relatively less anti-Semitism in Cincinnati and elsewhere in Ohio than in other American cities in the years before 1880.

Among the leaders that emerged from this first wave of Jewish immigration to Ohio was Isaac Meyer Wise (Figure 11.5), who arrived in Cincinnati in 1854. A native of Steingrub in Boehmia, who had spent some time in Albany, New York before coming to Cincinnati, Wise accepted a position as rabbi of Bene Yeshurun and built the congregation from 180 to 400 by the time he died in 1900. His success and fame, however, went far beyond Cincinnati. Wise had been instrumental in founding Reform Judaism, an Americanized version of the religion. He and others also founded the Reform umbrella organization, Union of American Hebrew Congregations in Cincinnati, where its head-quarters remained until after World War II. In 1875 Wise also helped found Hebrew Union College, which became a leading Jewish institution of higher learning in the United States. The tribute of Chicago's *Jewish Advance* newspaper was typical: "No other Jewish community accomplished so much good in the interest of Judaism and its people" as did Cincinnati.

German Jews had established themselves in a number of fields, most predominantly in the clothing and garment industry. Simon Lazarus and his family came to Columbus in 1851 from Prussia and established a thriving clothing business on High Street. Lazarus also became the first rabbi of Temple Israel, which began meeting upstairs in his store. In Cleveland, Jews prominent in the garment industry included Kaufman Koch and Moritz Joseph.

The arrival to Ohio of Jews from Southern and Eastern Europe after 1880 changed the group's composition and led to serious division within it as well as between Jews and non-Jews. For all their appearance of assimilation acceptance of Jews was still tenuous. Meanwhile, Cleveland's Jewish population outpaced that of Cincinnati's. The Jewish population in Cincinnati grew from 2,800 in 1850 to 28,000 by 1910. In Cleveland, by 1920, there were 75,000 Jews. The already established German Jews were highly Americanized followers of Reform Judaism, whereas the new arrivals were Orthodox, Yiddish in their culture, more liberal or radical in politics, and adherents of Zionism.

In Cleveland the East European Jews settled in neighborhoods with other recent immigrants, and from the beginning German Jews tried to assist them, combining humane concerns with self-interest and paternalism. Martin A. Marks, a prominent German Jew active in business and civic affairs in Cleveland noted the tenuous nature of Jewish assimilation, which new immigrants threatened. In 1891 he warned new arrivals that "no matter what one Jew does all Jews are blamed for it. The only way for you to overcome this prejudice is by becoming part of the country itself and to do this you must become supporters of its institutions." For his part, Wise urged Jews to abandon Orthodoxy, "the traditions of the long forgotten dead and buried past" and embrace Reform Judaism in order to "gain the esteem and confidence of your fellowmen."

Although they could be found in different trades, many Jews entered peddling, buying goods from stores and then traveling to other immigrant neighborhoods to sell them. Others entered the garment industry or cigar workshops. Relatively few Jews could be found working in heavy industry.

Like other immigrant groups, Jews established a variety of institutions as they began to establish a presence. Synagogues, benefit societies, and literary clubs blossomed in Cleveland, Cincinnati, and other Ohio cities. In 1894, Jewish women in Cleveland founded a chapter of the National Council of Jewish Women, which provided immigrants in the Woodland neighborhood with English-language programs, U.S. citizenship classes, and day nurseries.

African Americans

As a result of the Civil War and Reconstruction, African Americans had gained greater equality with whites through the Thirteenth, Fourteenth, and Fifteenth Amendments to the Constitution. As previously noted in chapters 9 and 10, white Southerners resisted the new situation tooth and nail. In the South, daily life for blacks became more treacherous, as state after state fell under the power of "Redeemer" governments that sought to restore race relations to their antebellum days. While many states in the nation adopted laws and customs to keep whites and blacks separate, in the South the system became most egregious. The system, called "Jim Crow" after a popular minstrel show at the time, constrained African American behavior, which the revival of terrorism in the form of lynching and other extralegal violence helped to enforce. Consequently, given their reputation as places of greater tolerance and increasing economic opportunity, states in the North like Ohio began to look increasingly attractive to African Americans.

While immigration from Europe increased dramatically, Ohio's African American population grew slowly during the late nineteenth century, rising from 79,900 in 1880 to 96,901 by 1900, representing less than 5 percent of Ohio's total population. The real growth came with the start of the World War I and accelerated during the 1920s. Ohio's African American population grew from 111,452 in 1910 to 309,304 by 1930, marking the beginning of a phenomenon known as the Great Migration, which lasted until 1970 and witnessed millions of African Americans streaming out of the South and into the North and West (see Table 11.2).

African Americans sought new opportunities not only in big cites but also in small communities in Ohio. The Anderson clan of Washington Court House, southwest of Columbus, shows some of the possibilities that were open to African American migrants. Husband and wife Bolding and Eliza Anderson were free blacks living in North Carolina who moved to Washington Court House during or just after the Civil War. While Eliza seems to have been literate, it is not clear if she was employed. Bolding, her husband, could not write and worked as a laborer. He joined the Second Baptist Church, which had been established by African Americans before the Civil War. Bolding and Eliza's household included two daughters, twenty-one-year-old Maggie, who worked as a domestic, and fourteen-year-old Eliza who was in school. Even as unskilled workers, the

Table 11.2   African American population in Ohio, 1880–1930

	White	Black
1880	3,117,920	79,900
1890	3,584,805	87,113
1900	4,060,204	96,901
1910	4,654,897	111,452
1920	5,571,893	186,187
1930	6,335,173	309,304

couple managed to obtain property, as each of them owned lots in town. Another member of the Anderson clan, Betsey, had come with her husband William, who would serve in the Union Army. William died in the early 1870s, leaving Betsey with five children. She did not remarry, and her only occupation was "keeping house," yet she, too, managed to accumulate a modest amount of property. One of her sons, Alonzo, made a life for himself as a barber. King Anderson served in the 42nd Regiment of the U.S. Colored Troops during the Civil War and had moved to Washington Court House. King held a variety of occupations, beginning as a butcher. He also joined the Second Baptist Church and became active in Republican Party politics. In an unusual move, he joined with John Keller, a German immigrant, to open a saloon. Temperance activists managed to close this bar down, but by 1880 King had opened another one. He then took up carpentry, a trade he practiced until his death in 1904.

In the small community of Washington Court House, African Americans managed to obtain small amounts of wealth, including a relatively high rate of home ownership and African Americans could be found in just about all sections of the city. Such dispersal was not uncommon in other Ohio cities during this time. The racially concentrated ghetto would not develop until the population surge that accompanied the demand for labor during World War I. Still, the trends toward greater segregation were emerging. Even though Ohio held greater potential for freedom and opportunity for the Andersons and the other African Americans who migrated north, the color line remained visible.

One could see the color line most clearly in employment. The political status of black men had improved and, among the wealthy, race relations were fluid in many parts of the state. However, the reality of labor for most African Americans meant confinement to lower-paid, lower-skilled, less-prestigious jobs. The 1890 Census showed that of the 28,000 working African American men in Ohio, about three-fourths were employed as laborers or service workers. In urban areas, blacks faced competition from foreign immigrants. In Springfield and Columbus, both with relatively fewer foreign immigrants, blacks in 1890 represented 11 and 7 percent of the workforce respectively, while in the immigrant strongholds of Cincinnati and Cleveland they were 4.5 and 1.5 percent respectively. In the burgeoning metal industries of Cleveland, for example, there were only three black workers in 1890. Moreover, in general, unionization did not help black workers, since the majority of labor unions restricted membership to whites. Black men did better in coal mining. Many black miners had migrated from the South where they had gained some experience. Blacks were sometimes used as strikebreakers, as in the case of the Hocking Valley strikes. By 1890 there were about 500 black miners or mine laborers in Ohio, making up 2.5 percent of the total employed in that field.

Black men and women were overrepresented in the domestic and personal-service industry. As one scholar has noted, most whites in Ohio only came into contact with African Americans when they "needed their shoes shined, their hair cut, their homes cleaned, or their clothes washed." While only 9 percent of white workers were engaged in domestic and personal service in 1890, 40 percent of blacks were. There were exceptions, of course, which makes the case of Walter Black so interesting (see Figure 11.6). He began

Figure 11.6 This 1920 photograph is of Walter Black, one of the first African Americans to be promoted to foreman in the Youngstown steel industry. Black began as most African American men did in the steel industry, as a laborer in 1915. He worked his way up through various positions until becoming a blast furnace foreman. He was typical of many black men in the industry, taking an unskilled job as the demand from World War I increased but atypical in that he was able to become a foreman while most blacks remained in lower skilled positions.
Source: Courtesy of the Ohio Historical Society (AL02994)

as a common laborer, but worked his way up to foreman in the steel industry. For black women, this type of employment was almost all they could obtain: 89 percent of black working women in Ohio were employed as service workers.

A small number of African Americans were represented among the middle and upper classes. Lighter-skinned, upper-class African Americans shared the basic conservative values of their white counterparts, as well as a religious faith that found them worshipping together as Episcopalians, Congregationalists, or Presbyterians. Most African American professionals worked in the traditional occupations of clergy and teaching. There were, however, other pathways. Fountain Lewis and his sons established and operated a famous barbershop in Cincinnati, as did George Myers in Cleveland. In the late nineteenth century some blacks found their way into the professions, including lawyers Charles Chesnutt, John Green, and George Washington Williams. Chesnutt was the first black member of Cleveland's chamber of commerce and he became a celebrated author.

Figure 11.7 This portrait of Harry C. Smith (1863–1941) was taken during his first term in the Ohio House of Representatives, 1894–95. He also served in the Ohio House in 1896–97 and 1900–1901. Smith combined politics with publishing, cofounding the *Cleveland Gazette* in 1883. He purchased the paper outright in 1886 and remained its editor and owner until his death. In his political life and through his journalism, Smith worked steadily for African American civil rights. *Source*: Courtesy of the Ohio Historical Society (AL03899)

Williams was a Civil War veteran and minister who became Ohio's first African American legislator by serving one term in the Ohio House, 1880–1901. He went on to become a respected historian. John Green of Cleveland became the second African American to serve in the Ohio House and the first to serve in the Ohio Senate, from 1892 to 1893. While in the House, Green introduced legislation to establish Labor Day in Ohio. Besides politics and law, owning a newspaper was another potential avenue for African Americans, and a small number of black papers flourished in late-nineteenth-century Ohio, including one by the poet Paul Laurence Dunbar published in Dayton by the Wright Brothers. The most notable paper was perhaps the Cleveland *Gazette* owned by Harry C. Smith, shown in Figure 11.7. Smith was a devoted Republican, serving as state oil inspector. He served three terms in the Ohio general assembly where he was instrumental in creating the Civil Rights Law of 1894 and the Mob Violence Law of 1896.

As Harry Smith understood, whatever their class status, all African Americans faced the threat of antiblack violence. While racially motivated violence is commonly associated with the post-Civil War South, the North was not immune from such actions. In Ohio, the state's largest cities did not report racial violence in the years after the Civil War, but there were reports of lynchings and mob violence in smaller cities and towns. It is most probable that the violence stemmed from the changing context of race relations after the Civil War. Blacks in Ohio and elsewhere were beginning to assert themselves politically, as well as economically and socially, competing alongside whites and new European immigrants for a place in society.

There were twelve recorded incidents of antiblack violence in Ohio between 1885 and 1910, including dramatic riots in Akron (1900) and Springfield (1904, 1906). In Akron, Louis Peck, an African American, had been arrested for and pled guilty to raping a six-year-old white girl, Christina Maas. News of the arrest and crime spread throughout Akron. Realizing the potential for violence by local whites, on August 22 Akron police removed Peck and another African American male from the jail and sent them to Cleveland. That evening, a mob formed in front of the city hall building that held the jail. With the crowd demanding Peck, the police allowed several committees from the crowd to search the building to verify that he was not there. This did little to assuage the crowd, which attacked the building. Police fired into the crowd, wounding some people and killing two children. Enraged yet determined, most of the rioters left for a short period and returned with dynamite stolen from a construction site, blasted the building and set it on fire. When firefighters responded, some in the crowd fired guns at them. Eventually, the Ohio National Guard restored order. Peck was rushed back to Akron the next day, tried, convicted and sent to the Ohio State Penitentiary in Columbus. In addition to the two white children killed, twenty-five people, including three police officers and six firefighters, were injured or wounded. None were African American.

In the first Springfield riot, March 1904, a crowd broke into the jail and seized and lynched African American Richard Dixon, who had been arrested for shooting a police officer. The next night, a crowd assembled and carried out an attack against a block of saloons owned mainly by African Americans in the "Levee," a district with a reputation for vice. In the second riot, when police and National Guardsmen intervened during the attacks on saloons, the mob unleashed its fury on African American homes outside the Levee. In addition to racism, there were class and sexual overtones to the violence as well. White women and men interacted with African Americans in the Levee, partaking in the music, gambling, drinking, and prostitution known to occur there. According to racial stereotypes of the time, whites believed blacks were predisposed to illicit if sometimes humorous behavior. As the white mob saw it, violence was a way to maintain social order. One of the National Guard officers noted that the Levee district "has been an eye-sore to the respectable element of the town for years." Even upper-class blacks were not sorry to see the Levee go. While deploring violence, a prominent African American in Springfield noted that the saloon district had "bred nothing but crime and thrown a disgrace on colored people who have regard for law and right." For whites involved in the riot, economic competition played a role, too. Destroying a saloon meant destroying one of the few avenues open to African American entrepreneurs. With more traditional, respectable pathways blocked, the vice trade remained one area in which blacks could try to gain a foothold. Moreover, the homes destroyed in the second riot were those owned by black industrial workers, who were competing with white men for jobs.

The irony for blacks is that the violence and segregated labor market came just as legal barriers to discrimination were falling in Ohio. In the decades after the Civil War, black men gained the right to vote, and the state legislature approved laws that barred discrimination in public accommodations and allowed black children to attend school with white children. In response to lynchings, and at the urging of Harry Smith, the state passed an antilynching measure as well. In practice, however, racism fed into a variety of written and unwritten rules that governed day-to-day activities, which served to harden the color line in late-nineteenth-century Ohio.

Within these parameters and in response to them, blacks carved out a vibrant cultural life in late-nineteenth-century Ohio. For those African Americans in the upper echelons of society, they sought respectability. As they shared conservative values and religious preferences with their white counterparts, they also adopted white forms of leisure, including classical music, dress balls, and dances such as waltzes and polkas. Working-class African Americans tended to hold closer to their African roots. They preferred dances such as the congo or juba, and were more likely to worship as Baptists or Methodists. Musically, African American clubs and bars gave birth to distinct forms of American music: the blues, ragtime, and jazz. As the cultural expressions and the incidents in Springfield make clear, African Americans in Ohio were not immune from the class divisions emerging at the turn of the twentieth century. Elite blacks, just like native whites or older immigrants, increasingly chafed at the condition, culture, and livelihood of their lower-class counterparts, sentiments that would soon find greater expression in the reform movements that erupted across Ohio and nation.

Industrial Work and the Rise of Organized Labor

For African Americans and new immigrants alike, the industrial urban experience became a defining one for most of them. As it was across the United States the trend in employment was away from artisanal and small-batch work to wage earning in large factories located in urban areas. By 1890, two-thirds of Americans worked for wages as opposed to being self-employed, or owning a farm or a business. Ohio's workers contributed to and benefited from the new industrial growth. Generally in the United States, wages were rising faster than prices, which helped workers. Indeed, real wages for workers in Ohio rose by 50 percent between 1860 and 1890, and they continued to increase until World War I.

However, there were also significant costs. While the ideal of hard work as the path to great wealth may have held power for many Ohioans, and defined men like Rockefeller, the reality for most industrial workers in Ohio was far different. As wage earners, all workers remained vulnerable to the boom and bust cycles of the economy. There was no social safety net to speak of and, during the depressions of the 1870s and the 1890s, thousands of workers in Ohio lost their jobs or faced deep cuts in wages. For many immigrants accustomed to rural life, adjusting to the routines, monotony, and dangers of unskilled work proved difficult. In many industries, ten-hour days, six days a week was the norm. Steel mills usually ran twelve-hour shifts. Dangers abounded in industrial workplaces. As one observer noted of a plant in Cleveland, workers faced "the roaring thunder, the flowing sea of flames, (and) the choking smoke," with "great red-hot furnaces" as they made steel. The state of Ohio sought to improve working conditions through the creation of a state inspector for workshops and factories in 1884. In his first report issued that same year, Ohio's first state inspector Henry Dorn noted that of the 173 shops and factories he inspected in Cleveland, only 27 were compliant with the state laws on safety. In Cincinnati, he noted the difficulty workers would have in escaping fires, since most of them toiled on the top floors of buildings from five to nine stories high. Two fires in 1885 had claimed the lives of twenty-five workers, mostly women, in Cincinnati.

Coal miners had a large amount of autonomy once in the mine, but they faced perhaps the most dangerous working conditions and were the most beholden to the whims of the company. The major area of coal activity by 1900 lay in the Hocking Valley, which spreads across Athens, Hocking and Perry counties. Other significant coal-producing counties were Jackson, Guernsey, Belmont, Stark, and Tuscarawas. Miners were most likely to be involved in the truck system of paying workers, which meant that they were not paid in national currency but scrip, a type issued by the company, which was only good at the company store whose proprietors charged what they wished. Workers in this system were also forced to live in company-owned housing. Finally, miners also had to buy their own tools and supplies. The number of deaths in mining increased over the course of the late nineteenth century. From twenty-six in 1884, there were 114 killed in 1903, with more than one hundred deaths each year through 1913, peaking at 165 that year.

The intensity of these dangerous conditions, wage rates, and insecure situations could vary from industry to industry, as well as within industries. For example, in 1880, the average annual wage in Cleveland's manufacturing industries was $391, while the national average was $386. Average annual earnings in Ohio in 1901 for workers in steel, iron, and tin was $636.13, for cigar makers $306.86. There were further variations nationally that were no doubt reflected in Ohio. For example, in 1900 an open-hearth melter in a steel mill earned about $32 a week working an average of 74 hours. A female examiner in the clothing industry worked about 58 hours a week for about $8. Generally, male skilled workers could command higher wages and more control over their employment. Miners, while working in some of the most dangerous conditions had significant autonomy while underground. While the percentage of skilled workers in the United States did not change dramatically from 1870 to 1910 (20 to 18.5 percent), the trend in many industries was towards a less skilled workforce. Whereas earlier an artisan might produce an entire product himself, in the new industrial Ohio workers only performed one part of the production process repeatedly for the entire workday. Moreover, inside the factory, authority shifted away from skilled artisans to foremen, who held authority on hiring and firing.

As unskilled work expanded, employers in several industries often hired women and children, whom they paid much lower wages than men. In the United States in 1900, women comprised 20 percent of all manufacturing workers. Women worked in all industries, but they were concentrated in domestic service and in the textile and garment factories. One of the most common work settings in the clothing industry was the "sweatshop," which developed apace with the new immigration from Europe in the late nineteenth century. In Cincinnati, for example, by 1890 there were 24,593 men, women, and children working in the clothing industry, the city's largest employer. Immigrant tailors, often Russian or Polish Jews or Italians, would take work from garment companies and craft clothes in their homes, typically small, dingy tenement flats that served not only as living space but a work space as well. The male tailor and head of household would then employ his wife and children and additional immigrants as needed to produce the clothes. After 1900, the industry shifted from cramped tenements to larger, loft buildings.

A Bureau of Labor Statistics committee formed to investigate the sweatshop practice noted the following in Cincinnati:

> A-S, a Polish Jew, was found making cloaks in the third floor rear of a Central Avenue tenement. The man and his wife cook, eat and sleep in the same room where the man was working two machines, assisted by a boy of 14, who made sleeves and did the binding, receiving $1.50 a week. The wife was lying sick on the bed and there was dirt and disorder on all sides, the room close and stuffy and cloaks littering the floor and bed. The house is one of the vilest four-story back tenements in town; bad ventilation and sewerage, decaying swill and rubbish fill the air with fetid odors.

By 1900 there were some 250,000 children under the age of fifteen working for wages in sweatshops, mines, and factories across the United States (see Figure 11.8). In 1878, Ohio's Bureau of Labor Statistics found that of the 64 mining companies across 23 counties responding to a survey, these mines employed 738 boys and 4,666 men. The men earned an average of $295.63 per year and the boys $147.05. The 1885 Bureau report noted that the state law preventing children under the age of sixteen from working was "being freely and persistently violated." Meanwhile, minor children were busy working in cigar factories, furniture, paper box, and match factories. Despite its illegality, many companies, and even some families routinely violated child employment laws.

For their part, business owners, especially those in industries undergoing the greatest changes in production were most active in joining national associations as a way to meet rising demands from disgruntled workers and from reformers in government. Workers often responded to their dangerous and low-paid working conditions with strikes and attempts to form unions. Most of these efforts were unsuccessful, reflecting the power of companies, the nature of the labor market, and divisions among workers along lines of skill, race, ethnicity, and gender. Moreover, although radical ideas associated with socialism were beginning to attract the attention of some workers, most of them did not advocate such positions. Like the miners in the Hocking Valley, most industrial workers and their unions sought only improved wages, shorter hours, and safer conditions along with a modicum of regulation of business behavior by the state or federal government. Most strikes centered on wages, which hardly meant that conflict was not serious or that violence did not occur.

Mining was perhaps the most conflict ridden of all of Ohio's industries in the late nineteenth century. Between 1886 and 1894, miners waged 295 strikes over wages, only a

Figure 11.8   Lewis Hine became famous for his photographs made for the National Child Labor Committee beginning in 1908. Hine used his camera to push for social reform, especially in areas of labor. He later made a series of work portraits and went on to document the work of the New Deal. A portion of Hine's caption for this 1908 photograph of sixteen-year-old Harry McShane of Cincinnati reads: "Had his left arm pulled off near shoulder, and right leg broken through kneecap, by being caught on belt of a machine in Spring factory in May 1908. Had been working in factory more than 2 years."
Source: Library of Congress Prints and Photographs Division (LC-DIG-nclc-05350)

handful of which were successful. Two major strikes in the Hocking Valley illustrate this. The first began on April 1, 1874, after coal operators cut production and tried to enforce severe wage cuts. Miners had created local chapters of the newly formed Miners' National Association, and they refused the new contracts and walked out. After two months, the companies brought in African Americans as strikebreakers and continued operations. The local newspapers attacked the companies and the use of black workers. "Our hills," declared the *Hocking Sentinel*, "vocal with independence and intelligence, were not formed to echo the crack of the negro driver's whip." The company strategy worked, as the majority of blacks stayed on the job despite intimidation from white strikers. Ultimately, the strike and union's efforts failed, and all of the workers had to sign contracts pledging no union activity.

Ten years later more violent conflict erupted in the valley. In 1883, several mining companies joined together to form the Columbus and Hocking Coal and Iron Company (or the

"Syndicate" as the miners called it) instituting deep wage cuts over the next several months. In June 1884 the miners, now represented by the Ohio Miners' Amalgamated Association, went on strike, idling 46 mines and some 3,000 workers. The operators responded by hiring hundreds of recent immigrants to break the strike. At first, the dispute remained peaceful, but that changed when the Syndicate went to court to enforce evictions of miners and their families from company housing. Strikers did not attack the immigrant "scabs," but sought to disrupt the operators' ability to mine coal by damaging hoppers, trains, bridges, and even setting fire to some mines (one of which still burned more than a hundred years later). In September, Governor George Hoadly dispatched the militia and made a personal visit to the valley. The presence of the militia cooled things somewhat. Leading the Amalgamated Association was John McBride. Born in Wayne County in 1854 to an Irish father and English mother, McBride had worked in mines from age of eight. In a speech to the union on October 29, 1884, he urged all Ohio miners to support the strikers: "Your liberty, your manhood is threatened." The *Hocking Sentinel* once again railed against the monopoly of the operators and the strikebreakers who were immigrants: "These pauper contract laborers are dirty, disease producing wretches." The strike lasted nine months, but it, too, largely failed. Following the strike, the Ohio legislature did, however, outlaw the practice of forcing miners to buy exclusively in company stores. Strike leader Chris Evans and McBride both would be part of the creation of what became the most powerful labor union for miners, the United Mine Workers (UMW) in Columbus in 1890, and McBride would become UMW president in 1892.

Industrial conflict in the urban centers of Cincinnati and Cleveland was also common. One of the first major national labor organizations active in Ohio was the Knights of Labor (KOL). Led by Terrence V. Powderly from 1879 to 1893, the Knights began in Philadelphia in 1869. According to Powderly, the new industrial system forced laborers to become "wage slaves" and that a new order could only come through the moral behavior and cooperation of all "honorable producers"; an end to the wage system; and the establishment of cooperative ventures owned and operated by laborers. Unlike the craft unions that dominated most industries, the Knights welcomed most laborers, regardless of skill, ethnicity, religion, gender, or race. They emphasized temperance and excluded "non-producers," including bankers, lawyers, liquor dealers, and stockholders. The Knights, however, also supported the exclusion of Chinese laborers. Moved by successful strikes in the southwest against powerful financier Jay Gould, workers flooded into the KOL. The height of the Knights' influence came as a result of the May Day strikes of May 1, 1886, when their membership swelled to some 750,000.

On May 1, some 350,000 workers walked off the job nationwide to demand an eight-hour day. The Knights officially opposed this work stoppage, but thousands of members joined in anyway, as did activists of various stripes. The general strike occurred nationwide, but the most activity occurred in New York, Chicago, Milwaukee, and Cincinnati.

In the Queen City, some 32,000 men and women participated in the protest, which played out over the course of a month. They were led mainly by the factory workers and lower-skilled laborers to the KOL banner. The city ground to a halt for most of May as freight handlers, garbage collectors, laundresses, streetcar workers, and a host of others went on strike. Workers in the furniture, coffin, and carriage industries also walked out, demanding the eight-hour day and a 20 percent increase in pay. Workers paraded through downtown, waving banners, American flags, and playing fife and drum music reminiscent of the American Revolution of 1776.

The strikes came on the heels of the Ohio legislature's approval of an eight-hour day law to take effect on May 1. The law may have given confidence and sanction to workers that the state now would support their organizing activities, however, the Haley Bill did not cover all workers and contained so many loopholes that it was largely ineffective. For example, there was no enforcement clause and it also failed to make clear whether workers would be paid the same rate or be forced to accept pro-rated wage cuts. Indeed, Procter and Gamble and other large factories answered the new law by switching their method of payment from daily to hourly.

The most famous events of the May Day strikes took place in Haymarket Square in Chicago, where as the crowd dispersed at the end of a peaceful rally on May 4, a bomb exploded amid a group of police officers. The officers responded by opening fire on the remaining crowd. In the end, the bomb killed one officer immediately and seven others died of their wounds. The gunfire killed seven or eight protestors and wounded thirty to forty others. The police also wounded about sixty of their own. General hysteria and weeks of police repression followed as officials cracked down on various leftist groups and labor unions. Ultimately, eight men were convicted of murder, seven of whom were sentenced to death in a trial that was anything but fair. Some protested the impending execution, including the nation's leading man of letters at the time, Ohioan William Dean Howells, novelist, playwright, one-time editor of *The Atlantic* magazine, and regular writer for *Harper's Weekly*. In a letter published in the *New York Tribune*, Howells wrote that the "justice or injustice of their sentence was not before the highest tribunal of our law, and unhappily could not be got there. That question must remain for history, which judges the judgment of courts." Howells' appeal and that of others had limited affect. In November 1887, four of the convicted men were hanged, one committed suicide, and two others had their sentences commuted to life imprisonment. The event affected Howells' writing, as he became increasingly concerned with social issues.

In Cincinnati, the strikes of May 1 were peaceful, but the violence of Haymarket Square frightened Mayor Amor Smith and other leading citizens into calling Governor Foraker for additional militia units. By May 9, several hundred troops were in the downtown industrial areas and another 1,400 waited on the outskirts armed with Gatling guns and artillery. After tense negotiations, the mayor ordered troops out of the city as Cincinnati's manufacturers mostly acceded to workers' demands. Although workers now flocked to join the Knights, the national repression of the group proceeded to end its influence. Employers began blacklisting members of the KOL, enforcing pledges by workers not to join unions, and spying on employees. Moreover, workers remained divided over race, ethnicity, skill, and gender. Finally, Powderly continued to push against both strikes and political action. Membership in the Knights declined so that by 1890 it was down to near 100,000.

As the influence of the Knights faded, another organization emerged. One of the leading organizations that had called for the general strike had been the Federation of

Organized Trades and Labor Unions. In December 1886, amid the fallout from the Haymarket bombing, the group reorganized at Druids Hall in Columbus as the American Federation of Labor (AFL). Dominating the group's philosophy was craft unionism as opposed to industrial unionism, which in practice meant a focus on skilled workers, mainly male, white, and of native birth or from Northern and Western Europe. As industrialization developed in the late nineteenth century, these men had been growing more separate from other members of the working class, a fact reflected in their unionization. Led by cigar maker Samuel Gompers, the AFL would grow to become the dominant labor federation in the United States.

Meanwhile, in Cleveland, ethnic cleavages and the power of employers proved difficult to overcome and played into the arguments made by Gompers and others that labor unions should focus solely on skilled workers. The most significant strikes in Cleveland occurred at the Cleveland Rolling Mill Company in 1882 and again in 1885. The expansion of iron and steel and other industries pulled migrants into the growing numbers of working-class residents. By this time the mill complex employed some 5,000 workers and was the city's largest manufacturing establishment. It was founded by Scottish immigrant Henry Chisolm, who ran the company until his death in 1881, when his son, William, replaced him.

As was becoming more common in manufacturing during these years, Chisolm had shifted from iron to steel, and within steel introduced open-hearth furnaces. This reduced the need for skilled workers and increased demand for lower paid laborers to perform physically demanding unskilled work. In a fiercely competitive, cyclical industry, steelmakers like the Rolling Mill Company usually cut costs through reductions in labor. Skill reflected ethnicity as well, in this case with English, Scottish, and Welsh Protestants having the most, and non-English-speaking, mainly Catholic Poles and Bohemians, having the least.

In 1882, most of the Rolling Mill workers were still either native born or of English-speaking immigrant backgrounds. They were represented mainly by the Amalgamated Association of Iron and Steel Workers, which focused on skilled workers. In the middle of a steel recession, on May 9 and 10, workers raised several demands, including recognition of the Amalgamated Association, union wages, and a closed shop. Chisolm refused and 3,000 to 4,000 workers walked off the job. Chisolm then shut down the entire complex.

In early June 1882, Chisolm announced he would reopen part of the complex with new, non-union workers, mainly unskilled Bohemian and Polish immigrants living near the mill. As these "scab" workers entered the plant, ethnic tensions erupted. A crowd of strikers, their female supporters, and teenage boys, the latter perhaps looking for excitement, met the workers with jeers, and then followed by hitting police with bricks and rocks. Officers responded by charging the crowd and beating both women and their male companions. After this, authorities beefed up protection of the mill, and Chisolm began an intensive effort to bypass hiring workers in Cleveland. He started recruiting from the Polish and Bohemian immigrants landing in New York who then traveled by train directly to Cleveland and began working in the mill. The strike ended by August, with some of the strikers rehired but all of the workers forced to sign a pledge that they would not join a union.

Violence erupted again at the Cleveland Rolling Mill in 1885. This time the issue was not union recognition by skilled, English-speaking workers but wage cuts that affected mainly unskilled non-English-speaking Bohemian and Polish workers. They had already seen two cuts of 17 and 20 percent when management announced a third in July. Leading this protest were the same Polish and Bohemian workers brought in by Chisolm to break the 1882 strike. A group that grew to several hundred, led by a man carrying an American flag, forced the entire mill complex to shut down. Days later some 1,500 strikers marched to Chisolm's office as well as to the mayor's, but Chisolm refused to restore wages and the mayor pleaded helplessness. The group followed this with a march to two other companies owned by the Chisolm family, forcing both to shut down.

Chisolm tried to reopen the plant but he immediately closed it when violence ensued as strikers, trying to prevent the opening, battled with the police charged with protecting the company. Newspapers in Cleveland had been more sympathetic to the English-speaking workers in 1882 than they had been to the immigrants of 1885, with editors calling the Bohemians and Poles "foreign devils" and "ignorant and degraded whelps." Among the workers, a shaky alliance developed, this time between the skilled and unskilled. Calls for moderation came from Father Francis Kolaszewski of St. Stanislaus, a Polish church, who warned the strikers that he would not give the rites of the church or Christian burial to any parishioners killed in the disturbance. After two months, Chisolm announced he would rescind the wage cuts. The irony was, however, that he refused to rehire many of the Bohemian and Polish workers he had brought in to end the 1882 strike. For its part, the Amalgamated Association would be crushed ten years later during the Homestead steel strike of 1892.

The state of Ohio responded to the continued labor tension by creating public employment offices in 1890 and a state Board of Arbitration in 1893, but this did not end the conflicts. Riots erupted in Cleveland in 1894 when thousands who were out of work forced the closure of several factories in the city and clashed with police and National Guardsmen. Then, in June 1899, a major streetcar strike broke out against the Big Consolidated line, one of Cleveland's two, which emanated from a forced speedup and increased hours of work. Once again strikers and their sympathizers clashed with strikebreakers, police officers, and members of the militia. Strikers succeeded in launching a boycott of the rail line, but by the fall, the strike and boycott had essentially ended. Nevertheless, these and other incidents in Cleveland and elsewhere across Ohio and the nation would prompt reforms that constituted part of the progressive movement.

In response to the pressure from workers, some companies in Ohio sought to improve conditions and stave off unionization through what has become called "welfare capitalism." Cincinnati's Procter and Gamble, for example, introduced a profit sharing plan in 1887 and other benefits. At NCR in Dayton, John Patterson responded to unionization efforts by designing factories to let in more light and landscaping the grounds. He added other benefits for workers including healthcare, recreational activities, and educational opportunities. Other companies did similar things. Led by Sam "Golden Rule" Jones, the future progressive mayor of Toledo, the Acme Sucker Rod Company provided picnics, a company band, a library, and allowed workers to keep track of their own time. The major rubber companies in Akron vied for creating the most welfare benefits for employees. Both Goodyear and Firestone went so far as to design and build neighborhoods for their workers in the 1910s, Goodyear Heights and Firestone Park. These neighborhoods were initially restricted to whites only. Following a 1916 steel strike in which portions of East Youngstown were burned to the ground, Youngstown Sheet and Tube in the Mahoning Valley began constructing worker's housing as well. In these cases, the companies offered separate neighborhoods for white American, foreign, and African American workers.

These labor disputes illustrate further how, between the end of the Civil War and World War I, Ohio and the United States underwent a momentous transformation, adding a significant urban and industrial presence to its rural and agricultural set up. Ohio stood at the forefront of these changes that profoundly affected virtually all aspects of life in the Buckeye State and others. Big business transformed Ohio into an industrial leader, pulled immigrants from across the world into the state, remade the environment and the economy, and drove urbanization. The speed and depth of these changes surprised, awed, excited, and even unnerved Ohioans as it did others in the nation. The industrial order opened new opportunities for millions of people and created a cadre of defenders of the system. It also generated demands for change, both moderate and radical, that would have an equally lasting impact on Ohio and the nation.

Further Reading

On Ohio's inventors see: Neil Baldwin, *Edison: Inventing the Century* (1995. New York: Hyperion); Mark Bernstein, *Grand Eccentrics: Turning the Century: Dayton and the Inventing of America* (1996. Wilmington, Ohio: Orange Frazer Press); Rayvon Fouche, *Black Inventors in the Age of Segregation: Granville T. Woods, Lewis H. Latimer & Shelby J. Davidson* (2003. Baltimore: Johns Hopkins University Press); Fred Howard, *Wilbur and Orville: A Biography of the Wright Brothers* (1987. New York: Knopf; Stuart W. Leslie, *Boss Kettering* (1983. New York: Columbia University Press). For industrialization, European immigrants, African Americans and labor, see: Jack Blocker, *A Little More Freedom: African Americans Enter the Urban Midwest, 1860–1930* (2008. Columbus: The Ohio State University Press); Raymond Boryczka and Lorin Lee Cary, *No Strength without Union: An Illustrated History of Ohio Workers, 1803–1980* (1982. Columbus: The Ohio Historical Society); David C. Hammack, Diane L. Grabowski, and John J. Grabowski, eds., *Identity, Conflict, and Cooperation: Central Europeans in Cleveland, 1850–1930* (2002. Cleveland: Western Reserve Historical Society); Leslie S. Hough, *The Turbulent Spirit: Cleveland, Ohio, and its Workers, 1877–1899* (1991. New York: Garland Publishing); Steven J. Ross, *Workers on the Edge: Work, Leisure, and Politics in Industrializing Cincinnati, 1788–1890* (1985. New York: Columbia University Press); and Henry Shapiro and Jonathan Sarna, eds., *Ethnic Diversity and Civic Identity: Patterns of Conflict and Cohesion in Cincinnati since 1820* (1992. Urbana: University of Illinois).

12

Urban Life, Leisure, and Political Activism

1880–1920

Four years after making a canoe voyage to locate the mouth of the Mississippi in 1881, popular author, explorer and Civil War veteran Willard Glazier penned a book about American cities, in which he included Cincinnati and Cleveland. He painted a vivid scene of portions of the transformation associated with rapid growth and industrialization. Of Cincinnati he wrote: "The city proper is occupied by stores, offices, public buildings, factories, foundries, and the dwelling houses of the poorer and middle classes, over all which hangs a pall of smoke, caused by the bituminous coal used as fuel in the city. Cleanliness in either person or in dress is almost an impossibility." He went on: "The smoke of hundreds of factories, locomotives and steamboats arises and unites to form this dismal pall, which obscures the sunlight, and gives a sickly cast to the moonbeams." Beyond, though "on the magnificent amphitheatre of hills which encircle it, are half a dozen beautiful suburbs, where the homes of Cincinnati's merchant princes and millionaires are found, as elegant as wealth combined with art can make them."

However, there was more to the new urban world than dirty industry. Glazier also described the opera houses, theaters, schools, synagogues, and churches. He described the various social groups in the city, noting especially the prominence of Germans, concentrated in the "Over the Rhine" district where in entering, "one seems to have left America entirely," where the "German tongue is the only one spoken, and all signs and placards are in German."

Glazier described Cleveland using similar language: "The old pasture grounds of the cows of 1850 are now completely occupied by oil refineries and manufacturing establishments; and the river, which but a generation ago flowed peaceful and placid through green fields, is now almost choked with barges, tugs and immense rafts." The area known as the Flats, Glazier observed, "though far from beautiful" was nonetheless "interesting." "There are copper smelting, iron rolling, and iron manufacturing works, lumber yards, paper mills, breweries,

Ohio: A History of the Buckeye State, First Edition. Kevin F. Kern and Gregory S. Wilson.
© 2014 John Wiley & Sons, Inc. Published 2014 by John Wiley & Sons, Inc.

flour mills, nail works, pork-packing establishments" and "multitudinous industries of a great manufacturing city." The whole valley in which Cleveland sits he noted was "lit up with a thousand points of light from factories, foundries and steamboats." Like Cincinnati, Cleveland showed its wealth and leisure activities. There were opera houses, theaters, parks and gardens, and Euclid Avenue, "lined with handsome residences, elegant cottages and superb villas, the grounds around each being more and more extensive as it approaches the country." It was, in Glazier's exaggerated prose, "the finest avenue in the world."

Glazier remained fixated on showcasing great industrial development and the signs of wealth. Despite the smoke and haze, for the adventurer both were signs of American pride and progress. In addition to the industrial growth and cultural aspects such as opera houses, theaters, schools, and parks, Glazier might have also mentioned other forms of commercial leisure growing in popularity in Ohio's cities. Amusement parks sprouted up as urban residents had more time and money to pursue entertainment. Ohioans also developed a deep love of sports, especially baseball and football, whose national professional development owes a great deal to the Buckeye State.

Glazier's brief mention of Germans in Cincinnati (and an even briefer set of comments on Jews there) remained the only exploration of the streaming immigrants making these and other cities in Ohio home during the late nineteenth and early twentieth century. The German presence in Ohio remained vibrant and significant although their migration had peaked before the Civil War. As Glazier made his way through urban America, new groups dominated the migration, mainly those from Southern and Eastern Europe. Ohio came to be a major destination point in this global movement of people. In the process, they diversified the state, transforming its culture and politics among other things.

Glazier was neither the first nor the last to be fascinated with the tremendous growth of urban industrial Ohio. More and more, the cities grew to exert great influence and command attention from writers, reformers, and political leaders. The new urban life had its benefits as well as its costs. Ohio was at center of a national, even a transnational, endeavor to address such issues as overcrowding, pollution, great disparities of wealth, harsh working conditions (including child labor), and a political system that appeared corrupt and unresponsive to the people. This chapter, along with chapter 13, considers urban and industrial Ohio and the reform sprit that emerged to address the great transformation from a predominantly rural state to an urban one. This chapter examines the local arena while chapter 13 discusses events at the state and national levels, including World War I and its immediate aftermath.

Urban Life and Leisure

Urban growth went hand-in-hand with industrialization. As Ohioans came under the influence of the factory, one of the most notable changes concerned time. For many, one's time became increasingly separated into that for labor and that for leisure. Except in rural areas, industrialization meant that increasingly more Ohioans were working outside the home and for wages. Although many found themselves working 10 or 12 hours, six days a week, Ohioans were earning more and looking for leisure activities outside home and work. Within the new urban landscape Ohioans developed new lifestyles that saw a growth in mass consumption and commercialized leisure activities. These activities took many forms, ranging from penny arcades, city parks, playgrounds, amusement parks, theaters and restaurants, to beer gardens, dance halls, gambling dens, and brothels. Interestingly, social divisions of work also divided Ohioans in leisure.

The emergence of high culture in Ohio's cities could be seen in museums of art, orchestras, and operas, to this day some of the finest in the world. Founded by wealthy families, these institutions were efforts to preserve fine works of art and instill order and civility among the growing urban population. Cincinnati had a museum association in 1881, with the Cincinnati Art Museum opening in 1886, the first permanent home of an art museum west of the Appalachians. With the philanthropy of the Libbey Glass founders, Toledo began its Museum of Art in temporary buildings in 1901. Two other renowned institutions began shortly before and after World War I, the Cleveland Museum of Art (1913) and Youngstown's Butler Institute of American Art (1919). Classical music developed as well with Cincinnati adding its symphony orchestra by 1895 and Cleveland's symphony orchestra was performing on a permanent basis by 1918. Cities also boasted new theaters. In 1896, Columbus opened the Southern Theater, which featured famous performers of the era, including Lillian Russell, Ethel and Lionel Barrymore, Sarah Bernhardt, and Maude Adams. In Cleveland, the Euclid Avenue Opera House opened in 1875. Following this were two more theaters, the Park Theater (renamed the Lyceum Theater in 1889), which opened in 1883 and the Cleveland Theater, which opened in 1885. An innovative, interracial organization, the Karamu House, began in Cleveland in 1915 and was dedicated to promoting positive race relations through the theater and arts.

Together with such exemplars of high culture came more popular forms of entertainment. One could take in a vaudeville or burlesque show at Cleveland's Columbia Theater, while the city's Hippodrome, built in 1907 and at the time the world's second largest, showcased operas as well as large spectacle shows. Such forms of entertainment would see a decline as motion pictures grew in popularity after World War I. More popular forms of music continued to grow in the late nineteenth century, especially through bands or singing societies identified with a particular ethnic or racial group. These types of concerts were held in various venues, including parades, parks, beer gardens, social clubs, and bars.

Characteristic of the forces shaping urban life and leisure was the appearance of a new form of commercial leisure, amusement parks, and Ohio boasted several. The nation's first, Coney Island in New York, inspired the creation of others. More well-heeled Ohioans looked down on amusement parks as dens of iniquity, but that did not stop the middle and working classes from attending. As cities spread outward, residents increasingly travelled by trolley or light rail lines. Frequently, owners of trolley systems invested in amusement parks as a way to expand their business. In Cleveland, the most popular park was Euclid Beach Park, which opened along the shores of Lake Erie in 1895. A trolley line with a terminus there enabled urban residents to reach the site, where they could picnic in the seventy-five acres of woods or bathe in the lake along the sandy beach. The park expanded rapidly after 1901 with new investments by the Humphrey family who, appropriately, had made a fortune as popcorn and candy magnates. In an effort to attract the middle and upper classes, Euclid Beach Park's slogan promised

"Nothing to depress or demoralize." The park had free admission but charged for attractions, which included a carousel, a roller coaster, a dancing pavilion, and a skate rink. The expansion of transportation networks allowed easy access to other parks as well. Cedar Point, on a peninsula near Sandusky, emerged as a recreation area once a rail line came to the area in 1867. The amusement park started in 1870 but saw greater expansion once the Cedar Point Pleasure Resort & Company purchased the site in 1897. In addition to rail travel, visitors came to Cedar Point by steamships from Detroit and Cleveland.

The steamship was instrumental in developing Coney Island, ten miles from Cincinnati. After receiving requests to use his land for picnics and leisure activities, James Parker realized that this was potentially more profitable than apple farming, so he began renting out his land, building a dining hall, dance hall, and merry-go-round. He sold "Parker's Grove" to a group headed by two steamship captains, who hoped to emulate the trolley parks by linking the park to their steamship business. In 1886 it officially opened as "Grove Park: The Coney Island of the West," but the Grove Park name was dropped the following year. For fifty cents, visitors bought a round-trip ticket on the steamship that included the price of admission to the park. Like other park operators looking to attract a certain clientele, Ohio Grove owners touted their venue as "Cincinnati's Moral Resort," a safe haven for women and children. Other parks included Idora in Youngstown, Buckeye Lake near Newark, and Summit Beach in Akron.

As amusements parks grew in popularity, so too did organized sports, especially baseball. Like other forms of leisure, the rise of baseball reflected trends transforming Ohio. The game spread among Civil War troops and became increasingly popular and began to professionalize in the decades following the war. Cities and towns across Ohio started baseball clubs, some with professional players but most without. These teams became sources of civic pride and served the interests of city boosters and business leaders. Ohio is famous for having the first all-professional baseball team, the 1869 Cincinnati Red Stockings (shown in Figure 12.1). That year under the leadership of player-manager Harry Wright, the club's ten salaried players went undefeated, in a season that included a cross-country tour from San Francisco to Boston that drew more than 200,000 spectators. The highlight of the year came in June, when the Red Stockings defeated the three New York teams and the Philadelphia Athletics, all four traditionally considered the best. Upon their return to Cincinnati from the East Coast tour, the team was met by some 5,000 home-town fans, complete with banners, songs, bands, firecrackers, and a parade. After defeating the New York Mutuals, the Red Stockings received a telegram on behalf of "all the citizens of Cincinnati" gushing that the "streets are full of people, who give cheer after cheer for their pet club. Go on with the noble work. Our expectations have been met." Later, the journal *Spirit of the Times* joined the excitement: "Full of courage, free from intemperance, they have conducted themselves in every city they visited in a manner to challenge admiration, and their exhibitions of skill in the art of handling both ball and bat call for unexampled praise." In 1881, the Cincinnati Red Stockings were reformed and joined with numerous other teams, including the Forest City team of Cleveland, to create the National Association of Professional Baseball. In 1886, this association became the National League. In 1892, the Western Association was formed in Cincinnati. This association eventually became the modern-day American League.

Figure 12.1   Here are the members of the Cincinnati Reds in 1869, with Harry Wright in the middle. The Reds earned fifty-seven straight wins before losing their first game in June 1870. The decision to pay players led to other teams doing the same, sparking the rise of professional sports.
Source: Courtesy of the Ohio Historical Society (AL06023)

Baseball was not just an urban sport; teams sprang up across rural Ohio as well. Similar expectations surrounded those men who played in smaller towns, where baseball "emanated from informal neighborly circles of men and boys at work and at leisure" and reflected the homogeneity, unity, and friendliness found in many of these communities. These men were expected to conduct themselves as "gentlemen" as they represented the class values and standards of the community in which they lived.

Nonetheless, the game of baseball revealed some of the tensions at work in late nineteenth-century Ohio. In the cities, the players were mainly of working-class backgrounds, but with the advent of professionalization they could potentially earn the same as the higher classes. Moreover, the game had begun as a way for upper-class men to engage in leisure as amateurs; these men bemoaned the shift to commercialized, professional organizations that the Red Stockings epitomized. Upper-class men worried about the corrupting influence of money in the game, a concern that has yet to diminish. Whether professional or amateur, baseball remained a masculine arena, nurtured by the Civil War and sustained by veterans and supporters as a public venue for men, whether on the field or off. In addition, in adopting a fully professional lineup, Wright and owner Aaron Champion ran the Red Stockings as a business enterprise and sought to appeal to the larger middle-class audience by working to enforce discipline, regular drills, and respectable behavior in the players. Wright himself avoided the use of tobacco and alcohol, yet the tension remained as baseball players and fans alike continued to smoke, gamble, and drink.

Unfortunately as the twentieth century opened, as in other areas of Ohio's public life, baseball and leisure were becoming more segregated activities. At least through the 1890s, it was common for blacks to visit most public spaces along with whites in Ohio. Wendell Dabney, prominent African American in Cincinnati observed: "Colored people used to go to Parker's Grove, the site of our Coney Island." But by the 1900s, that had changed. "In late years, however, the prejudice has grown by leaps and bounds." African Americans, excluded from essentially white public space in many areas, created their own arenas for leisure activities. There were black gambling dens and pool halls, saloons, and brothels. There were also more respectable venues that catered to a black clientele such as restaurants, dance halls, and theaters. Cincinnati had become a center for black vaudeville and it housed the Afro American Booking Company, which managed a circuit of black theaters and performers. Columbus had the Crown Garden Theater and Airdome, an outdoor recreation park. The largest black-operated and patronized amusement park in the nation was Dayton's Dahomey Park. The brainchild of African American real estate magnate Moses Moore, the park contained a zoo, roller rink, restaurants, and eventually a movie theater. Moore added the Marco Baseball Club, which became one of the many black Ohio teams that competed throughout the North after 1900 and Moore's team became one of the eight clubs that formed the Negro National League in 1920.

In the late nineteenth century, black baseball teams barnstormed the North, independent of white organizations but playing both white and black teams. African Americans also formed their own organization in 1887, the League of Colored Baseball Clubs, which included a team from Cincinnati. There were some exceptions to the color line. Blacks played on some minor league teams that were mostly white and Moses "Fleetwood" Walker became the first black player to play with a major league franchise when his otherwise white Toledo Blue Stockings team joined the American Association in 1884.

As baseball increased in popularity, so, too did football. The modern version of the game with eleven players began among the universities of the Ivy League but quickly spread west from there. As with baseball, football already tolerated a blurring of the lines between professional and amateur, with many of the best college players accepting money to play. Spreading the game beyond colleges were athletic associations that emerged in cities, the incubators of the modern professional football system. During the 1890s, the sport was chaotic and violent, not unlike the urban environment itself, with high schools, athletic clubs, and colleges often playing one another. The spirit of rationality and reform that would sweep into other aspects of life came to football, too, as separate and regulated associations emerged for high school, college, and professional teams. Reformers tried to make the game less violent but, even with the mandated changes, a typical year in the early twentieth century could see eighteen football-related fatalities.

College football could be directly tied to the movement labeled "muscular Christianity." This strain of religiosity emerged in the late nineteenth century, whereby the body could be used as an agent of societal uplift at home and abroad. The emergence of muscular Christianity also played into male concerns that Victorian Protestantism had become too feminized, that women had gained too much power. At the same time, among middle- and upper-class Protestants, fear grew that urban middle-class life had become too sedentary, and that white, Anglo Protestants were losing influence as foreign immigrants continued to flock to the cities. Those advocating the Social Gospel also espoused physical training as necessary to enable leaders to reform urban life. The new religious philosophy emphasized the unity of humankind and redefined salvation as no longer a private affair but a social one. The Kingdom of God was not something for the next world, but one to be fashioned in this one. Therefore many reformers came to see physical conditioning as a necessary foundation to restore certain values to Ohio and America.

Football thrived in Ohio, especially on college campuses. At Oberlin College, the connection between football, the Social Gospel, and muscular Christianity was palpable, particularly under the presidency of Henry Churchill King, who called for a religion to transform a "vacillating, flabby, self-indulgent generation." With faculty support, in the 1890s Oberlin hired John Heisman as their football coach. Heisman, after whom the Heisman Trophy is named, was born in Cleveland in 1896 and grew up among the oil fields of Titusville, Pennsylvania. He attended Brown University and went on to earn a law degree at Penn. He played football at both schools, and immediately upon earning his law degree in 1892 he launched his coaching career by coming to Oberlin. That year he coached the team to a seven and nil record that included two wins over Ohio State. He then went to Buchtel College (now the University of Akron) for the 1893 season and then split time in 1894 between Oberlin and Buchtel before leaving for Auburn. Among other innovations, Heisman is credited with legalizing the forward pass, introducing the center snap, the "hike" shouted by the quarterback, and breaking the game from two halves to four quarters. Oberlin was one of the "Big Six" teams that in 1902 founded the Ohio Athletic Conference, along with Case, Kenyon, Ohio State, Ohio Wesleyan, and Western Reserve. Ohio State would go on to join the Big Ten in 1913.

Ohio is home to the Pro Football Hall of Fame in Canton, and for good reason. Professional football emerged first in Pennsylvania, but as it faded there in the early twentieth century, Ohio became the center for the sport. Several teams played in the Ohio League, which lasted from 1902 to 1919, including the Akron Indians (Pros), Canton Bulldogs, Columbus Panhandles, Dayton Triangles, Massillon Tigers, and the Youngstown Patricians. In 1920 came the American Professional Football Association, formed in the showroom of a Canton auto dealership owned by Ralph Hay, who also owned the Bulldogs. Five of the APFA's first teams were from Ohio: the Akron Pros, Canton Bulldogs, Cleveland Tigers, Columbus Panhandles, and Dayton Triangles. Two years later, in 1922, the APFA reorganized as the National Football League. Ohio's teams were among the best and boasted significant players, including Knute Rockne, who played for the Massillon Tigers before going on to

Figure 12.2   Canton Bulldogs's general manager Jack Cusack signed Jim Thorpe in 1915 for the high sum of $250 per game. With Thorpe as coach and player the Bulldogs claimed championships in 1916, 1917, and 1919. Thorpe—whose Indian name as Wa-Tho-Huk ("Bright Path")—was of mixed French, Irish, and Sac and Fox Indian heritage and became world famous by winning the decathlon and the pentathlon in the 1912 Olympics.
Source: Photo courtesy Research Division Oklahoma Historical Society with thanks to Jim Thorpe Home

fame as coach of Notre Dame. Some of the best players were non-whites. Unlike baseball, football allowed African American and other minority players until the early 1930s. Jim Thorpe (Figure 12.2) of Native American heritage and the world's most famous athlete, played for the Canton Bulldogs, generating huge crowds (and revenues). He later coached the team, as well as served as the first president of the APFA. Charles Follis (the "Black Cyclone from Wooster") became the first African American professional when he played for the Shelby team in the Ohio League from 1902 to 1906. Paul Robeson, All-American from Rutgers, played for the Akron Pros as did Fritz Pollard, an All-American at Brown who went on to become the first African American coach in professional football for the Pros. Not all was positive, of course. Racist slurs and shouts could be heard in the crowds, and white players often made a point to go after African American opponents. Football was, therefore, relatively more open than other forms of commercialized leisure that were growing in popularity.

Urban Political Reform

As the reformers of the Social Gospel preached, Ohio's new landscape of leisure and consumption came at a price. In it were the ill effects of rapid expansion, including outbreaks of epidemic disease, air and water pollution, and a lack of adequate city services, including fire and police protection, sewerage, sanitation, and good roads. Cities also bore witness to the growing disparities of wealth, containing both neighborhoods of grand opulence and appalling poverty. City politics also came under fire as reformers set about tackling the corruption and inefficiency of city leaders. Reformers argued that the older doctrines of laissez-faire and Social Darwinism had led to injustice, disorder, and the concentration of power and wealth in relatively few hands, all of which threatened democracy. They maintained, however, that purposeful human action could improve society. Intervention could take many forms, but most reformers looked to government to play a central role in promoting social justice, expanding democracy and civic engagement, and bringing order and efficiency to Ohio. However, reform came with its own set of contradictions between social justice and social control.

Reformers looked to leisure as one area in which to rebuild public culture on a foundation of "education and morality." Politics became another and quickly overshadowed all others as the major arena for addressing the costs of progress. In city government, Toledo and Cleveland were held up by the national press as shining examples of enlightened mayoral administration. Perhaps the most colorful and unique progressive mayor was Toledo's Samuel "Golden Rule" Jones (Figure 12.3). Born in Wales, Jones came from an intensely Calvinist background. Initially, he believed in the idea that one's accumulation of great wealth evidenced one's living according to God's word. This belief stayed with Jones as he looked to make his way in the emerging oil business. He was the first person to strike a large well in Lima, Ohio, he joined with others to form in 1887 the Ohio Oil Company, which sold out to Standard Oil two years later, leaving Jones with a tidy profit. Widower Jones remarried Helen Beach of Toledo in 1892, and the couple moved to her hometown. There Sam started another oil company and began to work on improving the drilling process, which led to his patent on the first all-metal sucker rod. The production and sale of this innovation allowed Jones to leave the oil fields in 1894 and open his Acme Sucker Rod Company in Toledo.

As he attained great wealth, Jones grew ever more enamored of those advocating for reform, particularly those in the Social Gospel movement. Of these, no one stood out more than Washington Gladden, who would soon become one of Jones's personal friends. Gladden had been a Congregational minister in New York and Massachusetts before accepting the pulpit at the First Congregational Church in Columbus in 1882. Like other reformers of the day, Gladden was well-versed in European writings and aware of the social reforms taking place across the Atlantic. Religiously inspired reformers sought to reconcile Protestant Christianity with direct responses to the conditions of urban America. Gladden became a major proponent of the Social Gospel emphasis on fashioning perfection in this world, as opposed to waiting to achieve salvation in the next.

Figure 12.3 Samuel "Golden Rule" Jones (1846–1904) became an international symbol of the Progressive reformer in action. His childhood poverty combined with his religious upbringing to drive Jones to achieve wealth in the first part of his adult life and then divest it and work for social justice later.

Source: Courtesy of the Ohio Historical Society (AL03909)

For Gladden, selfishness lay at the root of all society's wrongs. "The good of life is not found by those who prey upon one another or plunder one another; it is found only by those who in friendship serve one another." "The stable and fruitful social order" will be one that obeys the meaning of Christ's law of life, "Good Will." To bring about this society, Gladden believed that the state was necessary to curb the excesses of industrialization. He advocated government ownership of national industries such as railroads and telegraphs, and city ownership of local gas, water, communication, and transportation systems. While serving one term on Columbus City Council from 1900 to 1902, Gladden managed to lower streetcar fares.

Although Gladden pushed for a greater role of government in the economy, he did not endorse socialism. For him, like other Protestant reformers and advocates of the Social Gospel, socialism—the belief that public ownership of large economic enterprises should replace private control in order to distribute more evenly the wealth produced—threatened individual transformation and private property. Moreover, Gladden continued to emphasize brotherhood and the common interests of capital and labor. His was mainly a spiritual concern, secondarily an economic one. He supported unionization but desired both business and labor to work cooperatively; he initially favored profit sharing over government ownership or unions. Gladden did not view society as permanently divided, but rather as an organic whole which industrialization had disrupted. Gladden himself never abandoned some of his more conservative views, including his temperance, anti-Catholicism and racism.

While Gladden sought a middle way between laissez-faire capitalism and socialism, Jones moved further to the left, shifting from the Social Gospel to Christian Socialism. Like Gladden, Jones held an optimistic belief that application of the Golden Rule could cure society's woes. Unlike his fellow Toledo business owners, who posted long lists of rules and regulations, Jones placed one tin sign on his sucker rod factory wall that read: "The Rule That Governs This Factory: 'Therefore Whatsoever Ye Would That Men Should Do Unto You, Do Ye Even So Unto Them.'" There were no other rules, no time clocks, and he paid wages 50 percent higher than other factory owners in Toledo. He also instituted profit sharing, paid vacations, and day care facilities.

Not content to transform lives only through business, Jones won the Toledo mayor's race in 1897 and served until his death in 1904. The call for reform had been growing along with Toledo's population. From roughly 81,000 in 1890 with 65 percent of the residents either born outside the United States or the children of foreign-born parents, the city reached in excess of 132,000 in 1900. In Toledo, as in other cities, the huge influx of people led to enormous challenges for which city governments were largely unprepared.

Government in Toledo and other cities had been run by so-called political machines. In the machine, power flowed from a political boss or small group, who often exerted behind-the-scenes control over city affairs and politics. The boss or small cadre of leaders dispensed patronage and jobs to supporters, steered city contracts to favored businesses, which in turn provided kickbacks, and offered various services to help the incoming population survive. The machine—whether run by Democrats or Republicans—rewarded their candidates by getting voters to the polls. In Toledo, the Republicans dominated politics. Their machine had come under fire from newspapers for its corruption and inefficiency, but not necessarily for its failures to help the city's growing working classes.

Into this fray stepped Jones, who became the Republican candidate for mayor in 1897. Party regulars assumed they could control Jones: they could not. He frequently argued for abolishing political parties at the local level and in 1899, he ran for re-election and won as an independent, which he would do for each campaign thereafter. He also made a bid for governor in 1899, coming in third but carrying Cuyahoga and Lucas counties. Jones loved campaigning, the crowds loved him, too and he fed off their energy. As mayor, Jones received countless letters from people in Toledo asking for help. He responded to most of them personally and sought to aid anyone he could. He donated his $800 annual salary as mayor and, when that was not enough, he used his own money, so much so that his wealth fell from close to $1 million in 1897 to some $333,333 when died in 1904. He mandated the eight-hour day for city workers, authorized the building of public parks, and established kindergartens. He advocated for "gas and water socialism," the public ownership of city utilities, and pushed forward civil service regulations to all city departments. He also fought for Toledo and other cities to establish "home rule," the ability of cities to exert greater authority over their own affairs as opposed to being under the control of the state government. To the consternation of many middle-class reformers, Jones refused to clamp down on vice. He did not see vice or poverty as endemic to immigrants or the poor themselves, but rather to the economic and social environment caused by rapid industrialization and urbanization. Jones himself was a teetotaler, but he knew that attacks on vice in Toledo carried with them strong anti-immigrant sentiments and class biases. Jones also needed the votes of ethnic, blue-collar workers to survive.

By the time of his death in 1904, Jones had become a national and international sensation. While he had achieved some of his goals as mayor most of the progressive reforms came later under Jones's protégé, lawyer, poet, and writer Brand Whitlock, born in Urbana, Ohio, in 1869. In 1897 Whitlock entered law practice in Toledo where he became an admirer and friend of Jones. Whitlock was a Democrat, but he ran on an independent ticket and served from Jones's death until 1913, when President Woodrow Wilson appointed him as minister to Belgium.

Whitlock campaigned successfully to amend Ohio's constitution to allow for home rule for cities and spoke out forcefully against capital punishment. Although he failed to create a publically owned streetcar or utility company, he did manage to pressure the Toledo Railway and Light Corporation to lower fares to three cents and offer free transfers. Later administrations would adopt a city charter modeled on progressive ideals put forward by Jones and Whitlock, and in 1916 the city bought out Toledo Railway and Light to own and operate streetcars.

Jones's and Whitlock's contemporary in urban reform was Tom Johnson of Cleveland (Figure 12.4). While not as religious or idealistic as Jones, Johnson shared a conviction to change how city government addressed the effects of rapid industrialization and population growth. Born in Kentucky in 1854 to a Confederate family, like "Golden Rule" Jones, Johnson, too, had risen from poverty to make a fortune in business. The family had befriended relatives of the du Pont's, a connection that saw Johnson land a job with the Louisville Street Railway Company. Johnson worked his way to superintendent and, possessing a great amount of mechanical skill, managed to invent several devices for street railways, using money from these inventions to purchase the Indianapolis Street Railway. He expanded his holdings into Cleveland and Johnson and his wife, Maggie, moved there in 1883, living in luxury along Euclid Avenue. In 1889 Johnson expanded his holdings further by building a rolling mill for manufacturing steel rails in Johnstown, Pennsylvania, which opened just as the Johnstown Flood devastated the city. Johnson helped coordinate the massive relief efforts there. Six years later he opened a steel mill in Lorain, Ohio, at the time a small village west of Cleveland.

Few in the 1880s expected that Johnson, a wealthy industrialist, would enter politics and earn an international reputation as a reformer. However, his reading of Henry George and a subsequent friendship he forged with the writer pushed Johnson in a new direction. George had been an antislavery newspaper editor in California in the 1850s and 1860s and had witnessed the rapid monopolization of land there. After the Civil War, George turned his talents and attention to addressing the growing disparity of wealth in the nation. In 1883 while riding the train between his new home in Cleveland and Indianapolis, the conductor persuaded Johnson to read George's *Social Problems*. At first skeptical, since he was

Figure 12.4 Tom Johnson (1854–1911) earned a reputation for reform during his time as mayor of Cleveland. Popular "muckraker," journalist Lincoln Steffens stated that "Johnson is the best mayor of the best governed city in America."
Source: Courtesy of the Ohio Historical Society (AL03917)

still looking for the "sure prospect of continuing to make money" Johnson, once he started the book, finished it almost without stopping. He then purchased all of George's writings, including his most famous work, *Progress and Poverty*. George saw monopoly as a social wrong, a chief cause of inequality. He argued for replacing the tariff and tax structure with a single tax on the unimproved value of land that would replace the private wealth accumulated through ownership of land. He also called for the regulation or state ownership of public utilities and the replacement of protectionism with open trade.

Johnson met George in 1885 and became deeply involved in George's political career. George narrowly lost the 1886 election for mayor of New York and Johnson ran George's unsuccessful 1897 mayoral campaign, the strain of which ultimately cost George his life. Persuaded and inspired by his friend, Johnson entered politics. In 1890 he won a seat in the U.S. House of Representatives representing Cleveland. He lost his bid for re-election in 1894, but during his four years in office Johnson advocated for lowering the tariffs, including those on the steel rails he manufactured.

Yet Johnson was not an entirely changed man. Between 1894 and 1899, he sought to undermine one of the most progressive mayors in the nation, Hazen Pingree of Detroit.

Through his position as general manager of Detroit's Citizens' Street Railway Company, Johnson tried to gain monopoly control over streetcars in the city and engaged in a battle over fares and control of lines with Pingree. Eventually, Johnson left his post, but not before he learned a good deal about progressive government from his battles with Pingree. After this episode and George's death, Johnson decided to tackle the problems of political economy directly by running for mayor of Cleveland. He won that office in 1901 and served in it until 1909.

Johnson's record was impressive. Although Johnson failed to get direct city ownership of streetcars, he did oversee the creation of a quasi-public corporation to run lines offering three-cent fares. His 1901 campaign came in the wake of Cleveland's bitter 1899 streetcar strike and, in a direct appeal to his working-class base, Johnson made reform of public transportation one of his key issues. As he would later write in his autobiography, *My Story*, "I had no conception of the character of the struggle I was engaged in then, but I know now that the cure for this evil with all its possibilities of terrible consequences to men individually and to society collectively is the municipal ownership of street railways. A large proportion of the political evils of our cities is due to private ownership of public utilities." When Cleveland annexed South Brooklyn in 1906, Cleveland owned the former South Brooklyn electric plant and later built and operated another plant. Johnson succeeded in revising the tax code to increase taxes on businesses, reforming criminal justice by separating juvenile from adult offenders and opening a rehabilitation facility. He oversaw the professionalization of the police and city government, expanded public health, revised and enforced building codes, paved streets, and created a regular program of street cleaning. Johnson also pushed ahead with the construction of new parks, public works, and playgrounds. Finally, he initiated the city's Group Plan, which constructed a mall of neoclassical public buildings in downtown, designed by noted architects that included Daniel Burnham. Johnson left office in 1910 and died the next year. Fittingly, he was buried next to Henry George in Greenwood Cemetery, Brooklyn.

Johnson brought in young reformers who themselves would go on to influential careers, including Frederic C. Howe and Newton Baker. Baker carried on with many of Johnson's ideas as he assumed the mayor's office. Baker had studied at Johns Hopkins, taking courses with future president and fellow progressive Woodrow Wilson. Baker came to Cleveland to practice law and became the city's law director in 1903. Baker fused the urban populism of Johnson with the expert-driven style characteristic of many progressive reformers. He continued Johnson's focus on expanding municipal services and oversaw the construction of Cleveland's second municipal power plant. Baker helped to write the successful Ohio constitutional amendment for city home rule and was influential in selecting the committee that wrote Cleveland's first city charter, which voters approved in 1913. Baker also worked more closely, than Johnson, with business leaders relying on business-dominated civic groups for advice and cooperation in city projects. Like other state leaders, Baker came to national attention. He served as Woodrow Wilson's secretary of war during World War I, responsible for the massive task of overseeing the drafting, organizing, and equipping of the nation's armed forces, as well as the awarding of war contracts.

Alongside reformers like Jones, Whitlock, Johnson, and Baker Ohio also saw more radical leadership. With its strong mix of industry (and wealthy industrialists), immigrants, and labor union activity, Ohio provided fertile ground for socialism. The Socialist Party of America formed in 1901 and in Ohio between 1910 and 1915 Socialists achieved substantial victories. The administrations of Jones and Johnson demonstrated the popularity of Socialist-backed ideas such as municipal ownership of utilities, as well as day-to-day concerns like streetcar fares, poor sanitation in urban neighborhoods, and workplace safety. Workers showed willingness for independent political activity outside the two major parties. In 1911, for example, Socialist candidates won mayoral races in Ashtabula, Barberton, Canton, Conneaut, Cuyahoga Falls, Fostoria, Lima, Lorain, Martin's Ferry, Mount Vernon, Salem, St. Marys, and Toronto. They also won city council seats in Akron, Columbus, Dayton, and Toledo. Nationally, Socialist presidential candidate Eugene Debs grew popular receiving over 900,000 votes in the 1912 presidential election. He received the most votes from Ohio, over 90,000, carrying 8.8 percent in the state.

In Cleveland were two of the most prominent Socialists, Max Hayes and Charles Emil Ruthenberg. Hayes, born in Havana, Huron County, in 1866, founded the labor paper *Cleveland Citizen* in 1891 and eventually joined the Socialist Party. Hayes ran for U.S. Congress in 1900 and for Ohio Secretary of State in 1902. He also was active in the AFL, challenging Samuel Gompers for the organization's presidency in 1911. Hayes's counterpart, Charles Ruthenberg, was born in Cleveland in 1882. An admirer of Tom Johnson, Ruthenberg became a Socialist, editing two local party papers, *The Cleveland Socialist* and *Socialist News*. Ruthenberg gradually became more radical, eventually joining the Communist Party in 1919 after serving a one-year prison sentence for his antiwar activities related to World War I.

The popularity of Socialist candidates shows the depth of the "fierce discontent" at the time in Ohio and across the country. It also demonstrates the power of workers and labor organizations, which formed the foundation for Socialist success. One result was to push some major party candidates further to the political left, and at the same time make reformers like Jones and Johnson seem less threatening to moderate or more conservative voters.

In addition to politics, urban reform at the local level included the settlement house. Borrowed from England and deeply influenced by the Social Gospel of Gladden and others, the settlement house saw reformers, so-called "settlement workers," living among those they sought to help. By gaining greater insight into the lives of the poor, settlement workers believed they could respond more effectively to the ills of urban life. Settlement houses were also an avenue of employment for middle- and upper-class women, who were increasingly becoming leaders in reform as they moved from the domestic sphere into more public roles in the late nineteenth century. Ohio's first settlement, Hiram House, was founded in Cleveland in 1896, its workers mostly female college students from Hiram College. The mission of Hiram House and other settlements comprised a mixture of altruism and social control. As they interacted with the mostly Catholic and Jewish immigrants they encountered, settlement workers also hoped to transform immigrants by setting a good example of Protestant middle-class behavior and values. In short, they sought to "Americanize" those they served. Settlements offered adult education, English language courses, healthcare and childcare, classes in personal hygiene, recreation, and advocated for improved living conditions for the urban poor. Typical of the immigrant who used Hiram House was a Russian Jewish woman "who lived in a one-room apartment on highly congested Cherry Alley" and regularly left her three children in daycare at Hiram House while she worked all day in the apartment sewing buttons on suits for one of Cleveland's garment manufacturers. Cleveland's wealthiest families donated money to keep Hiram House afloat and its director, George Bellamy, became increasingly conservative, adopting the lifestyle and outlook of his donors. As it was of other reformers, Bellamy's views shifted from emphasizing the need for social change to focusing on the individual behavior of the poor. As Bellamy became less optimistic about changing urban society, by 1906 Hiram House focused mainly on the children of immigrants, with an emphasis on playgrounds and other activities.

Women's Activism

As settlement houses spread from Cleveland to other Ohio cities, they became a major vehicle for white Protestant women's increased involvement in public affairs after the Civil War. This represented but one way in which women in general were playing a wider role in reform and in shaping public culture. Women, particularly Catholic and Jewish women, had already been active in the labor movement. Immigrant women, as mentioned, were already involved in establishing benefit societies and working through churches and synagogues to better their communities and respond to the social needs of urban life. With their husbands working in industrial jobs and therefore subject to swings in unemployment, work-related injuries or even death, married women, especially mothers, craved security. Moreover, if these women worked outside the home, they were mainly employed in some of the lowest paid and least secure jobs. Women's agitation for reform, combined with that of their husbands, pushed political leaders like "Golden Rule" Jones and Tom Johnson to come to the aid of working-class urban residents.

Middle- and upper-class women began to challenge the expectation that they should only remain in the home as wives and mothers, and women's clubs became a key institution for them. For example, the goal of those who formed the Cincinnati Woman's Club in 1894 was to provide an "organized center of thought and action among women to promote their social, educational, literary and artistic growth" and to aid the city in various ways. Many local women's groups were chapters of larger state or national organizations, such as the Ohio Federation of Women's Clubs and the national General Federation of Women's Clubs. Some were even international in scope, with Ohio women participating in conferences and activities in Europe and elsewhere. As they expanded, the focus of the women's clubs became more political, with members involved in issues such as factory labor, public schooling, pollution control, food safety and purity, and good government. For example, Cleveland's Book and Thimble Club had been organized by prominent women in 1890 as a literary group, but the members became instrumental in forming the Consumer's League of Ohio in 1900. The Consumer's League campaigned for ending child labor, as well as better wages and working conditions for industrial workers. It also discouraged patronage of businesses who failed to meet their standards.

A concern for the environment became a critical component of reform, one in which club women often led the way. As Glazier's earlier descriptions indicated, cities burned coal as their primary energy source, and thus smoke abatement became a major issue. In 1916 an estimated 217 tons of soot fell annually per square mile in Cincinnati's central business district. In Cleveland, soot and cinders fell like rain. Pollution was bad for business, as the costs of cleaning up ran to millions of dollars. More important, however, were the moral issues that connected public health to the character of the city and its people. Soot could be directly linked to asthma, bronchitis, and pneumonia: all fatal diseases. Many middle-class reformers saw a clear connection between health and morality: dirty air and littered streets led directly to immoral behavior. Clean up the city, clean up the character and morality of the people, especially the poor and their children. This connection to morality became sharper as women became leaders in initiating anti-smoke campaigns in Cincinnati and other cities. In these years, women often couched their entry into the public sphere as a form of municipal housekeeping, meaning that they were extending their traditional role as caretakers of the home outward into the city. If, as many women argued, they were the responsible for instilling proper values in their children, then women needed to lessen the impact of the evils of the outside world. It was the Woman's Club of Cincinnati that pressured the city's political leaders to enforce anti-smoke ordinances. Clubwomen, along with prominent physicians Julia Carpenter and Charles Reed, formed the Smoke Abatement League in 1906, which counted more than 200 of the city's most prominent citizens among its members. Smoke abatement, like other reforms, became a sign of enlightened civilization and culture.

Two other major reforms involving women's clubs and benefit societies also became imbued with references to morality and character: temperance and woman suffrage. The temperance issue re-emerged after a hiatus during the Civil War. Ohio played a leading role, as home to three-fifths of all those involved in the temperance crusades of 1873–74 and witnessing the founding of the two largest temperance organizations, the WCTU and the Anti-Saloon League. A number of factors fed into the movement. With many married women relying on their husband's income to manage the household, they feared the threat alcohol consumption placed on an already precarious financial situation. Women and children also bore the brunt of alcohol-induced domestic violence. Temperance advocates and much of the public linked alcohol to the many problems of urban Ohio, such as crime, vice, poverty, and delinquency. The temperance movement also had class and ethnoreligious overtones to it. Middle- and upper-class Protestants connected alcohol to the growing power of big business, as well as to waves of Europeans arriving in Ohio who were changing the state's culture and politics. Temperance, like other forms of progressive social legislation, aimed to remake Ohio society along native, Protestant, middle-class lines and, at the same time, curb the power of "the liquor interests" in Ohio political culture.

By 1900, temperance advocates had already formed the WCTU and with the addition of the Anti-Saloon League and activist churches, "drys" as they were labeled entered politics with a powerful statewide and national institutional base. The League maintained a ten-thousand-square-foot printing facility that turned out a weekly newspaper, *The American Issue* with a monthly circulation of 350,000 copies. Within Ohio, the Anti-Saloon League became especially active and successful. Under the leadership of Wayne Wheeler, the league worked to pass local option laws across the state. This drive culminated in the 1908 Rose law, which allowed counties to hold local option elections if 35 percent of the electors desired it. The Rose law allowed for review of the decision every three years. By 1909, sixty-three of Ohio's eighty-eight counties had outlawed the sale of alcohol. The momentum shifted some by 1912, such that eighteen counties that had originally voted dry under the Rose law switched back to "wet." But the battle raged on within Ohio and nationally, culminating in the Eighteenth Amendment.

As women became more active in public affairs, they soon ventured into pushing for the right to vote. Like many other reforms, woman suffrage was international in scope, and Ohio's leaders were part of the global effort to achieve women's rights. The trend towards greater equality for women was a slow one, but some progress had been made in the decades after the Civil War. From 1874 to 1887 Ohio passed fourteen new statutes on property, business, and contracts that expanded the independence of women (see Figure 12.5). And, as already noted, under the governorship of William McKinley the legislature managed to secure laws granting limited suffrage to women for school board elections and allowing married women to act as executors of estates. Nonetheless, the securing of full voting rights for women eluded reformers.

The right to vote soon trumped other reforms for women. The Ohio Woman Suffrage Association formed in 1885 with Frances Jennings Casement as president. Casement's views had developed in sympathy with those of her abolitionist father and husband, John (Jack) Casement, who had been a brigadier general in the Civil War and in charge of laying the Union Pacific Railroad in 1869. Jack was elected non-voting representative to Congress for the Wyoming Territory and had worked with Susan B. Anthony and Elizabeth Cady Stanton to secure Wyoming statehood and women's suffrage there. In 1883 Frances formed the Equal Rights Association in Painesville, Ohio, which became part of the Ohio Woman Suffrage Association (OWSA). Harriet Taylor Upton of Warren, Ohio, served for eighteen years as second president of OWSA as well as treasurer of the National Woman Suffrage Association (NAWSA); she was instrumental in Ohio and nationally. The group had been active in pressing the men of Ohio to allow full suffrage for women. Notable male leaders had endorsed the idea, including Tom Johnson, Samuel Jones, Brand Whitlock, Newton Baker, and John Patterson of NCR in Dayton, as were members of the Ohio Grange and the Ohio Federation of Labor.

Yet, organizationally, suffrage and other women's organizations were racially segregated, with separate organizations emerging for African Americans. Many white women were uneasy about accepting black women into their organizations, and blacks also sought to create their own groups in which they could act more freely. White leaders, including Susan B. Anthony and Harriet Upton, acquiesced in racial discrimination within states and national organizations such as NAWSA. Temperance, too, usually held the color line, with the WCTU advocating segregated local chapters. Women's clubs also developed separate white and black organizations.

Figure 12.5   This is a postcard from 1915 depicting the Seal of Ohio and a woman's face framed by the sun. Ohio women organized for suffrage in the 1870s at the local and county level, and then various groups merged at the state level to form the Ohio Woman Suffrage Association in 1885. The grandmother of noted feminist and Toledo native Gloria Steinem, Pauline Perlmutter Steinem, served as president of the Ohio Woman Suffrage Association from 1908 to 1911.
Source: Courtesy of the Ohio Historical Society (AL01124)

Among African Americans, perhaps no one became more influential than Hallie Quinn Brown (Figure 12.6). The daughter of former slaves, Brown graduated from Wilberforce in 1873, and after teaching in Mississippi and South Carolina, became Dean of Allen University in South Carolina from 1885 to 1887. Thereafter she returned to teach in the Dayton public schools and then served as Dean of Women at Tuskegee Institute from 1892 to 1893. Tuskegee Institute in Alabama, founded in 1881 as a school for African Americans and led at the time by Booker T. Washington, focused on vocational training (training for a job as opposed to liberal arts learning). After returning to Wilberforce to become a professor of elocution, Brown became more involved in temperance, as well as suffrage and civil rights. She traveled to Great Britain in 1895, speaking in London at the international Women's Christian Temperance Union, and again in 1899, among those representing the United States in London at the International Congress of Women. Brown led efforts to create separate women's clubs for African Americans, helping to form the National Association of Colored Women and serving as president of the Ohio State Federation of Colored Women's Clubs from 1905 to 1912, and the National Association of

Figure 12.6   Hallie Quinn Brown served in a number of the interlocking reform movements of the late nineteenth and early twentieth centuries, including civil rights, temperance, and suffrage. During her travels to London speaking on African American life in the United States and civil rights, she had several appearances before Queen Victoria. She also authored several books and prose collections.
Source: Courtesy of the National Afro-American Museum and Cultural Center

Colored Women from 1920 to 1924. She remained active in Republican Party politics and the African Methodist Episcopal Church, serving as representative of the Women's Parent Missionary Society at the World Missionary Conference in Scotland in 1910. Brown's life shows clearly the connections that developed between the push for temperance and woman suffrage (and among blacks for civil rights as well).

With Ohio having been a center for antislavery and abolitionist activity, and with many leaders supporting Reconstruction, it would seem that in an age of reform, white progressives would take up the cause of racial injustice. This was not, however, the case. Indeed, in the antebellum years support for abolition had been no guarantee of support for racial equality. In the late nineteenth century, many white, middle-class reformers, quick to expound on the inequalities endemic to industrialization, either remained silent on matters of race or sympathized with whites in the South who, as was popular at the time, condemned Reconstruction as a catastrophe and downplayed slavery as a cause of the Civil War. White Northerners also slowly accepted as inevitable *de jure* (meaning by law) segregation in much of the South, and *de facto* (by custom) segregation in the North that would last until the 1960s. Some, like Washington Gladden did not neglect the issue of race, but he could not fully escape the racial contradictions of white reformers. He could write passionately about the need for northerners to continue aiding African Americans in the South, out of "a sense of justice." He visited the South and spoke out against lynchings, and he supported efforts to educate African Americans. Yet, at the same time, he also believed that Reconstruction had inverted "the natural order of society" and based its measures on "the disfranchisement of the people of intelligence and character, and the enthronement of the illiterate and degraded." Eventually he acquiesced in the separation of the races, believing that racial hatred among whites was too powerful for blacks to demand full equality.

Education

Public schools and higher education underwent significant changes as a result of industrialization. Higher education met the needs of big business by developing a greater focus on training students in science and technology. Once content to leave higher education to the private, religiously affiliated colleges, state and city governments were now taking a greater role. This was a significant shift, with higher education now deemed an essential public responsibility, no longer solely in the hands of churches.

Using funds from the Morrill Land Grant Act of 1862, the General Assembly authorized the establishment of Ohio Agricultural and Mechanical College in 1870. Sitting a few miles north of the state capitol along the banks of the Olentangy River, the college expanded from its purely practical base to include a liberal arts curriculum and in 1878 it changed its name to the Ohio State University. In conjunction with a renewed focus on public schools, public colleges and universities also expanded their training of teachers. Programs for teacher training had been established by Ohio's private colleges, but in 1902 the state authorized and subsidized programs at Ohio University and Miami University. Additional programs were authorized in 1910 in Bowling Green and Kent, expanding training to all corners of the state. State-supported training for African American teachers had come in 1887 through Central State University in Wilberforce, despite opposition from its privately funded neighbor, Wilberforce College.

Municipal colleges emerged largely as partnerships with businesses. Local tax subsidies funded the creation of the University of Cincinnati in 1870, which in 1906 developed an innovative cooperative training program for engineering students in local businesses. In Toledo, the original University of Arts and Trades opened in 1872 but closed six years later. Reopening in 1884 under the control of the city, the institution was mainly a vocational training school that would expand in the first decades of the twentieth century. In 1913, the city of Akron assumed control of Buchtel College, and the new Municipal University of Akron patterned itself on the model established by the University of Cincinnati. Clevelanders rejected a new municipal university since they were already served with the Case School of Applied Science, founded in 1880 as the first school west of the Appalachians devoted solely to higher technical education.

As universities grew and expanded their curriculum to train professionals for the new industrial, urban world, the faculties became more professionalized. Academics emphasized the gathering of evidence and scientific investigation. Seeing themselves as dispassionate, trained experts ready to apply their knowledge and skills to meet Ohio's needs, academics created new standards and professional organizations devoted to their particular specialty. Their new expertise would be in demand as an important component of reform.

Within the public schools an intense battle for control emerged, reflecting the cultural and political tension in the cities between largely Catholic immigrants and native-born Protestant Ohioans. Overall, reformers sought professionalization of teachers and administrators and centralized authority in the hands of superintendents. They also sought to upgrade the physical condition of urban schools. Ohio schools were to become an integral part in creating an organic society, one in which citizens shared a common public culture and devoted themselves to the public good. What exactly defined the public good remained open for debate, and like other reformers, methods contained equal elements of altruism and social control.

In 1892–93, education reformer and muckraking journalist Joseph M. Rice wrote a series of scathing attacks on the condition of urban schools in the journal *The Forum*. Commenting on schools in Cincinnati, he deplored the rote memorization, the "crowded and poorly ventilated schools," the use of corporal punishment, "the professional incompetency of the teachers," and the control of the schools by politicians. He attacked the parents, too, for their "unjustifiable ignorance" and "criminal negligence" in allowing the conditions of the schools to deteriorate. Rice wanted schools to become more "scientific" in their approach to teaching, paying particular attention to "the laws of psychology" in understanding the "mind of the child." Instead of being "cold and harsh," teachers were to be "loving and sympathetic," with each school less like "a prison or a factory" and more like "a refined and refining home." Such sentiments reflected the growing expectation among the middle class that children were no longer simply an economic asset, but instead were to be nurtured (especially in the home by mothers who did not work for wages) and given an environment in which they could grow and mature as sensible and productive members of society.

Clearly, Cincinnati school leaders were listening, for they responded to Rice's expose. By the time of World War I, the city's schools had moved away from the pattern of "mechanical, highly formalized instruction demanding rote learning and memorization" and offered a wider variety of courses. The reformed schools stressed "efficiency, punctuality, regularity, obedience, order, industry, self-reliance" as well as habits of "cleanliness, awareness of health" and "aspects of civic responsibility." School boards gave greater control to superintendents, who in turn exercised greater control over teachers. Students participated in more athletic activities as well, with new schoolhouses proudly featuring baths, gymnasiums, playgrounds, and auditoriums for both school and community use.

In Cleveland, school reform revealed the sharp social and political divisions within the city. In 1892, reformers, mainly Republican Protestants, succeeded in changing the election of school board members from a ward-based system to an at-large one. In the time leading up to that year's election, Protestant clergy actively urged their congregations to vote for the reformers as a way to quell the influence of immigrant-dominated Catholic wards. One Protestant minister warned of the growing influence of "chicanery" and "priestcraft" in the schools. The Cleveland *Leader* echoed this, complaining of a "Popish conspiracy" in public education. For its part, the *Catholic Universe Bulletin* accused the reformers of partisanship, with the result of reform being "fresh, fat offices for prominent reformers." The reformers, businessmen, and lawyers, defeated the Democratic candidates of "Bohemian, German and Irish extraction" and ushered in their desired changes. For school superintendent, they chose Andrew Draper, judge and former head of the New York state schools. He assumed greater authority and independence from the Board. Draper dismissed inadequately trained teachers and pushed the remaining ones to increase their preparation in content and pedagogy. He forbade corporal punishment and managed to increase the number of students in the school system. Try as he did to claim neutrality in his leadership, it was clearly political. The Cleveland School Board became a one-party forum, with Democrats, who represented immigrant and laboring groups, excluded. Meanwhile, the Catholic Diocese of Cleveland moved ahead with its plan to build a private school system.

The Ohio legislature also played a role in transforming public education. In 1889 the General Assembly made school attendance mandatory for those between the ages of eight and fourteen. It also made several revisions to the state's school laws to establish greater uniformity and consistency to the school year, teacher examinations, and courses of instruction. Finally, in 1921, the Bing Law mandated all children between the ages of six and eighteen attend school, including high school. There were two exceptions: those who had already finished high school did not have to remain in school, and sixteen-year-old students who had passed seventh grade could work as farmers, this exception was an effort to help Ohio's farm families.

Conclusion

As Ohioans crafted a new society in which cities, mass consumption, and mass production came to exert greater influence, many enjoyed the benefits of this new world. However, the costs were enormous and reformers of various stripes sought to address them. The ensuing battles to control and shape this urban, industrial system exposed deep tensions and many contradictions. At times inclusive and democratic, white reformers often excluded African Americans. Among white suffragettes, for example, one of the main arguments these women made was that it was unfair for federal law to allow black and immigrant men to vote while denying white women the same right. In addition, as was the case with Tom Johnson and Samuel Jones, city leaders responded to the ill effects of rapid growth and industrialization, but did so in a way that shifted more authority to the executive branches in government and granted power to unelected experts and commissions, who could research problems, or manage organizations and people without direct influence from below.

Immigration sparked controversy, too. Schools, as they so often do, witnessed some of the most vocal clashes for reform. Higher education expanded to meet the growing demand for expertise and professionalization, but the tougher battles lay in the urban public schools. Authority shifted to superintendents and school boards, and Protestant middle-class reformers gained greater control over urban schools, whose populations contained large numbers of immigrant Catholics. Among settlement workers like George Bellamy, they achieved much needed changes that improved urban life, but their view of immigrants was often patronizing and condescending.

Full of idealism and contradictions, social control and social justice, this reform spirit, which many referred to as "progressivism," spilled out into state and national politics (chapter 13). Ohio maintained its central place as progressivism deepened its hold on national events and expanded its international reach. Eventually, the tensions within progressivism and within the nation led to violence and repression that only ebbed after the 1920 presidential election that featured two opposing Ohioans.

Further Reading

For further information on baseball and football, see Stephen D. Guschov, *The Red Stockings of Cincinnati: Base Ball's First All-Professional Team and Its Historic 1869 and 1870 Seasons* (1998. Jefferson, NC: McFarland) and Keith McClellan, *The Sunday Game: At the Dawn of Professional Football* (1998. Akron: University of Akron Press). On reform and radicalism see: Florence Allen, *The Ohio Woman Suffrage Movement* (1952. Cleveland: Committee for the Preservation of Ohio Woman Suffrage Records); Stephanie Elise Booth, *Buckeye Women: The History of Ohio's Daughters* (2001. Athens: Ohio University Press); Jacob Henry Dorn, *Washington Gladden: Prophet of the Social Gospel* (1976. Columbus: Ohio State University Press); Willard Glazier, *Peculiarities of American Cities* (1885. Philadelphia: Hubbard Brothers); Tom Johnson, *My Story*, edited By Elizabeth J. Hauer (1993. Kent: Kent State University Press); Marnie Jones, *Holy Toledo: Religion and Politics in the Life of "Golden Rule" Jones* (1998. Lexington: University Press of Kentucky); Richard Judd, *Socialist Cities: Municipal Politics and the Grassroots of American Socialism* (1989. Albany: State University of New York Press); Judith Trolander, "Twenty Years and Hiram House," *Ohio History* 78 (1969, pp. 25–37); and Hoyt Landon Warner, *Progressivism in Ohio, 1897–1917* (1964. Columbus: The Ohio State University Press).

13

Reform and the Great War
1912–1920

In his 1913 inaugural address, Governor James M. Cox captured the spirit of reform sweeping Ohio and the nation in the first two decades of the twentieth century: "The forces of human intelligence have carried us to a point of higher moral vision, and it would have been a distinct anomaly of history if government had not been carried on in the progress of the time." At the state level, Cox and other politicians were not alone in advocating change. As reform moved beyond the city, farmers and laborers became even more active in shaping Ohio's political culture. African Americans, especially after serving their nation in World War I, began to push more assertively for their civil rights. As a group, women, especially those from the middle and upper classes, expanded their movements for temperance and suffrage, as well as other causes. Joining them were middle- and upper-class white men, all of whom made up the self-named reformers called "progressives." Working alongside progressive citizens was a new class of professionals, "experts" in social science and management who sought to apply their academic training to address the many problems facing society. Continuing their involvement were religious leaders like Washington Gladden, who brought the Social Gospel to the reform spirit. Even some business leaders signed on to reform, hoping to bring stability and efficiency to both the economic and social system.

The passion and fury associated with domestic reform during the early twentieth century became intertwined with a new sense of patriotism and national pride brought on by World War I—The Great War as it was called at the time. Ohioans fully embraced the call to war and contributed to its outcome. However, in their quest for social unity during wartime, many progressives slid from supporting reform to repression. After a wave of violence in the immediate postwar period, by 1920, the tumult had subsided and in a presidential election that featured two Ohioans, Cox and Republican Warren Harding, voters opted for Harding and a return to "normalcy."

Ohio: A History of the Buckeye State, First Edition. Kevin F. Kern and Gregory S. Wilson.
© 2014 John Wiley & Sons, Inc. Published 2014 by John Wiley & Sons, Inc.

The 1912 State Constitution

Many of the issues outlined in the previous chapter coalesced at the state level during the Ohio Constitutional Convention of 1912. Of the 119 delegates chosen by voters in the fall of 1911, forty-six were lawyers, twenty-five farmers, fourteen bankers and businessmen, and ten labor leaders. The remaining delegates came from various other occupations, including education, medicine, the ministry, and newspaper editors. At least three-fourths were progressives who expected success as they assembled in Columbus on January 9, 1912; conservatives, on the other hand, feared the worst.

Heightening this sense of expectation (or fear) was the election of radical preacher Herbert Bigelow as president of the convention. As minister of the Vine Street Congregational Church in Cincinnati, the fair-haired, slender Bigelow favored among other reforms the single tax and woman suffrage. He also had opposed U.S. annexation of the Philippines. The pulpit, however, was too small to contain his desire for promoting change and Bigelow first sought to become Ohio's secretary of state in the 1902 election. He failed in that effort, but when time came for voters to decide whether to amend the state's constitution Bigelow crisscrossed Ohio in favor of change. He was joined by the Progressive Constitutional League, the leading organization in favor of amendments and led by Toledo Mayor Brand Whitlock. Only with such measures, Bigelow, Whitlock and other supporters believed, could change come to the corrupt, money-driven politics of the day.

As president of the convention, Bigelow had the power to select and organize the committees responsible for proposing amendments. There were nineteen committees, each with seventeen to twenty-two members. Each member served on three committees, with those serving on the committees covering education, equal suffrage, good roads, initiative and referendum, judiciary and the bill of rights, labor, legislative and executive, liquor traffic, municipal government, and taxation seeing the most work. His fair use of appointments mollified conservatives. While progressives chaired most key committees, such as initiative and referendum and suffrage, Bigelow placed his most vocal critics on the latter, and the liquor committee was evenly split between "wets" and "drys," with five others noncommittal. Any citizen could propose an idea and rules were adopted to ensure open debate and consideration of amendments. Finally, remembering the failure of constitutional reform in 1873–74, delegates rejected the idea of sending the entire document to the people for an up or down vote, and instead voted to submit each item separately.

The debates made state and national news and even drew the attention of scholarly journals. Dailies and weeklies covered the convention and in some Ohio communities, regular Saturday evening meetings sprang up to discuss the week's events and debate the issues. Since 1912 was an election year, all of the major presidential candidates except Woodrow Wilson spoke at the convention. It was a testament to the popularity and fervor of reform and the intense political interest of Ohioans that such attention came to the otherwise dull practice of amending the state's constitution.

The delegates came down largely on the side of reform, with some critical exceptions. The two issues that occupied most of the delegates' time were the liquor question, and initiative and referendum. As submitted to the voters, the liquor licensing amendment would have allowed licensing of saloons, but it came with a number of restrictions placed upon it by the "drys," including one that prohibited breweries from directly operating saloons, one mandating that saloon keepers had to be of good moral character, and one mandating that there could be only one licensed saloon for every 500 residents in a community. This amendment the delegates approved ninety to eighteen. The initiative and referendum amendment allowed for legislation and state constitutional amendments to be submitted by citizens either to the General Assembly or directly to the people through ballot initiatives. Amendments to make the direct primary (which opened up the choice of a party's candidate to the electorate) mandatory and for the recall of state officials also went forward to the voters.

Amending the state's suffrage laws led to vigorous debate as well. Ohio's constitution opened voting to "white, male citizens of the United States" who had been a resident of the state for a year and who were at least twenty-one years old. Since African American men had been legally allowed to vote in Ohio since the passage of the Fifteenth Amendment in 1870, delegates agreed without debate to remove the word "white." This was not the case with proposals to remove the word "male." Supporters of woman suffrage argued that Ohio's citizens needed to decide the issue. Head of the committee on suffrage William B. Kilpatrick, Democrat of Trumbull County, spoke at length in defense of giving women the right to vote: "Give them the right to say for themselves. No matter what the ability of a woman may be, or what the experience of a woman may have been, she has just exactly the same inalienable right that man has." The opposition often relied upon images of home and family, as well as arguments from the Bible. Farmer Allen M. Marshall of Coshocton expressed the biblical arguments in a lengthy speech, arguing that suffrage would assist women in making a "fatal leap from the highest pinnacle of the pedestal of creation down to its base, alighting in the seething cauldron of political corruption." A vote for suffrage, Marshall argued, would be to "commit treason against God." Franklin Stalter of Upper Sandusky argued that "we are a nation of families. The father is the natural head of the family" and by extension women were represented by the father as part of the family. Despite the opposition, the delegates agreed to send the suffrage amendment to the voters for approval, seventy-six to thirty-four.

In the end, eight amendments failed at the hands of voters: elimination of the word "white" from the Constitution; the use of voting machines; modification of injunction proceedings; the eligibility of women for certain offices; woman suffrage; good roads; regulation of outdoor advertising; and abolition of capital punishment. It seemed clear that Ohio still retained a sizable measure of racism; the removal of "white" would not come until 1923. Despite a massive grass-roots campaign and a parade that attracted some 5,000 marchers to Columbus, Ohio's men were determined to keep women from voting. As suffrage had also become wrapped up with the temperance issue the "wets" feared that women, given the opportunity, would likely vote for stricter temperance laws. There were also still a number of conservative women who argued against woman suffrage. Harriet Upton commented that "Two enemies are working against us—a band of ignorant and futile women, very few in number, and the federate forces of evil." Good roads failed because voters preferred not to fund them with bond issues, and companies that used outdoor advertising succeeded in convincing voters to reject regulation. Finally, voters still favored the death penalty.

On the other side, voters approved thirty-eight changes to the Ohio Constitution. In the constitutional voting, geography mattered, as it often does in Ohio politics. The northern, more urbanized part of the state generally favored reform, while the southern, more rural portion did not. Indeed, nineteen of the thirty-four amendments that passed would have failed were it not for the support of the large urban areas. The initiative and referendum won, as did home rule for cities and changes to the tax code. Voters also approved greater state management of forests and other natural resources. The state clarified its authority over the organization, administration, and control over the public school system, while allowing local school districts to elect boards of education. The convention also approved a number of protections for workers, including a provision that allowed the General Assembly to regulate work hours, set minimum wages, and provide for the general health and well-being of all employees. Again, here Ohio became part of an international trend, since Australia and European nations had been expanding the welfare state prior to various progressive measures adopted at the state or national level in the United States. The voters also approved an amendment giving the state the power to create a compulsory workers' compensation law, to establish an eight-hour day for public works, and to prohibit prison contract labor.

The battle over temperance and suffrage continued. Prohibitionists failed to make liquor illegal, but there were new restrictions and the local option remained. The adoption of the initiative and referendum allowed for an almost annual vote on temperance as both sides brought the issue to voters. Urban interests generally prevailed, which prompted groups like the Anti-Saloon League to shift their strategy to the rural-dominated federal Congress so as to gain national prohibition, which they finally accomplished (with the help of World War I) under the Eighteenth Amendment.

The 1912 Elections

In the midst of amending the state's constitution, Ohioans also had to choose the next governor and president. The 1912 contest came at the height of reform. Both major parties remained divided over many issues, but the split between so-called stalwarts and progressives within the Republican Party proved decisive. Teddy Roosevelt had assumed the presidency in 1901 following McKinley's assassination and in 1904 Roosevelt won outright. During his tenure, he earned the ire of stalwarts as he amassed a progressive record and remained widely popular. Although he came to regret this decision, Roosevelt had pledged not seek a third term, and as the 1908 election approached he selected Ohioan William Howard Taft as his successor.

Born in 1857, Taft ("Will" or "Willie" to his friends) grew up in Cincinnati in a close, large, energetic, and renowned family. His father, Alphonso, was a distinguished attorney, serving under Ulysses S. Grant as secretary of war then attorney general. Alphonso later served as minister to Austria-Hungary and Russia under Chester Arthur. William's mother, Louisa was the equal to Alphonso in energy and intelligence, active in the kindergarten movement, organizing art and book clubs, and traveling with her husband on his overseas trips. Young William always felt pressure to live up to the high expectations of his parents, perhaps contributing to Taft's struggle with obesity (he reached 300 pounds while president). Like his father, Taft attended Yale (joining the famous Skull and Bones fraternity that Alphonso helped found) and then studied law at the University of Cincinnati. In 1886, he married Helen "Nellie" Herron, a woman not unlike his mother. Nellie was independent and ambitious, and pushed the otherwise reluctant Taft to aspire to national office. While Taft served on the U.S. Sixth Court of Appeals, President McKinley asked Taft if he would become the governor general of the newly acquired Philippines. Taft reluctantly agreed, and served in that position from 1901 to 1903. While he believed that the Filipinos were incapable of self-government he nonetheless abandoned the harsh tactics of the U.S. military and built a viable civil government and expanded public works. He left that post to become Roosevelt's secretary of war.

As a candidate in the 1908 election, Taft pledged to continue Roosevelt's progressive ways and he claimed a decisive victory over William Jennings Bryan, who was seeking the presidency for a third and final time. Over the course of his term Taft's conservative tendencies rose to the surface and exacerbated the growing divisions within the Republican Party. Taft supported progressive legislation, including increased regulation of business under the Mann-Elkins Act, and the Sixteenth (income tax) and the Seventeenth (direct election of U.S. Senators) Amendments to the Constitution. Taft also broke up more trusts (99) than Roosevelt. After an initial period of activism, Taft backed away from trust busting. He also made two errors that drove a wedge between him and the progressive wing of the party. Taft had tried to revise tariffs significantly downward, but he gave in to the conservatives and backed away, ultimately signing the Aldrich-Payne Tariff that held only modest reductions. Taft also fired Roosevelt's beloved conservationist, Gifford Pinchot as head of the forestry. Pinchot had openly criticized the actions of Richard Ballinger, Taft's head of interior. Ballinger, a businessman, had reopened Western lands to development that Roosevelt had closed. By 1912, Roosevelt had returned from his trip to Africa and Europe, determined to take the nomination away from Taft.

Taking advantage of the new open primary in several states, including Ohio, Roosevelt won most of these, proving he was the popular choice and securing more delegates than Taft. However, Taft still controlled the Republican National Committee, which made the decisions on which delegates to seat. The Committee blocked most of Roosevelt's delegates, giving the nomination to Taft. Roosevelt and his supporters then left the GOP and formed the Progressive Party. Nicknamed the "Bull Moose" party, derived from Roosevelt's declaration that he felt as fit as a bull moose, the former president dubbed his and the party's platform the New Nationalism, which included a minimum wage for women, the eight-hour day, social security, direct election of senators, and a national health service.

With Republicans divided, Democrats sensed victory and nominated progressive governor Woodrow Wilson (over several other candidates including Ohio governor Judson Harmon). Wilson's platform, the New Freedom, called for tariff reductions, limits on campaign contributions by corporations, stronger antitrust laws, banking and currency reform, income tax and direct election of senators. Although both Wilson and Roosevelt were reformers, they differed over the extent to which the federal government should intervene in the economy. Roosevelt aimed for greater regulatory authority in federal hands while Wilson preferred a more decentralized approach. Wilson also favored breaking trusts, while Roosevelt believed that some trusts were inevitable and could be regulated by the federal government.

Taft largely retreated from the fray, spending more time on the golf course than the campaign trail. In the end, Wilson secured the victory, winning Ohio and the nation. Wilson secured 41.8 percent of the popular national vote, Roosevelt 27.4 percent, and Taft 23.1 percent. Eugene Debs, the Socialist candidate, earned just over 6 percent. The election left the conservative wing of the Republican Party, as represented by Taft, discredited and showed that reform was at its height. Ohioans supported this trend, going against Taft, their native son and favoring Wilson. Taft would eventually secure his dream of being on the Supreme Court, when in 1921 his fellow Ohioan, President Warren Harding, selected him as Chief Justice. This makes Taft the only person to serve as both President and Chief Justice.

It was a Democratic year in Ohio. In the governor's race Democrat James Middleton Cox (Figure 13.1) defeated conservative Republican Robert Brown and Progressive Party candidate Arthur Garford. Democrats also carried both houses of Ohio's General Assembly. Cox had made his career in journalism, becoming editor and publisher of the *Dayton Daily News* in 1898 and purchasing the *Springfield Daily News* in 1905. Cox had, since 1908, represented the Third Congressional District and had shown himself as a progressive in the House of Representatives, siding with those pushing to regulate railroads, for example. He endorsed Bigelow as president of the Ohio Constitutional Convention and supported the initiative and referendum. Cox had also been close to the political bosses in Dayton such that there remained an air of skepticism surrounding his progressive credentials.

Cox took up the governorship in January 1913 and with Democrats in the legislature set about pushing Ohio further along the path of reform. Their first major task was to address the approved state constitutional amendments but Cox also pushed to enact additional legislation. He followed Tom Johnson and Samuel Jones closely but he also had studied the state reforms in Wisconsin, which had become a model for many progressives across the nation. In state agencies, and where he could in the legislature, Cox placed into power fellow progressives who would draft bills and execute reforms. Not content with moderate change, in his first message to the Ohio legislature, Cox outlined his program of fifty-six measures he expected the legislators to enact.

All in all, between the regular session and a special one called by Cox in 1914, the legislature adopted a significant number of reforms during Cox's first term. The legislature enacted laws to put into practice the direct primary, initiative, referendum and a limited recall of public officials. While neither Cox nor the legislature reopened the question of votes for women, they did put forward a revised constitutional amendment to allow women to hold official positions in institutions charged with the care of women and children. Voters approved this easily. Meanwhile, suffragettes failed again in 1914 to open voting to women as voters rejected another proposed amendment. Home rule for cities

Figure 13.1   James M. Cox became nationally known for his progressive policies and along with Samuel Jones and Tom Johnson made Ohio a center for reform at the turn of the twentieth century. *Source*: Courtesy of the Ohio Historical Society (AL00567)

went into effect, but progressive mayors such as Newton Baker failed to gain broader powers to tax and operate public utilities. For laborers, Ohio enacted a workers' compensation law, modeled on the German plan. Cox urged delay on a minimum wage law, but supported laws for maximum hours. Provisions for eight-hour days on public works and limiting hours for minors went easily through the General Assembly. However, an impassioned discussion ensued over efforts to lower maximum hours for women workers from ten to eight, and to extend the restriction beyond factories to cover mercantile establishments and hotels. After several debates in the Senate and House, the legislature and Cox agreed on a nine-hour day for women in factories and mercantile establishments, but not hotels. Business did see greater regulation in the form of securities and banking legislation, but large brokerage houses approved of this as a means of stabilizing their industry and keeping out competition.

As approved in 1913, Ohio led the nation in adopting a comprehensive Children's Code. In 1911, under Governor Judson Harmon, Ohio became the first state to create a commission to investigate conditions of children and to recommend legislation. The commission submitted its report under Cox, who endorsed the report as did the General Assembly. This set of laws raised the minimum working age to fifteen for boys and sixteen for girls, mandated compulsory education with the same age guidelines, established a statewide juvenile court system and separate detention facilities for minors, and strengthened oversight of the state board of charities that handled the placement of children in private homes and public institutions. The state also created a new Bureau of Juvenile Research to aid in the research and policymaking related to children. The Code also included provisions for pensions to indigent mothers. This Children's Code was, like other progressive reforms, modeled upon legislation approved in Britain and other European nations.

Cox regarded penal reform as another key part of his efforts. He fought for and achieved legislation that reformed the prison system in Ohio, shifting its emphasis to rehabilitation. While the death penalty remained, new laws mandated that convicts be engaged in healthful labor (for the state, not private companies) and that they be compensated for this in the form of credits; the state also created a parole board and instituted intermediate sentencing.

Other reforms followed. The state approved a Rural School Code to consolidate districts under county supervision, as well as laws to provide graded courses of study and to mandate that teachers be college or normal school graduates. Ohio also established a state superintendent of public instruction. The reform of rural schools also fed into two other proposals, good roads and aid to agriculture. Cox had grown up on a farm and always held a special concern for rural Ohioans. He and others believed that good roads would improve rural life by making travel and transport of goods easier. He also remained concerned about the shift in population towards cities, and he hoped good roads would be one way to keep people on the farms. Cox also pushed for consolidating state activities in agriculture under a new agricultural commission, and increasing research in farming and forestry. It was quite a set of new legislation and brought Ohio into the heart of progressive reform.

The Flood of 1913

As though progressive reforms and the issues related to urbanization and industrialization were not enough to address, Ohioans also had to respond to what would be the greatest weather disaster in the state's history, the Flood of 1913. Over Easter weekend, March 21–23, a series of three storms battered the Ohio Valley. The first brought heavy rains with temperatures of 60 degrees. The second dropped temperatures to below freezing. The third brought more heavy rain. The last deluge fell upon frozen, saturated ground that was unable to absorb the water. Between six and eleven inches of rain fell in Ohio as massive runoffs overwhelmed streams and rivers, broke levees and led to devastating floods.

All of Ohio felt the effects, but Dayton saw the worst. Of the Easter storm, the *Dayton Daily News* commented, "It seemed as if the windows of heaven had been opened. The rain descended in floods." The Miami River flooded fourteen square miles of the city, with water upwards of twenty feet high running in swift currents through downtown. At the height of the flood, more water flowed through Dayton than Niagara Falls.

Figure 13.2   This photograph shows one of the rescue boats built by NCR employees under John Patterson's supervision in action in Dayton during the 1913 flood. In the background a watermark is visible showing the maximum height of the floodwaters. Numerous stories of tragedy and heroism emerged from the rescue operations in Dayton and elsewhere.
Source: Courtesy of the Miami Conservancy District

Not only were stores, businesses and homes destroyed by water, but also fires, as gas lines ruptured and firefighters were unable to stop the conflagration. With civil government overwhelmed, John Patterson head of the National Cash Register Company (NCR), took charge of rescue operations in the southern half of the city. He turned his factories (on high ground south of the floodwaters) into shelters and organized relief efforts, which included having his employees build boats (see Figure 13.2) and rescue stranded residents. In the northern half, stranded residents organized their own system. Despite these herculean efforts 123 were killed in the city. In the state capital, 100 died as the Scioto River ran upwards of seventeen feet deep through Columbus, forcing residents to find safety on rooftops and in trees. In Akron, flooding forced the city to dynamite the remaining locks from the Ohio and Erie Canal so as to release the water into the Cuyahoga River. Similar actions in other areas ended once and for all commercial boating on the canal system. Downstream in Cleveland, the flood destroyed trains, rail yards, and docks. Meanwhile, the Ohio River flooded cities like Portsmouth and Cincinnati.

   Once the flood was over, Ohioans assessed the damage. At least 428 people had died, 20,000 homes were destroyed and perhaps the same number damaged. Factories and other businesses faced major losses as well. Animals, too suffered; at least 1,400 horses were killed in Dayton. In just one of many stories of the flood, the Wright Brothers' Kitty Hawk glider, sitting disassembled in boxes at the Wright's shop was spared.

Leaders also sought to reform Ohio's flood control system. Since Dayton had suffered the most, the state focused efforts on flood control along the Miami River. Working with Governor Cox, Patterson raised $2 million to fund a study and hired engineer Arthur Morgan, a native of Cincinnati to supervise a new flood control system. Morgan exemplified many of the traits of the progressive age. As a self-taught engineer, he valued expertise, rational planning, efficiency and order. He also valued free inquiry and sought to remake society along utopian lines. Morgan believed that through right living, education, and planning, improvement in the human condition was possible. Morgan recommended the construction of a series of earthen dams on the Great Miami River, as well as modifications to the river channel in Dayton. Governor Cox supported the plan, but Morgan needed the state the authorize it. With intensive lobbying the General Assembly approved the Ohio Conservancy Act in 1914. The next year, the state authorized the creation of the Miami Conservancy District, the first major watershed district in the nation. Morgan's plan was a success and Ohio later created additional watershed districts to control flooding, including the Muskingum Valley Watershed District. Morgan would go on to national recognition as president of Antioch College, as the first chairman of the Tennessee Valley Authority, and as the author of more than twenty books.

Cox had battled the flood and pushed through several reforms. He hoped that this would be enough to win re-election in 1914. But he also faced a recession that had begun in 1913 and lingered into 1915. In Cleveland, a canvass of 16,851 families found 11.6 percent unemployment (2,358 jobless workers) who, with their families, totaled 67,787 dependent people. Moreover, it seems Cox's aggressive program had angered or disappointed enough voters to allow conservative Republican Representative Frank Willis to beat Cox in a close contest. Coming in third was the Progressive candidate, Secretary of the Interior James R. Garfield, son of the assassinated president. Voters also rejected woman suffrage and approved the local option for liquor. However, Cox was not finished. In the midst of the presidential election of 1916, Cox bested Willis for the governorship by fewer than 7,000 votes. Ohioans also gave their votes to Woodrow Wilson, without which the incumbent Democrat would have lost the presidency to Republican Charles Evans Hughes. By 1916, Cox had mellowed and took a more moderate course that focused more on running government efficiently and less on attacking special interests or big business. He also won again in 1918, becoming Ohio's first governor to serve three full terms. What dominated Cox's second and third terms was the entry of the United States into World War I in April 1917.

Ohio and the Great War

The war in Europe began in August of 1914, and quickly engulfed the continent and drew into the conflict much of the globe, earning the name "The Great War." The nations of Europe had been engaged in an arms race and developed a series of interlocking alliances that required one nation to come to the aid of another should there be an attack. In June 1914, Archduke Franz Ferdinand, heir to the throne of the Austro-Hungarian Empire, was shot and killed by a Serbian nationalist. In response,

Austria-Hungary declared war on Serbia, setting off a chain reaction that triggered one of the most devastating and bloodiest conflicts in history. As a result of the alliances in place, Russia, France, Great Britain, and Japan—calling themselves the Allies—were at war with the Central Powers, consisting of Austria-Hungary, Germany, and the Ottoman Empire, which included modern day Turkey and large parts of the Middle East.

When war began, President Woodrow Wilson declared the United States neutral. However, over the next three years and for a variety of reasons the United States pushed closer to the Allies, especially Britain. The United States insisted upon being able to continue trading with all nations involved; in practical terms, this gave Britain and the Allies an advantage since most trade went to Britain and that nation's navy dominated the sea routes to Europe. Britain used its navy to form a blockade. In response, the Germans utilized submarine warfare and began attacking vessels carrying armaments and passenger ships.

Wilson and the American public were especially outraged when in May 1915 the *Lusitania* was sunk off the coast of Ireland, killing 1,198 passengers including 124 Americans. Despite this, Wilson campaigned in 1916 on a slogan "He kept us out of war," and it was just enough to secure his win, but in 1917 tensions increased. Germany resumed submarine warfare, sinking a number of merchant ships. In March, British agents intercepted and made public a telegram from Arthur Zimmerman, Germany's foreign secretary, calling on Mexico to declare war on the United States. In exchange Germany would help Mexico recover land it had lost to the in the Mexican War. Also that month a revolution in Russia deposed the Czar and installed a constitutional government. This made it more likely that should the United States intervene in the Great War, it would be fighting with other democracies. Finally, on April 2, Wilson asked Congress for a declaration of war, to make the world "safe for democracy." It passed the Senate 82 to 6 and the House 373 to 50.

Direct U.S. involvement in World War I was relatively short. Troops did not arrive in large numbers until the spring of 1918, but when they did they made a large impact in the offensives that eventually turned the tide in favor of the Allies, who declared victory in November 1918. There were 225,000 draftees, volunteers, and National Guard troops from Ohio who served in the Great War. The press dubbed them "doughboys," like those in Figure 13.3. By war's end, some 6,500 Ohioans had been killed or died from disease. Of those who served, the most famous was Captain Edward V. Rickenbacker of Columbus ("Eddie"). Initially he was the staff driver for General John Pershing, head of U.S. forces in France, but in 1918 Rickenbacker transferred to the 94th Aero Pursuit Squadron. He became head of the squadron and earned the nickname "Ace of Aces" for shooting down twenty-two airplanes and four balloons during the war. There were other notable units besides Rickenbacker's in which Ohioans fought. The 37th Infantry Division, an Ohio National Guard unit, fought at Saint Mihiel and in the Meuse-Argonne. The 372nd Infantry was one of four segregated (or "Colored") units organized by the United States (see Figure 13.4). It was the only unit in which African American Ohioans served. Due to racism, American and British military commanders refused to allow these men to serve with white soldiers, so they served under French command. The 372nd fought with distinction during the Meuse–Argonne offensive, part of the final Allied push that

Figure 13.3 This is a group of "Doughboys" from Grove City at Camp Coëtquidan in France, 1918. They served in the 323rd and 324th Field Artillery regiments with the American Expeditionary Force fighting in the Meuse–Argonne offensive. All of these men returned safely from the Great War. The most commonly accepted reason for calling soldiers "Doughboys" is that the buttons on their uniforms resembled doughboys, flour dumplings cooked in soup.

ended the war in November 1918. Black soldiers felt liberated in France. Ralph Tyner expressed the feeling of many: "I feel free over here—absolutely … free." Such sentiments would help drive a post-World War I reassertion of African American identity in Ohio and challenges to the color line.

The war had a significant impact on Ohio. The war offered an opportunity for reformers to unite the people behind purposeful action, regulate society along state-guided, scientific lines, promote social justice, and expand progressive values to Europe and elsewhere. Hiram House leader Edward Bellamy captured this by referring to the war as "a cleansing wind blowing from the khaki strewn fields of France," that swept moral lassitude, selfishness, and dissension out of America. Mobilizing and organizing the United States for war demanded a strong national state. Urged on by Secretary of War Newton Baker, federal agencies formed to regulate many facets of American life. The War Industries Board supervised war production, while the War Labor Board supervised work. Other agencies included the Railroad Administration, the Food Administration and the Fuel Agency— all designed to promote efficient use of resources and production towards the war effort.

Figure 13.4   The 372nd Infantry Regiment, pictured here in a victory march held in Columbus in April 1919, was one of four African American regiments attached to the 157th Division of the French army. All of these men earned France's highest military award, the Croix de Guerre, and many earned U.S. awards, including the Distinguished Service Cross.
Source: Courtesy of the Ohio Historical Society (Om1341_1626879_001)

Ohio's leaders responded accordingly. The Ohio branch of the Council of National Defense supervised the state's response to the war, working closely with Governor Cox. The Ohio Industrial Commission organized labor and business on the state level, matching some 564,000 jobs with applicants and responding to other war needs. With Ohio's industrial might critical to the war, the Commission served a vital national need. Indeed, Ohio's industries benefited during the war. For example, Akron's rubber companies could not fill their need for workers, so they sent agents into Appalachia to recruit laborers as the rubber factories churned out tires, tubes, balloons, gas masks, and other war essentials. The expansion was so rapid, that between 1910 and 1920, Akron was fastest growing city in the nation, growing from 69,067 to 208,435 residents. Over the same decade, rubber companies expanded their payrolls. Firestone went from 1,000 employees to 19,800. Housing was in such short supply that laborers often slept in beds in shift patterns related to their work. The war helped to spur Firestone and Goodyear to build or expand company housing; parts of Akron's Firestone Park and Goodyear Heights respectively.

With men serving in the war, rubber companies and other Ohio industries brought more women in the factories. Women were now producing tires, making steel, and serving in other laboring capacities from which they had previously been restricted. Women deepened their traditional roles in wartime through serving as nurses in the military, organizing relief efforts, and running war bond campaigns. They also served on the Woman's Committee of the state's Defense Council. By answering the call for service and demonstrating their capacity to assist in multiple ways, women helped the cause of suffrage, too. With President Wilson arguing that the war was about democracy, it was harder to deny women political equality as they demonstrated their patriotism. In 1919, Congress approved legislation to add the Nineteenth Amendment to the Constitution. Ohio became the fifth state to ratify the amendment and it went into effect in 1920.

Wartime needs increased the migration of African Americans to Ohio. This migration was part of a larger one that began during the Civil War and lasted through the final third of the twentieth century. Over 1 million blacks left the South between 1910 and 1930, with over half between 1916 and 1918. The migration was almost exclusively an urban one. Industrial labor certainly helped pull these men and women north, but so too did family ties. Conditions in the South added other incentives, including the Jim Crow laws, the depression of 1914–15 that devastated farms, and the destruction of cotton crops by the boll weevil. During the war, businesses sent agents—both blacks and whites—to the South to recruit blacks. The state of Ohio did its part, organizing a Negro Workers' Advisory Committee to actively place black workers in industrial jobs. In Ohio, the African American population rose by 67 percent between 1910 and 1920, to 186,187. It was a dramatic and visible change. The *Cleveland Gazette* announced almost on a daily basis that train "carloads of Afro-Americans arrived in Cleveland and other cities." Cleveland would have the largest African American population, but the percentage of African Americans in all of Ohio's cities began a dramatic increase that accelerated into the twentieth century.

Alongside increasing wartime opportunities came an increase in racism. The color line hardened as blacks faced hostility and discrimination in seeking a new life in Ohio. The lynchings in Akron and Springfield were the most sensational demonstration of this tension and housing also became a critical issue. Blacks were increasingly confined to certain sections in Ohio's cities. The new company housing built in Akron's Firestone Park and Goodyear Heights, for example, was initially off limits to blacks. This came in the midst of a massive overall housing shortage during the war. In Cleveland, *Gazette*

Table 13.1   African American population in select cities, 1910–30

	1910		1920		1930	
	Population	*% black*	*Population*	*% black*	*Population*	*% black*
Akron	69,067	1.0	208,435	2.7%	255,040	4.3
Cincinnati	363,591	5.4	401,247	7.5	451,160	10.6
Cleveland	560,663	1.5	796,841	4.4	900,429	8.0
Columbus	181,511	7.0	237,031	9.4	290,564	11.3
Dayton	116,577	4.2	152,559	5.9	200,982	8.5
Toledo	168,497	1.1	243,164	2.3	290,718	4.6
Youngstown	79,066	1.8	132,358	5.0	170,002	8.6

editor Harry Smith reported that migrants were "living in old railroad cars, shanties, abandoned buildings, shacks and tents."

Still, despite the violence and discrimination, World War I helped forge a vibrant, African American culture in Ohio and an economically important segment of Ohio's population. As it was with migrants from Europe, African American men and women filled critical niches in the labor force, helping the war effort. They developed and expanded a set of cultural and economic resources, including newspapers, churches, self-help associations, businesses, and labor unions. By 1920, African American men were still overwhelmingly represented in unskilled factory work (73 percent of black male industrial workers in Cincinnati, 64 percent in Cleveland, and 59 percent in Columbus). For African American women, domestic service remained the major sector of employment. Increasing African American migration also spurred on a growth in the African American middle and professional classes. Hence, the increase in wages and opportunities was real, helping to establish a significant economic and cultural African American presence in Ohio's cities. The experience of war would also lay the foundation for greater African American political expression in the 1920s and 1930s.

As Ohioans responded to war, they also had to contend with the outbreak of influenza that began in 1918. The close quarters and massive movement of troops for the war hastened the spread of the virus, which killed 50 million people worldwide, far more than the 16 million killed in the war. In Ohio, Camp Sherman lost 1,200 men by the fall of 1918. Cleveland witnessed 682 deaths per week during the worst of the pandemic. Colleges and public schools closed and campus buildings became makeshift hospitals. Cities quarantined those affected and Cincinnati went so far as to outlaw spitting for fear that this might spread the disease. Lacking a cure, folk remedies abounded but none proved effective. Officials could only encourage people to avoid crowds, and transportation such as streetcars and railroads. After peaking in the fall, it gradually subsided and left Ohio by the summer of 1919, but not before killing thousands and striking fear and panic into Ohio's residents.

Fighting the war and the flu demanded unity but, like all Americans, when war began Ohioans were divided. With a diverse, polyglot population Ohioans had strong ties to all the belligerents. British Americans supported the Allies, as did many others who thought of Britain as an example of liberty and democracy, and considered the monarchy of Germany oppressive. Germans sympathized with their homeland and Ohioans of Irish descent supported the Central Powers, since Britain had imposed rule over Northern Ireland and suppressed uprisings that demanded Irish independence. Russians, Jews especially, had no sympathy for the Czarist state and with Russia an initial member of the Allies it made it difficult to argue that the war was a simple battle between democracy and autocracy. African Americans backed the war, but would use the experience to push for greater democracy. Finally, there was an active presence in Ohio among socialists, pacifist sects such as Quakers and Mennonites and various reformers who saw the war as either immoral or at odds with social reform.

With the entry of the United States into the conflict on the side of the Allies came the mission of Wilson administration and leaders in Ohio to promote unity. The war effort enhanced the drive for order and cultural homogeneity that had been part of progressive reform. One of the beneficiaries of this sentiment was temperance, which embodied both an effort to enforce cultural values as well as a drive to conserve agricultural products for the war. In 1918 Ohioans voted to go "dry," which was later reinforced by the Eighteenth Amendment with effect from January 1920, enforced by the Volstead Act.

Enforced unity had other consequences. With the passage of the Conscription Act in May 1917, men in Ohio were required to register for the draft. This proved controversial. Among the traditional peaceful churches of Quakers, Amish, Mennonites and others, these men and other conscientious objectors fulfilled their obligations through service in hospitals, in the ambulance corps, or through labor in areas deemed essential for the war. Some refused, and were imprisoned at Fort Leavenworth and other posts. Most objectors were treated fairly, but there is evidence of abuse.

Along with the draft, the federal government initiated a massive propaganda campaign led by the Committee on Public Information (CPI). To persuade the public to support the war, the CPI used pamphlets, posters, and advertisements. It also sent 75,000 Four-Minute Men around the nation to give short standardized speeches to the public. Greater coercion came through two additional laws. The Espionage Act of 1917 made it a federal crime to not only spy but also interfere with the draft or make false statements that might prevent military success. The list of offenses expanded through the Sedition Act of 1918, an amendment to the 1917 Act. Under this new law punishable offenses included: "false reports or false statements with intent to interfere with the operation or success of the military"; and attempts to obstruct "the recruiting or enlistment service of the United States." The 1918 law also made it a crime to "utter, print, write, or publish any disloyal, profane, scurrilous, or abusive language about the form of government of the United States, or the Constitution of the United States, or the military or naval forces of the United States, or the flag."

These two laws aided in the repression of radical activities. The most famous victim of these laws was Socialist Eugene Debs. Debs traveled to Canton in June 1918 and in front of the state gathering of the Socialist Party gave an impassioned speech against the war. He spoke glowingly of the recent Russian Revolution and charged that the war was waged at the expense of the workers. "The master class has always declared the wars; the subject class has always fought the battles." Debs was arrested, convicted, and given a 10-year prison sentence.

Coercive loyalty led to a fierce campaign to remove anything that seemed "foreign." The first manifestation of this was a statewide anti-German campaign (see Figure 13.5). With Ohio having such a strong German heritage, the campaign to wipe out all things German reached a fever pitch. German language newspapers shifted from supporting Germany to supporting the United States. By federal law all foreign language newspapers had to first submit a translation to the Postmaster General of the United States before being issued a permit to publish. This had the effect of forcing all foreign language newspapers to support the war or be shut down and the editors were threatened with fines or imprisonment. In addition to newspapers, colleges and schools were forbidden to teach the German language or use German literature. German teachers and professors were dismissed in many places, including Cincinnati and all teachers and professors had to swear a loyalty oath. Students succeeded in removing the president of Baldwin Wallace for not being anti-German enough. Libraries removed from circulation German publications. Street names were changed and the city of New Berlin

Figure 13.5   Propaganda posters like this one for Liberty Bonds were commonly used during World War I. Often employing dark, sinister imagery of Germans, these posters were a major tool for garnering support for the war effort. They also helped breed anti-German hysteria, especially in Ohio and other areas of the United States with large German populations.
Source: Library of Congress Prints and Photographs Division (LC-USZC4-2950)

changed its name to North Canton. The trend continued in 1919 with passage of the Ake Law, which forbade the teaching of the German language below the eighth grade in public schools.

Ohio's state and city leaders aided and abetted these federal activities. When war was declared in April 1917, several large cities created Americanization Committees. Under the state's Defense Council, Governor Cox approved professor Raymond Moley, already head of the Cleveland Americanization Committee to become the state's Director of Americanization. The state committee published pamphlets to be used by schools, local governments, churches and other institutions to assimilate immigrants. The Committee went so far as to recommend books and urged libraries to remove German writings (see Figure 13.6).

The tensions generated during the war spilled over in a Red Scare, prompting an extension of repression that lasted into 1920. A sharp recession hit the nation after the war, which added to tensions already evident in Ohio's manufacturing and mining industries. Pushed to keep up with war demands, workers had their hours extended and conditions grew more dangerous. Inflation during the war had cut into workers' earnings while the war boom enhanced corporate profits. Business and labor had been asked by

Figure 13.6   This poster is one of the items produced in Ohio during World War I to promote "Americanization" of immigrants. It is intended to encourage immigrants to attend Cleveland's public schools special classes in order to "Learn the Language of America" and "Prepare for American Citizenship." The words are printed in English and several other languages.
Source: National Museum of American Jewish History, Philadelphia. Dedicated in memory of Ronald Israelit by the Robert Saligman Charitable Foundation (1990.4.42)

the federal government to work together during the war. Afterwards, both groups sought to gain advantage. Labor organizers used the economic tensions and the increase in the number of workers to establish union recognition in a number industries, most notably steel. Meanwhile, business owners began to fight back by refusing to allow workers to meet, maintaining long hours even after the war, and refusing to increase wages to deal with inflation.

At the same time, a growing fear of revolution spread across the nation and in Ohio. The success of the Bolshevik revolution in Russia in 1917 was followed in 1919 by general strikes in Europe and the rise of anticolonial nationalism around the world. In January 1919, a massive strike in Seattle turned the city over to workers for five days. In Cleveland on May 1, 1919 some 30,000 people (most of whom were foreign-born) gathered to hear Charles Ruthenberg and other Socialist and labor leaders speak at a rally. Police responded by arresting participants and a battle ensued. Such tensions and fear prompted Cox and the General Assembly to recreate the Americanization Committee that had ended in December 1918.

The largest and most significant strike to impact Ohio came when steelworkers across the nation walked off the job in September 1919. In Ohio, workers walked out in Cleveland, Youngstown, Canton, and elsewhere. Production ground to a virtual halt and it seemed that steelworkers might gain the advantage. In Cleveland where upwards of 25,000 workers walked out, black and ethnic workers joined together in nightly meetings and in organizing. However, the strike came in the midst of the Red Scare and owners used divisions within the working class and the antiforeign and antiradical sentiment to their advantage. In Canton, for example, steel companies ran newspaper advertisements attacking the strike as un-American. Violence erupted between strikers—who were overwhelmingly foreign—and native white workers, who crossed picket lines. Owners also brought in strikebreakers. Meanwhile, police, private security and National Guard troops clashed with strikers. For its part, the Ohio Federation of Labor still held the color line among its unions and refused to organize unskilled workers. Within the black community, leaders were ambivalent about supporting strikers. By January 1920 the steel strike had ended as workers went back into the mills. Meanwhile, the federal government conducted raids on radical and labor organizations, which further undermined their ability to survive.

The 1920 Election

With Ohioans and the nation immersed in the Red Scare, presidential politics came to the fore as the 1920 election approached. With Wilson ending his two terms, the Democrats had no incumbent and the Republicans looked to recapture the White House. Both parties were sharply divided and in the end they turned to Ohio for their standard bearers. After forty-four ballots the Democrats nominated Governor Cox. As his running mate, convention delegates settled on the up-and-coming New Yorker Franklin Delano Roosevelt. The Republicans had difficulty settling on a candidate, and after ten ballots they chose Senator Warren G. Harding of Marion, Ohio. His running mate was the popular governor of Massachusetts, Calvin Coolidge.

Harding was born in Blooming Grove, Ohio on November 2 1865. In 1882 he graduated from Iberia College (Central Ohio College), which was little more than a secondary school, giving the commencement address to his graduating class of three. Like Cox, Harding was a newspaper owner. With a friend Harding bought the *Marion Star*, and rebuilt the daily into a success. He entered politics, winning a seat in the Ohio Senate in 1899 and then serving as lieutenant governor under Myron Herrick. Following this, Harding kept out of politics until 1914, when he won election to the U.S. Senate. Harding needed to be liked and he enjoyed meeting people. He did not seek to be a great leader, avoiding controversial issues as much as possible. Thus, he missed most of the debates in the Senate, including ones on suffrage and prohibition. Eventually, in 1919 he did vote for suffrage, but only when he was convinced most male Ohioans supported it. He also voted for the Eighteenth Amendment, but privately hoped it would fail. However, not taking a strong stand meant that he had no political enemies, thus he appealed to the various factions within the Republican Party and potential voters.

Harding's campaign theme was "America First" a return to what he called "normalcy." Harding promised higher tariffs and restrictions on immigration. His main tactic was to capitalize upon the weariness of Americans from war and social upheaval. He vowed to bring America back away from reform and involvement in foreign affairs. Harding had joined most Republicans by denouncing Wilson's conduct of the war and the Versailles Treaty, which among things, placed blame for the war on Germany and called for a League of Nations to police world affairs and work to prevent future conflicts. Until a stroke left him debilitated, Wilson campaigned hard for the Treaty and refused to allow any amendments offered by Republicans. Ultimately, the Senate refused to ratify it.

In campaign styles, the 1920 campaign echoed that of 1896. Harding conducted his campaign as had McKinley, from the front porch of his home in Marion. Meanwhile, Cox and Roosevelt stumped across the nation, speaking against prohibition, and in favor of the League of Nations and reconciliation between labor and industry. Ethnic voters remained divided on the Treaty; both German and Irish Americans opposed it, costing Cox critical support. In the end, Harding took Ohio and won a national landslide, beating Cox by over 7 million votes, with 37 states and 404 electoral votes. Harding won Tennessee, the first time since Reconstruction a Republican had won a Southern state. Election night was also the first to be broadcast on radio; KDKA of Pittsburgh read results over the air for those Americans who had just begun owning radios. Perhaps some of those listening sensed that they were hearing Ohio end its era as a leader in reform and begin another chapter in the state's history.

Summary

By 1920, Ohio had been through a tempest of change that had lasted at least since the Civil War. No longer was Ohio chiefly a rural state, its people and economy were industrialized and urbanized. Ohio had become more ethnically and racially diverse. Reformers had succeeded in crafting new forms of urban space, environmental, business and economic regulations, labor protections, suffrage, and civil rights laws. Education had been transformed and Ohio had joined the nation in going "dry." Ohio had contributed to the Great War, but also succumbed to the repression, fear, and violence of the postwar period. When Ohioans picked Harding over Cox they overwhelmingly chose to end their drive for reform. In the 1920s, many Ohioans would opt for pursuing the good life through new material prosperity, but at the same time work to contain the secular, urban, and diverse society they had created. They would move on to face the Great Depression and fight again in a global war, two crises that would have profound impacts on Ohio and the nation.

Further Reading

The two volume set *The History of Ohio Law*, edited by Michael Les Benedict and John F. Winkler contains over twenty essays (2004. Athens: Ohio University Press). On the 1912 Constitution see in *The History of Ohio Law* Barbara A. Terzian's "Ohio's Constitutional Conventions and Constitutions" (pp. 40–87). On the progressive era and World War I in Ohio see: Mark Bernstein, *Grand Eccentrics: Turning the Century: Dayton and the Inventing of America* (1996. Wilmington, OH: Orange Frazer Press); Lewis L. Gould, *Four Hats in the Ring: The 1912 Election and the Birth of Modern American Politics* (2012. Lawrence: University Press of Kansas); John Grabowski, "From Progressive to Patrician: George Bellamy and Hiram House Social Settlement, 1896–1914," *Ohio History* 87 (1978, pp. 37–52); James E. Cebula, *James M. Cox: Journalist and Politician* (1985. New York: Garland); The Ohio Historical Society, *The Governors of Ohio* (1969. Columbus: Ohio Historical Society); Kimberley L. Phillips, *Alabama North: African-American Migrants, Community and Working Class Activism in Cleveland, 1915–45* (1999. Urbana: University of Illinois Press); Kathryn Kish Sklar, "Ohio 1903: Heartland of Progressive Reform," in Geoffrey Parker, Richard Sisson, and William Russell Coil, eds., *Ohio and the World, 1753–2053: Essays toward a New History of Ohio* (2005. Columbus: The Ohio State University Press, pp. 95–128); and Wiliam E. Scheuerman, "Canton and the Great Steel Strike of 1919: A Marriage of Nativism and Politics," *Ohio History* 93 (1984, pp. 68–87).

14

Boom, Bust and War
1920–1945

During his successful campaign for the presidency in 1920, Warren Harding argued that "America's present need is not heroics, but healing; not nostrums but normalcy; not revolution but restoration; not surgery but serenity." Ohioans may have wished for "normalcy" after the tumult of the previous decades. But if the progressive era's concerns with the ill-effects of capitalism faded in the 1920s, then social and cultural conflicts took center stage. These ebbed only as Ohioans then faced the twin crises of the Great Depression and World War II. A brief snapshot at events in Akron illustrate some of the significant struggles and changes Ohioans experienced during this period.

During the 1910s, Akron was the fastest growing city in America, an effect of the demand for tires to accompany the skyrocketing sales of automobiles and trucks. However, south Akron residents, whose world revolved around working in the city's rubber plants, had long been angry at housing shortages and especially overcrowded conditions in their public schools. Making this worse was the seeming indifference shown by the Akron School Board, dominated by west Akron residents. West Akron held the city's economic elite, as well as many liberal religious congregations that differed from the more traditional Protestantism prominent in south Akron. In addition, south Akronites had also become frustrated with residents of north Akron, who were mainly Catholic and seemed unconcerned about the plight of public schools.

The school issue became a wedge that soon allowed for the rise of the Ku Klux Klan in Akron. The group appeared in 1921 and it was quickly condemned by the city's main newspaper, the *Beacon Journal*, as well as local NAACP leaders, west Akron's liberal religious leaders and north Akron's Catholic priests. However, the rubber workers in south Akron—many of whom had roots in Appalachia—proved receptive the Klan and by 1923, the group had managed to control the Akron School Board.

Ohio: A History of the Buckeye State, First Edition. Kevin F. Kern and Gregory S. Wilson.
© 2014 John Wiley & Sons, Inc. Published 2014 by John Wiley & Sons, Inc.

The city council too came under the influence of the Klan and by 1924 the "mayor, sheriff, county prosecutor, clerk of courts," and "two of three county commissioners" were all reputed Klan members. The Klan held massive parades and other demonstrations in Akron, with thousands of members in full regalia. At a July 4 parade in 1925, a national leader declared that the Summit County Klan was the largest in the nation with over 50,000 members.

No longer was the KKK a Southern phenomenon as the group's 1920s incarnation found its greatest influence in the Midwest. Among Ohio's cities, Akron was not alone in seeing the rapid rise of the Klan, as similar events happened in Youngstown, Niles, Columbus, and other places. The KKK's success symbolized the social and cultural conflicts that erupted in Ohio and the nation during the 1920s, with divisions over religion, education, alcohol, and sexual mores complicating those already stemming from race and ethnicity. In general, the modern values associated with Ohio's diversity, individual freedom, and mass consumption found opposition from those looking to hold to traditional ways or for whom a liberal, pluralistic culture seemed abhorrent.

The Klan, however, fell as quickly as it rose so by the late 1920s they had faded from influence. The feverish battles over social mores and customs also fell by the wayside after the stock market crash in 1929 helped precipitate the Great Depression of the 1930s. With the economic collapse, those Akron rubber workers who had been working nearly round the clock during the boom and supported the Klan in its drive for "100 percent Americanism" found themselves in a city with 60 percent unemployment. In the 1930s, instead of the KKK Akron's rubber workers found security and empowerment through the United Rubber Workers (URW). Using an innovative strategy of the sit-down strike, Akron's rubber workers joined Toledo's autoworkers, Youngstown's steelworkers, and others to create a new, vibrant, national organization, the Congress of Industrial Organizations (CIO). These workers formed a critical component of Ohioans who supported Franklin Roosevelt and the various federal programs that became part of the New Deal.

On the heels of this economic catastrophe and battles for union recognition Ohio and the nation then had to weather the storm of World War II. The war lifted Akron and the nation out of the depression. The city's rubber factories hummed again, churning out various goods needed for the war effort. Workers found near full employment, and this time women filled the ranks of the industrial army as Akron's "Rosie the Rubber Worker" joined the iconic "Rosie the Riveter" as a symbol of the wartime contributions of female workers. Women flocked into other industries across the state, too, and joining them were thousands of African Americans, men and women, able to obtain certain jobs once denied to them. Opportunities opened, but war also meant greater tensions on the home front, exacerbated by the strains of a two front war in which thousands of Ohioans fought and died. At the end of the war in 1945, Ohioans could look back at the previous quarter-century and realize that while some things may have remained constant, they had participated in a series of events that led to unprecedented social, economic, and political developments. Ohio was indeed a different place in 1945 than it had been in 1920.

The Economy and Politics in the 1920s

The new prosperity

The decade after World War I has been called "The Roaring Twenties" in part because of dramatic economic growth and low unemployment that came with vibrant mass consumption. After the recession of 1920–21, the American economy grew dramatically, so that by 1929 the United States produced 40 percent of the world's manufactured goods. From 1922 to 1929, the national rate of unemployment never fell below 5 percent and real wages grew by more than 15 percent. The boom caused stock prices on Wall Street to soar. The new prosperity meant that factories produced consumer items in mass quantities, which individuals and families often purchased on credit. As the number of homes with electricity grew, sales of American-made consumer goods such as radios, washing machines, telephones, and vacuum cleaners increased. To sell these new goods, manufacturers teamed with advertising firms to market each item as fulfilling consumers' psychological needs. However, ownership of big-ticket consumer items was not uniform. As late as 1929 75 percent of Americans did not own a washing machine and 60 percent did not own a radio.

Ohio played a central role in the boom. Manufacturing dominated most of Ohio's largest cities and employed some 991,000 of the state's 2.6 million workers. New industries emerged such as electronics, aviation, and chemicals, adding to the growth. None of these industries had the same impact as the automobile. Ford's Model T and Model A, along with models from General Motors and other American automobile manufacturers, captivated Ohioans who began to purchase a new car as soon as they could, almost always on credit or installment plans. Indeed, car registrations in Ohio were among the highest of all states. With more than half of all Americans owning a car by 1929, Ohio's automobile industry was central to the prosperity. There were spinoff effects as Ohio's industrial output became integrated into the auto craze, since the manufacture of automobiles drove sister industries such as rubber, glass, and steel.

As Ohio's industries expanded they also modernized, adopting more mechanized methods and reducing industrial employment in some areas. As a way to maintain the loyalty and undermine support for unions, more firms adopted "welfare capitalism," which had been pioneered in an earlier generation by NCR. Now, major companies, including Firestone, Goodyear, Procter and Gamble, and Youngstown Sheet and Tube created employee-benefit programs. Some employers built company housing and entire neighborhoods. Some also offered employees access to athletic clubs, libraries, cafeterias, and a host of other programs.

The politics of business: Warren G. Harding

The economic boom came along with a decidedly conservative shift in political culture that began with the election of Ohioan Warren G. Harding as president in 1920. The last of the nation's Ohio-born presidents, Harding swept into office in a landslide; Americans genuinely admired Harding and he relished the attention. Harding shifted the

Figure 14.1 In this image, Harding goes along on a camping trip in Maryland with Henry Ford, Thomas Edison, and Harvey Firestone in 1921. Ford, Edison, and Firestone took many of these trips and invited Harding along. The "vagabonds" as Ford, Edison, and Firestone called themselves, drove out of their campsite to meet Harding, who was traveling with an entourage from Washington, D.C. Hardly roughing it, the camp included family members, cooks, staff, drivers, horses, and members of the public angling to view these famous men.
Source: Courtesy of the Ohio Historical Society (AL01138)

concentration of the federal government away from the regulation of big business and the financial sector to wealth accumulation. Harding sought closer ties to big business, first appointing Andrew Mellon, one of the richest men in the world, as secretary of the treasury. Mellon worked with Congress and federal appointees in agencies to lower taxes on the wealthy and corporations, to oppose various reforms sought by organized labor, and to halt antitrust actions. In these ways, Harding fulfilled the promise of one his campaign pledges: "Less government in business and more business in government" (see Figure 14.1).

In addition to probusiness policies, Harding favored other conservative positions as well. He supported the Emergency Quota Act of 1921, the first in a series of anti-immigration measures that emerged in the 1920s. The Johnson act stipulated that annual immigration of a given nationality could not exceed 3 percent of the number of residents of that nation residing in the United States in 1910. This act and later ones were designed to limit the number of immigrants entering the United States from southern and eastern Europe. Harding revealed a few streaks of centrism. He supported aid for farmers and urged the steel industry to move to the eight-hour day. In accepting an honorary doctorate from the University of Alabama, Harding spoke against segregation. He also pardoned Eugene Debs, the perennial Socialist Party candidate for president who had been imprisoned for violating the Sedition Act during World War I.

In foreign policy, Harding moved away from Wilson's internationalism and free trade by keeping the United States out of the League of Nations and supporting the Fordney-McCumber Tariff of 1922 that raised taxes on imports. Although supporting tariffs had been identified with increasing international tensions and had been cited as one cause of World War I, Harding and his advisers desired to reduce the risk of inciting another such conflict. Secretary of State Charles Evans Hughes worked with Japan and European nations at the Washington Arms Conference to lower the number of naval vessels each nation could maintain. This also fit into Harding and Mellon's desire to reduce government expenditures. At the same time, Harding pursued economic diplomacy elsewhere, encouraging U.S. banks to loan money to foreign governments. This included Germany, which used the money to pay war reparations. Meanwhile, Harding, Mellon, and Hughes aided industries in Ohio and across the nation as they increased their presence in foreign nations through production facilities and ownership of raw materials.

Although at the time Americans deeply mourned Harding's death from a heart attack in 1923 his reputation has since suffered. When he died he was on a trip to San Francisco and the West, one taken to reassure the public amid investigations into the emerging scandals of his administration. He managed to appoint capable leaders, including Mellon and Hughes, as well as Herbert Hoover as secretary of commerce and former president William Taft as chief justice of the United States. Harding also selected the "Ohio gang," several men with whom he enjoyed drinking and playing poker, but whose corruption and malfeasance were the worst since the Grant administration. In what became known as the Teapot Dome scandal, Secretary of the Interior Albert Fall of New Mexico persuaded the U.S. Navy to give Interior control over the Navy's petroleum reserves on public lands at Teapot Dome, Wyoming, and Elk Hills, California. Previous presidents had authorized these emergency reserves in case of war, but many western politicians and oil interests had opposed these restrictions, arguing that oil companies could provide for the Navy. After gaining control from the U.S. Navy, Fall secretly leased the reserves to business associates for a personal payoff of $400,000. Harding never knew of the bribery, but as the Senate began investigating the sale Fall resigned in January 1923 and was eventually sentenced to prison in 1929. Another scandal involved Charles Forbes, head of the Veteran's Bureau, which had been established in 1921. Forbes used his position to enrich himself through kickbacks on construction projects and the sale of surplus alcohol and drugs to bootleggers and drug dealers. When Harding found out about this in 1923 he demanded Forbes's resignation. Forbes would serve two years in prison. As Attorney General, Harry M. Daugherty avoided punishment from allegations that he accepted payments for not prosecuting certain individuals and for defrauding the government in the sale of property seized from German nationals during World War I.

Harding was never implicated in the scandals and seemed genuinely surprised and hurt by them, yet he also seemed oblivious to his own behavior, flouting federal law by drinking during Prohibition and having two extramarital affairs. One was with Carrie Phillips, the wife of his close friend from Marion, James Phillips. The tryst began in 1905 and lasted until Harding became president. The Republican National Committee bribed the Phillipses with money to keep them quiet. The other affair began in 1917 with Nan Britton, then a teenager from Marion and thirty years his junior. Harding obtained a job for Britton in Washington, and the two of them continued the affair until his death. In 1919, Britton gave birth to a daughter, which she claimed was Harding's. The president never saw the child, but he made child-support payments that were hand delivered by the Secret Service. Harding admitted to his close friends that the job of president was beyond him. Like Grant, Harding trusted his aides and friends to a fault, for they ultimately brought scandal upon Harding's presidency and tarnished Ohio's political reputation.

Vice President Calvin Coolidge served out Harding's term and won election in his own right in 1924, carrying Ohio and the nation by wide margins. Coolidge's vice president was Charles Gates Dawes, born in Marietta, Ohio. Dawes' plan for restructuring Germany's war debts from World War I won him the Nobel Peace Prize in 1925. After Coolidge, Herbert Hoover won handily in Ohio and the nation in 1928. In the 1920s, all but three members of the House of Representatives were Republican and both Ohio Senators, Frank Willis and Simeon D. Fess, were Republicans.

State politics

Conservatism dominated Ohio politics just as it did the national scene. After the fever of the progressive era, little in the way of substantive change occurred at the state level during the 1920s. Some reorganization of executive authority occurred under Republican governor Harry Davis, who was elected in 1920 and stepped down after one term. Democrat Vic Donahey bucked the Republican trend by winning the governorship in 1922, 1924, and 1926. His tenure was noted for his penchant for vetoing bills from the Republican legislature, hence the nickname "Veto Vic." Like so many of Ohio's politicians, Democrat and Republican, Donahey was a fiscal conservative, in his case carefully monitoring Ohio's funds as state auditor and then continuing to do so as governor. Under Donahey the state made progress in reforming the court system and in paving roads, the latter a response to the growing numbers of cars and trucks in the state. In 1923 a state constitutional amendment finally removed the language that had restricted voting to white males. Donahey elected not to run in 1928, an auspicious decision. Winning the governorship over Democrat Martin Davey was Republican Myers Cooper who approved a revision of the state's tax code so that intangible forms of property such as stocks could be taxed. Cooper's administration would be remembered as the one that was in place when the crash of 1929 came, ushering in the Great Depression. Like Herbert Hoover in the White House, Cooper and other Republicans would earn the wrath of voters for the disaster, turning over the governor's mansion to Democrats in 1930 and supporting Roosevelt in 1932.

Social and Cultural Conflict

As the manufacturing economy boomed and politics embraced the status quo, conflicts emerged over several social issues. All of these stemmed from Ohio's shift to an urban, industrial, and diverse society that began in the late nineteenth century and continued into the mid-twentieth century. The 1920 census showed for the first time more Americans living in cities than in small towns. Americans also celebrated success through mass consumption of material goods and devoted more time and money to leisure activities, including the purchase of automobiles and the popularity of movies and radio. Unlike the nineteenth century, the new emphasis for Americans in the 1920s was self-realization as opposed to self-control, self-indulgence rather than self-restraint. Not all Ohioans looked favorably upon the trends of the day, and they fought back with a counter reaction. This reaction took several forms, including support for Prohibition, immigration restrictions, the Ku Klux Klan, and a renewed emphasis upon fundamentalist religion.

Prohibition

Although national Prohibition came with ratification of the Eighteenth Amendment, enforced nationally with the Volstead Act, Ohioans continued to remain divided over this issue into the 1920s. The Ohio General Assembly ratified the Eighteenth Amendment in 1919. However, just one year earlier, an amendment to the Ohio Constitution mandated that all amendments to the U.S. Constitution approved by the General Assembly must then be approved by voters through a state referendum. The referendum went forward, and by 479 votes, Ohio voters rejected the Eighteenth Amendment. This was the first time in United States history that a state referendum had been held on a Constitutional amendment, and voters in Ohio overturned the state legislature. Cincinnati attorney and prohibitionist George Hawke immediately challenged the constitutionality of allowing a state referendum on an amendment. Hawke and his attorneys argued that Article Five of the U.S. Constitution clearly specified that only state legislatures or state conventions could ratify amendments. While state courts ruled against Hawke, the U.S. Supreme Court in *Hawke v. Smith* reversed those decisions, supporting Hawke's argument and prohibition, and declaring Ohio's 1918 referendum amendment unconstitutional.

With this issue settled for the time being, Ohio enacted the Crabbe Act of 1921 to enforce prohibition. This was the second Crabbe Act, the first having been rejected in 1919 along with the Eighteenth Amendment. The new Crabbe Act compensated mayors, judges, police officers, and other law enforcement officials for arresting and convicting violators of prohibition. In 1927, in the *Tumey v. Ohio* case, the U.S. Supreme Court (in the opinion read by Chief Justice William Howard Taft) struck down the Crabbe Act arguing that paying judges and law enforcement officials violated due process. Prohibition would not end officially until 1933, when the Twentieth Amendment to the U.S. Constitution repealed the Eighteenth Amendment. In the meantime, alcohol consumption declined but corruption and criminal activity associated with liquor trafficking emerged. In urban areas, "speakeasies," underground bars, and drinking clubs, served liquor supplied by bootleggers who often obtained alcohol illegally, brewed or distilled it locally, or sometimes smuggled it in from Canada, shipping it across Lake Erie into Cleveland and other lakefront locales for distribution. Cleveland in particular became nationally known as a center for organized crime in the 1920s, with bootlegging and associated crimes part of most Ohio cities under Prohibition.

The "new woman"

As a result of another progressive era constitutional amendment, the Nineteenth, Ohio's women could now vote and enjoyed several "firsts" in the 1920s. Politically, the first women were elected to the statehouse in 1922, and in 1923 the legislature voted to extend full civil rights to women. Florence Allen won election to the Ohio Supreme Court in 1922, becoming the first woman in the United States to win election to a state's highest court. In 1933, Franklin Roosevelt would appoint her as the first woman judge to serve on the United States Circuit Court of Appeals. Despite these gains, women still faced severe limitations. For one thing, government leadership remained a male-dominated sphere. More Ohio women were now entering the workforce but even as they did, they still tended to find work only in certain sectors. If working for wages, the largest numbers of women still toiled in domestic service. There were high concentrations of working women among bookkeepers, typists, nurses, garment workers, telephone operators, and sales clerks. Additionally by this time relatively large numbers of women could be found in rubber, electrical machinery, and shoe manufacturing.

While women's political and economic gains may have been tempered, middle-class women were finding greater personal freedom and altering their behavior. Many adopted the "flapper" look—bobbed hair, make-up, short dress—and joined men as they drank in speakeasies, smoked cigarettes, went to movies, enjoyed live jazz in clubs, and engaged in premarital sex. These trends were especially prevalent among younger women and men. Women's pursuit of personal pleasure—a "lifestyle"—now became part of the advertising world, marketing items such as automobiles, cigarettes, clothing, and personal hygiene products. Another sign of these was the formation of the American Birth Control League, founded by Margaret Sanger in 1921. Spermicidal jellies and diaphragms became more widely available, especially for men and women of the middle class, as they sought reproductive control and sexual liberation.

The Ku Klux Klan

Trends such as these upset the self-appointed guardians of traditional values. Ohio's entry into the world of consumerism, urbanization, ethnic and racial diversity, and new roles for women added to the social tensions that had emerged in the late nineteenth century. Already evident in the support for immigration restrictions, white, Anglo-Saxon protestant Ohioans continued attempts to define Ohio on their terms in the wake of massive social changes. The most extreme manifestation of these beliefs came in the revival of the Ku Klux Klan. The Klan of the 1920s represented a continuation of the cultural conflict that came with rapid immigration, industrialization, and urbanization. The new KKK comprised white, Anglo-Saxon Protestants of all social classes who formed a nationwide fraternal order in opposition to the advancement of African Americans, immigrants, Catholics, and Jews. The Klan also took upon itself to enforce laws related to vice, especially in areas of sex and drinking and devoted itself to "pure

Figure 14.2   Akron held its centennial parade in 1925, which featured prominent floats by the Ku Klux Klan, including this one by women of the KKK. This came at the height of Klan influence in Akron and in the nation.
Source: Akron-Summit County Library, SC 1999-11-50

Americanism." The group was both rural and urban and more popular in the Midwest than in any other region of the nation, including the South (see Figure 14.2).

The Ohio KKK claimed to be the largest of any of the Klan's state organizations, with some 400,000 members whose list of enemies included not only African Americans but also "Rome, atheists … followers of the petty political bosses, defenders of the corruptionist methods in politics … the so-called liberal element, the ex-saloon keeper, the gambler, the scarlet woman and the bootlegger." Initially denounced by many officials across the state, Klan members by the mid-1920s served as members of city councils and school boards, and across Ohio mayors were elected either as open Klan members or with the open backing of the KKK. In 1921, the city council of Youngstown approved a resolution condemning the Klan as un-American and the mayor, Fred Warnock, reassured African American residents that the city would protect them. By 1923 Warnock was a Klan member and eventually became a grand titan, or district official. Klan members used mainly intimidation and public pressure to exert political and social influence. Opposition to the Klan emerged mainly from rival ethnic organizations, especially Catholics and Jews, as well as the NAACP. The battles between these rival groups sometimes turned violent, as in Niles in 1924. All that year, conflicts continued between the Klan and Catholic residents, led by the Italian-dominated group, Knights of the Flaming Circle (as a counter to the Klan's flaming crosses, the Circle used tires). Then the Klan held a three state meeting on November 1 just before the 1924 presidential election. To protect the right of the Klan to enter Niles for the meeting, Niles's mayor created a special police force controlled by the Klan and charged with enforcing order. Circle members armed with guns amassed downtown and fired upon Klan members who had to enter the city to reach the meeting. After first refusing to do so, Governor Vic Donahey eventually called in the National Guard to end the conflict. By 1925, opposition to the Klan as well as internal divisions and corruption led to a decline in Klan membership.

The Scopes trial

An Ohioan, Clarence Darrow, stood at the center of another event illustrative of the clash of cultures in the 1920s, the Scopes "Monkey Trial" of 1925 held in Dayton, Tennessee. Darrow, born in Kinsman Township, Trumbull County, had a long career as a labor lawyer, defense attorney, and civil libertarian. In the Scopes case, Darrow represented biology teacher John Scopes, accused of violating a Tennessee law that forbade the teaching of the theory that human beings had evolved from primates. During the trial, Darrow called William Jennings Bryan to the stand as an expert witness on the Bible. Darrow's interrogation destroyed Bryan's credibility, but in the end Scopes was found guilty and ordered to pay a $100 fine. Ohioans were not immune from the tension between "modernist" and "fundamentalist" views of the Bible. A movement similar to the one that created the Tennessee law had emerged in Ohio but did not result in a similar law. The issue has continued to resonate in Ohio, with tensions over "intelligent design" being the most recent manifestation.

Literary Critics of Ohio

The period that witnessed Ohio's great transformation from a largely rural, agricultural place an urban, industrial one brought forward some of the state's most celebrated and prolific writers. As Ohioans fought over how to define their state during this transformative period after the Civil War, these Ohio-born writers, several of whom had become expatriates, highlighted many of the central issues involved in those conflicts, including race, ethnicity, class, gender relations, and divisions between cities and small towns. In addition, their writings often critiqued what they saw as the confining nature of Ohio society, one symbolized most by the trends of the 1920s. For many it seemed that Ohioans had abandoned virtue and good citizenry and embraced the private pursuit of material gain and personal expression. At times nostalgic, their work could also offer a trenchant analysis of life in Ohio. They sought answers for what had happened to the place they both loved and yet from which they now found themselves alienated.

William Dean Howells

One of the first to capture this dichotomy was William Dean Howells, who paved the way for future Ohio literary expatriates. Born in Martin's Ferry in 1837, Howells grew up enthralled with reading and languages. After writing a biography of Lincoln, Howells gained appointment as American consul in Venice, Italy, where he stayed for the duration of the Civil War. After this, he returned to the United States and lived in New York and Boston. He eventually became editor of the *Atlantic Monthly* and a regular contributor to *Harper's Magazine*. Howells was a prolific writer, and while he gained international fame, his Ohio roots stayed with him. He is best known for promoting realism, and his most famous works are *The Rise of Silas Lapham* (1885) and *A Hazard of New Fortunes* (1890), in which he criticized the effects of industrialization. Howells's view of Ohio often shifted from critical to nostalgic. In a set of unpublished essays written in the 1850s, he lambasted the "meanness and hollowness of that wretched little village-life" in which he was raised. In *A Boy's Town* (1890) Howells recognized the limits of small-town life, yet wrote of his childhood in Hamilton as a happy one.

Sherwood Anderson

Coming into fame after Howells was Sherwood Anderson. Anderson's most famous work, *Winesburg, Ohio*, is a collection of short stories published in 1919. This work is not a direct criticism of Ohio, although it has often been seen as one. Anderson was born in Camden, Preble County, in 1876. When he was one year old, the family moved to Clyde, south of Sandusky, which became the model for Winesburg. Anderson made a living as a writer in Chicago and then Virginia. Set in the late nineteenth century, Winesburg appears to be a prosperous, if fairly typical small town of the era and the characters who live in this setting struggle to find happiness, to connect with one another. The reason for their discontent is their constant repression of self-expression. It is not Ohio per se that causes insecurity and loneliness, but people's own state of mind. Nevertheless, the work added to the sense that something had been lost in Ohio; even as the state's people drove themselves towards material progress and achieved it, they remained unfulfilled. In his 1920 work, *Poor White*, Anderson critiqued the industrialization of the Midwest. The construction of a factory near the small town of Bidwell along the Mississippi River brings the ills of industrialism to a town once nurturing and peaceful. While not specifically on Ohio, the book laments the emphasis so common by the 1920s on material possession and fulfillment of personal goals.

Louis Bromfield

Louis Bromfield followed Anderson and went further in condemning the decline of Ohio's rural life at the expense of industrial and urban development. Bromfield was born in Mansfield in 1896, the son of Charles and Annette Bromfield. Charles was a popular politician, and he made money as a city official and occasionally in real estate. The Bromfields had strong ties to the land, since Louis's maternal grandfather, Robert Coulter, owned a multigenerational family farm near Mansfield. Louis spent time on the farm as a child, but Annette refused to have the family live there. Having grown up on the farm, she knew all too well the difficulties of farm life and wanted none of it. That would change when family financial reverses in 1914 led Charles, Annette, and Louis to sell their home in Mansfield and move back on to the Coulter farm.

Annette, demanding something else for Louis, enrolled her son at Cornell University to study agriculture. Before he had completed his first year, grandfather Coulter died, and Louis had to leave college to work on the farm. He was too young to do much, and his father was no farmer, so, after several generations of being farmers, the Bromfields were forced to sell the land. The experience of the Bromfield family mirrored the larger Ohio one, as the agrarian lifestyle gave way to an urban, industrial one.

Louis Bromfield went on to serve in the ambulance corps in France during World War I, and later to return to New York to begin a career in journalism. While there, he published *The Green Bay Tree* (1924), a novel that drew upon his experiences growing up in Mansfield and centered on the forces upon which Bromfield would focus for much of his life: the city and country, the material and the ideal. The novel was a huge success, and Bromfield began his career as a literary figure, leaving New York to take up residence in Senlis, France, north of Paris. There he became acquainted with many of the other notable American expatriates there, including Gertrude Stein, Edith Wharton, Ernest Hemingway, and Sinclair Lewis. While there, his career blossomed and Bromfield won the 1927 Pulitzer Prize for *Early Autumn*, a novel about a wealthy, old-line white Anglo Saxon Protestant (WASP) family in Massachusetts facing a changing world. He enjoyed France, but he began to feel a longing for something that fame and wealth seemed unable to satisfy. He talked of buying a farm back in the United States; he twice visited India, in 1933 and 1935, and drew from those experiences a hope that India could modernize without the same kind of industrialization that Bromfield found so destructive to rural life in Ohio and the rest of the Midwest. The rise of fascism in Europe forced Bromfield and his family to leave France and return to the United States, and in 1939 this became a homecoming, as Bromfield came back to Mansfield and the land he had been forced to leave.

He used his wealth to acquire some 1,000 acres near Lucas, Ohio, which he called Malabar Farm, after the Indian coast. In coming home, he wrote, he was "sick of the troubles, the follies and the squabbles of the Europe which I had known and loved for so long. I wanted peace and I wanted roots for the rest of my life." He turned his attention to writing about agriculture, and it is this set of writings and his work at Malabar Farm that have endured. At Malabar, Bromfield (Figure 14.3) restored the land to its former richness and established what he considered a model of self-sufficient rural living. He believed that just as his land had been restored, so too could the values and lifestyle he associated with rural life.

Through the 1930s, Bromfield maintained both his critique of modern life and his optimism that society could change. He was critical of the New Deal, but passionate about soil conservation and renewing agriculture. As he wrote in *Pleasant Valley* (1933), "I believe one day our soil and our forests from one end of the country to the other will be well managed and our supplies of water will be abundant and clean." Bromfield went on to state "that the abomination of great industrial cities will become a thing of the past, the men and women, and above all else, the children, will live in smaller communities in which there can be health and decency and human dignity, and then when that time comes, the people then living will look back upon us and the stupidity of our times as we look back with unbelief at the squalor and oppression and misery of the Middle Ages." By the winter of 1944, though, his writing became somewhat darker: "If we can overcome

Figure 14.3   Despite what this picture may suggest, Louis Bromfield led an active life at Malabar Farm, working by day and socializing in the evenings with celebrities and dignitaries who came to see him and his work. Humphrey Bogart and Lauren Bacall were married there in 1945. Never afraid to speak his mind, in his later years Bromfield lectured around the nation on conservation earning an Audubon medal for his contributions.
Source: Photo by Joe Munroe

the evils, economic and social, which industry and great cities have brought us, we shall be making progress. That is the frightening element in the recent elections. A growing urban proletariat without economic security can wreck everything that America has been in the past and darken the whole of her future." By 1955, after living through two world wars, the Great Depression, and the onset of the Cold War, with his wife deceased and his daughters moved away, Bromfield's romantic spirit and hope had faded. In "Fifteen Years After," he wrote that "we at Malabar have not achieved these romantic dreams nor have I won the escape into the boyhood past which brought about the decision to return. A return to the past can never be accomplished and the sense of fortified isolation and security is no longer possible in the world of automobiles, or radios, of telephones and airplanes. One must live with one's times, and those who understand this and make the proper adjustments and concessions and compromises are the happy ones." At this point, Bromfield's optimism, which he had used to contrast himself with the more pessimistic of his contemporaries of the 1920s such as Lewis, had dissipated. He had become not only critical but pessimistic, a combination he had tried so hard to deflect. Bromfield died the next year at the age of fifty-nine.

James Thurber

Just as Bromfield was beginning to write and reflect on life in Ohio and the nation, so too was Columbus-born James Thurber. Like so many other writers, Thurber was ambivalent about his Ohio home. After he worked as a reporter for the *Columbus Dispatch* from 1921 to 1924, Thurber moved to New York to work for the *New York Evening Post*. He joined *The New Yorker* in 1927 and contributed to that magazine for the remainder of his career as both a writer and a cartoonist. In his 1933 memoir *My Life and Hard Times*, which consists of a series of short stories, Thurber revealed a middle-class life full of monotony and mindless conformity. He painted a complex social world, but one that only existed among those considered at the margins of middle-class life: white and black female servants. Although at this stage in his career Thurber saw Ohio as a place to leave, he realized that no matter where he went, Ohio and Columbus were always with him. While he lampooned the conservative culture of his hometown, he became sentimental regarding it as he grew older. Upon receiving the Ohioana Sesquicentennial Medal for the state's celebration in 1953, Thurber wrote that "I am never very far away from Ohio in my thoughts and…the clocks that strike in my dreams are often the clocks of Columbus." Since then, Columbus has honored the author with the Thurber House, Thurber Drive, and apartments and shopping centers bearing his name.

Paul Laurence Dunbar

More cutting in their critiques of Ohio were some of the state's more famous African American writers. As blacks continued to enter Ohio in the 1920s as part of the Great Migration there had already developed a pattern among black writers of celebrating African American culture all the while noting the limitations of discrimination. Paul Laurence Dunbar was born in Dayton in 1872 and attended school there. His parents, Matilda and Joshua, were both former slaves; Joshua had escaped slavery in Kentucky and served in the Massachusetts 55th Regiment during the Civil War. Paul absorbed the stories from his mother and father, becoming fascinated with oral tradition and African American folk experience. He used this folk experience and dialect, as well as traditional English, to craft poems, essays, short stories, novels, plays, and songs that celebrated black life and criticized racial injustice.

Dunbar's fame came from the publication of poems in *Majors and Minors* (1895) and *Lyrics of Lowly Life* (1896), the latter a collection of his earlier poems for which William Dean Howells penned the introduction. While Dunbar's influences were British Romantic poets such as John Keats and Percy Bysshe Shelley, as well as American regional writers such as James Whitcomb Riley, it was Dunbar's own efforts to create an authentic black dialect that drew most of the public attention. Dunbar was criticized for following too closely the racist depictions of blacks in the works of Joel Chandler Harris, Thomas Nelson Page, and Irwin Russell, all of whom used dialect to depict blacks as happy, if simple, plantation workers. The first lines of Dunbar's poem "When Malindy Sings" provide an example:

> G'way an' quit dat noise, Miss Lucy –
> Put dat music book away;
> What's de use to keep on tryin'?
> Ef you practise twell you're gray.

Even if Dunbar could not fully escape the fact that some African Americans criticized his dialect poems as a concession to racism, there is no doubt that overall he affirmed black success and pride and criticized racism. Consider the last stanza of "We Wear the Mask":

> We smile, but O great Christ, our cries,
> To thee from tortured souls arise,
> We sing, but oh the clay is vile,
> Beneath our feet, and long the mile;
> But let the world dream otherwise,
> We wear the mask!

Charles Chesnutt

Pride and frustration come through as well in the writing of Charles Chesnutt. Chesnutt was born in Cleveland in 1858 and after the Civil War his family moved to North Carolina, where Charles grew up, working in the family grocery store. When that store went out of business, Chesnutt supported the family as a teacher, eventually becoming principal of the Fayetteville State Normal School for Negroes in 1877. Chesnutt learned mathematics, literature, history, as well as Latin, German, and French. With his wife and children, Chesnutt relocated to Cleveland in 1884 and worked as a court reporter before passing the bar in 1887 and opening a law office and court-reporting business. He began to write literature and in 1899 published a collection of short stories, *The Conjure Woman*, which received critical acclaim. That same year he published a set of stories about Groveland (the fictional stand-in for Cleveland) in *The Wife of His Youth and Other Stories of the Color Line*. In his first published novel, *The House Behind the Cedars* (1900). Chesnutt tells the story of two light-skinned blacks who "pass" for white in the post-Civil War South, mirroring his own frustrations that even someone as talented and educated as he was could still not fully break the color line. Chesnutt's grandmothers were of mixed race and it is likely that his grandfathers were white. Chesnutt himself was light skinned and his works examine the question of skin color, class, and discrimination among blacks as well as between blacks and whites. His writing grew more pessimistic about the potential for Ohio and America in general to accept African Americans as equals. While he initially believed that through literature, as well as hard work, education and perseverance blacks could achieve equality, he became more politically active and until his death in 1932 spoke out against continued racism.

Toni Morrison

As far as the talented Toni Morrison is concerned, only by claiming their history and culture can African Americans find happiness and the tools to address discrimination. Toni Morrison grew up in Lorain in the 1930s, and her first novel, *The Bluest Eye* (1970) is set in her hometown. The novel deals not only with racism but also incest and child molestation. The main character, Pecola Breedlove, is a young black girl who believes that she can only find happiness if she has the blue eyes and blond hair of her Shirley Temple doll. The lives of Pecola and her family are torn apart by their search for happiness, often on terms set by whites—whether it is beauty or behavior or culture. In this novel, only the three prostitutes who live above the shabby apartment of the Breedloves are truly happy; Morrison's message is that contentment can only come to those blacks who fully embrace their own sense of self, heritage, and culture—as opposed to the mass culture whose normative values are those of middle-class whites. The obsession with respectability and beauty as defined by the mass culture created in Ohio and the nation destroys those characters who attempt it. The irony is that discrimination gave blacks the very tools necessary to fight against it. Through racial pride, faith, and family blacks could endure; after World War II, this perseverance would manifest in the form of the civil rights movement. Morrison would go on to win great acclaim for subsequent works, including the Pulitzer Prize for *Beloved* (1987).

The Great Depression and the New Deal

These cultural tensions did not disappear suddenly in 1929, but the context changed significantly with the stock market crash of that year that precipitated the Great Depression. Ohio had witnessed several depressions in the late nineteenth century, but all of them paled in comparison to the dislocations and transformations set in motion by the near economic collapse of the 1930s.

Underlying problems

Some observers in the 1920s saw trouble coming, but most Americans basked in the optimism and speculation of the economic boom. Yet the boom rested upon shaky ground. The foundation of the prosperity of the 1920s exhibited several interlocking characteristics whose weaknesses grew more significant as the decade wore on. Whether they knew it or not,

Ohioans played a part in a global economic system. As a result of World War I, the United States moved from being a debtor nation to the world's creditor. The Treaty of Versailles that ended the conflict mandated that Germany pay war reparations; the victorious Allied nations also needed capital to repay war debts and to rebuild, so Europe looked to Wall Street for financial assistance. The international economic structure of the 1920s relied on loans from American banks to stay afloat, and money sent to Europe often went not to rebuilding but into a cycle of debt repayments that flowed between the United States and Europe. Ohio's farms and factories sold their goods to others in the United States and increasingly to Europe. However, where before 1914 the flow of goods had been relatively open, in the 1920s the United States raised tariffs, restricting the flow of European goods and thus the one chief way European nations had of repaying their debts. People also moved freely across the Atlantic prior to 1914. The movement of workers, too, came under tough new restrictions with the immigration laws of the 1920s. This produced a new, more restrictive economic structure wedded to New York banks; one glitch in the system of credit could jeopardize it all.

With the prosperity of so many depending upon access to credit, Americans went into debt. The annual average household debt increased from $4,368 in 1920 to $10,506 in 1929; average annual household savings barely changed. Most of that went to mortgages, but installment loans were becoming more popular. Automobiles were both the symbol of the age and the harbingers of the limits of prosperity. Before 1914 the personal automobile was an expensive plaything for the wealthy. By the end of the 1920s, the automobile industry accounted for 10 percent of the nation's economy and employed some 4 million laborers. The average American would need nearly two years of wages to purchase a car before the war; by 1929 the price of automobiles—now mass assembled—had fallen so that one could acquire a car with about three months of wages. Car registrations increased so rapidly that there were 26 million cars in the nation by 1929, one for every five Americans.

However, while workers' wages rose in the 1920s, they did not increase enough to keep pace with the mass production of the U.S. economy. Meanwhile, wealth in the 1920s flowed disproportionately to those at the top; hence the consumer goods Ohioans and other Americans purchased on credit could only carry the economy so far. Automobile production began to slow as early as 1925 and business inventories swelled to some $2 billion by 1928. In addition to automobiles and other consumer goods, thriving housing construction fueled the 1920s economy. This, too, shifted downward in 1925. Without increased purchasing power at home or abroad, the consumer revolution of the 1920s neared the brink of collapse by the late 1920s. These new modern conveniences were mainly an urban phenomenon. After witnessing tremendous growth, Ohio's farms fell into decline after World War I as agricultural prices fell. Farmers who had expanded in good times now faced larger debts on lands whose values had dropped. A wave of farm bankruptcies and foreclosures loomed.

The crash and depression

Meanwhile, the stock market continued its dizzying climb. Only about 3 million Americans—less than 3 percent of the population—owned securities, but for consumers and businesses the market became a barometer that determined their individual and corporate economic decisions. Much of the money in the market went not into plant and machinery investments but into speculation. Instability came to the speculative bull market in September when shares fell dramatically then recovered. Then decline accelerated in late October and by mid-November stocks has lost a third of their value. The stock crash did not cause the depression, but it caused Americans to stop buying. Without spending, factories began to close and unemployment increased. Then, in 1930, a string of bank failures sent further shockwaves through an already weak system. The Federal Reserve held to conservative orthodoxy that allowed banks to fail as a correction to the economic system. The crisis hit Europe as Germany defaulted on war reparations, which in turn led Britain and France to default on their loans from U.S. banks. Banks continued to fail as depositors withdrew their funds. By 1932, U.S. Gross National Product had fallen by one-third, prices dropped by 40 percent and national unemployment reached nearly 25 percent, the highest rate in U.S. history.

The crisis hit hard in Ohio's urban areas, heavily dependent on manufacturing. Unemployment reached unfathomable rates: 80 percent in Toledo and 60 percent in Akron and Youngstown. All three of these cities were dependent upon automobiles in large measure: glass, rubber, and steel. Statewide the unemployment rate stood at 37.3 percent in 1932. Factory workers that did have jobs usually had their hours cut, which in turn lowered their income by a third or more. Akron's rubber workers went to a six-hour day in 1932. Some of Ohio's largest cities, including Akron, Cleveland, Toledo, and Youngstown lost population in the 1930s. As it so often has done, Columbus bucked the trend, growing by over 15 percent, perhaps because of its strength in education and other white-collar jobs, including government. Shanty towns of the destitute, acerbically dubbed "Hoovervilles" after President Hoover, sprang up in Ohio's major cities as families struggled to survive (see Figure 14.4). Those with some means survived by renting rooms in their homes, postponing buying new consumer goods, or moving in with relatives. Hiram House reported on one working-class neighborhood in Cleveland in 1931: 44 of 234 families had no means of support, with 22 living on garbage and another 11 surviving from gambling, theft, or prostitution. Schools suffered as tax collections that financed them fell; as a result, schools were forced to open later in the year and close earlier. Teachers' salaries were cut and some received no pay. The state lowered property taxes in 1933, which cut revenues even further. In 1935 the state acted to approve the School Foundation Bill, which diverted funds from Ohio's sales and other taxes to firm up schools around the state.

The unemployment crisis cut along racial and gender lines. Overall, the rates listed above reflected mostly male job losses. Among African Americans, at least 4 out of 5 men were unemployed in Cleveland through 1934. By 1934, some 80 percent of the city's African Americans were on direct or indirect relief. Companies openly fired blacks to make room for white workers. The Central area of Cleveland, home to some 90 percent of the city's blacks, had one of the highest concentrations of unemployment, especially among male industrial workers and building trades. Black women had long found work as domestics, but the need for work now pushed white women into that line of employment, displacing blacks. One family was forced to burn battery boxes for fuel; this led to severe lead poisoning for all five children, and two of whom subsequently died.

Figure 14.4 This image, taken by artist and photographer Ben Shahn in 1938 details a "Hooverville" in Circleville, south of Columbus. Farm foreclosures sent many farmers into nearby towns looking for work and housing, such that "Hoovervilles" became part of both the rural and the urban experience during the depression. Shahn worked as a photographer for the Farm Security Administration from 1933 to 1938, contributing to the rich documentary heritage of the New Deal and Great depression. Shahn later used these images, mainly of rural America, for his paintings, which were some of the most important to represent the "social realist" school of art. *Source*: Library of Congress Prints and Photographs Division (LC-DIG-fsa-8a18461)

As Ohio and its people dealt with the effects of the depression, the state also became the site for famous gangsters of the era, who were at once notorious criminals and folk heroes. John Dillinger and his gang robbed banks in Bluffton and Fostoria in 1933 and 1934 and several more in Indiana, South Dakota, and Illinois before Dillinger was shot and killed by police and FBI agents in Chicago in June 1934. In October that year, another infamous gang leader, Charles Arthur "Pretty Boy" Floyd, was killed in East Liverpool, Ohio as he tried to escape from FBI and local law enforcement agents.

As they read about, and in some cases witnessed, these criminal exploits, Ohioans could look around their neighborhoods and see the crisis deepening. Initially, any relief from the depravation was local and private but the crisis quickly overwhelmed these institutions. In March 1933, riots and demonstrations erupted in Canton, Cleveland, and Mansfield as people demanded relief allowances for food and rent. Akron's sheriff used force to evict people who could no longer pay their rent. In Athens County a group of male miners, each armed with a gunny sack, marched into the town of Glouster demanding food. Some cities created work relief projects and the state's major urban centers increased their spending on public relief, going from $619,000 in 1929 to over

$14 million in 1932. Pressure increased for the state government to do something. The response showed how firmly wedded the state's leaders remained to fiscal orthodoxy and traditional notions of relief. Throughout 1931, the Republican-led General Assembly refused to take action, insisting that relief was a local issue and maintaining that the economic downturn would be temporary. Even the Democratic governor, George White, continued to insist on a balanced budget and to limit the state's response. By 1932, with the situation worsening and elections approaching, state leaders voted to create a State Relief Commission (SRC). The SRC did not provide relief funds, but coordinated local efforts and distributed federal money from the Reconstruction Finance Corporation, the creation of which was President Herbert Hoover's major response to the crisis. In 1933 White finally requested the state provide relief funds, but the General Assembly, now with Democrats in charge of the lower house, continued to maintain that relief should be local. The relief that finally came to Ohio did so through the auspices of the federal government under the New Deal; state leaders remained resistant, a theme that would continue throughout the remainder of the Great Depression.

Ohio's New Deal

The New Deal was the name given to the collection of federal programs created during the administration of Franklin Roosevelt (FDR) designed to address the effects of the depression. In contrast to Hoover, FDR promised action during the 1932 campaign and voters responded by giving Roosevelt 472 electoral votes, including those of Ohio. The two major New Deal agencies that provided relief were the Federal Emergency Relief Administration (FERA), which lasted from 1933 to 1935, and the Works Progress Administration (WPA), operating from 1935 to 1943. It was FERA and then the WPA that provided the major means for Ohioans to survive the depression. Between 1933 and 1935, FERA provided direct relief and funded various works projects in the state. Direct relief went to about 1 million persons each month between July 1933 and October 1935. The WPA operated work relief, paying otherwise unemployed persons to build roads, schools, parks, playgrounds, and many other projects throughout Ohio. The New Deal also funded white-collar jobs for writers, artists, actors, and musicians, as well as health programs and various research and historical preservation projects. At its peak in 1938, the WPA employed over 279,000 men and women for a statewide average wage of $58.21 a month. Of course, these wages and jobs reflected the gender and racial biases of the day, with women and African Americans often earning less for the same jobs or restricted altogether from participation. However, Ohioans benefited from these federal efforts, and the state was second only to Pennsylvania in the number of WPA workers. In Summit County alone, among other projects, the WPA built seventeen new public buildings and reconditioned hundreds more, improved the municipal airport and 600 miles of roads, constructed two reservoirs, built the stadium that became the Akron Rubber Bowl, and performed plays and concerts.

Several other New Deal projects made a lasting impact on Ohio. The Civilian Conservation Corps (CCC), created in 1933 provided jobs to some 14,000 unemployed urban men between the ages of fifteen and eighteen. The goal was to bring these men out into "nature" and have them perform useful work such as building and upgrading trails, parks, and playgrounds, planting trees, and performing other jobs to enhance the public landscape. These workers and those on the WPA also aided in creating the dams and facilities of the Muskingum Watershed Conservancy District.

Relief and work were urban in focus, but with dust storms from severe drought and erosion on the Great Plains, and federal recognition of rural poverty, the New Deal also focused on rural Americans. The Agricultural Adjustment Act (AAA) of 1933 and the Soil Conservation and Domestic Allotment Act of 1936 both aided Ohio's farmers. The AAA used subsidies to encourage farmers to withhold crops and livestock from the market in order to raise prices. Declared unconstitutional in 1935, a second AAA came in 1938 to continue the practice of federal assistance to farmers. In between, the Soil Conservation Act provided aid to farmers by encouraging them to practice various methods of soil conservation. All three pieces of federal legislation pumped millions of dollars into rural Ohio. In addition, the Rural Electrification Act of 1935 enhanced the livelihoods of Ohioans, working through local cooperatives to bring electricity to rural areas.

As well as providing direct relief and jobs, Congress sought to reform the economic system. Key to this was an effort to stabilize the banking system and the stock market by creating the Banking Act of 1933 and the Securities Exchange Act of 1934. The Banking Act created the Federal Deposit Insurance Corporation (FDIC) to insure depositors and the Securities Act created the Securities Exchange Commission (SEC) to monitor and regulate the stock market. The National Housing Act of 1934 created the FHA to insure mortgages and the Home Owners Loan Corporation, which lasted from 1933 to 1936, purchased mortgages in danger of foreclosure and replaced them with more secure government bonds. In 1935 came the Social Security Act, which formed the foundation of further federal government social welfare programs.

Ohio voters supported FDR through the 1930s, shifting to Republican Thomas Dewey and Ohio's John Bricker in 1944, albeit by less than 12,000 votes. Yet at the same time, Ohio's government leaders continued to wrangle over the new federal presence in Ohio. Democrat Martin Davey replaced George White as governor in 1935. Davey operated the Davey Tree Expert Company in Kent, who "spouted Republican laissez-faire rhetoric almost as easily as Coolidge or Hoover." Despite the victory of FDR in Ohio and the apparent endorsement of New Deal programs by Ohio's voters, Davey held firm against what he viewed as the intrusion, waste, and corruption of the federal government in state matters. He was quick tempered and held grudges against those whom he believed had slighted him. The combination of his personality traits and beliefs led him into conflict with the Roosevelt administration. Davey hoped for a federal appointment when FDR came into office, but he failed to get one. Though he railed against the WPA, Davey tried to get his own political supporters hired on WPA programs in Ohio. Davey even used WPA employees to campaign for him and pressured workers to donate to his campaign. This led to public feuds between Davey and WPA head Harry Hopkins and even FDR himself. When Davey refused to authorize the state's share of relief funds, Hopkins had FDR grant direct federal control over the money. In 1935 federal officials brought criminal charges against Governor Davey. The investigation found political strong-arm tactics, but no criminal activity; and there was waste and inefficiency, just as Davey had charged. Meanwhile, Davey told a 1935 joint session of the state legislature that he had sworn out an arrest warrant for Hopkins, daring him to come to Ohio. Hopkins did, but Davey withdrew the charges. Davey did manage to support two state measures that extended aid, the School Foundation Law and the Unemployment Compensation Law. He also pushed the legislature to approve $17 million in direct relief aid in 1937. State Democrats rallied around Davey and voters sent him back to the governorship in 1936, although without FDR's 600,000 vote landslide in Ohio it is unlikely that Davey would have won. Davey lost reelection bids in 1938 and 1940.

Both of those elections saw Republican John Bricker win the governor's race. Bricker served as governor until 1945, when he was elected to the U.S. Senate. Bricker's base came from the traditional alliance of rural lawmakers and business leaders. By 1938, voters had tired of the flamboyant Davey and elected instead the unassuming, silver-haired Bricker, a man who exuded personal integrity. Apparently, FDR and the New Deal were also losing their luster, as Bricker railed against the Roosevelt administration. Bricker and the General Assembly, now in the hands of Republicans, continued to balance the budget, freezing relief expenditures at current levels. As it was for his Democratic predecessors, Bricker saw relief as a financial and political problem, not a human one. He promised economy in government and his was a caretaker governorship. In 1938 Bricker proposed $10 million in state relief, but with a requirement that local governments would need to match each state dollar. This put a heavy burden upon already strapped communities, especially large cities where the bulk of the unemployment existed. At the same time, in 1939 the WPA cut funds, weakening one of the major sources of income for Ohio's citizens. Bricker managed to cut government expenses further and in his first term he could boast that Ohio had eliminated its budget deficit. Bricker also benefited from the economic boom of World War II, and when he left office in 1945 to assume his seat in the Senate, Ohio possessed a $70 million budgetary surplus. After 1938, Republicans regained the momentum more generally. While Democrat Vic Donahey served one Senate term from 1935 to 1941, he was succeeded by moderate Republican Harold Burton. When Burton resigned to take a seat on the Supreme Court, the conservative Bricker won the special election. Meanwhile, Democrat Robert Bulkley lost to conservative Republican Robert A. Taft in the 1938 election.

Labor's upheaval

The fight over relief showcased the divisions between urban and rural Ohio. With the onset of the depression and the New Deal, urban areas had become more tightly identified with the liberalism of Roosevelt and the Democrats. Meanwhile, rural Ohio remained conservative, favoring leaders like Bricker. These divisions only grew in the midst of a massive uprising of organized labor, fed by a combination of grass-roots activism and a sympathetic federal government. Two pieces of New Deal legislation aided workers in their efforts to organize unions. Section 7(a) of the National Industrial Recovery Act of 1933 allowed for collective bargaining. When the Supreme Court found this law unconstitutional (this law also established codes of practice and prices for various industries) Congress authorized the Wagner Act in 1935. The Wagner Act, which withstood Supreme Court scrutiny, reaffirmed the rights of workers to engage in collective bargaining and created the National Labor Relations Board (NLRB).

As the federal government granted its support for organized labor in the 1930s, workers across the nation challenged business, sought to alleviate the conditions of the depression, and put into action the promises offered by federal laws. Ohio's mass production industrial workers were at the center of this. For years the American Federation of Labor (AFL), made up largely of skilled craft workers who were mainly white and male, had refused to organize the unskilled and semi-skilled workers. In the 1930s, workers themselves began to launch their own organizing drives. They were aided by the new Congress of Industrial Organizations (CIO) led by the United Mine Workers (UMW) leader John L. Lewis. In contrast to the AFL, Lewis and the CIO actively sought to organize all workers along industrial lines.

One of the first major labor strikes during the depression occurred at Toledo's Electric Auto-Lite company, which manufactured electric parts for automobiles. In April 1934 male and female workers, many of whom were of Polish background, walked off the job. Union leader Charles Rigby recalled that the strikers "were fighting for justice, fighting for just recognition." Radicals from various organizations, including the American Communist Party, the Socialists, and the Conference for Progressive Labor Action joined the workers, hoping the strike might lead to more dramatic change. Local courts issued an injunction limiting the number of picketers to twenty-five; meanwhile law enforcement deputies, whose salary Auto-Lite paid, patrolled the lines to enforce the ruling. When some of the organizers violated the injunction they were arrested and the company hired new workers to replace them, a recurring practice. These events led some 6,000 men and women to blockade the plant, trapping the replacement workers inside. Local law enforcement fired tear gas and turned water hoses on the crowd, setting off a riot. Governor White asked for the National Guard to disperse the crowd. In subsequent battles over several days in May, Guardsmen killed two protestors but failed to break the strike. Electric Auto-Lite temporarily shut down the plant, eventually recognized the local union, and rehired the strikers with a 5 percent pay increase. While radicals were disappointed, most of the workers were jubilant and the Auto-Lite strike, along with the massive sit-down strikes in Detroit auto factories led to organizing the automobile industry under the United Autoworkers.

There also were union rumblings in rural Ohio, not too far from Toledo. In the hot summer of 1934, the onion fields in Hardin County's Scioto Marsh were the scene of a violent strike by agricultural workers. For years, workers, many of them transients from Kentucky and West Virginia, had harvested onions in the marsh, once the center of the nation's onion trade, operating within a tenant farming system. As the depression hit, growers cut wages and hours so that the lives of the workers, never easy, became even harsher. In June, 210 workers met in the village of McGuffey and formed the first agricultural union chartered by the AFL, the Agricultural Workers Farm Labor Union, Local 19724. Now organized, they proceeded to strike. Thirty-seven-year-old Okey O'Dell led the strikers, and the leaders of Toledo's successful Auto-Lite strike came in to help. Sporadic conflicts between strikers and non-strikers continued through July; fist fights and gun battles between deputies and strikers became more frequent, as did dynamite blasts and fires set by strikers in attempts to inflict damage on property. Then, on the same day in late August, as replacement workers began harvesting the onions that had survived the extreme heat and inattention from the strike, a bomb damaged the home of McGuffey mayor, Godfrey Ott. Okey O'Dell was abducted, beaten, and warned not to return. He did so anyway but barricaded himself in his house along with his wife and brother as crowds outside reportedly shouted "Let's lynch O'Dell." Federal mediators stepped in to bring an agreement between the growers and the workers. In the end, several small growers agreed to raise wages to 35 cents an hour but not to recognize the union or alter work conditions. Larger growers refused to meet any union demands and continued to employ replacement workers. Soil exhaustion continued to be a problem and over the next several growing seasons production fell and fewer and fewer workers were needed; the Agricultural Workers Union dissolved.

In the same year that witnessed workers in McGuffey and Toledo organize and strike, rubber workers at General Tire in Akron developed a new tactic, the sit-down strike. In the past, workers on strike left the plant to join a picket line, which allowed owners to bring in replacement workers or "scabs." In the sit-down strike, workers remained inside the plant at their machines or place of work, making it more difficult for owners to use alternative labor and to use force to remove strikers inside the plant, since that might damage property. The 1934 sit-down at General Tire led to recognition of the local independent union. The next year these and other rubber workers joined together to create the United Rubber Workers (URW) as labor–management tensions continued to build. In February 1936, rubber workers again used the sit-down strike, this time at Goodyear Tire and Rubber, as part of the larger Akron rubber strike that year in which the URW sought official recognition from the rubber companies and contracts that would restore cuts in wage and hours and certain working conditions (see Figure 14.5). Picket lines and crowds formed outside Goodyear's plants in the city. To enforce a court injunction that barred intimidation of "scabs" entering the Goodyear plants and that set the number of pickets per gate at ten persons, Akron's police formed a "flying wedge" and attempted to break up the crowd of some 5,000 men, women and children blocking the entrance to Plant 1. The police chief called the officers back, however, before they made the charge. This strike remained relatively peaceful and after five weeks, Goodyear agreed to restore the six-hour day, and the thirty-six-hour week and rehire striking workers. It did not officially recognize the URW. Meanwhile, other confrontations had erupted in Akron. In some instances, women were central to the organizing efforts. A strike at the L.E. Shunk Latex Products Company in August involved mostly female URW workers who, armed "with small clubs," stood at the gates of the company to prevent strikebreakers from going to work after the URW women struck to protest layoffs. Strikes at Firestone in 1937 gave further success to the URW, as the union managed to negotiate contracts with both Firestone and Goodrich. Goodyear was the last to sign a contract with the URW, doing so in 1941. The sit-down strikes in Akron also inspired other workers, most notably autoworkers in Detroit who used the tactic in 1937 during their successful efforts to launch the United Autoworkers (UAW). Both the URW and the UAW were key unions in the formation of the CIO.

Another key CIO union, the United Steelworkers (USW) also came into being in the 1930s. In 1937, the largest company in steel industry, U.S. Steel had signed a contract with the USW. That done, and with growing success in the rubber and automobile industries, CIO head John L. Lewis then turned his attention to organizing the companies that made up

Figure 14.5   In this May 1938 picture Akron police clash with striking rubber workers from Goodyear. While the 1936 sit-down strike at Goodyear had been relatively peaceful, the 1938 strike was not. Workers walked out in protest when Goodyear violated seniority rules in transferring a number of employees. A massive street battle between police and workers erupted on the second day of the week long strike, when this picture was taken. It took three more years of cooperation between the new URW and Goodyear before the first formal contract was signed in 1941. *Source*: Courtesy of the Ohio Historical Society (AL00626)

"Little Steel," which included Inland, Republic, and Youngstown Sheet and Tube. The Steel Workers Organizing Committee (SWOC) called a strike against these three companies in May 1937, and more than 50,000 Ohio steelworkers heeded the call and walked off the job. Republic's leader, Tom Girdler became the most outspoken of the Little Steel group, vowing to "quit the steel business and grow apples" rather than sign an agreement with the USW. As the strike loomed and anticipating violence should workers walk out, he had already begun stockpiling munitions at various Republic plants to be used to defend the mills. Meanwhile, steelworkers borrowed the sit-down technique and also established picket lines to prevent replacement workers from entering plants. Violence broke out between police and picketers on June 19 at the Republic plant in Youngstown, killing two strikers. Governor Davey sent National Guard troops to Youngstown. After four days negotiations failed to result in an agreement and Republic and the other companies proceeded to bring in replacement workers. Davey instructed the National Guard to protect these strikebreakers. Violence

Figure 14.6   Little is known about the artist who rendered this remarkable mural in a Cleveland barbershop in 1952. It may have been Charles E. Harris. The painting depicts the movement of African Americans out of the South and into the city, part of the Great Migration. The artist features the Future Outlook League as taking charge of the process and ensuring a powerful voice for African Americans through the words on the pedestal, "Militancy," "Courage," and "Equal Economic Opportunity."
Source: Western Reserve Historical Society

again erupted, killing five strikers and injuring over 300 others. In July, in Massillon, a mis-understanding led police to fire upon a crowd that had been gathering nightly at the union headquarters, killing three men. A reporter commented that the "kitchen of the union hall was spattered and smeared with blood." By the end of the month, the Little Steel strike had been broken and workers slowly returned to the mills. Critics charged that the initials CIO stood for "Collapsed in Ohio." Nevertheless, as a result of subsequent federal rulings by the NLRB and the onset of World War II, Little Steel eventually signed union contracts in 1941.

In Ohio's urban areas many African American workers lay outside the major unions forming in the 1930s. Years of discrimination in hiring and resistance by white workers toward accepting black workers as fellow union members meant that black men and women often had to fight for better conditions through their own organizations. In Cleveland, African Americans formed the Future Outlook League in 1935. Led by Alabama migrant John Holly, the men and women of the FOL operated boycotts as well as pickets in an effort to get businesses to hire black workers and urged blacks to open and run their own businesses. The mural shown in Figure 14.6 depicts the Future Outlook League taking a leading role in shepherding blacks out of the South and into Cleveland, integrating them into black urban life, labor and politics. In time, the CIO began to open up more opportunities to African Americans, especially during the heavy labor demand of World War II.

World War II

As Ohioans struggled and fought one another in an effort to redefine themselves and the role of government in the Great Depression, a more ominous and far more violent struggle was emerging, one that would envelop most of the world. World War II would witness an ever greater role for the federal government in the lives of Ohioans, spur further debates and tensions over organized labor, race, and gender, and finally provide the economic impetus not only to end the depression but also to generate tremendous prosperity in the postwar decades. The war would draw in 839,000 men and women from Ohio to serve in the military, claiming the lives of some 23,000 of them. One of those serving was Paul Tibbets of Columbus, who piloted the *Enola Gay* as it dropped the first atomic bomb on the Japanese city of Hiroshima (see Figure 14.7). Overall, World War II was the most devastating conflict in history, leading to the deaths of 60 million people worldwide and over 418,000 Americans.

The coming conflict

The outbreak of World War II owed much to the end of World War I. Contrary to Woodrow Wilson's hopes, the Treaty of Versailles signed in 1919 did not sow the seeds of peace, but of future conflict. Italy and Japan came under leadership that sought to redress perceived slights at being denied the spoils of victory. Under Benito Mussolini, the Italians sought to recreate the glory of ancient Rome by extending their military power into Africa and the eastern Mediterranean. Militarists in Japan looked to China and Southeast Asia to fulfill their expansionist dreams. Fixed by the Versailles Treaty as being responsible for the Great War, Germany went through a troubled experience with democracy in the 1920s, only to see further instability from the economic crisis of the 1930s. The Nazis, under the leadership of Adolf Hitler, craftily exploited the Germans' economic desperation and lingering resentments from World War I.

In 1931, the Japanese invaded and occupied Manchuria and then invaded China in 1937. In 1935 Italy invaded Ethiopia and in 1936 the Spanish civil war erupted. Germany absorbed Austria in 1938 and in 1939 took over the Sudentenland in Czechoslovakia. Later that year, on September 1, the German military invaded Poland from the west and the Soviets, with whom Germany had signed a non-aggression pact, invaded from the east. By this time, Britain and France had begun rebuilding their militaries; they declared war on Germany after the Polish invasion. After taking Poland, German armies moved swiftly to take over Norway, Denmark, and the Low Countries. France fell in the summer of 1940, leaving Britain to stand alone against the Nazi war machine. Meanwhile, in Asia,

Figure 14.7 Paul Tibbets named the B-29 bomber *Enola Gay* after his mother. With Tibbets at the controls, the plane dropped the atomic bomb, code named Little Boy, over Hiroshima at 8:15 a.m. local time. For the remainder of his life Tibbets defended his mission to those who were critical of the decision to use atomic weapons. In an interview in 1970 he said "I would drop that bomb again without reservation, because it saved far more lives than it took."
Source: National Archives (535736)

Japan had moved troops into French Indochina (Vietnam, Laos, and Cambodia) and in 1941 the United States responded with an embargo against Japan. Under prodding from President Roosevelt and a slow but steady shift in public sentiment, Congress began to drift away from its non-interventionist policies.

The worsening situation, especially with the fall of France, led Congress to approve the Burke-Wadsworth Act in September of 1940, which established America's first peacetime draft. Ohio's National Guard mobilized in response, its men becoming soldiers in the U.S. Army, and leaving for basic training at Camp Shelby in Mississippi. After a fierce debate in Congress, U.S. neutrality technically ended with the Lend-Lease Act of 1941, which allowed the United States to lend or lease war materials to Britain or any nation deemed vital to the nation's defense. Roosevelt likened it to lending your water hose to your neighbor to fight a fire, to which Ohio's staunch isolationist senator Robert A. Taft quipped: "Lending war equipment is a good deal like lending chewing gum, you certainly don't want the same gum back." Only with the Japanese attack on Pearl Harbor on December 7, 1941, a day Roosevelt called "a date which will live in infamy," did the United States officially enter the global conflict. The United States declared war on Japan on December 8; Germany declared war on the United States and on December 11, the United States quickly reciprocated.

Politically, the deepening crisis also led President Roosevelt to defy tradition and run for a third term in 1940. He received substantial criticism for the move but nevertheless won Ohio and the national election over political newcomer Republican Wendell Willkie. Willkie had secured his party's nomination after GOP stalwarts such as Robert Taft were deemed too isolationist. Roosevelt's victory aside, Taft seemed to represent the majority of what Ohio's voters wanted in the state government and in Congress. John Bricker, another vocal isolationist and critic of FDR, remained as governor through 1945, and Ohio's voters kept Taft in the Senate and sent mostly Republicans of isolationist leanings to Washington.

Ohio at war

Despite his criticism of FDR, as governor, Bricker moved to put Ohio on war footing. He authorized the creation of a 2,200 member State Guard to replace the National Guard and worked with the legislature to create the State Defense Council. The council had broad powers over civil defense, industrial production, agricultural production, labor, training and mobilization of workers for various defense-related activities, finance, housing, and health. When war came, Ohio made the transition more easily than other states. The state's economy revived, with unemployment virtually disappearing, while personal and corporate income soared. Coal production increased by 82 percent, industrial wages went up 65 percent and farm income by nearly 200 percent. The number of workers in Ohio's basic industries increased from 754,886 to 1,268,685. Much of this came from migrations into Ohio, especially from Appalachia and the South, a trend that would continue into the 1960s. During the war, Ohio ranked fourth in the amount of money received from defense contracts, with a total of $18 million. The contracts benefited Ohio's industrial cities: Cleveland realized $5 billion, Cincinnati $3.4 billion, Akron $2.1 billion, and Dayton $1.2 billion. Ohio's basic industries contributed substantially to the war effort. Goodyear created plants to manufacture aircraft. Staffed with some 30,000 workers they built Corsairs and other aircraft parts. The rubber factories turned out a host of products for the war, as did the auto and steel plants. The federal government also created weapons manufacturing plants in Ravenna, and outside Columbus, Toledo, and other cities. The iconic Jeep came into being at Toledo's Willys-Overland site.

All of this activity increased the growing connections between business, national defense, and universities. This was most apparent in the race to create a substitute for raw rubber, a natural resource that had largely come under the control of the Japanese. By drawing together scientists, military leaders, industrial managers, and government officials, the Synthetic Rubber Program that began in 1942 resembled the Manhattan Project (which, at the same time, oversaw the development of the U.S. atomic program). The amount of rubber needed for wartime was immense: one battleship alone needed 75 tons. Without rubber, the military would come to a halt. According to the Baruch Committee in charge of reviewing the situation, "If we fail to secure quickly a large new rubber supply, our war effort and our domestic economy both will collapse." Akron was at the center of the national effort, with tire company personnel involved and the University of Akron playing important administrative and scientific roles. The university administered over $8 million in government funds and Akron's tire companies received millions of dollars to fund research as well. The result was GR-S synthetic rubber, and by 1945 the United States produced some 920,000 tons of it per year. While some hail the program as a success, others have criticized the delay and wasted resources stemming from needless battles between the government and the oil companies, both of whom sought to dominate the process of making synthetics.

For Ohioans still reeling from the effects of the depression, the war only added to the stress of daily life. Citizens not joining the military were compelled to help on the home front. Federal agencies helped with a massive advertising and propaganda campaign to enlist every citizen in the fight, especially women maintaining the home while husbands and sons were at war. Propaganda posters abounded, with titles including: "Waste Helps the Enemy" and "When You Ride Alone, You Ride with Hitler." To supplement the nation's food supply, Ohioans participated in the "victory garden" program, planting more than 1 million gardens in the state. Others collected metals and rubber in scrap drives and used coupons in their ration books to buy regulated goods and foods, such as tires, gasoline, nylon stockings, meat, and butter.

With so many men serving in the military, industrial labor was at a premium. Deaf workers, for example, were hired to work in the rubber plants. The most significant change in the labor situation, however, regarded women and African Americans. The government propaganda campaign was aimed at women in the home and used a variety of means to attract white women into the workforce, including posters with the iconic "Rosie the Riveter" image and ads that stressed the cleanliness and ease of defense work (see Figure 14.8). Women comprised about 30 percent of all industrial workers in Ohio. Employers placed women mainly in a variety of semiskilled positions, including the manufacture of parts, munitions, and electronics. In Akron, women entered the rubber plants to make various products including pontoons, life rafts, and tires. Cities employing women

Figure 14.8   Scenes like this one from a manufacturing plant in Cleveland were common during World War II as women flooded into the industrial labor force. This is almost certainly a photograph of workers (or "associates") of the Jack & Heintz company in Maple Heights and Bedford, near Cleveland. Jahco, as the company came to be known, earned praise for its efficiency in manufacturing aircraft parts and its generosity to its employees. In return for generous benefits, workers agreed to 12-hour shifts, seven days a week during the height of production.
Source: Courtesy of the Ohio Historical Society (AL00101)

offered some assistance: women with children often worked the night shift, public and private daycare centers emerged, and shopping hours were extended. Married women were still expected to take care of the home while working. Single women found city life empowering; wages and entertainment allowed them more freedom. While opportunities emerged, women were paid less than men and many unions refused to allow them to join. Black women found it more difficult than their white counterparts to gain access to industrial jobs, yet some did manage to work alongside white women at Akron's rubber plants and in other industries across Ohio. For women workers, the issue was to what extent they would keep their factory jobs once the war ended. Certainly companies and the federal government saw the labor situation as temporary and encouraged women to see it this way as well. Goodyear profiled female workers in its "The Real Miss Americas" series, all of whom made statements similar to Leila Fletcher's: "I have found the work…very interesting and I enjoy doing it. Of course, it's just a duration job and, like hundreds of other war wives, I'm looking forward to the day when I can again settle down to being a housewife." However, this image did not necessarily reflect the reality of work for women. Women had always worked in the rubber factories and other industries. Some women did return to the home after the war, others were laid off, and others stayed on the job. Tensions over gender roles and expectations would only remerge in postwar Ohio and America.

For their part, African Americans experienced equally ambivalent messages from government, business, and unions during and just after the war. Just as in World War I, the need for labor prompted another wave of migrants from the South and new employment opportunities did emerge on the home front and some improvement came by war's end. While some businesses and unions voluntarily ended their discriminatory practices, most refused to do so. Only pressure from blacks and those sympathetic to them led to these greater openings in Ohio's war industries.

In 1940 Governor Bricker established the Advisory Commission on the Employment Problems of the Negro. This was both a sincere effort to assist blacks in obtaining jobs as the war grew closer and a way to keep Ohio's African Americans in the Republican fold. It lasted two years and accomplished little. Moreover, it did not work with the Fair Employment Practices Commission (FEPC), the federal agency established in 1942 by FDR under Executive Order 8802 to enforce racial equality in hiring by businesses receiving federal contracts. The FEPC only came about after labor leader A. Philip Randolph threatened to organize a march on Washington, D.C. to protest unfair treatment. Not since Reconstruction had the federal government taken such a stance on racial equality. The FEPC investigated complaints across the state, yet enforcement of the order was uneven and the level of discrimination varied from place to place. There were exceptions, but despite FDR's order most companies still refused to hire blacks; as one reportedly told an NAACP investigator: "I don't care what Roosevelt says, I am not hiring any Negroes." In some cases, local officials of FEPC and other federal agencies worked with white business leaders and refused to refer blacks to jobs or to pressure companies to hire blacks.

In Cleveland John Holly's Future Outlook League organized picketing and filed court cases to pressure companies to hire black men and women. Another group, the Cleveland Metropolitan Council for Fair Employment Practice, made up of forty-five civic organizations, avoided direct action and tried working with FEPC to achieve results. The pressure, and a growing tight labor market by 1943, led to successes in opening several of Cleveland's major industries to blacks. In Columbus, the Vanguard League, a Congress of Racial Equality affiliate, used direct action protests and cooperation with FEPC to open jobs at the Curtiss-Wright plant and Ohio Bell Telephone. Unions moved slowly as well. Officially, groups like the AFL and the CIO stated a commitment to racial equality. However, at the local level integration proved difficult. The local CIO at Curtiss-Wright organized a strike in 1941 when the company hired skilled black workers and the day before D-Day, 5 June 1944, white workers staged a massive walkout at Wright Aeronautical in Cincinnati to protest about the upgrading of black employees.

Difficulties aside, African Americans came to Ohio and seized the opportunities open to them. By 1950, African Americans made up 6.5 percent of Ohio's total population (513,000) and they would be concentrated in the cities, especially Cleveland where some 28 percent of all black Ohioans lived. For women and African Americans the World War II experience proved to be a watershed. In the years that followed, blacks would use the experience to build a powerful foundation for the postwar civil rights movement.

While the wages workers earned were relatively good, industrial work had always been fraught with dangers and tensions, which the war simply exacerbated. Plants ran all day, every day. Housing shortages, rationing, and the stress from military deployments strained workers and their families. Divorce rates increased. Unions and business owners pledged to keep the peace for the war effort. Business reaped enormous profits while unions gained members and saw higher wages and benefits go to those who could join. The tensions still allowed for work stoppages and in some cases outright strikes. By 1943 Ohio workers were involved in 467 stoppages; on some occasions military officers had to step in to keep the peace. In 1943, John L. Lewis and the UMW came in for special condemnation as Lewis called half a million miners across the nation out of the pits over the refusal of mining companies to grant a wage increase of $2 a day. Lewis won the increase, but he lost in the public opinion polls and damaged organized labor's reputation. "If they don't want to work, draft them!" emerged as the popular sentiment. The American public's dislike of organized labor would linger into the early postwar years. Despite that organized labor gained in terms of membership so that by 1945 some 36 percent of all workers in Ohio were unionized.

The 839,000 Ohioans who served in World War II were scattered throughout different military units across the globe. One exception was the 37th Division, which was comprised mainly of former Ohio National Guard troops. The 37th Division fought in the Pacific campaign. Other notable units composed mainly of Ohioans were Company C of the 192nd Tank Battalion, the 112th Engineer Combat Battalion, and the 174th Field Artillery Battalion. Several black Ohioans also served as part of the famed Tuskegee Airmen, several of whom are shown in Figure 14.9. While the level of support for World War II was high, there were those who refused to serve, mainly as conscientious objectors. Ohio's traditional peace churches, Brethren, Mennonites, and Quakers, sent the bulk of those registered as objectors. While a few who refused to serve in the military on moral grounds went to prison, most agreed to serve in other capacities. Hundreds worked on farms, in hospitals, and in other areas depleted of labor. They also worked in Civilian Public Service camps, run by Quakers, Mennonites, and by the federal Soil Conservation Service. Just after the war, when the United States responded with aid for Europe, many of these men worked as "sea cowboys," managing livestock shipped over to replenish food supplies.

At War's End

Ohioans had weathered two major crises and like others around the world they celebrated Victory in Europe (VE) Day on May 8, 1945 and Victory in Japan (VJ) Day on August 14. With the Great Depression and World War II finally over, they could return to something approaching a normal life. After so much tumult and change it was unclear what 'normal' meant. The social and cultural tensions of the 1920s revealed the differences inherent in Ohio, among rural and urban, white and black, Protestant and Catholic, Republican and Democrat. These divisions continued into the 1930s and 1940s, exacerbated by the crises

Figure 14.9 African Americans had been barred from flying for the military, but pressure from civil rights organizations and black newspapers led to the formation of the Tuskegee Airmen in 1941. The Tuskegee fighter groups were some of the most highly respected of World War II. Pictured in this signed print are several of the men from central Ohio. The myth that the Tuskegee Airmen never lost a bomber they escorted held sway for many years, but recent research shows that they did, albeit at a lower rate than other fighter groups.
Source: Courtesy of the Afro-American Museum and Cultural Center

of the Great Depression and World War II. Ohio had become an urban and industrial state and the New Deal and the war had brought a greater federal presence into the lives of all Ohioans. By 1945, the state had recovered from the depression and its economy looked strong. Cities hummed and farms were once again prosperous. Like the nation itself, Ohio stood on the verge of a new wave of economic growth, and of the suburban expansion that would define much of the postwar years. The good life would come for many. However, if some Ohioans thought they were now immune from tension and trouble, or could simply ignore it, then the postwar years showed the folly of such naiveté.

Further Reading

For literary figures, see various individual biographies and collected works, as well as William Coyle, ed., *Ohio Authors and Their Books* (1962. Cleveland: World Publishing). For Ohio between the 1920s and World War II see: Raymond Boryczka and Lorin Lee Cary, *No Strength Without Union:*

An Illustrated History of Ohio Workers, 1803–1980 (1982. Columbus: The Ohio Historical Society); John Braeman, Robert H. Bremner, and David Brody, eds., *The New Deal: Volume 2, The State and Local Levels* (1975. Columbus: The Ohio State University Press); Richard O. Davies, *Defender of the Old Guard: John Bricker and American Politics* (1993. Columbus: The Ohio State University Press); Vernon Herbert, *Synthetic Rubber: A Project That Had to Succeed* (1985. New York: Praeger); William D. Jenkins, *Steel Valley Klan: The Ku Klux Klan in Ohio's Mahoning Valley* (1990. Kent: Kent State University Press); Steve Love and David Giffels, *Wheels of Fortune: The Story of Rubber in Akron* (1999. Akron: University of Akron Press); Daniel Nelson, *American Rubber Workers and Organized Labor, 1900–1941* (1988. Princeton: Princeton University Press); Kimberley L. Phillips, *Alabama North: African-American Migrants, Community and Working Class Activism in Cleveland, 1915—45* (1999. Urbana: University of Illinois Press, 1999); Eugene Trani and David Wilson, *The Presidency of Warren G. Harding* (2d ed. 1985. Lawrence: University Press of Kansas); and Frank P. Vazzano, *Politician Extraordinaire: The Tempestuous Life and Times of Martin L. Davey* (2008. Kent: Kent State University Press).

15

Affluence and Anticommunism

In 1953, Ohio's sesquicentennial, public events and published materials produced for the celebration emphasized Ohio's material progress and success, from the pioneer days through the present, and the unity of Ohio's citizens who had come from diverse backgrounds. At that year's state fair in Columbus, the sesquicentennial displays attracted some 500,000 viewers. Youth and education were of special interest to the sesquicentennial's planners. The celebration came at the height of the Cold War, and thus programs throughout the state emphasized understanding Ohio's past as embodying community participation and loyalty to the economic and political system of the United States. President Dwight Eisenhower reinforced these ideas when he spoke at Defiance College in October. In saluting the "builders of Ohio" Eisenhower praised them as helping to "construct a way of life—the American way of life, of which the cornerstone is an indestructible faith in man's dignity as a child of God." The sesquicentennial commission also authorized a pageant to tell the history of Ohio, which, according to one historian, crafted Ohio's story as "one, great, ongoing struggle for liberty." Another historian writing at the time, Carl Wittke, captured this essence as well: "From the hardy and heroic survivors of this courageous struggle with Nature, frontier Ohio was born. Conservative Southerners and New Englanders joined with reckless, lawless adventurers from many States to lay the foundations of a mighty commonwealth." Wittke looked around him and added that he saw an Ohio in which "men of many origins in many lands are participating, as equals, in the building of our great commonwealth. What we are doing in Ohio has also, happily, been going on elsewhere. It is part of the American way, and the average Ohioan is also the average American."

No doubt Ohioans had much to celebrate and reason for optimism as their state and nation appeared socially unified, politically stable, and economically strong. Optimism,

Ohio: A History of the Buckeye State, First Edition. Kevin F. Kern and Gregory S. Wilson.
© 2014 John Wiley & Sons, Inc. Published 2014 by John Wiley & Sons, Inc.

however, belied the tensions building within Ohio. The Cold War against communism led to a second red scare, while the narrative of progress ignored growing problems that would come to a head in the 1960s and 1970s.

The Postwar Boom

Undergirding the expressions of pride and optimism in the postwar decades was the unprecedented economic boom. The growth during World War II continued afterwards as employment remained high and cities and towns bustled with activity as mass consumption and mass production flourished. This prompted Cleveland's Chamber of Commerce to adopt the slogan "Cleveland, the best location in the nation." Crime rates remained relatively low as well and compared to the tumult and stress of the 1930s post-World War II Ohio seemed peaceful and prosperous. Yet tensions surfaced as early as the postwar transition.

Reconversion and labor strife

Ohio's postwar economic boom came after a rocky transition from the wartime economy. Demobilization caused problems as soldiers clamored to be sent home quickly. The military eventually developed a point system based on length service that brought some order to the process. By 1947 the number of men in the armed forces had dropped by 90 percent. To reward veterans and to further ease the transition out of war, the federal government established a generous welfare program for returning veterans in the form of the Servicemen's Readjustment Act, or the GI Bill, signed by FDR in 1944. The GI Bill provided one year of unemployment compensation, low interest loans for purchasing a home, farm or business, and tuition reimbursement up to $500 per year so veterans could enroll in higher education or technical training programs.

On the home front during the war, Ohioans had become frustrated at price controls and the lack of certain goods. Now, with the war over, demand for goods and for the removal of controls accelerated. There was also a severe housing shortage. The large migration of workers to Ohio's industrial cities during the war strained housing stock and the situation only became worse as veterans returned from service. At war's end, a sharp recession hit Ohio and the nation. With war contracts cancelled industries responded by cutting workers. The prevailing public assumption at the time was that any jobs that did open should be reserved for male veterans returning from service. One result was that in the immediate postwar years women were forced out of many companies. Even as women increased their role in the paid labor force, their overall wage levels dropped as companies pushed women out of higher paying factory jobs and into less lucrative clerical, sales, or light industrial jobs.

The economic difficulties of reconversion and organized labor's desire to capitalize on its wartime success led to massive nationwide strikes in 1946. More than 5 million workers were involved in nearly 5,000 work stoppages nationwide. The three major industrial unions at the time, the United Autoworkers (UAW), United Rubber Workers

(URW), and the United Steelworkers (USW) won wage concessions. In Ohio and across the nation organized labor reached its peak in terms of membership, helping propel the millions of Ohio's industrial workers into the middle class. Some 36 percent of Ohio's workers were unionized in 1945. Union power came with industrial growth. The automobile industry in Ohio became second only to Michigan's; plants expanded in cities and in rural areas like Lordstown, where General Motors built a new factory in 1966. As the automobile industry grew so too did Akron's rubber industry. In 1950 there were 12,000 hourly workers at B.F. Goodrich, 15,000 at Firestone, and 17,000 at Goodyear. And in the Youngstown area alone, in the early 1950s, more than 40,000 workers took home a paycheck for making steel.

However, union membership growth came at a cost. While unions won wage concessions, they failed to gain a seat at the governing board of major corporations. Strikes fueled a growing popular backlash against organized labor. This dovetailed with charges of communism as the Cold War began to intensify. With Democrats more strongly associated with organized labor, Republicans capitalized on the tensions and captured Congress in the 1946 elections. Ohio sent Republican John Bricker to the U.S. Senate that year and the state's other senator, Republican Robert Taft became senate majority leader. Using his new power and influence, Taft co-authored, with Republican Representative Fred Hartley of New Jersey, the Labor-Management Relations Act of 1947, better known as the Taft–Hartley Act. Taft–Hartley revised the Wagner Act of 1935 in several ways. It outlawed the closed shop (the practice of hiring only union workers) and secondary boycotts and prohibited the use of union dues for political purposes. It authorized the president to declare a cooling off period before a strike could begin. Union officials had to sign affidavits that they were not Communists. The act also permitted states to pass "right to work" laws that barred making union membership a requirement for employment. Congress approved the Act over President Truman's veto. Meanwhile, with Republican Thomas Herbert in the Governor's office and with large GOP majorities in the Ohio House and Senate, in 1947 Ohio approved the Ferguson Act, which barred public employees from striking.

Recovery and the affluent society

The backlash against labor ebbed a bit as the 1950s began, as did the economic tensions associated with demobilization and the immediate postwar recession. Nationally, between 1946 and 1960 the gross national product more than doubled and the federal government estimated that 60 percent of Americans enjoyed a middle-class standard of living in 1960. In 1953, the nation's average annual per capita income was $1,800. Ohio's was $2,028, tenth highest among the states. In global terms, this placed Ohioans well above the next highest nations, Canada, Great Britain, New Zealand, Switzerland, and Sweden. Throughout the 1950s, Ohio ranked fourth or fifth in industrial production, and second only to Michigan in exports. Ohio's population continued to grow during the postwar "baby boom," from 6.9 million in 1940, to 7.95 million in 1950, 9.7 million in 1960 and 10.65 million in 1970.

Growth and prosperity fueled civic optimism. Cleveland's industrial boom gave credence to the nickname created in 1944, the "best location in the nation." Clevelanders celebrated the city's 150th birthday in 1946, complete with parades and entertainment that drew national attention. An article in the *New Yorker* declared: "Clevelanders display an exuberant enthusiasm for their town and their way of life." Small towns felt the prosperity, too. In 1950 Camden, birthplace of Sherwood Anderson, had a population of just over 1,000. Having endured the depression and the war, postwar residents were anxious to "enjoy the benefits of good times." The editor of the local paper commented that Main Street was "a 'little Broadway' these days," as shoppers were "jamming the streets and stores." Three new restaurants opened in 1947. The Lions Club raised enough money to buy new uniforms for the high school band; there were good jobs in local industries such as Neff and Fry, which manufactured concrete silos and other storage structures. The local Ford and Chevrolet dealers could not keep up with demand. The first televisions arrived in 1948, and soon homeowners constructed antennas on rooftops to capture the signals that brought them professional wrestling (Gorgeous George and Don Mohawk were favorites), Cincinnati Reds baseball, and *I Love Lucy* episodes. Bars and restaurants bought televisions to lure customers and people began hosting "TV parties" with their neighbors.

Medical, technological, and scientific advances came in quick succession. As Ohioans celebrated their sesquicentennial they might have read about the discovery of the double helix for DNA or the creation of IBM's first computer. Ohioans certainly benefited from Jonas Salk's successful introduction of the vaccine for polio in 1955. In 1953 TWA began the first nonstop air passenger service between New York and Los Angeles. In the postwar decades, irradiation and nuclear power emerged. In 1958 the National Aeronautics and Space Administration (NASA) came into being and sent several Ohioans into space, including John Glenn of New Concord, Ohio, the first American to orbit the Earth in the Mercury spacecraft *Friendship 7* in February 1962 (see Figure 15.1), and Neil Armstrong of Wapakoneta the first human to walk on the moon with *Apollo 11* in July 1969. Akron's B.F. Goodrich built the spacesuits worn by astronauts in the Mercury program, including Glenn. With the space program, Ohio reinforced its ties to aviation history.

Optimism abounded in sports for Ohio during the 1940s and 1950s. The Cleveland Indians were regular contenders in the American League, winning the World Series in 1948. The roster that year included the first African American to play in the American League, Larry Doby (see Figure 15.2). In 1945, the Cleveland Buckeyes won the Negro League championship. The postwar era included the glory years of the Cleveland Browns. The team's first coach and general manager, Paul Brown led the team to four consecutive All American Football Conference titles from 1946–49, and then National Football League titles in 1950, 1954, and 1955. In 1951, Woody Hayes began his legendary twenty-eight-year coaching career at Ohio State, leading the Buckeyes to three national championships and thirteen Big Ten titles. In the 1960s, the Cincinnati Reds emerged as contenders as well, and by the early 1970s they became the "Big Red Machine," with such stars as Joe Morgan and Pete Rose. The rise of television helped solidify the prominence of professional and college sports in Ohio and national popular life.

The growing centrality of sports reflected the flowering of a mass consumption economy. In the context of the battle against communism in the postwar years, consumer spending on goods and services created by corporations came to define American freedom. Industrial workers joined the rising numbers of professionals and other white

Figure 15.1   Pictured here is John Glenn sitting outside the *Friendship 7* space capsule. Prior to becoming an astronaut Glenn served with great distinction as a Marine pilot in World War II and again in Korea (where he flew about half his missions with famed Boston Red Sox slugger Ted Williams as his wingman). Glenn became a hero for his 1962 flight and, following his long career in politics, returned to space in 1999 aboard the Space Shuttle Discovery.
Source: Courtesy of the Ohio Historical Society (AL00609)

collar workers in their desire for and ability to purchase many of the consumer goods flooding the market in the postwar years. Like most Americans, Ohioans were bombarded with advertisements on billboards, in magazines and newspapers, on radio and increasingly through television. By the end of the 1950s, nearly nine out of ten Americans owned a television; the frozen TV dinner came along in 1954.

The availability of goods emerged simultaneously with the growth of suburbs and the expansion of interstate highways in Ohio. Indeed, the engines of economic growth after World War II were residential construction and consumer spending. In the process the Ohio landscape began to change. Ohioans bought homes outside the central cities and small towns, commuted between the new houses and work in their cars, and outfitted them with consumer goods sourced increasingly in shopping centers. Cleveland opened its first shopping center in 1953, and others across the state quickly followed (see Figure 15.3). Driving to go shopping also meant driving to eat and fast food emerged in the 1950s. Two men in their twenties, Burt Rose and Jerry Islan, opened the first McDonald's in Ohio in 1958 in Toledo; the same city

Figure 15.2 Larry Doby was the American League's first black player, breaking the color barrier with the Indians only weeks after Jackie Robinson did so with Dodgers in the National League. He is pictured here in 1948 between Hall of Fame player/manager Lou Boudreau on the left and Hall of Famer Hank Greenberg, who had just retired from a stellar career to take an office position with the Indians. Doby endured the prejudice out of the spotlight that Robinson occupied, showing himself to be an excellent ballplayer, earning seven All Star trips in his career and a spot in the Baseball Hall of Fame.

claimed the company's 500th restaurant in 1963. Dave Thomas came to Columbus in 1962 to save four Kentucky Fried Chicken stores. He turned them around (becoming a millionaire in the process) and then in 1969 opened his own fast food restaurant, Wendy's.

The scale and scope of postwar suburban expansion made this one of the most notable transformations in Ohio and the nation. In defining the postwar good life, more and more Ohioans preferred the housing and amenities found in the new suburban areas. These communities sprang up around all of Ohio's major cities and larger towns, turning former farmland into what some commentators would later define as "suburban sprawl." These subdivisions usually featured tract housing, cheaply built but an improvement over small apartments in the city for growing families in a hurry to buy and developers anxious to do business. In the late 1940s, a new house typically cost between $7,000 and $8,000, affordable for the average family and even easier to buy for veterans under the GI Bill. Feeding, weeding, and watering the lawn in these houses would become staples of postwar life in Ohio and elsewhere across the nation. There to help was O.M. Scott and Sons of Marysville. Scott published its *Lawn Care* magazine, and provided seeds, chemical fertilizers, and weed

Figure 15.3 Shoppers crowd a recently opened Big Bear supermarket on Lane Avenue in Columbus in this 1952 picture. Supermarkets like this one spread across Ohio and the United States with the advent of suburbs and highway construction.
Source: Courtesy of the Ohio Historical Society (AL07664)

killers, all designed to give suburbanites the perfect lawn. The company, which soon exerted near monopoly control in the area of lawn care, also capitalized on the growing popularity of golf, another staple of the postwar good life for which Ohioans developed an obsession. Later, Ohio golf legend Jack Nicklaus would become one of the company's spokespersons. Moreover, unlike the "streetcar suburbs" of earlier years, these new communities were tied to new expressways and interstates whose construction came with significant federal help in the form of the Interstate Highway Act of 1956, strengthening the population shift out of central cities and into suburbs and deepening the dependence upon the automobile. Ohioans had approved bond issues to build highways but with the 1956 Act, states could obtain 90 percent funding for highway projects. This was a popular public works project. During his successful 1956 campaign for governor, Republican William O'Neill told members of the Cincinnati Transportation Club, with perhaps only slight exaggeration, that there "is no state problem more important to the ordinary citizen of Ohio than that of highways. Everywhere I go, everyone to whom I talk wants new roads, wide roads, safe roads."

  Forest Park outside Cincinnati typified some of the trends of suburban growth. The suburban development emerged out of the New Deal programs to create greenbelts around large urban areas. Originally called North Greenhills, it was renamed Forest Park in 1954 and the city's first subdivision opened two years later. Forest Park grew quickly, with 8,000 people by 1960 and over 15,000 by 1970. Developers, planners, and civic leaders in Forest Park maintained a vision of the suburb as "a conventional bedroom suburb, a static vision which saw Forest Park as a place with housing sufficiently high-priced to insure a homogeneous upper-middle class population." Rather than developing civic mindedness, by the 1970s, Forest Park residents worried more about personal and psychological issues. Residents did not see themselves as part of Cincinnati, but instead began to draw distinctions between themselves and the big city. They battled over zoning, traffic, and city services. Forest Park began as mostly white, but by 1975 some 12 percent of the residents were African American. White residents seemed to welcome integration and at the same time became concerned about the prospects of the "ghettoization" of their city.

The suburbs attracted increasing numbers of people from Ohio's small towns. So full of possibilities in the late 1940s by the 1950s the small town of Camden faced trouble. The same forces that amazed and excited the town's residents, especially the mobility of the automobile and the television, were the same ones now eroding Camden's social fabric. Young people looked for jobs in nearby Dayton or Cincinnati, often moving to one of the suburbs surrounding those cities. Rather than shop or look for entertainment in town, Camdenites drove their cars to the larger cities and shopped for goods that they saw advertised on their televisions. A bypass of Route 127 took motorists around the town, further devastating the downtown businesses. One resident noted years later that Camden was "dead compared to when I lived there."

Another aspect of the affluent society fraught with tension revolved around the increasing emphasis on traditional family life. The nuclear family became the ideal, touted in popular and scientific circles as able to meet all the postwar needs of Ohioans. In this ideal, men were the patriarchs, working for wages while women remained homemakers. Women were to subordinate their needs to those of the husband and children. Experts, religious and secular opinion leaders, and media outlets all reinforced the message. Popular television shows at the time, such as *Leave it to Beaver* and *Father Knows Best* featured this ideal family unit. A popular 1947 book, *Modern Woman: The Lost Sex* argued that women who sought paid employment were psychologically abnormal. There were, of course, women who embraced the role of wife and homemaker. Women married younger and had more babies than previous generations. Yet there were trends pointing in the opposite direction. Ohio native Erma Bombeck captured some of this in her newspaper writings. Bombeck had begun a career in journalism in the 1940s, but quit to become a full-time homemaker. After the birth of her second son, she resumed her writing career. In her humorous ways, Bombeck became a social critic, supporting the domestic ideal but satirizing it at the same time. Like Bombeck, by the 1950s, more women were working for wages than ever before. Those who felt overwhelmed, unhappy, or who challenged the idealized expectations of domesticity were labeled deviant. Tranquilizer use skyrocketed, and by 1959 Americans, mainly women, consumed some 1.15 million pounds a year. The 1950s led to the highest teen pregnancy rates in U.S. history, prompting one historian to note that in the 1950s young "people were not taught how to 'say no'—they were simply handed wedding rings."

Still another postwar consumer revolution daunted those attempting to enforce stability in postwar society—rock and roll. Rock appeared to threaten tradition, with its mixture of rebellion, sex, race, self-fulfillment, and consumerism. As the baby boomers became "teenagers," they also became the major consumers of this new form of expression, with the time, money, and desire to merge these threads together. In contrast with the romantic ballads and soothing sounds of pop music that featured crooning singers like Frank Sinatra, Perry Como, Nat King Cole, and Johnny Mathis, rock grew out of rhythm and blues (R&B). Music and recordings of R&B, dubbed "race records" because of the black artists who recorded them, drew on the musical traditions of African Americans, such as blues and gospel. Its singers grunted, growled, and yelled over the pounding sounds of pianos, guitars, saxophones, and drums that all played a vibrant dance rhythm. White artists, especially Elvis Presley, further blurred the social and musical barriers of the time, blending R&B, country, and even gospel. Rock was "body music" as one scholar put it; lewd, loud, and dangerous according to most adults and self-appointed arbiters of taste and social mores at the time.

The Rock and Roll Hall of Fame is in Cleveland, and for good reason. In the late 1940s, Leo Mintz, the Jewish owner of the Record Rendezvous, noticed that sales of jazz and big band music had dropped off in his store, but the teenagers who visited, especially the growing number of white ones, would dance when an R&B song played. At the time, area radio stations refused to play these "race records," but Mintz hoped to change that. He began calling the music rock 'n' roll, a term for sex that had been used in blues since the 1920s. Alan Freed, a white DJ from WAKR in Akron befriended Mintz and, impressed with how the teenagers reacted to the music, began using the term and playing the songs as novelties on his afternoon show. With Mintz's assistance in 1951 Freed moved to WJW in Cleveland. With Mintz as his show's sponsor and handing him records, Freed called himself the "Moondog" and became the first DJ to play and promote rock 'n' roll, playing recordings of black artists to the mainly white audience during his "Moondog Rock & Roll House Party" from 11:15 p.m. to 2 a.m. Building on the success of the radio show, Freed and Mintz then worked with promoters to host the first rock concert, the Moondog Coronation Ball in March 1952 at the Cleveland Arena that featured black artists including the Dominoes (see Figure 15.4). An interracial crowd filled to capacity the 10,000-seat arena, and when the music began thousands more who were waiting to get inside stormed the entrance. Fighting broke out in the audience and after one song the concert ended. It took the police and fire departments hours to clear the arena and stop the fighting. Afterwards, the story spread over the front pages of newspapers in Cleveland and then around the world. Rock had arrived.

Migration and the Changing Cities

It is no wonder that rock came together in Cleveland, which bustled with economic activity and possessed the largest African American population of any Ohio city, as well as a mixture of whites migrating in from rural Ohio, Appalachia, and the Deep South. In short order, rock became one of several precipitants that pushed race relations into the public arena. The experience of World War II transformed the relationship between whites and blacks. For veterans, the experience of fighting in a Jim Crow military to end fascism

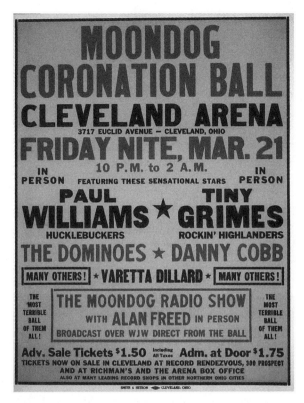

Figure 15.4 The "Moondog Coronation Ball" in 1952 is regarded as the first ever major rock concert. Freed was born in Pennsylvania, but grew up in Salem, Ohio. While other disc jockeys in the United States played R&B records, Freed was the one calling the music rock 'n' roll. Freed had promoted several dances in the northeast Ohio region before sponsoring the large show at the Cleveland Arena. After the concert, Freed's popularity soared and he moved to New York City, but in 1960 he was indicted on payola charges stemming from a national investigation into the recording industry. The legal battles took their toll on Freed, who died of kidney failure in 1965.

abroad only served to heighten their desire to end discrimination at home. Meanwhile, longer term trends also undermined segregation. The mechanization of agriculture in the South, coupled with urbanization, pushed African Americans out of the old rural system, which in turn provided a strong inducement for dismantling the Jim Crow social and political structure. In a continuation of the migrations that had begun in the early twentieth century, African Americans left the rural South for better opportunities and looser racial customs in Southern cities and eventually urban areas in the North and West.

Segregated Ohio

As they had been before, Ohio's cities became important destinations for black migrants. Ohio ranked fourth in states in which the nonwhite population increased in the 1950s. This migration of blacks, occurring in the post-World War II years, happened in conjunction with changes that distinguished this era of migration from earlier ones. Ohio's population grew from 7,946,627 in 1950 to 10,652,017 in 1970. By the 1960s, most of the economic growth lay in the burgeoning suburbs, not the central cities where most black migrants went. Using annexation, Columbus and Toledo managed to grow steadily in the 1950s and 1960s. Canton, Cincinnati, Cleveland and Youngstown all declined over the course of the postwar decades, while Akron and Dayton grew in the 1950s but declined in the 1960s. The postwar years saw an increase in segregation, too as the number of African Americans living in these cities increased and whites continued their transition to the suburbs.

Segregation occurred in several ways. Southern segregation mainly came through the law—*de jure*—as opposed to Northern segregation which was by custom—*de facto*. While different in form from the South, segregation and inequality were facts of the African American experience in Ohio and throughout the North. Indeed, after World War II the Midwest had become the most residentially segregated region in the nation, with Cleveland topping the list of most segregated cities. Real estate agents used various techniques that spurred this process along. In so-called "blockbusting," agents would sell a home in a largely white neighborhood to a black family. Then, the real estate agents would play on the fears of whites in that neighborhood to entice them to sell their homes at a lower price "before it was too late." In turn, the real estate agents would then sell the home at a higher value to incoming blacks, often at high interest rates. In addition, construction of interstate highways isolated and separated poorer, mainly African American neighborhoods from wealthier, mostly white ones. Other tactics included red-lining, whereby mortgage companies drew red lines on maps to designate areas (usually populated by African Americans) where those companies would often refuse to make loans, and neighborhood covenants to keep African Americans out of certain sections of the city and suburban communities. Techniques like this continued even after the Supreme Court ruled racial covenants legally unenforceable in 1948.

Two examples illustrate the trend. During the 1940s and 1950s, blacks that did settle in Cleveland lived mostly in the areas of Central, Glenville, and Hough. These Cleveland neighborhoods had been ethnic enclaves since the late nineteenth century, but by the postwar years they became populated largely by African Americans. Population density in these areas increased, and landlords subdivided homes into smaller apartments and increased rents. School segregation increased as well. Cleveland's growing combination of racial problems in housing, jobs, and schools could be seen in Ohio's other major cities.

In his memoir, *Dancing with Strangers*, Mel Watkins, who became a writer and editor for the *New York Times Book Review*, recalls his youth in Youngstown during the 1940s and 1950s as he became conscious of how race defined his life and that of whites. When he was a child he had friend, Al Bright, who was the only black member of the championship little league team. To celebrate, the team went to the South Side Park. As the team entered the swimming pool there, the lifeguard stopped Al and denied him entry, enforcing the customary ban on interracial swimming. While the rest of the team swam, Al was forced to stay outside the fence, sitting on his blanket as coaches and parents brought food and drinks to him. For Watkins, hearing about his friend's experience reinforced "a subtle seemingly inexplicable sense of outwardly imposed restraint and negation of self-worth." Ohio possessed a "congenial Midwestern atmosphere and surface tranquility that insistently suggested all was right with the world. Everyone was promised a bright future. Well, nearly everyone."

While segregation within the central city defined much of the postwar black experience, African Americans were not exempt from the postwar suburban story. In Chagrin Falls Park, outside Cleveland, African Americans crafted their own version of suburbia. To most whites, the community of some 900 people resembled a "shanty town." Magnolia Strickland and other African American residents praised the "open space, fresh air, gardens and the opportunity to own a home." She told a reporter: "I got five rooms; they all got heat from an oil furnace. I got an electric stove and hot and cold running water from my well—and it's all paid for...I couldn't have done all that in Cleveland." For these African Americans, the move to Chagrin Falls Park embodied a mixture of internal choice and external limitations. The experience tended to reinforce black identity in the suburban context and set the stage for the expansion of the black middle class.

In the 1960s, Ohio's white population grew by 8.3 percent but the African American population increased by 26.1 percent. This growth came not from new migrants into the state, but from births, which meant that people were now bypassing Ohio as they settled in other states to build their lives. Ohio had a net migration of –125,581 during the 1960s. The drop in white citizens of 191,401 was offset by the 68,820 new African American residents. Within the state, central cities had a net loss of 458,999 people, and rural areas a loss of 85,725. The winners in this scenario were suburban communities, which saw a net positive migration of 419,143. Combined with births, the suburban rings saw an increase of 893,563 people in the 1960s. Tables 15.1 and 15.2 show a variety of population statistics.

On a positive note, the increasing numbers of African Americans gave them greater influence and potential political power in the postwar years. Black-dominated organizations grew in strength, including branches of the NAACP, the Urban League, and the Congress of Racial Equality (CORE), as well as institutions such as churches and fraternal lodges. There were all-black schools of high-quality as well. These organizations maintained a strong sense of African American community against the negative trends inside Ohio's central cities.

The need to maintain a strong community became even greater as living conditions, schools, and employment prospects all began to deteriorate in the 1950s and 1960s.

Table 15.1 Total population, central cities

	1950	1960	1970
Akron	274,605	290,351	275,425
Canton	116,912	113,631	110,053
Cincinnati	503,998	502,550	452,524
Cleveland	914,808	876,050	750,903
Columbus	375,901	471,316	539,677
Dayton	243,872	262,332	243,601
Toledo	303,616	318,003	383,818
Youngstown	168,330	166,689	139,788

Table 15.2   African American population

	1950	Percent of population in 1950	1960	Percent of population in 1960	1970	Percent of population in 1970
Akron	23,762	8.7	37,636	13.0	48,205	17.5
Canton	7,102	6.1	11,055	9.7	13,766	12.5
Cincinnati	78,196	15.5	108,754	21.6	125,070	27.6
Cleveland	147,847	16.2	250,818	28.6	287,841	38.3
Columbus	46,692	12.4	77,140	16.4	99,627	18.5
Dayton	34,151	14.0	57,288	21.8	74,284	30.5
Toledo	25,026	8.2	40,015	12.6	52,915	13.8
Youngstown	21,459	12.7	31,677	19.0	35,285	25.2

Cleveland, with the state's largest concentration of African Americans, could not adequately house or teach its growing student population. From 99,686 students in 1950 the district grew to 148,793 by 1963. In 1960 the city ranked among the lowest in professional staff per pupil, 38 per 1,000. By contrast, the suburb of Beachwood had 63 per 1,000. Cleveland also ranked lowest in per pupil expenditures within Cuyahoga County and 90 of its 174 schools were over 50 years old. Some 93 percent of the city's elementary students, 78 percent of its middle school students, and 83 percent of its high school students attended either all-white or all-black schools. In 1960 the Cleveland school district placed 14,000 students, mainly on the black east side, on half-days because of a lack of space and shortage of teachers.

At the same time, a set of economic and political adjustments undermined the ability of Ohio to compete with other states and regions and exacerbated the racial dynamics of poverty and inequality. The fastest growing areas of the nation in the postwar years were in the South and West, where the Cold War fostered a strong economic connection between military contracts, job growth, and population expansion. The economy of Ohio and most of its large cities remained tied to traditional manufacturing. The greatest job concentrations were in six cyclically sensitive industries: primary metals, fabricated metals, electrical equipment, nonelectrical machinery, transportation equipment, and rubber. As late as 1980 these six accounted for 25 percent of Ohio's nonagricultural employment, as opposed to 14 percent for the nation as a whole. This was second only to Michigan and Indiana. Moreover, the overall employment in these industries began to decline, and those jobs that did remain began to demand higher skill levels. Discrimination prevented many African Americans from obtaining the training needed to obtain these dwindling manufacturing jobs and from getting the education needed for work in newer, growing industries such as services and technology. A job in manufacturing had once been an important rung on the ladder of success for immigrants and African Americans, but it was now vanishing. At the same time, Ohio's cities faced a host of social and economic problems centered on the interrelated issues of poverty, crime, housing, schools, and employment. This dual transformation for African Americans in urban Ohio—greater numbers and political influence coupled with segregation and limited opportunities—increased racial tensions and spurred political activism associated with civil rights and black freedom.

Nationally, there were a series of dramatic events during the 1950s that challenged some of the growing divide between white and black. In 1948 President Truman ordered the U.S. military to desegregate, and the Korean War would become the first in which troops fought in integrated units. The landmark Supreme Court case of *Brown v. Board of Education* in 1954 ruled that "separate but equal" held no place in public education. From December 1955 to December 1956 a boycott of city buses in Montgomery, Alabama ended segregation there on public transportation and brought to the public's attention Rosa Parks and Martin Luther King, Jr. Then in 1957, as whites across the South promised massive resistance to desegregation rulings of *Brown*, President Eisenhower was forced to send in federal troops to integrate Little Rock High School in Arkansas.

In Ohio, city and state leaders responded slowly to racial issues and the larger social and economic challenges. In 1950 Cleveland enacted the first fair employment practices law in the nation. Democrat Anthony Celebrezze became mayor of Cleveland in 1953 and served until 1962, when he resigned to accept an appointment in the Kennedy administration as Secretary of Health, Education, and Welfare. As mayor, Celebrezze recognized the growing issues within Cleveland and tried to address them. He supported the continued building of freeways through Cleveland, which improved the flow of goods and people, but had the negative effect of destroying housing and facilitating the loss of population to the suburbs. Other transportation improvements came to Cleveland's port and the Burke Lakefront Airport. Yet under Celebrezze, Cleveland's welfare rolls increased as did poverty and unemployment for African Americans.

One of the main techniques Celebrezze and other big city mayors used to remake the urban landscape came through projects funded with federal money and dubbed "urban renewal." Such projects revealed that the glimmering façade of postwar prosperity contained within it the makings of the rust belt. In the 1930s and early 1940s, studies of central Cleveland and Cincinnati concluded that each city already showed the markings of decline. The Queen City, one report noted, was at a crossroads "between becoming a static or retrogressive community" or becoming a "focal point for a large surrounding territory." These concerns brought about the first wave of urban renewal, funded primarily by the Housing Act of 1949, which allowed cities to receive federal money to regenerate their central core. Later federal programs added to this legislative foundation.

Cleveland's major project that received national attention was Erieview, a downtown redevelopment project initiated by Celebrezze in 1960 and designed by renowned architect I.M. Pei, which originally called for a mixture of high-rise buildings, low-rise structures, and parks. The centerpiece was Erieview Tower, a 40-story skyscraper finished in 1964. Little else followed, however, and most of the space cleared for the plan became parking surfaces. Sadly, most urban renewal money went to projects like Erieview, mixtures of commercial, light industrial, and apartment complexes for middle- and upper-income residents. Lower income residents, who were largely African American, were displaced into already crowded areas. The Kenyon-Barr project in Cincinnati followed this pattern. Trumpeted as part of making the Queen City the "city of tomorrow," the plan called for erasing the city's oldest black neighborhood, and replacing some 2,500 structures (many of which were truly decrepit) with a combination of expressway and mixed-use residential and commercial buildings. African Americans in the area supported the project, believing that they would be brought back into the renovated district. As the plan developed into the 1960s and early 1970s, however, most of the space was sold off to commercial interests. Some new housing did emerge but the once vibrant center of Cincinnati's black political and social life had been erased. Only about one-quarter of the area returned as residential. The city's white leaders called it a success. Black Cincinnatians saw it differently. This divergence of collective memory fed the growing racial tensions in postwar Ohio.

Meanwhile, at the state level under Democratic governor Michael DiSalle, Ohio approved the creation of the Ohio Civil Rights Commission in 1959. The Commission investigated the conditions of African Americans in a variety of areas and detailed extensive discrimination in housing, education, employment, and public facilities. Ohio also approved a Fair Housing Law in 1965, but its provisions and enforcement remained weak. It exempted one and two family buildings with resident owners, while local authorities often ignored it, allowing discriminatory practices to continue.

Appalachian migration

The growing numbers of African Americans mixed increasingly with Appalachians, who also migrated to Ohio in large numbers during and after World War II. Between 1940 and 1970 some 1 million mountain people left for the Buckeye State. Most were white, but about 50,000 were African Americans. They followed the highways to Ohio's cities in a general pattern, Kentuckians to Cincinnati and Dayton, and West Virginians to northeast Ohio cities such as Akron, Ashtabula, and Cleveland. Columbus took in migrants from both places. As it had been for millions of other migrants, Appalachians looked to Ohio for jobs and a better life. Ohio companies wanted them. For example, Buckeye Steel chartered buses to bring Appalachians to its steel plant in Columbus and other firms regularly advertised in Appalachian newspapers. Word of mouth worked, too. By the early 1970s, one-third of all industrial workers in Ohio were Appalachian.

The lives of many Appalachians had been centered on three major traits: familialism, Protestant fundamentalism, and individualism. They tended to bring these values with them as they moved. Most migrants were young men or young families who already had relatives in Ohio. The majority had an eighth grade education, with about one-third possessing a high school diploma or higher. Like other newcomers at times Appalachians faced a rough transition. They left behind family, friends, and social practices, and had to adjust to factory work, urban life, new customs, and a different landscape. Some harassment and ridicule came from their accent. Appalachians also brought musical traditions such as country and folk that reshaped Ohio and national culture. Dwight Yoakum moved with his family from Pikeville, Kentucky to Columbus in the late 1950s. He played rockabilly as he attended Ohio State before moving on to Nashville and Los Angeles. One of Yoakum's songs, "Readin', Rightin', and Rt. 23" refers to the main route between Kentucky and Columbus.

Appalachians also enriched Ohio's religious diversity, bringing new styles of worship and expanding Protestant denominations. Those that worshipped tended to prefer Pentecostal and Southern Baptist traditions, which emphasized emotional worship style, individual salvation, and literal interpretation of the Bible. As a result, Southern Baptists were the fastest growing denomination in Ohio during the 1950s. These new trends were reflected in the growth of such institutions as Dallas Franklin Billington's Akron Baptist Temple. Born in Kentucky, Billington moved to Akron in 1923 to work in the rubber industry. His church began with 14 people in 1934, but by 1949 the church claimed 15,000 members, which *Life* magazine described as the largest Baptist Church in the nation. The Akron area was also home to Ernest Angley and Rex Humbard, both of whom used radio and then television to become two of the most influential "televangelists." Their ministries now reach millions around the world.

Angley and Humbard joined Billy Graham as symbols of a broad trend in postwar American society in which Christianity became an important part of social life. Two-thirds of Americans claimed church membership by the end of the 1950s and 97 percent stated they believed in God. As they moved into their suburban retreats, more and more Ohioans looked for a postwar world that was homogeneous, safe, quiet, and free from controversy. Religion fitted these desires. Rather than emphasize doctrinal or theological differences religion served to unify society, particularly in the suburbs. Religion also became a measure of Americanism, fusing into a growing opposition to communism. In 1954, Congress added the words "under God" to the Pledge of Allegiance and ordered the phrase "In God We Trust" placed on all coins and currency. In 1956 "In God We Trust" became the national motto. Ohio followed these national trends, adopting a new state motto, "With God, all things are possible" in 1959.

The Cold War and Ohio Politics

As much as the issues of mass consumption, suburbia, and racial tensions occupied Ohioans in the postwar years, perhaps nothing was more pervasive as anticommunism and the Cold War. The struggle for global dominance between the United States and the Soviet Union in the years following 1945 dominated foreign policy and politics. The Cold War worked in tandem with various postwar economic and social trends and underscored the pressure for conformity, squelching challenges to the status quo and adding to the growing tensions at work in postwar Ohio.

The "Red Scare"

Each international incident in the Cold War deepened anticommunism across the nation. Of particular importance were the success of the Communists in China under Mao Zedong in 1949 and the outbreak of the Korean War in June 1950. In responding to the conflict in Korea, U.S. troops comprised the majority of a United Nations (UN) force that came under the initial command of Douglas McArthur. UN troops pushed North

Korean armed forces out of the South and back towards the Chinese border, but as they neared the border, Chinese forces entered to aid the North Koreans. The war ground to a stalemate by 1951, and lasted until an armistice was signed in 1953. During the conflict, Ohioans accounted for 1,777 dead and 4,837 wounded in what many have labeled "the Forgotten War," coming as it did between World War II and Vietnam.

At the time, the Korean War was anything but forgotten. The war and the success of Mao in China fed into a growing desire to root out communism at home. This dominated politics from the 1940s to the 1960s, spreading to cover all aspects of life in Ohio. This anticommunism fed what became the second Red Scare, more commonly known as McCarthyism after Senator Joseph McCarthy, a Republican from Wisconsin, led a series of investigations during the height of his power from 1950 to 1954. The remnants of the Communist Party (CP) in the United States as well as spies for the Soviet Union became the initial targets. Certainly there were spies in the United States, but it is clear that the threat posed by the 40–50,000 members of Communist Party was exaggerated. Moreover, while the CP and Soviet spies were the expressed targets, the effort to root out subversion quickly spread to include attacks against a much broader set of behaviors and beliefs that challenged the status quo. In addition, the government hearings and investigations that emerged served partisan political purposes, as conservatives used them to attack not only leftists but liberals as well, especially the Truman administration. In turn, many liberals turned on leftists and adopted strong anticommunist rhetoric and actions. Early actions at the federal level included Executive Order 9835, issued in 1947 by President Truman, which broadened the grounds for dismissal of federal employees to include not only treason and espionage, but also membership in, or sympathetic association with, Communists or other groups deemed subversive. Those active in civil rights or unions were vulnerable, as were gays and lesbians. For example, President Eisenhower revised the program in 1953 to tighten security investigations and for the first time in civil service law stated that federal workers could be fired or not hired for "sexual perversion."

Across the nation, organizations responded to fears of subversion through various means. State and local governments, as well as private employers, began to impose political tests on current and prospective employees. Public schools, colleges, and universities forced teachers and faculty to sign loyalty oaths. Ohio State University approved a series of regulations limiting what faculty could discuss and which groups could speak on campus. Other organizations used background checks or investigations. The Committee of Industrial Organizations (CIO) expelled leftist unions from its membership, and individual unions such as the UAW and USW in turn purged Communists and other leftists from leadership positions. George DeNucci, shown in Figure 15.5, head of the Cleveland CIO Council followed the instructions from CIO President Phillip Murray to drive out Communists and led the effort at the state level to oust left-leaning members of the Ohio CIO executive board. DeNucci would go on to fight Communists in CIO unions throughout the United States. Ironically, DeNucci himself was accused of being a Communist. He was denied a passport because his name was on the mailing list for the *Daily Worker* and an FBI agent in the Ohio River city of Portsmouth had reported DeNucci as attending a meeting at a cleaning establishment at 3966 Gallia Street, known to be a front for Communists. After two years he was finally able to clear his name. He

Figure 15.5   George DeNucci played a key role in organizing Ohio workers during the 1930s and in the divisive years of the early Cold War. Born in Italy in 1902 he moved with his family to join his father in Parkersburg, West Virginia who had secured work as a tailor there with a textile firm. DeNucci moved to Columbus when the company moved there and joined his father working at the firm. George became active in union activities during the 1930s, and rose rapidly from president of Local 245 of the United Garment Workers to one of the chief organizers for the CIO. As the Cold War fed strong anticommunism in Ohio and across the nation, DeNucci joined in efforts to oust radicals from the CIO. He remained active in union activities until his death in 1979.
Source: Courtesy of the Ohio Historical Society (AL02814)

had repeatedly requested that the U.S. Postal Service stop delivery of the unwanted pub-lications and it turned out that DeNucci had attended steelworkers meetings at the Eagles Hall, 3900 Gallia Street. The FBI informant's zeroes looked like sixes.

Within Ohio, the Red Scare peaked between 1950 and 1954. In 1950, the *Cincinnati Enquirer* ran an exposé on communism in the city and then invited the federal House Un-American Activities Commission (HUAC) to the city to conduct hearings, which came just weeks after start of Korean War. In the 1950 elections, voters put Republicans in charge of the Ohio House and Senate and the GOP used the power to put forward a stronger antisubversive program, the centerpiece of which was the Ohio Un-American Activities Commission (OUAC). With voting along party lines, Republicans succeeded in sending a bill to Democratic Governor Lausche, who went against his party and signed the bill into law. Chairing the OUAC for the first session, 1951–52 was Gordon Renner, Speaker of the House from Cincinnati, who according to fellow Republican William Saxbe, was "a nice little guy who drank too much, exerted little control, but followed orders." Samuel Devine of Columbus, who would go on to serve in the U.S. House of Representatives from 1959 to 1981, took over for 1953–54.

The pattern for the OUAC hearings like those in Congress was to subpoena "friendly" witnesses, usually people who had been working for the FBI and had infiltrated the Communist Party to provide evidence of various activities, or radicals in the labor movement and former CP members. Then, the commission would call individuals who had been named as subversives. Commission members already knew these individuals' backgrounds. The goal of the Commission was merely exposure for political gain and to apply pressure to get the individuals to name others. The Commission held hearings in Akron, Canton, Cincinnati, Cleveland, and Columbus and sought to identify the political beliefs and associations of various individuals. Among those who refused to answer these questions were a Cleveland schoolteacher who was fired for "unbecoming behavior" and Admiral Kilpatrick, an African American from Cleveland who was fired from his job at Westinghouse for being a member of the CP and the former head of a local 735 of the Mine, Metal and Smelters Union. A number of working-class women also appeared before the Commission, and like others, they largely refused to testify about their political affiliations. The male members of the Commission often assumed these women had been influenced by their husbands or other men, as opposed to being politically active and aware in their own right.

The investigations revealed no activity designed to threaten Ohio's government. The immediate results were to cite twenty-two people for contempt of court and the passage of further antisubversive legislation. Senate Bill 38 barred communists from public employment, House Bill 575 required public employees to testify about their communist activity and House Bill 308 confiscated funds from subversive organizations and appointed the state attorney general to maintain records on Communism in the state. Only a handful of people associated with the Communist Party were punished under these laws, but the real points of the hearings were to narrow political debate and enforce certain social and cultural norms.

Conservative political success

Such actions only reinforced the conservative trend in Ohio politics. As governor during this era, Democrat Frank Lausche was at the center of this activity. Lausche, the son of Slovenian immigrants from Cleveland is Ohio's only five-term governor, serving from 1945–47 and again from 1949 to 1957. His tenure is noteworthy as well since the state assembly and Ohio's members of Congress were overwhelmingly Republican. Lausche was popular for a number of reasons. In keeping with a dominant trend in Ohio's politics, he was a fiscal conservative and moderated himself on various issues including race. His ethnic background gave him strong support in Cleveland and other ethnic communities. He regularly endorsed Republicans and often battled against his own party and their allies, especially organized labor. With regard to anticommunism, Lausche generally supported these efforts more than he spoke against them. Lausche favored the creation of the OUAC, loyalty oaths, and rules regarding speakers at Ohio State, but vetoed anticommunist legislation that authorized jail terms and fines for the targets of OUAC investigations. In his veto message of July 30, 1953, Lausche stated that he could "see nothing but grave danger to the reputation of innocent people against whom accusations can be made on the basis of rumor and frequently rooted in malice." The legislature overrode his veto.

At the same time Lausche won re-election in 1954 against the up and coming Republican James A. Rhodes, Ohio voters approved an amendment extending the governor's term in office from two years to four, effective in January 1959, and limiting the governor to two consecutive terms. Sponsored by a Republican it was clearly an effort to stop Lausche. In 1956, the popular Lausche ran successfully for the U.S. Senate, where he served two terms. Ironically, the 1954 amendment later backfired on Lausche's 1954 opponent, Rhodes. After winning two terms, Rhodes had to sit out in 1970 before running and winning again in 1974 and 1978. He had to wait until 1986 to run again, when he lost to Democrat Richard Celeste.

At the national level, Ohio voters sided with the GOP in most presidential elections and though there were some exceptions, Ohio's delegation to Congress remained largely conservative and staunchly anticommunist. In presidential elections from 1944 to 1972, Democrats captured Ohio only twice, in 1948 when Truman scored his victory against Thomas Dewey and in 1964, when Lyndon Johnson won against Barry Goldwater. Republicans dominated Ohio's House delegation during the 1950s. Among those serving Ohio were Republicans Frances P. Bolton and Oliver O. Bolton. Elected in 1952, they were the first mother-son team in the House. Ironically, with Democrats in control of the House of Representatives from 1955 to 1994, the dominance of Republicans in Ohio's delegation meant that the state never had the clout to lead committees and gain influence. Liberal democrats Charles Vanik of Cleveland and Thomas Ashley of Toledo, both elected in 1954, were the exceptions to the conservative trend and there was some moderation among Ohio's Republicans in the House. Although conservative on other issues, Representative William McCulloch of Piqua strongly backed civil rights and cosponsored the landmark Civil Rights Act of 1964. His support was critical to the passage of the legislation and earned the moniker "Mr. Civil Rights of the GOP." He had fellow GOP allies on this issue including Clarence J. "Bud" Brown of Blanchester in Clinton County. Brown had worked closely with Virginia Democrat Howard W. Smith to block liberal legislation coming from presidents John Kennedy and Lyndon Johnson. However, in 1964 he supported the Civil Rights Act. Brown again broke with his conservative record to support the Voting Rights Act of 1965, checking himself out of the hospital to get the bill through Smith's Rules Committee. Brown died days after Johnson signed the bill into law in August.

Ohioans also gained political appointments from presidents. Former Republican mayor of Cleveland Harold Burton had been appointed to the Supreme Court by Truman. Potter Stewart of Cincinnati took his place under Eisenhower in 1958. In the Eisenhower administration was Michigan-born but Ohio resident secretary of the treasury George Humphrey, chairman of the board of M.A. Hanna and Company. Ohio-born and General

Motors president Charles Wilson served as secretary of defense, succeeded in 1957 by Procter and Gamble president Neil McElroy of Cincinnati. Arthur E. Flemming, former president of Ohio Wesleyan University, served in 1958 as Secretary of Health, Education and Welfare. Anthony Celebrezze, former mayor of Cleveland, served in that capacity under John F. Kennedy and Lyndon Johnson.

Ohio's U.S. Senators were also mainly from the GOP during the 1940s and 1950s. Robert Taft served until his death in 1953, and his seat went to Republican George Bender until 1957 when Lausche took over. Meanwhile, John Bricker served from 1947 to 1959, when he lost to the Democratic septuagenarian Stephen Young who served from 1959 to 1971, when Republican Robert A. Taft, Jr. took the seat.

O'Neill, DiSalle and the "right to work" controversy

Young's victory over Bricker in the 1958 election was an upset, for Bricker seemed invincible but in 1958 the Republicans miscalculated in supporting one of the key issues in postwar Ohio politics: the "right to work" amendment to Ohio's constitution. Labor organized across the state to defeat the law and Young was able to capitalize on this. So, too was Democrat Michael V. DiSalle who bested incumbent C. William O'Neill of Marietta to become the first governor to serve a four-year term under the state's new law.

O'Neill, a lawyer, seemed destined for political success. In 1938 at the age of twenty-two he became the youngest person ever elected to the Ohio House. At thirty he became the state's youngest Speaker of the House, and at thirty-four the state's youngest Attorney General, a post he held from 1950 to 1957. In his career, O'Neill staked out a moderate position, decidedly distinct from the conservatism of Taft and Bricker. As Attorney General, O'Neill gained attention for investigations that led to new legislation on drug trafficking, and forcing the state board of education to uphold the 1954 landmark Supreme Court decision on school desegregation in *Brown v. Board of Education*. He maintained a strong anticommunist stance, but distanced himself from McCarthy. In 1956, Eisenhower coasted to a second presidential term and O'Neill handily defeated DiSalle in Ohio's gubernatorial contest with 56 percent of the vote and winning eighty-three counties. O'Neill outspent his opponent $233,847 to $82,179. This included, for the first time, the wide use of television advertising, with O'Neill spending nearly $60,000 to DiSalle's $18,281.

As the state's youngest governor, O'Neill, of Irish background but Baptist in faith, maintained wide popular appeal. With the state's population growing and its industries expanding, he argued for more highway construction, increased services, and greater spending on mental health, education, and conservation. While these issues placed O'Neill in the moderate to liberal camp and earned the support of voters who might usually support Democrats, he argued vociferously against new taxes. O'Neill, like Lausche before him, opposed taxes on philosophical grounds, but they both also had the advantage of relying on the state's growing revenues to expand services.

With a record of success at each office, there seemed no reason to suspect that O'Neill would falter. But a series of events made him vulnerable. The energetic governor had promised action, but in 1957 little had been done and he appeared indecisive and failed to respond positively to various criticisms leveled by the press. Then, in January 1958 O'Neill suffered a heart attack and he was confined to rest through March. A recession in 1957 drove unemployment higher, hitting Ohio's manufacturing sector particularly hard. The state's economy was slower to recover than the rest of the nation and Ohioans still felt the effects of the downturn by the fall of 1958. In the midst of all this came the right to work amendment—Proposal 2 on the 1958 ballot—put forward by local chambers of commerce, retail merchants, industrialists, and conservative Republicans. Particularly popular in the South, right to work laws weakened union organizing by allowing workers in union shops to refuse union membership. Supporters believed Ohioans would easily approve the change. The anticommunist crusade had organized labor on the defensive. In 1955 voters had issued labor a stinging rebuke in refusing by a two-to-one margin amendments to reform the state's unemployment compensation system. Republican victories in the 1956 elections added to the growing sense that labor's influence could be further diminished. Apparently even the bookies on Cleveland's notorious Short Vincent Street were offering 7–5 odds on a right-to-work victory.

Yet several factors allowed organized labor to wield sufficient political muscle in 1958. One was the merger of the AFL and CIO in 1955. The AFL had always been the larger and more conservative organization, focusing on skilled trades dominated by white males, and eschewing most political activity to focus instead on securing good wages and benefits for its members through contracts with employers. The CIO, formed in the tumultuous years of the Great Depression, welcomed all workers regardless of skill and aligned itself with FDR and the New Deal. The AFL and CIO had competed fiercely for members, but a series of events brought them together. World War II inspired unity for the duration of the conflict and the passage of Taft–Hartley served to convince many union leaders that labor's divisions would only weaken the movement. Both the AFL and CIO came under new leadership in 1953, with George Meany taking the reins of the AFL and Walter Reuther the CIO. By 1955, they had worked out a merger agreement. State bodies still had to ratify and in Ohio the negotiations moved slowly. Unlike nationally, in the heavily industrialized Buckeye State the CIO was more numerous and powerful than the AFL and those in the CIO did not want to lose this influence within a new organization. At the same time, the more conservative unions, especially the building trades, still opposed joining with the more activist ones in the CIO. However, the "right-to-work" would affect the building trades especially, which were solidly union shop organizations. This, the political success of antiunion conservatives, and pressure from national leaders removed the remaining resistance. On May 7, 1958 Ohio representatives created the state version of the AFL-CIO and used the new found sense of unity to counter the "right-to-work". Unions put together their own campaign and voter registration drive to match that of business. Jane Adams, head of the new Ohio AFL-CIO Women's Activities Division, organized over a thousand housewives to make calls and send out letters. Unions reached out for help with leadership in other organizations. Leaders of the Ohio NAACP joined in opposing Proposal 2 and African American newspapers editorialized against it as well, equating those supporting "right-to-work" with those who supported segregation in the South. President of the Columbus CIO Harry

Figure 15.6 "Right-to-work" laws had been spreading amid Cold War tensions and in 1957 Indiana became the first northern state to approve one. Big business interests in Ohio took notice of this and sought to implement a similar law in Ohio in 1958. This pamphlet was part of the campaign to defeat the proposed "right-to-work law" and appealed to women as managers of the family budget. Women formed a key part of the coalition that successfully defeated the proposal. *Source*: Courtesy of the Ohio Historical Society (AL05056)

Mayfield wrote that "This is the time to start our campaign against the Chamber's 'right-to-work' program. This is the time to realize that your enemies mean business… Now is the time to start OUR fight!" (see Figure 15.6).

State Republican Chair Ray Bliss and John Bricker had urged supporters of Proposal 2 to wait until 1959 to put the measure through. Bricker warned business leaders that the issue would threaten all Republicans in the state during an election season, but he was met with "chortles of disbelief." Bricker and Bliss proved correct. O'Neill publicly endorsed the amendment and then tied his re-election bid directly to "right-to-work" in an effort to revive his chances. Meanwhile DiSalle stated that he was against the "right-to-work", but refused to make it a centerpiece of his campaign. In the end, DiSalle bested O'Neill in their rematch, capturing 57 percent of the vote. The amendment was defeated by an even larger margin, 63 percent. Indeed, more people voted against the amendment than for DiSalle. Overall, 1958 proved to be a good one for Democrats. Bricker lost in an upset to Stephen Young, and Democrats captured the Ohio House and

Senate and all statewide offices except secretary of state. Nationally, Democrats won twenty-two of thirty-two governorships and gained forty-nine seats in the House of Representatives. O'Neill never regretted his decision to support the amendment and his career continued to be notable. In 1960 he won election to the Ohio Supreme Court and became Chief Justice, serving until his death in 1978. Thus, O'Neill became the only Ohioan to serve in the top state posts in the legislative, executive, and judicial branches.

The first governor to serve a four year term, Michael DiSalle was born to Italian immigrant parents in New York City. His family moved to Toledo when he was three. DiSalle, like O'Neill, was short of stature but not ambition. DiSalle earned his law degree in 1931 and was elected to the Ohio House in 1936. After losing his re-election bid in 1938, he then served the city of Toledo in a number of positions, as assistant law director, member of city council, vice mayor, and then as mayor. As vice mayor he initiated a labor-management-citizens committee known as the Toledo Plan to ensure industrial harmony after World War II. As mayor he eliminated the city's debt, largely because of the enactment of a citywide 1 percent personal and business income tax, the first city income tax in Ohio and only the nation's second (the first was in Philadelphia in 1939). From 1950 to 1952 DiSalle chaired President Truman's Office of Price Stabilization during the Korean War, winning praise for his management of inflation during the conflict.

When he entered the governor's office in 1959, DiSalle put forward a program calling for $337 million in new taxes to help fund $2.1 billion in spending. The low-tax, pro-business stance of Ohio's leaders had left Ohio near the middle or bottom among states in spending on items such as education, transportation, hospitals, and social welfare. The state had relied on overall economic growth and a surplus in revenue left from the World War II years to cover increases in state spending. The Democratic legislature agreed with DiSalle's plan, and in June 1959 the package included an increase in the gasoline tax, cigarette tax, horse racing tax, and the corporate franchise tax. This increased state spending by nearly half a billion dollars. Conservatives pounced, accusing DiSalle of driving jobs out of the state. After working to get DiSalle into the governor's mansion and defeating the right to work issue, organized labor expected and received support for other items on their political agenda. One was a new law allowing workers to collect both supplemental unemployment benefits from their employer through a labor contract and benefits provided to all workers through the state unemployment system. Unions pushed this since employer contributions to the state's unemployment compensation fund were seventy cents per $100, while the national average was $1.31. The 103rd General Assembly produced increases in workers' compensation and approved a Fair Employment Practices Act that prohibited discrimination based upon race, color, religion, or national origin. DiSalle also advocated for an end to the death penalty and commuted the sentences of five men and one woman from death to life in prison. Six men were executed.

DiSalle faced a major crisis when in July 1959 some 500,000 steelworkers across the United States and 61,000 in Ohio went on strike. The strike affected 90 percent of the nation's steel output and became the largest single work stoppage in U.S. history. The strike came after industry leaders pushed the introduction of technology that threatened to end certain job practices and the elimination of jobs. During the fall, as the strike continued and workers' financial reserves dried up, steelworker families in cities like

Lorain, Niles, and Youngstown survived on union soup kitchens. In November, after 116 days and with no end in sight, President Eisenhower invoked the Taft–Hartley Act and ordered a cooling off period in which workers were required to go back to work. The Supreme Court upheld the decision and in January the strike was finally settled. The union gained a short-term victory, securing wage increases and maintaining some control on the shop floor. On the downside the strike led other industries to import foreign steel, which in the long run contributed to the contraction of the American steel industry.

DiSalle's record also includes the creation of the Department of Industrial and Economic Development, the Ohio Civil Rights Commission, and other improvements to social services in the areas of mental health and education. He authorized the creation of community colleges and university branch campuses and developed programs for gifted students and increased teacher salaries. The tax issue and DiSalle's stance against capital punishment became fodder for the 1960 elections, in which Republicans regained control of the Ohio House and Senate, and Richard Nixon won Ohio in the presidential contest that year while losing to John Kennedy overall. DiSalle pushed for greater spending in 1961, but the Republican-controlled legislature blocked his proposals, which prompted DiSalle to veto the entire appropriations bill. Eventually a smaller bill made it through and DiSalle signed it, but it left out many of his projects. DiSalle's campaign for re-election was a vigorous one, but in the end he lost by nearly 600,000 votes to James Rhodes, who would go on to become Ohio's longest serving governor and one of the state's most controversial.

James A. Rhodes

Rhodes was born in Coalton, Jackson County in 1909. His parents, coal miner James senior and his wife, Susan, had migrated to Ohio from Kentucky. In 1910, as output in the mines declined the elder Rhodes moved the family to Jasonville, Indiana to a more prosperous mining community where he became a mine manager and a Republican precinct committeeman. Rhodes's father died in 1918 during the influenza epidemic, at which time Susan took her son James and her two daughters back to Jackson in Jackson County, Ohio where they lived until 1923. Then, the family moved to Springfield where Rhodes attended high school. To help make ends meet, Rhodes worked a variety of jobs in Jackson, including collecting scrap metal, carrying newspapers, running errands, and according to Rhodes, trapping muskrats and selling them for forty cents each. As a teen in Springfield, Rhodes continued his hustling ways, selling suits and ties, booking bands, and running dances. While he and his mother worked a number of jobs, his two sisters provided the more steady income for the family, one a nurse the other a bookkeeper.

As the family struggled in the early years of the depression, Susan put the family's success in Rhodes's hands, and she urged him to attend Ohio State, where he could play basketball and possibly earn a college degree. Rhodes and family then moved to Columbus, but Rhodes soon gave up on basketball and the degree; in the one quarter he attended, Rhodes earned a "D" in English and Geography, while failing hygiene, physical education,

Figure 15.7 For some two decades no one dominated Ohio politics like James Rhodes. Voters elected him four times as governor in: 1962, 1966, 1974, and 1978. If he had been allowed by law to run in 1970 he likely would have won then as well. Rhodes is often remembered for his no nonsense approach and demeanor, as well as his ability in self-promotion. His legacy includes transforming state politics and policies to promote economic development, public works and education, and his involvement with the shootings at Kent State in May 1970.
Source: Courtesy of the Ohio Historical Society (AL04511)

and military science. As he always seemed to do, Rhodes busied himself with a variety of jobs, including being a clerk at the Ohio House of Representatives and eventually opening Jim's Place along North High Street, which became a popular hangout. With schooling and a professional career gone, politics was one way an energetic, ambitious person from the working and lower-middle class could get ahead. Rhodes credits his mother for the decision. "My mother wanted me to run for ward committeeman and in 1934 she put up six dollars. I bought six dollars worth of campaign cards and I walked every street in the ward, and knocked on every door. I defeated a man who had been committeeman for sixteen years." From this post Rhodes advanced to city auditor and then mayor of Columbus from 1944 to 1952. He became Ohio's auditor in 1952 and in 1954 sought the governorship but lost. He ran again in 1962 and won repeating this in 1966 (see Figure 15.7).

The 1962 campaign brought Rhodes into close collaboration with Ray Bliss, head of the Ohio GOP from 1949 to 1965. Rhodes adopted Bliss's vision of "New Deal Republicanism."

Bliss designed a campaign around support for more highway construction and parks, and the economy. Week after week, Rhodes delivered speeches addressing jobs and progress, punctuated with the slogan "profit is not a dirty word." An oft-repeated anecdote had Rhodes excusing himself from dinner saying he had to make his 300th speech. His wife then commented, "No, Jim, you're going to make the same speech for the 300th time." Reporters often bet on how many times Rhodes would say "jobs" in his speeches. Unfazed by the barbs, Rhodes saw jobs as the answer to all manner of social issues, including crime, divorce, and delinquency, a theme he would return to again and again during his first eight years as the urban crisis and the tumult of the 1960s grew. The Bliss-Rhodes strategy worked. In the 1962 contest, Rhodes defeated DiSalle winning 59 percent of the vote. Rhodes also made gains in traditionally Democratic areas; while in 1960 Nixon lost Cuyahoga and Lucas counties, Rhodes won them and Rhodes came within 100 votes of winning Mahoning County. Rhodes's message of no taxes, jobs, and economic security appealed to a wide range of voters, picking up enough working-class votes to cut into Democratic strongholds. He easily won re-election in 1966, carrying 87 of Ohio's 88 counties.

What frustrated Rhodes's opponents was that the governor remained popular despite offering few details on how he would create these jobs. In general Rhodes let his staff handle the details and take the political heat from reporters. Rhodes, meanwhile, played promoter-in-chief of all things Ohio. Rhodes attended the state fair every day while it ran each August. He urged Ohioans to drink more Ohio tomato juice, which he claimed would create 2,000 jobs. He organized "Rhodes's Raiders," a group of business and political leaders whose job was to travel the nation and world to attract industry to the Buckeye State, mainly advertising Ohio's low-tax environment for jobs. Once, while meeting with officials in China, Rhodes bragged about Ohio's aviation and space exploration heritage, supplementing his appeal by flapping his arms wildly and exclaiming "Wright brothers!"

While uncouth and raw, Rhodes had a vision and the energy, support, and political skill to transform most of that vision into reality. He enlarged the efforts of earlier governors who sought to put the state government to work in building Ohio's industrial capacity. Rhodes recognized that other states especially in the South and West benefitted from federal largesse in the form of defense and other government programs related to economic development. Rhodes sought to "create a financing system to facilitate capital investment, build a state bureaucracy to implement programs, emphasize the inherent relationship between education and economic growth, and cultivate R and D to stimulate prosperity." Rhodes transformed DiSalle's Department of Industrial and Economic Development (with the unfortunate acronym DIED) into the Department of Development (DOD). The renamed agency expanded from forty-two employees to seventy-four and tripled its budget to $1.8 million. The new DOD fostered plans to develop natural resources, work with the federal and local governments to promote economic growth, and collect information to generate business expansion. All of this required funds, and Rhodes's favored mechanism to raise revenue was the bond issue. He used his political popularity and skill to persuade the Republican dominated legislature and voters to go along with this massive accumulation of debt. All totaled, in Rhodes's first eight years, the state raised nearly $1.8 billion for industrial development, higher education, highways, parks, and many other projects. Of course, to maintain these facilities would require new taxes, but that was left to future governors and legislatures. In the meantime, Rhodes pushed ahead.

He aimed to create the Ohio Development Financing Commission to sell bonds and make loans to businesses. However, Rhodes's state Attorney General, William Saxbe, argued that the plan was unconstitutional and the state Supreme Court agreed. Most of the state's leaders and newspaper publishers sided with Rhodes. A few conservatives lambasted Rhodes. The *Springfield Sun* argued that the governor wanted to create a "socialized lending and credit agency to take the place of the state's, private and highly adequate, banking structure." Undaunted, Rhodes took the issue to the voters and in 1965 they approved an amendment to the state constitution that allowed the state to issue bonds and make loans for capital improvements that "directly or indirectly create jobs, enhance employment opportunities, and improve the economic welfare of the people of the state." Similar proposals would emerge again the 1990s and 2000s.

More than any other governor, Rhodes expanded the public university and vocational education systems in Ohio. In June 1963, the legislature approved his plan to create the Ohio Board of Regents to centralize authority over the state's public universities. Despite their initial opposition, the presidents of the six major universities went along with this, for Rhodes had promised $175 million in bond issues for higher education and capital improvements. Rhodes wanted a state university within 30 miles of every Ohioan, so that more Ohioans could receive a degree and, most important for Rhodes, get a job. As a result, at the end of Rhodes's first eight years instead of six state universities there were twelve. New medical schools and branch campuses were opened as were community colleges, technical, and vocational training schools. These institutions of higher learning were part of the new economy that focused upon white collar employment and were connected to the Cold War, which emphasized links between universities, industry, and government. By the 1980s and 1990s many of these universities would become the largest employers in their communities or in the state. Funding for new buildings could not mask the lack of funding for people. Ohio's rankings among states changed little under Rhodes. By 1970, the national average of per capita state spending was $35.99; Ohio ranked 41st at $30.52. In spending per full time equivalent student, Ohio ranked 30th, at $1,544. Thus, while under Rhodes Ohio invested in the physical improvement of higher education and expanded the number of institutions covered by the state, Ohio still ranked below the national average in spending. In terms of public schools, Ohio ranked 23rd in 1972, spending $871 per pupil and below the national average of $930. Under Rhodes, the state's share of support for K–12 slipped from 40 percent to 29 percent, prompting several school districts to close temporarily in 1968 and 1969.

Rhodes truly believed that his plan of jobs and progress would solve Ohio's larger economic and social issues. He focused on what he thought united Ohioans: economic security and material progress. As Rhodes saw it, "what people really want is security through a job. That's what this civil rights agitation, crime, and social problems all stem from—lack of jobs." To cure these ills, Rhodes advocated for a revamped system of education that emphasized technical education for most high school students, as opposed to a college preparatory program "which prepares many for nothing—except unemployment." This class baiting helped Rhodes politically. It secured him votes from the middle class and by constantly praising skilled workers and vocational education, he kept his support among unionized industrial workers as well.

For Rhodes, education existed to provide skills. These skills enable a person to get a job. He believed that jobs create self-sufficient, employed, satisfied citizens, who become the basis for a productive, successful society. Liberal arts programs held special opprobrium for Rhodes. He would write later: "It is significant that the uprisings plaguing our universities do not seem to be centered in the engineering, medical or scientific sections where students can gain a perspective of their future contributions to their own welfare and the welfare of people and our economy through their work. The student unrest seems to be centered in the so-called "humanities" and "social science" colleges or departments." Forcing students to take general education courses amounted to "intellectual snobbery." Behind the social problems lay snobbery, whose perpetuators could be found among those "pointy head intellectuals" that Rhodes's contemporary, Alabama governor George Wallace often railed against. Rhodes wanted a university within 30 miles of all Ohioans; but he wanted them to train "goal-oriented" students who worked hard, kept quiet, and did not question the system. Such sentiments fit well the context of Cold War Ohio.

Conclusion

The emergence and success of Rhodes, and political battles fought under his predecessors, Lausche, O'Neill, and DiSalle, reflected the Janus-faced nature of postwar Ohio. The state emerged from World War II with a strong economy and by the 1950s the public possessed a well-founded optimism about the present and future. Ohio possessed a growing population. Science and technological innovations provided advance after advance that seemed to improve the lives of many Ohioans. Overall employment remained high, especially for skilled workers and the white collar professionals earning degrees at the expanding number of colleges and universities. Unions showed their political clout by defeating right-to-work legislation and gaining a number of legislative victories. For their part, conservatives could take stock in the success of anticommunism and the Republican hold upon state government, even if Rhodes and O'Neill seemed too close to mainstream New Deal-style liberalism. New consumer goods, purchased in the expanding shopping centers near suburban homes, provided what many Ohioans defined as the good life. With highways upon which to ride, automobiles provided added status and the mobility to enjoy leisure activities, especially tourism. By many measures, there was much to admire in Ohio's postwar status quo.

Yet the status quo masked critical issues. The Cold War stifled dissent and enforced a level of conformity of behavior and ideas. Rock and roll challenged postwar mores and ideals, fusing the sensitive issues of sex, youth, and race. Tensions stemming from racial segregation and inequality increased as did those over gender roles. Finally, the state's manufacturing base, and the cities and people who relied upon it, began to undergo serious challenges and transformations that threatened economic security for millions of Ohioans. These and other tensions erupted in the tumultuous 1960s.

Further Reading

James T. Patterson's "Ohio 1953: Problems and Prospects," in Geoffrey Parker, Richard Sisson, and William Russell Coil, eds., *Ohio and the World, 1753–2053: Essays Toward a New History of Ohio* places Ohio in the larger context of national and international postwar events (2005. Columbus: The Ohio State University Press, pp. 129–48). For specific issues and people in post-World War II Ohio see: Deanna R. Adams, *Rock 'n' Roll and the Cleveland Connection* (2002. Kent: Kent State University Press); Glenn Altschuler, *All Shook Up: How Rock 'n' Roll Changed America* (2003. New York: Oxford University Press); William Russell Coil, "New Deal Republican: James Allen Rhodes and the Transformation of the Republican Party, 1933–1983." (2005. unpublished Ph.D. dissertation, Ohio State University); Stephanie Coontz, *The Way We Never Were: American Families and the Nostalgia Trip* (1992. New York: Basic Books); Richard O. Davies, *Main Street Blues: The Decline of Small Town America* (1998. Columbus: Ohio State University Press); Carl E. Feather, *Mountain People in a Flat Land: A Popular History of Appalachian Migration to Northeast Ohio, 1940–1965* (1998. Athens: Ohio University Press); James Gregory, *The Southern Diaspora: How the Great Migrations of Black and White Southerners Transformed America* (2007. Chapel Hill: University of North Carolina Press); W. Dennis Keating, David C. Perry, and Norman Krumholz, eds., *Cleveland: A Metropolitan Reader* (1995. Kent: Kent State University Press); Alexander P. Lamis and Brian Usher, eds., *Ohio Politics* (2d ed. 2007. Kent: Kent State University Press); Leonard N. Moore, *Carl Stokes and the Rise of Black Political Power* (2003. Urbana: University of Illinois Press); Zane L. Miller, *Suburb: Neighborhood and Community in Forest Park, Ohio, 1935–1976* (1981. Knoxville: University of Tennessee Press); Ted Steinberg, *American Green: The Obsessive Quest for the Perfect Lawn* (2007. New York: W.W. Norton); Warren Van Tine and Michael Pierce, eds., *Builders of Ohio: A Biographical History* (2003. Columbus: The Ohio State University Press); Mel Watkins, *Dancing With Strangers: A Memoir* (1998. New York: Simon and Schuster); Kate Weigand, "The Red Menace, the Feminine Mystique, and the Ohio Un-American Activities Commission: Gender and Anti-Communism in Ohio, 1951–1954," *Journal of Women's History* 3:3 (1992. Winter, pp. 71–94); Andrew Wiese, *Places of Their Own: African American Suburbanization in the Twentieth Century* (2005. Chicago: University of Chicago Press).

16

Rebellion and Reaction

The 1960s

If any one year defined the issues of the 1960s, it was 1968. In Cleveland, Carl Stokes took office in January as the first African American mayor of a major city, only months, after violent racial unrest there. In February, after months of investigations that included visits to Cleveland and Cincinnati, the National Advisory Commission on Civil Disorders, known as the Kerner Commission after its chair, governor Otto Kerner of Illinois, published its report that concluded: "Our nation is moving toward two societies, one black, one white—separate and unequal." On April 4, Martin Luther King, Jr. was assassinated, leading to urban unrest in some 110 cities, including Cincinnati. The next day, at the Cleveland City Club, presidential hopeful senator Robert Kennedy, brother of slain president John Kennedy, gave one of his most eloquent speeches, in which he stated that "violence breeds violence, repression brings retaliation, and only a cleaning of our whole society can remove this sickness from our soul." In June, Sirhan Sirhan killed Robert Kennedy in Los Angeles and in July urban violence came again, this time in Akron and Cleveland. That spring and fall, environmental activists were busy in Ohio and testifying before Congress on regulating strip mining and cleaning up the state's rivers. Feminists too had begun to organize, from small informal groups to creating chapters of the National Organization of Women and in Cleveland starting the Women's Equity Action League in October. There were student demonstrations on Ohio's campuses that year over the war in Vietnam and other issues. In November at Kent State University, for example, Black United Students (BUS) staged a massive walkout, joined by members of the Students for a Democratic Society (SDS), in protest against on-campus recruiting by the Oakland (CA) police department. Oakland was the home of the militant Black Panthers and the group had labeled the police as a key instrument of racial oppression. The year ended with a narrow victory in Ohio and the nation by Republican Richard

Ohio: A History of the Buckeye State, First Edition. Kevin F. Kern and Gregory S. Wilson.
© 2014 John Wiley & Sons, Inc. Published 2014 by John Wiley & Sons, Inc.

Nixon, who claimed he had a secret plan to end the war in Vietnam and promised more "law and order." His victory—and the strong showing by former Alabama governor George Wallace—reflected the hard work of conservative activists, many of whom emanated from Ohio. They had been busy in the 1960s challenging the prevailing liberalism of nation's politics so identified with leaders such as John F. Kennedy and Lyndon Johnson.

Such conflict prompted Ohio Governor James Rhodes to write in 1969 that "Ohio and the entire nation are heading directly, at breakneck speed, into social and economic catastrophe." The next year, four students were killed and nine others wounded when National Guard troops fired upon demonstrators during a protest at Kent State University. Clearly, if something like a consensus existed in Ohio in the 1950s, it had all but shattered by the early 1970s. With good reason the 1960s can be counted as one of the most tumultuous decades in Ohio history as public activism spread widely within the state and across the political spectrum. The challenges to the status quo—and its defense—began in the previous decade and lasted into the following one, but they all reached their peak in the 1960s. A number of events occurred, many overlapping and interconnected, some tragic and violent, whose legacy lingers in the lived experience of so many Ohioans. Indeed, rather than simply a backdrop, Ohioans occupied a central place in the rebellion and reaction of the 1960s.

The Struggle for Black Equality

Perhaps no movement of the 1960s was more significant than that of black equality. It challenged at all levels the meaning of freedom in Ohio and the nation, it drew together average people from all walks of life as well as heroes such as Martin Luther King, Jr., and Rosa Parks, and inspired several other significant social movements that came to reshape life for Ohioans and all Americans.

After the success of *Brown v. Board* in 1954 and the Montgomery bus boycott in 1956, the civil rights movement slowed considerably. In the South, white opposition grew under the banner of "massive resistance." In 1957 African American students sought to integrate Central High School in Little Rock, Arkansas. President Eisenhower was forced to call out the 101st Airborne Division to protect the "Little Rock Nine" as they entered the building and attempted to attend school. While some integrated easily, many school districts across the South closed rather than allow blacks to attend, so that by 1960 only 2 percent of Southern African Americans attended integrated schools.

In 1960 the momentum shifted and each year after brought another significant event and helped spur Kennedy, Johnson, and other political leaders to act. First, college students took the lead in pushing for equality. In February, Ezell Blair, Jr., Franklin McCain, Joseph McNeil, and David Richmond, four freshmen at North Carolina Agricultural and Technical State University in Greensboro staged a sit-in at the lunch counter at Woolworth's department store. Denied service, they returned the second day with some 20 students as whites heckled them. By the end of the week hundreds had joined the four and sit-ins spread across cities in the South. Sit-ins had occurred before, but never had they provoked such a reaction. Then, in 1961, freedom rides began as whites and blacks boarded buses to challenge segregated transportation. In 1962 President Kennedy sent troops to the University of Mississippi so that James Meredith could become the school's first black student. The March on Washington for "jobs and freedom" followed in the summer of 1963, at which Martin Luther King, Jr. gave his immortal "I Have a Dream" speech.

In the summer of 1964, two civil rights groups, The Congress of Racial Equality (CORE) and Student Non-Violent Coordinating Committee (SNCC) led a voting rights and educational campaign in Mississippi dubbed Freedom Summer. The project involved some 1,000 white students from the North, who were housed and trained at Western College for Women in Oxford, which is now part of Miami University. The first group left Oxford on Sunday June 20, 1964, one day after the Senate passed and President Johnson signed the Civil Rights Act. Among them, driving in a station wagon to Meridian, Mississippi were James Chaney, an African American from Mississippi, Andrew Goodman a new volunteer from New York City and Michael (Mickey) Schwerner, also from New York. Mickey's brother, Steven, attended Antioch College and was also active in civil rights efforts as was Goodman. Chaney had been working with CORE in Mississippi along with Mickey Schwerner and Mickey's wife, Rita. Upon arriving in Meridian, the three set out the next day to investigate the burning of a CORE Freedom school set up in the Mt. Zion AME Church near Philadelphia, some 50 miles north. The three never returned from the trip. Their burned-out station wagon was found several days later. The volunteers in Oxford watched the news reports with trepidation. A few left, but the majority stayed. "I saw fear turn into toughness, vacillation into quiet conviction," wrote one observer. After delays, the federal government eventually sent in FBI and Navy divers, who in August found the bodies buried in an earthen dam. The news shocked the nation but Freedom Summer went forward as did the movement for black equality (see Figure 16.1).

The use of Miami as a staging ground for civil rights protests is but one illustration of the growing activism within Ohio. CORE, the interracial group which had formed during World War II but faded by the 1950s, renewed small but dedicated affiliates in Cincinnati, Cleveland, Columbus, and Oberlin. In June and July 1963 CORE and other groups led sit-ins at the state house. As the legislature debated a fair housing bill, the leader of the Columbus CORE chapter, Reverend Arthur Zebbs, chained himself to a chair in the house gallery for over eight hours and Ruth Turner, head of the Cleveland chapter led an all-night vigil. Proposals in Cleveland to build new schools met with resistance by some civil rights leaders who argued that although they might be new, schools would remain largely segregated. In April 1964, at the construction site for a new elementary school, a group of five protesters gathered; four of them, including Turner, blocked a bulldozer's path in front of it. A fifth, Presbyterian minister Bruce Klunder, lay down behind. Trying to avoid those in front, the driver unknowingly backed up over Klunder, killing him. Blacks took to the streets in protest and police had to be called to restore order.

This incident revealed the extent to which schools had once again become battlegrounds for issues over equality. In this era, the main issues were segregation and inequality of resources. Even with the *Brown* decision of 1954, and without specific laws

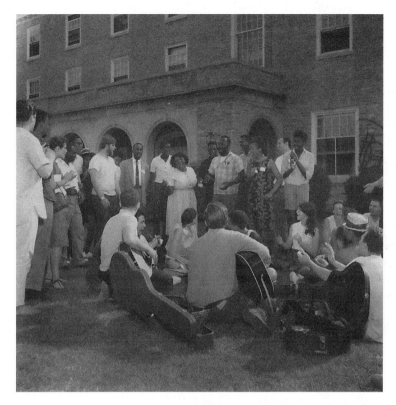

Figure 16.1 Leading this group of civil rights workers in song is Fannie Lou Hamer, the famed activist from Mississippi, who came to the Western College for Women in Oxford, Ohio to help train activists for Freedom Summer in 1964. Working with CORE and SNCC to coordinate Freedom Summer was the National Council of Churches Commission on Religion and Race, which aided in bringing resources, securing the cooperation of Western College to host the training, and introducing more white volunteers from the North into the civil rights movement. White college students who made it to Oxford had passed through a series of interviews led by SNCC at college campuses in the North over the spring.
Source: Photograph by George R. Hoxie. Courtesy of Smith Library of Regional History (Oxford, Ohio)

separating the races in Ohio, the problems of racial segregation and inequality remained deeply entrenched. Indeed, several Ohio court cases involving schooling were not settled until the 1970s, more than twenty years after *Brown*. In Cleveland, black students were often placed in classes with other blacks, scheduled to eat lunch at different times than white students, and could not participate in extracurricular activities. Finally, in 1976 judge Frank J. Battisti ruled in *Reed v. Rhodes* that Cleveland's schools were segregated and required officials to implement programs to desegregate.

Columbus also witnessed protests. Unlike most of Ohio's large cities, Columbus continued to grow in the 1960s, using its near monopoly on water and sewer services to annex territory. As those newer areas became part of Columbus, they were allowed to remain part of the suburban school districts; hence, the city's growth and the city's school district were divorced. With inequality and segregation growing, African American leaders became more assertive about demanding action from the Columbus school board. In 1967 parents of students at the mostly black Ohio Avenue Elementary organized a one-day student boycott. Other protests followed. In 1971 there were attempted firebombings at two schools and racial tensions temporarily shut down two others. Then in May at Linden-McKinley, a racially balanced school, white students resisted efforts by black students who were trying to replace the American flag on the school's stage with the red, black, and green one of black nationalism. Administrators closed the school for fear of a race riot. Police officers were stationed around the building so seniors could return for final exams. Finally, in the case *Penick v. Columbus Board of Education*, federal circuit court judge Robert Duncan ruled in March 1977 that the Columbus Board of Education had knowingly segregated its schools and that the Board had to implement a program to desegregate. Like many cities, Columbus decided upon busing. However, even when busing began in 1979, Columbus city schools remained largely African American. As one scholar has written, "the health of the city school district was sacrificed to preserve the expansion of the city itself."

The irony of the 1954 *Brown* decision is that today the most segregated schools are in the North and West, while Southern districts are the most integrated. For years, cities in Ohio and elsewhere in the North and West sought to remedy segregation, eventually adopting busing, which showcased vigorous and often vicious opposition from whites. For all the attention paid to the issues of segregation in the South, Ohio's urban schools and neighborhoods remain racially divided. Moreover, the issue of school inequality would emerge again in the 1990s.

While pressure grew over schools and neighborhoods, urban unrest exploded across the nation during the "long hot summers" from 1965 to 1969. The event that sparked the conflagrations was the uprising in the Watts section of Los Angeles, just days after Lyndon Johnson signed the Voting Rights Act into law in August 1965. With Watts, public and political attention now shifted from the demonstrations and sit-ins of the South to the problems of urban areas, mainly in the North and West.

After Watts, the U.S. Commission on Civil Rights began hearings in the nation's cities, coming to Cleveland in April 1966. In some forty hours of testimony the Commission heard from city leaders and residents on key issues, including education, housing, employment, police-community relations, health, welfare, and municipal services. As the Commission's chair, John Hannah noted at the opening session, the Cleveland hearing was "the first of a new series of hearings" to "seek the facts concerning civil rights problems affecting Negro citizens and other minorities living in the inner city." At the first hearing, Governor Rhodes testified briefly, continuing his mantra on job creation and vocational training as the keys to solving most problems. Cleveland Mayor Ralph Locher also testified and defended the city's record on addressing racial inequality.

Blacks offered a different view. The most powerful testimony of life in the urban core came from residents there. Hattie Mae Dugan lived with her daughter in a three-room apartment in Hough. Dugan was a member of the Citizen's Committee in Hough, and had been arrested in 1965 demonstrating at City Hall, demanding that poor people be represented on the city's Council of Economic Opportunity. As part of the federal War on Poverty, begun under President Johnson in 1964, in theory these councils were to be led by the poor themselves to provide services and improve life in the inner city. But local governments refused to do so, fearing that poor people would use the council to challenge city leadership. Dugan related her problems getting the landlord to repair problems with her sink and bathtub. She had called the city's health department but had received no response. Dugan also received money under federal aid for dependent children, but banks in her neighborhood refused to cash the checks. Like other inner city residents receiving aid, she had to cash her checks at a local store, which required Dugan to purchase items there before cashing the check. Rats were also common in the area. "The kids they play with rats like a child would play with a dog or something." She pointed to inadequate police protection and overcrowded classrooms in her daughter's school. Garbage collection was inconsistent, sometimes longer than two weeks between pickups. Dugan had been trained to operate powered sewing equipment for work in the garment industry, but could not find work in that field. Employers in other fields refused to hire her because she lacked experience.

Hough storeowner Morris Thorington pointed out the problems of trying to operate a successful small business there. He regularly extended credit to customers, but many could not pay him back or they just moved out. Thorington voiced a common complaint that urban renewal had been a failure. All the program had done was to "tear down a few houses, make the streets more deserted, fewer people and more vulnerable to hoodlums. As for urban renewal, this is a joke." Residents left the area and moved to nearby neighborhoods of Glenville, Central, or Mt. Pleasant. Urban renewal forced residents "into an area that is too small to hold them. They are being crowded into another ghetto." Thorington had seen the Hough and Central areas change. He had grown up in the area during the 1920s and 1930s with Italians, Polish, and Swedish residents. By the 1960s, the neighborhood had become almost totally African American.

Others continued the attack, including Carl Stokes, who would soon run for mayor. "The contemptuous, callous and inhuman disregard reflected in the Mayor's policy to perpetuate people having to live in hovels and shacks by not enforcing housing codes" could only be fixed by cutting off urban renewal funds until the city fixed the current housing issues. Stokes called on city unions and businesses to end discriminatory hiring. He called the federal War on Poverty in Cleveland "a failure," with money going to programs, bureaucracy, and academic studies rather than poor people themselves. Adding to these views was Ruth Turner, executive secretary of Cleveland CORE. In opposition to view of Cleveland's leaders, Turner argued that "Cleveland is not a progressive town under any stretch of the imagination." The attitude of those in the city's administration was one of "disrespect." She also made a connection that many in the civil rights movement and others on the political left would make by noting that "not too long ago, $14 billion was granted to the war in Vietnam for emergency use. I cannot, for the life of me, understand why the lives of our citizens are not considered an emergency use."

In the process of her work, Turner articulated a position that would become more common among civil rights and black freedom activists. Turner studied German at Oberlin, attended further training in Germany, and then earned her Master's in Teaching from Harvard. She returned to teach German in the Cleveland schools. However, the civil rights movement galvanized her and she left her job to lead the Cleveland CORE. "The events in Birmingham ... brought about the rather sudden decision. I felt that after what occurred there that I could no longer continue teaching German at a time like this." Turner sought to move beyond basic legal victories against segregation. "I feel that those who concentrate on integration and ending segregation have much too narrow a goal because I feel that the basic issue here is restoring to this country—well, maybe not restoring but implementing for the first time ... economic justice, social justice, political justice, and that goes far beyond the bounds of ... ending segregation per se."

In June 1966, the U.S. Civil Rights Commission issued its report, titled "Cleveland's Unfinished Business in its Inner City." It painted a bleak picture. In education, the report noted that 91.5 percent of Cleveland's public school students attended schools that were either 80 percent or more all white or 80 percent or more all black. Moreover, the dropout rates were higher in the mostly black high schools. There was an inadequate supply of low-income housing and what did exist confirmed the testimony of residents like Hattie Dugan. In employment, the report confirmed discrimination and that African Americans were concentrated on the lower rungs of jobs. In addition, the unemployment rate for blacks in Cleveland was 8.9 percent, while for whites it was 2.4 percent. Median black income was $4,768 in 1960 compared to $7,288 for whites. Police were discourteous to black residents, sometimes brutal. Blacks were often arrested without warrants or probable cause. Police also refused to crack down on prostitution and gambling. Blacks faced higher rates of infant mortality and premature births and there was a shortage of neighborhood clinics. Those on public assistance received payments from the state of Ohio that were 78 percent of the minimum standard needed to maintain health and decency. Food stamps required waiting for hours in long lines. Finally, the report noted inadequate municipal services in black neighborhoods. The city made little effort to eradicate rats and needed more frequent trash pickup. There were also too few play areas for children and a lack of street lighting.

Cleveland responded to the report. Between April and June, Mayor Locher announced plans to enforce building codes and improve city services. The Cleveland Metropolitan Housing Authority announced construction of more single family homes. The Cleveland Community Relations Board pledged to work more closely with companies and the building and trades unions to open up positions for blacks. The Cleveland Council of Churches, the Urban League, and various neighborhood groups continued various efforts to address inequality. Meanwhile, direct action protests continued. This time a new group, welfare mothers, organized a march of approximately 5,000 people from Cleveland to Columbus in June to dramatize their situation and demand an increase in state welfare payments. Then came the violence in Hough.

It began as a dispute over a glass of water on the night of July 18, 1966 at the Seventy-Niners Café. Tensions already existed between the white owners and black neighborhood residents. When the owner refused to give a black patron who had bought a carry out item a pitcher of water and a glass, the patron yelled to those inside that he had been refused water. Word spread within the neighborhood and a crowd began to gather outside the café. Police were unable to disperse the crowd; soon, arson, vandalism, and rock throwing spread throughout the Hough area. Gunfire erupted and more violence followed on the

Figure 16.2 Riots like the one in Hough in July 1966 occurred almost like clockwork in cities during the late 1960s. While the Hough riot helped elect Carl Stokes and draw greater attention to Ohio's cities, violent episodes like this also contributed to racial tensions, shattered the Democratic coalition and liberalism, and led many Americans to support calls for "law and order" in both Ohio and the nation.

second night, which prompted Mayor Locher to ask for the National Guard, who arrived on July 20. Violence subsided over the next several days and by July 25 the Guard began to leave. In the end, four African Americans were dead; two were innocent bystanders and two others were killed blocks away from the riots, one by three white men from the Little Italy neighborhood that bordered Hough. Over 40 people were injured, including police and firefighters, and close to 300 arrested. Estimates of property damage reached between $1 million and $2 million (see Figure 16.2). A grand jury investigation confirmed the beliefs of many whites that the riots had been the work of outside radicals. While there were certainly some, the riot began spontaneously, stemming from years of frustration and anger.

Violence erupted in Cincinnati in June 1967 after the arrest of Peter Frakes, who was protesting the death sentence of his cousin, Posteal Laskey, who had been charged as being the "Cincinnati Strangler." Some violence broke out after a community meeting called to address the arrest and longstanding issues similar to those in Cleveland and other major cities. The municipal judge charged the African Americans arrested for the violence with violating the Riot Act, punishable with up to one year in jail and a $500 fine. Whites meanwhile were charged with the lesser offense of disturbing the peace. African Americans in the city were incensed at the varying levels of punishment, and for the next several nights protests turned violent. Once again, the National Guard restored order.

The February 1968 report of the National Advisory Commission on Civil Disorders stated: "This is our basic conclusion: Our nation is moving toward two societies, one black, one white—separate and unequal." It highlighted as underlying causes many of the issues already made visible in Cleveland, Cincinnati and other cities, including police practices, unemployment, housing, lack of recreation and city services, discrimination, and a lack of political responsiveness to the situation in the mainly African American neighborhoods. Sadly, the unrest continued that year. Outbreaks occurred in the wake of the assassination of Martin Luther King, Jr., in April. Then in July, a six-day confrontation occurred in Akron. A crowd gathered in the largely African American Wooster-Hawkins section in the early morning hours of July 17, after police had broken up a fight between two African American gangs. Soon, police were battling residents. The National Guard came in the next day but the unrest continued until July 23. As the Akron disturbance ended, another began in Cleveland. A shootout in the Glenville neighborhood on July 23, 1968 between police and black nationalists left seven people dead, including three police officers. Looting and arson followed for three days and again, the National Guard came in to restore order.

Carl and Louis Stokes

It was against this backdrop that two of Ohio's most influential African American political leaders emerged, brothers Carl and Louis Stokes (see Figure 16.3). They drew attention to discrimination and poverty in Ohio and symbolized the transformation of African

Figure 16.3   Carl (right) and Louis Stokes became two of the most recognized African American political leaders in postwar Ohio and the nation. They both credited their mother with instilling in them the importance of education and hard work.
Source: Special Collections, Michael Schwartz Library at Cleveland State University

American protest to mainstream politics. Carl became the first African American member of the Democratic Party elected to the Ohio House and in 1967 the first African American elected as mayor of a major city, Cleveland. Louis was the first African American U.S. Congressman from Ohio, serving fifteen consecutive terms from 1969 to 1999.

The brothers were born in poverty in Cleveland, Louis in 1925 and Carl in 1927. Their parents, Charles and Louise had come from Georgia during the first Great Migration and they met in Cleveland. Charles died in 1929 and Louise worked as a domestic for white families while raising the two boys. In the 1930s the family moved to the Outhwaite Homes, Cleveland's first federally-funded public housing project. Both Carl and Louis served in the Army during World War II, and returned home to continue with their education. Louis graduated from Cleveland Marshall Law School in 1953, and Carl followed in 1956. Carl became assistant prosecuting attorney for Cuyahoga County then joined his brother to open the law firm of Stokes, Stokes, Character, and Terry in 1962. As he was making his way in law, Carl was also learning politics. In 1948 he supported Henry Wallace's Progressive Party, and later worked as John Holly's driver. Holly had organized the Future Outlook League in Cleveland during the 1930s and after the war continued to travel statewide organizing black Democrats. As Stokes wrote, listening to and being with Holly became his "primary-level education in politics." In 1962 Stokes was elected to the Ohio House of Representatives and served three terms.

Louis had mainly focused on his law career, becoming more involved in civil rights issues. He defended protesters who had staged a sit-in at the Cleveland School Board over segregated schools. He also argued for the defendant, John Terry, in front of the U.S. Supreme Court in the *Terry v. Ohio* case in 1968, in which the court defined reasonable searches by police officers and whether evidence gathered during such a search could be admitted into trial. Politics would lure Louis, too, and that year he won election to the U.S. House of Representatives, serving fifteen consecutive terms representing Cleveland's East side. Among his more important assignments were the chairmanships of the House Select Committee on Assassinations, which in 1976 undertook new investigations into the murders of John F. Kennedy and Martin Luther King, Jr., the House Ethics Committee, the House Intelligence Committee, and the Congressional Black Caucus. He retired from Congress in 1999.

Carl announced his campaign for the Cleveland mayor's office in June 1967, noting that if elected he would serve "all the people" white and black, rich and poor. Stokes first challenged fellow Democratic incumbent Locher in the September primary. The white business leaders threw their support behind Stokes, believing that electing Stokes might quell further violence, restore order, and improve Cleveland's image. Conservative whites, meanwhile, launched a campaign of fear. One group, the Save Our Homes Committee, distributed flyers in white areas of the city asking whether a Stokes victory would mean that city hall would open to "revolutionaries," that school children would be bused to integrate schools, that housing would be "forcibly integrated," and that Stokes would fire whites working for the city. Locher added to this, using the Democratic Party newsletter to claim that Stokes's victory would give Martin Luther King "the noted racist, control of his first city." Whites vandalized Stokes's headquarters on the West Side and his volunteers there were attacked. Despite all this, Stokes defeated Locher, sweeping the black vote and gaining 15 percent of the white vote. In the general election, Stokes, the great-grandson of a slave, now faced Republican Seth Taft, grandson of the former president. Many white Democratic leaders in Cleveland refused to endorse Stokes, and Taft and his supporters worked hard to turn out the white vote. In the end, Stokes achieved a narrow victory, 129,396 to 127,717. He won 95 percent of the African American vote, and 15 percent of the white vote.

Stokes took office and quickly set about addressing the city's problems. He managed to restore funds from the Department of Housing and Urban Development that had been frozen during the Locher administration. Stokes ensured that some 5,496 units of low- and moderate-income housing were built. He persuaded Cleveland's bankers to increase their loans to black businesses. He also prevailed upon city council to authorize an increase in the city income tax, and succeeded in gaining increased spending on schools, welfare, public safety, and public health. Voters also approved a bond issue to improve the city's sewage treatment and Stokes began efforts to address water and air pollution.

Cleveland stayed relatively calm as other cities erupted in violence after Martin Luther King's assassination in April 1968. Stokes walked the streets and used television to appeal to Clevelanders to react to the tragedy "in a peaceful manner." He also formed an all-black peace patrol to walk black neighborhoods and maintain order. Stokes, however, could not completely avoid conflict and controversy. After the Glenville shootout in July, it was revealed that the nationalist group led by Fred "Ahmed" Evans had received funds from the Cleveland:NOW! program, an ambitious plan that Stokes had launched in cooperation with business leaders and the federal government to raise money to rehabilitate the city. Despite the controversy, Stokes won re-election in 1969, but conflict with the police department after the Glenville shootout and city council persuaded Stokes not to run again in 1971. He went on to become a broadcaster with WNBC-TV in New York City, returning to Cleveland in 1980 to practice law. He was elected a municipal court judge in 1983 and in 1994 President Clinton appointed him U.S. Ambassador to the Seychelles. Carl Stokes died in 1996.

Resurgence of Women's Activism

The black freedom struggle inspired other social movements of the era and among them was a resurgent women's movement. A pattern emerged in the 1960s that was reminiscent of the nineteenth century—women who were active in the cause of racial equality developed their own consciousness and became active in the cause of sexual equality, too.

Cold War culture had emphasized an ideal that connected fighting communism to the maintenance of a male-headed household, with a wife who worked outside the home as little as possible. As we have seen, the ideal did not match the reality, as the daily lives of women continued to change. Nationally, the female participation rate in the labor force increased from 34.5 percent in 1960 to 41.6 percent by 1970. Women who were working for wages or attending colleges and universities were expected to defer to male colleagues and accept employment positions in the "pink collar" world as secretaries, clerks, teachers, and nurses. Despite the Equal Pay Act of 1963, which prohibited unequal pay for two people in the same job, women earned about 59 cents for every dollar a man earned in similar work. Women were restricted in their access to managerial positions in business and to professional schools such as law and medicine. Even with advanced degrees, women faced discrimination in hiring. Single women were often denied credit and married women's credit was often in the husband's name. During the 1960s, women and men began to marry later than they had done in the previous decade; divorce rates rose; and the number of female-headed households began to rise.

Publication of Betty Friedan's *The Feminine Mystique* in 1963 brought to light the growing frustration of millions of middle-class women. In story after story, these mostly college-educated women voiced their sense of repression and isolation in a postwar culture that had promised women happiness through family and consumption. According to Friedan, women remained trapped by a mystique that defined women solely by their sexual relationship to men, as sex object, housewife, or mother, thereby denying women full opportunities for self-fulfillment equal to that which men had always possessed.

This second wave of feminism also grew out of the experience with the civil rights movement and, later in the 1960s, the antiwar movement. Men assumed leadership roles in both the civil rights movement and the antiwar movement, and relegated many women to duties such as typing, copying, and making coffee. Within civil rights, the consciousness-raising, organizing, and protesting served as inspiration for women's own activism. So, too, did the growing contradictions of sex—that within a movement dedicated to equality and freedom women remained subservient. Not all women active in the feminist movement abandoned other social movements out of anger at male oppression. For many, it was simply time to devote oneself to the cause of women. This growing awareness led women to battle continued discrimination as well as a host of other issues, including sexuality, family, work, and reproductive rights.

Feminists sought not only to challenge laws and institutional practices, but also to reshape gender identity. Groups organized that emphasized one set of strategies and goals over others. Liberal feminist groups organized more at the national level, especially through groups like the National Organization of Women (NOW), which formed a chapter in Columbus in 1971. Unlike more radical organizations, NOW sought change primarily by raising money for political candidates, lobbying government, and seeking changes through the court system. Meanwhile, those who saw themselves as radical feminists operated in a less organized and hierarchical structure. These women shared many of the larger goals of groups like NOW, but radicals sought to transform society, not reform it. Radicals operated more local, grass-roots organizations that usually steered clear of mainstream politics. There were also moderate to conservative women like Elizabeth "Betty" Boyer who founded Women's Equity Action League (WEAL) in Cleveland in 1968. Boyer and others in WEAL objected to NOW's focus on abortion and direct action tactics such as picketing and demonstrations. Boyer explained, WEAL supported "economic advancement for women" in areas such as employment and education.

Figure 16.4 Toledo native Gloria Steinem became one of the most recognizable leaders of second wave feminism often appearing on news and talk shows and magazine covers. After graduating from Smith College, she entered journalism in the 1960s, reporting on issues like contraception, marriage, and work. She became politically active as well, working for the Equal Rights Amendment and legislation to end discrimination against women, and founding or cofounding several organizations including the Women's Action Alliance, the Coalition of Labor Union Women, and the Ms. Foundation for Women.
Source: Photo courtesy of Wright State University

As with black freedom and civil rights, Ohio does not initially come to mind as a center of feminist activism. However, like all social movements, feminism was "an immense, multifaceted grass-roots movement in a decentralized country." In fact, one of the most recognized leaders of the new feminism, Gloria Steinem (Figure 16.4), grew up in Toledo. Born in 1934 during the Great Depression, Steinem's mother suffered a mental breakdown such that she had difficulty keeping a job. Gloria's parents divorced as a result and the events had a profound effect on her. Years later she would recall how this showed her ways in which women lacked support and equality. As so many artists and intellectuals from Ohio have done, Steinem left Ohio when she could; in her case a degree at Smith College and then a career in journalism and eventually leadership in the women's movement. Steinem co-founded *Ms.* Magazine in 1972, and became active in a number of political and social causes.

Yet outside the national spotlight, Ohio women were pushing forward with women's rights. Dayton, home to Erma Bombeck, a city that sat "in the inexact geography of the national mind like a mirage, an unformed vision on the imagined expanse of flat Midwestern plains," became a center for the women's movement. In the fall of 1969, a modest advertisement in the radical newspaper *Minority Report* signaled the beginning of the radical women's liberation movement in Dayton: "Women's Liberation—Call Cheryl, 278-6271." The group that assembled met in Kathy Kleine's home in Dayton View, one of the few integrated neighborhoods in Dayton. They were white, between twenty-five and thirty-five, and half were married. Almost none were college students. Many of the early founders in Dayton had strong church connections—one was studying to be ordained, another was the wife of a Methodist minister, and others had become politically active through church activities. For Robin Suits, it "was just an explosion! I don't think there was one woman there who didn't feel that she, personally, had been oppressed all her life." They came away forming the Dayton Women's Liberation Movement, shortened later to the Dayton Women's Liberation (DWL). In Columbus, a number of radical women's groups had also emerged by the late 1960s. One of the first was the Columbus-OSU Women's Liberation. Like other groups, these women had experience with student demonstrations and civil rights activity, and adopted the language of black liberation. It included not only white, middle-class women, but also college students at Ohio State University.

Early media attention ignored the political nature of the groups. At a February 1970 rally to amend Ohio's abortion law, male reporters repeatedly asked the women activists if they were wearing bras, about their make-up, or their husbands. If they covered feminist activism at all, newspapers initially placed the story in the "women's pages." Editorials were uniformly hostile.

Activists sought to have Ohio create a state commission on the status of women, but Governor Rhodes refused, making the state the only one without a counterpart to the federal commission. Feminists went ahead and created their own, conducting research and pushing for legal changes, including passage of the Equal Rights Amendment. Ohio's feminists participated in the national Women's Strike for Equality on August 26, 1970, which came on the fiftieth anniversary of women's suffrage. Among other slogans, marchers used "Don't Iron While the Strike is Hot!" and "We Demand Equality" to draw attention to unequal pay and other issues. Media coverage was widespread and it was an international event, as women marched in Paris, Amsterdam, and other major cities. The next year Congress declared August 26 as Women's Equality Day.

Activists achieved notable successes as laws, customs and views began to change. With a flurry of activity courts and legislatures supported women's rights as individuals, and families as a collection of persons, not a unit headed by a man. These new views came as the so-called "sexual revolution" gathered momentum and moved from being a radical concept in 1960 into the mainstream by the early 1970s. The "pill" had been approved by the U.S. Food and Drug Administration (FDA) in 1960. In Ohio, in 1965 the legislature dismantled the Comstock Laws that dated from the 1870s, removing birth control from state obscenity statutes. That same year, in *Griswold v. Connecticut*, the U.S. Supreme Court ruled that such laws against contraception for married couples were unconstitutional.

In this ruling, the court developed the notion of a constitutionally-protected right to privacy. The court applied the same reasoning for allowing contraception use by unmarried persons in 1972 under *Eisenstadt v. Baird.* Building on this concept of privacy, in 1973 the court ruled in *Roe v. Wade* that a woman had the constitutional right to terminate a pregnancy. This overturned some forty-six state bans on abortion, including Ohio. In 1974, in the U.S. Supreme Court case of *Cleveland Board of Education v. LaFleur,* the court overturned a regulation requiring pregnant women to resign from their jobs after the fourth month of pregnancy. That same year Ohio ratified the proposed Equal Rights Amendment (ERA) to the U.S. Constitution. However, ratification fell one state short and the ERA was not adopted.

Emerging Environmental Issues

In addition to social issues related to race and gender, environmental concerns became more widespread in the United States and Ohio after World War II. Ohio's industrial heritage, compounded by World War II and the postwar boom, created serious environmental problems, from smoke and haze over industrial centers like Akron and Youngstown, to polluted waterways stretching from Ohio's southern coal country to the Cuyahoga River and Lake Erie. Driving the emergence of an organized environmental effort were several factors. Certainly, the liberal political context in the 1960s opened greater space for environmental politics. Deeper ecological awareness came from the popularity of works such as Rachel Carson's *Silent Spring,* published in 1962. Suburban growth and changes in Ohio's economy also made a difference. Rapid and widespread expansion beyond the central cities into suburbs awakened these residents to their natural surroundings and to issues such as the loss of open space, contamination in drinking water from septic systems, and increased energy use. Indeed, the suburban home of the postwar years came with a large environmental price tag, from appliances and air conditioning and heat, to highways connecting them, to the chemicals and fossil fuels used to care for the lawns. The growth of the service sector added to this. As fewer Ohioans made their living in manufacturing or in coal mining, environmental damage became harder to justify as a necessary and inevitable cost for economic development. Instead, when economic growth became more dependent upon recreation, tourism, and the so-called postindustrial sectors in the service and high technology areas, the change opened the possibility for more popular concerns with pollution.

In the postwar world, parks, unspoiled landscapes, clean air and water all became amenities sought for and supported by a growing number of Ohioans. In response, a number of environmental organizations increased their numbers and influence in the 1950s and 1960s. In Ohio, the National Audubon Society gained a larger presence just outside Dayton with the creation of its first nature center in the Midwest, the Aullwood Audubon Center. In 1957 and again in 1962, Marie Aull donated land to the Audubon Society to establish the center. Aull was the widow of John Aull, owner of Aull Brothers Paper and Box Company in Dayton.

Addressing the environmental damage from coal mining became a major issue in postwar Ohio. Better technology and increased demand after 1940 led coal companies to rely more and more on surface coal mining, or strip mining. With draglines and shovels, strip mining could gather more coal with fewer workers than underground mining. In 1956, a twelve-story excavator, dubbed the "Mountaineer" worked near Cadiz, while the 22-story "Big Muskie" debuted in 1969. Operated by the Central Ohio Coal Company, the Big Muskie dragline was the world's largest, with a 220-cubic-yard bucket that could remove 320 tons of earth, pivot and deposit it some 600 feet away. With a crew of five the machine operated around the clock. In its lifetime (it ceased operation in 1991) it aided in the removal of 20,000,000 tons of coal and twice the quantity of earth moved to build the Panama Canal. Operations like this provided the energy needed to fuel the postwar boom, but they also denuded millions of acres of land, causing loss of vegetation, soil erosion, increased flooding, and silting of streams. Acid mine drainage from coal operations also polluted waterways and wells throughout the eastern part of the state. The removal of "overburden," the earth above the sought-after coal, created landslides that sometimes buried people and buildings in the homes and towns below mining operations.

Just after World War II, a movement emerged to end, or at least regulate, strip mining. It began with farmers, local sportsmen, pastors, and other rural people—the types not usually associated with the environmental movement. The deputy master of the Morgan County Grange wrote in 1947 that "strip mining is a menace to the agriculture and the very life of our county." Others argued that strip mining went against the ideals of Christian stewardship of the land, and ruined the pastoral beauty of the rural landscape. Most, though, argued that strip mining damaged their private property. Opponents of regulation, as they would in subsequent debates over environmental legislation, often worried about jobs. Coal hauler Dale Brennon urged the governor to "protect my job from those outside the coal industry." But those favoring regulation received support from Governor Lausche and his Republican successor, Thomas Herbert, as well as the General Assembly, and Ohio's first law regulating surface coal mining went into effect in January 1948. Amendments followed, but by the early 1950s, critics charged that it was an ineffective law that regulators failed to enforce. Vague requirements to reclaim spoil banks, for example, allowed mining companies to leave the land in such a state as to promote continued environmental degradation. Efforts eventually led to the federal Surface Mining Control and Reclamation Act of 1977, which regulated active coal mines and mandated reclamation of abandoned ones.

Along with coal mining, Ohio's major waterways came under increased environmental scrutiny. The Ohio River had long been central to the culture and economy of Ohio and the region. By the time of World War II it supplied drinking water to millions, served as a major transportation link, and supported recreational activities. It was also severely polluted. Industries, farms, cities, and towns dumped wastes into the river and its tributaries. In 1948, Ohio joined seven other states to form the Ohio River Valley Water Sanitary Commission (ORSANCO), an interstate commission. ORSANCO created programs to monitor the health of the river and its tributaries and improve water quality. Sewage treatment and industrial waste regulation throughout the watershed were the early areas of focus. In 1948 only 1 percent of sewered communities along the Ohio River treated their waste. This had risen to 99 percent by the mid-1960s. Later efforts focused on industrial wastes and other sources of pollution. Beyond the Ohio River, in 1951 the Ohio legislature created a water pollution board that aimed to control the discharge of wastes into all state waters. However, industries continued to receive permits to dump and enforcement of prohibited activities remained lax throughout the 1950s and 1960s.

Both Lake Erie and the Cuyahoga River garnered international attention and became symbols for the combined urban and ecological crises of postwar society. As early as the 1900s Canada and the United States had begun joint investigations into Lake Erie pollution but they concluded that the sheer volume and vastness of the Great Lakes would absorb any damage. By the 1960s, further research had undermined that view. Continued population and industrial growth in the Lake Erie basin threatened the lake's multiple uses, from drinking water, to commercial fishing and recreation. The main issue with Lake Erie was a process called eutrophication, which is the buildup of phosphates in water that can lead to algae blooms. Algae washed up on the shores, closing beaches. Moreover, as the algae died, the decomposing organic matter depleted the oxygen in the lake, killing species of fish upon which commercial and recreational anglers relied. As a 1965 *Newsweek* article noted, "To live on Lake Erie is to know the stink of algae and dead fish." The phosphates came largely from synthetic detergents, flowing into the lake system as part of the postwar consumer revolution in automatic washers. Media reports like those in *Newsweek* called the lake dead or dying. In 1971, even Dr. Seuss used the lake as a symbol of environmental degradation, with a line in his environmental fable *The Lorax* that reads: "I hear things are just as bad up in Lake Erie."

Several Great Lakes states signed the Great Lakes Basin Compact in 1955, but Ohio did not join until 1963. Grass-roots pressure for more action continued. In October 1964, many of Ohio's League of Women Voters chapters joined their colleagues from the Lake Erie Basin Committee to issue a report on pollution in the lake. With Cleveland Press reporter Betty Klaric raising awareness through a series of articles, by February 1965 David Blaushild, a member of the Shaker Heights city council and auto dealer, had organized a petition drive that garnered some 180,000 signatures from the greater Cleveland area demanding governor Rhodes do more to prevent further pollution. Rhodes called for a conference of relevant governors, federal officials, and Canadian leaders to address the issue. Early resistance to banning phosphates came from business leaders, especially Cincinnati-based Procter and Gamble, whose company manufactured a number of detergents. Not until the 1980s did such legislation come into law. By then, phosphate levels had begun to drop and detergent manufacturers had been selling phosphate-free products.

Meanwhile, the United States and Canada were working together towards a broad agreement on water quality. The result was the 1972 Great Lakes Water Quality Agreement. It established specific water quality objectives and mandated programs to meet them. The agreement focused on point-sources of pollution—those from clearly identifiable industrial or municipal sources such as factories and sewage treatment facilities. Later amendments in 1978 and beyond strengthened the cooperation among the nations and sought to go further in reducing harmful pollutants entering the Great Lakes.

Figure 16.5 Although the Cuyahoga River fire of 1969 is the most famous one, no picture of that fire is known to exist, nor was it the worst in terms of damage. Yet news of the 1969 fire spread to national media outlets at the precise moment the environmental movement was gaining popularity and influence. This image is of the 1952 fire, and is often assumed to be of the 1969 conflagration. The 1952 fire was the largest in terms of damages, estimated at some $1,000,000.

As the movement to clean up Lake Erie gathered momentum, the Cuyahoga River became a national cause célèbre when it caught fire in June 1969 (Figure 16.5). Like other industrial cities, Cleveland's rise to prominence incurred significant environmental costs. Already by 1889, one immigrant described the Cuyahoga's water as "yellowish, thick, full of clay, stinking of oil and sewage." There had been earlier and more damaging fires on the river. Hence, initially the 1969 fire garnered little attention locally but, by the end of the year it had become a national and international story. In August 1969 *Time* Magazine described the river this way: "Chocolate-brown, oily, bubbling with subsurface gases, it oozes rather than flows." Then, as one scholar notes, "the 1969 Cuyahoga fire evolved into one of the great symbolic environmental catastrophes of the industrial era." The December 1970 issue of *National Geographic* featured the Cuyahoga in an issue titled "Our Ecological Crisis." The concern was not so much with the immediate damage caused by the fire (roughly $100,000 to two railroad bridges) but rather how the fire damaged the reputation of Cleveland and affected activities like fishing and recreation. In late 1970 Louis Stokes framed the issue as an environmental one, arguing that "the rape of the Cuyahoga River has not only made it useless for any purpose other than a dumping place for sewage and industrial waste, but also has had a deleterious effect upon the ecology of one of the Great Lakes."

The greater attention to the 1969 fire was a result of several threads coming together. Environmental concerns and awareness had grown, and emerged as Cleveland underwent a transition. The city lost 60,000 manufacturing jobs in the 1950s and 1960s, as riots and decay hit many of its neighborhoods. Its schools suffered as did its budget. Thus, by 1969 Ohioans and the world could see Cuyahoga River as "an ecological wasteland, not an economic engine." Somewhat paradoxically, deindustrialization and urban blight allowed the river to become a symbol of the costs of postwar economic expansion, something more than simply another industrial waterway.

The movement to cleanup Ohio developed like other social movements of the postwar era, at the grassroots level, and eventually involved the state and federal government in crafting new legislation and creating new bureaucratic entities to address various environmental concerns. At the federal level, a new Clean Air Act in 1963 allocated funds for state level pollution control agencies and the Water Quality Act of 1965 created federal standards for water quality. The Wilderness Act of 1964 designated some federal lands as wilderness while the Land and Water Conservation Fund Act in 1965 provided funds to maintain outdoor recreation areas. This Act would serve as an important foundation for the creation of Ohio's Cuyahoga Valley National Recreation Area in 1974, and eventually its designation in 2000 as a National Park, consisting of 33,000 acres between Akron and Cleveland. The park developed from grass roots activists, help from U.S. Congressman John Seiberling of Akron (grandson of F.A. Seiberling, founder of Goodyear) and the Cuyahoga River fire in 1969, which added to the desire to stem further development between Akron and Cleveland along the river valley. In 1970, President Nixon signed the National Environmental Protection Act, which led to the creation of the Environmental Protection Agency. April 1970 saw the first Earth Day celebration.

Escalation: Vietnam and Politics

Even more than other issues in the 1960s, the war in Vietnam polarized Ohioans and the nation. In 1960, few had heard of Vietnam, let alone understood its history and culture. By decade's end, the war had become a dominant issue in politics and in protests, fostering a vigorous debate between what was then mainstream liberalism and challengers from both the left and right. As American involvement in the war increased, Ohio's college and university campuses became the crucibles for debates, teach-ins, and demonstrations that pitted "hawks" (who supported the war) against "doves" (who opposed it). Political leaders responded to and helped fuel the growing rift. The acrimony ended in violence on several Ohio campuses, with particularly tragic results at Kent State in 1970.

The United States had been involved in Vietnam since at least the 1950s, but under President Lyndon Johnson that participation increased dramatically. After it appeared that two U.S. destroyers had been attacked, in August 1964 Congress approved the Gulf of Tonkin Resolution, which gave President Johnson authority to escalate the conflict if he chose to do so. During his 1964 re-election campaign, Johnson sought to appear more moderate than his opponent, Republican Barry Goldwater. Among other things Goldwater opposed the Civil Rights Act of 1964 and called for a more aggressive military campaign in Vietnam. In the end, Johnson took Ohio (winning eighty-three counties) on his way to a sweeping victory over Goldwater in November. Liberals supported Johnson on the war, at least for a time, and so too did most Americans. In February 1965, not long after his inauguration, Johnson made the decision to send ground troops into Vietnam. By 1968, U.S. troop levels had reached to over 500,000, as well as extensive naval and air force support. As the war continued, dissatisfaction among the public grew as troop levels and bombings seemed to have little effect. This would galvanize opponents on both the right and left.

The lack of progress in the war, the ascendancy of a liberal mainstream in American political culture, and challenges to traditional social mores and customs in the 1960s fueled a resurgent conservatism, led by a coalition of groups lumped together under the banner of the New Right. The Goldwater candidacy represented the emergence of this force in politics and he had received significant help from a new, critical group in the New Right, the Young Americans for Freedom (YAF). Formed in 1960 at the Sharon, Connecticut estate of William F. Buckley, Jr., the YAF espoused their vision in the "Sharon Statement." Among their ideals were the beliefs that "political freedom cannot long exist without economic freedom," that the Constitution's genius lay in reserving power to the states, that "the market economy…is the single economic system compatible with the requirements of personal freedom" and the United States must "stress victory over, rather than coexistence with" communism. The YAF spearheaded Goldwater's nomination and worked tirelessly for his campaign, in the process moving the Republican Party, and national politics, further to the right.

In Ohio the most prominent advocate of these ideas was Republican Congressman John Ashbrook (Figure 16.6). Ashbrook was born in Johnstown, Licking County in 1928, the son of Congressman William Ashbrook and Marie Swank. John served for two years in the Navy from 1946 to 1948, and then received an A.B. from Harvard and his J.D. from Ohio State University Law School in 1955. After law school, he became publisher of the weekly newspaper *Johnstown Independent*, founded by his father in 1884. Ashbrook served two terms in the Ohio General Assembly from 1957 to 1961. In 1960 he ran for and won a seat in Congress, serving the Seventeenth District for twenty-two years. Ashbrook earned a national reputation as a staunch opponent of communism and liberal domestic programs. In 1961, he praised the YAF as helping to prevent "national suicide" in the wake of the New Deal and communism. Ashbrook would go on to help form the American Conservative Union and chaired the organization from 1966 to 1971. He also served on YAF's national advisory board and was one of the leaders in getting Goldwater to run in 1964. The later success of Ronald Reagan in the 1980 presidential election owes much to Ashbrook's work in the 1960s and early 1970s. For his part, Governor Rhodes distanced himself from the conservatism of Ashbrook and the New Right. Rhodes did allow the Ohio delegates to endorse Goldwater in the 1964 Republican Party convention, but during the campaign against Johnson, Rhodes remained on the sidelines.

As the war escalated, Johnson faced a challenge not only from conservatives in the YAF, but also from radicals in a coalition of groups that fell under the banner of the New Left. One of the key campus groups making up the New Left was Students for a Democratic Society (SDS). In their 1962 "Port Huron Statement", the largely white members of SDS set themselves to speak for the "people of this generation, bred in at least modest comfort, housed now in universities, looking uncomfortably to the world we inherit." This comfort,

Figure 16.6   Ohio became a leading staging ground for the resurgence of conservatism in American political culture in postwar America, and one of the leaders was John Ashbrook. In 1982, he sought the Republican nomination to challenge incumbent Democrat Howard Metzenbaum. While campaigning in March he collapsed and a month later died. The Ashbrook Center at Ashland University is named in memory of the congressman and Ronald Reagan dedicated it in 1983.
Source: Ashbrook Center at Ashland University

though "was penetrated" by "the permeating and victimizing fact of human degradation, symbolized by the Southern struggle against racial bigotry," racial segregation in the North, and the potential for global nuclear war. The group expressed frustration at the status quo and put forward a commitment to "understanding and changing the conditions of humanity." Like their YAF counterparts, SDS emphasized personal freedom, a popular mantra of the 1960s. SDS wanted individuals to have the freedom to find "meaning in life that is personally authentic." Unlike their YAF counterparts, SDS attacked wealth and the power of corporations and sought to open major industries to "democratic participation" and make them subject to "democratic social regulation." In particular, SDS railed against the "authoritarian and oligopolistic structure of economic decision-making" of what President Eisenhower had called the "military industrial complex."

   The Port Huron Statement tapped into a well-spring of frustration for many college-aged Ohioans. The growth of universities led many students to complain of alienation, inattentive bureaucrats, outdated curriculum, and a sense that students had no voice in campus affairs. Students began to challenge policies over dress codes, visitation rights for members of the opposite sex to dormitories, library hours, and other items. By the late 1960s, these seemingly small issues became part of a more political stance associated with larger national issues. Blacks connected civil rights and black freedom to their protests for curriculum that included black history and culture and a greater voice in campus affairs. Women began to connect policies restricting their behavior with the emerging feminist movement and for many students, Vietnam became the lynchpin in general debates over the character of American society.

Reports from government and military leaders emphasized progress in the war in Vietnam. Those on the left, however, began to protest the war as immoral and unnecessary and cast doubt on the chances for success, while conservatives demanded stronger action to defeat communism. During 1968, support for the war and for President Johnson's handling of it eroded. In January, North Vietnamese soldiers staged a massive attack against South Vietnam in what became known as the Tet Offensive—occurring during the Vietnamese holiday of Tet and under a supposed cease-fire agreement. South Vietnamese and U.S. soldiers repulsed the attack, but the political and psychological effects of Tet were devastating. For years, the American public had been told of progress, that the enemy had been weakened, that the bombing campaign had been effective. The Tet Offensive called all that into question. The evening news, which had just switched from fifteen minutes of programming to thirty minutes, streamed images of fighting, and of dead soldiers and civilians. In February trusted CBS anchor Walter Cronkite expressed what it seemed most Americans were thinking.

> We have been too often disappointed by the optimism of the American leaders, both in Vietnam and Washington, to have faith any longer in the silver linings they find in the darkest clouds." He concluded that to "say that we are closer to victory today is to believe, in the face of the evidence, the optimists who have been wrong in the past. To suggest we are on the edge of defeat is to yield to unreasonable pessimism. To say that we are mired in stalemate seems the only realistic, yet unsatisfactory, conclusion.

Upon hearing this, President Johnson is reported to have said "If I've lost Cronkite, I've lost Middle America." That included Ohio.

Johnson was up for re-election and even with Tet it seemed in January that he might yet win in November. Events, however, shifted in ways unanticipated. The New Hampshire primary opened each presidential election season and Johnson faced Senator Eugene McCarthy of Minnesota, who in late 1967 entered the primaries as a direct challenge to Johnson's Vietnam policy. McCarthy attracted liberals and antiwar students, who cut their hair and went "clean for Gene" as they canvassed throughout the Granite State. McCarthy nearly defeated Johnson in the March primary, which prompted another liberal icon, New York Senator Robert Kennedy to enter the contest. Then, in a televised Vietnam speech at the end of March, Johnson stunned the nation by announcing that he would not seek another term as president. He threw his support behind Vice President Hubert Humphrey.

Further violence gripped the nation. In April Martin Luther King, Jr. was shot and killed in Memphis. Riots broke out in 125 cities. Then, in June Robert Kennedy was assassinated at the Ambassador Hotel in Los Angeles moments after winning the Democratic primary in California. In August, the Democratic Party convention in Chicago witnessed pitched battles between police and protestors as Humphrey won the nomination. In a much calmer affair, in Miami Beach the Republicans chose Richard Nixon on the first ballot.

In the middle of such chaos, Ohioans chose not only a president but a new senator as well. William Saxbe gained the Republican nomination. Born in Mechanicsburg in 1914, Saxbe was a tobacco-chewing gentleman farmer and lawyer. A World War II veteran and later a member of the Ohio National Guard, Saxbe served in the Ohio General Assembly, becoming House majority leader from 1951–52 and Speaker from 1953–54. He then became Ohio's Attorney General, serving first under Governor O'Neill and then Rhodes. Saxbe could be considered a moderate Republican. He supported the death penalty and maintained a strong legal stance in favor of police and prosecutors. Yet Saxbe supported civil rights and sought and received support from some in organized labor. He campaigned at many job sites and with his straightforward ways and chewing tobacco, Saxbe related well to blue-collar voters. In talking with voters during the 1968 campaign, Saxbe commented that the two major issues were Vietnam and crime and that voters wanted an end to both. Saxbe promised to do that if elected. He centered his critique of the war on his belief that it was being fought "with one hand behind our back." He had concluded that the war could not be won; but Saxbe did not support the antiwar protestors either. As he later wrote: "I felt such demonstrations cut the ground from under our troops serving in Vietnam."

Democratic incumbent Frank Lausche found himself in a primary battle against former college professor, Cincinnati City Council member and Representative John J. Gilligan. Gilligan was born in Cincinnati and a Silver Star veteran of World War II. After the war he taught English at Xavier University and then ran successfully for a seat on the Cincinnati City Council in 1953. He served there until 1963. He ran successfully in 1964 for a seat in the House, only to lose in 1966 to Robert Taft, Jr. In an unprecedented move in a decade filled with surprises, the Ohio Democratic organization pulled its support of the incumbent Lausche in favor of Gilligan. In his 1968 campaign, Gilligan captured the feeling of youth and brashness of the liberal 1960s. He criticized the leadership of the AFL-CIO for failing to support civil rights and allowing racism within its unions. He spoke out against the war in Vietnam, and charged up his youthful supporters with this rhetoric: "The greatest thing about this generation ... is that it is finally asking questions that should have been asked a long time ago." Despite the attacks against racism in the AFL-CIO, organized labor threw its support towards Gilligan; after all, Lausche regularly opposed labor's goals. Liberals blasted Lausche as a "dependent Republican" rather than a self-named "independent Democrat." Lausche supported the right-to-work legislation and voted with conservatives against poverty programs, Medicare, the nuclear test ban treaty, and other liberal legislation. He vigorously defended the Vietnam War. Overall, he disagreed with his party 74 percent of the time. In the end, Gilligan beat Lausche in the May primary.

For most white voters the phrase "law and order" often used by Nixon and Saxbe captured their concerns. Personal security had become a political issue. They had grown uneasy over black protests in the cities, student radicals, and rising crime rates. In Ohio, the violent crime rate rose from 80.9 per 100,000 in 1961 to 284.3 in 1970. It would keep rising generally until 1992. White voters found appeal in conservative condemnations of a "culture of permissiveness" and a decline in traditional values, embodied both by counterculture dress, sexual behavior, drugs, and music, and changes under the Supreme Court that included not only civil rights protections but also rights for criminal defendants and legalizing the sale of contraceptives. They were also leery of further federal involvement in local issues; conservatives decried the power of distant government officials over the lives of individuals in communities.

In addition to Nixon and Saxbe, third party presidential candidate George Wallace capitalized on these issues. Wallace was the former governor of Alabama and ran representing the American Independent Party. His running mate was Columbus native and retired Air Force General Curtis LeMay. On the campaign trail, Wallace defended segregation as a matter for local people to decide, promised to shoot student demonstrators, and argued that unrest had been caused by communists, aided and abetted by the Supreme Court and "bearded beatnik bureaucrats" from Washington, D.C. Wallace added further appeal to white, blue-collar workers when he promoted a higher minimum wage, job training, and protections for unions. Wallace maintained a vigorous defense of the Vietnam War with LeMay arguing that nuclear weapons could be used to achieve victory. However, such candor deflated some of Wallace's appeal. Both Saxbe and Nixon won close races; Saxbe edged Gilligan by some 114,000 votes and Nixon's margin over Humphrey was just over 90,000. Saxbe served in the Senate until 1973, when he became Nixon's Attorney General, appointed to replace Elliot Richardson at the height of the Watergate scandal. Wallace polled well for a third party candidate, winning 13.4 percent of the national total and capturing four states in the South. His 467,495 votes in Ohio were second only to California's 487,270 outside the South. In terms of percentages, Wallace garnered 11.8 percent of the vote in Ohio, the most among Great Lakes states and among the highest outside the South. Most of Wallace's votes would have gone to Nixon, showing that at least at the presidential level, voters were shifting away from the New Deal and towards the New Right.

On the whole, Ohioans kept Republicans in power during the 1960s, as national politics favored Democrats. Kennedy and Johnson held the presidency from January 1961 to January 1969 and Democrats held majorities in both the House and Senate. In Ohio, the GOP held the majority of seats for Ohio's delegation to the House of Representatives. In the Senate, while Democrats Lausche and Young represented Ohio from 1963 to 1969, only Young could be considered liberal. At the statehouse, Republicans dominated, controlling the General Assembly fourteen times between 1939 to 1974 (fifteen counting the 106th Assembly in which the Lieutenant Governor held the tiebreaking vote); Democrats were in power only twice. Meanwhile, aside from DiSalle's term from January 1959 to January 1963, Republican Rhodes held the governor's seat.

One of the key events of the 1960s that initially helped to bring Democrats back into power in Ohio the following decade was redistricting. This emerged as a result of the Supreme Court ruling in *Baker v. Carr* (1962) that set out the "one man, one vote" principal for representation. Passed in 1903, the Hanna amendment mandated that each of Ohio's 88 counties have at least one representative in the Ohio House. This meant that areas with lower populations, which were usually rural and conservative, had the same voice as more populous counties, which were usually urban and liberal. In the words of William Saxbe, then Ohio's attorney general, redistricting was "a political hot potato." A federal three-judge panel approved a temporary plan in 1965 that created the current system of 99 House districts and 33 Senate ones with roughly equal populations. The following year, voters approved an amendment to the Ohio constitution to this effect, giving the power to an Apportionment Board to redraw these districts every ten years based on census data.

There were short-term and long-term effects of this Supreme Court decision. Perhaps most important, the new process became a partisan one, since the Apportionment Board consisted of the Governor, Secretary of State, State Auditor, and one House and one Senate member, divided by party. Whichever party controlled the board controlled redistricting. Second, as one scholar has noted, this meant that "the diminished Cornstalk Brigade could no longer run roughshod over the metropolitan areas of the state." As legendary speaker of the Ohio House Vern Riffe recalled, *Baker v. Carr* "helped set the stage for Democrats to win the majority in the House but also enabled us [to] keep the House for a number of years." This did not happen, though, until after the 1970 elections, when Democrats won all three positions on the Apportionment Board. Able to redraw the lines based on the 1970 Census, Democrats took the Ohio House after the 1972 elections and then the Ohio Senate after 1974. Alongside the partisan nature of redistricting, as the population of Ohio shifted out of cities and rural areas, it would be the suburbs that gained the most. The legislators from these areas would be the new power brokers, forming blocs with their urban and rural colleagues on legislation. In addition, the new plan preserved a majority African American district in Cuyahoga County, the 21st, from which Louis Stokes would be elected in 1968.

Gaining control of the Apportionment Board became a key issue for the 1970 election. In addition, Ohioans had to choose a new Senator. Forbidden from running for a third consecutive term as governor, James Rhodes decided to enter the race for Senate. With Democrat Stephen Young retiring, this meant a primary campaign for candidates in both major parties. Rhodes's opponent in the Republican primary was Congressman Robert A. Taft, Jr., scion of the famous Cincinnati family. On the Democratic side, the Senate primary featured former astronaut and national hero John Glenn battling then-unknown liberal Jewish millionaire Howard Metzenbaum.

Meanwhile in the governor's race, John Gilligan secured the nomination for the Democrats as state auditor Roger Cloud gained the nomination for the GOP. Fortunately for Democrats, Cloud was no Rhodes; "awesomely bland" according to one scholar. Cloud's own press secretary even quipped that "To know Roger Cloud is to forget Roger Cloud." Gilligan's staff, meanwhile conducted an aggressive and skilled campaign, led by Mark Shields (who would become a nationally syndicated columnist and television commentator). Cloud also suffered from a scandal involving millions of dollars in illegal loans made during Rhodes's second term from the state retirement system. Gilligan, running on a campaign of "we can do better" and the need for a new state income tax, easily defeated Cloud, 56 to 44 percent, or 1,725,560 to 1,382,659. Gilligan's victory initiated the growing power of Democrats in Ohio during the 1970s.

The battle between Rhodes and Taft was a largely tame affair, despite Taft's effort to allude to the loan scandal and a *Life* magazine story that sought to make a connection between a reduced sentence for a mobster and a supposed payoff to Rhodes. Taft also accused Rhodes of environmental neglect when news reports of pollution in Lake Erie became widespread; Rhodes blamed Canada for the lake's condition. Rhodes attacked Taft's weak attendance record in Congress and his votes on legislation that may have favored his family's financial interests. In the end, Taft secured the nomination in a close race.

Waiting in the Democratic wings for Young to retire were two ambitious men: Glenn and Metzenbaum. After losing to Young in 1964, Glenn became an executive at RC Cola and made millions investing in Holiday Inns in Ohio and Florida. Metzenbaum, another millionaire, had little name recognition outside Cuyahoga County, but he quickly made up ground with a strong campaign that relied heavily on television advertising. Glenn had slipped in the shower and his slower-than-expected recovery led voters to question the former astronaut's health. In an upset, Metzenbaum gained the nomination by some 13,000 votes. In the general campaign, Taft edged Metzenbaum 49.7 to 47.5 percent to take Ohio's second senate seat, joining fellow Republican William Saxbe starting in 1971.

The election news of the 1970 Senate race was not so much that Taft won, or that Metzenbaum defeated Glenn, but that Rhodes lost. As governor, Rhodes remained hugely popular yet he had been behind for most of the race—why? One argument is that Ohio voters were perfectly willing to have a "wheeling-dealing, hard-sell promoter" like Rhodes as governor, but not as a senator. Republican primary voters preferred Taft's quiet style and demeanor. That may have been true, but Rhodes made the vote close in the last week of the campaign, most likely because of his tough response to the protests and shootings on the campus of Kent State University that occurred just before the primary vote.

Campus Unrest and the Kent State Shootings

The unrest in Ohio culminated in campus protests in May 1970. The largest and most violent were at Ohio State and Kent State. After demanding several changes to campus governance and curriculum, and receiving no response from the administration of Ohio State president Novice Fawcett, the Ad-Hoc Committee for Student Rights announced a campus-wide boycott of classes to begin on April 29. As former Ohio State student Mary Webster recalled years later, the student groups "decided that we had enough going on to do more than what had ever been done, and we could get the attention of the administration to get them to actually listen." Fawcett issued a statement that summed up the view of most university leaders, and most of the Ohio public: "From my own point of view, (the demands) appear to be drafted in such a manner as to elicit negative responses . . . These statements strike at the very heart of the university and attack institutional policies cooperatively developed over the years."

The strike began peacefully, but after students (or, as some believe, plain-clothed officers posing as students) closed the former wrought-iron gates to campus on 11th and Neil Avenue, Columbus police moved in to force the gates open. As police and students brawled, the Highway Patrol came in to try to restore order. The crowd had grown to some 3,000 and began throwing rocks, bricks, and bottles at the police. Webster recalls that at that point, the police "started charging in, in full riot gear," and "then they tear gassed us." Chaos reigned as students ran. Some broke into smaller groups that surrounded the Administration Building (today, Bricker Hall) and threw rocks and bricks at windows, others damaged businesses along High Street. By the end of the day, over 300 had been arrested and 70 taken to area hospitals. The National Guard then came to campus. For several days, students continued to boycott classes and hold rallies on the Oval at the center of campus. The Guard used more tear gas to disperse a crowd of 4,000 on April 30. Meanwhile, the Administration defended the use of Guard troops and made some effort to meet student demands. On the morning of May 4, the university announced efforts to hire more African American faculty members and to create a Black Studies program. The violence continued. A rally that morning of some 1,500 students turned ugly when the Guard advanced to drive them from the Oval. Students responded by hurling dirt, rocks, and insults and once again the Guard used tear gas but the strong breeze on that sunny day dispersed the gas without effect. Rather than attend class that morning, Forrest Brandt, a photographer for the campus paper *The Lantern* stayed to document the rally. As he said later, "I don't think [students] had any idea of just how dangerous the situation was." He left to go home to his wife, telling her "I can't believe this is really going on … somebody is going to get upset, and they're going to pull a trigger." The conflict continued through May 6, when Fawcett closed the OSU campus. It remained closed for two weeks.

Tragically, some Guardsmen did pull their triggers on May 4—not in Columbus but 130 miles northeast on the campus of Kent State University. The immediate cause of the protests at Kent stemmed from the evening of Thursday, April 30, when President Richard Nixon announced the incursion of U.S. troops into Cambodia. Nixon's goal was to destroy supply lines coming from North Vietnam; Cambodia was officially neutral in the conflict and Nixon had publicly pledged to de-escalate the war. Protests erupted at hundreds of campuses across the nation over the next few days. Kent State remained open as the protests there escalated. On the evening of May 1, a crowd assembled in downtown Kent during which time a bonfire was lit and the windows of several businesses were smashed. National Guard troops arrived on the KSU campus and in the city of Kent.

Fear gripped the city as Mayor LeRoy Satrom and police believed outside agitators and SDS were working together to cause chaos. Kent's police chief, Roy Thompson later would testify that he thought "Armageddon was at hand." Merchants reported receiving telephone threats telling them to put antiwar slogans in their windows or face further damage. Events on Saturday May 2 witnessed the burning of the ROTC building on campus. Governor Rhodes, in the midst of his primary battle against Taft, arrived on campus on Sunday morning May 3. As he often did in the wake of such disturbances, Rhodes gave a fiery speech in which he blamed outside groups for causing problems on Ohio's campuses. He pledged to "eradicate the problem" of such groups who he argued would "destroy higher education in this state." "These people just move from one campus to the other and terrorize the community. They're worse than the brownshirts and the communist elements and also the nightriders and the vigilantes. They're the worst type of people that we harbor in America." A crowd gathered that evening on campus; Guardsmen read the Ohio Riot Act and dispersed them with tear gas.

On a sunny, windy Monday May 4, as conflict continued at Ohio State, classes went on as scheduled at Kent; flyers and word of mouth announced a rally for noon. On the Commons, at the crossroads of several major buildings on Kent's campus, students began gathering, some to protest, some curious, others just moving across campus from class to

Figure 16.7   This picture was taken as the National Guard troops marched towards Taylor Hall in their efforts to disperse the rally on the Kent campus on Monday May 4, 1970. Although the Guard used tear gas, the wind made it relatively ineffective. Kent's mayor, Leroy Satrom had requested the National Guard after violent confrontations between police and crowds in the city of Kent on the evening of Friday, May 1. The shootings on May 4 came to symbolize the tensions and divisions over the Vietnam War and of the 1960s more generally.
Source: Kent State University, News Service, May 4 Photographs (705/4-1-34)

class. Under the command of General Robert Canterbury, National Guard troops armed with tear gas, live ammunition in M-1 rifles, .45 caliber pistols, and shotguns moved to disperse the crowd (see Figure 16.7). The troops were nervous, but they and the General were experienced with other disturbances, including those in Akron and in Hough. Indeed, since 1968 Rhodes had authorized the Guard some forty times to quell civil disturbances. As the crowd began to disperse, some students threw rocks and jeered at the Guard. The wind made tear gas largely ineffective and some students grabbed canisters and threw them back. Troops followed students across the Commons and up one side of Blanket Hill. At this point, Canterbury concluded it would be necessary to push the students beyond a football practice field that lay some eighty yards below the hill. Antagonism between the Guard and students only increased; Guardsmen thought students were disobeying orders to disperse and that they had shown their capacity for violence. For their part, students were already angry at the war and other campus issues, and now the Guard had taken over; their rights to assemble and speak freely on campus were being violated. As many students would later say about the rally on May 4, "We weren't doing anything."

The troops moved down Blanket Hill onto the practice field; they then retraced their steps back up the hill. At 12:25 p.m. they reached the crest of the hill, turned and began firing into the crowd. The shooting lasted for thirteen seconds; when it was over, sixty-one shots had been fired, four students lay dead or dying—Allison Krause, Jeffrey Miller, Sandra Scheuer, and William Schroeder—and nine others wounded, including Dean Kahler who was paralyzed from the waist down. Krause and Miller were involved in the protests; Scheuer was on her way to class; Schroeder, an ROTC student was an onlooker.

Almost instantly the shootings at Kent became icons of the 1960s, helped by the release only a few weeks later of the hit song "Ohio" by Crosby, Stills, Nash and Young. Neil Young's lyrics capture the raw directness of the experience:

> Tin soldiers and Nixon coming
> We're finally on our own.
> This summer I hear the drumming,
> Four dead in Ohio.
> Gotta get down to it
> Soldiers are gunning us down
> Should have been done long ago.
> What if you knew her
> And found her dead on the ground
> How can you run when you know?

The shootings seemed to split Ohioans even further. Rallies and protests erupted anew on campuses. At first peaceful, demonstrations at Ohio University in Athens turned violent and the school shut down for the remainder of the quarter. The news only intensified the existing conflict at Ohio State. Equally direct and vocal were voices of Ohioans who expressed their approval of the Guard. Although he lost, Rhodes's tough talk helped his flagging candidacy. Letters to Mayor Satrom and to newspapers, and editorials overwhelmingly supported the Guard, Rhodes, and the city officials. For weeks after, Kent's paper, the *Record-Courier* had to devote a full page each issue to community outpouring. Middle-America displayed its resentments, frustrations, and anger against the counterculture, students and higher education, but more so at the thought of disruption to an established social order:

I stand behind the action of the National Guard! I want my property defended.

We are paying a large percentage of our hard-earned money to support and educate these young people. For what? To let them burn and destroy property that more of our tax money has paid for?

If the slouchily dressed female students and the freakishly dressed, long-haired male students would properly dress and otherwise properly demean themselves as not to make show-offs of themselves, such trouble could be and would be avoided.

The National Guard made only one mistake—they should have fired sooner and longer.

Just as it did during the campaigns of Nixon, Rhodes, and Wallace, the phrase "law and order" came up frequently in these comments. Rhodes's statement at Kent was not out of the ordinary for him and the local reaction to campus unrest had remained fairly constant in supporting the forces of order. In December 1969, African American students took over an administration building at the University of Akron. Rhodes called these actions "a disgrace," called out the Guard and promised to restore order. This event ended peacefully, but locals reacted positively to Rhodes's tough stance. Lonzo Green, a retired Akron minister, thanked Rhodes for his "immediate and forceful dealing with the Black Power demonstration in Akron." Green went on to say that "a great many patriotic citizens, including myself, are pretty sick and tired of the coddling that has been going on in so many places—coddling of black anarchists by politicians who should seek their unholy votes."

Much of the memory of the 1960s is about social movements, student demonstrations, and public figures such as John and Robert Kennedy, Lyndon Johnson, and Martin Luther King, Jr. It may be that the most significant national domestic development of the 1960s was the resurgence of conservatism. In Ohio, that sentiment never faded. On the political level, the success of Rhodes showed this, as did the strength of Republicans in Congress and in the Senate. The views of those Kent residents who supported the Guard illustrate the depth of what Nixon would call the "silent majority" of citizens. They were not radical or liberal, but moderates or conservative whose influence shaped much of Ohio's political culture in the 1960s and who would come to dominate national politics in the decades following.

The search for truth and meaning over Kent continued in the immediate weeks and years and still does today. The President's Commission on Campus Unrest, led by Republican William Scranton visited Kent in August and its report spread blame among students, the Guard, and Kent administrators. "The actions of some students were violent and criminal and those of some others were dangerous reckless and irresponsible. The indiscriminate firing of rifles into a crowd of students and the deaths that followed were unnecessary, unwarranted and inexcusable." Meanwhile, a grand jury convened by Rhodes consisting of mainly Portage County residents made it clear they were interested in exonerating the Guard and punishing the students and Kent administrators and faculty. They issued their report in October and indicted twenty-five people, none of whom were Guardsmen. "What disturbs us," the jury said, "is that any such group of intellectuals and social misfits should be afforded the opportunity to disrupt the affairs of a major university." Courts rejected a criminal trial against the Guard, but a wrongful death and injury trial resulted in a 1979 settlement out of court between the families and the State of Ohio. A memorial on Kent's campus came in 1990, but it too was shrouded in controversy. Recently, new evidence has emerged from May 4 at Kent. Analysis of a cassette tape recording made that day indicates there may have been shots fired before the National Guard fired and that the Guard may have been given an order to prepare to fire. If followed with calls for new investigations, the tape may heighten the divisions of the tragedy and the issues related to the unrest of the postwar years.

Kent marked a tragic end to tumultuous decade that witnessed profound changes in many arenas. Politically, it became a decade in which liberals, radicals, and conservatives battled for control over Ohio's and the nation's policies, values, and institutions. What might be called the liberal mainstream of the era, crafted in the New Deal, came under attack from activists on both the political left and right. Social activism on the political left broadened the rights and freedoms for African Americans and women; challenged Cold War foreign policy; forged an environmental movement that redefined the relationship between society and nature; increased student influence in curriculum and governance on university and college campuses; and a fostered a counterculture that altered social mores and expectations. For their part, conservatives of various stripes gathered under the umbrella of what came to be called the New Right and would come to dominate politics in the decades that followed.

Further Reading

The literature on the 1960s is vast and growing. For some overviews and most Ohio specific events see: Judith Ezekiel, *Feminism in the Heartland* (2002. Columbus: The Ohio State University Press002); Michael W. Flamm, *Law and Order: Street Crime, Civil Unrest, and the Crisis of Liberalism in the 1960s* (2005. New York: Columbia University Press); Thomas Hensley and Jerry Lewis eds., *Kent State and May 4th: A Social Science Perspective* (2010. Kent: Kent State University Press); Gregory S. Jacobs, *Getting Around Brown: Desegregation, Development and the Columbus Public Schools* (1998. Columbus: The Ohio State University Press); Alexander P. Lamis and Brian Usher, eds., *Ohio Politics* (2d ed. 2007. Kent: Kent State University Press); Manning Marable and Elizabeth Kai Hinton, eds., *The New Black History: Revisiting the Second Reconstruction* (2011. New York: Palgrave); Doug McAdam, *Freedom Summer* (1990. New York: Oxford University Press); William McGucken, *Lake Erie Rehabilitated: Controlling Eutrophication, 1960s–1900s* (2001. Akron: University of Akron Press); Leonard N. Moore, *Carl Stokes and the Rise of Black Political Power* (2003. Urbana: University of Illinois Press); James A. Rhodes, *Alternative to a Decadent Society* (1969. Indianapolis: Howard W. Sams); William B. Saxbe, *I've Seen the Elephant: An Autobiography* (2000. Kent: Kent State University Press); David Stradling, "Perceptions of the Burning River: Deindustrialization and Cleveland's Cuyahoga River," *Environmental History* 13(3) (2008, pp. 515–35); Warren Van Tine and Michael Pierce, eds., *Builders of Ohio: A Biographical History* (2003. Columbus: The Ohio State University Press); United States Commission on Civil Rights, *Hearing before the United States Commission on Civil Rights: Hearing Held in Cleveland, Ohio, April 1–7 1966* (Washington, D.C.: United States Commission on Civil Rights).

17

Ohio since 1970

Former U.S. Poet Laureate Rita Dove grew up in Akron (Figure 17.1). Writing in the 1990s, she remembered a place full of excitement and possibility. "The Akron I grew up in was governed by two scents: the stench of the rubber factories and the smell of burning oats from the Quaker Oats silos." "Neither smell was pleasant," she noted, "but both aroused the imagination of children." For Dove and for many others in Akron "rubber brought to mind huge truck tires rolling out of Akron to travel the globe" that meant Akron "was a *happening* town." The "bitter aroma of Quaker Oats, on the other hand, enveloped me in a feeling of security." Rubber was the smell of money and importance that provided security for thousands of Akronites.

Yet by the time Dove wrote these words, something in Akron and Ohio had been lost. The rubber factories were gone, as were other signs of Ohio's industrial power and identity. From the Civil War through the mid-twentieth century, Ohio had been a leader, a symbol of progress and modernity. By the 1970s, Ohio had become part of the Rust Belt, a symbol of the collapse of the postwar dream. Frustration, torpor, and decline came to describe the Buckeye State. In her song from the 1980s, "My City was Gone," Akron native Chrissy Hynde, leader of the rock group The Pretenders, wrote that she "went back to Ohio," but that her "city was gone." The founders of the new wave group Devo, Jerry Casale, and Mark Mothersbaugh, lived and performed in Akron in the 1970s and described the city as possessing a "hellish, depressing patina" that formed the backdrop for their music.

However, Dove was optimistic, expressing hope that Akron, and all of Ohio, could bounce back. "Akron," she argued, was "one of the few old manufacturing hubs which has survived the loss of labor-intensive factory production by turning itself into a corporate center, a feat requiring perseverance, faith in human resources, and—last but not least—imagination." Dove joined a vibrant conversation in Ohio to redefine the state and restore

Ohio: A History of the Buckeye State, First Edition. Kevin F. Kern and Gregory S. Wilson.
© 2014 John Wiley & Sons, Inc. Published 2014 by John Wiley & Sons, Inc.

Figure 17.1 Akron native Rita Dove served as Poet Laureate of the United States and Consultant to the Library of Congress from 1993 to 1995 and as Poet Laureate of the Commonwealth of Virginia from 2004 to 2006. In 2011 President Barack Obama presented her with the National Medal of the Arts. Her father, Ray was the first African American chemist to work in the U.S. tire industry when Goodyear employed him in Akron. She began writing poetry as a child but kept the poems in a secret notebook because she was afraid her classmates would make fun of her.
Source: Photo by Fred Viebahn

a sense of leadership and possibility. Those conversations continue, driven by the ways in which industrial transformation intermixed with ever-present social and political changes that have come to define Ohio's history since the 1970s.

Stagnation and Decline

Population trends

In several key social and economic indicators, Ohio faced decline and stagnation that began in earnest in the 1970s and continues in many areas today. In terms of population, the state's population was basically stagnant from 1970 through 1990, growing 1.4 percent in the 1970s and 0.5 percent in the 1980s. There were approximately 10.6 million Ohioans in 1970 and 10.8 million in 1990. Slow growth continued so that by 2010 there were about

11.5 million Ohioans. One effect of this has been a drop in Ohio's clout in Congress. Ohio had twenty-four representatives in Congress in 1960, while in 2010 there were sixteen. The state's electoral votes have dropped, too, from twenty-six in 1960 to eighteen for the 2012 elections. Ohio's 1.6 percent growth rate in population was the third slowest among states between 2000 and 2010. Michigan was the only state to lose population in this decade. The Midwest generally has grown more slowly than other parts of the nation. From 2000 to 2010, the South and West continued to grow much faster (14.3 and 13.8 percent, respectively) than the Midwest (3.9 percent), and Northeast (3.2 percent). Within Ohio, since 1970, with the notable exception Columbus, Ohio's largest cities have lost population. Of Ohio's eighty-eight counties, thirty-four lost population in the 2000s (see Table 17.1 for detailed data).

Racially Ohio is still mainly white. In 2010, 82.7 percent of Ohioans were white, 12.2 were African American, and 1.7 percent Asian. Of those who were white, 3.1 percent were Hispanic. The Census asked respondents about multiracial identity; in Ohio 2.1 percent identified as being of two or more races—mainly white and African American. Although still the overwhelming majority, non-Hispanic whites declined as a percentage of Ohioans while all other groups grew. Data from 2010 show that in the United States as a whole, 72.4 percent identified as white, 12.8 percent African American, and 4.8 percent Asian. Among those listed as white, 16.3 percent were Hispanic.

Industrial transformation

Like the toppling statues of a defeated regime, in the early 1980s Ohio's old industrial symbols came down. In Akron, the wrecking ball felled one of Firestone's plants where thousands used to make tires. In Youngstown, down came the blast furnaces that had made steel. As one Youngstown resident commented: "The community's identity is up for grabs. People are confused, frustrated and bitter." Manufacturing had defined Ohio and shaped much of the state's economy, politics, and social structure. The state experienced what many have called deindustrialization, the widespread disinvestment in basic productive capacity, especially manufacturing. In the 1970s industries including steel, rubber, appliances, glass, and automobiles all experienced plant closures and job losses, contributing directly to Ohio's flat growth rate and reinforcing Ohio's rust-belt image. This transformation altered social structures built on certain conceptions of work and community that were forged in Ohio's industrial landscape. What once seemed solid began to collapse and disappear.

The problems were not just in Ohio or solely in manufacturing; the entire U.S. economy in the 1970s and early 1980s languished. Between 1969 and 1976 the United States lost 22.3 million jobs. In the 1960s, the U.S. economy had grown 4.1 percent. Between 1970 and 1973, it grew about 2.9 percent a year and between 1974 and 1980 there was virtually no growth. Purchasing power had declined for most workers. The 1973–74 oil crisis aided this, with OPEC increasing the price of oil in response to U.S. support for Israel in the Yom Kippur War. Stagflation became the dominant economic term of the 1970s. Usually when inflation is high, unemployment is low, suggesting a rapidly growing

Table 17.1 Total population, Ohio and central cities

	1970	1980	% change 1970–80	1990	% change 1980–90	2000	% change 1990–2000	2010	% change 2000–10	% change 1970–2010
Akron	275,425	237,177	–13.9	223,019	–6.0	217,074	–2.7	199,110	–8.3	–27.7
Canton	110,053	94,730	–13.9	84,161	–11.2	80,806	–4.0	73,007	–9.7	–33.7
Cincinnati	452,524	385,457	–14.8	364,040	–5.6	331,285	–9.0	296,943	–10.4	–34.4
Cleveland	750,903	573,822	–23.6	505,616	–11.9	478,403	–5.4	396,815	–17.1	–47.2
Columbus	539,677	564,871	4.7	632,910	12.0	711,470	12.4	787,033	10.6	45.8
Dayton	243,601	203,371	–16.5	182,044	–10.5	166,179	–8.7	141,527	–14.8	–41.9
Toledo	383,818	354,635	–7.6	332,943	–6.1	313,619	–5.8	287,208	–8.4	–25.2
Youngstown	139,788	115,436	–17.4	95,732	–17.1	82,026	–14.3	66,982	–18.3	–52.1
Ohio	10,652,017	10,797,630	1.4	10,847,115	0.5	11,353,140	4.7	11,536,504	1.6	8.3

economy but in the 1970s, both inflation and unemployment increased. Jimmy Carter, elected in 1976, created the "misery index" for economic data, adding inflation and unemployment rates together. By 1980 it had reached nearly 20 percent, three times its average in the 1960s. In Ohio, unemployment rates resembled a roller coaster. The annual rate for 1973 was 4.3 percent, jumping to 9.1 percent in 1975, falling back to 5.5 percent in 1978, and then back to over 13 percent during the recession of 1982–83. These were often higher than the national average. Ohio still maintained its strong manufacturing profile and those industries were often hardest hit during recessions. Nationally, the unemployment rate was 4.9 percent in 1973, 8.5 percent in 1975, 6.1 percent in 1978, and hovered just over 10 percent during the recession of 1982–83.

From the 1970s on, globalization has meant that more and more companies have been able to produce goods and deliver services without respecting political boundaries. Economic power has shifted to Asia, with consequences for Ohio and the United States. The United States's share of world manufacturing dropped from about 25 percent in the late 1960s to 17 percent by the early 1980s. The trade deficit grew, hitting manufacturing the hardest. With Japan alone, the deficit reached $10 billion in 1980. Based on dollar value, Japan's top exports to the U.S. were automobiles, "iron and steel plates, truck and tractor chassis, radios, motorbikes, and audio and video tape recorders. In contrast, America's top seven exports to Japan, in order of dollar value, were soybeans, corn, fir logs, hemlock logs, coal, wheat, and cotton." Examined this way, the United States had become similar to so-called "Third World" nations that imported their higher-value manufactured goods and exported lower-value agricultural products. In 2010 China overtook the United States as the world's largest manufacturing nation. China possesses many of the same factors that once benefited Ohio's rise to prominence, but on a much larger scale, including a large workforce, abundant resources, and a government committed to economic development through various incentives to businesses. China's labor costs are relatively low as well. In terms of transportation and location, the development of large ocean freighters (like the development of canals and railroads before) has made movement of goods easier and cheaper. China and other countries in Asia such as Japan, South Korea, and India have been able to invest more completely in new and more efficient technologies for producing goods, especially electronics. These nations have also benefited from favorable global trade policies and exchange rates for currency, which made exports competitive. As in Ohio, there have been high social and environmental costs to rapid industrial development in China and other nations. Calls for reform have been more frequent. To paraphrase a quote often mistakenly attributed to Mark Twain, when considering industrial transformation on a global scale, history may not be repeating itself, but it certainly rhymes.

In the face of increasing global competition, Ohio's steel, automobile, and tire companies, for example, adopted several strategies. Some firms stayed in Ohio and continued production of their original product, but decentralized locations, building new factories away from big cities and in favor of rural areas where they could pay lower wages and were more likely to attract a non-union workforce. In Ohio, this drove population numbers down in places like Cleveland and Cincinnati, but helped expand them in the surrounding suburbs. When the South and West rose in influence and population after 1945, manufacturing and other leading sectors shifted there. Others divested their original core industries and instead moved money into newer ventures. The older factories and plants across Ohio became obsolete and shut down.

Nationally, and in Ohio between 1970 and 2000, the absolute numbers of employees in manufacturing remained fairly steady, with some ups and downs, before plummeting to record lows in the most recent data from 2010. At the same time, thanks to innovations in technology, worker productivity has increased steadily, so that today fewer workers produce three times as much as they did in the 1980s. However, the percentage of workers in manufacturing has dropped regularly since 1945. At the beginning of 1970 there were 18,424,000 employed in manufacturing in the United States, with the number peaking at an all-time high of 19,553,000 in June 1979. In March 1989 the total was 18,060,000, and in July 2000 17,321,000. Since then the number dropped to 11,465,000 in January 2010 the lowest since March 1941, when the total was 11,409,000. As a percentage of employment, manufacturing has been dropping since 1945, when it was 38.5 percent. In 1970 it was 27.3 percent, 22.4 percent in 1980, 17.4 in 1990, 12.8 in 2002 to about 9 percent in 2010. Retail trade and services employment passed manufacturing in the 1980s, and government employment did so in the 1990s. By 2011, the services sector was the largest employment sector in the U.S. economy. Ohio has followed these trends in some ways, but it retains a higher portion of manufacturing than the nation as a whole. In 2008 manufacturing represented 9.8 percent of the U.S. economy. In Ohio it was 13.8 percent making Ohio the eighth highest among the states. Ohio also ranked third behind California and Texas in the number of production employees, at 496,000 in 2008.

Economic transformation also hurt organized labor. Ohio's workers had been among the most unionized in the nation. While that remains true, their overall numbers and percentages have dropped, and the industries in which workers are organized has shifted, so that today most unionized workers in Ohio and the nation are government employees rather than those in manufacturing. In 1983, the percentage of workers who were members of a union in the United States was 20.1. In 2010 it had dropped to 11.9 percent. In Ohio, there were 655,000 workers belonging to a union in 2010, or 13.7 percent of all workers in the state. This was down from 21.3 percent in 1989.

As plants closed most political and civic leaders in Ohio and elsewhere perceived the issue as local or at best a regional rather than national matter. Southerners and Westerners, benefitting from decentralization of factories and shops, refused to support national legislation that might have given workers and communities in Ohio and the traditional manufacturing belt advanced notice of plant closures or added benefits from job losses. Ohio legislators and business leaders also opposed such a move, fearing that such legislation might make things worse by encouraging remaining plants to close, and by keeping new businesses from opening. Opponents of legislation also argued that businesses had the right to open and close as they saw fit. National legislation did emerge in 1988 with passage of the Worker Adjustment and Retraining Notification Act, which requires employers of one hundred or more workers to provide sixty days advance warning of a plant shutdown or mass layoff.

This legislation did little to stop the process of industrial transformation. If in the 1930s workers fought to create their unions, then by the late 1970s and early 1980s many unionists seemed resigned to their fate. Plant closures seemed inevitable. Unions had little leverage against plant shutdowns. They could gain collective bargaining agreements for wages, hours, and benefits, but decisions on production and shifting of capital remained firmly in the management's hands. This had been part of the labor-business accord hammered out in early post-World War II years. Workers and their union leadership largely accepted management's argument that high wages were causing the problems and readily agreed to concessions in new contracts. Little wonder workers became disillusioned and bitter towards unions and that arguments against unionization, once voiced by lonely conservatives in the early postwar decades, became part of mainstream beliefs by the 1980s.

Several case studies illustrate the local experience of this broad process of industrial transformation. In Moraine, just outside Dayton, Frigidaire, a division of General Motors, had been making refrigerators there since the 1920s. In 1971, losing market share in the appliance sector, the company laid off several thousand workers. Company officials then orchestrated a campaign to gain concessions from the remaining unionized employees. This included having the public relations officer spread a rumor that the company would close, urging the formation of a "Save our Frigidaire for the Community Committee," and then having company executives make public comments about the possibility of moving the factory. Eventually, union workers bowed to the pressure, agreeing to wage cuts in exchange for calling back laid off workers and a commitment from GM to keep Frigidaire in Dayton. The workers had been the highest paid in the industry and the Frigidaire example showed how, in the context of industrial transformation businesses were able to marshal public opinion in their favor. Other companies formed similar committees to gain concessions from workers. GM sold Frigidaire in 1979 and then converted the 4.2 million-square-foot building to automotive parts. The plant continued to shed workers until 2008 when GM closed it in the wake of the company filing for bankruptcy.

Ohio, and especially Akron, had been the home for tire production in the United States. In 1947, 43 percent of all tire industry employees worked in Ohio. By 1972, it had fallen to 25 percent. From some 51,000 workers in Akron alone, employment by Firestone, General Tire, Goodrich and Goodyear fell to 37,000 in 1970. As their numbers declined, the union representing most of them, the United Rubber Workers (URW), became more aggressive under the leadership of Peter Bommarito. "The Bomber," as he was called, took over in 1967 and he was a force to be reckoned with. Lean, muscular, with charisma, energy, and talent for confrontation, The Bomber moved to Akron from Detroit where he had worked for U.S. Rubber. He served in the Marines during World War II and gained a reputation as a skilled fighter against the Japanese and his fellow Marines. In 1967, Bommarito led the URW out on strike, something he would do every three years when each contract expired, until 1976.

In the contracts, Bommarito and the URW won: in 1967 workers won additional supplemental unemployment benefits; and in 1970 they gained better pay, a study on carcinogens, and paid prescription drugs. In 1973 they gained a 5.5 percent increase in wages, the maximum allowed under President Nixon's price and wage control program. Inflation, though, had reached over 12 percent by 1974 and it was clear that the 1976 contract year would equal the massive fireworks displays planned for the nation's bicentennial. Nationwide, some 60,000 URW members went on strike in April, about 11,000 walked out in Akron. As the bicentennial celebrations went forward, the strike lasted through August, and only with the help of federal officials was there a settlement. The URW gained wage and pension increases, and cost-of-living allowances. However, the lengthy strike created divisions in the URW and dissatisfaction with Bommarito, who had promised even more. Workers "survived, but something was taken out of them."

Meanwhile, jobs disappeared. Between 1960 and 1979, thirty-one tire plants were built in the United States but none in Akron. In February 1978 Goodyear closed its Plant 2 and 1,200 workers lost their jobs. In June Firestone closed and demolished its Plant 2 and another 1,200 workers lost their jobs. Mohawk closed in November, with over 300 losing their jobs. Then, in early 1982, tire production essentially ended when General Tire closed its plant laying-off another 1,300 workers. By the 1990s about 6,000 worked for the rubber companies; nine of the top ten states making tires were in the South with Ohio ranked twelfth.

Many people blamed the union and its leaders for driving tire jobs out of Akron. "None of them were flexible enough," argued Don Stephens, Akron Regional Development Director. "Leaders chose only to do what was most politically expedient," said Goodrich executive Peter Pestillo. Former Goodyear pipefitter Jim Walker criticized the focus on wages, "We should have been looking at job security, retraining issues, transfer rights." In 1976 Goodyear offered to rebuild its Akron Plant 2 for the new radial tires then making inroads from Europe and Japan, but the URW refused to allow work concessions.

Companies also did not reinvest. As Goodrich president John Ong acknowledged, "[when] our stock price was going through the roof, and a lot of people were getting wealthy, we should have reinvested in the tire business if we were going to stay in it. We barely reinvested at all." By the late 1960s, Akron's tire companies had been building new plants in the South and West, to take advantage of new markets and new technologies, and to escape unions. Akron's companies failed to adopt radial technology until the 1970s. Conversion was expensive and radials required new technical skills workers did not possess. The buildings in Akron, moreover, were all built before 1917 and designed for bias-ply tires, not radials. Goodyear's offer in 1976 to rebuild was an anomaly. Those firms still making tires built factories elsewhere. In 1975 Goodrich ended its passenger tire production in Akron and its industrial tires in 1978. The company focused on its money-making invention of PVC as well as aerospace and chemicals.

In her memoir of growing up in Akron, *Gum Dipped*, author Joyce Dyer remembered the industrial transformation of her home town. "Over and over we watched the factories turn into empty buildings, the bricks and windows grow darker and more bleak. Finally saw them collapse and disappear." Like many other industrial cities in Ohio and the Midwest, over time Akron became a center for finance, high tech, medical, and education. "The machinery of production gave way to desks and little shelves, and the sounds inside grew light. They were hives with insects in them now, not hot slaughterhouses with roaming beasts."

If Ohio, as a state, came to symbolize deindustrialization, then Youngstown was ground zero. Black Monday in Youngstown, September 19, 1977, was when Lykes Corporation, a New Orleans-based company that had purchased Youngstown Sheet and Tube, announced it was closing most operations at the Campbell works of Youngstown Sheet and Tube.

Within weeks, 4,100 workers were out of work. This had been the city's largest producer and employer, but its production facilities were decades behind the current technology. Just a week before workers had set a production record and company officials had told union leaders that there were no plans to close.

The trouble in the steel industry had begun in 1959, when, for the first time, imported steel accounted for greater volume than domestic. As global competition increased, the steel industry failed to modernize. Older, open hearth methods were already outdated by the 1950s, when Japan and Europe entered the global steel business using the basic oxygen furnace (BOF) and continuous casting, which allowed for fewer steps in production and higher quality steel. From the 1960s to the 1980s, steel companies that did stay in the business tended to consolidate near Chicago and Gary, with easier access to cheaper water transport. Meanwhile, employment in the steel industry declined from 509,000 in 1973 to 240,000 in 1983.

A month after the closure of the Campbell Works, the Ecumenical Coalition of the Mahoning Valley formed with the goal of reopening the plant under new ownership—mainly the former workers and other community members. The group, which included former steelworkers and religious leaders, became in the words of one scholar "a band of daring, quixotic preachers, tilting at the corporate powers on behalf of their people." They were joined by experts and activists such as historian and lawyer Staughton Lynd who had moved to Youngstown in order to work with communities facing economic and social dislocation. Its religious leaders, led by Rabbi Sidney Berkowitz, Episcopal Bishop John Burt, and Roman Catholic Bishop James W. Malone issued a pastoral letter in November 1977. Overall it was a powerful, thoughtful document that went beyond the isolated closing in Youngstown to raise questions about the larger process of economic transformation underway in the 1970s.

The closing of the Campbell Works, the letter noted, generated "shock, anger and genuine fear," and raised "profound issues of corporate responsibility." It was not simply a private, economic decision; it was a "matter of public concern" since it affected so many people and there was a need to take into account "the moral and religious aspects of this crisis." "Our common religious tradition summons us to respond to our neighbors' needs and to work for justice," the religious leaders stressed. Although the letter acknowledged global competition and union demands, it largely framed the shutdowns as local issues and placed the blame mainly upon Lykes. "Corporations have a social responsibility to their employees and the community" as well as to their shareholders. "By their abandonment of Youngstown, the Lykes Corporation has neglected this corporate social responsibility."

Initially, the federal government supported the coalition with a research grant to develop plans and studies for operating the plant. National and international news media focused on the story as a unique response to plant closings then sweeping the Northeast and Midwest. For their part, Governor Rhodes and state leaders could offer little. Rhodes visited Youngstown and urged local mayors to apply for state loans that would help build new industrial plants to attract companies.

The Youngstown story prompted Congressional hearings on shut downs; some saw what was happening in Youngstown as a symbol for national problems in the post-Watergate era. Ohio Congressman Clarence Brown commented, "What happened in northeastern Ohio is a sad symbol of our total national decline." Despite the attention and energy, the coalition failed to keep the mills open. The group ended in April 1979 after loan guarantees from the federal government failed to materialize. President Carter himself had little sympathy for the issue, and he and his administration rejected calls for further assistance, including legislation requiring advanced notice of shut downs. They also considered the poor environmental record of the steel industry, which would make supporting its continued operation in the older methods a contradiction with calls for greater environmental stewardship.

Yet it was a vocal minority of locals who pushed the plan forward. Part of it was apathy or disinterest among the steel workers themselves. Marsha Peskin worked in the office as part of the campaign. "I would say that the response was disappointing." "But out of 5,000 that were laid off, you had 100 people that I knew about that were vaguely interested. Then, you only had no more than a dozen who were willing to come down and work." At the same time, the United Steel Workers Association (USWA) refused to get involved, citing the plan as unworkable and also fearing that a reopened plant might undercut wages elsewhere. The USWA leadership continued to blame imports and believed that shutdowns would reduce overcapacity in the industry, thus giving greater security to those workers remaining. Despite the media coverage, no coordinated national response came; it remained chiefly a local matter.

Lykes also closed the Brier Hill Works in December 1979 and in November 1979 U.S. Steel announced it would close the McDonald and Ohio Works in early 1980, eliminating another 3,500 jobs. Youngstown steelworkers traveled to Pittsburgh, occupying U.S. Steel's headquarters. They also participated in a legal fight led by Staughton Lynd against the corporation to keep the mills open. These failed, too. As one steelworker active in the campaign noted, "It makes me sick now to drive down Poland Avenue to see those empty spaces where the blast furnaces used to be" (see Figure 17.2).

The story of steel's apparent demise in Youngstown has been immortalized by Bruce Springsteen in the song "Youngstown," which appeared on the recording *The Ghost of Tom Joad* in 1995. Springsteen purposefully evoked the bitterness, hardship, loss, and resilience found in John Steinbeck's novel of the Great Depression, *The Grapes of Wrath* as well as Woody Guthrie's 1940 recordings on *Dust Bowl Ballads*.

> Well my daddy come on the Ohio works
> When he come home from World War Two
> Now the yard's just scrap and rubble
> He said, "Them big boys did what Hitler couldn't do"
> These mills they built the tanks and bombs
> That won this country's wars
> We sent our sons to Korea and Vietnam
> Now we're wondering what they were dyin' for

Springsteen also drew on the photographs and essays in the book *Journey to Nowhere*, which came out during the recession of the early 1980s, just after the collapse of the mills in Youngstown. The book chronicled the deindustrialized landscape of the Midwest, and it too evoked memories of the Great Depression.

Figure 17.2 U.S. Steel's Ohio Works in Youngstown contained the blast furnaces and open hearths needed to make steel. U.S. Steel closed its Ohio Works in 1980 and in 1983 the company had the plant demolished, a portion of which is pictured here. It became a symbol of deindustrialization and Ohio's history in this era.

Source: Courtesy of the Ohio Historical Society (AL04499)

Politics in the 1970s and 1980s

John Gilligan

Addressing industrial transformation and stagnation became the central problem facing Ohio's political leaders in the 1970s and 1980s as both Democrats and Republicans sought solutions. While there were some successes in job creation and other areas, overall the state failed to recover from the devastating losses. In the 1970 elections, Democrats swept the statewide offices, bringing John J. "Jack" Gilligan into the governor's mansion. Gilligan faced a number of issues. The state's share of spending on public schools had dropped and local taxes had increased to make up the difference. By 1970, local residents began voting down more levies, and schools had started to close. Mental health institutions and other social services were also in financial difficulties. Gilligan appointed a Citizen's Task Force on Tax Reform, made up of members from business, labor, civic, and academic circles. The group recommended a graduated personal income tax, lower property taxes, homestead exemptions for elderly homeowners, and a reduction in personal property tax. To get his tax plan through, Gilligan agreed to drop his opposition to the state lottery. During the battle, the state had to balance its books and Gilligan made cuts, including closing the state parks for several weeks. Finally, after nine months of wrangling, Gilligan signed the new budget and tax legislation into law in December 1971, Ohio's first major tax since 1935. Conservatives challenged the income tax, but in 1972 voters rejected a repeal effort. That year there were new laws for consumer protection, workplace safety, and revamped strip mining regulations. The revenues made possible the creation of the Ohio Environment Protection Agency (EPA) in 1972, the state Commission on Aging, and increased spending for schools, mental health facilities, and new separate departments for economic development and transportation. Ohio also created its first minimum wage law and there were updates to state campaign finance and ethics laws.

Gilligan later noted that the new tax and other laws "changed, in a relatively short period of time, the general approach to state government." Gilligan assumed he would win re-election with these achievements, and he was touted as a possible Democratic nominee for president in 1976. However, the sixty-five-year-old James Rhodes was ready for another try at the state's highest office, accusing Gilligan of taxing "everything in Ohio that walks, crawls or flies." Gilligan and his advisers were overconfident and unready for Rhodes's campaign attacks. Gilligan hurt himself, too. At the 1972 Ohio State Fair, as he headed for the sheep barn, the governor stopped to talk with the reporter at the radio booth broadcasting live from the fairgrounds. The reporter asked him: "Gonna shear a sheep?" "Nope," replied the governor. "I shear taxpayers, not sheep." To the surprise of even Rhodes, the ex-governor scored a narrow victory over Gilligan, 48.6 percent to 48.2 percent. Voters never warmed to Gilligan, whom they perceived as arrogant and aloof. Voters also reacted in their "traditional, almost visceral dislike of taxes and politicians who support them." Rhodes remained hugely popular. Further proof lay in the fact that John Glenn won easily in his Senate bid that year, and voters elected Democrat Richard Celeste as Lieutenant Governor.

Rhodes again

Democrats could take some solace in their control over the Senate, and continued control over the House. Rhodes's third and fourth terms coincided with the ascendancy of another powerful figure in recent Ohio political history, Vernal G. Riffe, Jr. a moderate Democrat representing Scioto County. He began his career in the Ohio House in 1959, serving as Speaker from 1975 until his retirement in 1994. Riffe was a practical, results-oriented political leader who worked with the opposition out of a belief in "the politics of coalitional pragmatism, not ideology." In the 1970s and 1980s, Riffe ensured House support for the Equal Rights Amendment and mentored and supported African American leaders. He also supported limits on abortion and reinstated the death penalty. Riffe worked with organized labor, but one United Auto Workers (UAW) leader expressed the view of many when he called Riffe "dictator of Ohio." His annual birthday party fund raiser funneled millions into the Democratic Party caucus, which Riffe used to support Democrats and to maintain his power.

As governor in the 1960s, Rhodes benefited from a growing economy; the opposite was true for his second set of terms as he battled Ohio's declining economy, the national energy shortage, and inflation. He also faced a Democratic legislature firmly under the grasp of Riffe. Rhodes had some successes, but much "of his second eight years was spent marking time, trying to keep the state afloat." For the issues of economic development in the central cities, jobs, housing development, energy and transportation improvements, and public construction—all of which Rhodes stated Ohio needed to make the state "Depression-proof"—Rhodes relied on his standard answer: bonds. Democratic legislators remained cautious as Rhodes proposed a massive $4.5 billion package he called his "Blueprint for Ohio," funded in part by proposed increases in gasoline and sales taxes (despite Rhodes's pledge against new taxes). Although the governor's opponents called it a "Blueprint for Bankruptcy," supporters gathered enough signatures to put the plan to the voters as a referendum. Voters rejected the plan by wide margins.

Meanwhile, Ohio struggled with the energy crisis. Cheap and plentiful gas and oil had fueled the postwar boom, feeding industrial growth, forming key parts of consumer goods such as plastics and fertilizers, and abetting the spread of automobiles and highway expansion in Ohio and across the nation. In the 1970s Ohio faced rising fuel prices, industrial transformation, economic stagnation, inflation and other economic difficulties. In Gilligan's last year as governor, the Arab nations of OPEC forced a spike in oil prices in response to U.S. support for Israel in the Yom Kippur War of October 1973. The price of a barrel of oil went from $3 to $11 by January 1974. In December 1973, independent truckers blocked the Ohio Turnpike in protest of higher fuel prices. As state leaders, Gilligan and then Rhodes struggled to respond to events and issues that were national and global in nature. Gas prices rose through summer 1974 and President Nixon called for a rationing program that saw most gasoline stations stop selling gas from Saturday night through Sunday. Lines formed during the weekdays as drivers filled up in anticipation of the closures. Congress enacted a nationwide 55 mph speed limit that year, followed by the creation of the Strategic Petroleum Reserve in 1975 and the cabinet-level Department of Energy in 1977. The energy crisis also helped the sales of more fuel efficient vehicles being imported from Japan, further undercutting Ohio's manufacturing base since U.S. carmakers continued to produce larger, less fuel efficient vehicles.

Further energy scares erupted in 1977 and 1978. In 1977, the issue was a natural gas shortage. Gas prices had been regulated and kept low, sparking greater demand from consumers in the midst of rising oil prices. Yet low prices provided little incentive to drill for more gas, thus supplies remained stable. The gas shortage came amid a fierce winter and forced Ohio schools to close in February. Rhodes declared a state-wide energy crisis, which among things allowed him to avoid federal clean air regulations and give industries authority to burn Ohio coal. Indeed, Rhodes engaged in constant battles over the EPA when it came to emissions from Ohio's coal-fired power plants, which used high sulfur coal that contributed to air pollution. Rhodes and other conservatives used the energy crisis to attack these and other regulations as killing job growth and the state's economy.

The issue of coal and energy emerged again with a nationwide coal miner's strike that began in December 1977 and ended in March 1978. Rhodes declared another energy emergency and met with governors of neighboring states in an effort to negotiate a separate agreement with UMW District 6 that covered eastern Ohio. Political opponents such as Democratic Lieutenant Governor Richard Celeste argued that Rhodes was "scrambling to get back on top of a situation over which he has lost control." Rhodes continued to ignore EPA regulations on air pollution from coal plants. "Blaming Ohio for acid rain is like blaming Florida for hurricanes," he quipped. To Rhodes, jobs were at stake and the dangers from air pollution were exaggerated.

The economic crisis of the 1970s fueled new debates over public education. Inflation led to rising assessments on real estate, which then led to higher property taxes. Voters expressed their growing unrest and demanded action. George Voinovich, then Cuyahoga County Auditor, came up with a plan to limit the growth of property taxes that eventually became law in 1976 under House Bill 920. The Bill, which received large bipartisan support in the legislature, prevented increases in tax receipts because of inflation and fixed the dollar amount that could be raised through property tax levies. Voters supported the measure and then went further by making it part of the Ohio Constitution in 1980. In doing this, Ohio became the first state to limit taxes in this way, providing a model for the more famous Proposition 13 approved in California in 1978. These measures and others like them became the foundation for a variety of proposals under the "taxpayer bill of rights" movement that became a key part of the conservative turn in politics.

House Bill 920 certainly helped individual and corporate property owners. Its effect on schools, however, has been a continuous source of controversy. Local property taxes are the primary funding mechanism for public schools. Since the law fixed the dollar amount from levies, this prevented revenues from rising due to increased property assessments from inflation. Schools faced declining revenues as costs increased, which led them to regularly ask for levies to maintain operations. Supporters saw the law as making schools accountable to voters and believed that schools could and should be able to cut costs while improving education. Opponents argued that constant preparation for levies would detract from the primary purpose of schools, which is education, that levies often fail, and that voters understandably suffer from "levy fatigue." Indeed, since implementation of the law, Ohio regularly has more school levies on the ballot than any other state. So while solving issues related to property taxes, House Bill 920 exacerbated the controversy over school funding and led to further court challenges.

Although overall the general public supported House Bill 920, teachers did not and school funding still remained a problem in many districts. In 1977 Ohio House leader Riffe pushed through a school loan law that took effect in 1978. Although it was available to all schools, Riffe intended it specifically for the Cleveland board that was in danger of closing due to a lack of funds. Funding, union recognition, and pay raises were among the factors leading to a series of teacher strikes in Ohio in 1978, including in Cleveland.

These and other economic problems abounded such that by the campaign season of 1978 Rhodes appeared vulnerable. By contrast, the fortunes of Democrats in Ohio seemed to be on the rise. In 1976, Howard Metzenbaum won his campaign against Robert A. Taft, Jr. and joined fellow Democrat John Glenn in the Senate. Democrat Jimmy Carter took Ohio (by only about 11,000 votes) in his successful presidential victory over Republican Gerald Ford. Democrats also took control of the Ohio Supreme Court for the first time since 1960 and elected enough legislators to have a veto-proof majority in the Ohio General Assembly.

Rhodes's opponent in 1978 was his Lt. Governor, Richard Celeste. Celeste was a formidable candidate. Born in the Cleveland suburb of Lakewood in 1937, he attended Yale and then

Oxford as a Rhodes Scholar. After serving in the Peace Corps and as the executive assistant to John Kennedy's ambassador to India, Celeste returned to Lakewood. In 1970 he won his first political campaign by earning a seat in the Ohio House of Representatives. He won again in 1972 and worked to organize white liberals and African Americans from Cuyahoga County, and with their support he earned the newly created position of House majority whip. In 1974 he sought and secured the nomination for lieutenant governor, expecting to join Gilligan for the incumbent's second term. At that point in Ohio political history, lieutenant governors were elected separately from governors. Gilligan lost to Rhodes, but Celeste beat Republican John Brown. Being lieutenant governor left Celeste few obligations but a lot of time and opportunity to travel the state and become the leading dissenter to Rhodes's plans. As the 1978 campaign got underway Celeste and his followers–dubbed "Celestials" for their starry-eyed, Kennedy-like optimism and devotion to their leader–seemed poised to unseat Rhodes. "James A. Rhodes, Pack Your Bags!" Celeste would shout at campaign rallies.

Rhodes, as he so often liked to say, hid "in the weeds" waiting to launch a blistering, last minute attack. First, Rhodes hammered Celeste by accusing the Democrat of "itching to raise taxes." Second, Rhodes used the growing popularity of single-issue campaign items to his advantage. In this case it was abortion. In 1973, the Supreme Court ruled in *Roe v. Wade* that abortion during the first trimester was constitutional, which galvanized both supporters and opponents of the ruling to enter the political fray. During the 1978 campaign, Rhodes's organization donated $7,000 to the Ohio Right to Life Political Action Committee, which printed antiabortion literature claiming that: "If James Rhodes wins, unborn children will win. If Richard Celeste wins, unborn children will lose." Celeste himself supported antiabortion legislation in the House, but refused to support the group's "human life amendment" that would have outlawed all abortions except those required to save the life of the mother. Finally, Rhodes also benefited from his earlier handling of the Blizzard of 1978, which struck before dawn on January 26 and lasted two days. National Guard troops worked long hours to clear roads, assist utility crews, and fly helicopters across Ohio rescuing stranded individuals and delivering medical personnel and attending to those with medical emergencies. When it ended 51 people had died, making it among the deadliest natural disasters in the state.

Seeking to avoid another divided executive branch, the Ohio legislature amended the state constitution so that after 1978 the governor and lieutenant governor would be elected as a team. Rhodes's running mate in 1978 was future governor and U.S. Senator George Voinovich (Figure 17.3). In 1978, Voinovich had made a name for himself supporting House Bill 920 and he was the popular auditor of Cuyahoga County—no small feat in a generally Democratic county. He used his ethnic roots to great political success. Voinovich was born in Cleveland to a Croatian Serb father and a Slovenian mother. Before becoming Rhodes's running mate, Voinovich had served as assistant attorney general for Ohio and in the Ohio House. Voinovich helped Rhodes cut into Celeste's normally Democratic base in Cleveland. Voinovich, local issues, and Rhodes's strong popularity were enough to withstand Celeste's challenge. Rhodes won a close race, 49.3 percent to 47.6 percent. Meanwhile, Democrats won the other state races so that they continued to control the Apportionment Board for the upcoming 1980 Census. Celeste would later quip that after the 1978 election he became a "Rhodes' scholar."

Figure 17.3 Pictured here, left to right, are Ohio governors George Voinovich, Richard Celeste, James Rhodes, and John Gilligan as they gathered at the Ohio Historical Center for Ohio Politics Day in 1994. There were many political connections and scars between the four men who were at the center of Ohio politics from the 1970s through the 1990s.
Source: Courtesy of the Ohio Historical Society (AL03587)

As Rhodes entered his fourth term, serious economic issues continued to plague the state. In December 1978, Cleveland became the first city since the Great Depression to default on its financial obligations when it went defaulted on its loans from local banks. Problems in Cleveland led Voinovich to leave his post as lieutenant governor and run for mayor of his hometown, winning in November 1979. He went on to serve as mayor of Cleveland until 1986, during which time he helped stabilize Cleveland's financial footing. A national energy crisis occurred again in 1979 following the Iranian revolution that ousted the Shah and installed Ayatollah Khomeini. Gas shortages appeared and drivers were forced to locate an open station and then wait in line to fill up. Truck drivers went on strike to protest high diesel prices and in some places striking truckers fired shots at those choosing to drive. Police were called out to maintain order in many communities.

As this was going on, a bright spot came with the opening of Honda's manufacturing plant in Marysville. Rhodes and the legislature agreed to provide property tax abatements, and over $3 million in funds for water, sewer, and railroad improvements. The plant opened in 1979 with 64 employees making dirt bikes. Today, Honda employs some 13,000 workers at four separate facilities in and around Marysville. To compete with other states for factories, Ohio joined the trend of offering cheap land, tax incentives, and state-funded development of the factory site. Rhodes and his Democratic opponents supported these measures in the wake of economic challenges associated with industrial transformation, inflation, and stagnant growth.

Meanwhile, labor unrest with teachers continued and Ohio became famous for the then longest teacher strike, when teachers in Ravenna remained out from November 1980 to April 1981. School boards obtained court orders in Ravenna and other communities, including Boardman, Brunswick, Dayton, and Youngstown to force teachers back to work and those that defied the orders were jailed. At stake for Ravenna and other school districts was the power between school boards and teachers to control issues including recognition of teacher organizations as bargaining units, wages, healthcare, hiring and firing, and performance evaluation. Boards relinquished some power and teachers gained some greater benefits, but communities remained divided.

More economic challenges emerged, especially in Rhodes's last two years as Ohio struggled during the 1982–83 recession. Ohio's unemployment rate reached 13.8 percent in 1982. Rhodes's budget director Howard L. Collier stated it was the state's worst crisis since the 1930s. Despite his pledges to the contrary, Rhodes agreed to tax increases along with cuts to balance the budget. Despite this the state ended up with a $540 million deficit.

When he left office in 1983, Rhodes had become the longest serving governor in U.S. history (later tied by George Wallace). Rhodes retired and became a private business consultant based in Columbus. He died in March 2001 and thousands paid their respects when his body lay in state in the Rotunda at the state capitol—only the fourth to receive that honor since Lincoln in 1865. Rhodes's legacy was a large one and he left his mark throughout the state. His role in Kent State, his resistance to funding public schools, social welfare, and environmental protections were matched with his support for economic development, the physical expansion of higher education, highway construction, and the growth of the state's park system.

With Rhodes again barred from running in 1982, Republicans turned to Congressman Clarence J. "Bud" Brown from Urbana as the nominee. However, Celeste ran a solid campaign and Brown had trouble gaining support. Celeste effectively argued that it was time for a change, time to "get Ohio moving again" in the wake of budget deficits, a recession, labor strife in education, and a weakening manufacturing base. Celeste crushed Brown, winning 59 percent of the vote to Brown's 38.8.

Richard Celeste

In his 1983 inaugural address, Celeste noted Ohio's deep economic trouble. There were 750,000 people out of work, and the state's basic industries such as rubber, automobiles, and steel were in decline with factories closing. Celeste, however, sounded hopeful. Ohioans, he said had led the nation before and must now come together and prepare for "global competition which is unrelenting." "Stand with me because we can do together what we can't do alone." Immediately setting a different tone from Rhodes, Celeste appointed six women and four African Americans to his cabinet. The average age of the group was thirty-five, while under Rhodes it was fifty-one. Celeste's wife, Dagmar, also announced that, unlike Rhodes who lived in his Columbus home and left the Governor's Mansion vacant, Celeste would restore the building and live in what they called the "Residence." Dagmar would become more politically active than most first ladies of Ohio had been. She played a significant public role advocating for a number of issues related to families, women, children, mental health, substance abuse, and conflict resolution.

Governor Celeste's first main task was to get the state on a firmer financial footing. "Ohio's condition is critical," he told the General Assembly in a special joint session in February 1983. The state's unemployment rate had hit 14.5 percent. The projected $540 million deficit threatened to undermine an already weak economy. He ordered some $280 million in budget cuts, including savings in healthcare. Medicaid costs also skyrocketed, growing from $182 million in 1972 to $1.2 billion in 1982; healthcare costs had become the single largest line item in the budget.

After consulting with major business leaders in Ohio and others, Celeste proposed making permanent the temporary 50 percent increase in the state income tax approved by Rhodes, and adding an additional 40 percent increase. Predictably Republicans denounced the move and newspaper headlines proclaimed a 90 percent tax increase. Celeste had failed to show how other tax cuts he proposed meant it was in reality a 27 percent hike; Celeste's chief adviser Jerry Austin later recalled: "If we had labeled it '50 percent Rhodes, and 40 percent Reagan' early in the game, it might have helped." In the House, Riffe steered passage through with the solid Democratic majority. In the Senate, Democrats held the chamber by one seat. In a dramatic scene, Senate leader Ocasek flew in from Florida where his wife lay in the hospital recovering from a serious automobile accident. With a whisper he voted "yes" and the bill passed with his vote. Conservatives immediately used a referendum to place the law before voters, but Ohioans supported the increases by a two-to-one majority. The new taxes aided state services, including education, mental health (in which the state ranked among the worst), and social welfare. In time, though, the tax vote hurt Democrats, for Republicans used it successfully to gain support and take over the Ohio Senate in 1984.

Another significant aspect to Celeste's record was the support he gave to Senate Bill 133, legislation spearheaded by state senator Harry Meshel of Youngstown allowing collective bargaining for public sector employees. Twice under Rhodes, Democratic legislators had approved such a measure, only to see each vetoed. Opponents argued that the law would undermine public control, lead to more strikes, that there would be greater costs to local districts and that the new State Employment Relations Board would have too much power. Opponents also argued against the proposal that required all teachers pay union dues. However, public employees, such as teachers, police officers, and firefighters generally favored the plan. With Celeste in office and Democrats controlling the legislature, a new bill became law in 1983.

Fortunately the severe recession eased by 1983, thanks in part to a sharp decline in oil prices and the tight-money policies instituted by Carter and continued by Reagan. After reaching over 14 percent the unemployment rate began to decline. By the end of Celeste's first term it had fallen to just below 8 percent and near the end of his second the rate fell to nearly 6 percent. Of course these numbers included wide variations, as they always have in Ohio's history. Relatively prosperous and growing Delaware County had a

1990 rate of 3.4 percent, while Meigs in Appalachian Ohio remained 13.2 percent. The rate in Cleveland remained high at 14 percent while in the state's capital of Columbus it was 5.9 percent.

Celeste also garnered praise during the national savings and loan crisis of the 1980s that resulted in the failure of nearly 750 Savings and Loan Associations (S&Ls) across the nation and a price tag of $124 billion for bailing out depositors. In Ohio, Celeste focused on the collapse of Home State Savings Bank that was owned by Marvin Warner, one of Celeste's major supporters. Ohio was one of the few states at the time that operated an insurance fund for savings and loans, the Ohio Deposit Guarantee Fund that did not have federal insurance. When Home State collapsed, it threatened some 88,000 depositors with potentially unrecoverable losses of $1 billion, and toppled the state's guarantee fund. Celeste acted quickly, using an executive order to close all seventy state-chartered S&Ls, which became the largest national "bank holiday" since the Great Depression. Working with just enough supportive Republicans, Celeste crafted legislation that resulted in the institutions either reopening or merging, and the state recovering its losses and those of depositors. Warner and other Home State executives were found guilty of mishandling depositors' money.

Despite his pledge to end the "cronyism" of the Rhodes years Celeste's record suffered from some bad political appointments. Several heads of state agencies came under investigation. Legislators and the media alleged that businesses looking for state contracts, and higher level state employees looking for promotions, were expected to make political contributions to Celeste. They also claimed that county campaign coordinators screened potential businesses and workers.

Despite the allegations, Celeste ran a strong reelection campaign in 1986. In his 1986 State of the State address in January, Celeste declared "Our pride is back in Ohio." He cited the drop in unemployment, job training programs, highway programs, a clean coal bond issue (1985), business-university enterprises and partnerships through the Thomas Edison progam, lower personal property taxes, and a large increase in state support for education. Celeste's opponent was none other than James Rhodes. Rhodes had his own problems with allegations of cronyism and it became clear that his administration had done little to monitor the growing problems at Home State and other S&Ls. The Republican leadership hoped someone else could beat Rhodes in the primaries, but the seventy-six year old came out the winner. Rhodes attacked Celeste's ethics and Celeste focused on his own accomplishments. In the end, Rhodes never gained ground and Celeste captured 61 percent of the vote, becoming the first Democratic governor since Frank Lausche to win re-election.

His second term lacked the verve and achievements of the first. Further problems surfaced for Celeste when the *Cleveland Plain Dealer* published an article in June 1987 alleging the Celeste had a series of extramarital affairs; this ended any plans Celeste may have had for a 1988 presidential run. In policy, Celeste went along with reducing some of the taxes set in the 1983 law. In 1990 he spoke at the twentieth anniversary of the Kent State shootings and offered an apology from the state to those who were killed.

The scandals and personal failures tarnished an otherwise positive record as governor. Economic growth of the 1980s helped lower unemployment, even if the manufacturing sector still found itself in transition with fewer workers than before. State services and education received needed funds, but many Ohio communities still struggled. For example, Ohio's poverty rate remained 12.5 percent in 1990, but this, like unemployment rates, varied considerably across the state. Lake County's rate was 4.9 percent. In Ohio biggest cities, the poverty rate was higher, in some cases double the state average. Dayton's was 26.5 percent, Cincinnati's 24.3, and Youngstown's 29 percent. On average poverty rates remained even higher for African Americans.

Among his last actions were to commute the death sentences of several prisoners to life without parole and to issue pardons to twenty-five female prisoners who were "battered" women who, he argued, would not have been convicted had they been allowed to raise the issue of abuse as a new law provided. After leaving office, Celeste never returned to the campaign trail. President Bill Clinton named former Governor Celeste Ambassador to India in 1999. After leaving this post in 2001, Celeste served as president of Colorado College from 2002 to 2011.

Towards the Future: Ohio since the 1990s

Conservatives in power: Voinovich and Taft

During the 1970s and 1980s, apart from Rhodes's return, Democrats were successful in Ohio. They controlled the Ohio legislature, had eight years of the governorship with Celeste, and Metzenbaum and Glenn remained U.S. Senators. Outside Ohio, though, the nation's political culture shifted towards the conservatives and by the 1990s, the Republicans had regained control over Ohio's government. The majority of Ohioans supported Nixon and Gerald Ford continued the GOP hold when he took over in 1974 after Nixon resigned in the wake of the Watergate scandal. Democrat Jimmy Carter gained a narrow victory in Ohio in the 1976 election, but he sought a moderate stance on many issues and avoided the kind of liberalism common in the 1960s. Ohioans turned back to the GOP and supported Ronald Reagan in 1980 and 1984. Reagan's election signaled the arrival in power of the New Right, which had begun in the 1960s with leaders such as Barry Goldwater, Phyllis Schlafly and Ohio Congressman John Ashbrook. His vice president, George H.W. Bush took Ohio on his way to victory in 1988. Republicans put together a coalition of voters in securing their victories, consisting of "white blue collar workers, southern white foes of civil rights, Republicans who opposed big government, and social conservative Catholics and evangelical Protestants." In Ohio, with its urban and rural mix, the GOP found large numbers of these voters. A key group was male white blue collar voters—so called "Reagan Democrats" that had once been part of George Wallace's base. These voters still largely supported liberal economic programs, but they were worried about rising crime rates and opposed issues such as affirmative action, busing, gay rights, feminism, and environmentalism.

The GOP took control of the Ohio Senate in 1985 and in the 1990s wrested control of the state government from the Democrats. For sixteen years (1991 to 2007) Republicans George Voinovich and Bob Taft controlled the governorship. Democrat Ted Strickland broke that stretch when he served from 2007 to 2011, but Republican John Kasich returned the governorship to GOP hands. The GOP gained control of the Ohio House in 1994—the same year that conservatives under Newt Gingrich gained control of the House of Representatives in Washington. Republicans also captured both of Ohio's Senate seats. Voinovich's lieutenant governor Mike Dewine left office in 1995 to take the seat held by Metzenbaum, and Voinovich himself entered the Senate in 1999 taking John Glenn's former seat. The 1990 election also gave Republicans control of the Apportionment Board and thus control over redrawing congressional districts. Democrats had controlled the Board since the 1970s and since 1990 the GOP has used the process to maintain its power. The new districts drew together Republican-leaning rural and growing suburban districts at the expense of declining, Democratic-leaning urban centers mainly in the Northeast. Republicans did not all speak with one voice, however, as battles between moderates and conservatives continued. Still, through the first decade of the twenty-first century, the GOP had achieved considerable success in Ohio.

After the recession of 1991–92, for the remainder of the decade it seemed that problems with the state's economy and its cities had been solved as Ohio benefited from national economic growth, driven by the so-called "Dot Com" boom in information technology. It was the longest peacetime boom in U.S. history. Adjusted for inflation, Ohio's Gross State Product grew 2.8 percent annually in the 1990s and its per capita income grew by 13.3 percent. (However, both were still below national averages of 3.5 percent and 14.3 percent respectfully). After a sharp recession in 1991–92, Ohio's unemployment rate fell from above 7 percent to 4.3 percent in 2001. This was below the national average, which was 4.8 percent in 2001. Yet manufacturing employment declined still, and services continued to lead employment growth, along with construction, finance, insurance, and real estate. Of course this image of growth varied within Ohio. Counties in Appalachia and most central urban areas struggled as the suburban rings around the cities (and Columbus more generally) prospered. The patterns evident in Ohio's farming continued, as the number of farms declined as yields per acre increased.

Amid the economic growth, the focus of the state's politics shifted to other matters. In creating and responding to these, Ohio's Republicans maintained their vehemence against taxes on individuals or corporations and continued to pursue balanced budgets. They also upheld their commitments against abortion and greater social welfare spending. Education emerged again as a critical issue. Republicans resisted calls to equalize outlays among the state's school districts and instead shifted money to charter schools, which included religious ones. All of these issues dominated Ohio's political agenda in the 1990s beginning with the governorship of George Voinovich.

George Victor Voinovich was a well-known candidate for governor in the 1990 race to replace the outgoing Celeste. After being elected lieutenant governor in 1978, he left the office after one year to run a successful campaign as Cleveland's mayor. Voinovich defeated Dennis Kucinich in 1979, whose tenure had been riddled with financial and political controversy. The city had defaulted on its loans, and Voinovich worked with local banks and the Rhodes administration to restructure the debt so that by the late 1980s the city had come out from under that cloud. New optimism, construction, and neighborhood revitalization programs all contributed the media calling Cleveland the "comeback city" during Voinovich's ten-year stint as mayor. Left out of the media blitz was the fact that Cleveland's poverty rate remained among the highest in Ohio. Nevertheless, in the 1990 governor's race, Voinovich defeated then Ohio Attorney General Anthony J. Celebrezze, Jr.

In his inaugural address, Voinovich touched on themes he would repeat throughout his two terms as governor: "The new realities dictate that public officials are now judged on whether they can work harder and smarter, and do more with less." Yet, with Ohio facing another recession Voinovich proposed spending cuts and—contrary to his campaign pledge—tax increases to balance the state's budget. The legislature followed, albeit after a tough battle. Voinovich also supported a popular proposal for term limits of eight years for legislators and those in executive offices. This came into effect in 1992.

Voinovich remained quite popular and he easily won re-election in 1994. That year witnessed some historic firsts in Ohio politics, all under the auspices of the GOP. Conservative Kenneth Blackwell became the state's first African American to win state-wide office when he secured the Treasurer's post. Nancy Putnam Hollister of Marietta became the state's first female elected lieutenant governor and Betty Montgomery the first female elected as Attorney General. When the GOP took the Ohio House, the party made Jo Ann Davidson the first female speaker. This ended the long career of Vern Riffe, who retired.

One of the first issues conservatives placed on the legislative agenda was abortion. In their first session after taking over the Ohio legislature, conservatives gathered support to pass a bill with Voinovich's signature making Ohio the first state to ban certain late-term abortion procedures. Ohio's "Right to Life" political action group played a key role in this effort, showing the new power of that organization in the state. The U.S. House and Senate would also pass similar legislation, but neither Ohio's law nor the federal one survived initial constitutional challenges. This changed, though as a state ban and a federal ban went into effect in 2004.

Voinovich joined with conservatives in having Ohio create the nation's first law that allowed public money to pay tuition at church-affiliated schools. The law tested the voucher program in Cleveland's school district as a pilot project. Opponents fought this, but the law withstood constitutional challenges. One of the leaders in the charter school movement, Akron businessman David L. Brennan, argued that using public money for charter schools was "the best answer, ever, to the issue of decrepit schools in the state, most of which are in the cities." He used his wealth to found White Hat Management, which operated some thirty-one charter schools across the state. Yet reports have shown that on average Ohio's charter schools are neither more nor less effective than public ones.

Another conservative success was amending the state's welfare law to a system that shifts aid recipients toward work. Less punitive than some other state proposals, (*Time* Magazine called it "among the most intelligent in the country") Voinovich signed the law in 1995, saying "It's fair. It's tough love." Ohio's law came one year before President Clinton signed national legislation on this issue, the Personal Responsibility and Work Opportunity Reconciliation Act. The laws ended the system of welfare that had been created in the 1930s and expanded in the 1960s. The new Ohio law placed a three-year limit that most recipients can spend on public assistance, and combined incentives and sanctions to encourage those individuals to find work, to promote two-parent families, and to discourage out-of-wedlock births.

Education returned again to the spotlight when in March 1997 the Ohio Supreme Court ruled 4-3 that Ohio's method of funding public schools was unconstitutional. In writing the majority opinion for the Ohio Supreme Court in 1997, Judge Francis Sweeny declared: "Upon a full consideration of the record and in analyzing the pertinent constitutional provision, we can reach but one conclusion: the current legislation fails to provide for a thorough and efficient system of common schools, in violation of Section 2, Article VI of the Ohio Constitution." The case, *DeRolph v. State of Ohio*, began in 1991 with a complaint filed in Perry County on behalf of Sheridan High School freshman Nathan DeRolph and 550 districts by the Ohio Coalition for Equity & Adequacy of School Funding. It challenged the state's funding system that relied primarily on local taxes. Voinovich and other Republican leaders attacked the decision as "judicial activism," vowed to challenge it and did. Democrats defended it. Initially the Court affirmed its earlier ruling. Veteran statehouse reporter Lee Leonard of the *Columbus Dispatch* captured the view of many when he said that "anecdotal evidence showed they're in violation of common sense. You can't ignore textbook lotteries, classes held in coal bins, and school buildings sliding down hills." All of this and more had come out during the hearings. Republican majorities on the Court finally ended the skirmish. In 2003 the Court ended its jurisdiction in the matter and forbade further challenges to the constitutionality of the funding system. Critics still remain active in forcing changes to the system.

The results that stemmed from the *DeRolph* case made a difference but Ohio still lagged behind in many areas of education. The state created the Ohio School Facilities Commission and directed new spending on facilities in many of the neediest districts (including those in Perry County). The state created a system of parity aid to less wealthy districts and has increased the percentage of funding from the state to above 40 percent, where it was in the late 1970s. *Education Week* ranked Ohio 11th overall and graded it at a B–, up from a D– grade in the early 2000s. Without factoring in new standards and accountability, Ohio ranks average to below average in other categories, including spending, college readiness and opportunity for student success. The state ranked 42nd in public revenue per student in 2009. Higher education found Ohio below average as well. At $680, the state ranked 34th in per capita state and local spending, with the U.S. average at $734. In general, Ohio ranked 32nd in general expenditures of state government in 2008.

Voinovich's popularity and the state's strong economy allowed him to win a U.S. Senate seat in the 1998 elections. Ohio voters supported William J. "Bill" Clinton for president in the 1992 and 1996 elections, although both were three-way contests and Clinton won them with less than 50 percent of the vote. However, they maintained their preference for the GOP at home by electing Robert A. "Bob" Taft II as governor that year. He served two terms, from January 1999 to January 2007. Taft was the great-grandson of former president and Supreme Court Justice William Howard Taft and grandson of former Senator Robert A. Taft. His election came exactly 90 years after his great-grandfather had been elected president in 1908. With such a long family pedigree and political experience, many believed Taft would serve well as governor.

Economic growth continued, inspiring Taft in his 1999 inaugural to state that it was now "time to dream about the future, to be inspired by a vision of what lies ahead for our children." The federal budget ran surpluses from 1998 to 2001 and Ohio enjoyed a $1 billion income tax surplus in 1999. Taft persuaded his Republican colleagues in the legislature to use some of the surplus for schools as a way to respond to the *DeRolph* case. The rest went back to taxpayers in the form of tax cuts. He also increased per pupil funding and proposed a new plan that used money from lawsuits against tobacco companies to improve school facilities.

Taft focused attention on Ohio's economic base, which still remained tied largely to the manufacturing sector that continued to lose jobs, some 200,000 during Taft's two terms. Looking for alternatives to the state's reliance on manufacturing had been part of the political agenda since the 1960s and there had been some shift towards growing sectors. To continue this, voters in 2005 approved the Third Frontier program that used state funds to invest in high-tech startup ventures. As of 2010 the plan had attracted over 600 high-tech companies to Ohio.

In addition conservatives moved ahead on other issues. They succeeded in getting term limits in Ohio, which went into effect in 2000. In 2001 most legislators would be brand new; departing were "forty-five House members with a total of 578 years of experience," including Robert Netzley of Miami County with a record of forty years. The group was more conservative, more partisan, and with only a short stay allowed, more interested in single-issues, less on long-term solutions and compromise. In 2004, conservatives succeeded in approving legislation that allowed concealed hand guns, expanded charter schools, and banned same-sex marriage.

Conservatives were in power when again the nation went to war. On September 11, 2001, nineteen al-Qaeda terrorists hijacked four commercial passenger jets. They crashed two into the twin towers of the World Trade Center, killing everyone on board the planes, and thousands of others as both towers collapsed. A third plane hit the Pentagon and the remaining hijackers attempted to redirect the fourth jet to Washington, D.C., targeting either the Capitol or the White House. It crashed with no survivors in a rural area near Shanksville, Pennsylvania, after passengers on board tried to retake control of the plane.

The attack ignited panic and led the United States to declare a "war on terror," which among other things created a sweeping new federal and state bureaucratic system devoted to "homeland security" under the national Patriot Act. When it was discovered that the hijackers had trained in Afghanistan under the rule of the Taliban, the United States led a NATO coalition attack on that nation. The attacks of 9/11 (as the events are now commonly called) also served as a pretext for the United States to lead an attack on Iraq to oust dictator Saddam Hussein and to install a government friendlier to American interests. At the time, President George Bush and members of his administration argued that there was a connection between the hijackers of al-Qaeda and Hussein, although that had been refuted. Ohioans again served in both conflicts. As of 2010, out of the 1,083 U.S. troops killed in Afghanistan, 30 were Ohioans and of the 4,400 U.S. soldiers killed in Iraq, 182 were Ohioans.

As the wars began, Ohio and nation again faced a serious recession, as the 1990s boom ended. The state faced a serious shortfall. In response, in 2003, Taft signed a $3 billion tax hike, the largest in the state's history. In 2005, the legislature approved a major overhaul of Ohio's tax system, something Taft had been pushing for. The new law lowered income taxes by 21 percent over five years and lowered corporate taxes by replacing both the intangible personal property tax and corporate franchise tax with a new commercial activity tax.

Taft ran into deeper trouble, however, as in August 2005 near the end of his second term, he became the first governor in Ohio history to be convicted of a crime. He had failed to report on his annual financial disclosure form some $6,000 worth of free golf, meals, hockey tickets, and other gifts. It was part of what the press dubbed "Coingate." Most of the gifts came from Thomas W. Noe, a rare coin dealer from Maumee, former chair of the Lucas County Republican party, and major GOP campaign contributor. Taft had appointed Noe to the Ohio Board of Regents and the Ohio Turnpike Commission. Noe had received two investment contracts from the state's Workers' Compensation Fund, one in 1998 and the other in 2001, both for $25 million. This came about in part because in 1996 the state ended the law that only allowed the state to invest in bonds. The money went into high-risk investments run by individuals like Noe and other large donors close to the Republican Party. Tom Noe was convicted of running a criminal enterprise, the theft of $13 million from the fund, and of keeping false records.

A Democratic interlude: Ted Strickland

Taft's troubles helped elect Democrat Ted Strickland as Ohio's 68th governor in 2006. He was born in Lucasville and was one of nine children. He was the only one of his siblings to attend college and went on to earn a Master of Divinity from Asbury Theological Seminary in Kentucky and a doctoral degree in counseling psychology from the University of Kentucky. He worked as an ordained Methodist minister, a psychologist, and a professor before entering politics. He won a seat in the U.S. Congress in 1992, lost it in 1994, and then won it again in 1996. In his run for governor, Strickland rode to victory on a wave of voter frustration with the GOP, as well as voter reluctance to support the Republican nominee, secretary of state Kenneth Blackwell, who professed highly conservative views on a number of issues. Strickland captured 60 percent of the vote.

Strickland emphasized economic development and education. Of immediate concern throughout Strickland's term was the state's unemployment rate, which went from 5.4 percent in January 2007 to 10.6 in January 2010. It began to drop steadily throughout April 2011, although it remained high at 8.6 percent. Ohio had been losing jobs since January 2000, mainly in manufacturing. The recession ended the trend under Taft of lowering taxes and increasing spending. With Ohio facing a budget shortfall, Strickland and the legislature made cuts in various areas and agreed to freeze the last of the tax cuts promised under Taft. As a result of the lower taxes begun under Taft and continued (despite the freeze) under Strickland, as well as Strickland's own efforts to streamline business regulations, business magazines and various trade associations began to look more favorably upon Ohio, despite the recession. Also, Strickland supported efforts to make Ohio a so-called "green energy" leader in solar and wind energy production.

In education, Strickland reorganized the state's public institutions of higher learning into a new University System of Ohio and made the Chancellor of the Board of Regents, which oversees the system, a cabinet level position. The goal was to eliminate duplication of programs, increase enrollment and graduation numbers, and stop the "brain drain" by keeping more college graduates in Ohio. In the arena of K–12 education, Ohio's rankings in some areas improved. The number of schools rated "Effective" or higher on the state's annual education report card increased. Strickland pushed through increases in school funding and for school construction. He also implemented a new, evidenced-based model for the state's public schools and worked to address the weaknesses in overall funding put into place by House Bill 920.

Back to the Right: John Kasich

Despite Strickland's efforts, the recession still plagued Ohio and this hurt the governor's re-election bid in 2010. Strickland's main opponent was former Republican U.S. Congressman John Kasich. After leaving Congress, Kasich landed a job working as a commentator for the Fox News Channel. He also worked as a managing director for Lehman Brothers investment banking. Strickland made up ground pointing out that Lehman Brothers, which had filed for bankruptcy in 2008, played a major role in the global financial crisis that led to the recession. Kasich promised what he called a "jobs budget" with spending cuts. In the end, voters chose Kasich, who collected 49 percent of the vote in a close contest. Republicans also captured both houses in the General Assembly and all statewide executive offices. The GOP held on to retiring senator Voinovich's seat with Rob Portman's win and controlled thirteen of Ohio's eighteen congressional seats.

With a Republican controlled state government, Kasich began with an aggressive, thoroughly conservative agenda. One of the first items he signed was Senate Bill 5, a measure designed to end the collective bargaining rights for public employees (see Figure 17.4). Its popularity with Republican legislators did not match that of the general public, and opponents rallied to have a measure placed on the November 2011 ballot to repeal the law (see Figure 17.5). Voters defeated the measure decisively. To plug a deficit that varied between $5 billion and $8 billion and balance the state budget, Kasich supported a plan that cut funding for various state services, public education, and local governments. Kasich and the legislature also added new restrictions on abortion.

As Rhodes had done, Kasich opted to stay in his own home rather than the Governor's Mansion, which his critics argued was not fiscally responsible since it demanded additional security. More criticism mounted when he became the first governor since 1962 to not appoint an African American and to have five women in the twenty-two cabinet positions. Kasich's aggressive approach combined with a still weak economy led the public to sour quickly on the governor in his first months in office, as polls revealed only a 35 percent approval rating by mid-2011, the lowest since Celeste in 1983. Even with Kasich's troubles, Ohio voters have largely favored the GOP since the 1990s. Yet, as it has been clear throughout this book, Ohio politics has shifted so that precisely where the

Figure 17.4 This political cartoon captures the popular view in Ohio of Kasich's plan to end collective bargaining for public employees. Kasich, of Croatian ancestry, was born in the industrial city of McKees Rocks, Pennsylvania. He graduated from Ohio State University and at the age of twenty-six, he was elected to the Ohio Senate, the youngest person ever. He then ran successfully for Congress in 1982 and served until 2001, where he developed a strong reputation for being a fiscal conservative.
Source: Used by permission, Kirk Walters/The Toledo Blade

state's sentiments will lead is far from certain. Whichever political party gains control of the state they will need to craft a response to the challenges facing Ohio at the beginning of the twenty-first century.

Ohio at the crossroads

The most recent recession simply underscored the fact that Ohio continued to struggle to regain its role as a leader in the United States and that the things that had come to define the middle class were slipping out of reach for millions of Ohioans. Since the 1980s, the disparity of wealth in Ohio has increased. For example, between 1979 and 2006, wages for Ohio's wealthiest workers increased 14.9 percent, while those in the middle saw their wages fall by just under 1 percent. Ohioans' median household income has remained below the national average and has fallen further behind. In 2000 it was $40,956 and national average was $41,994 whereas in 2009 it was $47,144 and national average was $51,425. Adjusted for inflation, Ohio's median income in 2010 was about the same as it was in the late 1980s, but the state's ranking had dropped from eighteenth to thirty-second.

Figure 17.5   Kasich's plan to end collective bargaining rights for public employees in Ohio met with strong resistance. These rights had been put into place in the 1980s under Richard Celeste, after a decades-long battle by unions and their supporters. This image comes from a rally against the proposed measure, Senate Bill 5, in February 2011. The law passed, but opponents then collected signatures to put the law on the ballot as a referendum—Issue 2. In November, 2011 those voting to repeal the law garnered 62 percent of the vote.
Source: Jason Perlman/Ohio AFL-CIO

Poverty has also increased. Between 2002 and 2009 the state's population grew by 1.2 percent while the poverty rate increased by 41.7 percent to reach 13.7 percent in 2009. Poverty rates hit all classes of people in the latest recession, but as always rates were higher in the cities. Youngstown's 2008 rate of 33.5 percent was the state's highest, with Cleveland following at 30.5 percent and Dayton third at 29.2 percent. Even Columbus, with its seemingly recession-proof economy of education, medical, and services, registered 20.1 percent. The groups with the highest rates were single female-headed households (41 percent), African Americans (29 percent), Hispanics (25 percent) and children (23 percent). Whites (11 percent), older adults (9 percent), and married persons with children (5 percent) were the lowest. All regions of the state had poverty rates above 10 percent. Appalachian Ohio had the highest (as it always has) at over 18 percent. Northeast Ohio had historically had one of the lowest in the state, but the loss of manufacturing jobs among other things has led to a rate of 14.5 percent, a rate 84 percent greater than in 1969.

Women's participation in the Ohio labor force has increased since the 1970s. Whereas in 1979 only about half of women over 16 were part of the labor force in 2006 more than 61 percent work for wages. At the same time, however, men's participation rate has declined steadily. In 1979, about 80 percent of Ohio men over 16 were in the labor force by 2006 the rate had fallen to 73.1 percent.

Ohio also still struggles with educational achievement. As most jobs now require at least a four-year degree economic progress has become even more challenging. As of 2009, the state ranked thirty-ninth in the percentage residents with Bachelor degrees (24.1 percent). Since the postwar boom in higher education began, Ohio has dropped further behind. The state ranked thirtieth in 1960 with 7 percent of its residents having a Bachelor's degree. In 1970 the state ranked thirty-fourth with 9.3 percent, slipping to forty-first in 1980 with 13.7 percent, fortieth in 1990 with 17 percent and fortieth in 2000 with 21.1 percent. Spending on higher education has lagged as well. Educational appropriations per full time equivalent student dropped between 2005 and 2009, from $4,986 to $4,293; Ohio ranked thirty-forth in per capita spending on higher education in 2008. Meanwhile, enrollments have increased. On average, between the mid-1990s and 2010 Ohio's tuition revenues went up by roughly 10 percent but state appropriations dropped by over 25 percent.

The recent trends in Ohio contribute to a larger sense of loss, of stagnation, of a lack of larger public purpose that has plagued the state and the nation since the 1970s. The nation, like Ohio, seems to have lost its way. Such sentiments have their roots in history, for much of the last two centuries Ohio has been "perhaps the nation's most representative state." Although its representation in Congress has dropped in the last fifty years, as Figure 17.6 shows, Ohio remains a battleground and a bellwether state as its citizens work through the present challenges alongside much of the country.

Summing Up: Ohio as America

Ohio has been, and in many important respects remains, a composite of the nation. Figure 17.6 reflects the political breakdown of the state in recent elections. As recent observers of the state have done, if one were to think of Ohio as being made up of regions—"Five Ohios"—then it becomes clear how each one reflects a larger part of the United States and showcases the state's internal complexity.

Northeast Ohio reflects its origins as the Western Reserve, today resembling the Northeastern and Mid-Atlantic portion of the United States. Despite the effects of being in the heart of the rust belt, Northeast Ohio has a large number of cities, and is the state's most populated region. Unions remain although the decline in manufacturing has damaged them. The postindustrial knowledge economy has made some inroads into the region, especially in medical and technical employment. Northeast Ohio is also the most ethnically diverse region, yet sharp divisions remain between the urban, suburban, and rural populations. There are a higher proportion of Catholics in the Northeast than anywhere else in the state. It remains a stronghold for the Democratic Party as it has been since industrialization took root there.

The Northwest of Ohio resembles much of the Midwest. The Northwest is an agricultural region, a legacy of the Wisconsin Glacier that created the rich, flat lands, although Toledo and smaller cities like Findlay and Lima provide some industry. Toledo has

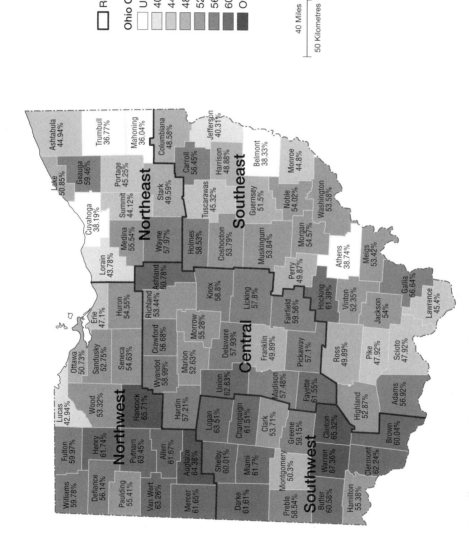

Figure 17.6 Overall percentage of votes for Republicans in the 1980–2010 elections.

Source: The Ray C. Bliss Institute of Applied Politics at the University of Akron. www.uakron.edu/bliss/research/biop-2-the-five-ohios.dot

some ethnic and racial diversity but the Northwest as a whole remains largely white, with strong German and northern European ethnic ties. Farming has given the region a strong conservative trend in political affairs. While the inland counties are Republican the areas along the Lake Erie shore are Democratic, making it mixed politically.

Southwest Ohio was one of the earliest areas of the state to be settled, with Cincinnati becoming an early industrial, cultural, and population center. Dayton and Springfield contribute the urban character as well, as do the surrounding farmlands. This region has a strong similarity to the upper South, partly due to its settlement patterns and its connection to Kentucky. Cincinnati's population decline since the 1970s translated into strong growth in the suburban and exurban areas of the region. These areas, which were among the highest in the nation, tended to be wealthier, less diverse, and more conservative than other parts, helping to make Southwest Ohio akin to the South, reliably conservative politically and socially.

Southeast Ohio was among the first areas settled in Ohio, but its unglaciated topography meant there would be fewer large farms, cities, and industrial centers than other parts of the state. However that same geology gave the region coal, which has been a mainstay of the region's economy since the 1800s. It is the least populated region in Ohio. The region is part of Appalachia, and poverty and unemployment rates are among the highest in the state. In 1965 a federal agency created the Appalachian Regional Commission that seeks to promote economic development there through business loans, job training, and infrastructure improvements. Southeast Ohio is the least diverse region in the state, with whites making up more than 96 percent of the population. Traditional religion adds to the socially conservative political culture there. However, there has been stronger support for liberal economic policies in the region, making it more of a swing region than the Southwest.

Central Ohio resembles in some measure the West. Thanks to Columbus, which had become Ohio's largest city, the region has developed a strong base in the new postindustrial knowledge economy. It has remained one of the few areas in the state with relatively strong job growth, wealth, and employment. As in the West, Central Ohio's residents are younger than average and possess the highest percentage of college degrees. Yet Central Ohio has the second lowest percentage of Catholics among the five regions and the second highest percentage of Evangelical Protestants. Like the areas surrounding Cincinnati, Central Ohio's suburbs and exurbs, extending outward from Columbus, have grown remarkably and shaped the character of the region. In Columbus the voting trends have been Democratic but in the exurbs, in places like Delaware County, Republicans have been dominant.

Ohio's blend of the nation has created among some people a sense that the state lacks anything distinctive; it is simply "flyover country." As one scholar had remarked, it seems for many people that Ohio serves simply as a bypass, a "perennial midpoint between desired ends, an entire state as Middletown." Perhaps, as writer Jeffrey Hammond comments, Ohio's destiny today is to take pride in being the "roving cultural ballast," the "counterweight to whatever seems unusual."

Hammond and others are certainly correct to see Ohio as a great crossroads. While today it may signify blandness, Ohio's history suggests something profoundly more interesting, complex, and significant. In 2003, Ohio celebrated its bicentennial. Like the

1953 events, which were filled with patriotic fervor stemming from the Cold War, those in 2003 witnessed an infusion of nationalism related to the war on terror and in Iraq. Ohioans were also justifiably proud as they reflected on the history of Ohio. Native peoples came to Ohio as the glaciers melted some 13,000 years ago, giving rise to two world-renowned cultures, Adena and Hopewell. As these and other prehistoric cultures faded, Indians moved in, finding a rich land full of resources. The Miami, Shawnee, Lenape, Mingo, Wyandot, and others gave the state its name, and soon found themselves facing Europeans and then Americans for control of the land. With American military victories and statehood achieved, the new settlers of Ohio came to define the state in their terms, building cities, towns, farms, and industries that made Ohio the third most populous state by the time of the Civil War. In the Civil War the state showed its importance to the Union victory with its industries, farms, soldiers, and citizens.

After the Civil War, Ohio remained at the heart of the national transformation into an industrial powerhouse, with the Buckeye State providing seven presidents, a host of inventors and entrepreneurs, and the natural resources needed to make the United States a global power. Ohioans found themselves at the heart of the debates over the meaning of this transformation, as reformers, workers, political leaders, and citizens engaged in struggles to address the effects of rapid growth and expansion, both at home and abroad. Ohioans weathered the Great Depression and once again provided critical resources— and witnessed tremendous sacrifice—during World War II. Slowly at first, but with increasing rapidity after the 1950s, the sense of Ohio's purpose and importance eroded. Debates over policies and identities grew harsher and violent as the 1960s witnessed tremendous social and political upheaval. Afterwards, the state entered a long period of economic and demographic stagnation, if not decline, and its citizens and their leaders have been struggling to recover.

With serious challenges facing the state at the dawn of the twenty-first century, what does the future hold for Ohio? Certainly the transformation at work in Ohio and the nation, since the 1970s, has led to sharp economic, social, and political divisions. Ohioans have certainly been divided before, and perhaps a reflection on the past will lead to new ideas and innovations that will inspire greater cooperation and less conflict. We close with a poem from Ohio native James Wright who, in his work, showed that while desperation and brutality can often define a place hope and beauty also reside there.

Beautiful Ohio

Those old Winnebago men
Knew what they were singing.
All summer long and all alone,
I had found a way
To sit on a railroad tie
Above the sewer main.
It spilled a shining waterfall out of a pipe
Somebody had gouged through the slanted earth.

Sixteen thousand and five hundred more or less people
In Martins Ferry, my home, my native country,
Quickened the river
With the speed of light.
And the light caught there
The solid speed of their lives
In the instant of that waterfall.
I know what we call it
Most of the time.
But I have my own song for it,
And sometimes, even today,
I call it beauty.

Further Reading

On Ohio's very recent history see: Robert Bruno, *Steelworker Alley: How Class Works in Youngstown* (1999. Cornell: ILR Press); Daniel J. Coffey, John C. Green, David B. Cohen, and Stephen C. Brooks, *Buckeye Battleground: Ohio, Campaigns, and Elections in the Twenty-First Century* (2011. Akron: University of Akron Press); William Russell Coil, "New Deal Republican: James Allen Rhodes and the Transformation of the Republican Party, 1933–1983," (2005. unpublished Ph.D. dissertation, The Ohio State University); Jeffrey Hammond, *Ohio States: A Twentieth Century Midwestern* (2002. Kent: Kent State University Press); Alexander P. Lamis and Brian Usher, eds., *Ohio Politics* (2d ed. 2007. Kent: Kent State University Press); Sherry Linkon and John Russo, *Steeltown U.S.A.: Work and Memory in Youngstown* (2002. Lawrence: University of Kansas Press); Steve Love and David Giffels, *Wheels of Fortune: The Story of Rubber in Akron* (1999. Akron: University of Akron Press); Bruce Meyer, *The Once and Future Union: The Rise and Fall of the United Rubber Workers, 1935–1993* (2002. Akron: University of Akron Press); and James Wright, *Above the River: The Complete Poems* (1990. New York: Farrar, Straus and Giroux).

Index

Page numbers for illustrations are in *italics*; those for tables are in **bold**.

1st Michigan Cavalry, 214
1st Ohio Volunteer Infantry, 223
2nd Ohio Volunteer Infantry, 223
4th Ohio Volunteer Infantry, 230
7th Cavalry, 245
8th Ohio Infantry, 214, 216, 230
9th Ohio Infantry, 214, 216
37th Infantry Division, 350, 393
54th Massachusetts Infantry, 215, 216
55th Massachusetts Infantry, 215, 216, 232, 374
127th Ohio Volunteer Infantry (5th U.S. Colored Infantry), 215, 216
372nd Infantry Division, 350

Abenaki Indians, 57
abolition, 142–143, 145, 147–148, 155–158, 226, 236, 239–240, 245; abolitionists, 125, 139, 149, 208–210, 215–221, 231, 333, 335
abortion, 437, 439–440, 468, 471, 477–478, 482
acid rain, 17, 470
Adams County, 13
Adams, John, 121, 194

Adams, John Quincy, 203–204, 206
Adelphia, 114
Adena, 21, 30–36, 39–42, 45–46, 488
Adrian, Michigan, 182
Afghanistan, 480
African Americans: in the arts, 374–376; and civil rights, 426–436, 447, 450, 452, 455–456; and the Civil War, *216*, 220–221, 223, 226, 227, 229, 232; in contemporary society, *458*, 459, 468, 471, 473, 476, 478, 482, 484; in early Ohio, 122, 134, 137, *147*, 148, 152, *190*, 198; in early 20th-century political reform, 333, 335, 336; in the era of industrialization, 302–307, 310, 321, 333, 335; and the Great Depression, 378, 386–387; and the "Great Migration," 353; and late 19th-century politics, 266, 275, 278; and post-World War II society, 404–410, 414, 417; in sports, 321, 323, 399; and Reconstruction, 240–241, 244, 246; and World War II, 392–393
African Methodist Episcopal Church, 149, 335
Agricultural Adjustment Act (AAA), 381
agricultural tile, 15

Ohio: A History of the Buckeye State, First Edition. Kevin F. Kern and Gregory S. Wilson.
© 2014 John Wiley & Sons, Inc. Published 2014 by John Wiley & Sons, Inc.

agriculture: crops, 31, 41–42, 176–178, 223, 381; in early Ohio, 114, 130–132, 161–163, 166, 180, 183–184; in the early 20th century, 347, 372, 441; in industrial-era Ohio, 248, 273, 281; livestock, 130–131, 162, 177–178, 223, 381; and Ohio geography, 1–2, 18; in prehistory, 21, 24, 28–29, 35, 41;

Agushiway, 96

airplanes, 286–287, 291–292, 350, 374

Akron Beacon Journal, 361

Akron Indians, 322

Akron, Ohio, 10, 15, 128, 147, 158, 183, 217, 232, 254, 330, 336, 348; and canals, 169, 173, *174*; in contemporary society, 457, 458, 459, **460**, 463–464; and education, 151, *152*, 208, 322, 336; and environmental issues, 440, 444; as an example of early 20th-century change, 361–362; and the Great Depression, 378–380, 384–385; in the industrial era, 180, 282, 285–290, 315, 352; in the post-World War II era, 398–399, 404, 406, **407–408**, 410–411, 414; and racial unrest, 306, *353*, 369, 426, 434, 453, 455; and sports and leisure, 319, 322–323; and World War II, 390–391

Alabama, 23, 157, 234, 334, 365, 386, 409, 424, 449

Alaska, 22

Albany, New York, 167, 300

alcohol, 53, 69, 73, 154, 161–162, 174, 244; beer, 179, 252, 296, 316, 318; wine, 176–177, 179, 281; *see also* Temperance movement; Prohibition

Alcoholics Anonymous, 154

Alger, Horatio, 258

Alger, Russell, 278, 89

Algonquian language groups, 51, 55, 57

Allegheny Mountains, 7

Allegheny Plateau, 1, 13, 17

Allen, Florence, 368

Allen, John, 150

Allen, William, 245

Alligator Mound, 44

amaranth, 31

American Anti-Slavery Society, 155, 157

American Federation of Labor (AFL), 274, 313, 330, 383, 392, 417, 448

Americanization, 356, *357*

American ("Know-Nothing") Party, 218–219, 222

American Professional Football Association, 322

American Revolution *see* Revolutionary War

American System, 20

Ames, Ohio, 150

Amherst, Jeffrey, 64–65, 69, 71–72

Amish (people), 126, 130, 136, 355

amusement parks, 317–318

Anabaptists, 136

Anderson Phase, 44

Anderson, Sherwood, 371, 399

Andrews, Clark & Co., 215

Angley, Ernest, 411

Angouriot, 57

anti-Catholicism, 79, 140, 154, 218, 261, 326

anticommunism, 411–415

Antioch College, 148–149, 349, 428

Anti-Saloon League, 252, 332–333, 343

antislavery, 149, 155, 157, 178, 209, 217–219, 221, 223, 230, 238, 250, 327, 335

Appalachia, 1, 134, 352, 361, 389, 404, 410–411, 475, 477, 484, 487

Appalachian Mountains, 7, 11, 13, 58, 71–72, 104, 122, 150, 155, 161, 177, 288, 318, 336

Appalachian Plateau, 7, 13, *181*

apples, 176, 319

Appomattox Court House, 234

apportionment, 208, 210–211, 450, 471, 477

aquifer, 8, 18

Arbuckle, Matthew, 81

archaeology, 22

Archaic period, 24–32, 35, 39–40, 42

architecture, 44, 135

Armstrong, John (soldier), 91, 113–114

Armstrong, John (Wyandot lawyer), 139

Armstrong, Neil, 399

Army of Northern Virginia, 226, 230, 232

Army of the Ohio/the Cumberland, 225, 232, 259

Army of the Potomac, 226, 230, 232, 259

Arnold, Benedict, 112

arrowheads, 41, 44

Arthur, Chester A., 267–268, 270, 343

Articles of Confederation, 90, 101, 103, 105

Ashbrook, John, 445, *446*, 476
Ashland College, 149, *446*
Ashley, James, 242
Ashtabula County, 157, 235
Ashtabula, Ohio, 174, 330, 410
Asians, 22, 294, 459
assassination, 21, 234, 240–241, 268, 270, 277, 343, 434–436
assembly line, 179
Athens County, 32, 308, 379
Athens, Ohio, 126, 149, 454
Atlanta, Georgia, 232, 234, 259
Atlantic Ocean, 11, 28, 33, 39, 49–50, 167, 324, 377
atlatl, 25, *26*, 41
atlatl weights, 29
attorney general: Ohio, 212, 285, 414, 416, 423, 448–449, 471, 478; U.S., 205, 343, 365, 414, 449
Atwater, Caleb, 151, 202
Auglaize River, 95
Aullwood Audubon Center, 440
Aupaumut, 93
automobile industry, 178, 282, 285, 290, 298, 363, 368, 377, 378, 383–384, 398, 459, 473
automobiles, 280, 283, 285, 290, 361, 363, 367, 377, 402–403, 461, 469
autoworkers, 362, 383–384, 397
Awl, William, 146

Babcock, Orville, 244
baby boom, 398, 404
Bailey, Gamaliel, 125, 157, 217
Bainbridge, Ohio, 150
Baker, Joshua, 75, 78
Baker, Newton, 329–330, 333, 346, 351
Baker v. Carr, 449–450
Baldwin, Michael, 121, 187
Baldwin Wallace (University), 149, 355
Baltimore and Ohio Railroad, 181, 266–267
Baltimore, Maryland, 150, 178, 185, 222, 266
banking, 141, 200, 208, 212, 236, 431, 436, 472, 475, 477, 482; and the Bank of the United States, 164–165, 200–201, 203, 206; and foreign policy, 365, 377; and the Great Depression, 377–379, 381; and the Panic of 1837; 182–183, and Progressivism, 344, 346

bannerstones *see* atlatl weights
Baptists, 136, 143, 149, 302–303, 307, 411, 416
Barber, Ohio Columbus, 282
Barberton, Ohio, 14, 330
Barclay, Robert, 198
barns, 130–131, 135
barter, 161, 163, 183
baseball, 267, 317, 319–321, 323, 399, *401*
battleground state, 247, 278
Battle of Antietam (Sharpsburg), 226, 230, 259
Battle of Bloody Run, 71
Battle of Blue Licks, 87–88
Battle of Buffington Island, 215, **233**
Battle of Bull Run (Manassas), 224, 238
Battle of Bushy Run, 71
Battle of Chancellorsville, 230
Battle of Chickamauga, 232, 238, 259
Battle of Corrick's Ford, 224
Battle of Fallen Timbers, *91*, 96–98, 193–194
Battle of Gettysburg, 214–215, 230, 232, 238
Battle of Lake Erie, 197–198, *199*
Battle of Little Bighorn, 245
Battle of Missionary Ridge, 238,
Battle of Moraviantown, 198
Battle of Philippi, 224
Battle of Phillips Corners, 205
Battle of Point Pleasant, 76–77, 79, 194
Battle of Rich Mountain, 224
Battle of Shiloh, 225–226, 238, 259
Battle of Stone's River, 238
Battle of the Thames, 198, *207*
Bäumler, Joseph (Bimeler), 144–145
Baum Phase, 44
Baynton, Wharton, and Morgan, 73
beans, 42, 461
bears, 32, 36, 130–131
beaver hats, 47–48
beavers, 23, 51
Beaver Wars, 51–52, 55–56
Bedford Shale, 5, 15
Bedini, Gaetano, 140
Beecher, Lyman, 126, 142, 153–155, 157
Beecher, Philemon, 189
Bell, John, 222
Bellamy, Edward, 351

Bellamy, George, 331, 339

Bellevue, Ohio, 181

Belmont County, 134, 145, 231, 308

Beloved (Morrison), 220, 376

Berea, Ohio, 16, 145

Berea sandstone, 5, 16

Beringia, 22

Bestor, Arthur, 143

bicentennial: Ohio, 15, 487; U.S., 463–464

Bickerdyke, Mary Ann, 226

Big Bottom, 92, 138

Bigelow, Herbert, 341, 345

Bill of Rights: Ohio, 341; taxpayer, 470; U.S., 105

Billington, Dallas Franklin, 411

bimetallism, 249, 274

Bingham, John, 240–242

Bing Law, 338

Bird, Henry, 84

Birney, James G., 157, 208–210

birth control, 368, 439

Black, Walter, 303, *304*

Black Brigade, *216*, 225

black codes, south, 241

black diamond region, 1

Black Hand sandstone, 5

Black Hoof, 193,

Black Laws, Ohio (1804, 1807), 139, 188–189, *190*, 203, 210, 212

Black River, 128

Black River limestone, 15

Blacks *see* African Americans

Black Swamp *see* Great Black Swamp

Black United Students (BUS), 426

Blackwell, Kenneth, 478, 481

Blair, Frank, 243

blast furnace, 1–2, 180, *304*, 459, 466, *467*

"Bleeding Kansas," 217, 219

Blennerhasset Island, 192

blimps *see* dirigibles

Bliss, Ray, 418, 421–422

Blizzard of 1978, 471

Bloodhounds, The, 187

Bloomfield, Ohio, 149

Blooming Grove, Ohio, 358

Bluffton College/University, 149

Bluffton, Ohio, 379

boats, 192, 195, 316; canal boats, 169, 172–174, 182, 280, 284; and early Ohio trade, 73, 160, 162–163, 166, 175–176, 180; gunboats, 197, 214, 232; rescue, 348; steamboats, 125, 159, 166–167, 226, 232, 297, 316–317, 319

Bolivar, Ohio, 83

Bolton, Frances P., 415

Bolton, Oliver O., 415

Bombeck, Erma, 403, 439

Bommarito, Peter, 463–464

bonds: canal, 173; city, 436; Liberty, 353, *356*; state, 218, 342, 402, 422–423, 469, 475, 481; surety, 189, 252 U.S., 236, 255, 381

Boone, Daniel, 82, 88

Boonesboro, Kentucky, 88

boosterism, 129, 165, 168, 202, 319

Booth, John Wilkes, 234

Boston, Massachusetts, 16, 79, 108, 154, 198, 290, 319, 371

Bouquet, Henry, 69–72, *73*

bow and arrow, 41

Bowling Green, Ohio, 129

Bowling Green State University, 336

Bowman, John, 84

Braddock, Edward, 63, *64*

Bradstreet, John, 72

Brady, Samuel, 138

Brant, Joseph, *see* Thayendanegea

Brassfield Formation limestone, 15

Breckinridge, John C., 222, 227

Breslin, John G., 218

Bricker, John, 381–382, 389, 392, 398, 416, 418, 451

bricks, 2, 14–15, 285, 287, 313, 451

Brinkerhoff, Jacob, 209

British government, 74, 79, 96

Brock, Isaac, 195–196

Brodhead, Daniel, 84–85, 113

Bromfield, Louis, 371–374

Brook Farm, Massachusetts, 143

Brough, John, 227, 231–232

Brown, Clarence J. "Bud," 415, 465, 473

Brown, Ethan Allen, 201–202

Brown, Frederick, 218

Brown, Hallie Quinn, 334–335

Brown, John, 158, 178, 217–218, 240

Brown, John Jr., 220–221
Brown, Oliver, 221
Brown, Owen, 158
Brown, Paul, 399
Brown County, 134, 157, 212, 238
Brownstown, 89
Brown v. Board of Education, 409, 416, 427–430
Brush, Charles, 290
Bryan, William Jennings, 273–275, 277, 344, 370
Buchanan, James, 219, 221, 235
Buchtel College *see* University of Akron
Buckongahelas, 92, 95, 96
"Bucktown," 139
Buell, Don Carlos, 225, 238
Buffalo, New York, 160, 168, 175, 277, 285
burials *see* mortuary practices
Burke-Wadsworth Act, 389
Burning Tree Mastodon, 23
Burnside, Ambrose, 229
Burr, Aaron, 192
Burton, Harold, 382, 415
Bushnell, Asa, 254, 276
Bushnell, Simeon, 220
business, 15; and contemporary society, 461–465, 475, 481; in early Ohio, 129, 139, 141, 160–166, 169, 173–175, 178–180, 183; in the early 20th century, 326–329, 336, 364, 377; and the Great Depression, 377, 383, 386; in the industrial era, 282–284, 287–290, 295–299, 309, 315; in late 19th-century Ohio, 248–250, 262–263, 271, 274–275, 278; and the post-war era, 397, 403, 418–419, 422–423, 435–436; and regulation, 344–346; and war, 352–354, 356–357, 390–393; *see also* specific businesses
busing, 430, 476
Butler County, 149
Buttermilk Creek, 22
butternut, 136, 157, 229, 238
buzzards, 131
Byrd, Charles Willing, 122

Cabot, John, 49
Cadiz, Ohio, 241, 441

Cahokia, 40, 42, 72, 84
calendar post, 44
calumet (peace pipe), 53
Cambrian period, 4–5
Cambridge, Ohio, 135, 282
Camden, Ohio, 371, 399, 403
Cameron, Simon, 235
Campbell, James, 263
Campbell, William, 96
Campbell, Ohio, 464–465
Camp Charlotte, 77
Camp Chase, 232–233
Camp Dennison, 232
Camp Greene Ville (Greenville), 97
Campus Martius, 114
Canada, 16, 102, 112, 161, 294, 367, 398; and the Civil War, 215, *228*, 229; and the environment, 442, 451; and the Middle Ground, 49, 59–60; and prehistoric Ohio, 34, 39; and the Underground Railroad, 157, 220; and the War of 1812, 194–195, 198
Canal Dover, Ohio, 173
Canal Fulton, Ohio, 173
Canal Fund Commission, 169, 173
canals, 17, 128–129, 137–138, *144*, 145, 159–161, 183, 237, 258, 283, 461; construction, 167–172; decline, 181–182, 223, 280, 284, 348; funding, 173; life on the canal, 172–180; political struggles over, 151, 165, 169, 202–204
Canal Winchester, Ohio, 173
Canton Bulldogs, 322–323
Canton, Ohio, 129, 180, 282, 330, 355, 358, 379, 414; population changes in, 406, **407–408, 460**; and professional football, 322–323; and William McKinley, 254, 262, 273, 277
Canton Repository, 262
Capital College/University, 149
capital (of state/territory), 112, 115, 117, 120–121, *186*, 191–192
capital punishment, 327, 342, 420
captives, 56; and the Civil War, 227; and the Middle Ground, 69, 71–72, *73*, 77, 82, 85–86
Captive Town, 84
Carey, Ohio, 86

Carter, James Earl, 461, 466, 470, 474, 476

Carthagena, Ohio, 140

Cartier, Jacques, 49

Case Western Reserve University (Western Reserve University), 149, *253*, 322

Cass, Lewis, 196, 200, 210

Casson, Francois Dollier de, 52

Castalia, Ohio, 58

Catawba grape/wine, 176–177

Catholicism (and Catholics), 1, 79, 313, 361, 393, 465, 485; and higher education, 149; and immigration/migration, 126, 137, 140, 174, 295–297, 330, 337, 339; and politics, 298, 338, and reform, 154, 331; 476; *see also* anti-Catholicism

cattle (cows), 177–178, 180, 223, 237, 316

caves (rock shelters), 23, 25, 41

Cayton, Andrew, 141, 158

Cayuga Indians, 50, 75

Cedarville College/University, 149

Celebrezze, Anthony, 409, 416, 478

Celeste, Richard, 415, 468–477, 482, *484*

Celina, Ohio, 10

Céloron, Pierre-Joseph de Blainville, 60, *61*

celts, 36

Cenozoic Era, 7–8

Central America, *43*, 272

Central State University, 326

ceramics (pottery), 1–2, 14–15, 180, 282, 287; and Native Americans, 14, 28–29, 31–32, 35–36, 44

ceremonialism, 24, 27–30, 32–33, 35–36, *38*, 39–42, 44, 53, 74

Chagrin Falls Park, 407

Champaign County, 17

Chapman, John (Johnny Appleseed), 176

Charleston Harbor, 215, 222

Charleston, South Carolina, 222, 265

Chase, Salmon P., 125–126, 157, 210, 218, 221–222, 248, 278; and the Civil War, 224, 233, 235–236, 239, 242–243

Chattanooga, Tennessee, 232

cheese, 223

Cherokee Indians, 56, 92

Chesnutt, Charles, 304, 375

Chicago, Illinois, 16, 297, 301, 371, 379; and the economy, 160, 178, *286*, 288, 290, 465;

and labor issues, 266, 311–312; and politics, 222, 243, 270, 273, 447

Chief Justice: of Ohio, 260, 419; of the United States, 219, 236, 242–243, 276, 278, 280, 345, 365, 367

Chiksika, 194

child labor, *181, 310*, 317, 332

Children's Code, 346–347

Chillicothe Faction, *119*, 120

Chillicothe, Ohio, 30, 33, 37, 116, 165, 177, 185; and Ohio politics, 112, 119–121, 187, 192, 201, 242

Chillicothe (Shawnee town), 82, 84, 87

China, 295, 387, 411–412, 422, 461

Chiningué (Logstown), 57, 62

Chippewa Indians, 55, 57, 60, 72

cholera, 172, 211

Church of God, 149

Church of the Brethren, 74, 136, 149, 393

Cincinnati, 125–126, 146, 148, 348–349, 355, 367; and African Americans, 134, 139, 294, 304, **353**, 354, **408**, 428; and the Civil War, 215, 217–220, 223–226, 229, 231–232, 239, 245; and de-urbanization, **460**, 461, 476, 487; and early statehood commerce, 162–166, 169, 180, 183; and early statehood politics, 187, 194, 201, 203, 208, 210–211; and early 20th-century politics, 343–344; and education, 142, 150–151, 153–154, 336–337; and immigration, 137, 140–141, 296, 299–301, 303; and industrialization, 281, 283, 293, 308–312, 314; and late 19th-century politics, 254, 257–261, 264; and late 20th/early 21st-century politics, 448, 450; and meatpacking, 177–179; and political activism, 331–332; and post-World War II society, 399, 402–403, 406, **407**, 409–410, 414–416; and reform, 154–155, 157–159, 250, 341, 442; in the territorial period, 93, 95, 109, 116–117, 120–121; and urban life, 316–321; and urbanization, 128–129; and violence in the 1960s, 426, 433–434; and wine, 176–177; and World War II, 390, 392

Cincinnati and Whitewater Canal, 159, 175

Cincinnati Arch, 5, 13

Cincinnati Enquirer, 125, 413

Cincinnati Law School, 150

Cincinnati Reds, 399

Cincinnati Red Stockings, 319–321

Circleville, Ohio, 77, 151, *379*

civil disturbances: ethnic clashes, 140,
369–370; political protests/riots, 121, 187,
229, 255–256, 379, 426–430, 432, 435, 444,
447–448, 451, 454, 469; race riots, 139–41,
227, 239, 306–307, 426, 432–34; strikes/
labor riots, 141, 263, 266–267, 303,
309–315, 329, 357–358, 362, 383–386,
392–393, 397–398, 419–420, 432–434, 436,
439, 463–464, 469–470, 472–474; *see also*
Kent State shootings

Civilian Conservation Corps (CCC), 380

civil rights: during the Civil War and
Reconstruction, 240–241, 249, 261,
265–266, 278; in the late 19th/early 20th
century, 305, 334–335, 340, 359, 368, 393,
394; post-World War II, 376, 409–410,
412, 415, 420, 423, 427–432, 437, 439,
447–449, 476

Civil Rights Act of 1964, 444

Civil Rights Bill, 241

civil service reform, 267–268, 278

Civil War, 14, 129, 136, 139, 143, 148,
157–158, 182–183, 185, 374–375, 457, 488;
Ohio and the, 214–240; and the post-war
economy, 280–283, *289*; and post-war
politics, 245, 247–249, 254, 256–261, 266,
278; and post-war society, 294, 302–303,
305–307, 315–317, 319–320, 332–333, 353

Clark, George Rogers, 84–85, 87–88

class, 74, 139, 141, 273, 306, 320, 355, 370, 376;
black middle, 407, 294; black upper, 304,
306–307; middle, 126, 141, 267, 289, 321,
374, 376, 398, 403, 421, 483; middle and
reform, 141, 145, 154, 330–332, 335, 337,
339, 340; and politics, 187, 211, 248,
267–268, 327, 329, 424; middle (women),
330, 368, 437, 439; working, 266, 294, 297,
307, 313, 320, 322, 331, 358, 368, 378, 422;
working (women), 414; upper, 268, 304,
306, 320, 322, 330–332, 340; upper
(women), 330

clay, 2, 6, 10, 14–15, 375, 443; and industry,
180, 282, 287; prehistoric uses, 31–32, 36

Clay, Henry, 201–204, 206, 209, 217

Cleaveland, Moses, 112

Clermont County, 209

Cleveland, Grover, 253, 270, 272

Cleveland Board of Education v. LaFleur, 440

Cleveland Browns, 399

Cleveland Buckeyes, 399

Cleveland Call, 294

Cleveland Gazette, 305, 353

Cleveland Indians, 399, *401*

Cleveland Medical College, 150

Cleveland, Ohio, 10, 14, 269–270, 348; and
African Americans, 151, 303–306, 353–354,
386–387, 392, 406–410; and the arts and
entertainment, 318–319, 375, 404, *405*; and
the civil rights movement, 426, 428–432;
and the Civil War, 215, 226, 235; and the
Great Depression, 378–379; and
de-urbanization, **460**, 461; and economic
development, 161, 169, 175, 180–181; and
education, 150, 336–338; and
environmentalism, 442–444; and football,
322; founding and urbanization, 112, 128,
129, 141, 174, 223; and immigration, 137,
296–301, 356–357; and industrialization,
271, 281–282, 284–285, *286*, 288, 290,
293–294, 308, 316–317; and labor, 311,
313–314, 358, 412, 484; and politics, 272,
349, 414–417, 470–472, 475, 477–478, 484;
and postwar society, 397–400, 404, 406, 410;
and Prohibition, 367; and racial violence,
306, 433–434; and reform, 148, 251, 324,
327–332, 437; and the Stokes brothers, 426,
434–436; and World War II, 390–391

Cleveland Plain Dealer, 475

Cleveland Rolling Mill strikes of 1882, 1885,
313–314

climate, 8, 23–24, 27, 40, 42, 55, 176

Clinton, DeWitt, 167–169

Clinton, William Jefferson, 436, 476, 478–479

Clinton County, 415

Clovis (Paleo) Points, 23

coal, 2, 6, 282, 284–285, *289*, 461, 487; miners,
303, 308, 310–311, 420, 469; mining and
production, 1, 16–17, 180, *181*, 237, 281,
287, 389; and pollution/the environment,
316, 332, 440, 441, 469–470, 475

Coal Measures, 6, *181*

Coercive Acts, 79

Coffin, Levi, 158

Cold War, 373, 396–398, 408, 436, 456, 488; and Ohio politics, 411–414, *418*, 423–424

Colfax, Schuyler, 243–244

college lands, 109, 116

College of Wooster, 149

colleges and higher education, 126, 142, 152–153, 235, 290, 330, 337, 424, 475, 482; and campus protest, 427, 444, 446, 451–456; and civil rights, 427–429; and the Cold War, 412; denominational affiliation, 148–150, 301; and the Ohio presidents, 257–260, 358, and sports, 321–322, 399; state and municipal colleges/universities, 109, 149–150, 235, 260, 336, 420, 423–424; and World War I, 354–355; and World War II, 390

colonial charters, 49, 79, 101

Columbia, 116

Columbiana County, 8, 10, 100, 137, 215

Columbiana, Ohio, 290

Columbus Crisis, 231

Columbus Dispatch, 374, 479

Columbus (Franklintown), Ohio, 128, 129, 132, 292, 348, 350, 362, 374, 420–421, 449, 451; and African Americans, 303, 306, *352*, **353**, 354, 392, 428–430; and the arts and entertainment, 318, 321; as capital, 186, 192, 211, 284, 341–342, 396, 432, 474; and the Civil War, 223, 231–234; and contemporary society, 459, **460**, 473, 475, 477, 484, 487; and the Great Depression, 378; and education, 149–150, 260; and immigration, 137, 301; and industry, 282, 286; and labor, 141, 266, 311, 313, 417; and post-war society, 401, 402, 406, **407–408**, 410, 414; and reform, 252, 324–325, 330, 437, 439; and sports, 322; and transportation, 163, 169; and World War II, 387, 390

Columbus Panhandles, 322

come-outers, 143

Committee on Public Information (CPI), 355

common pleas courts, 211

communication, 24, 28–29, 34–35, 325; telecommunication, 222, 224, 280, 284, 290, 293

communism, 267–268, 397–399, 411–415, 424, 436, 445, 447

Compromise of 1850, 216–217

Compromise of 1877, 265

Conchake, 60

Confederacy, The, 214–215, 222, 225, *228*, 229, 234, 238

Congo, Ohio, 1

Congregationalists, 136, 143, 145, 158, 304, 392, 412, *413*, 417, 448

Congress of Industrial Organizations (CIO), 362, 383, 384, 386–387

Congress of Racial Equality (CORE), 392, 407, 428, *429*, 431–432

Conklin, Joseph, 180

Conneaut, Ohio, 128, 285, *286*, 330

Connecticut, 101, 112, 125–126, 132, 135–136, 142, 155, 176, 248, 292, 445

Connecticut Land Company, 112

Conscription Act (1917), 355

conservatism, 280, 366, 416, 445, *446*, 455

Constitution, 103, 105, 205, 219; Ohio (first), 134, 139, 188, 190, 201; Ohio (second), 241–242, 253, 260, 327, 366, 416, 423, 450, 470–471, 479; U.S., 90, 109, 220, 229, 240, 244, 246, 260, 275, 344, 353, 355, 367–368, 440, 445

Constitutional Convention of 1802, 122–123, *186*, 189, 204

Constitutional Convention of 1851, 147, 210–213

Constitutional Convention of 1873–1874, 250

Constitutional Convention of 1912, 329, 341–343, 345

Constitutional Union Party, 222

container revolution, 28–29

Continental Congress, First, 78–79; and land policy, 101–106, 108–110, 112–113, 117; Second, 80, 83, 88, 99

continental divide, 11, 175

continental soldiers, 86, 127

Contrecoeur, Claude-Pierre Pecaudy de, 62

Cooke, Jay, 234, 236

"Coonskin Library," 150

Cooper, Myers, 366

Copeland, John A. Jr., 220–221

Copley, Ohio, 154

copper: and industrial Ohio, 316; and Middle
   Ground Ohio, 53; and prehistoric Ohio, 28,
   33, 36, *37*, 39, 45

Copperheads (Peace Democrats), 215, *221*,
   228–231

Corbin, Abel, 244

corn (maize), 19; and the Civil War, 223; in
   contemporary agriculture, 461; and early
   statehood, 154, 160, 162, 176–177; in
   Middle Ground Ohio, 50, 53, 88; in
   prehistoric Ohio, 35–36, 41–43;

Cornwallis, Charles, 85

corporations, 2, 5, 281–282, 287, 398–399;
   corruption and big business, 284–285; and
   deindustrialization, 464–466; economic/
   political power of, 245, 260, 271, 289, 344,
   446; and Harding, 365, 381; and the Ku
   Klux Klan, 369–370; late 19th-century, 245,
   249, 254, 257, 264, 267–268, 278, 288; laws
   concerning, 212, 364, 477; and political
   reform, 324, 326, 342; and the New Deal,
   381; and Prohibition, 36; and reform, 327,
   329, 380–381

Coshocton chert, 6, 25

Coshocton County, 6, 23,

Coshocton, Ohio, 60, 72, 74, 83, 84,
   128, 342

Cottawamago (Blackfish), 80, 82

cotton, 166, 237, 353, 461

cougar, 32,

county seats, 118, 120, 129, 200

coureurs de bois, 53

cows *see* cattle

Cox, George "Boss," 254–256

Cox, Jacob D., 241

Cox, James M., 278, 340, 345–347, 349, 352,
   356–359

Cox, Samuel, 229

Coxey, Jacob, 255

Crabbe Act, 367

Crawford, William, 76, 78, 83, 86–87

Credit Mobilier, 244

Creek Indians, 194

cremation, 23, 27, 32

crime, 246; in industrializing cities, 249, 296,
   306, 332; organized, 367; and post-World
   War II society, 397, 408, 422–423, 448, 476,
   481; and World War I, 355

Crimean War, 219

Croghan, George (soldier, War of 1812), 197

Croghan, George (trader), *54*, 58–59, 75

Crooksville, Ohio, 2

crops *see* agriculture

"Crowbar Law," 201

cultural complex, 28, 30, 33–35, 42

Cumberland, Maryland, 163

currency, 175, 411, 461; depreciated, 106, 108;
   late 19th/early 20th-century reform of, 249,
   261, 268, 273–274, 344; paper/scrip,
   200–201, 235–236, 249, 398; scarcity of
   hard, 162–165, 183

Custer, George Armstrong, 214, 234, 238, 245

Cutler, Ephraim, 150–151, 202

Cutler, Manasseh, 108

Cuyahoga County, 14, 137, 258, 326, 408, 435,
   450–451, 470–471

Cuyahoga Falls, Ohio, 330, 457

Cuyahoga River/Valley: in early statehood,
   128, 138, 169; and industrialization, 281,
   297, 348; and Native Americans, 57, 59, 82;
   and pollution, 440, 442–444

Cuyahoga Valley National Park, 444

Czechs, 296–298

Czolgosz, Leon, 277

Daily Cleveland Herald, 215

dairy farming, 136, 178

Dalyell, James, 71

Darrow, Clarence, 370

Davey, Martin, 366, 381–382, 385

Davidson, Jo Ann, 478

Dawes, Charles Gates, 366

Day, William R., 278

Dayton College/University of Dayton, 149

Dayton Daily News, 345, 347

Dayton, Ohio, 112, 128–129, 137, 141, 169;
   and African Americans, 305, 321, 334, **353**,
   374, **408**; and the Civil War, 228, 229; and
   the Flood of 1913, 347–349; and
   industrialization, 281–282, 286, *289*,
   290–293; and labor, 314; and post-World

War II society, 403, 406, **407**, 410, 439–440, **461**, 463, 473, 476, 484, 487; and sports, 322; and politics, 330, 333, 345; and World War II, 390

Dayton Triangles, 322

Dayton Women's Liberation Movement (DWL), 439

Debs, Eugene, 330, 345, 355, 365

debt: French, 47; individual/family, 165, 201, 271, 273, 295, 377; municipal, 250, 419; state governmental, 173, 211–212, 422, 477; U.S. national, 103, 108, 260, 377; World War I, 366, 377

deer, 23, 41, 84, 130–131

Defiance College, 396

Defiance Democrat, 227

Defiance Moraine, 10

Defiance, Ohio, 10, 128

deindustrialization, 444, 459–466, *467*

Delaware County, 137, 223, 232, 474, 487

Delaware Indians *see* Lenape

Delaware, Ohio, 81, 215, *216*, 257

DELCO, 281, 290–291

demobilization, 397–398

"Democracy of Ohio," The, 204, *227*

Democratic Party (Jeffersonian Republicans, Democratic-Republicans): and African Americans, 249, 435–436; and the Civil War, 215, 217–224, 227–229, 231, 234–235; in contemporary society, 467–471, 473–477, 479, 481, 485, 487; and the Great Depression, 366, 380–382, 393; in early statehood period, 157, 183, 187–188, 191–192, 200–201, 203–204, 206–211; and early 20th-century political reform, 326–327, 338, 342, 344–345, 349; and late 19th-century politics, 248, 250, 253–254, 260–261, 268, 270, 272–274, 279; and the 1920s, 358, 366; and the 1960s, 426, *433, 446*, 447–451; and post-World War II society, 398, 409–410, 413–419, 422; and Reconstruction, 240–245, 264–266; in territorial period, *118*, 119–123

Denison College/University, 149

Dennison, William, 223–224, 238, 240

Denny, Ebenezer, 90

dental schools, 150

DeNucci, George, 412–413

Denver, Colorado, 16

de Peyster, Arent, 85

depressions, 469; of 1819, 164–166; of 1837, 127, 183, 207; of 1857, 219; of 1873, 245, 250, 261, 264, 266, 307; of 1893, 255–256, 263, 271, *277*, 307; of 1914–1915, 353; Great, *255*, 285, 359, 361–362, 373, 376–387, 390, 393–394, 399, 417, 420, 438, 466, 472, 475, 488

DeRolph v. State of Ohio, 479–480

desegregation, 409, 416

Detroit, Michigan, 177, 195, 285, 319; and Tom Johnson, 328–329; and labor, 383–384, 463; *see also* Fort Detroit

de Villiers, Joseph Coulon, 63

de Villiers, Louis Coulon, 63

Devo, 457

Devonian period, 2, 5, 15

Dewine, Richard Michael, 477

Diamond Match Company, 282

Dick, Charles, 254

Dillinger, John, 379

Dingley Tariff, 274

Dinwiddie, Robert, 58, 62

direct primary, 342, 345

dirigibles (blimps), 286–287

DiSalle, Michael, 410, 416, 418–420, 422, 424, 449

Disciples of Christ, 136, 149, 258

discoidals, 44

discrimination: and African American writers, 374–376; and the Civil Rights Movement, 410, 419, 432, 434, 437, *438*; in the early statehood era, 140; in the industrial era, 293–294, 307, 333; and labor, 386, 392, 405, 408; and World War I, 353–354

disease: and canalworkers, 172; and the military, 92, 95, 216, 223, 276, 350; and Native Americans, 50–53, 55, 69; and reform, 311, 324, 332; and World War I, 354; *see also* specific diseases

district courts, 211,

diversification, 24, 29–30, 42

DNA, 22, 35, 40, 42, 46, 399

Doby, Larry, 399, *401*

dolomite, 13, 15

Donahey, Vic, 366, 370, 382
Donation Tract, 112
doughface, 219
Douglas, Stephen, 217, 222
Dove, Rita, 457, *458*
Dow Law of 1886, 254
draft: and the Civil War, 227, 229–230, 232; and World War I, 350, 355; and World War II, 389, 393
Dred Scott Case, 219
Dresden, Ohio, 75
drought, 40, 43, 139, 381
Duck Creek, 180
Dunbar, Paul Laurence, *293*, 305, 374–375
Dunmore, Lord (John Murray), 76–78; *see also* Lord Dunmore's War
Duquesne, Ange de Menneville, Marquis de, 62
Dutch (people), 51
Dyer, Joyce, 464

earspools, 36
earthworks, 1, 20–21, 30, 32, 36–39, 41
Eastern Agricultural Complex (EAC), 31–32, 35, 40–42, *43*
East Liverpool, Ohio, 106, 128, 282, 379
economic development, 2; early statehood, 161, 184, 202, 204; post-World War II, *421*, 422, 440, 461, 468–469, 473, 481, 487
economy/economics: and the Civil War, 216, 219, 222–223, 231, 236–237; and deindustrialization, 440, 444–445, 458–462, 468–470, 472–475, 477–485; early regulation of, 200–204; in early statehood, 130, 132, 136, 154, 160–184, 212; geological basis of, 1, 2, 15, 18; and the Great Depression, 376–378, 380–382; and industrialization, 283–286, 307, 315; and late 19th-century politics, 263, 273–274; in the Middle Ground period, 48–49, 53; and the 1920s, 362–363; and post-World War II society, 396–397, 399–400, 406, 408, 417, 422–424; and reform, 325, 327, 340, 345; and World War II, 387, 389–390, 394
Ecumenical Coalition of the Mahoning Valley, 465
Edison, Thomas A., 161, 245, 290, 292–293, *364*

education (and schools), 316–317, 361, 376, 378, 396, 412, 422, 473, 484; and Americanization, 298, 331, 355–356, *357*; charter, 477–478; decreased spending on, 150, 444, 467, 470, 479, 482, 485; for the disabled, 146; early 1800s reform of, 141, 145, 150–154, 202–203, 208; early 20th-century reform of, 314, 324, 341, 343, 347, 349, 362; increased spending on, 151, 211, 416, 419–420, *421*, 423, 436, 468, 474–476, 480–482; inequality in, 152, 210, 307, 406–410, 416, 427–432, 435, 437, 477, 479; late 19th-century reform of, 218, 232, 249, 254, 260–262, 266, 268, 331, 333, 337–339; level of, 116, 150, 202, 290, 410, *434*, 485; one-room schoolhouses, 152; parochial, 140, 155, 261, 295–298, 338, 478; public lands to support, 100, 104–105, *107*, 109, 112, 116, 123; and sports, 321; standardization of, 126, 153, 158; *see also* colleges and higher education
effigy mounds, 44
Eighteenth Amendment, *253*, 333, 343, 355, 358, 367
Eisenhower, Dwight David, 123, 396, 409, 412, 415–416, 420, 427, 446
elections, national: of 1800, 121; of 1824, 187, 203–204; of 1828, 204, 208; of 1832, 204, 208; of 1836, 206, 208; of 1840, 207–208; of 1844, 209; of 1848, 209; of 1854, 218; of 1856, 218–219; of 1860, 221–222, 231; of 1862, 228–229, 235, 261; of 1864, 233–234, *236*, 260; of 1866, 241, 260; of 1868, 243–244; of 1872, 244; of 1876, 245, 257, 261, 263–265; of 1880, 268; of 1884, 253, 270; of 1888, 270; of 1892, 255, 270, 272; of 1896, 254, 257, 272–274; of 1900, 254, 257, 277; of 1904, 343; of 1908, 343–344, 479; of 1912, 330, 344–345; of 1920, 278, 339, 340, 358–359, 363; of 1924, 366, 369; of 1928, 366; of 1932, 380; of 1936, 382; of 1938, 382; of 1940, 389; of 1946, 398; of 1948, 415; of 1956, 415–417; of 1960, 420; of 1964, 415, 444; of 1968, 447–448; of 1976, 476; of 1980, 445, 476; of 1984, 476; of 1988, 476; of 1992, 479; of 1996, 479; of 2012, 219
elections, Ohio: of 1807, 188; of 1808, 191; of 1809, 188; of 1810, 192; of 1826, 200, 208; of

1828, 208; of 1830, 208; of 1842, 209; of
1844, 209; of 1846, 209; of 1848, 209; of
1849, 211; of 1853, 218; of 1855, 140, 218; of
1857, 218; of 1861, 224; of 1863, *228*, 231; of
1865, 241; of 1867, 242; of 1869, 244, 260; of
1871, 245; of 1883, 253; of 1885, 254; of
1887, 254; of 1891, 255; of 1895, 254–255; of
1912, 345; of 1914, 349; of 1916, 349; of
1918, 349, of 1920, 366, of 1922, 366; of
1924, 366; of 1926, 366; of 1928, 366; of
1930, 366; of 1932, 366; of 1934, 381; of
1936, 382; of 1938, 382; of 1940, 382; of
1950, 413; of 1952, 415; of 1954, 415; of
1958, 416–418; of 1960, 419–420; of 1962,
420; of 1966, 421; of 1970, 415, 450–451,
467; of 1972, 450; of 1974, 415, 468; of 1978,
415, 471; of 1982, 473; of 1984, 476; of 1986,
475; of 1990, 477; of 1994, 477, 478; of 1998,
479; of 2006, 481; of 2010, 482; frequency
of, 122, 188, 212
elections, territorial, 120–121
electoral college, 222
Electric Auto-Lite, 282, 383
Elinipsico, 81
Elyria, Ohio, 128
Emancipation Proclamation, 217, 226, 227
Emergency Quota Act of 1921, 364
Emerson, John, 219
Enabling Act, 121–123, 163
energy crisis, 469, 472
English: early settlers and traders, 49, 51,
53–55, 58, 72–74, 112; immigrants, 135,
137, 311, 313; speech and language, 136,
295–296, 301, 313–314, 331, *357*, 374
environment, 10, 17; and early 20th-century
reform, 332, 359; in the industrial era, 315;
late 20th-century issues, 426, 440–444, 450,
456, 461, 466, 468, 473, 476; prehistoric,
22, 24
Episcopalians, 136, 143, 149, 304
Equal Rights Amendment, *438*, 439–440, 468
equinox, 39, 44
Erie and Kalamazoo Railroad, 182
Erie Canal, 128, 167, 169, 174–175
Erie Indians, 52
Erie, Pennsylvania, 197
Erieview, 409

Espionage Act of 1917, 355
ethnicity: of early Ohio immigrants, 135–137,
175; and early Ohio politics, 202–204; and
early 20th-century society, 362, 368–370;
and industrialization, 294–305, 309,
311–313, 358; and late 19th-century
politics, 250, 274, 327; and late 20th-century
politics and society, 414, 427–436, 471, 485,
487; among Native American groups, 57,
59, 193; and the Treaty of Versailles, 359;
see also specific ethnic groups
Europe, 331, 344, 357; and commerce, 172,
184, 215, 292, 377–378, 464–465; and
immigration to Ohio, 137, 140, 155,
248–249, 294–295, 297, 300–302, 309, 313,
317, 331, 364; and relations with Native
Americans, *48*, 49–50, 54; and World War I,
349–351, 354, 357, 377; and World War II,
372, 393
Evangelical United Brethren, 136
ex parte Milligan, 229
extension of slavery, 136, 209, 212

Fairchild, James, 220
Fairfield County, 189
family life, 130–132, 403
farmland, 15, 18, 100, 108, 114, 120, 129, 132,
165, 184, 401, 487
farm machinery, 132, 180, 290
farms and farmers, 100, 183, 223; and the Civil
War, 231; and early 19th-century economic
development, 132, 160–163, 180; and early
20th-century society, 340–342, 347, 353,
364, 371–373; in early U.S. settlement
period, 106, 116, 127–132, 139, 141, 154;
and the Great Depression, 377, *379*, 381,
383; and immigration/migration, 136–137,
140, 144–145; and industrialization,
280–281, 284–285, 290–291, 307, 319, 338;
and late 19th-century politics, 248–249,
252–255, 257–258, 262, 268, 271, 273–274;
and the Market/Transportation Revolutions,
166, 169, 175–178; and post-World War II
society, 397, 401, 441, 477, 487, 488; in
prehistory, 41; and World War II, 389,
393–394; *see also* agriculture
fast food, 400–401

Fearing, Paul, 121

Federalists, 118, 120–121, 187–188, 192, 195, 200

feminism, 437–438, 476

Ferguson Act, 398

Feurt Phase, 44

Fifteenth Amendment, 244–245, 260, 302, 342

"Fighting McCooks," 214, 230, 238, 245

Fillmore, Millard, 219

finance and capital: and the Civil War, 233–244, 235–237; in early Ohio, 163–166; 173, 182–183, 200–201; in the early 20th-century, 363–364, 377–379; and industrialization, 281, 284, 288–294 and the late 20th-century, 422–423, 467–468, 474

Findlay, James, 196

Findlay College/University of Findlay, 149

Findlay Jeffersonian, 227

Findlay, Ohio, 18, 129, 149, 227, 282, 287, 485

Finney, Charles Grandison, 142–143, 157

Fire Nation, 51

firearms, *228*, 379, 480; and assassinations, 268, *269*, 277, 447; and civil disorder, 140, 306, 312, 370, 383, 432, 453–455, 472; hand guns, 480; and Indian trade, 51, 53, 57, 65, 69, 73; and U.S.–Indian conflict, 68, 81–82, 84, 86, 88, 91

Firelands, 109, 112, 132, 135

Firestone, Harvey, 290, *364*

Firestone Corporation, 282, 290; and deindustrialization, 459, 463–464; and housing, 315, 352–353, 363; and labor issues, 384, 398

First Charter of Virginia, 49

First Reconstruction Act, 241–242

fish and fishing, 5, 27, 41, 43, 442–443

Fisk, James, 244

Five Nations of the Scioto Plains, 72

"Five Ohios," 485–487

flappers, 368

flax, 176, 223

flint, 1–2, 6, 14, 19, 23, 25, 28, 180; flint tools and weapons, 32, 36, 39, 41, 43

Flint Ridge, 1, 2, 6, 14, 23, 25, 32, 36, 39

floods, 4, 7, 18, 43, 327, 441; of 1913, 284, 347–349

Florida, 39, 264–265, 451, 470, 474

flour, 160, 162, 223, 317

Floyd, Charles "Pretty Boy," 379

Follis, Charles, 323

football, 317, 321–323, 399, 453

Foraker, Joseph, 253–254, 312

Forbes, Charles, 365

Forbes, John, 63

Ford, Gerald, 470, 476

Ford, Henry, 178, 290, *364*

Ford, Seabury, 209

foreclosure, 165, 201, 377, *379*, 381

Forest Park, 402–403

forests: and conservation, 271, 343–344, 347, 372; early geological eras, 5–7, 23, 181; and early U.S. settlement, 106, 130–131, 177, 180; and Ohio prehistory, 27–28

Fort Adams, *89*

Fort Ancient Complex, 44, 46

Fort Defiance, 95

Fort Deposit, 96

Fort Detroit: under British control after 1783, 89–90, 96, 102; under French control, 58–60; and Resistance of 1763, 70–72; and Revolutionary War, 80–85; and War of 1812, 195–198

Fort Donelson, 238

Fort Duquesne, 62–64

Fort Finney, 87–88, 106

Fort Gower, 76, 78–79

Fort Hamilton, 92–93

Fort Harmar, 90, 106, 113–114, *115*, 116

Fort Henry, 238

fortifications, 197, 215, 224, *225*, 259

Fort Jefferson, 93

Fort Laurens, 82–84

Fort Le Boeuf, 62

Fort Machault, 62, 64

Fort Mackinac, 195

Fort McIntosh, 86–87, 90

Fort Meigs, 197, *207*

Fort Miami (Indiana), 59

Fort Miamis, 96

Fort Necessity, 63

Fort Niagara, 64, 72

Fort Pitt, *65*, 67, 69–71, 76, 80, 82–86

Fort Randolph, 81

Fort Recovery, 92, 95–96, 193

Fort Sandoské, 60, 70

Fort Sandusky, 70–71, 197
Fort St. Clair, *89*
Fort Stephenson, 197
Fort Steuben, 113–114, *115*
Fort Sumter, 222–223, 227, 259
Fort Washington, 92, 109, 116
Fort Wayne, 59, 90, *91*, 97, 194, 196
"Forty-Eighters," 140
Foster, Charles, 253
Fostoria, Ohio, 330, 379
Fourteenth Amendment, 241–242, 245
France, 87, 122, 267, 292; and American
    territories, 47–49, 52, 55, 57–60, 62; and
    World War I, 350–352, 372, 378; and World
    War II, 387, 389
Franklin College, 149, 152
Franklin County, 15, 137
Freed, Alan, 404, *405*
Freedmen's Bureau, 241, 261
Freedom Summer, 428, *429*
Free Soil Party, 136, *190*, 209–211, 218
Fremont, John C., 218–219
Fremont, Ohio, 128, 197, 257, 261, 267
French Crescent, 49
French Grants, 112, 137
French (people), 47, 49, 51–53, 55, 57–65,
    68–70, 72, 75, 87, 114, *323*; Canadians, 79;
    immigrants, 112, 137
French Revolution, 112
Frenchtown, 197
Frigidaire, 463
"Frostbitten Convention," 206
fruit, 176, 231, 299; *see also* apples; grapes
Fugitive Slave Law, 217, 220, 224
Fulton, John A., 205
Fulton, Robert, 166
Fulton County, 205
Fulton Line, 205
furs (skins), 47–49, 51, 60, 71, 96
Fusionists, 218, 220
Future Outlook League, 386, 392, 435

Gage, Frances Dana, 147–148
Gage, Thomas, 72
galena, 39
Galena, Illinois, 238
Galinée, Rene de Bréhant de, 52
Gallia County, 134, 137

Gallipolis, 112, 137
Gallipolis Journal, 227
Gambier, Ohio, 257
Garfield, James Abram, 173, 216, 244, 247,
    257–259, 261–262, 265, 267–270, 278
Garfield, James R., 349
Garner, Margaret, 220
Garrison, William Lloyd, 155, *156*
gas mask, 293–294, 352
gas: natural, 1–2, 5, 17; gas industry, 18–19,
    282, 287; utility, 325–326, 348
gasoline, 290–291, 390, 419, 469, 472
Geauga County, 10
Geddes, James, 169
Geghan Bill, 261
Gelelemend (Killbuck), 81–83
General Assembly *see* Ohio General Assembly
General Order No. 38, 229
General Tire, 282, 384, 463–464
Genius of Universal Emancipation, The,
    155, *156*
geographer, 103, 106, 185
geology, 1–7, 13, 19, 487
George II, King, 58
George III, King, 72, 80
George, Henry, 327–329
Georgetown, Ohio, 238
Georgia, 232, 234, 259, 435
German Baptists (Dunkers), 137
German Reformed Church, 136, 149
German Society of Separatists (Zoarites), 144
Germans: and anti-German sentiment, 140,
    296, 350, 354, *356*; and arts and culture,
    296; as immigrants, 126, 135, 137, 140, 298,
    316–317; and temperance, 250, 252; and
    World War II, 387
gerrymandering, 208, 211; *see also*
    apportionment
giant ground sloth, 23
GI Bill, 397, 401
"Gibraltar Brigade," 230
Gibson, John, 75, 78, 83–84
Gibson, William H., 218
Giddings, Joshua, 157
Gilded Age, 288–289
Gilligan, John J., 448–450, 467–469, 471, *472*
Girty, Simon, 82, 84, 86, 92, 95
Gist, Christopher, 62

Gist, Samuel, 134

Glacial Kame tradition, 28–30, 32

glacial till (till), 7, 9–12, 19

glaciation (glaciers), 1–2, 7–14, 16–19, 22–23, 32, 129, 485, 487

Gladden, Washington, 324–326, 330, 336

Gladwin, Henry, 71

Glaize, The, 95

glass, 45, 50; industry, 15–16, 18, 282, 318, 363, 378, 459

Glazier, Willard, 316–317, 332

Glenn, John, 399, *400*, 450–451, 468, 470, 476–477

Glenville Shootout, 434, 436

globalization, 47–48, 461

Gnadenhutten, 67–68, 74, 85–86, 99, 112, 198

Goldwater, Barry, 415, 444–445, 476

Gompers, Samuel, 274, 313, 330

Goodrich, Benjamin Franklin, 282, 288–289, 384, 398–399, 463–464

Goodyear Tire and Rubber, 444, *458*; and airships, 287; and deindustrialization, 463–464; and industrialization, 282, 288, 290; and labor issues, 384, *385*, 398; and welfare capitalism, 315, 352–353, 363; and World War II, 390–391

goosefoot, 28, 31

GOP *see* Republican Party (modern)

gorgets, 29, 53

Goshachgunk, 83–85

Gould, Jay, 244, 311

gourds, 28, 31

governorship, 249, 261; in Constitution of 1802, 122; in Constitution of 1851, 212, 260; election of lieutenant-governor, 471; term limitations of, 212, 415; in territorial period, 105, 117, 120; and veto power, 105, 122, 212, 250

grain, 160–163, 176, 178

Grand River, 10

Grange, 268, 285, 333, 441

granite, 4, 25, 299

Grant, Ulysses S.: as general, 214, 216, 225–226, 230, 232, 234, 238–240; political career, 242–248, 257, 259, 261, 264, 266–267, 274, 278, 288, 343, 365–366

Granville, Ohio, 132, 284

grapes, 176

grave goods, 29, 32–33, 36, 45

gravel, 9–10, 16, 36, 285

Great Black Swamp (Black Swamp), 11, 15, 97, 129, 195

Great Britain (England): and immigration, 137, 179; and North American empire, 48–49, 55, 57, 59, 62, 63, 72, *73*, 113; and reform, 330, 334, 347; and World War I, 350, 354, 378; and World War II, 387, 389, 398

Great Circle, 39

Great Depression *see* depressions

"Great Hinckley Hunt," 131

"Great Hopewell Road," 37

Greathouse, Daniel, 75, 78

Great Lakes, 295, 449; in the early statehood period, 136, 193–194, 197; and environmental issues, 442–443; formation of, 11; and industrialization, 168, 272, 283, *286*, 295; and Middle Ground Ohio, 47, 49, 51–52, 54–55, 59–60, 65, 70–72, 79, 87, 89; and prehistoric Ohio, 28, 33, *37*, 39

Great Lakes Water Quality Agreement, 442

Great Miami River, 59, 87, 108, 113, 121, 347, 349

Great Migration, 302–303, 374, *386*, 435

Great Railroad Strike of 1877, 266–267

Green, John, 304–305

Green, Shields, 220

greenbacks, 235–236, 249, 260

Green Bay, Wisconsin, 137

Greenwich, Ohio, 112, 135

Greer, James, 214

Grenville Mountains, 4

grinding stones, 25

ground-stone tools, 25

Gruenwald, Kim, 184

Guernsey County, 282, 308

Guilford, James, 151, 202

Guiteau, Charles, 268–269

Gulf of Mexico, 8, 11, 28, 33, 39, 49, 167, 172, 194

gypsum, 5, 17, 287

Hamilton, Henry "Hairbuyer," 81, 84

Hamilton County, 8, 10, 100, 134, 254

Hamilton, Ohio, 177, 371

Hancock County, 10

Hand, Edward, 82

Hanktown, Ohio, 140

Hanna, Marcus, 254, 272–274; and Company, 415

Hardin County, 100, 383

Harding, Warren G., 247, 278, 288, 340, 345, 358–359, 362–366

Harmar, Josiah, 90–93, 95, 97, 113–114

Harmon, Judson, 344, 346

Harper, John L., 201

Harpers Ferry, Virginia, 178, 220

Harris, Chapin, 150

Harris, John, 150

Harris, William, 204

Harris Line, 205–206

Harrison, Benjamin, 247, 257–259, 261–262, 266, 270–272, 275, 278

Harrison, William Henry, *98*, 194; as Indiana territorial governor, 193–194; as Ohio politician, 120–121, 201, 206–208; and Tippecanoe/War of 1812, 195–198

Harrison Land Act *see* Land Acts

Hawke v. Smith, 367

Hay, John, 276, 278

Hayes, Lucy Webb, 226, 257, 259, 267

Hayes, Max, 330

Hayes, Rutherford Birchard, 257–258; as congressman, 260; as governor, 242, 244–245, 260–262; as president, 215–216, 240, 247–248, 257, 263–268, 278; as soldier, 226, 259

Hayes, Woody, 399

health: education, 337; environmental, 441; mental, 146, 416, 420, 467–468, 474; in prehistory, 27, 29, 43, 45, 50; public, 329, 331–332, 343, 380, 389, 430–432, 436, 473; and reform, 250, 254, 314, 344, 372; *see also* disease

Heaton, Dan and James, 180

Heckewelder, John, 74, 85, 99

Heidelberg College/University, 149

Heisman, John, 322

hemp, 176

Henry, Patrick, 81

Henry VII, King, 49

Heth, Henry, 224

hickory, 32, 40

High Banks Earthworks, 37, 39

Highland County, 13

Hillsboro, 250, *251*

Hiram College, 149, 258, 261, 330

Hiram House, 330–331, 351, 378

Hively, Ray, 39

Hoadly, George, 253–254, 311

Hockey Hall of Fame, 16

Hocking County, 308

Hocking River/Valley, 76, 263, 284, 303, 308–311

Hocking Sentinel, 310–311

Hoge, James, 294

Hokolesqua (Cornstalk), 75–76, 80–82

Hollister, Nancy, 478

Holly, John, 386, 435

Holmes County, 229

"Holmes County War," 229

"home rule," 265, 266, 326, 329, 343, 345

Homestead Act of 1862, 112, 235

Honda, 472

Hooker, Joseph, 230

Hoover, Herbert, 365–366, 378, 380–381

Hoover's Gap, 214

"Hoovervilles," 378, *379*

Hopedale Normal School, 149

Hopewell, 21, 30, *34*, 39, 42–44, 46, 53, 488; cultural complex, 35; decline, 40–41; interaction sphere, 39; mound group, 36–37

Hopewell Furnace, 180

Hopkins, Harry, 381–382

Hopocan (Captain Pipe), 82–83, 85–86, 93

horizontal integration, 288

Horn, Robert, 39

Horner, John S., 205

horses, 125, 348; as form of transportation, 122, 151, 172, 182, *256*, 280, 364; Ohio production of, 178, 223; military uses of, 71, 85, 92–93, 237; racing, 419

Hough Riot, 432–433

House Bill 920, 470–471, 482

House of Representatives, Ohio: and early statehood, 122, 187, 188, 191, 201, 206, 211; and early 20th century, 299, 305, 346, 380; and late 19th century, 250, 253, 260; since 1970, 468, 470–471, 474, 477–478, 480, 482; post-World War II, 398, 413–416, 418–421, 428, 435, 449–450

House of Representatives, U.S.: and the Civil War and Reconstruction, 229, 234–235, 242–245; early 1800s, 121–122, 185, 203, 206; early 20th century, 345, 350, 366, 414, 418–419, 435, 448–449, 477; late 19th century, 259, 261, 263, 265, 270–272, 277, 299, 328

houses (housing): and early U.S. settlement, 114, 130–131; architectural styles of, 135; for industrial workers, 295, 308–309, 311, 315, 363; prehistoric, 31, 35–36, 44–45; regional shortages, 352, 361, 389, 393, 397; suburban, 400–401, 403, 409; and Underground Railroad, 158; urban, 316, 353, 406, 408, 410, 428, 430–432, 434–436, 469

Howells, William Dean, 312, 370–371, 375

Hudson, Ohio, 135, 158, 217

Hudson River, 166–167

Hughes, Charles Evans, 349, 365

Hughes, Langston, 220

Hulett Ore Unloader, 285, *286*

Hull, William, 195, 196

Humbard, Rex, 411

Hungarians, 298

hunter-gatherers, 25, 31, 33, 41

hunting: in the Middle Ground period, 47, 51–53, 55, 69, 77, 81, 84; in prehistory, 21–27, 31–33, 35, 41, 43; *see also* "Great Hinckley Hunt"

Huntington, Samuel, 190–191

Huron County, 330

Huron River, 128, 160

Hutchins, Thomas, 103, 106, 108

hydrocarbons, 17–18

Hynde, Chrissy, 457

Iapetus Ocean, 4

Iberia College, 149, 358

Iberia, Ohio, 149

Illinois: and the Civil War, 217, 219, 222, 235, 237–239, 248; in early national period, 130, 135–136, 160, 202, 206; in early 20th-century, 379; in late 19th century, 265; in "Middle Ground" period, 52, 55, 72, 84; in prehistory, 8, 25, 28, 34, *37*, 40, 42

immigration/migration: and the Civil War and Reconstruction, 217–218, 223, 227, 245; and early 19th-century economic developments, 163, 174–175, 177; and early 19th-century politics, 188–189, *190*, 202–203, 210, 212; and early 19th-century society, 136–137, 139–141, 154; and the early 20th-century, 353–354, 356–357, 359, 364, 367–368, 377; and industrialization, 281, 283, 294–303, 307–309, 311, 313–315, 317; and late 19th-century politics, 248–250, 264, 266, 268, 274; and late 20th-century society, 404–408, 410–411; in prehistory, 21–22, 40, 52; and reform, 322, 327, 330–332, 337–339; and regional origins of early settlers, 132–136; in the territorial period, 97, 113–117; and World War II, 389, 397; *see also* Great Migration

impeachment: of Justices Tod and Pease, 191; of Andrew Johnson, 240, 242, 261

income: corporate, 389; from educational and ministerial lands, 104, 109, 151; family and personal, 2, 297, 332, 378, 382, 398, 409, 420, 432, 436, 477, 483; income tax, 273, 344–345, 419, 436, 450, 467–468, 474, 480–481

Indiana: and Civil War/Reconstruction, 215, 230, 237, 243; early statehood, 125, 130, 143, 136, 202, 206; early economy, 163, 173, 175–176; geology, 5, 8; and the Great Depression, 379; and industrialization, 292, 295; late 19th-century politics, 248, 258–259, 261–262, 266, 270, 272; in the Middle Ground period, 59–60, 90–91; post–World War II society, 408, 418, 420; in prehistory, 25, 28, 33; Territory, 121, 194; and War of 1812, 193

"Indian Republics," 57, 59–62, 64, 72

Indian Reservations, *97*, 112, 139, 189, 199, 271

industrialization, 184, 281–307; and the Civil War, 245; geological base of, 14, 17; and the Industrial Revolution, 166, 183–184; and late 19th-century politics, 248–249, 264, 266, 268, 273; and society, 317, 325–327, 335–336, 338, 368, 371–372

industry *see* business; industrialization; manufacturing; and under specific industries inequality: economic, 328; in prehistoric societies, 45; racial, 406, 408, 424, 428–430, 432

influenza (1918–1919), 354, 420

initiative, 341–343, 345

in lots, 114, 116, 295

internal improvements, 173, 203, 208, 212–213, 262

Interstate Commerce Commission, 285

Interstate Highway Act, 402

interstate highway system (interstates), 400, 402, 406

"Intolerable Acts," 79

invention/innovation, 28, *236*, 269, 318, 322, 336, 327, 362, 488; economic effects of, 178, 180, 462, 464; and industrialization, 178, 180, 248, 281–283; *286*, 288–293, 324; and Market Revolution, 166; and public lands, 104, *107*; and Transportation Revolution, 161, 167, 181

Iowa, 125, 130, 135

Iraq, 480, 488

Irish (people): and canal construction, 137, 169, 174; heritage, 311, 323, 338, 354, 359, 416; and immigration, 137, 139–141; and reform, 155, 250, 274

iron industry: in early statehood era, 180–181, 237, 258; geological basis of, 1–2, 15, 17; and industrialization, 281–282, 284–284, 308, 310, 313, 316; iron ore, 1, 2, 17, 180, 282, 284–285

Iroquois (Haudenosaunee): and Anglo-American conflict, 72, 81, 84, 87, 89; and Anglo-French conflict, 60, 62–63; and the early U.S. National period, 101, 106, 199; hegemony, 50–52, 55–58; in prehistory, 40

Irvine, William, 86

Italians, 369, 387, 431; and immigration, 296–299, 309, 419

Jackson, Andrew, 199, 229; and the economy, 182–183; and presidential elections, 203–204, 206–208; and Toledo War, 204–206

Jackson County, 14, 137, 180, 308, 420

Jay Treaty, 96

Jefferson, Thomas, 78, 103, 105, 119; as president, 121–123, 278

Jefferson County, 86, 134, 149, 164

John Carroll College/University, 149

John Hancock Mutual Life Building, 16

"Johnny Appleseed" *see* Chapman, John

Johnson, Andrew, 240–242, 244, 261

Johnson, Bushrod Rust, 214, 216

Johnson, Lyndon, 415–416, 427–428, 430–431, 444–445, 447, 449, 455

Johnson, Tom, 327–331, 333, 338, 345, *346*

Johnson's Island, 232

Joliet, Adrien, 52

Joncaire, Sieur Chabert de, 60

Jones, Samuel "Golden Rule," as Toledo mayor, 326–327, 330–331, 333, 338, 345, *346*; and welfare capitalism, 314–315, 324, *325*

Jones v. Van Zandt, 126

Judaism (Jews), 126, 354, 404, 450; and Americanization, 330–331, *357*; and immigration, 137, 295–300, 309, 317; and the Ku Klux Klan, 368–369; Wise and Reform Judaism, 300–301

judges (judiciary), 267, 312, 367–368, 419, 449; and Black Laws, 188; and civil rights, 429–430, 433; and controversy over judicial jurisdiction and tenure, 187, 189–192; and education, 479; and judicial reform, 200, 210–212, 260, 341; and judicial review, 201, 253; in the territorial period, 105, 117, 119–122

Junction City, 1

kames, 10, 13, 16, 29, 32; *see also* Glacial Kame tradition

Kanawha River/ Valley, 76, 81, 224

Kansas, 35, 125, 158, 199, 217, 219, 227

Kansas–Nebraska Act, 217–218; *see also* "Bleeding Kansas"

Kasich, John, 477, 482, *483*, *484*

Kaskaskia, 84

Kekionga, 59, 90, 97; *see also* Fort Wayne

Kelley, Alfred, 183

Kelley Bank Law, 183, 208

Kelleys Island, 10, *11*

Kendal, 145, 178

Kennedy, John F., 409, 414–416, 420, 427–428, 435, 449, 471

Kennedy, Robert, 426, 447, 455

Kent, Ohio (Franklin Mills), 158, 217, 381
Kenton, Simon, 88
Kent *Record Courier*, 454
Kent State shootings, *421*, 427, 444, 451–455, 473, 475
Kent State University, 336, 426
Kentucky, 481, 487; and American conflict with Indians, 88, 90, 96; and Anglo-American conflict, 81–82, 84; and the Civil War, 220, 222, 224–225, 229, 237–238, 374; and early American settlement, 113, 116–117, 119; and early national period, 125, 127, 133, 136, 138, 141, 157, 188; and economic development, 162–163, 176–178; geology, 5, 10, 13; and labor/Appalachian migration, 383, 410–411, 420; and late 19th-century politics, 259, 293, 327; in prehistory, 33; and War of 1812, 196–197
Kenyon-Barr, 409
Kenyon College, 149, 257, 322
Kerbel Delta, 4
Kerner Commission, 426
Kettering, Charles, 288–291
Kettering, Ohio, 144
kettles (geological feature), 10, 13–14, 17
Key to Uncle Tom's Cabin, 217
Kickapoo, 40, 46, 55–56
Kilbourne, James, 132
Killbuck *see* Gelelemend
Killbuck Creek, 10
King, Henry W., 151
King, Martin Luther, Jr., 409, 426–428, 434–435, 447, 455
King George's War (War of the Austrian Succession), 54
King William's War (War of the League of Augsburg), 54
Kirk, William, 139
Kirker, Thomas, 191
Kirk/Palmer tradition, 25
Kirtland, Ohio, 145
Klunder, Bruce, 428
Knights of Labor, 274, 311
Knights of the Flaming Circle, 369
knives, 23, 32, 43, 53, 73
knotweed, 31
Knox, Henry, 92

Knox County, 226
Korean War, *400*, 409, 411–413, 419, 466
Krause, Allison, 454
Ku Klux Klan (KKK), 361, 367–369

labor, 273; and anti-communism, 412–414; child, 152, 309, 317, 332; Chinese, 266, 268, 271, 275, 311; and deindustrialization, 457, 461–463; disputes, 263, 266–267, 272, 274, 309, 314–315, 419–420, 473; in early Ohio economy, 166, 169, 172, 178, 184; in early Ohio society, 113, 130, 141, 148; free, 210, 226; and the Great Depression, 382–384; and immigration, 294–301; and industrialization, 245, 284, 307–315, 377; organizations and unions, 141, 187, 248, 262, 268, 307, 311–313, 364, 398, 415, 448, 468; in prehistory, 29, 31, 36, 39, 44; racial issues, 188, 227, 232, 275, 302–304, 307, 358, 392–393; and reform, 251, 325–326, 330–332, 340–341, 343, 346–347; and "right to work" controversy, 416–419; women in, 390–392, 436–438, 484–485; and World War I, 351–358; and World War II, 387, 389–393; *see also* American Federation of Labor; civil disturbances; Congress of Industrial Organizations; Knights of Labor; workers
Lake County, 14, 145, 476
Lake Erie, 487; and the Civil War, 237; in early national period, 121, 128, 137, 150; and early Ohio economy, 161, 163, 165, 167–169, 172, 174–175, 177, 180, 182; and environmental issues, 440, 442–443, 450; geology, 8, 10–12, 14, 16, 18; and industrialization, 280, 284, 285, 294; in Middle Ground period, 47, 51–52, 62, 72, 85; in prehistory, 27, 41, 44; and Prohibition, 367; and recreation, 318; and state boundary, 204; and War of 1812, 197–198
Lake Maumee, 11
Lake Michigan, 52, 121
Lake Plains, 204
Lake Superior, 52, 284
Lake Tight, 10
Lakewood, 470–471

Lamme, Benjamin, 290

Lamme, Bertha, 290

Lancaster, Ohio, 135, 225, 235, 238, 266

Land Acts: of 1800 (Harrison), 120, 128, 194; of 1804, 120, 128; of 1820, 128, 165

land claims, 47; colonial/state, 49, 101, *102*, 109, 112; individual, 76, *111*, 112, 165; Native American, 72

land grants, 110, 123, 235, 260, 336

land grant universities, 109

Land Ordinance of 1784, 103

Land Ordinance of 1785, 103–106, *107*, 150

land sales, 13, 103–114, 151, 163–165, 173, 200

Lane Theological Seminary, 142

Langham, Elias, 187

Langlade, Charles, 60

Langston, Charles, 220

Langston, John Mercer, 215, *216*, 220, 245–246

La Salle, René Robert Cavalier, Sieur de, 52

Late Prehistoric period, 42–45, 50–51, 176

Latter Day Saints (Mormons), 145

Laurentian Archaic period, 28

Laurentide Ice Sheet, 8, 10–11

Lausche, Frank, 413–416, 424, 441, 448–449, 475

law and order, 115, 252, 263, 427, *433*, 448, 455

Lawrence, James, 198

Lawrence County, 145

Lawrence (ship), 198, *199*

Leary, Lewis Sheridan, 220–221

Lebanon, Ohio, 144

Lecompton Constitution, 219

Lee, Ann, 144

Lee, Robert E., 226, 230, 234, 238–239, 243

Leesburg, Ohio, 135

legal system, 114, 125, 139, 189, 220, 307, 432, 439; *see also* judges

Legion of the United States, 95–96, 194

Legislative Council, 105

Lenape (Delaware) Indians, 2, 160, 488; and Anglo-American conflict, 67–69, 72–76, 80–87; and Anglo-French conflict, 56–58, 63–65; and removal, 136, 138–139; and the War of 1812, 194, 198–199; and the Western Confederacy, 87, 92–93, 112

Lewis, Andrew, 76–77, 83

Lewis, Diocletian, 250, *251*

Lewis, John L., 383–384, 393

Lewis, Samuel, 151

Lexington and Concord, 79

Lexington Plains (Bluegrass region), 13

Libbey Glass, 282, 318

liberalism, 382, 424, 427, *433*, 444, 476

Liberator, The, 155

Liberty Party, 157, 208–210

Lichtenau, 74, 85

Licking County, 23, 36, 137, 445

lieutenant governor, 81, 212, 358, 449, 468–469, 471–472, 477–478

Lima, Ohio, 129, 282, 287, 324, 330, 485

lime, 1–2, 15

limestone, 2, 5–6, 11, 13, 15, 17, *68*, 180, 287

Lincoln, Abraham, 136, 157, 215–217, 220, 269, 370, 473; and the Civil War, 222–236; and Reconstruction, 240–245, 248–249

"Little Africa," 139

Little Miami Railroad, 159

Little Miami River, 84, 108

"Little Steel" strikes, 385–386

Little Turtle *see* Mishikinakwa

livestock *see* agriculture

local government, 105, 116, 118–123, 131, 200; in the 20th century, 356, 382, 412, 422, 431, 482; *see also* home rule

Locher, Ralph, 430, 432–433, 435–436

Lochry, Archibald, 85

lock, 169, 172–173

Lockbourne, Ohio, 173

Locke, David Ross, *221*, 227–228

Lock Seventeen, Ohio, 173

loess, 7, 19

Logan, 75, 78, 86

Logan, Benjamin, 88

Logan County, 232

"Log Cabin and Hard Cider Campaign," 207–208

log-rolling, 202, 210

Logstown *see* Chiningué

London, England, 58, 161, 334, *335*

London, Ontario, 139

Long, Alexander, 229

Longfellow, Henry Wadsworth, 177–178

"Long Knives," 68, 76, 78, 88, 193

Longview State Hospital, 146
Longworth, Nicholas, 176
Lorain, Ohio, 128, 174, 285, 327, 330, 376, 420
Lord Dunmore's War, 75–80, 83, 86, 101, 194;
    see also Dunmore, Lord
Lordstown, 398
Losantiville, 116–117
Loudon, James, 212
Loudonville, Ohio, *291*
Louisiana, 35, 60, 102, 143, 230, 264–266
Louisville, Kentucky, 162
Louis XVI, King, 47
Lowell, Ohio, 225
Loyal Company, 58
Lucas, Robert, 205
Lucas County, 326, 422, 481
Lucas, Ohio, 372
Lucasville, 481
Lundy, Benjamin, 155, *156*, 157
Lutherans, 137, 143–144, 149
Lynchburg, Ohio, 135
Lynd, Staughton, 465–466
Lyons, Ohio, 205

Madison, James, 190, 196, 200
Madisonville, 44
Mad River, 84, 87–88
Mad River and Lake Erie Railroad, 182
Mahoning County, 422
Mahoning River/Valley, 180, 282, 315, 465
malaria, 106, 172, 268
males, 368, 414, 439, 476; and citizenship, 105,
    120, 342, 366; and the Civil War, 226,
    238–239; and immigration, 295; and labor,
    308–309, 311, 313, 354, 378–379, 383, 397,
    417; and masculinity, 322, 436–437; and
    reform, 250, 333, 358
Malone College/University, 149
mammoths, 23
Manchester (Massie's Station), 116
Manitoba, 39
Mansfield, Ohio, 129, 371–372, 379
Mansfield, Sandusky, and Newark
    Railroad, 161
manufacturing, 2, 16–17; and the Civil War,
    237; and deindustrialization, 444, 457, 459,
    461–462, 469, 472–473, 475, 477, 480–481,
    484–485; in early statehood, 132, 166,

178–179, 183, 213; and the environment,
    440; and the Great Depression, 378, 383;
    and industrialization, 250, 281–282,
    285–287, *289*, 290, *293*, 294, 308, 312–313;
    and post-World War II society, 399, 408,
    417, 424, 442; and the 1920s, 356, 363, 366,
    368; and urban life, 316–317, 327, 331; and
    World War II, 390, *391*
Maple Creek Phase, 28
marble, 15
Marblehead Peninsula, 70
Marbury v. Madison, 190
"March to the Sea," 234, 254
Marie Antoinette, 47, 114
Marietta, Ohio, 14, 366, 416, 478; and early
    American settlement, 92–93, 100, 114–117,
    129, 132, 138; and early statehood society,
    147, 150, 162, 166, 176, 185; and territorial/
    early statehood politics, 121, 187
Marin, Pierre-Paul de la Malgue de, 62
Marion, Ohio, 129, 358–359, 365–366
Marion Star, 358
Market Revolution, 161, 166–167, 175–176,
    182–184
Marshall Town, Ohio, 140
Martin's Ferry, Ohio, 330, 370, 489
Maryland, 126, *256*, 266, *364*; and the Civil
    War, 226, 259; and early statehood period,
    133, 163, 185; and prehistory, 34
Marysville, Ohio, 401, 472
Mascouten Indians, 46, 55–56
Mason, Stevens, 205
Mason–Dixon Line, 233, 249
Massachusetts, 79, 206, 241, 258, 261, 358,
    372; and early American settlement, 108,
    132; and reform, 143, 150–151, 154, 324; *see
    also* 54th Massachusetts Regiment; 55th
    Massachusetts Regiment
massacres: Big Bottom, 138; Gnadenhutten,
    67–68, 85–86, 99; Logan's family, 75, 78
mass consumption, 284, 318, 338, 362–363,
    367, 397, 399, 411
Massie, Nathaniel, 115–116, 120–121, 128
Massillon, Ohio, 128, 145, 148, 175, 178, 180,
    255
Massillon Tigers, 322, 386
Mast Forest, 28
mastodons, 22–23

Matthews, Stanley, 278
Maumee Bay, 204
Maumee River, 72, 95–96, 197, 204
Maxville limestone, 15
Maxville, Ohio, 1
maygrass, 31
Maysville, Kentucky, 162–163
McArthur, Duncan, 128, 200, 208
McBride, John, 311
McCarthyism, 412
McClellan, George, 223–224, 226, 229, 233–234
McConnelsville, Ohio, 147
McCook, Alexander, 214
McCook, Daniel, 230
McCook, George, 245
McCook, John, 230
McCorkle College, 149
McCulloch, William, 415
McCullough v. Maryland, 201
McCuneville, 1
McDowell, Irvin, 223, 238
McGary, Hugh, 88
McGuffey, William Holmes, 126, 153–154
McGuffey, Ohio, 383–384
McGuffey's Readers, 126, 153–154, 158
McIntosh, Lachlan, 82–83, 87
McKee, Alexander, 75, 82, 86, 95
McKee, Robert, 180
McKinley, William, 282, 333; assassination of, 21, 257, 277, 343; election, 257, 272, 274, 359; life, 258, 262–263, 270; as president, 247–248, 254, 274–279, 344; as soldier, 215–216, 259
McKinley Tariff of 1890, 263, 270–271
McLean, John, 218–219, 222
McPherson, James B., 214, 238
Meade, George G., 230
Meadowcroft Rock Shelter, 23
meatpacking, 177–179
Medary, Samuel, 231
medical colleges, 150
Medina County, 131
megafauna, 23–24
Meigs, Return Jonathan Jr., 192, 200
Meigs County, 137, 475
Mellon, Andrew, 364–365
Memeskia (The Dragonfly, la Demoiselle, Old Briton), 59–60

Mennonites, 136, 230, 354–355, 393
mental illness, *see* health, mental
Mequachaka, 88
Mercer County, 8, 140
Merry, Ebenezer, 160, 178
Merry's Mill *see* Milan
Mesozoic Era, 7
meteorites, 39
metes and bounds, 103, 110, *111*, 134
Methodists, 126, 136, 143, 149, 158, 250, 307, 439, 481
métis, 53, 60
Metzenbaum, Howard, *446*, 450–451, 470, 476–477
Mexican-American War, 209, 216, 238, 350
Meyer, Elias, 70–71
Miami and Erie Canal, *170*, 173
Miami Conservancy District, 349
Miami Exporting Company, 163, *164*
Miami Indians, 55–57, 59, 77, 87, 91–92, 95–96
Miami River *see* Great Miami River; Little Miami River
Miamisburg Mound, 32, *33*
Miami University, 109, 153, 235, 258, 336, 428
mica, 33, *37*, 39
Michigan, 161, 214, 265, 415, 459; and industrial society, 287, 290, 398, 408; and the Middle Ground period, 51, 55; Territory, 200; and Toledo War, 204–206; and transportation, 173, 182; and War of 1812, 195, 197
middens, 29, 41
middle class *see* class
"Middle Ground," 49, 52–54, 63–65, 68, 72, 78, 80, 87, *97*, 98, 193
migration *see* immigration/migration
Milan Canal, 160
Milan (Merry's Mill), Ohio, 135, 160–161, 174, 178, 290
militia, 105, 195, 221, 227, 232; African Americans and, 189; Canadian, 96; Kentucky, 84, 88, 90–93, 96, 196–198, 205; Marietta, 114; Ohio, 192, 223, *225*, 266–267, 276, 311–312, 314; Pennsylvania, 67–68, 76, 82, 85–86, 90–93; Virginia, 62–63, 76, 81, 90–93
Mill Creek, Ohio, 220

Miller, Adam, 126

Miller, Jeffrey, 454

Mills, Lisa, 40

mills and milling, 139, 178, 282; grist/flour, 160, 174, 179, 317; paper, 316; saw, 160; stones, 16; and waterpower, 128, 160; *see also* steel industry

minerals, 13–17

mines and mining: and the environment, 426, 440–441, 468; geological basis of, 1–2, 14–15, 17; and industrialization, 282, 284, 287, *289*, 356; and labor, 303, 308–311, 383, 393, 414; and mine work, *181, 281*, 308

Mingo Bottom, 86, 113–114

Mingo Indians, 56–58, 63, 72, 75, 77–78, 80–81, 83–84, 92, 488

ministerial lands, 100, 109, 123

Mintz, Leo, 404

Mishikinakwa (Little Turtle), 91–92, 95–96, *98*

missionaries, 53, 73, 141, 335; Catholic, 52; Friends (Quaker), 139; Moravian, 20, 40, 63, 74, 113; Tenskwatawa (Shawnee Prophet), 194; Swedenborgians, 176

Mississauga Indians, 55

Mississippian period, 2, 5, 7, 14–16, 180; in early national period, 101, 105, 199

Mississippian tradition, 40, 42, 44

Mississippi River (Valley), 316, 371; and the Civil War, 214, 230; and commerce, 162, 166, 172; geology, 8; in Middle Ground period, 49, 72, 87, *97, 98*; in prehistory, *34, 35, 42*

Missouri, 39, 243; crisis and compromise, 200–202, 217, 219

Mobile, Alabama, 234

mobilization: Civil War, 224; World War II, 389

Mohawk Indians, 50, 55, 85, 89

Mohican Indians, 57, 93

Moluntha, 88

money, 280, 457, 464; and charity/donation, 226, 231, 299, 326, 331, 399; consumer spending of, 90, 317, 367, 404; and corruption, 112, 218, 254, 320, 341, 366, 475, 481; earning/saving, 154, 283, 288, 295, 321, 328, 371, 454; government collection of, 47, 103, 150, 108–109, 201, 231, 436; government expenditures of, 100, 129, 151, 163, 173, 202, 206, 208, 260–261, 284,

380–381, 389, 409, 431, 474, 477–478, 480; investment/financing, 165, 182, 280, 288, 292, 327, 378, 462; and loans, 365, 377; raising, 109, 112, 273–274, 437; *see also* currency

Monongahela River, *64*, 69, 75

Monongahela Woodland Complex, 44

Monte Verde, Chile, 22

Montgomery, Betty, 478

Montgomery County, 32, 44

Montreal, 55, 64

moon: Armstrong and, 399; Hopewell astronomy, *38*, 39

"Moondog," 404, *405*

moose, 23

Moraine, Ohio, 463

moraines, 8, 10, 13, 16, 129

Moravian Tracts, 112

Moravians (Church of the Brethren), 20, 63, 113, 136, 230; and Ohio Lenape villages, 67, *68*, 74, 82, 85, 99, 160

Moravians (ethnicity), 297

Moraviantown, 198

Morgan, Arthur, 349

Morgan, Garrett, 293–294

Morgan, George, 80

Morgan, John Hunt, 215, 230

Morgan County, 441

Morgan's Raid, 216, 230–231, *233*

Morrill Land Grant Act of 1862, 235, 260, 336

Morrill Tariff of 1861, 235

Morris, Thomas, 157, 209

Morrison, Toni, 220, 376

Morrow, Jeremiah, 169, 185, 195

mortuary practices, 13, 27–29, 32–33, 36, 39–42, 44, 45, 99

"Mother of Presidents," 249

Mound City Group, 36

mounds: geologic, 1, 10, 13; prehistoric, 20, 30, 32–34, 36–41, 44, *45*, 68, 99

Mount Pleasant, Ohio, 155

Mount Union College/University, 149

Mount Vernon, Ohio, 229, 330

Muddy Creek, 75

mules, 172, 258, 280

Munsee Indians, 57

museums, 1, 318

Muskingum College/University, 149

Muskingum County, 134

Muskingum River/Valley: and early economic development, 169, 180; in early national period, 106, 113–115; in Middle Ground period, 20, 57, 60, 75, 90, 92–93, 138

Muskingum Valley Watershed District, 349–381

mussels, 27

Nasby, Petroleum V., *221*, 227

Nash, George K., 285

Natchez Trace, 162

National Association for the Advancement of Colored People (NAACP), 294, 361, 369, 392, 407, 417

National Association of Colored Women, 334

National Banking Act, 183, 236

National Cash Register Company (NCR), 281, 288, 290, 348

National Era, 125, 217

National Organization of Women, 426, 437

National Republicans, 204

National Road, 163, *168*, 203

National Woman Suffrage Association, 333

Native Americans (Indians), 20, 22, 47, 49–53, *54, 56,* 57–60, *61,* 62–65, 68–72, *73,* 74–76, *77,* 78, 80–85, 87, 88–96, *97, 98,* 99, 125, 130, 138–139, 161, 163, 169, 192–195, 198–199, 244, 271; *see also* specific battles, groups, and persons

Nativism, 140; *see also* Americanization; Ku Klux Klan

Nekeik (Little Otter), 96

Neolin, 69, 194, 271

Netawatwees (Newcomer), 69, 74–75

Neutral Nation, 51–52

Newark Earthworks, 1, *34,* 36–37, *38,* 39

Newark, Ohio, 14, *34,* 128, 135, 169, 183, 267, 284, 319

New Athens, Ohio, 149

New Concord, Ohio, 399

New Deal, 310, 362, 379, 380–382, 402, 417, 421, 445, 449, 456

New England/New Englanders, 34, 104, 114, 115, 117, 119, 127, 132–136, 138, 151, 176, 178, 195, 203, 210, 295, 396

New France, 49, 55, 60, 62

New Hampshire, 125, 157, 447

New Harmony, Indiana, 143

New Haven, Ohio, 135

New Jersey, 134–135

New Left, 445

New Lexington, Ohio, 2

New London, Ohio, 112, 135

"new measures," 143

New Orleans, Louisiana, 162–163, 166–167, 172, 175, 230, 265, 464

New Philadelphia, Ohio, 15, 74, 135

New Right, 445, 449, 456, 476

New Salem, 160

New Schoenbrunn, 85

New Straitsville, Ohio, 1

New Wakatomika, *77,* 87

New York, 151, 155, 157, 161, 167, 172, 173, 174, 175, 178, 183, 206, 209, 218, 222, 223, 229, 238, 239, 244, 248, 264, 267, 268, 270, 277, 338

New York City, 284, 288, 290, 298, 311, 318, 319, 372, 374, 377, 405, 419, 436

Niagara, 198, *199*

Nicklaus, Jack, 402

Niles, Ohio, 258, 362, 369, 420

Nineteenth Amendment, 353, 368

Nixon, Richard, 420, 422, 426–427, 444, 448, 449, 452, 454, 455, 463, 469, 476

Noble County, 18, 180, 212, 287

Nobles Pond, 23, 24

Noe, Thomas, 481

nomadism, 29

North America, 4, 7, 8, 11, 14, 23, 24, 37, 47, 49, 50, 54, 57, 58, 62–64, 68, 71, 180

North Bend, Ohio, 194

North Canton, Ohio, 356

North Carolina, 7, *37,* 136, 145, 155, 158, 234, 291, 302, 375, 427

North Coast, 11

North Dakota, 39

North Fairfield, 112

North Union, 144

Northwest Indian War, 88

Northwest Ordinance, 103, 105, 109, 114, 120–122, 134, 150, 204

Northwest Territory, 1, 105, 115, 117, 120–121

Norwalk, Ohio, 112, 129, 135, 161

Noyes, Edward, 245

nuts, 23, 25, 27, 28, 31, 32, 40

Oaxaca, 42

Oberlin College, 142, *148,* 149, 157, 253, 322, 431

Oberlin, Ohio, 145, 227, 241, 245, 252, 428

Oberlin–Wellington Rescue case, 220, *221*

obsidian, 39

oceans (prehistoric), 2, 4, 5

Octagon, The, 37, *38,* 39

O'Dell, Okey, 383–384

Ohio and Erie Canal, 128, 144–145, 165, *168,* 169, *170, 174,* 175, 180, 181, 203, 258, 348

Ohio Anti-Slavery Society, 157, 158

Ohio Board of Canal Commissioners, 169, 173, 202

Ohio Civil Rights Commission, 410, 420

Ohio College of Dental Surgery, 150

Ohio Company of Associates, 108, 109, 112, 114–117, 127, 130, 138

Ohio Company Purchase, 108, 109, 112, 114–117, 119, 120, 121, 127, 132, 134, 135, 136, 149, 150, 162

Ohio Company of Virginia, 58, 62, 79

Ohio Constitution of 1802, 122, 139, *186,* 189, 190

Ohio Constitution of 1851, 147, 210–213

Ohio Constitution of 1912, 341

Ohio (Crosby, Stills, Nash, and Young), 454

Ohio Department of Development, 422

Ohio General Assembly, 146, 148, 149, 151, 163, 186, 188, 190–192, 200, 202, 208–212, 218, 241–242, 244, 245, 305, 336, 338, 342, 343, 345–346, 349, 357, 367, 380, 382, 419, 441, 445, 448–449, 470, 474, 482

Ohio Life Insurance and Trust Company, 219

Ohio Loan Law of 1837 (Plunder Law), 173, 182, 208

Ohio Northern College/University, 149

Ohio River/Valley, 7, 8, 10, *12,* 18, 28, 34, 42, 47, 52, 57, 58, 62, 72–77, 79, 80–81, 85–86, 88, 90, 95, 105–106, 112, 116–117, 129, 139, 158, 162–163, 165–166, *167,* 176, 192, 215, 217, 220, 223–224, 229, 237, 280, 283, 285, 347–348, 412, 441–442

Ohio River Valley Water Sanitary Commission (ORSANCO), 441

Ohio School for the Deaf, 146

Ohio School Law, 151, *152,* 153, 208

Ohio Statehouse, *98, 186, 199*

Ohio state motto, 411

Ohio State School for the Blind, 146

Ohio State University, 235, 260, 290–291, 322, 336, 399, 410, 412, 415, 420, 439, 445, 451, 452, 454, 483

Ohio Un-American Activities Commission, 413–414

Ohio University, 126, 149, 153, 235, 336, 454

Ohio Wesleyan College/University, 149, 322, 416

Ohio Woman Suffrage Association, 333, *334*

oil/oil industry, 1, 2, 17, 18, 184, 215, 254, 271, 281–282, 287–288, 322, 324, 365, 390, 459, 469, 474

Ojibwa, 40, 70, 87, 90, 92

Old Betsy, 197

Old Chillicothe, *56,* 82, 84, 87

Old Wakatomika, 75, *77*

Oneida Indians, 50, 55

Oneida, New York, 143

O'Neill, William, 402, 416–419, 424, 448

one-room schoolhouses *see* education

Onondaga Indians, 50, 55

Ontario, 25, 44, 51, *34, * 139, *196,* 198

OPEC, 459, 469

orchards, 176

orchestras, 296, 318

Ordovician period, 3, 4, 5, 15

Oregon, 125, 264

orogeny, 7

Orontony (Nicholas), 57–58, 60

Osawatomie, Kansas, 218

Osborn, Charles, 155, *156*

Osborn, Ralph, 201

Osborn v. Bank of the United States, 201

Oswego, 58

Ottawa County, 17

Ottawa Indians, 55, *56,* 57, 60, 69, 71–72, 87, 90, 92, 96

Otterbein College/University, 149

out lots, 114, 116, 134

Over-the-Rhine, 126, 137, 140, 296

Oxford, Ohio, 149, 428, *429*

Pacific Ocean, 50, 104

Pacific Railroad Act, 235

pacifism, 67, 74, 139, 145, 345

Packard, James and William, 290

Paine, Halbert, 214

Painesville, Ohio, 129, 333

Paleo-Indian period, 22–24

Paleo-Indians, 22–23

Paleozoic era, 4, 5, 7, 16–18

Palmer House, 16

Palmyra, New York, 145

Pangea, 7

panics *see* depressions

paper money *see* currency

Parliament Building, Ottawa, 16

Parsons, Samuel Holden, 117

patent medicine, 17, 180

Patterson, James, 281, 288, *289*, 314

Pauli, H.C., 71

Payne, John H.B., 232

Peace of Montreal (Grand Settlement), 55

peace pipe *see* calumet

pearls, 36

Pease, Calvin, 190, 191

peccary, 23

Pendleton, George H., 229, 234, 260, 267

Pendleton Civil Service Reform Act
    of 1883, 267

Penick v. Columbus Board of Education, 430

Peninsula Campaign, 226

Penn–Ohio Canal, 175

Pennsylvania, 18, 23, 28, 33, 44, 57–60, 63, 67,
    71, 74, 76, 78, 81, 85, 86, 90, 101, 106, 116,
    119, 126, 128, 134–137, 146, 158, 163, 175,
    183, 189, 197, 222, 230, 237–238, 241, 258,
    266, 281, 284, 287, 322, 327, 380, 480

Pennsylvania Dutch, 135, 203

Pennsylvanian period, 2, *3*, 5–7, 14, 16, 17, 180

People's (Populist) Party, 254–256, 273, 285

Peré, Jean, 52

Perkins, Simon, 173

Permian period, *3*, 7

Perry, Oliver Hazard, 197–98, *199*

Perry County, 1–2, 19, 137, 238, 308, 479

Perrysburg, Ohio, 197

Petersburg, Virginia, 232, 234

Petquotting, 160

Phalanx Mills, 145

Philadelphia, Pennsylvania, 73, 92, 161, 167,
    178, 223, 311, 419

Philanthropist, The, 125, 139, 155, *156*, 157

Philippines, 276, 341, 344

Pickawillany, *56*, 59, 60, 62

Pickett's Charge, 215, 230

Picote, Marie Francois, 60

pigs (hogs, pork), 177, 178, *179*

Pike County, 185

Pinckney's Treaty, 162

pine, 23

pipes (effigy pipes), 32, 36, *37*

pipestone, 32, *37*

Piqua, Ohio, 59, 128, 140, 415

Playfair, William, 112

Plea for the West, A, 154–155

Pleistocene period, 8, 13

Pluggy's Town, *77*, 81

Plukkemehnotee (Pluggy), 80

Plunder Law *see* Ohio Loan Law

pluralism, 186

Point Pleasant, Ohio, 225

Poland, Ohio, 258

Poles/Polish people, 296–97, 313–314

political machine, 254, 267, 326

politics, 117–123, 185–192, 199–213, 217–222,
    224, 227–229, 231–235, 240–246, 247–279,
    324–336, 341–347, 349, 354–359, 363–367,
    380–382, 398, 410–424, 434–440, 442–451,
    455–456, 467–483; and the Middle Ground,
    59–63; and Ohio's regions, 485–487

Polk, James K., 209

Pollard, Fritz, 323

pollution, 17, 316–317, 332, 436, 440–444,
    450–451, 466, 468, 469

Pond Bill, 1882, 252

Pontiac, 69–72, 194; *see also* Resistance
    of 1763

Pontifical College Josephinium, 149

"popular sovereignty," 217

population: African American, 134, 188–89,
    302, 303, **353**, 354, 392, 404, 405–407, **408,**
    459; of Akron, *174*, 282, **353**, 378, 406, **407,**
    408, 460; of Cambridge, 282; of Camden,
    399; of Canton, 282, 406, **407, 408, 460;** of
    Cincinnati, 126, 129, 176, 281, 296,
    299–300, 303, **353**, 406, **407, 408, 460;** of
    Cleveland, 281, 296–99, 301, 303, **353**, 378,
    392, 404, 406, **407, 408, 460;** of Columbus,
    282, 303, **353**, 378, 406, **407, 408, 460;** of
    Dayton, 282, **353**, 406, **407, 408, 460;**

population (*cont'd*)
  of East Liverpool, 282; and ethnicity, 137, 176, 203, 250, 295, 296–99, 326, 356; Jews, 299–301; of Milan, 160; Native Americans, 139; of Ohio, 126–127, 129, *133*, 134, 141, 175, 185, 206, 222, **294**, 398, 405–07, 458–59, **460**, 484, 485–87; prehistoric, 22, 24–25, 27–29, 30–31, 35, 40, 42–44, 50–51; of sheep, 178; of Springfield, 303; of Toledo, 282, 326, **353**, 378, 406, **407, 408, 460**; and topography, 13; of Youngstown, 282, **353, 378**, 406, **407, 408, 460**; of Zanesville, 282
populism *see* People's (Populist) Party
"Porkopolis," 178, *179*, 237
portage, 62, 169
Portage County, 10, 17, 137, 154, 157, 180, 455
Portage River, 128
Port Clinton, 128
Port Hudson, 214, 230
Port Huron, Michigan, 161
Portsmouth, Ohio, 128, *133*, 140, 169, 173, 181, 231, 348, 412
Post, Christian Frederick, 63, 74
Potawatomi Indians, 70
Pottawatomie Creek, Kansas, 178, 218
pottery, 15, 28, 29, 31, 32, 35, 44, 180, 282, 287,
Powderly, Terrence V., 274, 311, 312
Powell, William Henry, *199*
Precambrian era, *3*, 4
prehistoric peoples, 14, 16, 20–46, 51
Presbyterians, 136, 143, *148*, 149, 153, 155, 158, *251*, 258, 304, 428
Presque Isle, 62, 64, 197
Price, John, 220
"primary forest efficiency," 27
prisoners: in Civil War, 232–233; the Middle Ground, 60, 62, 67, 85–88, 97; and War of 1812, 197; *see also* capital punishment; crime
Proclamation of 1763, 72, 74, 79
Procter and Gamble, 281, 312, 363, 416, 442
Proctor, Henry, 197, 198
Pro Football Hall of Fame, 322
Progressive (Bull Moose) Party, 344, 345
progressivism/progressive era, 314, 324, *325*, 327–329, 332, 335, 340–341, 343–347, 349, 351, 354
Prohibition, *253*, 343, 358, 365, 367–368

projectile points, 23, 24, 25, 29, 39, 41, 43; *see also* arrowheads
Prophet, The/Lalawethika *see* Tenskwatawa
Prophetstown, Tippecanoe, 193, 195
Protestantism and Protestants, 67, 74, 137, 140, 141, 145, 149, 154, 248, 250, 261, 283, 296, 299, 313, 322, 324–325, 330–332, 337–39, 361, 368, 372, 410–411, 476, 487; *see also* specific denominations
Providence College, 149
Prussia, 59, 296, 297, 301
public land system, 13, 100, 102–112, 120, 123, 127, 184
public schools *see* education
public works, 173, 255, 329, 343, 346, 380–381, 402, 421
Puckeshinwa, 76, 194
Puerto Rico, 254, 275–276
Purcell, John Baptist, 140
Put-in-Bay, 198
Putnam, Rufus, 93, 99, 108, 114, 117, 130
Putnam Hill limestone, 15

Quaker Bottom, 145
Quakers (Friends, Society of Friends), 136, 139–140, 145, 149, 155, 178, 195, 217, 230, 354, 355, 393
quarry/quarries, 1, 14, 16, 23, *255*, 287
quartz, 39,
Quebec, 49, 51, 60, 64
Quebec Act of 1774, 79
Queen Anne's War (War of the Spanish Succession), 54
Queen City *see* Cincinnati
Quequedegatha (George White Eyes), 75, 80, 83

raccoons, 23, 130–131, 150
race: cities and, 404–410, 430–436; and Civil War and Reconstruction, *225*, 226, 229, 232, 239, 240, 241, 242–246, 265–266; in contemporary Ohio, 459; in early Ohio, 139–140, 148; in industrial Ohio, 302–307, 309–312; and laws, 419; and McKinley, 275; and progressives, 335; rock and, 404; schools and, 429–430; and writers, 375–376; *see also* African Americans
race riots *see* civil disturbances

Radical Republicans *see* Republican Party (modern)

radio, 359, 363, 367, 374, 404

radiocarbon dating (carbon-14), 22

railroads, 17, 129, 160, 181–182, 223, 224, 263, 266–267, 273, 275, 280, 281, 283–285, 288, 325, 345

Randolph, John (of Roanoke), 140

Rankin, John, 149, 158

Ravenna, Ohio, 129, 390, 473

Ray, Joseph, 152, *153*

Reagan, Ronald, 445, *446*, 476

recession, 313, 349, 356, 363, 397–398, 417, 461, 466, 473–474, 477–78, 480–482, 484

Reconstruction, 240–246, 250, 265–266, 302, 335–36, 392

reconversion, 397–398

rectangular survey, 104, 106, 109, 112, 116

Red Hawk, 81

Red Ochre tradition, 28, 29

Red Scare: during Cold War, 411–414; after World War I, 356–358; *see also* anticommunism

Reed v. Rhodes, 429

referendum, 341–343, 345

Refugee Tract, *110*, 112

regional origins (northeastern, mid-Atlantic, southern), *133*, 134–135, 151, 202

Regular Republicans, 187, 191–192

regulatory power, 183, 200–201, 249, 250, 253, 262–263, 268, 271, 273, 309, 328, 342, 344, 346, 364, 441, 446, 468–469, 481

Relief Act of 1821, 165

religion/religious diversity: and African Americans, 304, 307; and antislavery, 158; Appalachians, 361, 411; and civil rights, 428–429; and Cold War era, 411; in early statehood and settlement, 126, 136–137, 148–149, 203; and ethnicity, 137, 140, 298, 300–301, 332; Native Americans, 193–195; Northwest Territory and, 105, 109; prehistoric, 23, 32–33; and public schools, 140, 477, 478; and reform, 141–146, 322, 324–327, 332, 340, 465; and social conflict, 154–155, 250, 362, 368–370; *see also* Second Great Awakening; Social Gospel; temperance movement; and specific denominations

Republican Party (Jeffersonian) *see* Democratic Party

Republican Party (modern), 218–219, 220–224, 226–227, 231–236, 241–245, 247–250, 253–254, 258–267, 270, 272–275, 277, 283, 326, 337, 343–345, 358, 365, 380–382, 389, 392, 398, 412–418, 420–22, 444–446, 448–451, 455, 476–477, 479–482, *486*, 487

Resistance of 1763, *65*, 68–75, 197

Revolutionary War, 79, 83, 88, 106, 110, 112, 114, 116–117

Rhodes, James A., 415, 420, *421*, 422–24, 427, 429–430, 439, 442, 445, 448–449, 450–455, 465, 468–471, *472*, 473–475, 477

Richland County, 8

Richmond College, 149

Richmond, Virginia, 226, 232, 234

Rickenbacker, Eddie, 350

Riffe, Vernal G., Jr., 450, 468, 470, 474, 478

right to work, 398, 416–417, *418*, 419, 448

Rio Grande College/University of Rio Grande, 149

riots *see* civil disturbances

Ripley, Roswell, 215–216

Ripley College, 149

Ripley, Ohio, *133*, 158, 240

Rittman, Ohio, 14

Raisin (river), 197

Riverton, Ohio, 28

roads, 100, 134, 163, *168*, 175, 283, 285–286, 324, 341–342, 347, 366, 380, 402; *see also* National Road

Roaring Twenties, 363

rock and roll, 404

Rock and Roll Hall of Fame, 404

Rockefeller, John Davison, 215–216, 271, 281, 283, 288–289, 299, 307

Rocky Mountains, 39

Roe v. Wade, 440, 471

Roosevelt, Franklin Delano, 249, *255*, 358–359, 362, 366, 368, 380–382, 389, 392

Roosevelt, Theodore "Teddy," 254, 271, 275–276, *277*, 343–345

Rose, John (Gustave Rosenthal), 86

Rosecrans, William S., 214, 223–224, 232–233, 238, 259

Rose Law, 1908, 333

Roseville, Ohio, 1

Roseville Pottery, 1, 15

Rosie the Riveter, 362, 390

Ross, Alexander Coffman, 208

Ross, Joseph, 113

Ross County, 13, 36, 150, 186; courthouse, *186*

Rossville, Ohio, 140

Rotch, Thomas, 178

Royal American Regiment, 70

rubber industry, 15, 282, 286–287, 288–290, 315, 352, 361–362, 368, 384, 390–392, 398, 457, 459, 463–464, 473; *see also* synthetic rubber

rubber workers, 362, 378, 384, *385*, 391–392, 397, 463

Rumley, Ohio, 140

Rural Electrification Act, 381

Russell, Rev. Howard Hyde, 252

Russian Revolution, 355

rust belt, 409, 457, 459, 485

Ruthenberg, Charles, 330, 357

"Sack of Lawrence," 217

St. Clair, Arthur, 90, 92–93, 108, 110, 117, *118*, 119–123, 187, 188, 211

St. Clair Expedition, *89*, 93, *94*, 95, 193

St. Clairsville, Ohio, 155, 163

St. Joseph's Church, 1, 2

Saint Lawrence River/Valley, 27, 28, 49

St. Mary's, 198

Salem (Moravian Indian town), 85, 112

Salem, Ohio, 67, 147, 164, 330, *405*

Salineville, Ohio, 215, 230

salt and salt mining (halite), 1, 2, 5, 14, 17, 180, 287

sand, 4, 5, 6, 10, 13, 16

sandstone, 4, 5, 6, 15, 16, 44, 287

sandstone spools, 44

Sandusky Bay, 70, 232

Sandusky, Ohio, 161, 174, 177, 236, 319

Sandusky River, 57–59, 70, 72, 85, 86, 169, 197

Sandusky tradition, 44, 46, 51

Sanitary Commission, 226, 231

Sargent, Winthrop, 108, 117, 118, 120

savings and loan associations, 475

Saxbe, William, 414, 423, 448–449, 451

Scheuer, Sandra, 454

Schoenbrunn, 74, *77*, 85, 112

School Foundation Bill, 378, 382

schools *see* education (and schools)

Schroeder, William, 454

Scio College, 149

Scio, Ohio, 149

Scioto Company, 112, 132

Scioto County, 8, 468

Scioto Marsh, 383

Scioto River/Plains/Valley, 10, 57, 72, 76, 78, 110, 121, 134, 140, 169, 187, 348

Scopes Trial, 370

Scots, 137

Scots-Irish, 58, 136, 203, 204

Scott, Winfield, 224

Scott Law, 1883, 253–254

Searles, Mary, 231

Secession, 215, 221–222, 241

Second Battle of Bull Run (Manassas), 226

Second Confiscation Act, 227

Second Great Awakening, *142*, 143, 145, *147*, 157–158

Second Treaty of Fort Stanwix, 87

sectionalism, 186–192, 201–204, 208–210; *see also* "Five Ohios"

sedentarism, 29, 31, 35

Sedition Act of 1918, 355, 365

Seekunk (Salt Lick Town), 78

segregation, 151, 210, 303, 335–336, 365, 405–409, 416, 424, 428–430, 432, 446, 449

Seiberling, Frank, 288, 290, 444

Seiberling, John, 444

Seip Mound, 36

Senate Bill 5, 482, *484*

Senate, Ohio, 151, 188, 191, 244, 253, 260, 305, 346, 398, 413–414, 420, 450, 468, 474, 476, 478, 482

Senate, U.S., 79, 122, 235, 242, 265, 271, 276–277, 350, 358–359, 365, 428, 449, 478

Seneca County, 10

Seneca Falls, New York, 147

Seneca Indians, 50, 52, 57, 69, 80, 81, 138

September 11, 2001, attacks, 480

Serpent Mound, 44, *45*

sesquicentennial, 396

settlers, 11, 14–15, 17–18, 53, 58, 68–69, 73–75, 82, 88, 90, 97–98, 108, 113–119, 123, 128–132, *133*, 134–141, 162–163, 176, 180, 192, 194, 198, 202, 235, 271

Seven Ranges, 13, 106, *107*, 108, 109, *110*, 114

Seven Years' War (French and Indian), 47, 62–65, 68, *73*, 82, 102

Seventeenth Amendment, 344

sewer pipe, 15, 282, 287

sexuality, 231, 306, 368, 404, 412, 436–437, 439, 448, 480

Seymour, Horatio, 243

Shahn, Ben, *379*

Shaker Heights, Ohio, 442

Shakers, 144–145

shale, 5, *6*, 14–15

Sharon Conglomerate, 5, 16

Shawnee Indians, 40, 46, 56–59, 63, 72, 75–77, 80–84, 86–88, 90, 92, 95, 98, 106, 139, 192–194

Shawnee, Ohio, 1

sheep, 178, 223

shellfish, 27

shells, 2, 4, 5, 15, 28, 31, 33, 39, 43, 53

Shemenetoo (Blacksnake), 86

Shenandoah Valley, 234, 259

Sheridan, Philip, 234, 238, *239*, 278

Sheridan Cave, 23

Sherman, John, 209, 233, 235, 241–242, 248, 254, 267, 270–272, 278, 280

Sherman, William Tecumseh, 214, 225, 232, 234, 238, *239*, 248, 259, 278

Sherman Antitrust Act of 1890, 271, 274, 288

Sherman Silver Purchase Act of 1890, 271

Shingas, 63

shinplaster notes, *164*, 183

Shipherd, John J., *148*

shipping, 166, 168, 223–224, 272, 280, 285, 295

Sidney, Ohio, 140

Siebert, Wilbur, 158

Silurian period, 2, *3*, 5, 14–15, 17, 180

silver, 39, 165, 183, 249, 263, 271, 273, 274

Sioux Indians, 244, 271

Sippo Creek, 77

Sixteenth Amendment, 344

Slaughterhouse Cases, 245

slavery, 103, 105, 122, 125, 134, 155, 157–158, 203, 209, 212, 216–223, 226–227, 232, 234–235, 241–242, 250, 254, 257, 261

Slavery As It Is (Weld), 157

Slavs, 296–297; *see also* Czechs; Poles

smallpox, 60, *65*, 71, 83, 172

Smith, Harry C., *305*, 307, 354

Smith, Joseph, 145

Smith, Kirby, 224, *225*

soap, 131, 176, 281

soapstone, 28

Social Darwinism, 283, 324

Social Gospel, 322, 324–326, 330

socialism, 267, 309, 325–326, 330

social stratification (prehistoric), 33

soil, 2, 7, 11, 13, 18–19, 42, 176, 372, 381, 384, 441

Soldiers' Aid Society, 215

solstice, 39

Somerset, Ohio, 1, 2, 135, 137, 234, 238

Sonnontio, *56*, 57, 60

South Bass Island, 198

South Carolina, 63, 215, 222, 234, 259, 264–265, 334

South Dakota, 244, 271, 379

Southern Baptists, 411; *see also* Baptists

Soviet Union, 411–412

Spain, 49, 102, 113, 162, 254, 257, 275, 276

Specie Circular of 1836, 183

speculation: land, 58, 79, 183, 201; market, 378

speech patterns, 135–136

Springfield, Ohio, *3*, 163, 254, 290, 303, 306, 345, 353, 420, 423, 487

Springsteen, Bruce, 466

spruce, 23

squash, 28, 41–42

squatters, 69, 88, 90, 113–114, 141, 161

Squaw Campaign, *77*, 82, 86

Squire and Davis, *38*

"squirrel hunters," 224, *225*

squirrels, 130–131

stagflation, 459

Standard Oil, 254, 271, 281, 288, 324

Stanton, Edwin, 235, *239*, 242, 278

Stark County, 23, 262

Starling Medical College, 150

State Bank of Ohio, 183

statehood, 105, 120–123

State Penitentiary, 146, 230, 306

State Relief Commission (SRC), 380

State Treasury, 218

steamboats *see* boats

steel industry, 15, 17, 281–282, 284–285, 297, 304, 308, 313–315, 357, 358, 362, 363–364, 378, 384–386, 398, 410, 419–420, 459, 461, 465–66, *467*, 473

steelworkers, 358, 362, 385, 398, 410, 413, 419, 465–466

Steinem, Gloria, *438*

Steinem, Pauline Perlmutter, *334*

Steubenville, Ohio, 75, 113, 128, 129, 155, 188, 230, 235, 266–267

Stevens, Thaddeus, 241

Stewart, Philo P., *148*

Stewart, Potter, 415

Stickney, Benjamin, 205

Stickney, Two, 205

stock market, 362–363, 376–378, 381

Stokes, Carl, 426, 431, *433*, *434*, 435, 436

Stokes, Louis, *434*, 435, 443, 450

storage pits (prehistoric), 28–29, 31

Stowe, Harriet Beecher, 125–126, 153, 157, 217

Stow, Ohio, 138

Strickland, Theodore, 476, 481–482

strikes *see* civil disturbances

Struthers, Ohio, 180

Student Non-Violent Coordinating Committee (SNCC), 428, *429*

student protests *see* civil disturbances

Students for a Democratic Society (SDS), 426, 445–446, 452

suburbs, 316, 400–403, 406–408, 411, 429–430, 440, 450, 461, 477, 487

suffrage: African American, 212, 241–242, 260; women's, 147, 212, 231, 263, 297, 332–333, *334*, *335*, 338, 340–342, 345, 349, 353, 358

Sullivan, Samuel, 201

Summit County, 10, 154, 362, 380

Sumner, Charles, 241

sumpweed (marsh elder), 28, 31

sunflowers, 28, 31

Sunwatch Site, 44

Supreme Court, Ohio, 210–212, 220, 242, 252–254, 261, 285, 368, 419, 423, 470, 479

Supreme Court, U.S., 190, 201, 219, 229, 245, 261, 274–275, 345, 367, 382–383, 406, 409, 416, 420, 435, 439–440, 449–450, 471; *see also* specific cases

Surface Mining Control and Reclamation Act, 441

surveying/surveys, 99, 101, 103–104, 106, *107*, 108–110, *111*, 112–13, 115–116, 128, 134, 169, 204–205

swamps, 5–6, 7, 11, 13, 129, 172

Swan, Joseph, 220

Swayne, Noah, 278

Swedenborgians, 149, 176

"Sweeping Resolution," 191

"swing state" *see* battleground state; "Five Ohios"

Symmes, John Cleves, 108, 109, 117–118, 194

Symmes Purchase, 109, *110*, 114, 116, 117, 134, 136, 149

synthetic rubber, 390; *see also* rubber industry

Taber Opera House, 16

Taft, Alphonso, 278

Taft, Robert A., 382, 389, 398, 416

Taft, Robert A., Jr., 416, 448, 450–451

Taft, Robert A. II, 476, 479–481

Taft, Seth, 436

Taft, William Howard, 247, 254, 271, 276, 343–345, 367

Taft–Hartley Act, 398, 417, 420

Tallmadge, Ohio, 145

Tamaqua, 63, 69

Tammany Society, 191–192

Tanacharison (Half-King), 85

Taney, Roger, 219

tanneries, 180

Tappan, Arthur and Lewis, 155

Tarhe (The Crane), *98*

tariffs, 202, 249, 262, 273, 278, 328, 344, 359, 365, 377

taxes, 103, 121, 140, 151, 195, 201–202, 212, 231, 235, 244, 249, 252–254, 262–263, 273, 328–329, 336, 341, 343–346, 364–366, 378, 416, 419, 420, 422, 436, 450, 467–473, 474–475, 477–481

Taylor, Zachary, 209–210

Teapot Dome, 365

Teays River, 7–10

technology *see* innovation/invention

tectonic activity (earthquakes), 4, 7, 19

Tecumpease, 194

Tecumseh, 77, 95, 98, 192, 193–195, 197–198

television, 399–400, 403, 411, 416, 436, 451

temperance movement, 147, 154, 231, 249–251, *252*, 253, 254, 303, 311, 326, 332–334, 340, 342–343, 355; *see also* alcohol; Prohibition; Woman's Crusade; and specific organizations

Templeton, John Newton, 149

Tennessee, 39, 125, 127, 155, 158, 194, 206, 214, 222, 225, 230, 232, 238, 240, 241, 259, 359, 370

Tennessee Valley Authority, 349

Tenskwatawa, *193*, 194–195, 271

Tenure of Office Act, 242

teosinte, 43

Territorial Assembly, 120–121, *186*

territorial division, 103, 105

Terry v. Ohio, 435

Tertiary period, 7

Texas, 22, *34*, 206, 209, 287, 462

textiles, 29, 166

Thayendanegea (Joseph Brant), 85, 89–90, 93

theaters, 318, 321

Thebes tradition, 25

Thirteenth Amendment, 234, 302

Thomas, Dave, 401

Thompson, Eliza Jane Trimble, 250, *251*

Thorla, Silas, 180

Thorpe, Jim, *323*

Thurber, James, 374

Thurman, Allen G., 242, 260, 261, 265

Tibbets, Paul, 387, *388*

Tiffin, Edward, 120–122, 128, 187, 191–192, 204

Tilden, Samuel, 264–265

till, 7, 9–12, 19

Till Plains, 11, *12*

timber, 169, 172–173, 176, 180, 237

Timken, Henry, 282

"Tippecanoe and Tyler Too," 207

tobacco, 36, 135–136, 176, 281, 321, 480

Tod, David, 215, *216*, 224, 226, 231

Tod, George, 190–191

Toledo Blue Stockings, 321

Toledo, Ohio, 128, 151, *170*, 182–183, 223, 242, 282, 298, 314, 318, 324, 326–327, 330, *334*, 336, 341, **353**, 362, 378, 383, 384, 390, 400, 406, **407**, **408**, 415, 419, *438*, **460**, 485

Toledo Strip, *196*, 205

Toledo War, 122, 204–206

topography, 7–19

Toronto, Ohio, 330

towpath, 169, 172

trade/traders: in Civil War era, 223; in industrial era, 268, 273, 275, 328, 350, 365; and Middle Ground, 47, 49–51, 53, *54*, 57, 58–60, 63–65, 69, 71, 73, 75, 80; prehistoric, 14, 21, 24, 28–29, 33, 39, 44–45; in recent past, 461; in territory and early statehood, 117, 138, 139, 161–162; 166, 168, 173, 175, 183

Transcontinental Railroad, 217, 235, 244, 265

transportation, 18, 128, 132, 150–151, 159, 161–163, 166–82, 204, 208, 211–212, 237, 283–286, 319, 329, 354, 402, 408, 409, 419, 461, 468; *see also* canals; railroads; roads

Transportation Revolution, 166–182

Treaty of Easton, 63, 69

Treaty of Fort Finney, 87–88, 106

Treaty of Fort Harmar, 90

Treaty of Fort McIntosh, 87, 90

Treaty of Fort Stanwix, 77, 80, 87

Treaty of Fort Wayne, 194

Treaty of Greenville, *91*, 97, 98, 99, 118, 138, 194

Treaty of Lancaster, 58, 62

Treaty of Maumee Rapids, 198

Treaty of Paris (1763), 68, 70

Treaty of Paris (1783), 87, 101, 102

Treaty of Paris (1898), 276

Treaty of Pleasant Plains, 198

Treaty of Sandusky River, 198

Treaty of St. Mary's, 198

Treaty of Upper Sandusky, 198

Treaty of Versailles, 359, 377, 387

Treaty of Wapakoneta, 198

trilobite (*Isoletus*), 5

Trimble, Allen, 139, 169, 181, 200, 208

trophy skulls, 33

Troy, Ohio, 129, 140
Truman, Harry, 398, 409, 412, 415
Truman and Smith, 153
Trumbull County, 145, 342, 370
Truth, Sojourner, 147
Tullahoma Campaign, 238
Tupper, Benjamin, 108
turkeytail points, 29
Turner, George, 117
Turner, Ruth, 428, 431–432
Tuscarawas County, *144*, 173, 308
Tuscarawas River/Valley, 67, 83, 85, 99, 169, 180
Tuskegee Airmen, 393, *394*
Tuskegee Institute, 334
Twentieth Amendment, 367
Twinsburg, Ohio, 135
Tyler, John, 209
typhoid fever, 172, 262, 292

Uncle Tom's Cabin (Stowe), 125, 153, 157, 217
Underground Railroad, 157, 158, 220–221, 239
unemployment, 2, 249, 255, 349, 362–363, 378, 382, 389, 409, 417, 419, 432, 434, 459, 461, 463, 473–477, 481, 487
Union Village, 144
unions, 262, 267–268, 273, 285, 303, 309, 311–313, 326, 354, 358, 362–363, 382, 384, 386, 391–393, 397–398, 412, 417, 419, 424, 431–432, 448–449, 462–464, 484–485
Unitarians, 136, 149
United Autoworkers (UAW), 383, 384, 397, 412, 468
United Brethren, 74, 136, 149, 393
United Mine Workers (UMW), 311, 383, 393, 469
United Rubber Workers (URW), 362, 384, *385*, 397, 463–464
United States Civil Rights Commission, 430, 432
United States Military District, *110*, 112, 127, 128, 132
U.S. Steel, 384, 466, *467*
United Steelworkers (USW), 384, 398, 419
Universalists, 149
universities, 149, 235, 321, 336–337, 390, 412, 420, 423–424, 444, 446, 451, 456, 475, 482; *see also* specific institutions

University of Akron (Buchtel College), 149, 322, 336, 390, 455
University of Cincinnati, 336, 344
Upper Mercer flint, 1, 19, 23
Upper Mercer Limestone, 6
Upper Peninsula, 205
Upper Sandusky, 86, 139, 342
Upton, Harriet Taylor, 333, 342
Urbana College/University, 148–149
Urbana, Ohio, 195, 327, 473
Urbana Union, 227
urbanization, 50, 128–129, 223, 249, 264, 266, 315, 327, 368, 405
urban renewal, 402, 431
Ursuline College, 149
utopian communities, 143–145

Vallandigham, Clement, 215, *228*, 229, 231
Van Buren, Martin, 205–207, 210
Vance, Joseph, 208
Vanport Limestone, 6, 14–15, 23
Van Zandt, John, 125–126
Varnum, James Mitchell, 117
Venango, 62
Venice, Ohio, 70
Vermillion, Ohio, 128
Vermillion River, 128
Verrazano, Giovanni, 49
vertical integration, 288
Vicksburg, Mississippi, 214–215, 230, 232, 238
Vietnam War, 426–427, 431, 444–445, 447–449, 452–453, 466
Vincennes, 84, 121
virgin soil diseases, 50
Virginia, 5, 49, 58, 62–63, 71, 75–76, 78–79, 81, 84, 86, 90, 101, 106, 109–110, 116–117, 119, 127, 133–136, 162–163, 176, 188, 203, 207, 220, 224, 226, 230, 232, 234, 238, 247, 278, 371, 458
Virginia Military District, *111*, 112, 114–117, 119, 127–128, 133–135, 177
Voinovich, George, 470, 471, *472*, 476–479, 482
Volstead Act, *253*, 355, 367
Vorhis, Alvin, 232
Voting Rights Act of 1965, 415, 430

vouchers (schools), 478
voyageurs, 53

Wabash Moraine, 10
Wabash River/region, 88, 92, 93, 95, 193–195
Wade, Benjamin, 234, 235, 240–243, 248
wages, 249, 267, 270, 307, 308, 326, 332, 343, 363, 377, 389, 461, 483; child labor and, 309; immigrants and, 141, 275, 297–298; and race, 139, 141, 354, 380; and strikes, 266, 309, 314, 357, 383–384, 473; unions, 141, 309, 313, 383–384, 393, 417, 463–464, 466, 473; women and, 295, 297, 308, 309, 368, 380, 391, 403, 484
Wagner Act, 382, 398
Waite, Morrison, 278, 280
Wakatomika *see* New Wakatomika; Old Wakatomika
Walker, Timothy, 150
Wallace, George, 424, 427, 449, 473, 476
Wallace, Lewis, 224
wampum, 53, 69, 76, *98*
Wapakoneta, Ohio, 399
War of 1812, 163, 185, 192–200, *207*
Warren, Ohio, 145, 241, 290, 333
Washington, George, 58, 62–63, 76, 82, 86, 90, 92–93, 95, 113, 115, 117, 127, 239, 278
Washington County, 137
Washington Court House, 129, 250, 302–303
Washington, D.C., 121–122, 223, 226, 230, 252, 255–256, 480
water resources, 10, 11, 14, 18, 128, 167, 169, 325, 381, 429, 436, 440–444
Watervliet, 144
Watkins, Mel, 406
Wayne, Anthony, 95–97, *98*, 116, 193, 194
Wayne County, 231, 311
Weaver, James B., 255
Webster, Daniel, 206
Weizel, Godfrey, 214
Weld, Theodore Dwight, 155, 157
welfare, 343, 381, 397, 409, 419, 430, 432, 436, 473–474, 477–478
"welfare capitalism," 314–315, 363
Weller, Samuel, 282
Wellington, Ohio, 220
Wells, William, 95, *98*

Wellsville, Ohio, 158
Welsh, 132, 137, 313
West, Benjamin, *73*
West Milton, Ohio, 140
West Virginia, 5, 10, 33, 44, 76, 224, 266, 284, 383, 410
Western Basin tradition, 44, 51
Western Confederacy, 87–99, 163
Western Reserve (Case-Western Reserve) College, 149, 322
Western Reserve (Connecticut Western Reserve), 109, *110*, 112, 119, 132, 134, 136, 138, 157, 175–176, 178, 187, 203–204, 210, 221, 245, 485
Wetmore, William, 138
Weyapiersenwah (Blue Jacket), 76, 90, 92, *98*
wheat, 160, 161, 165, 175, 176, 237, 461
Wheeler, Wayne, 252, *253*, 333
Wheeling, Virginia (West Virginia), 113–114, 145, 162–163
Whig Party, 183, 206–211, 218, 223
Whiskey Ring, 244, 261–262
"White River" Indians, *56*, 57, 59
White, George, 380–381
White, Hugh Lawson, 206
White, Richard, 49, 52, 66, 99
Whitlock, Brand, 327, 330, 333, 341
Whittlesey focus/tradition, 44
Wilberforce College/University, 149, 334, 336
Wilberforce Colony, 139
Willard, Ohio, 128
Williams, George Washington, 304–305
Williamsburg, Ohio, 135
Williams County, 17
Williamson, David, 67, 85, 86, 198
Willich, August, 214
Willis, Frank, 349, 366
Willoughby College, 150
Willys-Overland Company, 282, 390
Wilmington College, 149
Wilmot Proviso, 209
Wilson, Amanda, 231
Wilson, Charles, 416
Wilson, Woodrow, 327, 329, 341, 344, 349–350, 387
Winchester, James, 196–197

Winton, Alexander, 290

Wisconsin, 35, 52, 137, 219, 237, 345, 412

Wise, Isaac Meyer, *300*, 301

Wittenberg College/University, 149

Wolf Plains group, 32

wolves, 130–131

Woman's Crusade, 1873–1874, 250–252

women: African American, 148, 303, 334, 354, 378; and the Civil War, 226, 231; and Cold War era, 397, 403, 414, 417–418, 436–437; in early Ohio, 131–132, 138; and education, 148; and the Great Depression, 378, 380, 386; immigrant, 295, 297–299; Jewish, 301; and the Middle Ground, 82; and 1920s, 368, *369*; and politics, 272, 342, 344–346, 473–474, 478, 482; and poverty, 484; and public sphere, 322, 330, 331–332; and settlement houses, 330–331; and strikes, 311, 313, 383–384; and Underground Railroad, 158; and World War I, 352–353, 354; and World War II, 362, 390, *391*, 392; *see also* sexuality; suffrage; temperance movement; women's rights

Women's Christian Temperance Union (WCTU), 251–252, 332–333

women's clubs, 331–334

Women's Equity Action League, 426, 437

women's rights, 145, 147–148, 250, 333, 345, 368, 426, 437–440

Women's Rights Convention of 1850, 147

Wood, Eleazor, 197

Woodland period (Early, Middle, Late), 1, 13, 24, 28–42, 44, 50

Woods, Granville, 292

Woods, William B., 278

Woodward High School, 126, 153

wool/woolen industry, 178–179, 223, 237

Wooster, Ohio, 128, 323

workers/working conditions: African American, 303, 307, 310, 353–354, 358, 362, 378, 386, 392; Appalachian, 410; and canals, 137, 139, 169, 172–174; and Cold War era, 412–413, 417; in early Ohio, 141, 178; ethnicity and, 295, 297–299, 312–313, 358; in Great Depression and New Deal, 378, 380, 382–385; industrial era,

307–315, 326, 349; in mining, 308, 309–311, 441; in 1920s, 363, 368, 377; and politics, 248–249, 255, 262–263, 267, 273–274, 312, 314, 327, 330, 343, 346, 362, 381, 383, 392, 398, 417, 419, 424, 449, 462, 476, 482, *484*; in post-World War II years, 397; railroads, 284–285; since 1970s, 459, 461–466, 483; women, 290, 295, 299, 303–304, 308–309, 311, 352–353, 354, 362, 368, 378, 390, *391,* 417, 484; in World War I, 352–353, 356–358; in World War II, 362, 389–390, 393; *see also* child labor; civil disturbances; deindustrialization; unions

Works Progress Administration (WPA), *255*, 380–382

World War I, 287, 294, 296, 329, 340, 349–358, 365–366, 372, 377

World War II, 362, 382, 387–394, 404, 410, 417, 435, 440, 448, 463

Worthington, Thomas, 30, *119*, 120–122, 128, 187–188, 190–192, 195, 199–200

Worthington, Ohio, 132

Wounded Knee, 271

Wright, Harry, 319, *320*, 321

Wright, James, 488–489

Wright, Orville, 281, 289, 291–292, *293*, 305, 348, 422

Wright, Wilbur, 280–281, 283, 289, 291–292, *293*, 305, 348, 422

Württemburg, 144

Wyandot County, 23

Wyandot (Huron, Petun) Indians: and Anglo-French conflict, 51, 55, *56*, 57, 59–60; and Anglo-American conflict, 67, 70–72, 80–81, 83–87; and the early U.S., 92, 96, 138–139, and removal, 125–126, 159, 199, 488

Wyandot Reservation, 139

Xavier College/University, 149, 448

Xenia, Ohio, 82, 84, 129

Yellow Creek, 75, 180

Yellow Springs, Ohio, 145

Yellowstone, 39

Yoakum, Dwight, 410

Yorktown, Virginia, 85, 87

Young Americans for Freedom (YAF), 445–446

Young, Neil, 454

Young, Stephen, 416, 418, 449–451

Youngstown, 224, 252, 363, 406–408, 440; and African Americans, **353**; and deindustrialization, 459, *460*, 464–467, 476, 484; and industrialization, 282, *304*, 315; and the Ku Klux Klan, 362, 369; and labor, 358, 362, 378, 385, 398, 420, 473–474; and urban life, 318–319, 322

Youngstown Patricians, 322

Youngstown Sheet and Tube, 315, 363, 385, 464–465

Zane, Ebenezer, 163

Zane's Trace (Trail), 163

Zanesville, Ohio, 128–129, 209, 229, 266, 280; and early Ohio economy, 163, 180–181; as state capital, 191, 282

Zeisberger, David, 20, 40, 74, 85, 99, 198

Zoar, Ohio, 144–145